PITCHFORK BEN TILLMAN

South Carolinian

B R Tillman
1906

Francis Butler Simkins

PITCHFORK BEN TILLMAN

South Carolinian

LOUISIANA STATE UNIVERSITY PRESS

First paperback printing 1967
Copyright © 1944 by Louisiana State University Press

Printed in the United States of America by
Edwards Brothers, Inc., Ann Arbor, Michigan

To

MARGARET LAWRENCE SIMKINS

PREFACE

Ben Tillman led the most significant transformation in the political life of South Carolina since Reconstruction. He took the control of the state from Wade Hampton and the Bourbons and gave it to himself and his farmer friends. There is danger of overemphasizing the social importance of this transfer of power, for both Hampton and Tillman were ever loyal Southerners who believed in the Confederate tradition, white supremacy, and the Democratic party; nevertheless, there were important social differences which made the rivalry of the two leaders something more than personal. Hampton believed in the rule of white democracy through a leadership derived from a social system which had existed before the Civil War; whereas Tillman believed in the rule of white democracy through a leadership which had arisen as the result of social changes after 1865.

Beginning life as a "simon-pure" farmer, Ben Tillman unconsciously prepared himself for the career which was to give him importance. He became familiar with the problems and difficulties of the agricultural majority of the state's population; he developed his imagination and powers of expression by reading the English classics; he imbibed the legends of his own province and learned to understand its sectional, class, and race rivalries. So, when he and other South Carolina farmers suffered from the distress which overtook the American farm population in the 1880's, he executed a minor revolution with mathematical precision. By using his unmatched ability as a pamphleteer and debater he won the loyalty of a majority of the voters of his state, appealing to their hates and hopes. Victorious in the 1890 canvass, he then executed a program of educational, constitutional, and administrative reform so moderate that conservative traditions were scarcely violated. Those who expected important social and economic changes were disappointed. The career of the farmer-statesman culminated in 1896 when he made an unsuccessful bid for national leadership.

The remaining twenty-two years of Tillman's career were mostly anticlimax. His was the story of a United States senator who at first divided his time between gradually failing attempts to dominate his state and unsuccessful efforts to impose his peculiar South Carolina mannerisms and doctrines upon the nation, but who later was wise enough to make peace with inevitable trends; he acquiesced in the decline of agrarianism in state politics and accepted the Senate as it was. Yet, until illness cast its shadows, Ben Tillman was ever a vivid personality with interesting ideas expressed in flaming words.

Perhaps the scholar will be disappointed in the degree to which this book is a contribution to knowledge; for it is not fully nurtured by the many private letters from which the authoritative biography is usually drawn. Such sources are not available in ample quantities. Nevertheless, as the scholarly paraphernalia of this book shows, the sources used have been extensive. Millions of words have been recorded by and about Ben Tillman; they were diligently digested.

For the arousal of my interest in the Southern agrarian movement I am indebted to the inspiring lectures of Professor Benjamin B. Kendrick, formerly of Columbia University and now of the Women's College of the University of North Carolina. Mr. Benjamin R. Tillman, Jr., has kindly permitted access to the Tillman Papers in the South Caroliniana Library, University of South Carolina. My good friends, Mr. Max Revelise of Columbia, South Carolina, and Professor James W. Patton of North Carolina State College, have helped me solve many problems of style and content. The late Professor Holland Thompson of the College of the City of New York has, in the light of his experiences as a seasoned writer on Southern history, helped me in difficult matters. Among the many who have given me firsthand information concerning events, or have pointed out sources of information, the following should be mentioned: John E. Swearingen, nephew of Ben Tillman and former South Carolina state superintendent of education; Professor Robert M. Kennedy and the late Professor Yates Snowden of the University of South Carolina; the late Eugene B. Gary, chief justice of South Carolina; the late Colonel John R. Abney of New York City; the late Thomas J. Kirkland of Camden, South Carolina; Mrs. Agatha A. Woodson and the late Dr. Francis W. P. Butler and Dr. C. Prescott De Vore of Edgefield; Alexander S. Salley and Francis M. Hutson of the South Carolina Historical Commission; and Professor James E. Walmsley of Farmville, Virginia. Many of the illustrations were reproduced through the kindness of Adjunct Professor Frank H. Wardlaw of the University of South Carolina. The execution of the final phase of the book was made possible by a grant-in-aid from the Southern Regional Committee of the Social Science Research Council. What accuracy and clarity of expression this book may possess are in no small measure due to the careful reading of the manuscript by Dean Wendell H. Stephenson and Dr. Fred C. Cole of Louisiana State University, and the Staff of the Louisiana State University Press.

F.B.S.

Farmville, Virginia

CONTENTS

Chapter I

MANNERS OF AN AGRARIAN SENATOR

BENJAMIN RYAN TILLMAN of South Carolina entered the United States Senate in 1895 with a reputation for flaming words and bad manners. These qualities, far from preventing him from leading the most significant political revolution South Carolinians have ever imposed upon themselves, had been partly responsible for his success. This fact confirmed him in his ways. Consequently, in his first words in the Senate he boorishly declared that he did not wish to adjust himself; and, as the Pharisee is wont to do, proclaimed himself more virtuous than other senators. Any other course would have been a confession of weakness, an admission that he wished to sacrifice one of his chief titles to fame in order to become an innocuous gentleman. He preferred notoriety to vacuity, but he was no mere poseur; his uncouthness was the natural heritage of a genuine rustic; his self-righteousness was rooted in his temperament and nurtured by the reading of some of the sturdier English classics.

Senator Tillman's appearance testified to his rudeness and crudeness. It is true that he was not of ordinary mien. "His face," said a sympathetic observer, "would compel attention in any gathering of distinguished men." [1] His head seemed Napoleonic in its strength and symmetry and in the high and defiant manner in which he carried it. The firm mouth and chin unmistakably indicated intellect and strong will; his shambling gait and generous proportions

[1] Charles A. Macauley, in Spartanburg *Herald,* April 2, 1908.

gave distinction of a sort. But there was little to suggest
kindness or refinement. The gleaming single eye, the empty
left socket above a pudgy cheek, the dark skin, the high
cheek bones, the snarling mouth, the great, flat head covered with a thick growth of short tousled hair, created an
aspect as sinister as it was arresting. Little wonder one commentator said of the severe, scowling Tillman: "Above this
gigantic man there gleams the fiercest face ever seen on a
public man."

His dress exaggerated the unfavorable demeanor. Conspicuous untidiness befitted one who said, "I am a rude
man and don't care." Although in winter he affected the
piccadilly collar, Ascot tie, and Prince Albert coat conventional to politicians, his coat dangled like a dressing sack,
often his collar yawned and his tie strayed outside his vest,
and sometimes his shoes were unpolished and his trousers
uncreased. His broad-brimmed plantation hat was dinted
from overuse and pulled down to shade his face. During
the warm months formalities of dress were largely forgotten.
Then an alpaca coat, often rusty with age, displaced the
Prince Albert, and a shapeless panama supplanted the felt
hat. Colored galluses were exposed and summer shirts were
often travel-stained.[2]

This strange legislator's appearance grew menacing
when he flung himself into the Senate debates. His one
eye glared, his index finger threatened, and his jaw snapped
in a whirl of exclamations. His distinctive voice compelled
attention. In it were a note of savagery and a strange combination of shrillness and loudness which penetrated every

[2] For descriptions of Benjamin R. Tillman, see James Creelman, "A Defender of the Senate," in *Pearson's Magazine* (New York), XV (1906), 622;
Clifford Howard, "Tillman, A Study from the American Soil," in *Appleton's Magazine* (Philadelphia), VIII (1906), 348; New York *Times,* January
17, 1909. Clippings of these and many other articles are in the Benjamin R.
Tillman Scrapbooks, Benjamin R. Tillman Papers (South Caroliniana
Library, University of South Carolina, Columbia). The Tillman Scrapbooks
in this collection will be referred to without indicating their relationship
to the whole collection.

corner of the Senate chamber. His vocabulary, stinging like a whiplash, was loaded with the crudities of the South Carolina stump by a speaker who regarded formal eloquence as so much trumpery. The climaxes, especially when the Negro question was broached, were so explosive that the observer almost expected to see pieces of the orator hurled in the air and deposited on the heads of the senators.

"Going up to the Senate to hear Tillman make a speech was like running to a fire," remarked one observer.[3] When it was noised about that he would talk, the doorkeepers were on hand hours in advance to handle the crowds who wished to enter the galleries; and when, without previous notice, his strident voice filled the Capitol corridors, there was a rush to vacant seats. Writers in the press gallery moved to the front; senators put down their newspapers and craned their necks. "The only thing that ever happens in the Senate," said a newspaper writer, "is Senator Tillman."[4]

From his seat directly in front of the presiding officer, the South Carolinian heard everything and consequently was frequently stirred into action. He chronically interrupted other speakers in violation of their rights to the floor, overcoming opposition by use of his obtrusive personality and powerful voice. He frequently talked at length on irrelevant subjects, turning debates on the colonial question into agitations of the American Negro issue, or discussions of domestic problems into tirades against the President. Often, for want of a juicier topic, he ranted about himself and his political problems. When Senator Joseph B. Foraker of Ohio tried to stop one of his endless excursions into the extraneous by asking what was the question before the Senate, the speaker, unembarrassed, said,

[3] Brooklyn *Eagle*, cited in *Literary Digest* (New York), LVIII (1918), 32.
[4] For descriptions of Tillman's oratory, see Zach McGhee, "Tillman, Smasher of Traditions," in *World's Work* (New York), XII (1906), 8013; Arthur Warren, in Boston *Herald*, March 27, 1906; and Howard, "Tillman, A Study from the American Soil," *loc. cit.*, 348.

"I am before the Senate." When the inquiry was pressed a second time, the resourceful talker cried triumphantly, "I want to finish a few little remarks by way of getting rid of some of the yellow blood in me." [5]

He frequently indulged in what he called "the discursive and expanding seductions of extemporaneous talk"; denounced as "gag rule" limitations on debate; and would not, he said, "crawl around like a whipped cur" before a presiding officer as members of the House of Representatives did.[6] He viewed with profound suspicion efforts of the Senate majority to substitute action for talk. "When only one side cares to discuss a question . . . ," he affirmed, "there is always devilment afoot." Senators loved speech too well to keep silent "unless there is something rotten in Denmark." [7] He confessed that he joined other senators in the "habit of loading down the *Record* with dead speeches or dull, dry utterances, and an immense amount of nonsense and rot." [8] But he believed himself right on every issue, and hoped, by a repetition of a few basic ideas, to arouse the people against the conduct of their supposed representatives in Congress. The presence of seemingly invincible Republican majorities never discouraged this Democrat.

Tillman's churlish language was more objectionable than his forensic mannerisms. To say, as one writer did, that he was "heedless of decorous speech" is an understatement. He was often rude and abusive, priding himself on his "brutal frankness" and on his use of "Saxon adjectives which leave a bad taste in the mouth." He decried the avoidance of statements calculated to wound feelings; to one senator who was temperate of speech he confessed, "I have always considered this a weakness and acted on the contrary principle." [9]

"Those bad words," he explained to one who lectured

[5] *Congressional Record*, 59 Cong., 1 Sess., 4324–25.
[6] *Ibid.*, 54 Cong., 2 Sess., 2559–60.   [7] *Ibid.*, 55 Cong., 2 Sess., 6529.
[8] *Ibid.*, 59 Cong., 1 Sess., 225.   [9] *Ibid.*, 63 Cong., 3 Sess., 301.

him on the quality of his language, "are my safety-valve. All men must have one vice as an outlet for the Old Adam in them." [10] Under the cloak of this quaint rationalization he freely indulged in his "verbal licentiousness." Thus, he was so unparliamentary as to say that a decision of the House was motivated by "sectional animosity"; that the state of a certain senator was a desert unattractive to white men; [11] and that senators who had been "bought" for "dirty work" justified themselves by "hypocrisy." [12]

On the subject of the Negro, he indulged in reckless truth-telling shocking to his colleagues. Once when the Senate was considering in secret session the appointment of a black man to office, Tillman grew livid, swung his fists, and cried, "You can keep up that kind of thing until you compel the people of the South to use shotguns and kill every man you appoint." "What!" exclaimed George F. Hoar, "the senator from South Carolina would not admit that in open session?" "Open the door right now and see whether I will admit it or not," shouted Tillman. "Your predecessors never acknowledged it," suggested the astonished Massachusetts senator. "Maybe not," replied the South Carolinian, "but if they didn't, they concealed the facts. We do not intend to submit to negro domination and all the Yankees from Cape Cod to hell can't make us submit to it." [13]

Amusingly enough, Tillman, despite avowals of frankness and simplicity, craftily couched his accusations of corruption and dishonesty in such nebulous language that he usually managed to escape embarrassment when outraged disputants called him to account. He then prudently reinterpreted *double-entendres* from their better sides. But his lurid "suspicions" made the headlines of the muckraking

[10] "Tattler," "The Broken Pitchfork," in *Nation* (New York), CII (1916), 694.

[11] *Cong. Record*, 56 Cong., 2 Sess., 2185; 57 Cong., 1 Sess., 4806.

[12] See interchanges between Tillman and John C. Spooner, *ibid.*, 56 Cong., 1 Sess., 3216–17.

[13] Cited in Creelman, "A Defender of the Senate," *loc. cit.*, 622.

press and helped sustain a popular belief that the Senate was corrupt.[14]

Attacks on others were interpolated with tedious dinnings of his own sanctity. Again and again he edified weary senatorial ears with dissertations on his purity and honesty. Such Pharisaism was conveniently based on the contrast between his occupation and that of the lawyer-senators. He asserted that he was the only simon-pure farmer in the Senate, that he was a veritable Cincinnatus who had abandoned the plow to become the sole true representative in the Senate of the agrarian half of the American people. The fact that he had achieved considerable knowledge of the law by methods different from those of the professional lawyers led him to boast: "I imbibed my knowledge of jurisprudence and human liberty with my mother's milk." This wisdom of his, which he aptly called "cornfield law," offered, in his opinion, better solutions of the national problems than the learning of the legal profession. He held the lawyers in contempt for their "little technicalities," their "hairsplitting" obscurities. He charged that lawyers, and even lawyer-senators, besides being obscure, were incapable of honest judgments since their moral sense was blunted by their taking either side of a case for money. A man who was not a lawyer, he contended, could have "a broader and more comprehensive view" of a legal question than a member of the profession. When challenged, he said that lawyers were downright dishonest, "pettifoggers and shysters," "dirty creatures" who "crawl out" to manipulate political conventions for selfish corporations.[15]

Tillman's vivid denunciation of the legal profession delighted the galleries and a large section of the outside public, but won the odium of lawyer associates. Joseph W. Bailey of Texas called him a grudge-bearing demagogue

14 *Cf.* Warren, in Boston *Herald*, March 27, 1906.
15 *Ibid.; Cong. Record*, 56 Cong., 2 Sess., 2365; Benjamin R. Tillman to Augustine T. Smythe, March 6, 1912, in Tillman Papers. Hereafter, Benjamin R. Tillman will be alluded to as Tillman.

unable to get the antilawyer cobweb out of his mind, and John C. Spooner lectured him for discourteously questioning lawyers' motives.[16] But the farmer-senator held his ground. He knew many lawyer-politicians who were prospering in the service of corporations, and he compensated himself verbally at the expense of colleagues with whom he was not professionally qualified to share such profits.

Republican leaders—Hoar of Massachusetts, William E. Chandler of New Hampshire, Foraker of Ohio, Spooner of Wisconsin—frequently lectured the incorrigible South Carolinian on his unparliamentary manners. But they were amused or even pleased at his indiscretions; for his vehemence, they felt, did them little damage. Secure in their majorities, they were not excited by the onslaughts of this sworn enemy of their party. Democrats, many of them Southern Bourbons, on the other hand, were chagrined that one of their number should repudiate the Southern tradition of good manners and expose the weakness of their position on the Negro. Usually, they glumly ignored Tillman's outbursts, but sometimes their feelings were so abraded by his mordant tongue that they could not restrain themselves.

When Tillman accused John T. Morgan of Alabama of wishing "to gobble up" for his state all the public lands within its borders, the wounded senator cried, "I am not a gobbler, Mr. President, and therefore the rules of decency that apply to gobblers do not apply to me. . . . This is the first time that anyone has ever attempted to take me off the floor by interjecting remarks that were personally objectionable." [17] On another occasion, Morgan, nettled by Tillman's habit of obtruding himself into the remarks of others, pointedly refused to let the South Carolinian interrupt his discourse. Tillman was hurt! "No Republican," he loudly grumbled, "would have denied it to me, because

[16] *Cong. Record*, 59 Cong., 1 Sess., 1430, 9648.
[17] *Ibid.*, 55 Cong., 1 Sess., 857–58.

there is no man on the other side so lacking in courtesy!" [18]

On Washington's Birthday, 1902, Tillman was guilty of one of the most flagrant examples of unparliamentary conduct ever known on the Senate floor: physical assault upon his colleague, John L. McLaurin.

The difficulty arose in this manner: Senator Spooner, in urging Democrats to support the Philippine tariff, reminded them that William J. Bryan had been influential in making possible the annexation of the Asiatic islands. Tillman took this as an opportunity to correct a Republican and to humiliate McLaurin, a former ally with whom he had quarreled. Bryan's influence, said Tillman to Spooner, had not been sufficient to secure enough votes to ratify the Philippine treaty. Shaking his finger at the Wisconsin senator, he added, "You know how you got them." Spooner professed ignorance. The South Carolinian continued, "I have reason to believe from the circumstantial evidence and from things that have been told to me in confidence by men on the other side that improper influences were used."

"Name the man!" was the cry from all parts of the Senate. Spooner searchingly rejoined: "That is due to the country, and due to the man who you suspect, and by innuendo charge. Who was it? Let him answer for himself if he is still a member of this body."

Tillman, with characteristic evasiveness, refused to call a name given in confidence. Spooner, amid applause from the galleries, scornfully commented, "Oh, in confidence. A man who would impeach another man in confidence is a coward." Then Tillman explained in words which turned all eyes to the vacant seat of McLaurin, who was attending a committee session. The absent senator, said Tillman, "after having made a speech in this body two weeks before, replete with cogent arguments and eloquence, against the ratification of the treaty, and after having told us in confidence that he would not vote for it, he did; and since then he has been

[18] *Ibid.,* 56 Cong., 1 Sess., 2031, 2183.

adopted by the Republican caucus and put upon committees as a member of that party, and has controlled the patronage in South Carolina. I did not expect to bring this in in this way, but I do not dodge or flinch from any responsibility anywhere. I simply know what I believe."

When the news of the accusation of "improper influences" reached McLaurin in the committee room, he rushed into the Senate, pale with anger: "I desire to state, Mr. President—I would not use as strong language as I intend to had I not, soon after the Senate met, replied to these insinuations and said that they were untrue—I now say that that statement is a willful, malicious, and deliberate lie."

Immediately Tillman, who had been sitting near-by, sprang at the speaker with tiger-like ferocity. McLaurin met the attack courageously. Tillman's blow landed just above his colleague's left eye; McLaurin's counterthrust spent itself on Tillman's nose. There followed a flurry of thrusts, part of which fell upon the doorkeeper who was trying to separate the combatants. Finally that official, assisted by several senators, wrenched the two men apart. As they took their seats, a large red welt appeared on McLaurin's forehead and Tillman wiped away the blood that flowed from his nose. So intense was the excitement that everyone was on his feet, and when the encounter was over the silence of extreme consternation prevailed. The Senate had not witnessed a similar scene since Senators Thomas H. Benton and Henry S. Foote had engaged in fisticuffs some fifty years before.

The Senate immediately went into secret session to discuss the punishment of the pugilists. After more than two hours of deliberation, the assembly unanimously declared the two South Carolinians "in contempt of the Senate on account of the altercation and personal encounter between them this day in open session," and the problem of their future status was referred to the Committee on Privileges and Elections. The two offenders were allowed to apologize.

Tillman, with his ability at self-criticism, confessed that his background unfitted him, in a measure, for a proper regard of the rules of the Senate. His apology was not without qualifications: "I was ready to do that two minutes after I had acted; but under the provocation, which was known to all of you, I could not have acted otherwise than I did; and while I apologize to the Senate and am sorry that it has occurred, I have nothing more to say."

McLaurin was even less apologetic. Unable to suppress his bitterness, he said that he could never have held his head erect had he not "in the strongest and most forcible terms" resented "a most brutal assault" upon his honor. Only the urgent solicitation of another senator prevented him from repeating the statement that provoked the fray.[19]

Extensive obloquy was visited upon Tillman for his temerity. His and McLaurin's apologies failed to effect the removal of the "contempt" penalty the Saturday it was imposed. The following Monday, by direction of the presiding officer, the names of the two senators were omitted from the roll call, and they were forced to maintain a dejected silence while the Senate debated their fate before a distinguished audience that included Prince Henry of Prussia. To their discomfiture was added the condemnation of the press for this "brutal exhibition," the "outrageous assault" before the Senate.[20] Tillman was deeply hurt that some of his "own people, Democrats . . . should stab me in the back" by such criticisms.[21] The cup of humiliation was filled when Theodore Roosevelt withdrew an invitation to dine at the White House with Prince Henry.[22]

Four days after the fight President Pro Tem William P. Frye, after allowing Tillman to insert in the *Congressional*

---

[19] For the encounter, see *ibid.,* 57 Cong., 1 Sess., 2081, 2087, 2089–90; R. M. Larner and others, in Charleston *News and Courier,* February 23, 1902; Tillman to David H. Magill, March 3, 1902, in Tillman Papers.
[20] Charleston *News and Courier,* February 24, 1902.
[21] Tillman to Magill, March 3, 1902, in Tillman Papers.
[22] For a full discussion of this incident, see below, p. 408.

Record a protest against further exclusion, ordered the restoration of the two senators to the Senate rolls. In his protest Tillman took the sound position that it was unconstitutional to deprive a state of its representation in the Senate, and that expulsion was the only legal action possible. He knew that the necessary two-thirds vote for that action could not be had because of Democratic opposition.[23] On February 28, six days after the fisticuffs, the Committee on Privileges and Elections made its report. A majority asserted that Tillman's offense was graver than McLaurin's, whose misdeed was adjudged to be only "the use of unparliamentary language for which he had unusual provocation." Curiously enough, both were considered worthy of the same punishment. It was decreed that the two senators "for disorderly behavior and flagrant violation of the rules of the Senate . . . deserve the censure of the Senate, and they are hereby censured"; but that after the adoption of this recommendation "the order adjudging them in contempt of the Senate shall be no longer in force and effect." Tillman's constitutional objections had led to the abandonment of a recommendation for suspension or material punishment.[24]

Official censure did not cure the South Carolina senator of unparliamentary conduct. He remained convinced that he had acted wisely in striking McLaurin. "Had I taken the lie," he wrote a friend, "my self-respect would have gone and my services here in the Senate of no effect." [25] He believed that he had "the approval of the Democrats of both Houses" [26] and knew that his constituents were delighted that he had "punched Johnny McLaurin." [27]

[23] *Cong. Record,* 57 Cong., 1 Sess., 2195–96.
[24] The vote of censure was 54 to 12. *Ibid.,* 2203–2207. For comments, see Augusta (Ga.) *Chronicle,* March 1, 1902; *Outlook* (New York), LXX (1902), 591–93.
[25] Tillman to Magill, March 3, 1902, in Tillman Papers.
[26] See newspaper opinion, in Charleston *News and Courier,* February 27, 1902.
[27] J. P. Buzhardt to Tillman, July 29, 1902, in Tillman Papers.

An unapologetic senator resumed his duties, a Tillman who did not care to change his manners or his language. Indeed, crude manners and rough language were needed in the battles ahead involving "Republican rascality and Democratic imbecility." Out of the McLaurin fight had grown the feud with Theodore Roosevelt which was destined to make Tillman's actions more offensively aggressive. As late as 1907 he would still be called with justice "the untrimmable Tillman," the confirmed egotist and Pharisee still proud of his clattering tongue and still thanking God that he was different from other men.[28]

On January 21 of that year he was aroused to a display of humor when the New York *Sun* called him "a burnt cork artist of the Senate." He told his colleagues that they had "given evidence of shining minstrel talent in wholly unexpected places." If he were "Pitchfork Ben" at one end of the line of showmen, "Fire Alarm Joe" Foraker would be at the other end. Strung in between would be "supple, sly and foxy" Spooner of Wisconsin; Alexander S. Clay of Georgia, "the pompadour artist"; "Smiling Tom" Patterson of Colorado, the representative of a state bought at auction by the Guggenheims; "Gum Shoe Bill" Stone of Missouri; George W. Daniel of Virginia "who works his rhetoric overtime"; and the consecrated Henry C. Lodge of Massachusetts, who was "a negro preacher." These characterizations were made in the best of humor and from most of the victims provoked real or simulated laughter. This, however, was not true of Edward W. Carmack of Tennessee who was characterized as "once a knight . . . whose spear had rung true on the visor of the usurper in the White House. But his spear had broken off. He has been unhorsed." Properly perhaps this characterization should have been regarded as a bit of pleasantry, a mere prelude to the lengthy speech on the Negro which followed. But Carmack, supersensitive because of his recent defeat by "Bob"

28 New York *Globe*, January 22, 1907, in Tillman Scrapbooks.

Taylor, interpreted it otherwise. In his opinion Tillman had committed a flagrant breach of etiquette; he had ridiculed a colleague for failure to be re-elected.

The Tennesseean was bitter and personal in his reply to the Pitchfork senator. The South Carolinian's remarks, he said, were the "studiously offensive" effusions of one who did not know how to speak with courtesy. He reminded Tillman that his spear, broken or unbroken, had "never been dipped in the filth of the gutter," and that he was sure that his retirement caused more regret among the senators than would Tillman's. Before Tillman had time to reply the Senate went into secret session, and behind closed doors the tactless South Carolinian was lectured by the graver senators of both parties.[29]

So much for Tillman at his worst. Inelegance and turbulence are not necessarily an accurate index to a man's character. Certainly Pitchfork Ben displayed his darker side to the public. Behind the harsh countenance, the vituperation and the vulgarity, were hidden many admirable qualities. There was another Tillman beside the Goth who, in the accentuated light of publicity, brandished a pitchfork in debate. Those who met him in private discovered that a shaggy exterior concealed an engaging personality; that he was a devoted husband and father, sober in his personal habits without being puritanical; that he was a man who lived as plainly and as economically as he had before he was touched with the accolade of fame. His careless but simple dress, his informal manners, and his utterly unaffected way in receiving both the great and the obscure were proofs that neither success nor notoriety had turned his head. Among his South Carolina friends he forgot that he was a celebrity, talking and acting like a plain farmer among fellow farmers. If he was not a pious Christian, he was in all but the most obvious sense a true gentleman, respectful and hon-

orable toward ladies and thoroughly imbued with the code
of honor associated with Southern gentlemen. Newspaper
writers reported that in private he was "as good a fellow,
as sensible and decent a citizen and as wise a man as one
could meet." [30] It was discovered that he was filled with the
precepts of the best literature; that he loved flowers and
sentimental music; that his public passion for righteousness
was based on a wholesome patriotism and a sincerely experienced social consciousness; that his handshake was warm;
and that he listened tolerantly and patiently to opinions
different from his own. It was likewise discovered that the
fierceness of his public convictions was softened by a sly
humor, by the absence of fanaticism and bigotry, and by a
personality which many found engaging. If there was an
opportunity for a jest, he seized it; if there was a chance to
inject a story, he never missed it. [31]

His most objectionable private traits were a noisy fussi-
ness and a constant indulgence in profanity. These characteristics were part of his nature and nurture; they expressed
the inevitable impatience of a poorly disciplined man of
action who never learned to control himself in the presence
of persons less energetic than he. But they were not the fail-
ings of a true tyrant. His outbursts were restrained before
they resulted in serious injustices to subordinates. His dis-
tempers left room for warm friendships and for devotion
from those who served him. The indiscriminate manner in
which his oaths were bestowed is proof that rancor was not
a guiding principle of his nature; he fumed at friend and
foe alike—at his beloved wife and family as well as at clerks
and servants. [32]

[30] Washington correspondent of New York *Times,* cited in [anonymous],
"The Most Extraordinary Compound in the United States Senate," in *Current Literature* (New York), XLI (1906), 154.

[31] W. A. Lewis, "The Tillman of the Armchair," in *Success Magazine*
(New York), IX (1906), 396; [anonymous], "Men & Work—Tillman without
the Pitchfork," in *Saturday Evening Post* (Philadelphia), CLXXVIII (1906),
15; New York *Sun,* March 30, 1906.

[32] Tillman to Walter M. Riggs, February 26, 1903, in Tillman Papers.

Religious people often complained of Tillman's profanity. He admitted that it could not be controlled, that it was "bred in the bone and must come out of the mouth." But from his viewpoint it was not a major defect; it was the only sin of Honest Ben, proof that he was not a hypocrite; quite harmless compared with the drunkenness and adultery of the truly sinful politician. He joked about "the hot times I am going to have in the hereafter for my wickedness"; and shortly before he died his wit triumphed magnificently: "I am still enjoying an honest damn once in a while." [33] Gambling, smoking, and drinking, he asserted to a reproving woman missionary, were infinitely worse physically, mentally, and morally. "I assure you, my dear young lady, I made a careful comparison of the whole list of vices before I chose one for myself." [34]

Tillman's most substantial virtue was the accomplishment of hard and purposeful work. His sobriety, his impatient energy, and his restrained living made possible a maximum dedication to duty. He demonstrated as marked a capacity for routine as he did for noisy oratory. Despite a professed contempt for parliamentary subtleties, he learned all the tricks of the trade. He had not been in the Senate many years before it was easier to prove him wrong on a principle of agriculture than on a point of law or legislative procedure. No senator was more attentive to the debates; none more conscientious in answering letters and interviewing visitors.[35] Truthfully he told his constituency, after six years in Washington, that he had not gone there merely to draw his salary, but to perform "hard, very hard work" which made him feel "more like going out in the grass than anything else." [36]

Moreover, a careful reading of most of Tillman's speeches

[33] *Id.* to George S. Legaré, December 18, 1912, *ibid.*

[34] "Tattler," "The Broken Pitchfork," *loc. cit.,* 694.

[35] McGhee, "Tillman, Smasher of Traditions," *loc. cit.,* 8020.

[36] Orangeburg speech, reported in Charleston *News and Courier,* June 15, 1900.

in the Senate proves that he was radical only in the choice of words and in the injection of personalities. A sensational press deliberately exhibited the South Carolinian at his worst and distorted his intentions. His speeches were more restrained, more convincing and less fervid in the reading than in the usual inflammatory delivery. In cold print his vigorous flow of words revealed a mind that could think clearly and comprehensively and that was, in actual expression, conservative and even reactionary. His patriotism was narrowly conventional; he had a wholesome respect for private property and aversion for more than a limited application of the principle of public ownership. His hatred for Wall Street was not irresponsible; it was the logical counterpart of his love for the agrarian South. If he pioneered the modern reactionary attitude toward the Negro, he did not abuse other racial or religious minorities, even admonishing those who attacked Jews and Catholics. Violent in his attacks on certain men and institutions, he carefully limited his field. He had no program of comprehensive reform.

When Tillman cried at the Republican senators, "In politics you are the most infamous cowards and hypocrites who ever happened," there was general laughter.[37] His Pickwickian sense of humor made it possible for him to be the best of friends privately with senators against whom he raved mightily in public. He often laughed with an antagonist over words just uttered.[38] At times he assumed the role of a minstrel. But levity did not crowd out serious obligations. "If they think I am going to be the clown in this circus, they are mightily mistaken," he said of those who laughed when he assumed management of the railroad rate bill of 1906.[39]

If hot temper frequently led him astray, no senator more

[37] Charleston *News and Courier*, February 23, 1902.
[38] Larner, *ibid.*, June 10, 1900.
[39] Cited in [anonymous], "Men & Work—Tillman without the Pitchfork," *loc. cit.*, 15.

quickly made amends. He allowed harsh phrases to be stricken from the *Congressional Record,* apologized for bad conduct, and graciously accepted corrections from better disciplined colleagues. He harbored few grudges.[40]

Contemporary critics recognized distinct values in Tillman's tempestuous manners. Someone was needed, they said, to put direct questions, to shake dry bones, to cut red tape, and to rip veils; someone was needed on occasion to "make a few remarks on the general cussedness of the situation." Tillman supplied this need abundantly. Daunted by nothing, he possessed the necessary brute force and pungency of phrase to make his courage effective. He courted debate with Spooner, Foraker, Nelson W. Aldrich, and Boies Penrose, the ablest debaters of their generation. His tough hide absorbed unflinchingly the sharp counterthrusts to his bold assaults. Discreet senators had a sneaking fondness for this Huckleberry Finn of debate.[41] They crowded the Senate chamber when he "broke loose" because he said things, sometimes grimly, sometimes humorously, but always interestingly, which they thought should be said but dared not utter. They were at heart delighted that this outspoken farmer tore through conventions to make smashing assaults upon the great and the powerful. Tillman was not one of the unpopular members of the Senate.

Senatorial colleagues recognized the peculiar virtues of the senator from South Carolina. Although they could not unreservedly admire a man so blatantly unparliamentary and so destructive in criticisms, they were not old ladies unable to distinguish between unessential vices and essential virtues. As successful politicians they were masters of the art of getting on with others, tolerant, gracious, able to extract the kernel of usefulness from the most refractory. They learned to use effectively whatever in Tillman was

---

[40] Gilson Gardner, "The Real Senator Tillman," in *Independent* (New York), XLI (1906), 68–70.

[41] Springfield (Mass.) *Republican,* cited in *Literary Digest,* XXXII (1906), 147.

pleasing and serviceable: his industry, his good humor, and his searching frankness. They allowed him to become actually as well as officially a member of that fraternity of gentlemen known as the Senate.

George F. Hoar, a mild-mannered representative of New England's best and the unofficial keeper of the dignity of the Senate, naturally regarded Tillman at first as "a wild man from Borneo," fit only for the company of Bryan and John P. Altgeld. The New Englander's face was often crimsoned by the Southerner's indiscretions, and he often assumed the duty of correcting him. Nevertheless, Tillman had not been in Washington more than two or three years before a mild friendship developed between the two men. The Southerner, despite his boasted democracy, was quick to pay undisguised fealty to the aristocracy of breeding and learning. Hoar, for his part, was moved to a revision of judgment when he learned Tillman's merits. They exchanged literary experiences; the cultured New Englander was pleased to find the Southerner a ready learner. As old-fashioned patriots they engaged in friendly arguments on the relative importance of South Carolina and Massachusetts in the building of the nation.[42]

Tillman's best friend among the senators was another New Englander, as different from him as Hoar. This was William E. Chandler of New Hampshire, as uncompromising a Northerner and Republican as Tillman was a Southerner and Democrat. In the South Carolinian's youth Chandler had been known as "Old Bill" Chandler, and had been despised because of his part in Reconstruction.[43] Yet Tillman and this man learned to love each other. Thrown together on the Senate Committee on Naval Affairs, the

[42] Tillman to Thomas P. Ivy, February 24, 1917, in Tillman Papers. For comments on the relations between the two senators, see Creelman, "A Defender of the Senate," loc. cit., 622; "Tattler," "The Broken Pitchfork," loc. cit., 694.

[43] Tillman to William E. Chandler, September 30, 1912, in Tillman Papers.

New Englander was attracted by Tillman's humor and industry, and the Southerner admired Chandler's sincerity
and parliamentary skill. He was the senator who called
most frequently at the Tillmans' Washington apartment.[44]

Another friend was John C. Spooner, ablest among the
debaters and constitutional lawyers who controlled the
Senate. This Wisconsin senator clashed with the South
Carolinian more frequently than any other senator. He
usually got the better of the argument. His rapier was more
flexible than the bludgeon of his burley antagonist. But
Tillman enjoyed nothing better than to cross arms with this
brilliant swordsman. A sly humor always pervaded their
mightiest clash of principles. After battles they often retired arm-in-arm, and Spooner was numbered among the
few who passed evenings in the Tillman apartment.[45]

Among the Democrats Tillman's close friend was Augustus O. Bacon of Georgia. Here again the attraction was
between opposites. The Georgian was a Bourbon aristocrat
as refined and conventional as Tillman was homespun and
nonconforming. They took long walks together and discovered mutual satisfaction in conversations about books, music, and politics. They were known affectionately to each
other as "My Lord Bacon" and "the Old Man." [46]

By 1906 Tillman had adjusted himself to the Washington environment sufficiently to express admiration for the
Senate as an institution. When he first came to Washington, he said that he had honestly believed "the Senators
were generally corrupt or corruptible" but now he was
convinced "that, with rare exceptions, the Senators are
honest and patriotic personally." [47] He extolled the Senate

[44] *Id.* to *id.*, November 25, 1911, *ibid.; Cong. Record,* 64 Cong., 1 Sess.,
236. *Cf.* Leon B. Richardson, *William E. Chandler, Republican* (New York,
1940), 540–45, 646.

[45] Charleston *News and Courier,* July 4, 1918; R. H. Faxon, in Hutchin-
son (Kans.) *Daily News,* March 3, 1906; unidentified Washington newspaper,
1906, in Tillman Scrapbooks.

[46] Tillman, in *Cong. Record,* 63 Cong., 3 Sess., 300.

[47] Tillman statement, in Tillman Papers.

as "the most august deliberative assembly in the world" and as "the last forum of freedom in this country." Invoking the platitudes of Madison and Hamilton, he called it a balance wheel, "the only bulwark against revolution." [48]

After Tillman had served in the Senate some six or eight years, journalists commonly asserted that he had changed; that association with gentlemen had tamed him; that he was no longer the fiery farmer brandishing the pitchfork; that the onetime Bombastes Furioso had become a champion of traditions. There was truth in these claims. Experience had taught the senator that screams, threats, and imputations accomplish little. He had learned to seek and enjoy the esteem that distinguished colleagues were willing to give him and had discovered the advantages of the reciprocation of charity. He relished the prestige of Senate membership; the salary meant much to one of his modest antecedents and tastes. Literally, the senator grew fat, as his pictures show, gradually acquiring the sleekness of the conventional statesmen. And he fattened intellectually; he became reconciled with things as they were; in a moderate but certain fashion he was getting his share of the swill at the public trough and was satisfied.[49]

But it is a mistake to press the thesis of a fundamental change in the senator's nature. Perhaps the Senate and the public had changed rather than Tillman. To hint corruption in high places was no longer profanation. The age of the muckrakers had come. Moreover, as time passed, Tillman's better qualities received more adequate recognition. His explosive remarks and boorish manners were soft-pedaled, and his honesty of purpose and solidity of character were emphasized. Yet, until illness incapacitated him, he remained the rough and tumble fighter with waving arms and snapping jaws; he continued to denounce the great

---

[48] Unidentified Sunday newspaper, April 29, 1916, in Tillman Scrapbooks.
[49] Undated statement, *ibid.*

corporations, to snarl at the President, and to fulminate against the Negro.

Whether or not Tillman's comportment improved with years, he certainly became more respected. As early as 1900 the Springfield *Republican* discovered that he was "a decent sort of man," and the New York *Evening Post* extolled his honesty, ability, and wit.[50] It is significant that in 1902 the press was by no means unanimous in condemning him for striking McLaurin. At that time the Washington *Post* declared that he was "as honest as he is bold, as sincere and incorruptible as he is aggressive." [51] When in 1906 he was placed in charge of the railroad rate bill, the newspapers made him into a minor hero. Immediately before his first illness in 1908 he was at the apogee of his fame as a senator. He was suggested for Vice-President; he was called one of the three most popular men in the country; mention of his name on the streets of Washington brought comments about his honesty and fearlessness; [52] and when illness forced his absence from his Senate seat, there was almost universal regret.[53]

Such was Tillman. Some assert his behavior was a bid for stage effect. Like most politicians, he knew that the ears of the groundlings were tickled by the tragicomic role of a bad, blunt man. But it is not fair to say that the parliamentary behavior of so serious a man was mere affectation. His bad manners were as true to his nature and upbringing as his good qualities. His one eye, his menacing countenance, rasping voice, rough tongue, careless dress, and impulsive acts were genuine Tillman traits, which found expression without pose or artifice. Association with polished gentlemen softened him somewhat, but as long as his health permitted he remained basically the same.

[50] Cited in Charleston *News and Courier*, October 8, 1900.
[51] *Ibid.*, February 27, 1902.
[52] "T. D. H.," in Spartanburg *Herald*, February 12, 1908.
[53] *Id., ibid.*, April 5, December 12, 15, 1908.

Perhaps Ben Tillman's failure to develop the usual good manners of a statesman prevented an unconscious betrayal of the tradition he represented. Would not Honest Ben of the South Carolina farmers have become a sort of Dishonest Ben had he grown conventional and mannerly? The tendency to be a colorless gentleman crept upon him, but he did not succumb to the tempter, did not allow himself to grow "too big for his breeches." Faithful to the plain rough people who had elevated him, he willed to remain the Honest Barbarian who would win respect on his own terms. That he succeeded was due to his solid integrity and to the discriminating tolerance of the Senate.

Chapter II

THE EDGEFIELD TILLMANS

BENJAMIN RYAN TILLMAN was born on August 11, 1847, at Chester, the country seat of his parents, Sophia Ann Hancock and Benjamin Ryan Tillman I, in Edgefield District, South Carolina.

Edgefield was then an extensive area lying beside the Savannah River, halfway between the mountains and the sea. It had been settled by pre-Revolutionary migrants from Virginia. Among its inhabitants the South Carolina character was "more intense, more fiery" than elsewhere, and men sometimes spoke and acted too quickly.[1] Certainly they possessed a reputation for lawlessness. "Another murder in Edgefield!" cried Parson Mason L. Weems. "The Lord have mercy upon Old Edgefield! For surely it must be Pandemonium itself, and a very District of Devils!" [2] Two hundred cases were reported in the district's criminal docket for one year; [3] there was complaints of much card playing, Sabbathbreaking and profanity; one "did not have to go far to find either a fight or a frolic." [4]

The energies of the men of Edgefield were not entirely absorbed by pointless passions. They were restrained by a substantial prosperity based on the cultivation of new cotton lands and on diversified industries which included the

---

[1] William W. Ball, *The State that Forgot: South Carolina's Surrender to Democracy* (Indianapolis, 1932), 22.

[2] Mason L. Weems, *The Devil in Petticoats Or, God's Revenge Against Husband Killing* (New Ed., Saluda, S. C., 1935), 1.

[3] J. Belton O'Neall, cited in John A. Chapman, *History of Edgefield County from the Earliest Settlements to 1897* (Newberry, S. C., 1897), 174.

[4] *Ibid.*, 73, 74.

Graniteville cotton mills. They were given a sense of direction by a coterie of planters and lawyers who formed an aristocracy of good manners and culture. "No interior bar of South Carolina," wrote Judge J. Belton O'Neall of an ante-bellum decade, "presented abler counsellors than there appeared in the Edgefield courts." [5] There were academies in which one could acquire the rudiments of English and Latin,[6] and many of their graduates had both the means and the will to attend Northern colleges. Fine houses were plentifully equipped with books which did not molder on their shelves. The early volumes of the Edgefield *Advertiser* were filled with essays so cultured and bookish that, were they not dominated by local prejudices, the reader could scarcely believe they sprang from so rural an environment.

This combination of passion and learning made Edgefield the home of veritable galaxy of leaders of the type that flourished in the South during the "fire-eating" years of proslavery aggressiveness. The district, says a flattering historian, "had more dashing, brilliant, romantic figures, statesmen, orators, soldiers, adventurers, daredevils, than any county of South Carolina, if not of any rural county in America." [7] There lived George McDuffie, leader of nullification; and thence went James Bonham and William B. Travis, defenders of the Alamo; Pierce Mason Butler, the commander of the Palmetto Regiment in the Mexican War; and Louis T. Wigfall, a manslayer who, as United States senator from Texas, was the most fiery of the secessionists. Edmund Bacon, the "Ned Brace" of Judge Augustus B. Longstreet's *Georgia Scenes*, was an Edgefield man, as were Andrew P. Butler, the senator whom Charles Sumner arraigned so bitterly; Preston S. Brooks, who exacted vengeance upon the person of Sumner for his impudent words;

[5] J. Belton O'Neall, *Biographical Sketches of the Bench and Bar of South Carolina* (Charleston, 1859), II, 279.

[6] Chapman, *History of Edgefield County,* 26–29.

[7] Ball, *State that Forgot,* 22.

and Francis W. Pickens, the governor who led South Carolina through the fateful ordeal of secession.

The men of Edgefield supported enthusiastically the aggressive attitude of their leaders. They blustered over nullification, vindicated Brooks with their unanimous vote, left the Union in 1860 with a shout, and, in the war years which followed, struggled as one man against the Northern invaders. Yet there was an important cause of social cleavage. Conscious of a superior urbanity, the courthouse cluster built a somewhat disdainful social fortress against both the planters and the lesser folk of the surrounding countryside. Even the wealthier rural families did not indulge in much hospitality, because distances were great and the red-clay roads were almost impassable. The country people remained rustics without the graces necessary for the courthouse society, and the more resourceful among them returned suspicion for disdain.

The Tillmans were products of this Edgefield environment. Like many of their neighbors, they migrated from Virginia before the Revolution, fought on the patriot side in that struggle, received land grants and, in the flush times of the first decades of the nineteenth century, became extensive landowners. They combined the characteristic lawlessness of "bloody Edgefield" with more than their share of the local intellectuality. They were readers who were capable of debating vehemently on political and literary topics. In a sense they were as aristocratic as any of their neighbors; they owned slaves and broad acres. But the Tillmans were country people, as free and lawless as they were strong-minded and proud. Isolated from the polite circle of Edgefield Village by miles of hills miry with red clay, they were not social climbers and expressed no open resentment against that group. Their situation, however, was one of potential opposition.

The various branches of the Tillman family stem from

an Englishman named Christopher Tilghman or Tillman, who established himself in Accomac County, Virginia, at the early date of 1638. His ancestors are reputed to have come to England from Germany; they settled in County Kent and possessed a coat of arms. The descendants of Christopher scattered in all directions. Those who remained in Virginia became substantial if not distinguished citizens. One branch settled in Somerset County, Maryland, where, apparently in imitation of the distinguished and aristocratic family of Queen Anne and Talbot counties, they retained the spelling of the name as Tilghman; but they were only remotely related to the Tilghmans of Queen Anne and Talbot counties.[8] Others settled in Tennessee, Alabama, Arkansas, Georgia, and various sections of South Carolina, where, as is often the case with a Southern family above the rank of "poor whites," a goodly number became men of distinction.

George Tillman, a grandson of the original Christopher Tillman, was in the eighteenth century an extensive planter and slaveholder in Brunswick County, Virginia. George's grandson was George Stephen Tillman who, after some years' experience on lands inherited from his grandfather in Brunswick, moved in 1750 to the region later known as Edgefield District. According to family tradition he joined the patriot side in the Revolution as a captain under Colonel William Washington, and was killed in 1781 at the Siege of Ninety Six. Three of his sons, Fred-

---

[8] Christopher Tilghman, or Tillman, and Richard Tilghman, the first of the distinguished Maryland family of his name, had as their latest common ancestor an Englishman named Nicholaus Tilghman. Christopher was the sixth in direct line of descent from Nicholaus, and Richard was ninth in this direct line. This means that the progenitors of the two American families were only remote cousins and that their respective descendants were only very, very remote cousins. The illuminating work of Stephen F. Tillman, *Records and Genealogy of the Tilghman, Tillman, Tilman, Tilmon Family, 1225–1938* (Ann Arbor, Mich., 1939), 1–2, 8–9, 33, 123, 273, clears up the confusion of the Maryland relationship. Ben Tillman was caught in this misunderstanding, never clearly knowing whether or not he was kin to the Tilghmans of Queen Anne and Talbot counties.

erick, Littlebury, and Stephen, likewise served the patriot cause; they were privates in Captain John Ryan's company of South Carolina Rangers.[9] In 1785 they received land grants from the state of South Carolina along Horne's Creek in Edgefield.[10] Littlebury moved to another state, leaving Stephen and Frederick behind to become the founders of the Edgefield branches of the Tillman family. Frederick's grant consisted of 391 acres in the heavily wooded and unusually hilly region on the stage road midway between Edgefield Courthouse and Augusta, Georgia. Here he established himself as a farmer and took as his wife Annsybil Miller, who was unable to sign her name to the will of her modest estate.[11] He named the youngest of his five sons for Benjamin Ryan, a friend and neighbor who was a brother of Captain John Ryan.[12]

On May 14, 1823, thirteen years after his father's death, Benjamin Ryan Tillman I married Sophia Ann Hancock, the granddaughter of Dionysius Oliver, a distinguished Revolutionary leader who had commanded a privateer and served under General Benjamin Lincoln at Savannah. From his home in Elbert County, Georgia, his daughter Martha had in 1792 ridden away as the bride of Thomas Hancock, an Edgefield farmer. Sophia was the daughter of this couple. At the time of her marriage she was fifteen and her husband was twenty.[13]

The young couple established themselves on the hereditary lands of the Tillmans and began a married life of

[9] This was shown by Frederick's military compensation receipt for £368, September 30, 1785; Stephen's for £442, September 28, 1785; and Littlebury's for an unspecified sum, January 6, 1786. Revolutionary Stubs (Library of the South Carolina Historical Commission, Columbia).

[10] South Carolina Grant Books (Office of the South Carolina Secretary of State, Columbia), 1784–1786, XII, 577; XLII, 98; LVI, 78, 214.

[11] This, however, may have been due to absence or illness instead of illiteracy. Edgefield County, South Carolina, Record of Wills (Edgefield Courthouse), II, BC (1817–1835), 437.

[12] See complete genealogy, in Tillman, *Records and Genealogy*, 51.

[13] *Ibid.*, 63; James E. Saunders, *Early Settlers of Alabama* (New Orleans, 1899), 428–30.

twenty-six years which, measured by practical standards, was emphatically successful. In 1840 they purchased as the family homestead a house and farm of 1,864 acres, adjoining their original lands and costing $8,035.[14] Chester, as the house was called, was a plain but dignified story-and-a-half structure of twelve rooms, with narrow halls and stairs. Although it possessed none of the legendary splendors of the ante-bellum Southern mansion, it was both in quality and size above the modest average of the Tillmans' landholding neighbors. Its one concession to beauty was a yard of roses, evergreen shrubs, and bulbous flowers.[15]

Instead of making their home a center of hospitality in the fabulous Southern manner, the master and mistress of Chester used it for commercial purposes. It became an inn for the accommodation of passengers at the halfway stops of the triweekly stage between Edgefield Courthouse and Augusta. But this thrifty couple was still more absorbed in the problem of increasing their slaves and improving their lands. They became the owners of fifty slaves [16] and the producers of a hundred or more bales of cotton annually. The Tillmans were highly pleased with their goodly acres. "I have," wrote a son who had traversed the Southwest, "seane no lands that eaquals Chester, . . . which is the garden spot of the world. It has many advantages, and is so well sittuated, and such a good out let for stock. And it is so well wartered that I would not give it for no sittuation that I have seane." [17] Benjamin Ryan Tillman I was, according to the standards of the times, a rich man—a planter with

14 Deed of the executors of John Fox to Benjamin R. Tillman I, Edgefield County, South Carolina, Deed Book (Edgefield Courthouse), BBB, 430.

15 For descriptions of Chester, see Royal G. Shannonhouse, in Columbia *Record*, July 14, 1918; Frances Miller Tillman to Tillman, May 25, 1864, in Tillman Papers; Tillman to Shannonhouse, December 12, 1916, *ibid.*

16 Actually 49 in 1850. United States Census of 1840, South Carolina, Edgefield District (Bureau of the Census, Washington).

17 Thomas F. Tillman to Benjamin R. Tillman I, Vera Cruz, Mexico, April 10, 1847, in Tillman Papers.

numerous slaves and broad acres, self-made, but a potential aristocrat.

For several reasons this man did not take the place in the polite society of Edgefield Courthouse to which his wealth seemingly entitled him. Much of his energy was utilized in the care of his large family of three daughters and seven sons.[18] Instead of falling under the influence of one of the prevailing faiths of his community, he isolated himself from his neighbors by espousing a strange creed. He was a Universalist amid orthodox Baptists and Methodists.[19] Additional energies of this versatile man were absorbed, strangely enough, by lawlessness. He was so fond of gambling that he felt constrained to take an oath not to practice this diversion.[20] In 1847 he killed a man, a deed which might have led to punishment had he been less wealthy or lived in a community less violent.[21] He was something of a dandy in manners and dress and was fond of reading religious books. Moreover, he had cultural ambitions for his sons. He sent one to Harvard, and by precept and liberal provision in his will attempted to educate the others. He died November 6, 1849, of typhoid fever, aged forty-six.[22] Ben, his youngest son, was then only two years old, too young in fact to retain a tangible impression of his father.[23]

Sophia Ann Hancock Tillman, who spent a long widow-

[18] The three daughters were Martha Annsybil, born August 5, 1828; Anna Sophia, born December 28, 1837; and Frances Miller, born April 16, 1840. Another daughter, Harriet Susan, born February 11, 1831, died in infancy on May 5, 1832. See Tillman, *Records and Genealogy*, 63.

[19] There were only three Universalist churches in South Carolina in 1850.

[20] This curious record was seen by the author and others in the courthouse at Edgefield, but the author in a second search for identification was not able to rediscover it.

[21] See brief record of the expenses of the trial, in Tillman Papers.

[22] His will of July 15, 1846, Edgefield County, South Carolina, Record of Wills, II, D, 407–409. The description of the elder Tillman is partly based on an interview with John E. Swearingen, a grandson, at Columbia, December 25, 1938.

[23] Tillman to his sister, Mrs. Frances Miller Tillman Simpson, March 3, 1914, in Tillman Papers.

hood of twenty-seven years as mistress of Chester, was amply able to assume the burdens of plantation and family which her husband left behind. "My mother," Ben afterwards wrote, "had a commanding figure, was about five feet, eight inches high, well proportioned and stately. She had a correct carriage with her shoulders thrown back; and a more queenly woman I have never seen. She was a very Juno." [24] Sophia was energetic and ambitious, accomplishing everything expected of the woman of the ante-bellum plantation as well as many tasks expected of the man. She nursed ill slaves, supervised the education of her children, taught her daughters to sew, and personally managed extensive planting and lumbering operations. She worked so hard that her children were concerned over her health. [25] Withal, she was a niggardly and sagacious businesswoman. As rich as she was, on her business trips to Augusta she hitched her horse in Hamburg and walked across the bridge into the city to avoid paying toll. By 1860 she had increased her slaves from fifty to eighty-six [26] and her landholdings from 1,800 to 3,500 acres. She was among the wealthiest persons in Edgefield District; she was the richest farmer in her neighborhood. Thirty of her slaves were African-born Negroes who had been smuggled into the interior in 1858 from the ship *Wanderer*. [27]

Ben was the favorite child, the "petted darling of his mother's heart." "She was," he often declared in later life,

---

24 *Id.,* "My Childhood Days," *ibid.*
25 Anna Sophia Tillman to Tillman, n.d. (sometime during the Civil War), *ibid.*
26 United States Census of 1860, South Carolina, Edgefield District, I, 434 (Bureau of the Census).
27 Tillman, in *Cong. Record,* 57 Cong., 2 Sess., 2565; *id.,* in Spartanburg *Herald,* November 22, 1906; *id.,* "My Childhood Days," in Tillman Papers; *id.* to Sallie Mae Tillman, September 14, 1913, *ibid.; id.* to Mrs. George T. McKie, August 23, 1916, *ibid.* Between 1850 and 1860 Mrs. Tillman's lands increased from 2,200 to 3,500 acres and the value of her total farm properties from $16,950 to $39,160. See United States Census of Agriculture, 1850, South Carolina, Edgefield County, Hamburg Township, 41 (State Library, State House, Columbia).

"the strongest minded, best balanced woman I ever met, and to *her* I owe whatever of ability and judgment I have in life." She taught him habits of thrift and industry; to be ambitious; to despise shams, hypocrisy, and untruthfulness; to bear trouble and sorrow with resolution. "She used to slap my jaws for telling a lie, and she switched me everytime she caught me 'shenanoging.' " [28]

It was well that this mother was so strong, for she was visited with enough sorrow and tragedy to break any but the stoutest heart.

Her oldest son, Thomas Frederick, against his mother's will, joined Captain Preston S. Brooks's company of the Old Ninety Six Boys of the Palmetto Regiment for service in the Mexican War. He suffered many difficulties in Mexico, among which was a threatened court-martial for taking horses from the natives; he was killed at Churubusco on August 20, 1847, nine days after the birth of Ben. His name, along with those of three other Tillmans, appears on the monument in the State House grounds in Columbia honoring the dead of the Palmetto Regiment.[29]

Two years and forty-eight days later Mrs. Tillman's husband died prematurely.

George Dionysius, her second son, brought trouble on himself. He was twenty-one years older than Ben and acted as a second father to the Tillman children. Their pet name for him was "Bud Nashe." Erratic and brilliant, he eagerly took to books, and after preparatory training in Penfield, Georgia, entered Harvard in the autumn of 1845 but left before the first Christmas. The bells of Harvard, this rustic bookworm complained, interfered with his studies! He would direct his own education. This he did by reading law

[28] Tillman, "My Childhood Days," in Tillman Papers; Saunders, *Early Settlers of Alabama*, 430.

[29] Chapman, *History of Edgefield County*, 511; interview with Swearingen, December 25, 1938; Thomas F. Tillman to Benjamin R. Tillman I, Vera Cruz, Mexico, April 10, 1847, in Tillman Papers; *id.* to *id.*, 1847, originally published in Pendleton *Messenger* and copied *ibid.*

at Edgefield Courthouse in the office of Chancellor Francis
H. Wardlaw and by accumulating a miscellaneous library.
"There was hardly a subject you could mention," Ben later
wrote, "he did not know something about." But it could
scarcely be claimed that he was well educated. His mind
was a storehouse of disjointed information; his speech was
a quaint mixture of pedantry and plantation vulgarity; and
his many plans, political, industrial, agricultural, or otherwise, were a curious confusion of the realistic and the
prophetic.

George D. Tillman began the practice of law at Edgefield
Courthouse in 1848. His large stature and interesting if
homely face differentiated him. His rough congeniality, his
aggressiveness, and his loud and careless manner made him
popular among the country people. They gave him a large
practice and in 1854 elected him to the legislature.[30] But
he was disliked by the upper circle of Edgefield Village.
This was partly the natural aversion of a well-mannered
group for a boorish countryman whose views on public
questions were unconventional and disturbing if not revolutionary. The dislike was also personal. In good humor he
was congenial enough, but he grew contentious and dangerous when angered, which led him into "numerous personal encounters." [31]

The first of these encounters was with John R. Wever, a
brigadier general of militia and popular spendthrift and
politician to whom George gave a "dangerous pistol wound
in the side." [32] Next came the wounding of a man named
Wells and a fight with Preston S. Brooks. Then, a few days
after George announced as a candidate for re-election to
the legislature, in a passion induced by a game of faro, he

[30] Edgefield *Advertiser*, October 12, 1854.
[31] Chapman, *History of Edgefield County*, 203, says, "When George D.
Tillman first went to Edgefield Court House to live and to practice law,
he made himself very unpopular in the town . . . and had many enemies."
[32] *Ibid.*, 75, 203.

shot and killed Henry Christian, an unoffending mechanic who was a mere bystander at the game. Although the crime was unpremeditated, the culprit fled the country, vainly pursued by proclamations calling him "an unprincipled wretch." [33] As Ben said, he literally "became a wanderer on the face of the earth," first visiting California and later joining William Walker's unsuccessful filibustering expedition to Nicaragua. After suffering from imprisonment and tropical diseases, he accepted the first opportunity to return home. The winter of 1858 found him once more under his mother's roof, a disillusioned adventurer. During the day he hid himself upstairs amid his books, emerging at night to take long walks with Ben. Tired of hiding and repentant of his crime, he surrendered to the sheriff of Edgefield, and at the March term of court, 1858, was convicted of manslaughter and sentenced to two years in the Edgefield jail and to a $2,000 fine.[34] The jailor treated him more like an honored guest than a felon, allowing him comfortable quarters, overnight visits from his brother Ben, the pursuit of a courtship, and the resumption of those phases of his practice not requiring attendance at court. When, in March, 1860, he completed his sentence, he was welcomed back into the Edgefield court by the presiding judge. In sincere remorse over his crime, he helped support the daughters of his victim. Seven months after leaving jail he married Margaret Jones, an heiress of the masculine type as capable as George's mother of managing her broad acres. His reputation was seemingly restored, for Edgefield was not intolerant of one who repented of an unplanned homicide.[35]

Sophia Tillman had scarcely recovered from the anguish

---

[33] Edgefield *Advertiser,* July 23, 30, August 20, 1856.
[34] *Ibid.,* March 10, 17, 1856.
[35] Tillman, "My Childhood Days," in Tillman Papers; Edgefield *Advertiser,* March 13, 1861; discriminating obituary by Narciso G. Gonzales, in Columbia *State,* February 3, 1901; interview with Swearingen, December 25, 1938.

of George's misdeed before other troubles befell her. In 1859 Henry Cummings, described as the brightest and most bookish of her sons, died of typhoid fever in his fifteenth year. John Miller, her third son, was described as "handsome as an Adonis"; but he possessed "a very ungovernable temper and was naturally tyrannical in his disposition," and as a consequence developed into a wild and dissipated man. While George was away on his wanderings, said Ben, John "lorded over my mother and the other children to his heart's content." Of what happened after George's return from Nicaragua, Ben related, "I recall as yesterday a scene I witnessed between the two sons. . . . George was the natural protector of my mother and the children. . . . He resented John's tyranny. . . . When George took him to task about it, he threatened to kill him [George], and went and got his pistol. George tore his shirt open and said, 'Shoot, you damned coward. You are afraid to shoot, for no brave man ever treated a widow and orphans as you have done.' After waiting for a minute with his bared bosom open, he turned and walked upstairs, and John slunk off." [36] This was in 1858. Two years later John met death at the hands of two brothers, the honor of whose family he had impugned.[37] In the same way Oliver Hancock, another son, not so brilliant as John but more levelheaded, was killed in Florida during a quarrel over a domestic difficulty.[38] A sorrowing mother inscribed the following defiant dirge upon the tomb of the slain boys:

Now is done thy long day's work
Fold thy palms across thy breast,
Fold thine arms, turn to thy rest.
Let them rave.

[36] Tillman, "My Childhood Days," in Tillman Papers.
[37] He was killed May 6, 1860, by John C. and George R. Mays. Edgefield *Advertiser,* October 10, 1860.
[38] He was killed December 29, 1860. Tillman, "My Childhood Days," in Tillman Papers.

On the heels of these tragedies, Sophia Tillman was confronted with the risk of every patriotic mother: the possible sacrifice of her three remaining sons in the maw of war. Ben, not yet fourteen at the outbreak of the Civil War, was too young to be expected to enter the army immediately. But warlike Edgefield expected service of George and his brother James Adams, aged thirty-five and nineteen, respectively. George, however, argued against enlistment. "Three of our family," he reminded Ben and James, "have been food for bullets. Let us try at least to avoid a similar fate." Besides, considering the youth of the two boys, he felt that they should continue in school for the time being and wait until a later phase of what he believed would be a protracted struggle "to fight and act like men, patriots, citizens, and soldiers." As for himself, he submitted that he had only recently assumed the responsibilities of a family, and knew, from Nicaraguan experience, what war was.[39] It was natural that his mother and sisters should echo these words. The war, his sister Anna wrote James, "is a great calamity to befall us now, and many a poor mother's heart is wrung with anguish. . . . Jimmie, my dear brother, we have had enough of our family's blood spilled, and you have an old mother and sisters who are dependent on you for protection." [40]

The result was that not one of the Tillman brothers answered the first call to the colors. But a year after the beginning of hostilities, the two older ones assumed the inevitable duty of patriots. George joined the artillery operating near Charleston. Fortunately for his family's peace of mind, his services were uneventful and were interrupted by his election to the legislature in 1864.

The Tillmans enjoyed no such emotional peace out of James's services. On March 20, 1862, he joined Ellison Capers' regiment as a private, and within two years was so

39 George D. Tillman to Tillman, May 5, 1861, *ibid.*
40 Anna Tillman to James A. Tillman, April 14, 1861, *ibid.*

liked by the soldiers that he was made commanding officer of his company. His eager participation in the bloody battles of the Hood-Johnston campaign in Tennessee and Georgia caused his mother grave anxiety. When in May, 1864, she received news that he had been wounded,[41] she and Ben rushed to Atlanta, where they found him after a weary search of many hospitals. They nursed him back to health. Fresh exposures caused the mother such additional concern that she was made positively ill.[42] The Tillmans were elated by the news that Colonel Capers had cited James for "gallant conduct" on November 29, 1864, in the Battle of Franklin. Observing that Capers had fallen wounded in the charge of his regiment against the position of the Ninety-seventh Ohio Volunteer Infantry, young Tillman, after crying to his commander, "Put your hat on your sword and wave it, and your men will go over the ditch," led his company over the works and captured the Ohio regiment's flag and some forty prisoners.[43] The war over, he returned home with both arms shattered and stiffened from terrible wounds, to die within the year.[44]

Thus in the course of two decades a full measure of sorrow had befallen Sophia Tillman. Death, violent death in three or four instances, had taken husband and five sons from her, and tragic misfortune had seared the life of her son George. Only Ben among seven sons remained untouched by life-destroying mishap. As a member of a proud clan Mrs. Tillman felt deeply aggrieved that the Edgefield authorities should have seen fit to impose a sentence on a man of George's standing; her resentment was doubled by the fact that the local lawyers did not favor his unconditional

---

[41] *The War of the Rebellion: A Compilation of the Official Records of the Union and Confederate Armies,* 129 vols. and index (Washington, 1880–1901), Ser. I, Vol. XXXVIII, Pt. I, 713. Cited hereafter as *Official Records.*

[42] Fannie M. Tillman to Tillman, May 25, 1864, in Tillman Papers.

[43] *Official Records,* Ser. I, Vol. XLV, Pt. I, 737–38; Chapman, *History of Edgefield County,* 372.

[44] The inscription on the tomb reads: "Died June 8, 1866, of a disease contracted in the army."

pardon.[45] But she kept steadfast to industry and duty, sustained by her own will and the devotion of Ben.

[45] Francis W. Pickens and other lawyers proposed that he be pardoned on condition that he leave the state. "But Bud Nashe," commented Ben, "scorned any such condition." Tillman, "My Childhood Days," in Tillman Papers. According to George D. Tillman, Pickens as governor in 1861 removed his fine. George D. Tillman to Tillman, May 5, 1861, *ibid.*

Chapter III

AN EDGEFIELD CHILDHOOD

Ben TILLMAN'S youth stamped him indelibly with his Edgefield environment. He participated in the normal activities of his family and neighbors, thoroughly imbibed their legends and prejudices, and was moved profoundly by his community's experiences in war and politics. He took a wholesome part in the recreational life of his neighborhood. He learned to associate freely with Negroes on the master-and-servant basis considered proper in the South. His social and political attitudes were modified by the maturity of years and experience, but to the end of his days he remained fundamentally true to the convictions of childhood. "I am from Edgefield," he was always able to boast.

"I grew up wild as a jimpson weed," was the manner in which Tillman recalled participation in the rough sports of the Edgefield countryside. There were calmer games of course: a primitive type of baseball called bull pen, foot races, and marbles. "I was fine at marbles," he later recalled. "I could knock out the middle man . . . several times hand-running, and was always sought as a partner." There was swimming in a neighboring millpond and a limited amount of fishing in near-by brooks. Hunting in the spacious fields and forests surrounding Chester was the diversion which absorbed the boy most extensively. He became skilled with rifle and shotgun, bagging squirrels in the late summer and rabbits and partridges in the autumn and winter. His greatest delight, however, was 'possum hunting with trusted Negro friends. He had "one of the best 'possum dogs that ever barked up anybody's branch." Armed with bright lightwood torches, young Ben and the Negroes were in the habit of wandering sleepily half the night over field and through thicket until "the well known deep-throated bark" indicated to these experienced hunters that the dogs had treed their quarry. Then, there was a spirited rush forward, the felling of the tree, and the inevitable capture. The next day came the savory reward of roasted " 'possum and 'taters." [1]

Intimate association with his mother's Negroes fixed in this young slaveholder the prevailing attitude toward the darker race: a patronizing kindliness in which emotions of pity and contempt were freely mixed. He was dictatorial in his contacts with the subject race, brooking no contradictions and expressing his opinions in curt and profane sentences. That he thought the Africans a very inferior race is conveyed by his opinion of the slaves his mother acquired in 1858. They, he felt, were "the most miserable lot of human beings—the nearest to the missing link with the monkey—I have ever put my eyes on." [2] The limited but definite improvements of which he believed the slaves capable could be had only through contact with the white race; without this beneficent influence the blacks would lapse into barbarism. Yet he was too good a Southerner not to appreciate the virtues of the slaves. He associated with them cordially, especially the older ones. Fixed in his memory were tales of genial black hunting companions, faithful servants, and skillful carriage drivers—good men for whom he felt affection despite their black skins. "There is a thronging of names and faces: Old Dave, Sam, Stan, Charles, Mike, Luke, and scores of others," he later asserted in retrospect.[3]

---

[1] Tillman recounts his boyish diversions in "My Childhood Days," in Tillman Papers; in Tillman to H. E. Gray, November 20, 1917, *ibid.;* and in *Cong. Record,* 57 Cong., 2 Sess., 2564.

[2] *Cong. Record,* 57 Cong., 2 Sess., 2565.

[3] Tillman, "My Childhood Days," in Tillman Papers.

Patriotic legends fed his pride in family and class. Recounted by his mother over many nights, they concerned the "miserable rapine and outrage and murder" perpetrated by the British and their Tory allies. Women were robbed, beds were cut open and their feathers spread over yards, and chickens and hogs were shot to cause privation. There was the story of the Ryan neighbor who escaped from his Tory captor and shot him in a forest retreat. There was the "murder field" on his mother's plantation where a Tory had been hanged, and deep in the forest was the Shelving Rock under which Ben's grandmother, Annsybil Miller, nursed her brother while he was ill of smallpox and hiding from the British.[4] More immediate if less extensive were the tales of the services and sacrifices of the Tillmans in the Mexican War, which gave a confirming intensity to the boy's patriotism. Then in the middle of childhood came the stirring actualities of secession and civil war. Thereby was developed a love of country as strong as that of any of his associates.

Ben's formal education supplemented the outlook on life derived from the normal associations of his early years. There was no overeducation in the sense of training inconsistent with the narrow cultural heritage of his folk; there was no thought of painting, sculpture, or other arts strange to his rural environment, but only a little dancing and enough music to allow a modest tenor in a neighboring church. There was a touch of Greek and more experience with Latin grammar and literature. The intenser passions of the boy were reserved for English literature, both prose and poetry. His rural environment did not preclude a normal understanding of the great writers of the mother country. Edgefield was too English for that.

In the absence of a public school in the Tillman community, Ben's mother co-operated with two neighboring

---

[4] *Cong. Record,* 57 Cong., 1 Sess., 1118–19; Spartanburg *Herald,* November 22, 1906; Shannonhouse, in Columbia *Record,* July 14, 1918.

families in establishing a private school. Mrs. Tillman provided the schoolhouse and shared with the neighbors the payment of the teacher's salary. Following a prevailing habit of Southern planters, they secured teachers from the North. The first was Miss Annie Arthur, a graduate of Miss Emma Willard's Seminary at Troy, New York, and a sister of the man who was later to become a President of the United States. This "sweet, mild, gentle-faced woman" taught Ben how to read. The next teacher was Miss Lucy Mills, also a graduate of the Troy institution. "I loved her very dearly," Ben recalled, "and we used to take long walks together after school was out," through woods in which there were hummingbirds and squirrels and buckeye blossoms. The third teacher was an old man named Eli Sego, whose log schoolhouse was located two miles from Chester on the Augusta road. He was described by Ben as "the typical old-field schoolmaster." He taught the boy reading, writing, and arithmetic, and the beginnings of algebra.[5]

This early schooling was often retarded by the irregularity of the sessions and even by the complete absence of a teacher. At the age of thirteen, Ben tells us, he had never looked into an English grammar and had progressed in arithmetic only as far as long division, knowing nothing of fractions. But in compensation for these deficiencies, he early developed an intensive reading habit. There were two bookcases in the Tillman house, one containing the religious books of Ben's father, and the other, English classics belonging to John Tillman. The latter group, particularly Bulwer, Scott, and Marryat, Ben eagerly read. His greatest delight was Robert Bonner's weekly story paper, the New York *Ledger*, whose "thrilling novels" by Mrs. Southworth and Sylvanus Cobb, Jr., he devoured "with avidity and eagerness." "I and one of my brothers," he later recalled, "would race down the road for three miles to meet the stage and then slowly walk home, one doing the reading and

[5] Tillman, "My Childhood Days," in Tillman Papers.

the other listening." The result of these readings was the development of a vocabulary and an understanding of literature more extensive than those of most better-schooled boys of Ben's age.[6]

Recognition of the boy's ability and literary interests induced his mother to take a radical step to remedy his obvious educational deficiencies. In 1860 she sent him to Bethany, a modest boarding academy at Liberty Hill in the western part of Edgefield District which his brother James already was attending. Bethany was more deeply buried in the woods than Chester, but it had a solid repute due to the ability of its master, George Galphin, a graduate of the South Carolina College and a skilled and well-educated teacher. He was partly responsible for the education of such Edgefield celebrities as Matthew C. Butler, Martin W. Gary, and John C. Sheppard.

In two years of uninterrupted study under Galphin, Ben's progress brought satisfaction to himself and his family. With surprising facility he mastered the subtleties of advanced arithmetic, algebra, and geometry, and became proficient in the technicalities of English grammar and composition, a sound foundation for his vigorous prose of later years. With an enthusiasm almost as great, he triumphed over the intricacies of Latin, mastering the grammar and reading the works of Caesar and Sallust and the elegiacs of Virgil. He also began the study of Greek.

The Tillman family was proud of the progress of "my little Bud," as a sister affectionately called him. One wrote: "Don't relax in your efforts to gain an education. School days are precious golden moments and I want you to be an ornament to your family." [7] But as practical people they felt that material well-being must take precedence over education. So in 1863 Ben was ordered home for a year to

[6] *Ibid.*
[7] Unidentified sister to Tillman, May 8, 1862, in Tillman Papers. *Cf.* Anna Tillman to *id.,* September 16, 1860, *ibid.;* James A. Tillman to *id.,* May 8, 1862, *ibid.*

help his mother pay off debts incurred through the speculative adventures of her sons John and George. She had backed their somewhat promiscuous purchases of lands and slaves by endorsing their notes to the extent of $20,000, and in 1863 John was dead and George had joined James in the army. Ben, his mother's sole masculine support, busied himself with her affairs, riding about the country collecting old lumber debts and trying his skill in selling butter and eggs in the Graniteville and Augusta markets. Within a year he reduced the debt to $5,000. His success was due to his tireless efforts and to the fact that he dealt in the greatly depreciated currency of the Confederacy. At the same time he was not too preoccupied to neglect literary matters. During his year out of school he continued to read novels, especially those of Scott.[8]

In March, 1864, Ben returned to Bethany for what was supposed to be his final year of preparation for entrance into the South Carolina College but actually proved to be his last five months of formal schooling. Confident in his ability, the family urged him with hopeful advice. "Do, Bud," one wrote him, "study hard and make good use of your time. . . . I want you to do something for the Tillman name." [9] He lived in Galphin's home, where, because of the privations of war, conditions were hard. His lunch consisted of corn muffins and sorghum molasses, and his only lights were tallow candles and lightwood torches. He "thought of the hams, chickens and good things at home and was hungry, but was not unhappy." He found great pleasure in his studies, taking full advantage of the skilled guidance the master willingly bestowed upon him. Lying on Galphin's floor with his head resting upon a pile of books, he soon recovered what he had forgotten in his year's absence from school and was ready for rapid progress in un-

[8] Tillman, "My Childhood Days," *ibid.;* Spartanburg *Herald,* November 22, 1906.
[9] Anna Tillman to Tillman, April 10, 1864, in Tillman Papers; Fannie M. Tillman to *id.,* April 10, 1864, *ibid.*

familiar fields. He rushed through six books of the *Aeneid,*
much of Horace, and the *Anabasis* and progressed in advanced mathematics. He learned to read Latin without a
lexicon.[10]

His last day at Galphin's school was not a moment of triumph. As "the brag scholar" he was scheduled to be the
feature performer at the customary all-day commencement
exercises. His sister sent him the only broadcloth coat in
the family,[11] and he carefully rehearsed his projected recita-
tions in the woods. At the appointed time he read a selection
from Horace with fine effect. He had thought himself so
perfectly prepared to recite James Otis' "Sink or Swim"
that he had shipped his copy home. But he had not pro-
ceeded far when his treacherous schoolboy's memory went
blank. There could be no more speech. He fled from the
hall and was away for home on horseback before there
could be explanations. This childish humiliation was not
without significance in the life of a man who was later to
obtain fame as a public speaker.[12]

On the day in early July, 1864, when Ben quit school, he
lacked one month of being seventeen, an age at which the
law, if not patriotism, put a young man into the Southern
army. For reasons already enumerated, he had not followed
the example of those thousands who at fifteen or sixteen
had entered the regiments of the hard-pressed Confederacy.
In 1862 his remaining brothers had volunteered, and he
alone of seven sons remained to support his mother. But
neither Ben nor his mother could ignore the sacrificial call
of a nation struggling for existence. He was too good a South
Carolinian and too orthodox a slavemaster not to be stirred
by the mighty events around him. He had experienced the
excitement of secession and mobilization, and believed like
a true Rebel that all the courage was in the South and all

[10] Tillman, "My Childhood Days," *ibid.;* Spartanburg *Herald,* November
22, 1906.
[11] Fannie M. Tillman to Tillman, May 25, 1864, in Tillman Papers.
[12] Tillman, "My Childhood Days," *ibid.*

cowardice in the North. He shared his mother's anxieties over the fate of James and got his first view of the realities of war while accompanying her on the search for the wounded boy in Georgia. He endured the inconveniences of Confederate train service and witnessed the horror of almost endless rows of wounded men in the hospital wards. Observing a group of Federal prisoners on their way to Andersonville, he was filled with hatred for "these invaders of our homes and destroyers of our liberty." "They ought to be shot," was his first reaction. He had left school to join the army, and following the advice of his brothers,[13] sent his name to a certain Captain Dixon to be enrolled as a member of a company of artillery operating on the South Carolina coast.

An unfortunate visitation prevented the boy from fulfilling this obligation of patriotism. Six days after leaving school, he was attacked by violent pains in the left eye as he walked home in the hot sun after a three-hour swim in a millpond. Previously he had suffered from weakness of the eyes caused by study under Galphin's crude lighting conveniences. The bath and the walk in the sun were all that was needed to make the illness acute. The actual trouble was an abscess in the left socket, but a country doctor said it was erysipelas. The affected eye became inflamed and the patient was physically prostrated. "For two months," he later wrote, "I suffered the tortures of the damned. I was paralyzed on the left side for a week and suffered untold horrors and agonies." Then early in October while seemingly convalescing he was seized with convulsions caused, Tillman afterwards related, "by a sore at the base of the brain."[14] Two nights later Dr. H. H. Steiner, an army surgeon from Augusta, by candlelight, removed the inflamed eye and inserted a seton in the patient's neck. These heroic

[13] James Tillman to Sophia Tillman, July 15, 1864, *ibid.*
[14] It was a fibroid tumor caused by injudicious applications of tartar emetic and lard.

remedies, Tillman always believed, saved his life; but actual recovery was slow. Five months later Dr. Steiner reported that the patient was still experiencing "repeated attacks of epileptic convulsions," and it was not until August, 1865, that the seton was removed. Thereafter, he gradually recovered his natural good health.[15] Illness had had two permanent results. One, of course, was the loss of an eye; the other was the prevention of young Tillman's entering the war. In fact, the Confederate armies had disbanded many months before he was fit for even the lightest field service.[16]

Ben Tillman's boyhood had not been exceptional. He had participated in the diversions and labors common to his associates; his educational experiences had been traditional; he had shared the common patriotic and political emotions of the time and place. It is true that there had been death, tragedy, and illness in his life, but they were parts of the normal vicissitudes of existence. It is also true that his talents and industry gave promise of a career above that of the average boy of his neighborhood, but there was nothing in his experiences or aspirations tending to make him other than the country youth he was born. Ben Tillman was an Edgefield boy, with all the virtues and limitations characteristic of that typical area of the Carolina of the Civil War period.

[15] Tillman's account of his illness is best related in letters to Smythe, January 25, 1913, and to Shannonhouse, December 12, 1913, in Tillman Papers. See also, Shannonhouse, in Columbia *Record*, July 14, 1918.

[16] See Dr. H. H. Steiner's certificate of disability, March 15, 1865, in Tillman Papers.

Chapter IV

THE EDGEFIELD FARMER

THE end of the Civil War in April, 1865, marked a break in the life of Ben Tillman. To him, as to thousands of other Southerners, the news of Lee's surrender seemed to indicate "that the crack of doom had sounded." [1] The defeat also brought to him a mingling of relief and disappointment that military service was no longer possible. It marked the definite beginning of recovery from the illness which had prostrated him nine months before. Likewise, it was the point of transition from childhood into adulthood. Ben was eighteen on August 11, 1865.

At this time he might readily have carried out à previous resolution by joining the little stream of matriculates at the South Carolina College when that institution reopened in January, 1866. He was the youngest and favored son of a purposeful mother who had not been ruined, as had thousands, by her share of the tragedies of sad years. Although she had lost five of her seven sons and her hundred slaves, she was unbent and without gray hairs. As the mistress of broad acres and of free Negroes she had before her eleven more years of fruitful endeavor.[2] Yet Ben was not sent to college. Educational ambitions were subordinated to considerations more immediate and practical. A new society was developing out of the ruins of the old. Material reconstruction was the main objective with the Tillmans, as with most Southern families.

[1] *Cong. Record,* 64 Cong., 1 Sess., 11, 787.
[2] She died in 1876, aged sixty-eight. Tillman to Mrs. George T. McKie, August 23, 1916, in Tillman Papers.

There was endless work for Ben. To the old difficulty of maintaining red and hilly lands against erosion was added the new trouble of using free Negroes as farm laborers. His mother, urged by the erratic and restless George, was considering leaving Edgefield for fresher lands. "I enjoin you," George had written Ben, "to press Ma to emigrate. Anywhere is better than here." [3]

In 1866 the Tillmans purchased a plantation in Marion County, Florida, and early in the following year Mrs. Tillman sent Ben and his sister Frances Miller to take possession. The plan was for the rest of the family to follow as soon as the venture proved practical. Visions of large profits from the growing of sea-island cotton were seductive, and Ben had no time for formal education.

The Florida experiment proved abortive. Ben remained there only two years, returning to Edgefield at the end of the growing season of 1868. The weevils ate up his corn in that unaccustomed climate. His hope of a dollar a pound for the yield of the ten bales of sea-island cotton which he expected from the thirty acres he planted proved illusory. The caterpillars came early in July. "On Saturday evening," he later recounted, "I rode over the field, and, like the milkmaid with the pail on her head, I calculated my profits. On Monday morning there was not a leaf or a square or a boll that had not been stripped clean. I made just 1 bale on the 30 acres." His agricultural difficulties were capped by a severe onset of malaria. Experience thus taught him the wisdom of remaining on the ancestral acres in Edgefield. [4]

In the meantime, other circumstances were calling him back to Edgefield—or at least in that direction. In 1865 he and Frances Miller, fearing Sherman, had refugeed in Elbert County, Georgia, with relatives who were descendants of their maternal great-grandfather, Dionysius Oliver.

[3] George D. Tillman to Tillman, April 10, 1864, *ibid.*

[4] The best account of the Florida experiment is given by Tillman, in *Cong. Record*, 61 Cong., 1 Sess., 3885. See also, Thornwell Haynes, *Biographical Sketch of Gov. B. R. Tillman* (Columbia, 1894), 4.

There Tillman met Sallie Starke, the daughter of Samuel Starke, a native of Longtown, Fairfield District, South Carolina. Less than three years later, on January 8, 1868, Ben, aged twenty, and Sallie, aged eighteen, were married.

This courtship was more than the story of a realistic farmer, with practical considerations uppermost, successfully bargaining for a wife. In fact, it illustrated many of the conventions of the contemporary Southern novel. There was the early love for Mamie Lewis, a girl with golden curls whom Ben had met at Bethany Academy. Then just as the war was over he met Sallie and fell in love at first sight. His heart sang, "Sallie is the gal for me." She was to him "a demure little russet hen, as good as gold, . . . a sweet buxom lassie." There followed a summer of gaiety in Elbert County—games of chess, picnics, and "such nice dinners." But like conventional true love, all did not run smoothly. There was a passing flirtation with a prettier girl. The Starkes, as if to retaliate, drove by a picnic Ben was attending, and the lovesick Ben saddled his horse and threatened to leave unceremoniously for Florida. But difficulties were ironed out, and Ben, with his heart comforted, could return to Florida in the autumn of 1867 fondly to await letters from Elbert concerning the marriage planned for a few months later. They journeyed to Edgefield after that event—"I," said Ben, "driving old Penny at the head of the procession of buggies and carriages, and once in a while speeding up to get out of sight so we could kiss." [5]

This marriage proved to be entirely felicitous. Sallie, simple and frugal in her habits, was appropriately without social pretentions, being content with her role as wife of a successful farmer and respected landowner. She performed cheerfully and competently the multitudinous chores of the wife and plantation mistress. Field work was beneath

[5] Tillman to his sister, Mrs. Frances M. Tillman Simpson, February 25, 1918, in Tillman Papers; *id.* to Mrs. Hill (a Georgia relative), February 14, 1917, *ibid.*

her social position, but in the early morning she hoed beside her husband in their vegetable and flower gardens. Ben responded enthusiastically to the kind fortune which had given him such a wife. For the rest of his days he remained romantically in love with her. She reciprocated this devotion without the servility one would imagine a husband of Ben's imperious disposition would demand. Despite her lack of intellectuality and her reverence for his talents, she was no mere shadow of the masterful male. She dared to differ from him in matters great and small, and she maintained her side of arguments with spirit and intelligence. This nettled him, but he was basically a person of too much tolerance and good humor to be seriously offended. He was capable of admitting that he was wrong and his wife right. Indeed, he learned to love her more dearly because of her sagacious criticisms of his often hasty judgments. His success in life, he always felt, was in great measure due to her.

In 1869 the youthful couple settled on 430 acres of the Tillman family lands given to Ben by his mother. There he began farming with four plows operated by Negro laborers, and there he built a humble residence. It was a one-story house of three unceiled rooms arranged in the shape of an L. The outer boards were placed in a perpendicular fashion and were weatherboarded with small strips. The main chimney was a large but primitive affair of rough stones, and the poorly-joined floors were raised high above the ground. This house was smaller and ruder than that of the average white landowner in the Edgefield area; in fact, it was not much better than the cottages of many tenant farmers. But it sufficed the plain farmer and the plain wife to whom it belonged. There Ben and Sallie Tillman lived for twenty-odd years marked by the birth of all but one of their seven children.[6]

Two circumstances seemed to indicate that Ben Tillman

<hr />

[6] Shannonhouse, in Columbia *Record*, July 14, 1918; Thomas J. Kirkland, "Tillman and I," in Columbia *State*, June 30, 1929.

would abide for the remainder of his days as a busy but un-
distinguished husbandman. The first was the stabilizing
influence of his family. His wife was merely a modest home
builder, practical and prosaic, serenely untroubled by visions of horizons beyond the high hills of Edgefield. Then
in 1876, eight years after their marriage, children began
arriving to give Tillman additional stability. Ben was a good
father, enjoying to the full the duties and diversions of par-
enthood. "I can never forget to the day of my death," he
later wrote, "the thrill caused by the cry of my first born." [7]

The second condition which seemed to anchor him
permanently to his land was the passionate manner in which
he followed his chosen profession of farming. He found un-
ending interest in planting, germination, growth, cultivation, and harvesting. Farming was his window to reality, an
emotional satisfaction as well as a means of making a living
and possibly of accumulating wealth. He was as deeply devoted to the practice of farming as an artist to his poetry or
his painting. It was the main interest of his lustiest years.
He never understood how a husbandman could be ashamed
of farming or could desert it for another occupation. Leaving the farm would always mean a great emotional sacrifice
to him.

It was well that he put so much energy and thought upon
his profession, for his problems were not easy. His lands
were red, unusually hilly for middle South Carolina, easily
eroded, and isolated from Edgefield and Augusta by many
miles of rough and muddy roads. The labor problem was
baffling. The former slaves were so crude, lazy, and irresponsible that young Tillman's contempt for the black

[7] Tillman to William T. C. Bates, February 13, 1915, in Tillman Papers.
The Tillman children were Adeline, born January 21, 1876, died July 15,
1896; Benjamin Ryan, born March 13, 1878, married Lucy Frances Dugas,
1901; Henry Cummings, born August 14, 1884, married Mary Fox, 1906;
Margaret Malona, born 1886, married Charles S. Moore, 1911; Sophia
Oliver, born November 26, 1888, married Henry W. Hughes, 1911; Samuel
Starke, born 1892, died 1894; Sallie Mae, born August 26, 1894, married
John W. Schuler, 1916. See Tillman, *Records and Genealogy*, 71–72.

race became ever more deeply engrained. But the available substitutes proved even less satisfactory. They were what he contemptuously called "these damned factory people," white cotton mill operatives recruited from near-by Graniteville. "Some," he said, "were just as mean and unreliable as could be. They would come to me in January, make a contract for a year, stay till June and hot weather, and then leave me with a crop on my hand." [8] Added to these problems was the cyclone of March 20, 1874, which came while Tillman and his Negro laborers were at dinner. Many of his fences, trees, and Negro cabins were destroyed.[9]

But he surmounted these obstacles and developed into a successful farmer, devoting himself tirelessly to the cultivation of his crops and the broadening of his acres. He subscribed to agricultural journals and learned the practice of progressive farming. An example of his energy was the manner in which he overcame the damages of the storm of 1874. "I sent to Augusta," he recounted, "and got some whiskey and some money, and the neighbors from all the surrounding country came to the rescue. . . . In four or five days we had gotten things in such a shape that we could plow again. . . . I made the usual good crop." [10]

He learned to make effective use of Negro laborers by overseeing them closely in yard and field and by constantly admonishing them with violent oaths. "You cannot work free negroes without cussing" was his grim philosophy.[11] Moreover, he gave his laborers the example of something more concrete than good advice; he supplemented his managerial functions with actual manual labor. A neighbor wrote of Ben, "He sowed oats broadcast, dipping his hands in the sack and letting fly the seeds; he shucked corn in the corn-crib, covering his clothes with silks, and fed his own stock; he arose before sun-up, rang his farm bell, and sent

8 Tillman to E. D. Miller, August 29, 1892, in Tillman Papers.
9 *Id.* to Mrs. M. N. Morton, August 7, 1892, *ibid.*
10 *Id.* to *id.*, August 12, 1912, *ibid.*
11 Kirkland, "Tillman and I," in Columbia *State*, June 30, 1929.

his farm hands out to work; he saw to the milking of the cows, and if necessary took a hand himself. . . . I have seen him jump out and take hold of a sack of flour and help his negro man swing it into the wagon." [12]

Ben indulged neither in whiskey drinking nor in tobacco smoking, neither in fine clothes nor in expensive recreations. His one concession to the appetites was indulgence in plentiful foods, inexpensive because home-grown. A true son of the rural South, he was largely satisfied with pork, both fresh and salted. He relished the chitterlings, the chine bones, the spareribs, the sausages, the bacon, the hams, vegetables made greasy with pork, and chicken fried in deep lard. At this time he suffered no thought of striving after the uncertain profits of politics. Such indiscretions he left to less purposeful neighbors.

Ben Tillman supplemented the customary dependence of his community on cotton and corn by bold adventures in diversification; he was in a very true sense an experimental farmer. He grew his own wheat and other grains, built a silo, and produced excellent crops of silage corn. He specialized in hog raising, curing thousands of pounds of pork each year for the use of his family and tenants. He fed his hogs on barley, rye, potatoes, sorghum, beets, and other unusual substances. [13] He established "a fine vineyard" from which grapes were marketed and wine pressed. He gradually acquired a herd of Jersey cows, established a dairy, and produced large quantities of butter, which in the warm months was refrigerated in a spring. [14]

Diversified farming required effective marketing. Every Saturday, in a wagon loaded with the products of his farm, Tillman joined the procession of his neighbors moving to the Augusta markets. While they generally sold only cotton and purchased foodstuffs for themselves and their stock,

[12] Hugh C. Middleton, "Ben Tillman: A Character Sketch," 1896, in Tillman Scrapbooks.

[13] Tillman, in Charleston *News and Courier,* July 28, 1887.

[14] Kirkland, "Tillman and I," in Columbia *State,* June 30, 1929.

he marketed corn, oats, hay, eggs, and butter, as well as the fleecy staple. It was his habit to walk up and down the streets of the Georgia city with a basket of eggs or butter on his arm while his wagon, driven by a Negro, followed. Thus he was able to dispose of his commodities at the best possible prices.[15]

In Augusta, Ben Tillman was called "a progressive citizen" and "a farmer with brains" whose "dairy and vineyards are marvels of thrift and skill." [16] At Edgefield Courthouse "his heavy agricultural strokes" were considered worthy of emulation. "It would be well," said the Edgefield *Chronicle*,[17] "if there were a hundred such pushing men as Ben Tillman in five miles of this place." Although he earned the respect and confidence of his neighbors, few imitated his progressive ways.[18]

The profits of his endeavors were invested in expanding acres. By 1874 his lands demanded the attention of twenty Negro laborers and one white man. Four years later he inherited 170 additional acres from his mother, and shortly thereafter he purchased 650 acres at Ninety Six, some thirty-odd miles north of his Edgefield holdings. By 1881 he was operating thirty plows. He had become an extensive and rich farmer.[19]

Farm and family did not prevent Ben from taking part in activities normal to a man of repute. He was full of humor; he did not need the stimulus of drink to be vivacious and even boisterous. Loud speech and a rude joviality were Tillman family characteristics. "Though the Tillmans," as

15 Middleton, "Ben Tillman: A Character Sketch," in Tillman Scrapbooks.
16 Augusta *Chronicle*, cited in Charleston *World*, March 15, 1890.
17 Edgefield *Chronicle*, April 1, 1885.
18 Haynes, *Biographical Sketch*, 16.
19 Tillman to Charleston *News and Courier*, March 21, 1886. In 1880 Tillman had 500 acres of tilled lands, 20 acres in woods, and 507 acres of unimproved lands in his home farm. This farm, including implements and livestock, was valued at $9,900. The 195 acres planted in cotton produced 65 bales. The total annual production of the farm was estimated as $4,700. United States Census of 1880, Agriculture, South Carolina, Edgefield County, Meriwether Township, 6–7 (State Library, State House).

one neighbor phrased it, "steer wide of the social tide," that is, avoided high society, Ben had certain socializing tastes. His passionate love of reading was supplemented by a deep fondness for flowers; and he appreciated sentimental music and moderately enjoyed singing and dancing. Indeed both Ben and George "can be gay; no men more gay than either of them as a host with a crowd of young people around them." [20] These gaieties remained vivid memories to the younger brother. Years later he wrote his brother-in-law recalling "The dances we used to go to at the Academy and any and everywhere else where the house was large enough; the dare-deviltry and scorn of consequences; the tilting with saber, with the two John Butlers and Jack Holder nearly always leading and excelling the rest of us." [21]

Ben Tillman was never pious or even orthodox in his religious views. In later life his skepticism, which was fundamental, expressed itself in deliberate avoidance of the church. It may therefore be surprising to learn that, during his early married life, he was a frequent churchgoer. Seemingly, he sought to indulge an inclination later satisfied by political gatherings. Churchgoing to him, as to many others in rural Edgefield, was a major social diversion. His mother was a Baptist, his wife a Methodist; but Ben never formally joined a church. He attended the near-by Baptist churches, and in 1882 he and his sisters aided the Reverend S. L. Morris, a personal friend, in building a Presbyterian church on Tillman lands near the family graveyard. This church was dedicated in November, 1883, by the Reverend John L. Girardeau, a famous preacher. In the new edifice Mrs. Tillman played the organ while Ben led the singing. The Reverend Mr. Morris on his regular visitations was always a guest in the Tillman cottage.[22]

[20] Hugh C. Middleton, in Charleston *World*, July 16, 1890.
[21] Tillman to John W. Bunch, March 31, 1916, in Tillman Papers.
[22] Shannonhouse, in Columbia *Record*, July 14, 1917; Middleton, "Ben Tillman: A Character Sketch," in Tillman Scrapbooks; Tillman to Deets Pickett, April 28, 1917, in Tillman Papers; Chapman, *History of Edgefield County*, 300–301.

Thus in the ten years after the Civil War did Tillman establish himself as a citizen of Edgefield. He had married, settled as an industrious farmer, was becoming the father of a growing family, and was able to spare some time from his agricultural chores for participation in the social diversions of his community. In 1876 a crisis developed in South Carolina political affairs which gave him opportunity for public service.

Chapter V

THE CAMPAIGN OF 1876

BEN TILLMAN believed that a reformed Republican was no better than a corrupt Republican; both were guilty of the intolerable crime of attempting to endow blacks with social functions forbidden by the immutable bonds of caste. Consequently, as one of the white men of Edgefield who accepted such ideas on race and politics, Tillman did yeoman's service in the struggle to rid South Carolina of Negro and Carpetbag rule. He shared with his neighbors the conviction that the participation of the Negro in politics under Carpetbag direction was the worst imaginable of civic evils.

About 1876 Matthew C. Butler and Martin W. Gary, two Edgefield lawyers who had been generals of the Confederacy, conceived a plan that once more put the Edgefield imprint upon the destiny of South Carolina. They believed that eight years' experience had demonstrated the futility of the white man's attempt to overcome a Negro majority of thirty thousand voters by ordinary political methods. Therefore they counseled, as the hard necessity of a still harder alternative, the use of intimidation and fraud as the only means of forcing the blacks into subordination. As the first step in this plan, the bold Edgefield leaders urged the organization of secret military companies. Only thereby could white social and moral superiority vanquish black numerical superiority. This plan was called the Straight-out, the Shotgun, or the Edgefield policy.

Nothing in the traditions of Ben Tillman prevented him from enthusiastically embracing the realistic creed of Butler and Gary. From actual experience in his community he knew that, under a free ballot, a black majority of six hundred out of a total vote of one thousand meant Negro rule. But he also knew that this majority could be cowed by high-handed methods. Nursed in a tradition of violence and experienced in the management of Negroes, he felt no compunction in applying lawless tactics to the political situation. Was he not a patriot willing to make any sacrifice to preserve accepted ideas of racial integrity? Necessity prompted the full use of all powers, legal or illegal, at the command of the whites.[1]

Ben Tillman was one of the most enthusiastic of the forty-five white men of Meriwether Township who, in 1873, organized themselves into the Sweetwater Sabre Club under the captaincy of Andrew P. Butler, a former officer of the Confederate army.[2] The men, unable to secure equipment from the Federal government, provided themselves with mounts, uniforms, and arms. A cleverly arranged system of alarms made possible the assembling of the company at a given point within a two-hour limit.[3] The enemy was the regiment of Negro militia organized in Edgefield County with arms and equipment supplied by the Federal government. Two companies of this regiment operated in Meriwether Township under the captaincies of Richard Bullock and Ned Tennant, local Negroes. The members of the Sweetwater company, confident that they could triumph over black bluster and numbers, were eager for a show of force.[4]

An opportunity almost came on the night of July 4, 1874, on the occasion of what Tillman, with exaggeration, calls the First Ned Tennant Riot. Captain Tennant, "a dashing

[1] Benjamin R. Tillman, *The Struggles of 1876: How South Carolina Was Delivered from Carpetbag and Negro Rule* (n.p., n.d.), 46.

[2] This was not United States Senator Andrew P. Butler, who was associated with the Brooks-Sumner affair.

[3] Tillman to Captain Joseph M. Moorer, March 4, 1912, in Tillman Papers.

[4] *Id., Struggles of 1876*, 40–43.

character" in long ostrich plume, who was especially hated by the whites, had spent the holiday drilling his company to the sound of drum and fife. A neighboring assembly of young whites were so angered that they resolved to give the bumptious black leader "a warning and frighten him or precipitate trouble of some kind so as to bring on a conflict." Consequently the young whites "emptied their pistols in front of his [Tennant's] home, shooting into the door." The black leader, as soon as he recovered from his fright, ordered his drummer to sound "the long roll," the signal for the gathering of his company. By daybreak several hundred blacks had assembled. But the whites had also heard the drum. There were rumors that "the negroes threatened to kill all whites from the cradle to the grave and burn as they went," and couriers sped through the night proclaiming a black uprising.

Milledge Horne, one of the couriers, reached Tillman's house at seven on the morning of July 5, and the "dreaded intelligence" of Tennant's conduct filled this race-conscious farmer with "anxiety, alarm and anger." He sent his wife and the family of his lone white tenant to his mother's house, and after telling his twenty black tenants "in very plain language that if anything happened . . . there would be something to pay for it," he hurried to the rendezvous of the Sweetwater company. There he found assembled sixty or seventy men. Scouts were sent to Tennant's house to demand an explanation of "the unheard of and outrageous assemblage in such a threatening attitude," and to warn him that if the blacks were not immediately dispersed, the whites would attack. The black leader, completely cowed, pointed to the bullet marks on his door, proclaimed a purpose no more sinister than self-preservation, and agreed to dismiss his men. This incident intensified the feeling of resentment against the black militia.[5]

One result of Tennant's activities was the circulation of

5 *Ibid.*, 42–45.

a petition among the landlords of the Meriwether area pledging them not to rent land or give employment to any of the two hundred black militiamen. The pledge was signed and rigidly kept by Tillman and most of his neighbors. The three or four who failed to comply suffered ostracism, and many blacks had to move away because of unemployment.[6]

Another manifestation of white prowess was the carrying of Shaw's Mill Precinct in Meriwether Township by the Democrats in the election of November, 1874. Although the Negro voters outnumbered the whites five to one, the white manager of the election and his white clerk, "by some manipulation which nobody ever clearly understood," turned the trick in the face of the two bewildered colored managers. Tillman approved this demonstration of prowess.[7]

Three months later the Meriwether whites seized another opportunity to strike at the militiamen. General Matthew C. Butler's residence was burned, and although only "circumstantial evidence and suspicion" pointed to the blacks as the incendiaries, "warrants were issued for Tennant and several of his leading men." When the constable who was sent to make the arrests did not find the militia captain at home, the whites applied "drastic measures." They prevailed upon the local magistrate to call a *posse comitatus* consisting mostly of members of the Sweetwater Sabre Club. As this little group searched the woods for Tennant and his men, there was an exchange of shots by which two Negroes were wounded. When a physician came to attend the wounded men he was fired upon. This attack upon a white man was the signal for the gathering of one thousand whites, "all armed and determined to make an end of such disturbances." They scoured the countryside for Negroes, but not a single one was to be found; all had fled in terror. Tillman and the other whites learned that Tennant and his men, skillfully evading their white pursuers, had escaped to Edge-

6 *Ibid.*, 45–46.   7 *Ibid.*, 46.

field Courthouse and abjectly surrendered their arms to the colored colonel of militia. The intrepid Meriwether whites marched to the town and seized the arms.[8]

The experiences of Tillman and his neighbors in 1874 and 1875 confirmed their faith in the Butler-Gary dictum that "one ounce of fear was worth a pound of persuasion" and that physical terror and political fraud were the only effective methods of overcoming great black majorities. Ben was an intimate friend of Gary, "one of his trusted lieutenants," and had "personal knowledge" that Gary, Butler, and his brother George D. Tillman had "agreed on the policy of terrorizing the negroes at the first opportunity, by letting them provoke trouble and then having the whites demonstrate their superiority by killing as many of them as was justifiable." [9]

Opportunity for bloodshed came in July, 1876, at a crucial moment in the history of the state. At that time white sentiment was balanced between a policy of compromise with Republican reformers under Governor Daniel H. Chamberlain and a policy of no compromise as advocated by the Edgefield leaders. Thirteen miles from the Tillman farm on the Savannah opposite Augusta was Hamburg, a once prosperous town which had degenerated into a refuge for Negro criminals and politicians. There a militia company under the command of a certain Dock Adams had its headquarters, and it was reputed to be "dangerous for white men to go through the town unless they were well armed." On the afternoon of July 4, two young white men, Henry Getzen and Thomas Butler, on their way home in a buggy, attempted the perilous passage. They found the main street blocked by the company-front parade of Dock Adams' company. "Charge Bayonets!" cried Captain Adams with a view of humiliating the two whites in the presence of the black

[8] *Ibid.*, 47–50.
[9] This, it was believed, would strike terror among the blacks and at the same time forestall the tendency of white moderates to compromise with reforming Republicans. *Ibid.*, 17, 27, 28.

multitude assembled to witness the parade. The young men, true to their pride of race, did not turn and flee, but drew their pistols and shouted, "We will shoot the first man who sticks a bayonet in that horse." The ranks were opened and the young men were allowed to pass. But this was not the end of the trouble. Adams swore out a warrant for the two disturbers of his drill, and they retaliated with warrants charging him with obstructing the highway. According to Southern standards, a serious wrong had been committed. Negroes had attempted to interfere with the prerogatives of white men.

Accordingly, on July 8, the day set by the Negro trial justice at Hamburg for the adjudication of the differences, the atmosphere was enveloped in ominous gravity. General Matthew C. Butler appeared as the lawyer for the two white youths, and seventy armed white men stood by to see that the black magistrate decreed justice according to white standards. Among the armed men were Ben Tillman and the other members of the Sweetwater Sabre Club. "It was our purpose," said the Edgefield farmer, "to attend the trial to see that the young men had protection and, if any opportunity offered, to provoke a row, and if one did not offer, we were to make one." Sensing this attitude, the trial justice ordered the cases postponed. But an opportunity for complaint and possible action soon presented itself. It was discovered that Dock Adams and his men had stationed themselves in their armory. The whites ordered them to surrender their arms. When they refused to do this, the whites, although outnumbered and outarmed, advanced to enforce the order, confident that "the difference in blood and the color of the skin far more than made up the odds in the armament." At sunset the firing began, and the attackers, aided by a large mob from Augusta, surrounded the armory. The black militiamen, after some desultory firing which resulted in the death of a white man named McKie Meriwether, fled in terror under the cover of darkness. Two were killed while attempting to escape. One of these was Jim Cook, the town marshal who cherished a "brutal and fiendish hate" for whites. He was slain by a squad to which Tillman belonged. That aroused farmer fired one shot at the Negro culprit and had the satisfaction of witnessing the killing of the other Negro. In all, some forty blacks from among the militia were taken prisoners.

The killing of Meriwether infuriated the whites. Two cousins of the dead man asked Tillman and others if it were proper that the lives of only two blacks should pay for the death of the one white. The answer was an emphatic negative. An execution party, to a member of which Tillman surrendered his loaded pistol, was organized, and five "of the meanest characters and most deserving of death" among the prisoners were shot. The whites, suggested Tillman, may have grown "sick of the bloody work." When the inhabitants of Hamburg returned home next day "the ghastly sight which met their gaze of seven dead negroes lying stark and stiff, certainly had its effect." The prestige of the white race had been re-established.

Tillman saw more clearly than other participants the significance of the bloody event. To him it was "like a fire bell in the night" calling the white men of South Carolina to "make one desperate fight to gain their lost liberties." He felt justified morally because of the many alleged crimes of the Hamburg Negroes. The dead blacks, he affirmed, "had been offered up as a sacrifice to the fanatical teachings and fiendish hate" of the Radical leaders. That the entire North as well as liberal Southern circles condemned the so-called Hamburg Massacre caused him no heartaches; he was contemptuous of such opinions. As he neared home that morning, he stopped at a neighbor's house and ate heartily of watermelon; he felt elated.[10]

Defiance and derision greeted the attempt of the Radical state government to bring the Hamburg rioters to justice.

[10] *Ibid.,* 14–26, 51.

The charge was murder and conspiracy. The sheriff of Aiken County prudently made no direct attempt to execute the warrants, but the accused men agreed to meet this official at a designated place and follow him to Aiken Courthouse. Accordingly, on September 4, 1876, a strange procession was led by the sheriff to the outskirts of the town. Here the men encamped to await the trial scheduled for two days later. They were "armed to the teeth."

While in camp these so-called defendants resolved upon a spectacular demonstration of their unrepentant and even aggressive intentions. Since the Republican newspapers of the North were at that time, because of the Hamburg incident, waving "the bloody shirt with such frantic energy," George D. Tillman, who accompanied the party in the capacity of lawyer, suggested that a long procession be organized to "wave the bloody shirt in reality as a token of defiance." The members of the Sweetwater company eagerly accepted the idea.

Ben Tillman, who had a strong liking for mixing the grim with the ridiculous, actively participated in the preparations for the parade. He was a member of the committee who induced the ladies of Aiken to make forty homespun shirts and who gathered a supply of turpentine, oil, and Venetian red with which to bedaub these garments. With two masks, a kinky chignon, and a large shirt hung upon a cross, he made the image of a giant Negro, and covered it with threatening legends and the marks of bullet holes.

The parade of Tillman and his friends, wearing their bizarre shirts and bearing aloft their grotesque effigy, was a triumph of white strategy. They passed in long file before the houses of the women who had made the garments; then they galloped through the streets of the town. The whites cheered; the Negroes, woefully frightened, remained in hiding; the garrison of Federal troops responded to the friendly greetings of the paraders with quiet applause—an evidence of what Tillman regarded as the instinctive solidarity of race. So successful was this demonstration that the "bloody shirt" of homespun and paint was soon transformed into the red flannel which became the uniform of all South Carolinians who in 1876 and 1877 battled for white supremacy.[11]

The success of the parade put the Sweetwater men in an even more defiant mood when, on the next day, they appeared in court. Supported by a corps of lawyers and by an ample supply of concealed weapons which made ominous thuds as their bearers took seats, the so-called prisoners turned the attempted reckoning of Republican justice into "a laughable travesty on law." The court officials wisely resolved to grant bail to all defendants. "If they had attempted to put us in jail," Tillman remarked, "I am sure few or none of us would have acquiesced; and we would have probably killed every obnoxious radical in the court room and town and gone to Texas or some other hiding place." When the clerk of court decided to wait until the next morning to execute the bonds, the sheriff whispered, "You had better let these men get out of town tonight else they may burn it and hang you before morning." Immediately the clerk awakened to realities and hastily handed out the bond blanks. The men went on each other's surety; great amusement was caused by the fact that a man known to be penniless signed bonds to the extent of $20,000. This was the end of the legal phase of the Hamburg trouble, for there were no judicial authorities in South Carolina with the temerity to reckon with Ben Tillman and his neighbors.[12]

Rapid events heightened the significance of Tillman's participation in the existing political struggle. Butler and Gary captured the Democratic State Convention and effected the nomination of Wade Hampton and the adoption of the Edgefield policy of no compromise with Governor

[11] *Ibid.*, 33–37. *Cf.* Alfred B. Williams, *Hampton and His Red Shirts: South Carolina's Deliverance in 1876* (Charleston, 1935), 133–34.
[12] Tillman, *Struggles of 1876*, 38.

Chamberlain and other reforming Republicans. Andrew P. Butler was elected to the position of colonel in the rapidly expanding Red Shirt regiments, and Tillman took his place as captain of the Sweetwater Sabre Club.

Scarcely two weeks after his election, the new captain was given opportunity to test his leadership. On the morning of September 22 he was informed of a riot in the Ellenton section of Aiken County in which Colonel Butler's command had been ambushed and members of both races killed or wounded. He hastily assembled his forty men and in stern elation set out for Ellenton, thirty miles away, to help frustrate the supposedly bloody intentions of the blacks. These unfortunate creatures had been surrounded in a swamp by irate whites who killed several scores of them and threatened a general massacre. Tillman and his command came too late to participate in bloodshed; Federal troops had arrived and induced both races to disperse. The Edgefield leader, however, enjoyed some of the ghastly phases of the aftermath of the riot. He was excited by the sight of a dead Negro. "It was," he says, "a rather grewsome [sic] object as it lay by the side of the road in a plain pine coffin. . . . The reason he had not been buried was that the negroes were afraid to be seen handling the coffin." Another savage incident was the execution of Simon Coker, the mulatto state senator from Barnwell, who was accused of making "a very incendiary speech." Captain Nat Butler, the one-armed brother of the general, selected two of Tillman's men as executioners. The victim was shot as he was on his knees in prayer; one of Tillman's men put another shot in the head of the prostrate form for fear the mulatto was "playing possum."

The murderous business at Ellenton was not without its festive phase. On the march Tillman and his men had devoured with "keen relish" a ham which a comrade had broiled on a ramrod over coals and the substantial meal of barbecued shoat, coffee, and corn pone which Tillman's kinsman, George Bunch, had prepared for them. On their way home they gladly accepted an invitation to dine with Captain Paul Hammond on broiled bacon, corn pone, and collard greens. "The fat meat and corn bread," commented Tillman, "were keenly relished." [13]

Hampton's victory in the crucial election of November, 1876, by a narrow margin of 1,134 votes was made possible by the fact that Edgefield turned a potential Negro majority of several thousands into a Democratic majority of 3,134 by a flagrant use of fraud and violence. Tillman's success as minority manager at Landrum's Store Precinct was spectacular. At 6 A. M. on the day of election, he and one of the Negro managers opened the polls. When at a later hour the second Negro manager appeared, the white manager passed upon his right to act. "Miles," said Tillman, "you are too late; but wait until I see what the election law says about your coming up here this time of day." The Negro, frightened by the ominous tone of these words and by the armed Democrats massed around the polls, abandoned his post of duty. Another black, who attempted to distribute the Republican ballots, fled when threatened by the pistols and the yells of Tillman and the other Democrats. "Benny Tillman," this Negro testified, "said that they [the whites] had been rulers of Carolina, and they intended to rule it." Individual Negroes were kept from voting by the white mob, while the white strangers were allowed to vote. The result was the return of 211 Democratic and only 2 Republican votes, in place of the 180 Republican and 104 Democratic votes of two years previous.[14]

During the eight or nine years following the re-establishment of white supremacy in 1877, Tillman played a vigorous but not unusual part in the life of Edgefield County.

---

[13] *Ibid.*, 56–66.
[14] See H. T. Tankersley and Robert Chandler testimony, in *House Miscellaneous Documents*, 45 Cong., 1 Sess., No. 11, pp. 332, 337, for quotations. See also, Chandler testimony, in *Senate Miscellaneous Documents*, 44 Cong., 2 Sess., No. 48, Pt. II, 137–38; Aaron Miles statement, in *House Documents*, 44 Cong., 2 Sess., No. 31, Pt. I, Appendix 61.

He was respected by his neighbors for his industry, his sterling character, his pure domestic life, and the useful if modest role he had played in 1876. He became a member of the Edgefield Huzzars, the leading military organization of the county, and in 1882 was honored with the captaincy of the company. He directed its drills and its annual barbecue and dance given at Lanham's Spring, a woodland near the Tillman lands.[15] In open approval of the tactics employed against the Negro voters in 1876, he denounced those who maintained that the subordination of the blacks could be effected less ruthlessly.[16] Tillman gained a thorough knowledge of public questions through reading and conversation. The common saying about him in Edgefield was: "It is a pity for such a man to go to seed." Twice urged by influential friends to run for the legislature, he twice declined because of pressure of farm work. But he did participate in the councils of his party, becoming a member of the executive committee of the Edgefield Democratic party, Democratic county chairman in 1880, and a delegate to the Democratic State Convention in 1882. In 1880 he expressed the will of the people of Edgefield by championing in the county convention the candidacy of Martin W. Gary for governor, and two years later he espoused in the state convention the ambition of General John Bratton for the same office.[17]

At that time Ben Tillman was thirty-five years old. There had been nothing in his career to indicate a future in any sense distinguished. Practical and material, his success as a progressive farmer tended to make him content with the world as it was, a complacence augmented by fruitful marriage and fatherhood. Moreover, his adjustment was accentuated by his participation in the social activities of his community; and when he left home to perform the duties

---

[15] Chapman, *History of Edgefield County*, 369–73.
[16] Tillman, *Struggles of 1876*, 32.
[17] Haynes, *Biographical Sketch*, 16–21.

of the patriot and the citizen, it was merely to join neighbors in the traditional battle against the Negro and the meddlesome Northerner. Ben Tillman in 1882 was a hidebound conservative. No one could have predicted that he was destined to play a role little short of revolutionary in the history of the state he loved so well.

Chapter VI

THE BACKGROUND OF TILLMANISM

"UP to the period of Reconstruction," asserted Ben Tillman, "South Carolina never had real popular government." Under the constitution of 1790, the parish system gave the low-country areas a preponderance of seats in the legislature; the major officers of the state were elected by this oligarchical body instead of by the people. This insured "the absolute domination of the city of Charleston" and created a government "as nearly aristocratic as has existed anywhere in America." The great slaveholding families held sway and made the white masses "mere puppets to register their will." "A prouder, more arrogant, or hot-headed ruling class never existed," concluded the analyst.

Reconstruction, Tillman explained, brought reforms in the machinery of government but no permanent changes in the distribution of political power. After that period "the newly emancipated white men" followed "with almost blind idolatry" the leaders who had driven out the Carpetbaggers. These leaders formed an oligarchy closely resembling the ante-bellum aristocracy. This new clique operated through political rings with headquarters in Columbia and Charleston and with ramifications in the county seats. The convention system of party nominations denied the common people an effective voice in the choice of their governors. Dissent from this system was ineffective because of established prejudices against partisan politics. Shortly before the Civil War the people had become unfamiliar with the machinery of party divisions, because of the enforcement of the unity necessary to meet a great crisis. During the sixteen years of war and Reconstruction this condition devolved into a veritable "paralysis of citizenship." After Reconstruction the necessity of white unity in the face of a feared resurgence of the Negro caused political insurgency to be regarded as treason. " 'Independentism'—division among the whites," said Tillman, "was abhorrent to every good Carolinian." Wade Hampton himself reviled the independent as "worse than a Radical"; and the people re-echoed this sentiment.[1]

The essential accuracy of Tillman's analysis has been confirmed by observers less partial than Tillman is reputed to have been. It is true, as one writer remarks, that for eighty years before the Edgefield farmer raised his voice all white South Carolina males had the vote and that consequently no class or ring could have monopolized political authority without the consent of the white democracy. "Yet," this writer accurately adds, "custom seems to have forged an intangible chain whereby the socially elect only were eligible to higher promotion." [2]

In the 1880's a series of social and political changes, aftermaths of the Civil War, made possible radical modification of the aristocratic politics Tillman censured. The war, to a large degree, destroyed the physical basis of South Carolina prosperity. Stores and other businesses had been closed; highways and railroads had been thrown out of repair. Charleston became a "city of ruins, of desolation, of vacant houses, of widowed women, of rotted wharves, of deserted

---

[1] See Tillman's brilliant interpretation of South Carolina history, in his eulogy of United States Senator Joseph H. Earle. *Cong. Record,* 55 Cong., 2 Sess., 3309–10.

[2] Kirkland, "Tillman and I," in Columbia *State,* July 28, 1929. Professor David D. Wallace in his monumental history of the state has much to say about low-country arrogance; about South Carolina as "the most aristocratic State in the Union, with less intercourse between the rulers and the ruled and less sympathy between rich and poor than any other commonwealth"; and about the inevitability of conflict between aristocracy and common people. Wallace, *The History of South Carolina* (New York, 1934), III, 97–101, 105–106, 108–109, 343–44.

warehouses, of wild-weed gardens, of miles of grass-grown streets." [3] Columbia was made a wilderness of ruins; and Ashley Hall, Middleton Place, Porcher House, and the houses of William Gilmore Simms and Wade Hampton had been reduced to ashes.[4] Slaves were free; Confederate money and securities had become worthless; and land had fallen almost to one third its former value.[5] Poverty was the lot of the formerly wealthy. The three traditional elements of the population—the former slaveholders, the white masses, and the Negro masses—began the task of rebuilding a shattered commonwealth on a basis nearer equality than had existed since pioneer days.

The disintegration of the old social order was accompanied by the emergence of new classes of whites. The pronounced increase in the number of farms [6] indicates the partitioning of great estates into small rentals and perhaps the actual increase of small proprietorships. The old slave-holding families, unable to adjust themselves to new conditions, in many instances deserted the land.[7] Many men of distinguished names preferred the overstocked professions of law and politics to the difficulties of land management.

Others, however, who before the war had been unable to compete with the planter and his slaves, took advantage of these changes. This new element found landownership less

---

[3] Sidney Andrews, *The South Since the War* (Boston, 1866), 1.

[4] *Ibid.*, Chaps. I, IV.

[5] The value of South Carolina farm lands averaged in 1860, $8.62 an acre; in 1870, only $3.70 an acre. Calculated from figures in *Ninth Census of the United States, 1870* (Washington, 1872), *Wealth and Industry*, 81, 86.

[6] Between 1860 and 1870 the number of farms (not the number of land-owners) increased from 33,171 to 51,889, while the average size of farms fell from 488 to 233 acres. *Ibid.*, 340–41; J. F. Duggar, "Changes in the Agricultural Methods and Plantation Systems of the South," in Julian A. C. Chandler *et al.* (eds.), *The South in the Building of the Nation* (Richmond, 1909–1913), VI, 25.

[7] The most striking example of this type of "broken-down aristocrat" was Wade Hampton, "one of the richest men in the South in 1860, and grandson of one of the most successful fortune-builders in the country," who, after the war, "went through bankruptcy and was never able to regain prosperity." Wallace, *History of South Carolina*, III, 232.

difficult because of the prevailing low prices, the elimination of the necessity of large capital investments in slaves,
and the expansion of credit facilities for the carrying on of
farm operations. There was a great development of small-
farm cotton culture, especially in the Piedmont region,
marked by an increased use of commercial fertilizers.[8]

After the war, towns and villages multiplied strikingly at
strategic points along the railroads, and in these settlements
a significant new mercantile class emerged. These merchants
became the wealthiest men in South Carolina by charging
high interest rates on crop liens and other types of advances.
Their wealth often gave them dominant positions in bank-
ing, in the church, and in political life. They ruled the community as supremely if not as glamorously as ever did the
ante-bellum planters.[9]

Another evidence of aristocratic decay was the rise of the
more democratic upcountry at the expense of the low country where the devastation of war and the demoralization of
the Negro had been greater. Rice, before the war the chief
staple of the low country, had, by 1883, declined to one third
its former value,[10] and was soon abandoned altogether. In
the upcountry, on the other hand, the extensive use, after
1865, of commercial fertilizer turned exhausted sand and
hill lands into valuable cotton fields. Likewise, there was a
rapid increase of cotton manufacturing in the upcountry,[11]
while the one great industry of the low country, the mining
of phosphates, had only a temporary prosperity. Charleston,
the commercial center of the low country, suffered a relative

[8] Duggar, "Changes in the Agricultural Methods and Plantation Systems
of the South," in *South in the Building of the Nation,* VI, 19–20; Matthew B.
Hammond, "Cotton Production in the South," *ibid.,* 89–90; Alfred H. Stone,
"The Influence of the Factorage System," *ibid.,* 347.

[9] Stone, "Influence of the Factorage System," *ibid.,* 349–50.

[10] *South Carolina Resources and Population, Institutions and Industries*
(Charleston, 1883), 58.

[11] Between 1872 and 1886 the capital invested in the industry rose from
ten to thirty-two millions. Victor S. Clark, "Modern Manufacturing Development in the South, 1880–1905," in *South in the Building of the Nation,*
VI, 282.

decline. This was due to the absence of water power suitable for factories, to the decentralization of cotton marketing, and to the use of rail routes to ports farther north by interior industrial centers.[12]

These economic and social changes did not cause the immediate overthrow of the traditional political leadership. Conditions existed, however, which were preparing for the rise of a new and more democratic leadership. Consider the political reforms achieved during Reconstruction; the nature of the Hampton victory in 1876; the unsatisfactory solution of the problem of Negro suffrage; the failure to solve acute problems of agricultural distress; and the manner in which public offices were distributed. All these factors served either to create unrest or to make easier the assertion of discontent.

The constitutional conventions of both 1865 and 1868 [13] facilitated a wider degree of popular participation in government. The first body apportioned legislative representation to the advantage of the upcountry and abolished property qualifications for officeholding. The second provided for the popular election of most officers, for the reapportionment of legislative representation every ten years, and for the principle of universal education.[14]

The methods by which the campaign of 1876 was won were not in all respects satisfactory to the Bourbons who gained the offices. Contrary to the advice of the low-country conservatives, the contest was directed along lines of mob violence by bold upcountry leaders. Hampton was "woefully mistaken" in believing that his policy of persuasion swung enough Negro voters to account for his election.

[12] Between 1870 and 1880 Charleston's population increased only 1,028; there was an actual decline of 59 in white population. *South Carolina Resources and Population*, 678.

[13] The former was composed of leaders in the old order and the latter of a Negro majority.

[14] Francis B. Simkins and Robert H. Woody, *South Carolina During Reconstruction* (Chapel Hill, 1932), 37–43, 95–103.

This was really won by the rifle clubs keeping blacks away from the polls. The white masses who composed these organizations, knowing that they had done the work, would at a later date transfer to their own shoulders the toga of political control.[15]

Notwithstanding the fact that all sorts of successful expedients were adopted to lessen the influence of the Negro in politics,[16] the degree of reaction did not satisfy the riotous white public consciousness created by the victory of 1876. A resolution calling for a constitutional convention, through which the stigma of living under a Negro-made constitution could be removed, was defeated at successive sessions of the legislature. The only plan of suffrage restriction which that body could be induced to enact, as a substitute for the necessity of white men standing over the polls with their guns,[17] did not entirely exclude the Negro from office. Black South Carolinians could still be seen in Congress and the legislature as representatives of the coastal counties, and it was deemed necessary to allow them a limited part in the councils of the Democratic party.[18] A full

[15] Tillman, *Struggles of 1876*, 27–28; Francis B. Simkins, "The Election of 1876 in South Carolina," in *South Atlantic Quarterly* (Durham), XXI (1922), 225–40; XXII (1923), 35–51.

[16] Among them were the following: the increase of the dubious white majority in the legislature of 1877 by the expulsion of Negro members from Charleston; the banishment of Negro political leaders; a control of election machinery so rigid that the Republicans deemed it useless to contest the election of 1878; the adoption of a gerrymandering scheme that concentrated 25,000 of the state's 30,000 Negro majority in one Congressional district; and the publication of the *Report of the Joint Investigating Committee on Public Frauds . . . , 1877–1878* (Columbia, 1878), a bulky indictment of the Reconstruction government. See articles entitled "South Carolina," in *Appleton's Annual Cyclopedia and Register of Important Events*, N.S. (New York), 1877 to 1884; Ball, *State that Forgot*, 169–70.

[17] This curious system was known as the Eight Box Law. By its provisions, as many boxes as there were contests were placed at each polling place; the voter, unassisted, was required to deposit a ballot in each box. If he could not read, he was almost certain to invalidate his ballots by depositing them in the wrong boxes. *Acts and Joint Resolutions of the General Assembly of the State of South Carolina*, 1882 (Columbia), 1117–19. Cited hereafter as South Carolina *Acts*.   [18] Ball, *State that Forgot*, 174.

policy of anti-Negro reaction was prevented by a sense of responsibility to the Negro, whose suffrage Hampton had promised to protect; by fear of Federal intervention; and by the timidity of the overdiscreet leaders of the black counties.

The white masses desired a system of government which completely excluded the Negro from politics. Unashamed of their anti-Negro opinions, they were dissatisfied with the halting manner in which their leaders stated their position. When opportunity came to justify South Carolina race attitudes, ample evidence was advanced to prove the venality of Negro government, without a word concerning the methods used to restore white supremacy.[19] Cautious leaders were reluctant to expose practices to which they felt they had been driven by necessity. The cultured upper classes disapproved of the violence with which the lower classes disciplined the blacks. The press and the pulpit, motivated by the patriotic desire to have South Carolina live up to the standards of the more civilized communities, cried for "law enforcement" and stridently exposed the doings of lynchers, duelists, murderers, and other men of violence.[20] The legislature outlawed dueling and tried to suppress lynching and pistol toting. The thousands who participated in or were sympathetic toward ruffianism were irritated by these harsh criticisms. They wanted a leader who would justify what they considered necessary oppression of the blacks.

In the 1870's the South Carolina farmers met with economic reverses. The fall in the price of cotton, the great increase in the number of liens on unharvested crops, and the purchase of farm supplies on credit from usurious merchants at prices 20 to 100 per cent above cash charges,[21]

[19] Representative John J. Hemphill, "Reconstruction in South Carolina," in Hilary A. Herbert (ed.), *Why the Solid South? or, Reconstruction and Its Results* (Baltimore, 1890), 85–111.

[20] The campaign culminated in the denunciation of Colonel E. B. C. Cash for killing Colonel William M. Shannon. Ball, *State that Forgot*, 170–71.

[21] Harry Hammond, in Charles H. Otken, *The Ills of the South; or, Related Causes Hostile to the General Prosperity of the Southern People* (New York, 1894), 84–85.

caused much complaint and a searching for remedies. Many
farmers between 1872 and 1875 joined the National Grange
of the Patrons of Husbandry,[22] an organization of national
extent which, through its co-operative program of buying
and selling and its demands for state regulation of railroads,
promised relief. But as may have been expected, the Grange
was of little practical benefit to the South Carolina farmers.
The attempt at co-operative trading was wrecked by faulty
management and the impatience of the average farmer with
such slow means of betterment. Although Governor Hampton and his successors were sympathetic toward the demands
of the farmers, they were able to do little. Their theories of
the limited functions of government prevented notable
ventures in paternalistic legislation. They did, however,
create a department of agriculture and the office of railroad
commissioner, and laws regulating the railroads were
passed.[23] Officers of mediocre ability were placed in charge
of these agencies; the earning power of the railroads did not
warrant such reductions of rates as would have materially
lightened the burden of the farmers. After 1875 the Grange
rapidly declined in membership; what was left of it joined
hands with the conservative Agricultural and Mechanical
Society to hold summer meetings in the various villages of
the state.[24]

But the Grange was not without lasting effects. It taught
the farmer to be class-conscious and to turn to the government for the redress of his ills. This in connection with the
decline in value of staple crops in the 1880's, the failure of
efforts to establish a cash basis of tenancy, and the forfeiture

[22] In 1875 there were 342 local Granges with a membership of approximately eleven thousand in the state. Solon J. Buck, *The Granger Movement:
A Study of Agricultural Organization and Its Political, Economic, and Social Manifestations, 1870–1880* (Cambridge, 1913), 58.

[23] South Carolina *Acts*, 1879, pp. 72–76; 1882, pp. 791, 843.

[24] "Seldom," said the principal leader of the Grange, "have we [the farm-
ers] experienced or seen any substantial benefit resulting from a convention
of farmers." D. Wyatt Aiken, in Charleston *News and Courier*, August 10,
1877.

by 1887 of over one million acres of land for nonpayment of taxes,[25] created an atmosphere of unrest and resentment. Between 1875 and 1885 there was a drop of six cents a pound in the price of cotton; and this measured the difference between easy living and the pinch of poverty.

Of course, this condition was caused by circumstances for which no particular group should be held responsible. Overproduction of cotton resulted in ruinous prices; and one-crop specialization meant the purchasing of foodstuffs and other commodities which should have been produced at home. As a consequence the farmers fell in debt to merchants who took liens on their crops. These were uncertain risks naturally bearing high interest charges. Bad debts were numerous, and only the shrewdest merchants avoided losses.[26]

The discomfited farmers turned on the merchant-creditors as the authors of their woes. Interest on loans ranged from 10 to 15 per cent, and the high prices charged for corn, bacon, clothing, farm tools, fertilizers, and even mules and horses purchased on credit or under the crop lien system were equal to interest charges of 25 to 100 per cent. The farmers, while enduring their own impoverishment, witnessed the enrichment of the merchants. They even saw merchants acquire mortgaged farms and operate them with Negro labor for whose services they outbid the older class of farmers. No wonder the prevailing credit system was regarded as "commercial extortion or legalized robbery of the farming, and, in general, the poorer class." [27]

The merchants of Charleston became the special butt of

[25] The Charleston *News and Courier,* in its economic survey of January 1, 1886, said an increase in cotton acreage of nearly 20 per cent between 1880 and 1885 was accompanied by an actual decrease of nearly 15 per cent in the money value of the crop. On the forfeitures, see Governor John P. Richardson, in *Journal of the House of Representatives of the General Assembly of the State of South Carolina,* 1887 (Columbia), 10. Cited hereafter as South Carolina *House Journal.*

[26] Holland Thompson, *The New South* (New Haven, 1921), 64–65; Ball, *State that Forgot,* 266.

[27] John L. M. Irby, in Otken, *Ills of the South,* 72–73.

the upcountry farmers. To inherited prejudice against that ancient center of supposed social and political tyranny was added envy of the profits of the city's bankers and cotton and fertilizer merchants. It was the "money center" whose usurers mulcted the country merchants, who in turn mulcted their farmer-debtors. Through the "endless tolls in one way or another" it was said that Charleston cotton factors, without the mediation of the country merchants, extorted great gains from the farmers. And this city was the seat of the profiteering fertilizer industry.[28]

Likewise, the farmers complained against the conduct of their state government. They said taxes were too high; they suspected corruption and believed that a state officer's salary of $2,100 was flagrant robbery. These accusations were supplemented by more convincing charges of sins of omission. The farmers called their rulers Bourbons, men who neither learned nor forgot anything; and indeed the hidebound South Carolina leaders adhered to the theory that the state should be content with a minimum of intervention in social and economic matters, discoursing in the meantime on their heroic services in the cause of the Confederacy, on the time-honored doctrine of tariff-for-revenue, and on economy in expenditures, and "viewing with alarm" the encroachments of the Federal government upon spheres of action marked out for the states.[29]

In another sense, however, they were not Bourbons. They were attuned to the progressive sentiments expressed in Henry W. Grady's definition of the New South. Without sacrificing their party or Southern principles, they wanted closer union with the North and the suppression of the crasser Southern prejudices. They fostered the growth of business and industry by low taxation, by a careful maintenance of the state's credit, and by avoiding restraining social

[28] See incisive articles in Charleston *American*, July 4, 1918. *Cf.* New York *Times*, November 8, 1894; Ball, *State that Forgot*, 266.
[29] Thompson, *New South*, 26–27.

legislation. Unlike Georgia's leaders,[30] they did not corruptly mix business in politics; most of them remained almost pathetically poor; but they did participate in a sort of "Little Barbecue" not unlike the "Great Barbecue" attended by politicians and businessmen in more opulent commonwealths. They allied themselves with the business leaders of the day, lending them the prestige of aristocratic names and glamorous reputations gained in war and politics. They were wined and dined by the rich men of Charleston and Columbia; they served as corporation lawyers; and by acts of omission encouraged the growing power of industry.

Although this alliance was too subtle for the farmers to recognize, they saw obvious injustice in the office-grabbing tactics of the Bourbons who granted appointments exclusively to themselves and their friends as though public salaries were their private property. Perhaps the Bourbons discharged public trusts with more than average merit. Yet farmers and others, in times of economic distress, were envious of their positions and capable of developing the emotions necessary to give a righteous bias to efforts to oust them from office.

Even during the early years of the Hampton regime there were "mutterings of discontent," "one or two spasmodic efforts to overthrow ring rule . . . where there was a majority of white voters." [31] The Greenback party in 1880 made a slight dent in the solid wall of Democratic strength, and noisy protests were made against the Fence Law, by which the landless were forced to confine their stock. In 1882 a legislative candidate in the upcountry won a large vote by attacking useless offices and the appropriations for state colleges.[32]

Thus in the 1880's were circumstances prepared for a

[30] C. Vann Woodward, *Tom Watson: Agrarian Rebel* (New York, 1938), 52–72.

[31] Tillman, in *Cong. Record*, 55 Cong., 1 Sess., 3310.

[32] Ball, *State that Forgot*, 174–75.

revolt from Bourbon control of South Carolina. The Civil War had shattered the social and economic bases of aristocratic privilege. The reforms of Reconstruction removed legal barriers against popular government, and the manner in which the Reconstruction regime was overthrown proved that the white masses of the state were capable of effective exercise of their franchise. Economic distress coupled with the ineptitude of the Bourbon government made the farmers discontented. All that was needed for this discontent to find expression was for a leader of intelligence and courage to emerge.

Chapter VII

THE FARMER EMERGES

CONFORMITY was destined to remain a constant reality in Ben Tillman's career. He never lost his passionate devotion to the soil, to his family, and to South Carolina, nor did he modify his prejudices against Negroes and Republicans, against groups and attitudes that were not American in the Southern sense. His conservatism was supplemented, not contradicted, by behavior and belief that distinguished him from his neighbors and early gave him, in limited spheres, the temperament of the innovator. For in truth Ben was no ordinary farmer. He was a passionate thinker and doer, a man of dreams in political and economic matters if not in the exalted substance of poetry; he was one who understood the historic trends of his state and was possessed of the necessary energy of mind and body to act upon convictions. He would remain quiet so long as the world served his purposes, but woe unto those who disturbed his peace of mind and body!

What sort of farmer was this successful husbandman who increased his holdings from four hundred to twenty-two hundred acres? He worked hard, but his labors were not those of the ordinary yeoman. They were intense—the almost profound concentration of the man of genius who for the moment sought nothing more significant than material prosperity. The speculative cast of his endeavors was unusual. He read farm magazines, wrote an occasional article for the *Southern Cultivator*, boldly gambled in lands, and, without the resources of the gentleman farmer, courageously experimented with new crops. Moreover, he was sharply critical of his own farm methods as well as those of others.[1]

His pronounced literary habits were not, as would have been the case in a more normal man, stifled by absorption in the practical obligations of family and farm.[2] During his early married life it became his fixed custom each day, after starting the farm routine, to stretch himself on his porch, with the back of an overturned chair as a head rest, and spend many hours reading. By afternoon he was surrounded by a barricade of the day's accumulation of books and newspapers which he had carelessly cast aside in the eager search for new materials. His reading habits were too well established to be shattered by such inconveniences as the call of farm work and the rompings of his children.[3]

His literary materials were limited but sound. Through subscriptions to several good publications, including the Charleston *News and Courier* and the *Southern Cultivator,* he developed an intense interest in public affairs and agricultural progress. But his major absorption was the English classics: Smollett, Fielding, Bulwer, Thackeray, Dickens, and, above all, Scott. He read and reread the great poets— Shakespeare, Ben Jonson, Milton, Dryden, Pope, Tom Moore, Burns. He did not neglect history—English, Roman, and American—taking special pride in the annals of his own beloved South Carolina. His readings were not indiscriminately broad. He did not investigate the economic theories current in his day. Unlike some of his neighbors, who tried to absorb the mysticism of the English Bible, he mastered only a limited portion of its literature. The narrative rather than the subjective and the lyrical in the great

[1] "I very soon knew from experience and observation," he declared, "that my education had been woefully neglected in so much as I knew nothing of practical affairs." Tillman to J. Wilson Gibbes, February 21, 1916, in Tillman Papers.

[2] "My education," he once told his son, "only began when I left school." *Id.* to Henry C. Tillman, July 18, 1912, *ibid.*

[3] Middleton, "Ben Tillman: A Character Sketch," in Tillman Scrapbooks.

greed for office, the lack of free discussion, the sycophancy of the plebeians, and the parish system through which the wealthy and aristocratic Charleston area achieved undue representation. The "ambitious plebeian," or interloper, he complained, instead of attaching himself to "what ought to be," waits, "with the cunning of the fox," for opportunity to be admitted into "the oligarchical club." He achieved this "by always going for the powers that be," that is, by supporting the candidates of the ruling clique.[6]

George had his day of revolutionary triumph. In the constitutional convention of 1865 he directed the destruction of the parish system.[7] On his election to Congress in 1878 he became a conservative so far as practical action in state politics was concerned, but his active mind continued to develop novel and erratic ideas. He stored up ample reserves for possible use by a brother who was to prove more intelligent.

While George was growing into a purposeless conservative, the development of Ben's political ideas was quickened by contacts with Gary, a man of action rather than doctrine. Gary developed a spasm of fury based almost entirely on personal disappointment. He wanted to be one of South Carolina's two senators, but in 1877 Matthew C. Butler beat him to the first vacancy, and the following year, Wade Hampton to the second. Then came a ruinous quarrel with Hampton and defeat for the governorship in 1880 by Johnson Hagood, a Hampton lieutenant. Within a year the fiery Edgefield politician was dead, with the imputation of a threatened party bolt hanging over his memory.[8]

[6] George D. Tillman's speech of December 7, 1855, on "Electors of President and Vice President," in *The South Carolina Legislative Times: Being the Debates and Proceedings in the South Carolina Legislature at the Session Commencing November, 1855* (Columbia, 1856), 97–101.

[7] Andrews, *South Since the War*, 81–82.

[8] See the dispute on this point between George D. and Ben Tillman, in Charleston *News and Courier*, September 17, 1895. Gary is defended by William A. Sheppard, *Red Shirts Remembered: Southern Brigadiers of the Reconstruction Period* (Spartanburg, S. C., 1940), *passim*.

Gary's distinguished services in the Confederate army and in Reconstruction commended him to all white South Carolinians. But his hasty and lawless disposition, his bold and profane language, his opposition to payment of the Reconstruction debts, his championship of a usury law, and his frank statement of the manner in which the victory of 1876 had been won, made him *persona non grata* to as moderate and discreet a leader as Hampton.[9]

Gary's attitude was expressed before the Democratic Edgefield County Convention of 1880. After telling of his desire "to put in the hands of every honest man a whip to lash the rascals [i. e., the Republicans] naked through the world," he launched into an attack upon the "aristocratic oligarchy," saying: "Do they want every office? Was one of them ever known to decline an office? . . . Is there not some way to satisfy their greed for office? Parties are made for the advancement of individuals and families. The door must be left open for all. . . . The autocratic and aristocratic leaders will be driven to the wall whenever the issue is made between them and the masses of the people." [10]

Had this bold speaker lived, he might have carried out the threat of the last sentence. As events happened, the memory of his actions and disappointments lived in the hearts of thousands who felt that he had been deprived of deserved rewards. Ben Tillman was among those who held this conviction, believing that Gary was more responsible than anyone else for the Hampton victory of 1876, and that he had been "swindled and cheated by Hampton, Butler and Hagood and that crowd." "I was his staunch friend, conferred with him often, and was one of his lieutenants in Edgefield." [11]

With the ideas of George D. Tillman and Martin W.

---

[9] Wallace, *History of South Carolina,* III, 328–30.

[10] Charleston *News and Courier,* May 5, 1880.

[11] Tillman to Francis W. P. Butler, June 7, 1918, in Tillman Papers; *id.,* in Charleston *News and Courier,* September 17, 1895; John K. Aull, in Charlotte *Observer,* January 3, 1933.

Gary as a beginning, Ben Tillman evolved a theory of South
Carolina history which later proved to be a practical basis
for the political reconstruction of the commonwealth. But,
unlike his two mentors, he was not a professional politician;
he was a farmer who was restrained from entering public
agitations by the common obligations of his calling. In order to act he needed political issues directly connected with
personal problems. How such issues grew out of his common
difficulties is best described in his own words:

"I had cleared money every year until 1881, and bought
land and mules right along. In 1881 I ran thirty plows,
bought guano and rations, etc., as usual, and the devil
tempted me to buy a steam engine and other machinery,
amounting to over two thousand dollars, all on credit. My
motto was that, 'It takes money to make money, and nothing risk, nothing have.' To have been entirely free from
debt would have made me feel 'like a kite without a tail.'
So I struck out boldly in deep water. Ben Jonson says:

> We are all mortals
> And do have visions.

I had mine, and they were rose-hued. Uninterrupted success had made me a fool. I was 'like the little wanton boys
who swim on bladders,' but I did not know how much of
'a bladder' cotton was on land impoverished of vegetable
matter in a dry year. The latter part of July began to give
me an inkling of what a frail support it was. The drought
came. It did not rain from July 10 till late in September,
and when I settled up I had 'tail' enough to my kite. I was
in the 'Red Sea,' but did not know it. . . . I thought I
knew how to farm and was a cotton 'planter' still.

"Nothing daunted, in 1882 I struck out boldly for the
shore. But I thought my kite's tail was lacking a little
weight, so I bought 250 acres more land, not doubting that
it would rain and that I would be all right again in a year
or two. Eighteen hundred and eighty-two was a good year

and I made good crops, but there was a small margin of profit as expenses were so heavy—corn was $1.50 per bushel and meat 14 to 16 cents per pound—so I only made the payment on the land I bought and had 'nothing for interest' on the debt of 1881."

Then he began to diversify and retrench. "Sickened" by high-priced provisions, he grew enough corn and oats for his own use, acquired a herd of cows, and butchered annually from six to eight thousand pounds of pork. But he did not prosper. The years 1883, 1884, 1885, and 1886 were "poor years for cotton." The land was "sick" and the rainfall irregular. Tillman's pocketbook was "like an elephant had trod on it." "The tail to my kite," he explained, "began to grow intolerably heavy. . . . I have felt the waters rising higher and higher, and looked forward without hope, as failure after failure in the cotton crop left nothing with which to pay interest." [12]

In other words, the Edgefield farmer had gone through an experience typical of many Americans of his profession. He had become absorbed in the passion for making money. Although he was experienced, industrious, sober and close-fisted, his road to fortune had not been smooth. He had been led into debt in order to expand his cotton lands and had suffered losses. Like most farmers, he was a bad loser, and gave "deep study" for "many, many months" to the causes of what, with exaggeration, he called the "grinding poverty" of himself and other farmer-capitalists in his class. In answer to those who called him "a self-confessed failure in the management of my own farms," he made thrusts at "the damnable lien law" and at the credit merchants who, by "successful farming," were "able to pick a large crop of cotton whether they grew it or not." But with a capacity for sharp self-criticism, he admitted that the main cause of the distress of himself and his class was ignorance. "I discovered

[12] Tillman, in Charleston *News and Courier,* March 30, 1887; address before the first Farmers' Association, *ibid.,* April 30, 1886.

that not only 'I do not know how to farm,' but that very few
of us in the hilly part of South Carolina do. We are land
butchers, not farmers. We are overseers far worse than Irish
landlords, and the negroes are eating us out of house and
home, while we follow the old ante-bellum system, and
strive after money to *buy* a living, instead of *making* a living
at home. Our lands, too, are going down the rivers and
rapidly deteriorating in intrinsic value by false farming."
To remedy this condition he was convinced that it was his
duty to advocate agricultural education.[13]

This diagnosis of the weaknesses of the South Carolina
farmer was prophetically sound. It gave birth to an idea
destined to motivate Tillman for many years; for he had
great confidence in his convictions and tenacity in holding
to them. But his remedy was not yet sufficiently comprehensive to encompass the significant agrarian and political
changes he was destined to effect.

Tillman's first move in the achievement of his objective
of agricultural enlightenment was the organization, in
1884, of the Edgefield Agricultural Club. Among the quite
unintellectual farmers of Edgefield, the vigorous academic
program he advocated made little appeal. The club failed
before it had begun to function.[14] Tillman, however, was
not the man to surrender after a single effort. In January
of the following year he revived the organization under the
name of the Edgefield County Agricultural Society.[15] Sixty
members were recruited, and the enterprising farmer was
made president. Indifference and dissension, originating in
the exacting personality of the leader and his no less exacting demands, soon reduced the membership by half.[16]

This organization, however, gave Tillman opportunity
to advance his ideas. Without compromise, he expressed

---

13 *Id., ibid.,* March 30, 1887; *id.,* "The Origin of Clemson," in Tillman
Papers.
14 *Id.,* "Origin of Clemson," *ibid.*
15 Edgefield *Chronicle,* January 5, 1885.
16 *Ibid.,* April 8, May 20, June 18, 1885.

himself fully on agricultural reform. Instead of the usual
rosy oratory about the greatness of the past and the hopes
for the future, he chided the farmers of Edgefield for failure
to attend the meetings in larger numbers, and bluntly asserted that to engage in efforts to help the farmers was a
thankless task. He castigated those who cried prosperity in
the face of "land butchery" by ignorant farmers and Negroes. "The farmer," he said, "is the creator of wealth. Yet
we are not enjoying the independence and freedom from
care which the tillers of the soil the world over who own
the land, naturally enjoy and which was once the most striking character of our people." [17]

Tillman's vigorous assault on ignorance engendered "a
manifest increase of interest in the welfare of the society,"
and he was elected one of Edgefield's three delegates to the
joint summer meeting of the State Grange and the State
Agricultural and Mechanical Society.[18] The president of
the Agricultural Society invited Tillman to be one of the
speakers. Accordingly, in the first week of August, 1885,
with a prepared manuscript in his possession, the Edgefield
farmer journeyed to the little town of Bennettsville, where
the two societies were to meet. He was supremely confident
in his own integrity and fearlessness and in the belief that
he was "perhaps the best posted man in South Carolina." [19]

[17] *Ibid.,* June 24, July 1, 1885.
[18] *Ibid.,* June 17, 24, 1885; Charleston *News and Courier,* July 20, 1885.
[19] Tillman to Gibbes, February 21, 1916, in Tillman Papers.

Chapter VIII

THE FARMER TURNS AGITATOR

THE ninth annual joint session of the State Grange and of the State Agricultural and Mechanical Society opened in the courthouse at Bennettsville on August 5, 1885, with 155 men of influence in agriculture and politics present. The courtroom was sprinkled with sawdust as a protection against farmers noisy in step or careless with tobacco juice. The rostrum was festooned with cedar, wild olive, and ivy; against the walls were vases of flowers and specimens of corn and tobacco plants; and in the yard were exhibitions of farm machinery and cattle. The mayor of Bennettsville gave the usual "eloquent speech" of welcome, to which President D'Arcy P. Duncan of the Agricultural Society responded with the usual "force and humor." Then the serious business began. The best minds of South Carolina agriculture read well-chosen and dull (for a warm day) essays on the details of correct farming. Under this soporific influence, the two societies closed their first day's deliberations.

The situation was changed on the second day when it was rumored that "the brother of Congressman Tillman" was going to say something out of the ordinary. The courthouse overflowed with an expectant throng when Ben Tillman arose to speak. In appearance and manners, as well as in words, he differed from the sort of speakers to which South Carolina conventions were accustomed. Instead of the typical gentleman with long hair and pleasing face, here was a farmer whose appearance was a mixture of the plain and the uncouth and whose one eye flashed ominously. He read his manuscript in a high, rasping voice with the hesitancy of a schoolboy. "As soon as you put a farmer upon his feet," he said apologetically, "he loses fluency," for his ideas and words are "like a pair of unbroken colts which never work kindly together." Eschewing the alleged achievements of the past and the rosy hopes of the future, he voiced hard historical truths and anxious forebodings. The diction was that of the masterful amateur disdainful of the glib euphuisms of the professional orator. He replaced the usual jokes with dry humor and the usual prolixity with the terse coarseness of a Swift and with illustrations drawn from the soil. Yet his words were choice. The paper bristled with literary references without pedantry. Phrases calculated to stir the complacent and to tickle the curiosity of the untutored were mixed with the hot passions of the righteously indignant. President Duncan's hospitality was repaid with the audacity of cross words and a questioning of motives.

The speaker drew a gloomy picture of what he described as the decline of the agricultural well-being of the state. At least half of the white farming population, he said, was compelled to mortgage crops in order to get supplies; half the landowners were merely "hewers of wood and drawers of water." "The yoke of the credit system that used to gall no longer frets. The decay of that sturdy independence of character, which once was so marked in our people, is rapid, and the lazy 'descent into hell' is facilitated by the state government, which has encouraged this reliance on others. . . . The people have been hoodwinked by demagogues and lawyers in the pay of finance."

The agricultural department of the South Carolina College, which was designed to give the farmers the information they lacked, was "just a sop to Cerberus, a bribe to maintain the support of the farmers in the legislature." Although he did not favor the abolition of the college as a place for the education of lawyers and scholars, he did believe that many of its graduates were "drones and vagabonds."

The agricultural and political activities of the state were grotesque. Six or eight "disreputable politicians," he asserted, were among the members of the Agricultural Society; yet the farmer members should not attempt their expulsion lest they prove strong enough to expel the farmers. With biting humor he described the evolution of a farmer-legislator into a politician: "He enters the State House a farmer; he emerges from it in one session a politician. He went there to do something for the people. After breathing the polluted atmosphere for thirty days he returned home intent on doing something for himself. The contact with General This and Judge That and Colonel Something Else, who have shaken him by the hand and made much of him, has debauched him. He likes this being a somebody; and his first resolution, offered and passed in his own mind, is that he will remain something if he can."

The fiery farmer embodied the constructive portion of his address in a series of resolutions designed to promote agricultural education. He asked that the Agricultural Society request the legislature to compel the trustees of the South Carolina College to execute "in good faith" the Federal laws giving funds for agricultural education; [1] to appropriate money to establish an agricultural experiment station and to aid in the holding of farmers' institutes; and to enlarge the state board of agriculture by adding a farmer from each Congressional district.

The Tillman address and resolutions electrified the convention. The speech, said the Columbia *Daily Register,* "was the sensation of the meeting. Almost every sentence was responded to with prolonged applause, showing that the farmers were *en rapport* with the scathing irony which he dealt out to the political close corporation." However,

---

1 The reference here was to the act of 1862 setting aside the proceeds of land sales "in order to promote the liberal and practical education of the industrial classes," and the act of 1887 giving $15,000 to each state for the establishment of an agricultural experiment station.

the applause was given by a minority of the delegates and by the nonvoting farmers behind the rails. The officers and a majority of the assembly were angered by what they considered Tillman's insulting words. Four of his five resolutions were rejected. Yet the impression of the speaker had been profound. His resolutions were not tabled until after there had been "a long and desperate fight" on the floor of the convention between him and the friends of the South Carolina College, in which, once again, he displayed "hard sense, keen satire, and good-humored badinage." The fact that his extreme tactlessness angered his opponents had its advantage: it made him the leader of the discontented; it convinced him and his friends that their wrongs could be redressed only by an agricultural organization different from that before which he spoke. He was satisfied that he had turned an attempt to laugh away his agitations into "anything but a comedy," and he frankly admitted, "I did not go to Bennettsville to pass resolutions but to explain to the farmers how they are duped and robbed." [2]

Tillman returned to the busy seclusion of his Edgefield farm and made no immediate attempt to act upon his words. Some tried to explain away "the fun" he had stirred up, saying that his essay was just another unconventional but harmless attack upon the established order by his well-known brother. Yet the address had actually created a stir, even in the most conservative circles, making Ben better known than the veteran George. Many frankly said that "a new deal" in state politics was necessary; the *News and Courier,* powerful conservative daily of Charleston edited by open-minded Francis W. Dawson, flirted with fire when it asked for an open discussion of the nature of the "ring" which Tillman said dominated the state. Other newspapers

[2] For this meeting, see Charleston *News and Courier,* August 5-8, November, 19, 1885; Columbia *Daily Register,* August 7, 8, 1885. The text of Tillman's address is in Tillman Scrapbooks, I, which is missing from the South Caroliniana Library.

spoke acrimoniously of the oligarchy of a dozen families supposed to control affairs; and there was talk of a "panic party" among state officials.[3]

The Edgefield farmer was stirred into action by these repercussions of his Bennettsville effort. To secure information he corresponded with General Stephen D. Lee concerning the merits of the agricultural college in Mississippi of which Lee was president. Then, as had been his custom while reading, he propped himself with a pillow and inverted chair, and composed the first of his memorable letters to the Charleston *News and Courier*.[4]

He began by scolding those who had ridiculed him for his alleged failure at Bennettsville. His facts, he asserted, had not been controverted, and he had not been "crushed or silenced." He then announced his constructive wish: not, as at Bennettsville, the reform of the South Carolina College, but the establishment by the state of a separate agricultural college on the Mississippi model. "I may be a crank," he continued; "I acknowledge being an enthusiast on the subject of agricultural advancement and enlightenment—but, if so, I am satisfied with my company." The reference was to General Stephen D. Lee who, in Tillman's opinion, was doing more for the farmers of Mississippi "than all the Confederate brigadiers from Virginia to Texas." The writer drew an unenviable comparison between the Mississippi college and "the pitiful, contemptible, so-called agricultural annex to the South Carolina College, a classical and literary kite with 'agricultural' written on its tail." The South Carolina College, in a state whose lands were worse worn than those of Mississippi, was "an admirable place" to add to the "ghastly heap of skeletons at the foot of the professional ladder," while it left "our agriculture in the deadly grip of imbecility and ignorance." He prophetically warned, as "the humble opinion

---

[3] See Charleston *News and Courier*, August 20–September 9, 1885.
[4] Stephen D. Lee to Tillman, October 21, 1885, in Tillman Papers.

of a backwoodsman, who is simply a farmer," what would happen to the state college unless "the lawyers of the state, who govern us," dig up the corpse of agricultural education which has been buried at Columbia and establish a separate college. "They had better compromise the matter," he explained, "ere the storm, which is brewing, shakes the foundation of their beloved college and, perhaps, topples it to the ground." [5]

In the letters to the *News and Courier* which immediately followed this initial outburst, the politicians, the agricultural bureau, and the Agricultural Society, as well as the state college, were victims of the Edgefield backwoodsman's irony. "Each and every one of these 'aids to agriculture,' " he sweepingly affirmed, "is permeated, saturated— I might almost say are rotten—with politics." The farmer sees the money which "might go far to revolutionize our benighted agriculture, divided, frittered and wasted, or boldly appropriated to other uses. He sees himself contemptuously pushed aside to make room for men who are really his inferiors." The Agricultural Society was accused of using an appropriation of $2,500 to foster a fair "where gambling is one of the chief attractions." The supporters of the state college "worship the past, and are marching backwards when they march at all." The $25,000 given the agricultural bureau was wasted in lawyers' fees, junketing tours, useless expositions, an absurdly bulky handbook of the state's resources, and "a monument of folly and extravagance" called the new agricultural building. In place of "information and enlightenment" the farmers were given "a pile of brick," and for internal reform was substituted a vain attempt to attract Northern capital and immigrants. The head of the agricultural bureau, the same Colonel Andrew P. Butler under whom Tillman had served in the Sweetwater Sabre Club, was accused of irresponsibility and of writing re-

[5] The first letter, November 16, 1885, appeared in Charleston *News and Courier*, November 19, 1885.

ports so dull that they were the "terror of any intelligent reader." [6]

These letters were unlike anything Tillman's generation had ever read. The discriminating asked, "Who is this abusive pamphleteer, this master of an emphatic style, who mixes so well the classic with the homely, and who has such constructive ideas of educational and agricultural reform?" The fact that he questioned motives and called names excited the attention even of many not interested in abstractions or constructive programs. On the other hand, it would be a mistake to confuse virulent language with extreme ideas. Tillman's views were moderate enough not to repel so fundamentally conservative a commonwealth as South Carolina. There was no attack upon private property, nothing other than scorn for the state's submerged Negro majority. Nor did the writer engage in the precise sort of slander which might have been the basis for summary retaliation by the proud gentlemen of South Carolina. He merely indulged in irritating hyperbole, metaphor, and innuendo. Charges of actual dishonesty were avoided in favor of accusations of stupidity and negligence.

The enlightened Conservatives of the state tried to be conciliatory. Dawson, the powerful and very intelligent editor, instead of silencing the literary farmer by refusing to publish his letters, gave a guarded approval of what in them he considered constructive.[7] President Duncan of the Agricultural Society invited Tillman to join that group and courteously offered to show him the agricultural exhibits at the state fair.[8] The trustees of the South Carolina College asked the establishment of the agricultural experiment station,[9] and the legislature took from the control of the agri-

---

[6] Tillman, *ibid.*, November 30, December 3, 7, 1885.

[7] *Ibid.*, November 20, December 4, 1885.

[8] D'Arcy P. Duncan, *ibid.*, December 14, 1885.

[9] *Reports and Resolutions of the General Assembly of the State of South Carolina*, 1885 (Columbia), I, 848–49. Cited hereafter as South Carolina *Reports and Resolutions*.

cultural bureau the money Tillman said that body had been squandering. The rude farmer, however, astonished his adversaries by publicly refusing to join the Agricultural Society, and to those who offered to escort him through the state fair he said, "Damn the fair; I'm hunting figures on you fellows." He roundly scored the legislature for its acts of omission and said that its attempt to correct the alleged abuses of the agricultural bureau was a "stultifying" confession.[10]

Such an attitude invited retaliation. Commissioner of Agriculture Butler replied indignantly to the farmer's "excessively personal" attacks,[11] and President Duncan said that the farmer's charges were "wild and imaginative" and that his insinuation of "political rottenness" was "a wilful, malicious slander." Tillman was derided as an "Agricultural Moses," who, "like Jonah's gourd, has sprung up in the night" to show the state how things ought to be done anew.[12] The college trustees rejected the separate agricultural college idea; the legislature refused to establish the experimental station or to investigate the expenditures of the agricultural bureau, and it re-elected the incumbent members of that body. The tactless farmer had infuriated the lawmakers.

The war was on, and Tillman welcomed it. "Singlehanded and alone" he had written his letters to the *News and Courier* in language obviously not intended to make peace. "Opposition and abuse," declared this tough-skinned man, "have only made me more determined." [13] He knew that by antagonizing those in authority he would win support among the more numerous group who did not hold office. He received letters of commendation from hundreds of sources; [14] letters commenting upon his ideas appeared in

10 Tillman, in Charleston *News and Courier*, December 14, 1885.
11 Butler, *ibid.*, December 9, 1885.
12 Duncan, *ibid.*, December 14, 1885.
13 Tillman, *ibid.*, April 30, 1886.
14 *Id.*, "Origin of Clemson," in Tillman Papers.

the press; [15] and a pro-Tillman minority in the legislature, a farmers' bloc, fought for the reduction of expenditures and renewed the traditional battle between the upcountry and the low country over the apportionment of legislative seats.[16]

Aroused by enemies and sustained by friends, Tillman assumed the title of Agricultural Moses assigned him in derision. He declared: "I have touched a chord which vibrates from Oconee to Georgetown. The pent-up indignation of the farmers has found a voice through me . . . I should be a coward to refuse to lead . . . I have waked you [the farmers] up and shown some of the wrongs and impositions." It was true that he had "mortally offended many of the leading and most progressive farmers"; that "cajolery, misrepresentation, ridicule, deception and every artifice" were used to divide the farmers; and that the political ring was united; but he would give "instructions like a general" in order that the farmers might be organized. "Like Moses of old," he was willing to die before he reached the Promised Land of office. "Make me a trustee of a genuine agricultural college, . . . and I ask no more. . . . I thank God I can make my living, even as a farmer, without scrambling for place at the public crib." It is not true, as some have claimed, that he permanently eschewed political ambitions. "If I ever get in office," ran his qualifying statement, "I will walk to it like a man, not crawl like a spaniel, and it will seek me, not I it." [17]

An address written by Tillman and signed by him and ninety-one other farmers called for the agriculturists to meet in a state convention at Columbia on April 29. The farmers, said the address, composed 76 per cent of the state's population, and "may justly claim that they constitute the state, although they do not govern." Notwithstanding the

---

[15] Charleston *News and Courier*, November 24, December 4, 1885.

[16] *Ibid.*, November 29, 30, December 2, 9, 1885.

[17] *Ibid.*, January 28, 1886; Tillman, "Origin of Clemson," in Tillman Papers.

fact that the legislature of 1885 consisted largely of agriculturists,[18] Tillman was dissatisfied with the type of agrarian consciousness these farmer-legislators manifested. He would have class-conscious and aggressive farmers—a type new to the decade: farmers who would not longer be content to be the "mudsill of society," but who would organize in such a manner as to dominate the state politically through the simple force of numbers.[19]

In response to Tillman's suggestion, county conventions representing community agricultural clubs were held on April 5 to elect delegates to the state convention. The Edgefield assembly praised the local leader and made him the head of its delegation. Some county assemblies, however, suspected his motives, accusing him of selfish political ambitions.[20]

At noon of the appointed day, the Farmers' Convention assembled in the state agricultural building with 300 delegates present, representing all but 5 of the state's 35 counties. The excellent attendance was proof of the far-reaching effect of Tillman's agitations. Among the 300 only 12 were members of the legislature, 2 were lawyers, about a dozen were doctors, 3 or 4 were editors, and several combined farming with merchandising. The remainder were simonpure farmers tasting for the first time the delights of a large political gathering. "It is," said Narciso G. Gonzales, the Columbia correspondent of the *News and Courier,* "a convention of intelligent South Carolina farmers, with a few black sheep [men of alleged Republican affiliations] among them."

The demeanor of the Agricultural Moses, when he arose from behind a simple pine table to call the convention to order, failed to impress Gonzales. From appearance one "did not suppose that he is the author of those incisive let-

[18] Seventy-one per cent of the House were farmers, while the Senate was composed of eleven farmers, fourteen planters, and ten lawyers.
[19] See address, in Charleston *News and Courier,* March 9, 1886.
[20] *Ibid.,* April 6, 1886.

ters to the *News and Courier*." In fact, continued the journalist, "he is a very ordinary looking man. He is of medium
height, spare build and rather swarthy complexion. His
single eye sparkles and snaps, it is true, when he begins to
'whoop up things,' but his face in repose is neither attractive
nor handsome. It certainly gives no indication of the brain
power which it undoubtedly conceals." He wore a double-
breasted coat, black pants, a black slouch hat, and a silk scarf
which "rode up" and showed a narrow standing collar. He
was revealed as he really was, a farmer attempting to appear
before the public with some show of grace.

The vivid personality behind this unprepossessing exterior was apparent as soon as Tillman began to read his
address. His rasping voice rang through the hall with a
strange resonance, and his points of emphasis were made
effective by cunning halts and gestures. The choicest English was deftly mingled with the familiar Tillman realism,
which evoked roars of laughter. The paper achieved unity
by utilizing the device of the caged starling in Laurence
Sterne's *The Sentimental Journey*.

"We can't get out! We can't get out!" cried farmers caged
by the evils of slavery and wasteful methods of cultivation.
The door was opened by the abolition of slavery and the
events of 1876, but still the farmers cried: "We can't get
out! We can't get out!" Mental slavery "is more helpless
than physical bondage." Physical slavery had been dead
twenty-one years, but "not only do we cling to the dead past
and follow the old slave system of farming, but we aggravate
that system by doing many things our fathers would not do."
There were the evils of speculation, the overproduction of
cotton, and "the damnable lien law" by which the farmers
were bound to the merchant-creditors. Unless the farmers
remedied these evils by an assertion of their potential liberties, there would be no space for them in the New South
replacing the Old South, "which now stalks about like a
ghost in its shroud." Unless this were done, the sons of slave-

holders would become hewers of wood and drawers of water for "alien" capitalists and merchants.

In reassuming the title of Moses, Tillman affirmed that he was willing to lead despite the fact that he had been called a crank, a demagogue, a dreamer, and a disrupter of the Democratic party. Opposition, he said, had made him more determined and the convention to which he spoke proved that Moses was able to gather the Israelites. He knew he had fanned the smoldering fires of discontent into flame. The agitation for a farmers' college "has broadened" into "a grand reform movement, looking to a general overhauling of the entire government and a thorough washing of dirty linen." Although he promised not to split the Democratic party, he called it "an old lady" who had shown favoritism to those of her children grown lusty and arrogant from pulling at her teats.

This playful sally was followed by a savage attack on those who questioned his motives. He snarled: "Little greedy men, office-seekers and their satellites, judging me by their own low standards of selfishness . . . , have cried, 'Office, office, he only wants office.' Oh, it is pitiful that in a short space of ten years the purity of motive, ardent patriotism, and useful devotion to duty which made possible the redemption of the state in '76, should be succeeded by this political leprosy which now permeates our entire governmental fabric."

Although he had thrown away the scabbard at Bennettsville, he quaintly denied that he had personal political ambitions: "I have told the devil to get behind me. I commenced this fight pure and honest and 'only a farmer.' I will end it as I began, and for reward I only ask your good opinion and confidence."

Yet he repudiated the advice of those who warned the farmers of the dangers of politics, crying: "Say, you men who own the soil of South Carolina . . . , how do you like this wet-nursing, this patronizing, this assumption of superiority, this insufferable insolence? What freeman has not felt his heart swell with indignation . . . at the idea that we know not what we want and must get on our knees and beg for it?" He concluded that the farmers must agree on a program and enter the approaching Democratic conventions and primaries so that men favorable to their views would be elected.

The Farmers' Convention, both in feeling and action, carried out Tillman's will. Governor Thompson was refused an invitation to speak on the grounds that "the work of the convention should not be overshadowed by one who has recommended wrongful appropriations." Although this "insult" to the chief executive was rescinded, his address received only formal courtesy, and he was forced to listen to one of Tillman's talks on the "robbery" of the farmers. Only twenty-seven votes could be mustered in opposition to Tillman's resolutions, all of which were adopted. They provided for a convention, to be known as the Farmers' Association, to meet each November; for a committee, of which the Edgefield farmer was chairman, to appear before the legislature to further the projects of the farmers. These projects consisted of an agricultural college with a tax on fertilizer to support it; the repeal of the lien law; the abolition of The Citadel, the state military academy; the establishment of an industrial college for girls in its buildings; and the calling of a convention to make a new constitution. The Farmers' Convention had been a success. A numerous and representative group of landowners had become acquainted with their designated leader, and an organization to change the policies of the state government had been created. The gathering had been a personal triumph for the Edgefield farmer. The address, his second before a state convention, had delighted his hearers and given him self-confidence. His bold assumption of single-handed leadership was not premature. On the evening before the convention he had called prospective leaders to his hotel room and had induced them to approve his resolutions after eliminating his designation of The Citadel as "that military dude factory" and of the cotton mills of the state as a "moral graveyard" for young women. On the floor of the convention his will was law. His opponents were "hooted down," "cut off" with furious denunciations; his measures were approved in summary fashion. "The convention," he explained, "needed no arguments, other than I have already made in the *News and Courier*, to convince it." "It was Captain Tillman's convention all the way through," dolefully admitted one commentator. "What he wished was done. That more was not done was because he did not wish it done." [21]

[21] For proceedings of the convention, see *ibid.*, April 29, 30, May 1, 1886; Columbia *Daily Register*, April 29, 30, May 1, 1886.

Chapter IX

THE FARMER ENTERS POLITICS

THE Farmers' Convention was the first move in the political canvass of 1886. Tillman and his followers wished to capture the machinery of the Democratic party to insure the election of a governor and legislature favorable to their program. Two major obstacles stood in the farmers' way: lack of political experience, and ignorance of the type of class-conscious political action to which they allowed Tillman to pledge them.[1] The leader himself was too absorbed in farm work and too inexperienced in politics to give the maximum effectiveness to his first adventure in such matters.

Having abjured political ambitions for himself, he hesitated long in designating a candidate for governor. Of the ten men suggested by the press as possibilities—among whom were both George D. and Ben Tillman—John C. Sheppard and John P. Richardson loomed largest. Sheppard had had a notable career in the legislature, had been elected lieutenant governor in 1882, and had become governor in 1886 when Thompson resigned. He was a man of eloquence and caution. Richardson's qualities commended him to those who opposed change. His family had already given the state four governors. Competent in routine matters and possessed of excellent manners, he was the last man in South Carolina to disturb the political peace.

Tillman favored Governor Sheppard, a citizen of Edge-

[1] See Alfred B. Williams' explanation, in Greenville (S. C.) *News*, March 18, 1886.

field, a former schoolmate, and endorsed by the same county convention which sent the farmer as the head of its delegation to the state nominating convention. Sheppard had, according to Tillman, committed himself to the separate agricultural college idea and other farmer principles. When it was apparent that the more hidebound Conservatives were drifting to Richardson, Tillman attempted to form a coalition with the more progressive Conservatives. On June 21, six weeks before the nominating convention, he met the editor of the *News and Courier* in conference at Augusta. They agreed that Dawson should use his powerful editorial pen in favor of a separate agricultural college, while Tillman should withdraw his opposition to The Citadel. Although, according to both men, nothing was said about the Sheppard candidacy, these two were the governor's staunchest supporters in the nominating convention.[2]

Meanwhile, the pro-Tillman farmers developed into active politicians,[3] and Tillman himself made addresses in various parts of the state, defending from a manuscript the work of the Farmers' Convention and answering personal attacks. At Tirzah, in York County, on July 27, before a gathering of twenty-five hundred people, he cast aside his notes and demonstrated talents as an extemporaneous speaker.[4] Conservatives were alarmed at these activities. "The farmers," wrote a member of the Democratic executive committee, "took the bit by their teeth and seemed opposed to everybody who tended to sustain the University and The Citadel." [5] The result was that in the state convention of August they lacked only thirty votes of a majority.

[2] Tillman to Greenville *News*, August 24, 1886; Charleston *News and Courier* (editorial), August 11, 1886.

[3] The farmers of South Carolina, said an outsider, have "come out of the shades of private life" to capture as many Democratic conventions as possible. Augusta *Chronicle*, May 14, 1886.

[4] Yorkville (S. C.) *Enquirer*, July 28, 1886.

[5] James F. Izlar to R. Means Davis, July 24, 1886, Robert Means Davis Papers (in possession of Professor Henry C. Davis, University of South Carolina).

On the eve of the convention, however, the strength of the Tillman-Dawson coalition was weakened by Sheppard's declaration against a separate agricultural college, a constitutional convention, or the repeal of the lien law.[6] The governor, by temperament and association a Conservative, shrank from a program of reform. As a consequence, the farmer delegates refused to endorse his candidacy, and Tillman, in seconding his nomination, said that he did so in the capacity of delegate from Edgefield and not as a representative of the Farmers' Association. This scattered the farmers' votes and led to Richardson's nomination by a majority of twenty-seven. Had Sheppard accepted the Tillman program, the support which Tillman and Dawson could have given him would have led to his nomination.[7]

The farmers failed to win endorsement of even a portion of their program. Proposals for a constitutional convention, for the apportionment of representation in Democratic conventions according to population, and for the nomination of state officials by direct primary, were voted down. Tillman took these defeats in gloomy silence.

Between this convention and the scheduled Farmers' Association meeting in November, 1886, the Edgefield farmer kept himself before the public eye by a wordy controversy with the officials of the agricultural bureau. Members of the official clique advised the unwisdom of controversy with him. It "will only serve to increase his popularity and give him greater notoriety." But some sensitive gentlemen could not restrain themselves. Tillman's sarcasm provoked uncontrollable anger, and the refutation of his sweeping charges was often too easy for silence. The answers gave him opportunity to pour vituperation on his antagonists. Analytical souls argued that the controversies he created were mere tempests in a teapot, an indulgence

---

[6] Charleston *News and Courier*, August 5, 1886.

[7] *Ibid.*, August 4–7, 1886; Tillman, "Origin of Clemson," in Tillman Papers.

in a mass of petty personalities; but beneath the trivialities there were issues which attracted the serious. Tillman never allowed his constructive program to recede far into the background.

When the farmer-leader said that the employment of a chemist by the agricultural bureau was unnecessary because the professor of chemistry at the South Carolina College had offered to do this work without charge, Major L. A. Ransom, a journalist employed as the clerk of the bureau, replied that this was "an unfair and untrue statement," and when the farmer retorted with exasperating insinuations, the clerk threw discretion to the winds. Wrote Ransom of Tillman, "He lied, l-i-e-d. No insinuation about that I hope, Benjamin?" This gave the Edgefield landowner his chance to indulge in patronizing belittlement. To create a chemist's position, he asserted, was merely to furnish another berth at public expense. "Public pap," he railed, "is so sweet it is hard to resist the appeals of friends for another gimlet-hole to be bored in the treasury and another teat stitched in for these pets to suck." Ransom himself was merely "Colonel Butler's clerk," "the tail, not the head of the agricultural bureau," "a Hessian," "a mercenary scribbler fighting for his clerkship." "Someone will say," concluded the farmer, " 'Go to Columbia and fight him.' Here again he has the advantage. Physically he is not my equal, and I would as soon strike a woman; should I leave home to seek a quarrel with him, and use arms to put us on an equality, if I killed him it would be murder . . . ; while if he killed me it would be justifiable homicide." [8]

The bold scribbler from Edgefield was soon to have better opportunity to follow brave words with brave deeds. On November 11, Commissioner of Agriculture Butler met him in a railroad station, and with his pistol at hand, responded to Tillman's friendly salutation "by giving vigor-

[8] Tillman and L. A. Ransom, in Charleston *News and Courier*, September 22, 28, October 4, 1886.

ous expression to a decidedly unfavorable opinion of the Edgefield leader." He was enraged by Tillman's long war against his bureau—a campaign waged "without proper regard for truth, honesty and fairness." And he had been "stung to the quick" because Tillman had accused him of signing his name to letters which had been prepared by clever subordinates and which he himself could not explain. Was it not most humiliating for a brave gentleman to be called a fool by a clever knave? If the brave man could not defeat the clever knave in argument, he could humiliate him and possibly kill him. But the Edgefield controversialist remained calm in the face of insult. He later explained that his pistol was in his satchel during Butler's verbal assault. He saved his bluster for a less dangerous moment. "Any gentleman," he said, "who thinks I am a hatrack upon which to hang insults, can risk it if he sees fit." The truth of the matter was that, despite bold words, he was not foolish enough to have a bloody encounter. Such risks would sooner or later have led to his death. "I am not of a fussy nature," he slyly confessed, "and can say with Falstaff, 'God keep lead out of my bowels.' " [9]

The Farmers' Association met according to schedule in November, 1886. There was an absence of the enthusiasm of the previous session. The coldness of the hall and the rival attraction of the state fair reduced attendance. In the principal address of the occasion, Tillman warned his enemies not to regard his movement as a failure. He had lost the August Democratic convention only because of suspicions against himself; the farmers were being slowly educated to look after their own affairs; and they had a goodly representation in the coming legislature. They should guard against letting the board of agriculture and the proposed agricultural college become an "asylum for broken-down politicians and superannuated Bourbon aristocrats, who are thoroughly incompetent, . . . but are ever ready

[9] *Ibid.*, November 12, 17, 22, 23, 1886.

to put in their claims for every position of honor and profit."
The vein of hopefulness in his address did not conceal a
lively appreciation of the ignorance of friends and the greed
of enemies. "To combat," he philosophized gloomily, "the
ignorance, the prejudices, the apathy, and the egotism of
our agricultural population is a difficult and wellnigh hopeless task."

Despite the decrease in attendance and enthusiasm, the
convention accomplished the work for which it was called.
The demands upon the legislature were precisely stated in
ten points, and Tillman and two others were approved as
the committee to present the demands. He and nine others
were nominated as members of the board of agriculture
which the legislature was asked to create.[10]

At the opening of the new legislature in November,
Representatives John L. M. Irby of Laurens and James E.
Tindal of Clarendon, and Senators W. Jasper Talbert of
Edgefield and Jefferson A. Sligh of Newberry appeared on
the floor as active champions of the farmers' program. Tillman, aided by Eli T. Stackhouse of Marion and Milton L.
Donaldson of Greenville, the two other members of the
farmers' legislative committee, was busy about the lobbies
preparing bills and holding conferences with members.[11]
Yet neither the outgoing nor the incoming governor encouraged his activities. Sheppard praised the work of the
agricultural bureau and of the agricultural annex of the
South Carolina College, but did not commit himself on
the constitutional convention issue.[12] Richardson contented
himself with a eulogy of South Carolina as "among the
most advanced and progressive of the States." [13]

The Tillman program had little chance of success. To
reduce salaries was deemed unwise for the sound reason

[10] *Ibid.*, November 10–12, 1886; Augusta *Chronicle*, November 10–12, 1886.
[11] South Carolina *House Journal*, 1886, p. 9; Charleston *News and Courier*, November 24, 25, 26, 1886.
[12] South Carolina *House Journal*, 1886, pp. 36–41.
[13] *Ibid.*, 118.

that salaries were already quite low. The attempt to repeal
the lien law was defeated by a large vote,[14] and the bill for
the reorganization of the agricultural board, after passing
the House, was defeated in the Senate because of "a determination on the part of the various agricultural senators
not to consent to what they consider 'Tillman dictation.' "[15]
The constitutional convention idea was defeated because it
was interpreted as "but an evidence of the fever and fer-
ment in the public mind, which is in itself the best reason
why the convention should not be held." [16] The measure to
double the phosphate royalty was postponed for fear of killing the goose that laid the golden egg and because no way
could be found to void existing contracts with the mining
companies.[17] The agricultural college bill was abandoned
in favor of Tindal's proposals for the establishment of agricultural experiment stations and for the appointment of a
commission to investigate agricultural colleges in other
states. Both measures passed the House, but only the experiment stations bill received the approval of the Senate.[18]
Lawrence W. Youmans, the anti-Tillman senator from
Barnwell, ridiculed the Mississippi agricultural college as
an institution whose merits were not worth investigating.[19]

Thus, only one constructive measure designed for the
benefit of the farmers became law; Tillmanism had been
temporarily routed. The source of the failure was resentment against Tillman's blustering and dictatorial manners.
There was no other reason why a body of legislators dependent upon a predominantly agricultural constituency should
have rejected a program of reform so moderate as that pro-

14 *Ibid.*, 186–87.
15 Narciso G. Gonzales, in Charleston *News and Courier*, December 22,
1886; *Journal of the Senate of the General Assembly of the State of South
Carolina*, 1886 (Columbia), 310–11. Cited hereafter as South Carolina
Senate Journal.
16 A Charleston legislator's speech, in Charleston *News and Courier*,
December 18, 1886.
17 *Ibid.*, December 6, 9, 1886.
18 South Carolina *Senate Journal*, 1886, pp. 383, 402.
19 Charleston *News and Courier*, December 24, 1886.

posed by the Farmers' Association. "Those whom Captain Tillman has singled out at different times," explained Dawson, "can hardly be expected to look upon his propositions with as much favor as though he himself had always been studiously moderate and just." [20] The fiery pamphleteer was quick to understand, but he did not take the editor's advice to "look more charitably upon opposing views," so that he might "find the road to reform easier to travel." Tillman made no effort to soften the asperity of his pronouncements; he refused to become a member of the legislature in order to convince a majority of his good intentions through extended personal contacts; and, likewise, he refused to resign his leadership of the Farmers' Association in favor of someone more tactful. He continued the difficult role of public censor from the isolation of his farm.

In this spirit, two weeks after the adjournment of the 1886 legislature, he resumed his letters to the *News and Courier*. The enemy of the farmers was now the Senate. The so-called "Tillman dictation," he said, was "a pitiful excuse" for that body's rejection of measures for which two farmers' conventions asked. An "oligarchy of lawyers" had planted "a sly dagger in Tillman's side" and slapped their agricultural constituents in the face. If the farmers were not the "dogs they were taken for, they will . . . see to it that the men who thus contemptuously put this indignity upon them are properly rewarded." On his visits to Columbia he had kept his eyes and ears open and learned that the Coosaw Mining Company wanted no changes in the laws. "This gigantic octopus" snapped its fingers in the face of a legislature of Carolina farmers, for it had "stockholders and paid attorneys in both houses." [21]

Youmans, the leader of the Senate, replied in kind. The Edgefield farmer was "a miserable failure in the management of his own farm" and "a chronic faultfinder and universal grumbler" whose ugly adjectives had become too

[20] *Ibid.,* January 6, 1887.   [21] Tillman, *ibid.,* January 6, 1887.

common, and who conceitedly imagined that his failure equipped him to establish the perfect commonwealth. His false claim that the farmers could be saved by government action sounded to Youmans "like the ravings of a fanatic" guided by the heresies of Henry George.[22]

This pointed attack gave the Edgefield controversalist his opportunity. "Our bosses at Columbia," he began, "have grown so arrogant that they resent criticism." Youmans was accused of being "a brazen and unblushing" indulger in "slanderous tirade," an egotist who had "brass enough to gild a church steeple" and whose brain was addled by the commissioner of agriculture's "good liquor." The charge that Tillman was a failure as a farmer came with poor grace from a merchant "who had waxed fat off his store by selling goods to his poor farmer neighbors" and whose "successful farming" consisted of "picking cotton" raised by the so-called unsuccessful. "This little tom-tit who accident had made Senator from Barnwell" and who had "the insufferable arrogance to twit his betters" may have had his vanity tickled by claiming that he had killed Cock Robin, but the farmers knew that his braying was that of an ass.[23]

Tillman debated with Youmans at Barnwell on October 31, 1887, the first of hundreds of such occasions which demonstrated the intense popular enthusiasm he had aroused for himself and his cause. In challenging the Barnwell senator to debate in the senator's community, the Edgefield farmer boasted, "If I don't start a farmers' movement there, I will 'shut up.' "[24] Youmans was as competent in speech as he was in writing, but Tillman's "fearful stabs" so stirred the audience of three or four hundred half-drunken farmers that they refused to allow their own senator to speak. The partial quiet which Tillman was at times able to secure for his crestfallen rival was not lasting, for the naturally angry

22 Lawrence W. Youmans, *ibid.*, February 15, April 18, 1887.
23 Tillman, *ibid.*, February 23, March 30, May 5, 1887.
24 *Id.*, *ibid.*, February 23, 1887.

retorts of the would-be speaker provoked pointed interruptions from Tillman. These interruptions in turn caused so many howls from the audience that the frustrated Barnwell leader was forced, after two hours of effort, to leave the stand unheard, "howled down" by his own people.[25] Thereafter, in South Carolina the brute strength of noise supplanted reason as a means of settling political issues. It was a reversion to the days of Chamberlain.

Conservatives again warned reputable gentlemen of the folly of debating Tillman. "Too much notice" was taken of his "demagogical harangues," and it was "undignified" for state officials to answer his "unwarranted attacks." [26] This argument, however, was ineffective. How could the traditional leaders of the people fail to accept the challenge of a man who threatened to deprive them of their following? Tillman's speeches were so galling and apparently so full of error and innuendo that their victims were led, even against their wills, to answer. Soon there was a second debate between Tillman and Youmans at Edgefield, followed by debates between the farmer-agitator and Chancellor William D. Johnson and others.[27]

In the meantime, official South Carolina held at Spartanburg the so-called Interstate Encampment of the State Grange. Exhibits were prepared to entertain and instruct farmers and to attract immigrants and Northern capital. The leading political and agricultural lights were solicited to speak. There was to be a farmers' institute of the type Tillman had advocated at Bennettsville, and the Edgefield critic was invited to be present. But, instead of accepting the invitation, he stood afar and indulged in criticisms as ungracious and uncharitable as they were true. The Spartanburg gathering, he said, was only an assembly of the "elders and high priests of the oligarchy," a "rendezvous of

25 "E.W.B.," *ibid.*, November 1, 1887.
26 Darlington *News*, cited in Robert Means Davis Scrapbooks.
27 Edgefield *Chronicle*, November 23, 1887; Charleston *News and Courier*, November 8, 14, 1887.

all men who shut their eyes to the present and worship the past," a disreputable means of enticing farmers from their homes "by the fanfaronade and grand promise of the well-advertised 'show.' " The exhibits were scarcely worth seeing; "the real, practical farmers" were spectators, not speakers; and the promoters—Bourbons, lawyers, doctors, and politicians—lacked the intelligence to manage a farmers' fair. He turned to fundamentals. Immigrants could not be attracted by false promises, and it was better for South Carolinians to develop their own resources than to try to attract Northern capital. Such investments, he held, were already coming in too large quantities in the form of loans on lands at extortionate rates of interest. "Owning our railroads, 'Northern capital and brains and Southern Shylocks,' " this agrarian patriot warned, "are rapidly absorbing our farms." [28]

Tillman's letters and addresses were followed in December, 1887, by the third gathering of the Farmers' Association, with only ninety-seven delegates present, since little was expected of the approaching holdover session of the legislature.[29] A faction of about forty delegates attempted to have the convention "throw Tillman overboard and thus put an end to him." He himself took no prominent part in the proceedings, not even replying to his opponents. Secure in his power, he frustrated those who wished to destroy his leadership and impelled the majority to vote for the measures he advocated.[30]

Notwithstanding this apparent lull in the Tillman Movement, the legislature of 1887 was the scene of a long battle between the friends and the enemies of the farmers' program. Strenuous efforts were made to reform the board of agriculture. The majority, however, merely enlarged that body, electing as its new members men not endorsed by the

28 Tillman, in *Charleston News and Courier*, September 16, 1887.
29 *Ibid.*, December 1, 2, 1887.
30 *Ibid.*, December 2, 3, 1887; Columbia *Daily Register*, December 2, 3, 1887.

Farmers' Association.[31] A resolution for a popular vote on the issue of a constitutional convention failed; [32] and after a bitter struggle, a proposal to reapportion legislative representation was defeated by the Senate.[33]

The most outstanding accomplishment of the session was the renaming of the South Carolina College as the University of South Carolina, and the creation of a college of mechanical arts and agriculture as the first of a series of new colleges proposed for the rechristened institution. Governor Richardson said that the scheme was "a true development" which would be "approved by the great bodies of our citizens." [34] The Tillman leaders, before hostile galleries, vainly tried to have the agricultural college excluded from the new arrangement. They pointed out that a state declared to be "too poor to try the costly experiment of an agricultural college" was asked to contribute nearly $100,000 to the new university.[35] The evident purpose of an act making into a "university" a college which only 192 students attended was to frustrate the ambitions of Tillman for a separate agricultural college.[36]

The only victory which the farmers won at this session was of a negative character: they prevented the reassignment of the state's phosphate franchises to five mining companies for the royalty of $2.00 a ton.[37]

Tillman was exasperated over the legislature's second failure to enact a fair share of his program and expressed

[31] South Carolina *Senate Journal*, 1887, p. 376; South Carolina *House Journal*, 1887, p. 239; South Carolina *Acts*, 1887, pp. 802–803.

[32] South Carolina *House Journal*, 1887, pp. 206–207.

[33] This measure aroused the traditional rivalry between the upcountry and the low country, as it involved the sacrifice of representation by the latter. Charleston would have lost four seats to the gain of Beaufort and counties above Columbia. South Carolina *Senate Journal*, 1887, pp. 205–206; Charleston *News and Courier*, December 10, 14, 1887.

[34] Charleston *News and Courier*, November 23, 1887.

[35] William H. Wallace, in Newberry (S. C.) *Observer*, December 29, 1887.

[36] South Carolina *House Journal*, 1887, p. 220; South Carolina *Senate Journal*, 1887, p. 194; Edwin L. Green, *A History of the University of South Carolina* (Columbia, 1916), 118.

[37] Charleston *News and Courier*, December 16, 1887.

his disappointment in his so-called Farewell Letter. The general assembly, he said, was composed of "political harlots" and "how-dye-do-statesmen" who wanted reform but did not know how to free themselves from "the same old hands." "The Columbia Club with its free liquors and entertainments had so won the good-natured farmers that they could not say nay to them." Such "malleable and complacent material" should be returned to private life.

Concerning the newly-created university with its added mechanical and agricultural college, he spoke words of warning: "Let its friends crow lustily over the great victory they have won," but the poor farmers, who could not afford this institution, would show these "lordly planters" that they were not satisfied with "the weak and contemptible agricultural tail which had been attached to the literary kite" and that they would have their separate college. Because he was not elected to the board of agriculture he ironically called his writings "the mutterings of a ghost, the howl of a disappointed office-seeker." How mortified he was not to be able to go on the annual junketing tour of the board to inspect phosphate deposits in no wise connected with farming! "The Bee-man from Spartanburg, the Sheepman from Chester, the Jersey-man from Anderson, and their brethren, must get out their water toggery . . . and go to sea to develop South Carolina's farming interest."

He bade Charleston not to risk the possibility of a return of the Negro to power when and if the political unity of the whites were destroyed. The city had better lose some of her representation than tolerate the refusal of "our imbecile statesmen" to draw the fangs of the Negro monster by making a constitution containing property and educational qualifications for voting. He was confident that he had on his side the numbers necessary for the success of his plans, and that he lacked only organization. Although "the 'Ring' newspapers" were declaring that "Capt. Tillman is a dead duck," he was certain that the farmers "will be on hand 'to make Rome howl' " in the next election.

Tillman went into temporary retirement, placing the management of the Farmers' Association in the hands of others. He said that unlike more fortunate rivals, he had no "big salary," and could, therefore, no longer afford "the costly luxury" of neglecting the material interests of his family. "I told you not to go into this thing," Mrs. Tillman had already remarked concerning his agitations; "you can't do any good, and you had much better be attending to your own business and looking after me and the children." [38]

So, with a declaration of faith in his own integrity and in the permanency of his good work, and with much praise from relieved opponents for "his honesty of purpose, his energy of expression, and his intelligent work in arousing the farmers of the state to better methods of farming," [39] he resolved to keep the peace by returning to his farm. "I am no politician," he explained, "trained to 'crook the pregnant hinges of the knee.' " But this retirement was not irrevocable. He was by nature too restless, and he felt too deeply the justice of his program, not to be active again when more fortunate circumstances might arise. Or as Dawson expressed it, "He had not lagged superfluous on the stage; he could with grace permit himself to come upon the scene again."

[38] Cited, *ibid.*, April 30, 1886.
[39] Dawson editorial with Tillman letter, *ibid.*, January 26, 1888.

Chapter X

THE AGRICULTURAL COLLEGE ISSUE

SCARCELY more than three months after the publication of the Farewell Letter, an opportunity for the Edgefield agitator to fulfill Dawson's prediction of returning to the stage presented itself. On April 2, 1888, Thomas G. Clemson, a son-in-law of John C. Calhoun, died, leaving Fort Hill, the Calhoun estate of 814 acres, and a cash endowment of $80,000, for the establishment of a separate state agricultural college. Under the Clemson will, Tillman and six others were named life trustees of the proposed college with power to name their successors, and the legislature was empowered to elect six other trustees. The making of a majority of the trustees independent of the legislature insured the execution of the will according to Clemson's specifications. The college would be kept out of politics, and if the Negroes should gain control of the state its future would not be subject to their rule.[1]

Tillman, elated over material reinforcement of his most cherished idea, immediately ended his retirement and began agitation for the acceptance of the bequest. By tactful persuasion perhaps it would not have been difficult to influence the mild-mannered gentlemen who controlled the state to accept the conditions under which a philanthropist wished to add to the public resources. But finesse was not a part of the Tillman strategy. He could enter the citadel of the enemy only by a frontal attack. Then, too, he saw

[1] Tillman, "Origin of Clemson," in Tillman Papers. The Clemson will as taken from the records of Oconee County is published in Alester G. Holmes and George R. Sherrill, *Thomas Green Clemson: His Life and Work* (Richmond, 1937), 193–201.

in the Clemson issue an opportunity to further a comprehensive program, of which the separate agricultural college was only an important part.

Accordingly, two weeks after the death of Clemson, Tillman published an address demanding, among other things, that the state establish the college at Fort Hill. "Fortune has unexpectedly smiled upon us in the form of the munificent bequest of Mr. Clemson." To avoid violating pledges against the increase of taxes, he insisted, in a bombardment against "that wonderful ten-student agricultural annex of the so-called university," that that school be divested of all subsidies for agricultural and industrial education. Since he anticipated that attempts to convert those in power to the separate college idea would be vain, he urged the people to "arouse themselves from their lethargy" in order to elect a new legislature pledged to the Clemson project.[2]

The Federal government, long before Tillman raised his voice, had done much, through the Morrill Act of 1862, for the advancement of agricultural education, and many states had established separate colleges for this purpose. Clemson proclaimed the notion that South Carolina should follow the example of these states. A native of Pennsylvania who had identified himself with South Carolina by marrying Calhoun's daughter and by espousing the cause of the Confederacy, he was well qualified to preach the gospel of agricultural education to his adopted state. Beginning in 1866 with articles in newspapers and addresses before farm societies, he had urged South Carolina to establish an agricultural school as a means of recovery from the disasters of war. In 1871, 1883, and 1886 he had made wills devoting his not inconsiderable estate to the endowment of the proposed school.[3]

But he did not possess the qualities necessary to convince

[2] Address of the executive committee of the Farmers' Association, in Charleston *News and Courier*, April 26, 1888.
[3] Holmes and Sherrill, *Thomas Green Clemson*, 1–5, 145–50, 157–59.

an unprogressive state of the wisdom of progress. He was looked upon with suspicion as a Northerner by a people noted for their provincialism. His odd personal habits and his fatuous notion that the body of Calhoun should be removed from Charleston to Fort Hill accentuated the distrust. With age, he developed into a neurasthenic recluse about whose religion and morals unflattering tales were circulated.

Impressed by Tillman's published letters, Clemson, in the fall of 1886, invited the Edgefield farmer to confer with him and two of Clemson's neighbors, Richard W. Simpson and Daniel K. Norris. The four men spent the day discussing the agricultural college. According to Tillman's version, Clemson was uncertain whether to turn Fort Hill into a Calhoun memorial or to use it for a college, until committed by his three visitors to the college idea with the scheme for seven life trustees. The three guests were named by him as members of this group, together with one man whom Tillman did not know and three others prominent in the Farmers' Association.[4]

Ben Tillman undoubtedly overemphasized his influence in the making of the Clemson will. That document had been given definite form three years before the Edgefield farmer had his one interview with the Fort Hill recluse. On the other hand, it should be remembered that it was not necessary for Tillman to visit Fort Hill to discover the need of an agricultural college; his published writings proved that he already knew it. The meeting at Fort Hill, instead of being the enlightenment of one leader by another, was really a merging of forces in common cause for the sound principle to which both individuals were already converted. Clemson's special contribution was the land and money; Tillman's, the force of his agitations.

[4] Tillman, "Origin of Clemson," in Tillman Papers. This version is partly contradicted by Richard W. Simpson. See Holmes and Sherrill, *Thomas Green Clemson*, 157–59.

Tillman's letters to the *News and Courier,* despite their fury and personalities, prove that their author had an authoritative understanding of the problems of agricultural education. When confronted with a fair and informed antagonist, as in 1887 when he˙debated Professor R. Means Davis of the South Carolina College, he was able, in a large measure, to lift the discussions above the irrelevant to the plane of fact and reason. He agreed with Davis that they should be "serious, candid and dispassionate." Unlike some who supported him in the debate, he did not become impractical or pedantic, going no further afield for illustrative material than the experiences of General Stephen D. Lee in Mississippi.

Tillman felt that it was first necessary to destroy in order to rebuild. Hence he began the debate with Professor Davis by a devastating attack upon the South Carolina College and its agricultural department. In the first place, the college was failing to develop the statesmen necessary "to rebuild our shattered commonwealth." Was it an accident that "the only Carolinian of world-wide fame" was educated outside South Carolina? [5] Did the college not tolerate "provincialism, stagnation, and self-idolatry"? Did not South Carolina as an agricultural state already have enough half-starved graduates in law and divinity? Second, he contended that the college lacked scientifically trained professors and the facilities in practical farming necessary to produce other than "mere theorists and cranks," or "book farmers." Third, he submitted that, granting the college's technical equipment for agricultural education could be rendered sufficient, such education could not be had successfully there because "the very atmosphere of the place" was "tainted with contempt for farming." Consequently, a separate college was needed.

A detailed description of the proposed agricultural college followed. Besides instruction in English, the theoreti-

[5] Doubtless a reference to John C. Calhoun, a Yale graduate.

cal sciences, and the practice of agriculture and mechanics, there should be an experimental farm in whose fields the students should actually work.[6] Although the plan of organization of the institution was largely gleaned by Tillman from his readings, he was original in the description of the spirit which he felt should motivate the new campus. He believed that the greatest obstacle to the success of the college was not cultural or physical but psychological: the fear that agricultural students would develop an attitude of inferiority. Hence came the insistence that the agricultural college should be placed at a distance from other types of schools and that the students should be required "each day to hoe, to ditch, to fork manure, to make butter, to feed stock, to graft, to bud, to prune." [7]

The most notable event of the Democratic State Convention of 1888 was the Edgefield leader's speech in favor of the primary method of nominating public officials. Although he knew that the majority was against him, he spoke as sharply in the direct presence of the enemy as he had written in his letters to the *News and Courier*. The convention, he bluntly began, represented only small cliques, but he represented a majority of the people. For twenty years the people had "fallen in the apathy of death" because of the necessity of maintaining white unity in the face of the Negro. "Putrefaction" had developed "in certain sections." "Two years from now when there is full head on," he warned the hostile delegates, "you will be swept before the flood." When interrupted by cries of "Questions!" he yelled, "You may gag me here, but I will meet you before the people. . . . When I think of the outrages which have been committed in this hall [the House of Representatives] I shudder to enumerate them—financial extravagances, tricky

[6] Tillman's plans for an agricultural college were first published in Charleston *News and Courier,* December 4, 1886.

[7] Tillman, *ibid.,* September 16, 27, October 10, 1887.

practices." The members had been "bamboozled or affected in some way by Columbia water or whiskey or by Charleston brains."

The speech was adjudged "discreditable both in matter and manner," and the primary plan was lost by vote of 207 to 83. Yet Tillman's proposal that the candidates for state offices be given opportunity to address the people was granted; definite dates and places for such occasions in each Congressional district were established. Moreover, the Tillman harangue helped undermine popular confidence in the convention system and demonstrated that the farmers' leader was as aggressive in the hall of the enemy as in the isolation of his farm.[8]

In inaugurating the practice of joint debates between candidates for public office, the convention of 1888 added a distinctive institution to the political life of South Carolina. These meetings, or "one ring circuses" as they have been derisively called, filled a genuine recreational need in the life of rural South Carolina in the period after the decline of the camp meeting and before the rise of commercial amusements and the automobile. Around an improvised rostrum, partly shaded from the summer sun by a grove of oaks, most of the white men of a given neighborhood, and such women as dared risk the possibility of coarse language from immodest speakers, would gather to hear jests and denunciations from favorite candidates and even to receive advice and information concerning affairs of state. If there was a chance that the opposing candidates would engage in hot debates, buggies, surreys, and wagons converged on the meeting place in seemingly endless lines. Not the least attractive features of the gatherings were the feasts of barbecued shoat and lamb prepared in roasting pits. The campaign meeting was a rural festival.

[8] For proceedings of the convention, May 17, 1888, see *ibid.*, May 17, 18, 1888; Columbia *Daily Register*, May 17, 18, 1888.

While the joint debates gave opportunity for vitriolic demagogues to arouse prejudices and evil passions,[9] it cannot be denied that such occasions had civic virtues. There the people could meet their prospective rulers in a pitiless conflict of debate calculated to expose their strength and weakness. In the rough and tumble of the joint discussions the candidates were tested for mental agility, loyalty to tribal prejudices, statesmanlike intelligence, and even physical courage. By means of these debates Tillman and others stirred the whites masses into political consciousness. He was not wrong when, in a calm moment of later life, he declared that the lively interest in public affairs which these meetings stimulated gave South Carolina "in a way the purest democracy in the United States." [10]

The Edgefield leader, though not a candidate for office, participated in the first of the scheduled debates of the 1888 canvass. This was held at Hodges Depot in Abbeville County on July 20. His forensic opponents were Governor Richardson and Lieutenant Governor William L. Mauldin, who were, up to that time, unopposed for the offices they held. Seven hundred enthusiastic admirers of Tillman gathered in a grove of oaks upon a semicircle of hewn log benches to await their idol and the feast which was to follow the addresses. Richardson was the first speaker. Tillman, in reply, used words and gestures which delighted his hearers. He opened with ironic regret over being forced to follow "the silver-tongued Governor, whose glowing words in praising South Carolina have stirred my heart." To make the contrast between the governor and himself seem ridiculous, he blurted out: "I am nothing but a barnyard rooster. . . . I am chock full of rocks and want to chunk some." A rapid succession of burning denunciations were cleverly interspersed with insinuating pleasantries. He designated Dawson, who in an editorial had attacked Tillman's Demo-

9 Wallace, *History of South Carolina*, III, 348.
10 Tillman to Judge F. M. Annis, June 21, 1914, in Tillman Papers.

cratic convention speech, as "some buzzard who had escaped from the market house in Charleston and gone into
the *News and Courier* office, where it was spewing its slime
all over me." [11] He spoke of his visit to the Columbia Club,
a gathering place of upper-class gentlemen. It was "a monstrous nice place," and "no wonder the corn and bacon
fellows [in the legislature] like it." As for himself, he had,
while on a visit to the club, refused strong drink in favor of
lemonade. The inclusion of such talk did not obscure emphasis on his constructive program. He wanted a legislature pledged to the establishment of the separate agricultural college. The Conservatives declared that he "had
injured himself greatly by his vulgar and bitter speech," [12]
but the Hodges audience was delighted, so expressing itself
by a vote of thanks.[13]

At the other meetings of the canvass Tillman was the
main issue. He was not invited to the Greenville meeting,
where each of the speakers commented upon his "foul slanders," and where Dawson appeared to answer the Hodges
speech.[14] The Edgefield tribune, before "a genuine Tillman audience" at Chester, refuted charges of conspiracy
against the integrity of the Democratic party. "I hurl the
imputation in their teeth and declare it a lie," he told his
excited auditors. The crowd applauded when he rejected
criticisms of Governor Richardson by saying that he respected him as chief executive but not as a man. The newspapers interpreted this as an insult, the like of which had
not been visited upon a governor of South Carolina since
Chamberlain.[15]

At Sumter, Tillman was opposed by three jeering speak-

[11] At that time buzzards were allowed to hover around Charleston's
famous market and eat the refuse.
[12] Greenville account in Charleston *News and Courier*, July 22, 1888. The
term Conservative, first used during Reconstruction to designate the party
of white supremacy, was revived in the 1880's to embrace the anti-Tillman
faction of the Democrats. The Tillman faction was called Reformers.
[13] Gonzales, *ibid.*, July 21, 1888.   [14] Greenville *News*, July 25, 1888.
[15] Charleston *News and Courier*, July 31, 1888.

ers and an insulting audience, but he was bolder than usual. He began: "Some come here to see what sort of an animal I am. I have neither hoofs nor horns, but I am a plain, simple farmer like yourself." Criticizing Sumter County for electing delegates to the state nominating convention before he had spoken, he said: "I wish I had those ten delegates here to tell them my mind." In his zeal to create popular distrust of those in authority, he repeated, without endorsement, the slander that Governor Thompson, on leaving the governor's mansion, had taken part of the furniture with him.[16]

The meeting at Blackville was featured by a dangerous dispute between Tillman and Gonzales, the testy correspondent of the *News and Courier* who, because of the failure of the governor to combat the sardonic speaker from Edgefield, undertook the novel and risky experiment of supplementing his fiercely partisan but accurate reports of the campaign meetings by interruptions from the reporters' desk. When the farmer accused the irascible journalist of misrepresentation, Gonzales cried: "If you say I misrepresented you, you are an infernal liar." The friends of the two men mobilized and for a moment bloodshed seemed imminent. But Tillman, as he had done under similar circumstances when challenged by Butler, prudently explained the situation away. Again he was too wise to allow rash acts to follow rash words.[17]

The canvass of 1888 culminated in Tillman's two speeches in Charleston, where he went to debate Dawson. The brilliant editor had done much to further the farmer's agitations by publishing his letters and subjecting his ideas to intelligent criticism. The two men had affected a sort of an alliance in the summer of 1886. But both soon discovered that co-operation between persons so dissimilar was impossible. So the understanding was broken. Tillman resumed

16 *Ibid.*, August 2, 3, 1888.
17 Gonzales, *ibid.*, August 7, 8, 1888.

his attacks on Dawson and the urbane journalist retaliated with severe criticisms of the boorish farmer.[18]

Tillman first appeared before a Charleston audience on August 3. Dawson was unavoidably absent attending to his duties as a member of the National Executive Committee of the Democratic party. Nevertheless, the Edgefield man, under the very shadow of St. Michael's Church, achieved a personal triumph. Through subtle humor he won a hearing from an inimical audience, and then ridiculed his hearers for "running like a parcel of turkeys" when they mistook a drumbeat for a repetition of the disastrous earthquake of 1886. He was able to say that he had "come to Charleston not to make friends but to brush the cobwebs from the people's eyes." [19]

More remarkable, however, was his return to Charleston three weeks later in response to the "prayer" of the element in the city hostile to Dawson and the local politicians. Appearing once more across the street from St. Michael's, he spoke for more than two hours before several thousand bristling but interested persons. Boldly and rudely, the up-country farmer expressed his suspicions of the low-country city of aristocratic conservatism and rich cotton merchants. He began thus: "You Charleston people are a peculiar people. If one tenth of the reports that come to me are true, you are the most arrant set of cowards that ever drew the free air of heaven. You submit to a tyranny that is degrading to you as white men. . . . God have mercy on your pusillanimous souls. . . . If anybody was to attempt that thing in Edgefield, I swear before Almighty God we'd lynch him. . . . You are the most self-idolatrous people in the world. I want to tell you that the sun doesn't rise and set in Charleston." The fact, he continued, that the city was over-

---

[18] For comments of Alfred B. Williams, see Greenville *News*, August 31, 1888.

[19] Charleston *News and Courier*, August 4, 1888.

represented in the legislature and was sending there "fat lawyers," who were agents of "fat railroads," was "burning the hearts of the country people."

And as for Dawson: "You [the Charlestonians] are binding yourselves down in the mire because you are afraid of that newspaper down the street. Its editor bestrides the state like a colossus, while we petty men, whose boots he ain't fit to lick, are crawling under him seeking dishonored graves. . . . He is the Old Man of the Seas, clinging around the neck of South Carolina, oppressing its people and stifling reform."

The rustic orator had scarcely finished his words when Dawson mounted the platform and with spirit denounced "the defamer from Edgefield." After he had finished, Tillman regained control of the audience for a full hour by the use of anecdotes made vivid with cunning gestures. Then he drove away amid cheers.[20]

The Tillman performance in Charleston had a lasting effect upon his career. He had proved his mettle under circumstances which would have frightened one less bold or more sensitive; the reward was no effective interruption of his unsparing words. Aware of the traditional prejudices of the upcountry majority against Charleston, he had deliberately antagonized the city as a means of marshaling these prejudices on his side. Charleston struck back venomously. Several thousand local patriots marched to the *News and Courier*'s office to hear Dawson excoriate the upcountry "invader"; and Charleston County elected a solid anti-Tillman delegation to the approaching state convention. A *News and Courier* editorial denounced the farmer as the leader of the Adullamites, those who were opposed to "the better classes, . . . to the people of education, intelligence, and civilized habits." These Adullamites, or Tillmanites, were "people who carry pistols in their hip pockets, who

[20] *Ibid.*, August 29, 1888; Kirkland, "Tillman and I," in Columbia *State*, June 30, 1929.

expectorate upon the floors, who have no tooth brushes, and comb their hair with their fingers." [21]

Whatever the remainder of South Carolina might do, Charlestonians resolved to wait many years before looking with favor upon one who had so crassly characterized their city. Undoubtedly they found moral satisfaction in their indignation; but in so expressing themselves they fell deeper into Tillman's craftily contrived trap. They were but adding fuel to the flames of sectional and social discord lit by the Edgefield man's hot words. He, not they, would profit by the conflagration.

The canvass of the state had been a personal triumph for Tillman. Had the May convention of the Democratic party adopted the primary system of nominations, or even postponed the election of delegates to the nominating convention until after the campaign meetings, it is likely that anyone whom Tillman supported would have become governor of South Carolina. In the resulting situation, the farmer had to content himself with greatly increased personal popularity. Many counties had chosen delegates before he had been heard,[22] and before the leaders of the Farmers' Association had developed sufficient experience to capture a majority of the county conventions. By July, Tillman had given up hope of dominating the nomination convention.[23] But this did not prevent him from controlling a strong minority of the delegates and a majority of the party's nominees for the legislature.

A necessary question at this point is, Why was Tillman able to exert such influence upon the white masses? An explanation is that the farmers for the first time in the history of South Carolina were given the opportunity of being

[21] Charleston *News and Courier,* August 31, 1888.
[22] Fifteen counties had chosen their delegates before Tillman made his second speech. *Ibid.,* June–July, 1888.
[23] He told Gonzales on July 20 that Richardson would win the nomination because the cards were stacked in favor of the governor. *Ibid.,* July 31, 1888.

led by one who looked at life from their angle, who was like them in personal appearance, speech, and manners, and who expressed their ideals and prejudices. His humorous and coarse speech appealed to a majority no more delicate than he in matters of taste. Although he was as unconventional in personal behavior and as abusive in speech as a Jacobin, his ideas, stripped of impertinencies and expletives, were sufficiently constructive to give the farmers hope and sufficiently moderate not to frighten naturally conservative landowners. His radicalism was not directed at property.

In the Democratic convention of 1888, as in 1886, the Tillmanites, without a candidate of their own for governor, supported the least objectionable candidate from among the officeholding group to oppose Governor Richardson, who sought a second term. Their choice was Attorney General Joseph H. Earle of Sumter. This was despite his defense of the Richardson administration in the summer canvass and his declaration for Richardson's re-election; [24] he was slated by the Conservatives to succeed the governor in 1890. Although his conduct was for a time somewhat ambiguous,[25] on the eve of the convention he commanded the withdrawal of his name if it should be presented. Nevertheless, the Tillman floor leader presented his name, believing that he would not refuse the honor if it were literally thrust upon him. This gesture was answered by an explicit declaration from Earle's brother that the attorney general would under no circumstances accept the governorship. But even in the face of these adverse happenings, the Tillman partisans gave the Sumter man 114 votes as compared with Richardson's 191. Had Earle been willing to serve, his

[24] Governor Richardson to Patrick H. Nelson, August 30, 1888, in John Peter Richardson Letter Books (Library of the South Carolina Historical Commission).

[25] The antagonism to Earle among the anti-Tillman delegates, said Gonzales, "was at a boiling point when the convention met." Charleston *News and Courier*, September 7, 1888.

nomination would have been assured. Tillman, although much discouraged by what he regarded as his "betrayal" by Earle, gracefully acknowledged defeat by moving that Richardson's nomination be made unanimous.

The Edgefield leader, though once more defeated in an attempt to secure the primary for the nomination of state officers, victoriously championed a resolution requiring Democratic county chairmen to invite candidates for state offices to speak in their respective counties. Thus the system of joint debates, which had already been inaugurated in each Congressional district, became a county-to-county affair.[26]

Tillman's second failure to capture the governorship filled him with discouragement which approximated demoralization. There were exaggerated rumors that he "went home, moped in the house for six weeks without going out of doors."[27] It is true that he retired from public view for more than a year, being absent from the meeting of the Farmers' Association of November, 1888. Only 75 delegates were present at the listless deliberations.[28] "It seemed as if the whole movement was in a dying condition," a Tillman leader remarked.[29] The Farmers' Alliance, a rival organization with national ramifications, had already won the active support of many South Carolina farmers of the class-conscious type to whom Tillman appealed.[30]

Despite the discouragement of their chief and the apathy in their organization, the Tillmanites made the acceptance of the Clemson will the leading issue before the legislature of 1888. They had good reason to hope for success because they commanded a majority of ten in the House and lacked

26 For accounts of the convention, see *ibid.*, September 6–8, 1888; Kirkland, "Tillman and I," in Columbia *State*, June 30, 1929; Earle, in Sumter (S. C.) *Watchman and Southron*, November 21, 1888; Charleston *World*, June 27, 1890.
27 Kirkland, "Tillman and I," in Columbia *State*, June 30, 1929.
28 Charleston *News and Courier*, November 15, 1888.
29 Kirkland, "Tillman and I," in Columbia *State*, June 30, 1929.
30 Charleston *News and Courier*, July 12, 1888.

only two for a majority in the Senate. Yet the opposition was able and formidable, consisting of the friends of the state university, The Citadel, and the church colleges. It was said to be unwise for the state to become a partner in an undertaking over the majority of whose trustees it had no authority. It was also argued that the Clemson property rightfully belonged to Floride Isabella Lee, a granddaughter of Clemson and a great-granddaughter of Calhoun. Gideon Lee, the girl's father, struck a popular note when he accused Clemson of wishing to deny Clemson's granddaughter the heritage of her illustrious ancestor and of being a vainglorious and demented old man seeking to erect a monument to his own vanity.[31] When this appeal failed to stop the movement to accept the bequest, Lee, in the name of his daughter, brought suit against the execution of the will just as the legislature met. "We simply stand before the world," said John C. Haskell, who along with his brother Alexander C. Haskell distinguished himself as an enemy of Tillman, "fighting for the only living descendant of John C. Calhoun's favorite child for the patrimony of her forefathers. . . . For God's sake let's not take this property until the courts have decided the case." Haskell and other anti-Tillman legislators exceeded such an appeal to sentiment when they accused Clemson of a type of "licentious living" which had made the visiting of Miss Lee to his home morally obnoxious.

Despite these arguments and the opposition of excited galleries filled with friends of the state university, the bill for the Clemson bequest passed the House by a substantial majority and the Senate by the casting vote of Lieutenant Governor Mauldin. The pro-Tillman legislators stressed the advantages of nonpolitical control of the college. They proved that the Clemson endowment was the endeavor of a distinguished patriot and agricultural scientist, not the whim of a senile egotist; that he was disposing of property

31 *Ibid.*, April 26, May 2, 1888.

purchased with his own funds and not inherited from his Calhoun in-laws. The charge that Clemson's alleged immoralities made him unworthy of being a patron of education was weakened by the fact that the University of South Carolina had put its moral and cultural approval upon him by giving him an honorary degree.[32]

The putting into operation of the law accepting the Clemson bequest was subjected to serious delay. Governor Richardson, taking advantage of the fact that the legislature had adjourned within three days of the time the bill was presented to him, exercised his constitutional right of holding it in suspense until the next annual session of the legislature. He justified the delay on the grounds that the Lee contest was still in court. In the meantime, however, events worked in favor of the proposed college. The delay of the governor subjected him to damaging criticisms; he was derided as "the figurehead who sits in the gubernatorial chair and obeys the bidding of the bosses." [33] On May 21, 1889, the Federal Circuit Court of Appeals decided that the will was valid.[34] The governor, impressed by these facts, signed the bill at the opening of the legislature in November, 1889.[35] Although Floride Isabella Lee had forfeited her right to her grandfather's inheritance by contesting the will, the legislature granted the $15,000 which Clemson wished her to have.[36]

The principal task of the legislature of 1889 was to frame a law which would give the proposed Clemson College full-

[32] For the debate, see *ibid.*, December 14–19, 1888. The House vote was 67 to 48; the Senate vote, 16 to 16. South Carolina *House Journal*, 1888, pp. 250–51; South Carolina *Senate Journal*, 1888, p. 262. A comprehensive discussion of the issue is available in Holmes and Sherrill, *Thomas Green Clemson*, 170–88.

[33] Florence (S. C.) *Farmer's Friend*, cited in Charleston *News and Courier*, January 8, 1889.

[34] Lee *v.* Simpson, 39 Federal Reporter 235; affirmed, April 7, 1890, by United States Supreme Court, 10 Supreme Court Reporter 631. Holmes and Sherrill, *Thomas Green Clemson*, 176.

[35] Act of November 20, 1889, in South Carolina *Acts*, 1889, pp. 277–80.

[36] Holmes and Sherrill, *Thomas Green Clemson*, 176, n. 22.

est opportunity to develop with least injury to the state university. William Christie Benet, a talented Scotch schoolmaster who had become a lawyer at Abbeville, skillfully accomplished this task. But, of course, the university was deprived of all Federal funds provided for industrial and agricultural education. Adequate support for the new agricultural college was secured by giving it these funds and the benefit of a sales tax on fertilizer. After a spirited contest, the measure passed the House without a record vote. In the Senate, Clemson College was declared to be "the biggest humbug" of Tillman, "the defeated Moses," and of Clemson, "a poor, vanity-stricken, miserable agnostic," [37] but the measure passed that body by a two-to-one majority and immediately received the signature of Governor Richardson.[38]

The pro-Tillman element in the legislature of 1888–1889 made various attempts to force into law projects of the Farmers' Association. Over the protests of the railroad interests, a law was passed giving the railroad commission authority to fix freight and passenger rates.[39] However, the bill to prohibit members of the legislature from receiving free railroad passes failed.[40] Efforts to reduce the salaries of public officials were likewise unsuccessful. A bill specially designed to reduce the salaries of judges was strongly favored by farmers. It passed the House but failed in the Senate.[41] An abortive resolution protesting against the salaries paid the professors in the state university was championed by those who felt that the institution had more teachers than the number of its students justified.[42] The attempt to take the fertilizer tax away from the board of

[37] Senator Fitz W. McMaster, in Charleston *News and Courier,* December 20, 1889.

[38] South Carolina *Senate Journal,* 1889, p. 485; Act of December 23, 1889, in South Carolina *Acts,* 1889, pp. 299–302.

[39] South Carolina *Acts,* 1889, p. 378.

[40] South Carolina *House Journal,* 1889, p. 60 and index.

[41] South Carolina *Senate Journal,* 1889, pp. 141–42.

[42] In 1888 there were 25 professors and only 170 students.

agriculture was frustrated, as was the proposal to elect Tillman and other members of the Farmers' Association to that body.[43] Although the constitution of 1868 was declared "unfit for white men to live under," and its retention an evidence of "pandering to Yankee sentiment," once more the resolution for the calling of a constitutional convention did not win the necessary two thirds of the Senate.[44]

Before considering Tillman's plunge into politics as candidate for remunerative office, it is well to summarize the results of his four years of political agitations. By means of his talents as a letter writer he had evoked an interest in public questions not often equaled in the history of South Carolina. And then by means of public speaking he had aroused a devotion to his personality and program, and a corresponding suspicion of, or hatred for, the personalities and programs of his enemies. His agitations had made possible the realization of a prized idea, the agricultural college, and had prepared the way for the profoundest political revolution from internal causes which South Carolina had ever experienced. But, at the same time, the Edgefield agitator had suffered disappointments. His rough manners and opprobrious speech had aroused bitter personal resentment. This was the overt reason why his enlightened program, with the exception of the agricultural college, had been voted down at four successive sessions of the legislature. Out of the realization that his displeasing personality had been responsible for his defeats had grown his so-called retirements after the legislative session of 1887 and the Democratic convention of the following September. Yet no defeat could destroy his belief in the justice of his cause or in the ability of the farmers to capture the state government. His agile brain continued to evolve plans and he retained the energy necessary to carry them out.

[43] William A. Ancrum was elected over Tillman by vote of 101 to 38. South Carolina *House Journal*, 1888, p. 225.
[44] South Carolina *Senate Journal*, 1889, p. 142.

Chapter XI

THE MARCH CONVENTION

AT the first convention of the Farmers' Association, Tillman had said: "I commenced this fight pure and honest, and 'only a farmer'; I will end it as I began, and for reward I only ask your good opinion and confidence."[1] The sincerity of this profession is attested by his repeated refusal to become a candidate for office. Naturally, he was severely criticized when his later action seemingly belied this pledge of self-abnegation.

In his defense it should be remembered that this self-denying ordinance was never designed to cover his active participation in politics in behalf of others; that he refused to grant his opponents the right to interpret his political ethics; and that he had modified the pledge long before he violated it. "If I 'go into the political mill pond,' " he had said less than a year after the first convention of the Farmers' Association, "it will be with pure motives."[2] In the summer of 1888 he had told Gonzales: "Give me a state primary and I'll run for governor myself."[3] These words were public notice that the leader of the farmers understood that a change in circumstances might necessitate a change in resolutions; that the successful reformer, as he becomes more and more involved in public issues, easily develops into the practical politician. Such considerations should have prevented the surprise and disappointment which many experienced when "the simple farmer" became "the selfish

---

[1] Charleston *News and Courier*, April 30, 1886.
[2] *Ibid.*, February 23, 1887. [3] *Ibid.*, July 31, 1888.

officeseeker": when, in the words of a friend who became one of Tillman's severest castigators, "the Farmers' Movement, for the farmers, of the farmers, and by the farmers, has been twisted into a Tillman Movement, for Tillman, and by Tillman." [4]

Circumstances surrounding Ben Tillman in 1890 made his candidacy for governor a practical necessity. Twice he had failed to bestow the honor upon others because his candidates failed him. He now turned to himself; for he had enough self-confidence to know that he would not himself fail the cause to which he had devoted five passionate years. In 1890 he was aged forty-three and in the prime of physical and mental vigor. Through both the spoken and written word he had become a seasoned political agitator who enjoyed the intense devotion of the South Carolina voters. He understood the sectional and class divisions of his state better than any other public figure and knew how to exploit these schisms for political purposes. Moreover, this farmer, who for years paid rather than received tax money, was undoubtedly as capable of developing avidity for the emoluments and honors of public office as "the broken-down aristocrats" he criticized. There was an element of envy in the incisive manner in which he analyzed the greed of those who preceded him in office. Once he got his mouth to the public teat he found the milk so sweet that he did not let go as long as he lived.

Personal difficulties made Ben Tillman hesitate before becoming a candidate for office. He knew that the hard words he had used against men of influence would stir an opposition far more pitiless than that which a less hated man would provoke. "What have I had to stand," he was soon to say, "in the way of misrepresentation, abuse and slander? Do these people suppose that I have got no sensibility?" [5] Moreover, there were financial embarrassments:

[4] Williams, in Greenville *News*, March 29, 1890.
[5] Charleston *World*, May 4, 1890.

debts from land speculations and crop failures.[6] He was faced with the necessity of borrowing campaign money and hiring an overseer, whose anticipated mismanagement of his lands would cause more financial trouble. Such difficulties appeared very serious to a man who for many years had striven for gain and who felt fully his obligations to his large and growing family.

Nevertheless, he consented to imperil personal comfort and security for chances of political success. No small factor was the persuasive influence of the coterie of advisers who, by 1889, had gathered around him. This group had seen him twice or thrice stir the white masses by the use of his almost magic pen and oratory, only to see him lose effectiveness because of personal discouragement or the exigencies of private business. Not one of his advisers was sufficiently gifted in language, personality, or principles to nourish a revolution; Tillman alone possessed these qualities. They knew that they could shine only in the light of his reflected glory. They were willing to serve him well, for they were ambitious, hungry for the offices his enemies held. Should he, after keying the masses to high tension, allow them to return to their traditional calm while the farmers' program was unachieved? Should not the Agricultural Moses lead the farmers and their friends into the rich pastures? Tillman accepted the responsibility.[7]

A conference was held in the spring of 1889 at the house of Daniel H. Tompkins at Ninety Six. The leaders were Tillman and John L. M. Irby, a popular politician of Laurens County. It was agreed that a convention of farmers should be called early in 1890 to present the Edgefield farmer as a candidate for the Democratic nomination for governor, and plans were formulated for writing a program for the proposed gathering.[8] At Columbia in November,

---

[6] See above, pp. 87–88.   [7] Cf. Ball, *State that Forgot*, 229–30.

[8] See Irby statement, in Charleston *News and Courier*, February 27, 1895. A few months later there was another meeting at Pendleton, where Tillman, G. Wash Shell, Daniel K. Norris, and other leaders of the Farmers' Associa-

sixteen members of the executive committee of the Farmers'
Association gave final approval to a statement of policy,[9]
and this document was published in the newspapers on
January 23, 1890, under the name of the Shell Manifesto.
It bore the name of the president of the Farmers' Association, but its language indicated unmistakably that it had
been composed on the porch of the same Edgefield farm-
house from which the people of South Carolina had received
so many similar pronouncements.[10]

The Shell Manifesto asked "every true Carolinian" to
join the farmers in electing delegates to a convention scheduled for the following March 27. This body was to designate
candidates for the Democratic nominations to be made that
summer. In order to anticipate the charge that such a gathering had as its purpose the disruption of the party, the
manifesto asserted that its signers would abide by the decisions of the party's convention even if adverse. "We have
shown our fealty to race by submitting to the edicts of the
party," the signers declared, "and we intend as heretofore
to make our fight within the party lines, feeling assured that
truth and justice will finally prevail." A preconvention assembly was declared necessary in order that the issue could
be joined squarely between "the common people who redeemed the State from Radical rule" and "those, who
wedded to ante-bellum ideas but possessing little of the
ante-bellum patriotism and honor, are running it in the
interest of a few families and for the benefit of a selfish ring
of politicians."

Since the days of the Lords Proprietors, the historically-
minded author of this paper dogmatized, South Carolina
had been controlled by "an aristocratic oligarchy" who

tion confirmed the decision reached at Daniel H. Tompkins' house. Gonzales, *ibid.*, August 13, 1889.

[9] See Shell address before the March convention of 1890, *ibid.*, March 28,
1890.

[10] Tillman, when asked about the authorship, said at first that he had
"something to do with it" and in 1896 confessed that he wrote it. Ball,
State that Forgot, 219.

had heretofore purchased every champion of the people or destroyed him through misrepresentation and slander. This clique operated through such "existing institutions," or "pets of the aristocracy," as the university, The Citadel, the agricultural bureau, and the Columbia Club, greedy organizations which "intended in the future, as in the past, to get all they can and to keep all they can get." A long list of abuses was ascribed to the state government. It was claimed' that the agricultural bureau wasted money which rightfully belonged to Clemson College, and that it had been "the best friend of the fertilizer companies" because it had not prosecuted them for swindling; that corporation attorneys in the legislature had prevented an increase of the phosphate royalty, and that it was "an open question" whether or not bribes had been passed around; that the legislature had been "bamboozled and debauched" because of its failure to protect South Carolina against the greed of Northern-owned railroad companies; that the railroad commission was weak, having been " 'tamed' so to speak" by the companies, and that the Senate was the stronghold of an extravagant aristocracy dominated by "Charleston's rich politicians." Among other counts in the indictment were mismanagement of the penitentiary, failure to reapportion legislative representation or to call a constitutional convention, neglect of the free schools, and the inadequate enforcement of laws.

Thousands of South Carolinians received the Shell Manifesto with profound misgivings. Although it was scarcely more than a summary of the complaints Tillman had been publishing for several years, moderates were outraged by its caustic phrasing and by its sweeping innuendo and borderline slander. Although it invited all Democrats in sympathy with the Farmers' Association to participate in the assemblies called upon to select delegates to the March convention, its rasping and even insulting language seemed designed to proscribe all who were not in sympathy with the blunt-spoken Edgefield agitator. Its expression of party loyalty was unconvincing to many who held in utmost horror the possibility of a return to Negro rule through a break in the solidarity of the Democratic party. James A. Hoyt, the Democratic state chairman, spoke of the "stubborn fact" of the presence of a Negro majority,[11] and perhaps a majority of those who attended the county conferences was opposed to nominations.[12]

Notwithstanding these difficulties, G. Wash Shell, at the appointed hour of noon on March 27, called the convention to order. Thirty-one counties were represented by 233 delegates. Tillman, as in all previous conventions which he had inspired, was the dominating force of the gathering, the man whom each of the 233 regarded as leader or enemy. He had come to Columbia the day before with the convention's platform in his pocket, and had formed a close alliance with Irby and others who wished to make the Edgefield farmer the gubernatorial nominee.

Gonzales, inclined no longer toward the patronizing charity with which he had described previous Tillman assemblies, said that the March convention "was in many respects one of the queerest deliberative bodies ever assembled in the State House. There was plenty of new material, men whose faces have not often been seen in such assemblages. There was but a slight sprinkling of the old war horses of Democracy." Yet the hint that the body would radically depart from accepted norms of South Carolina political conduct was quieted by Shell's assertion that it was an insult to suggest that a bolt from the Democratic party was contemplated by a convention whose leader was a man who had done his duty in 1876.

The convention's matter of principal concern was, of course, whether or not there should be immediate nominations for governor and the other state officers. The forces

11 Charleston *World,* March 15, 1890.
12 Analysis of Charleston *News and Courier,* March 5, 1890.

in support of nominations were led by Irby, with Shell and Senator W. Jasper Talbert as active lieutenants. The opposition, poorly organized because of an unjustified belief in its own weakness, was led by John J. Dargan of Sumter, who had already won recognition in several farmers' conventions as a vigorous opponent of Tillman's plans. Irby won the first victory by effecting the election of Talbert as permanent chairman and by persuading the convention to instruct its committee on credentials not to admit delegates opposed to its objects. The committee, however, fearing a partisanship which might be construed as independentism, recommended the seating of all delegates who had been elected by the county conferences, including some anti-Tillman contested delegations and the Sumter delegation which had vigorously denounced the Shell Manifesto. In accepting this decision the convention toyed with the very purpose for which it had assembled; as finally constituted it came dangerously near having a majority opposed to nominations.

As a preliminary to the main work of the assembly, Tillman presented a platform which he openly acknowledged having written. It reiterated the criticisms made in the Shell Manifesto, and stressed the demand that the people not select their rulers before they had heard them speak.

Then came the crucial battle of the day. Augustus E. Padgett, a delegate from Edgefield, moved "that for the purpose of educating and arousing the masses we will proceed to suggest candidates for governor and lieutenant governor . . . and we ask that those who disagree with us to do likewise. . . . Let us have a full and fair discussion, and a free fight, within the party lines, and let the majority rule." This motion caused two hours of confused debate featured by Dargan's denunciation of the alleged disruptive influences of Tillmanism. This provoked deafening cries for the Edgefield leader to defend himself and his plans.

"There are men here," cried Tillman, "who are so narrow, so prejudiced, so poisoned that they are ready to say that I am speaking for myself." He denied that he had initiated his candidacy for governor and asserted that his preferment would be at a great personal sacrifice. He defended his loyalty to the Democratic party, saying, "I am a simon-pure Edgefield Democrat." Then he climaxed his address by declaring in impassioned language that he would be a candidate for governor:

"If you ask me to fight for it, I will fight as long as I have a dollar left and the health with which to fight. . . . I put myself against the combined intelligence of the ring. . . . The Reform element of South Carolina has reached the Rubicon. If you don't cross it now, you may as well go home and better never come back here. If you ask me to lead this fight you call on me to lead a forlorn hope, but you will have at your head the only man who has the brain, the nerve and the ability to organize the common people against the aristocracy." [13]

After this address the vote was taken on the Padgett resolution. According to the tally of the newspaper reporters the noes won by the narrow margin of 117 to 116. There was great consternation, and for a moment it seemed as if Tillmanism were doomed. But Chairman Talbert withheld the announcement of the result for fully five minutes, spending this time, in very unparliamentary manner, shouting to the mob below him: "Come over, come over, everybody come over to our side!" Two delegates from Beaufort, who had not previously been enrolled, voted "yea," and Irby circulated around the floor and by the weight of his positive personality induced three delegates to change their votes from "nay" to "yea." Thus was Chairman Talbert able to announce victory for nominations by a vote of 121

[13] On account of the element of self-praise in these remarks, much controversy arose concerning their exact nature. The version of the Charleston *News and Courier,* March 28, 1890, is here followed. Tillman gave his own version, which was somewhat different, in a letter to this newspaper, published April 1, 1890.

to 114. The loud protests of the opposition leaders were ignored by the presiding officer. Had they been as dexterous as Irby and Talbert, they might have won; overestimating their opponents' strength, they had failed to co-ordinate their own forces. Their only recourse was to withdraw from the convention. This gave Irby a free hand to "suggest," in a voice that rang high and clear, the name of Tillman for governor. The nomination was carried by acclamation.[14]

The Conservatives were indignant over the manner in which the March convention had been controlled. Their wrath was expressed by hisses from the galleries, and by a mob of university students who followed the nominee to his hotel, singing: "We'll Hang Ben Tillman on a Sour Apple Tree," and "Pass Around Tillman and We'll all Take a Kick." [15] Undoubtedly, Talbert's and Irby's conduct had been highhanded and perhaps defeated the free will of the majority.[16] Yet they did only what wise political strategists usually do: they suppressed those who tried to have a voice in a convention called for a purpose with which those dissenters were not in sympathy. This element was not denied the opportunity, which it promptly exercised, of expressing itself politically against Irby, Talbert, and Tillman outside the bounds of the March convention but within the confines of the Democratic party, just as elements expelled from Democratic and Republican conventions express themselves in general elections.

Tillman in calling his cause a "forlorn hope" had underestimated his strength. The Farmers' Association—generally known after the March convention as the Reform Movement—was an effective political organization with

---

14 For proceedings of the convention, see *ibid.*, March 28, 1890; Columbia *Daily Register*, March 28, 1890; Charleston *World*, March 28, 1890. See also, comments of Gonzales and a Sumter delegate on the counting of the vote, in Charleston *News and Courier*, April 3, 4, 1890.

15 Charleston *World*, March 28, April 2, 1890.

16 "We were defeated by one vote. I cheated the question of nomination" to save Tillman, Irby later admitted. Speech at Manning, in Charleston *News and Courier*, August 28, 1897.

ramifications in every county of South Carolina. It was, said its opponents with justice, a more insidious political machine than the so-called "ring" which Tillman stigmatized. Irby, the chief lieutenant of the gubernatorial candidate, was as artful a political manipulator as the state had ever known. In his countless political intrigues the Laurens leader had the aid of many enthusiastic farmers now turned politicians, as well as a minority of the state's lawyers who saw in Tillmanism an opportunity to better themselves. The ablest among these farmers and lawyers were selected to run for the various state offices on the Tillman platform. They compared favorably in education, experience, and gentility with the so-called aristocrats who opposed them.[17] A daily newspaper, the Charleston *World,* founded by the Charleston faction which had invited Tillman to speak in 1888, was enlisted in the farmers' cause. Although this newspaper during its four years of existence did not challenge the *News and Courier*'s supremacy among South Carolina journals, it was an effective adjunct to Tillman's other means of getting his opinions before the public.

Another aid to the candidate was the Farmers' Alliance, an association of national importance which had been introduced into the state in 1887;[18] by 1889 it numbered 20,000 members organized in 745 sub-Alliances. Although the ostensible purpose of the organization was to make farm life more attractive and to promote co-operative buying and selling, the Alliance could not withstand the temptation of politics. The average Alliance farmer, sedulously taught

[17] Eugene B. Gary, nephew of Martin W. Gary, was a candidate for lieutenant governor; James E. Tindal, a wealthy planter who had been educated in Germany, candidate for secretary of state; Young J. Pope, a member of an old Newberry family and a distinguished officer of the Confederacy, candidate for attorney general; William D. Mayfield, an experienced educational administrator, candidate for superintendent of education; William T. C. Bates, a veteran banker, candidate for state treasurer; Hugh L. Farley, Confederate soldier and trusted companion of Martin W. Gary, candidate for adjutant general.

[18] The first South Carolina sub-Alliance was organized in Marion County, in the fall of 1887. Charleston *News and Courier,* July 12, 1888.

that the government could be the author of benefits as well as evils, naturally sought the control of the state. But this sacrifice on the altar of politics of the original ideals of the order transformed it into a noisy political machine sure to go out of existence as soon as the leaders got office and the rank and file were no longer interested in current political issues.

Tillman, fearing the Alliance as a rival to his own political machine, urged it to steer clear of politics.[19] But when he saw that his advice was not going to be taken, he, as a sensible opportunist, joined forces with it and became first president of the Edgefield branch.[20] The organization was a very effective adjunct to Tillman's candidacy in 1890. Often, as that leader later recalled, a group of farmers would at one hour constitute themselves as a unit of the Alliance, adjourn, and then at another hour, without a change of place, reconstitute themselves as a pro-Tillman political club.[21] Both organizations were political; both were powerful influences in promoting the class consciousness of the farmers.[22] Yet to say, as does a historian of the Alliance, that Tillman's election in 1890 was due to that organization,[23] is to ignore the unique social forces which gave discontent in South Carolina its peculiar turn, to ignore Tillman's personality, and to ignore the fact that his movement had been under way two years when the Alliance entered South Carolina. Indeed, Tillman later welcomed opportunity to reduce its influence.

A month after the March convention the Tillmanites

---

19 Edgefield *Chronicle,* May 4, 1891.

20 Charleston *News and Courier,* October 8, 1889.

21 Tillman, in *Cong. Record,* 59 Cong., 1 Sess., 447.

22 For the history of the Alliance in South Carolina, see W. Scott Morgan, *History of the Wheel and Alliance* (New York, 1891), 326–27. For a full discussion of the national movement, see Solon J. Buck, *The Agrarian Crusade* (New Haven, 1921).

23 Henry R. Chamberlain, *The Farmers' Alliance: What It Aims to Accomplish* (New York, 1891), 28.

won their first victory over the regular Democratic organization. Under pressure of public opinion, the executive committee of the party granted the Tillman demand for a joint debate at each county seat between the several candidates for state offices, and for a state nominating convention to meet after the canvass.[24] These steps, a Conservative leader ruefully remarked, placed a "plume in Tillman's cap" of which "he may be justly proud." [25]

The Conservatives, as Tillman's opponents were called, took energetic steps to contest in the county-to-county canvass for the control of the Democratic nominations. "An organized movement had begun," declared a typical Conservative, to force upon the party as its candidate for governor "a man who has surpassed its open enemies in bitter and reckless criticism of its aims and acts." [26] Anti-Tillman farmers met in conference and declared that the March convention had adopted "an innovation pregnant with great danger" by organizing a party within a party and that it had degraded the honorable profession of farming with a spoilman's machine. For the Tillman Movement to succeed, it was asserted, was to "declare slander truth and to reward the slanderers." [27] The Tillman opponents made no formal nominations, as such procedure was declared to be disloyalty to the Democratic party. Nevertheless, by tacit agreement, they united on Joseph H. Earle as their candidate for governor. His selection was a necessary reward for the sacrifice he had made in 1888 in favor of Governor Richardson. A second candidate of the Conservative group was General John Bratton, a planter whose outmoded ideas, distinguished war record, white head, and athletic bearing symbolized the romantic past. But measured according to the standards of 1890 General Bratton was ineffective. "He sees," was Till-

[24] Charleston *World*, May 17, 1890.
[25] General John Bratton to Davis, May 9, 1890, in Davis Papers.
[26] "Old Guard," in Charleston *News and Courier*, April 8, 1890.
[27] *Ibid.*, April 24, 1890.

man's accurate if cruel disposal of the old warrior, "through
ante-bellum spectacles. His gaze is toward the grave." [28]

Earle, on the other hand, was a redoubtable antagonist.
His rise from poverty to prominence, his zealous prosecution of Republicans after Reconstruction, and his defense
of the Richardson administration against Tillman's attacks,
gave him great prestige. Possessed of a high forehead, curly
locks, deep-set eyes, and an imposing figure, he was personally most attractive. Being a man of measured terms and
quiet dignity, he forced a hearing from hostile audiences
and wisely refused to lose his temper in the face of Tillman's
clever onslaughts. He was, said a Tillman lieutenant who
knew him well, the "strongest man the Conservatives could
have run" against the Edgefield debater; [29] indeed, he was
the ablest antagonist Tillman ever had on the South Carolina hustings.

But he was no match for his tigerish opponent. His very
capabilities worked against him. He carried his moderation
to such extremes that he failed to combat Tillman's accusations with spirit, contenting himself for the most part with
criticisms of the farmer's bad manners. In fact, his failure
to question the justice of his opponent's demands leads one
to suspect that he was halfhearted in his loyalties. His cool
dignity was no fitting substitute for constructive convictions. His subtle reasoning and his zeal for the welfare of
South Carolina were ineffective retorts for the Tillman sarcasm. Earle's polished manners and handsome face were not
what the turbulent South Carolina democracy wanted. It
wanted the Tillman qualities. The Edgefield man's one
eye, his homely sunburned face, his informal manners, his
country dress, and his plain and even vulgar language
created the belief among the common people that he was
one of them. Yet his distinctive qualities were not unappre-

[28] Tillman speech at Laurens, 1890, in Tillman Scrapbooks; John E.
Wannamaker to Hinson, May 27, 1890, in William Godber Hinson Papers
(Charleston Library Association, Charleston).
[29] John L. McLaurin, in *Cong. Record*, 55 Cong., 2 Sess., 3303.

ciated. The people admired his boldness in debate, his practice of preferring charges and defying his opponents to disprove them. His picturesque manners and brazen speech
created the lively sort of interest which the clown inspires.
But he did not fail to present principles of statecraft and to
offer constructive remedies. He gave both entertainment
and hope. "He is one of us, but wiser and more learned than
we are." [30]

[30] See Tillman and McLaurin characterizations of Earle, *ibid.,* 3303, 3309–
11; L. A. Patillo characterization of Earle and Tillman, in Augusta *Chronicle,*
June 15, July 6, 1890. For Earle's life, see *An Historical and Descriptive
Review of the State of South Carolina* (Charleston, 1884), III, 289–90.

Chapter XII

THE CAMPAIGN OF 1890

THE county-to-county canvass of 1890 opened in the up-country towns in an innocent holiday mood centering around Tillman, now a full-blown popular hero like Hampton in 1876. There were the rostrums garlanded with flowers and evergreens; signs marked "Tillman and Reform," and "Tillman, the People's Choice"; the feast of savory barbecue; and the gathering of hundreds of farmers, anticipating a festive occasion. Amid cries of "Hurrah for Tillman and Reform" and "Bring Out the One-Eyed Plowboy," the object of these adulations appeared enthroned upon the hard board seat of a farm wagon decorated with pea vines, cotton stalks, corn tassels and other bucolic symbols. This rustic chariot was drawn by "a hundred or more horny-handed sons of toil," while other hundreds of "wool hat and one-gallus boys" brought up the rear, lustily cheering their champion.[1] "Our Noble Leader" mounted the stand, and doffing his plantation hat, confirmed this symbolic mixture of the homely and the heroic.

He confessed: "I am glad of the opportunity for you to look me in the eye, and see what sort of man I am. . . . Judging from the newspaper reports I know that many of you do not realize that such an insignificant man can be Tillman. Some of you expected to see hoofs and horns. . . . I have some peculiarities. If I had none perhaps I would be

---

[1] McGhee, "Tillman, Smasher of Traditions," *loc. cit.*, 8017; accounts of meetings at Anderson, Greenville, and Edgefield, in Charleston *World,* May 12, June 1, 19, 22, 1890.

an insignificant and unknown man. I'm what I am, and God made me what I am, and, therefore, if this conglomeration of flesh and bones becomes a factor in South Carolina, it will be by reason of the peculiarities with which my Creator endowed me. I am left-handed, and have written with my left paw. I am one-eyed. Some say I can see more with that one eye than some men can see with a dozen." [2]

In the first speech of the canvass at Anderson, on May 11, Tillman proposed no less than nine positive reforms. They were public debate on political issues; eradication of the influence of corporation lawyers in the legislature; reapportionment of seats in that body; the elimination of extravagance in the agricultural bureau; maintenance of the South Carolina College as a seat of liberal culture; establishment of a state women's college; support of Clemson College; the energizing of the railroad commission; and reform of the public schools. All this was summarized in a fervent plea for a greater degree of popular participation in government.[3]

Conservatives were so blinded by Tillman's indulgence in "false issues, unfair charges and unjustifiable innuendos" that they asserted he had discussed no principle of government and postulated no reform.[4] Indeed, the Edgefield leader, in the Anderson speech alone, insinuated that the influence of corporations in the legislature was built on bribery; that Democratic conventions were "manipulated" by his enemies; that the failure of individual legislators to obey the constitutional mandate for legislative reapportionment was "perjury"; that the "greedy old city of Charleston" and Beaufort, "that niggerdom," had prevented this reform; that the professors at the state university inculcated "aristocratic doctrines and ideas of divine right"; that the public schools were "an abominable humbug"; and that there were other examples of "corruption and extrava-

2 Tillman address at Anderson, in Charleston *World*, May 12, 1890.
3 *Id., ibid.*
4 Charleston *News and Courier*, June 10, 1890.

gance." [5] At subsequent meetings he indulged in similar tactics. Persons better mannered than he said that he ignored committees appointed to direct the order of the speaking,[6] and bade his hearers "spit out of your mouths" candidates for office who would not declare their opinions. He gloried in the accusation that he and his followers were of the lower classes. "I am simply a clod-hopper like you are," he told the Abbeville audience, "and that's what's the matter with Hannah." [7] He repeated once more the canard about Governor Thompson making away with the furniture at the governor's mansion,[8] and interpreted the assertion of a Columbia judge that Tillman would never enter the governor's office as a threat of assassination. "The aristocracy are absolutely and utterly desperate," he confided artfully; "they will stop at nothing." [9]

This playing upon the emotions of excited audiences had several notable effects. Instead of evoking popular wrath against Tillman, it created in his behalf an unparalleled wave of enthusiasm. His constructive promises had awakened the hopes of the disinherited; now his appeals to class prejudices and his implications against the motives and morals of the privileged aroused hatred. His journey through the upcountry counties was a triumphant progress, while the anger of his enemies grew greater and greater. His language was declared to be "essentially coarse and vulgar"; ladies were warned to stay away from the campaign meetings lest "they have their modesty shocked and their sex insulted"; the applause which South Carolinians gave him was declared a disgrace to an honored commonwealth.[10]

The pro-Tillman demonstrations in the upcountry culminated at Laurens, the home of Irby and Shell and long a

[5] Charleston *World*, May 12, 1890.
[6] General Bratton to Davis, May 9, 1890, in Davis Papers.
[7] Charleston *World*, May 5, June 19, 1890.
[8] Charleston *News and Courier*, June 15, 1890.
[9] Charleston *World*, June 19, 1890.   [10] *Ibid.*

center of avid Tillman sentiment. A great crowd arrived early for the speaking, and when the object of their admiration arrived, they cheered and danced with joy and bore him on their shoulders to the rostrum. "If mortal man," said an observer, "can arouse his fellow beings to a higher pitch of enthusiasm than Tillman did, it would be a plain act of worship." [11] Amid cries of "Give us Tillman," General Bratton vainly tried to be heard. Deafening shouts greeted Earle's attempt to arraign the farmer's record. Although Tillman and Shell attempted to restore order, the meeting adjourned without the opposition being heard. Earle and Bratton had been "howled down," a type of conduct white South Carolinians were in the habit of visiting only upon Carpetbaggers.[12]

Enraged at the discourtesies shown Earle and Bratton, the Conservatives resolved to humble Tillman when he arose for his scheduled speech at Columbia, a city which Tillman said was "saturated with hatred" for him.[13] Accordingly, a crowd of fifteen hundred, 90 per cent of whom were hostile to the farmer, gathered at the fair grounds on June 24 to humiliate him. Many bore arms, believing that a man of questionable services to the Confederacy was so cowardly that he could be frightened by a show of force. Senators Hampton and Butler [14] and other leaders of opinion were invited to speak. With such a show of "free and full discussion," said John C. Haskell, one of two brothers who were uncompromising enemies of the Edgefield farmer, "the people of the State will spew this vile thing [Tillman] out of their mouths, this creature who has slandered his

11 Charleston *Sun*, June 13, 1890.

12 Ball, *State that Forgot*, 205. Three newspaper accounts of this canvass have been used: Charleston *News and Courier*, anti-Tillman; Charleston *World*, pro-Tillman; Augusta *Chronicle*, neutral. The Laurens meeting is described in these journals, June 13, 1890.

13 At Anderson, in Charleston *World*, May 12, 1890.

14 Both were invited by the local Democratic authorities. Butler did not accept.

mother State and accused falsely the white people who served her in '76." [15] Tillman's only supporters were the stalwart Irby and a contingent of "red-shirted, guano-horned volunteers" from Edgefield in the crowd.

The contrast between Hampton and Tillman, the two men who were contending for the good will of the people on that day, was as sharp as possible. Hampton, possessed of the polish of three generations of aristocratic culture, was handsome, erect and smartly dressed, and given to fervent yet moderate expositions of Southern principles; a benign countenance radiated kindness even toward the humble Negro; his love for the state had been expressed in heroic services on battlefields, in an uncomplaining loss of great wealth, and by the successful leadership he gave in 1876. The people had been taught to regard him as a veritable Grand Old Man of South Carolina and had rewarded him with the highest and most remunerative office in their gift, a United States senatorship. Tillman, in contrast, seemed an ill-mannered rustic, fierce of countenance, vulgar in speech, mercenary and complaining in money matters, pos-sessed of no war record and only inconspicuous services in 1876. Although it was not evident at the beginning of that memorable day, he was more than a match for Hampton in the game which the senator elected to play with him.

It was a moment of crisis in South Carolina history, a junction unfavorable for Hampton's obvious virtues, but opportune for Tillman's calculating intelligence. Hamp-ton's understanding was ordinary; he was without compre-hension of the methods by which he had been made gover-nor, without insight into the new social and political forces which the Edgefield farmer represented, without the critical ability to realize that South Carolina, for all its passionate traditionalism, needed new remedies for new conditions. The problems of the day, Hampton felt, could be solved by a rededication to the glorious tradition he represented. In

[15] Charleston *World,* June 20, 1890.

abandoning the role of moderator of South Carolina affairs in order to cross swords with an innovator, he acted from a high sense of civic duty; but his action resulted in his own undoing.

The address of General Hampton, despite its cold moderation, revealed unmistakably the senator's belief that the Edgefield farmer was an enemy of the weal and dignity of South Carolina. He deplored the outrage against the code of Southern chivalry—the "howling down of honored gentlemen." "When I saw that a South Carolina audience could insult John Bratton, I thought, good God! have the memories of '61, of '65, have they been obliterated?" The prince of the aristocrats presented his own naïve heart as proof of the falsity of the charge of oligarchy. "The people of South Carolina have been free from all wrong, from all misrule, from all oligarchy. . . . I don't know what aristocracy is, God knows I do not know. . . . I treated the man in the ragged jacket as well as I treated the man with the stars on his coat." Then came the cardinal accusation: the Tillmanites were threatening a division in the ranks of the whites similar to that which the notorious William Mahone had imposed upon Virginia. "It is useless to contend that you are Democrats," warned the illustrious veteran in imploring that Tillman not divide the whites, "when you do anything to divide your own, the Democratic party."

Tillman, in reply, struck at his audience. The flood gates of popular wrath, he said amid harrowing interruptions, "are open and this little Columbia dam won't stop the flood." This town, he added, was "the head center of devilment," and its citizens were more ill-mannered than the Tillman farmers of the upcountry. Amid hisses he contrasted the sins of the Columbia politicians of 1890 with the virtues of the ante-bellum leaders. He ridiculed Hampton's and Bratton's denials of the existence of an aristocracy. "Two innocent lambs, they never saw an aristocrat!"

The most dramatic moment of the day, and perhaps the

most trying moment of Tillman's career, befell when Colonel Alexander C. Haskell,[16] whose empty left eye socket was a symbol of the bravery he had shown on battlefields, attempted to convict Tillman of a crime which all patriotic South Carolinians, including Tillman himself, regarded as more reprehensible than Mahoneism. This was the failure of an able-bodied Southerner to bear arms in defense of the Confederacy. Above the great confusion Haskell rasped:

"What age were you when the war ended; honest now, true age?"

"Seventeen," replied the hard-pressed Tillman.

While many in the audience brandished weapons through sheer excitement or through the belief that such a ruse would frighten Tillman into cowardly conduct, Haskell shot back triumphantly:

"The law called him at sixteen and patriotism put thousands in the army at fifteen."

The Edgefield farmer rose in a defiant rage. Shaking a finger in the face of his interlocutor, he explained how illness resulting in the loss of an eye had prevented his joining the colors, and then added:

"I can call upon a better general than you, Haskell, to tell what part the Tillman family took in the War."

The general was Ellison Capers, the beloved rector of Trinity Episcopal Church, Columbia, who sat among those whose presence was designed to chasten Tillman. Although taken by surprise by the call of one whose cause he despised, this chivalrous Christian without hesitation sustained the memory of one of his officers, saying:

"When I am asked to bear testimony to the heroic gallantry of one of my brave men who followed the standard of the Twenty-Fourth South Carolina, God forbid that I should keep silent. Jim Tillman of Edgefield was the oriflamme of my regiment."

This relieved the tension and left Tillman triumphant;

16 A brother of John C. Haskell.

for in South Carolina, where family ties are strong, one's actions may be identified with those of a brother. The victor was free to close his address with slings at his opponents. To Hampton he said: "The grand mogul here who ruled supremely and grandly cannot terrify me. I do not come from any such blood as that." To the audience he said: "Two thirds of you want office. . . . Politics has sunk down to a plain level of dollars and cents. . . . It is leprosy." At Haskell he directed the final shot: "When any man comes here and talks about my record, I simply spew him out of the mouth."

Protected by Irby, he left the fair grounds. Although the day had not been his, he had proved his mettle. No sensible man could thereafter make the ugly insinuation that Ben Tillman was a coward. There were mournings and regrets in high Conservative circles. "In the very presence of Hampton," cried a prominent Columbia lawyer,[17] "I have heard this man strike with poisoned tongue at the vitals of our civilization. It is incumbent upon us to take this man by the throat and choke him until his lips are livid and until he retracts his infamous insinuations." But it was too late to do this.[18]

On the other hand, it was within the power of Tillman and his followers to get immediate vengeance, and that against no less a personage than "the grand mogul" himself. When Hampton, on invitation from local Democratic authorities, rose to speak at Aiken, three days after the Columbia meeting, he was greeted by indecorous cries of "Put him out," and when he intimated that the Tillman agitation would destroy white unity, the howls became so great that he was forced to sit down.[19] This behavior was stigmatized as "a display of disgraceful blackguardism," but the Till-

[17] Judge Andrew Crawford.
[18] For the Columbia meeting, see Charleston *World*, June 25, 1890; Charleston *News and Courier*, June 25, 1890; Augusta *Chronicle*, June 25, 1890.
[19] Augusta *Chronicle*, June 28, 1890.

manites refused to apologize, saying that it was the inevitable consequence of the old leader's participation in a factional fight.[20]

Retaliation for the dishonor to Hampton and Bratton was sought at Winnsboro in Bratton's home county. Because of the howls of his enemies, Tillman was forced to take his seat. His partisans rushed to the rostrum and lifted him upon their shoulders, swearing that he must be heard. This provoked a counter rush from the anti-Tillmanites. For a time there was threat of violence. "At no meeting in the past series," remarked an observer, "has such bad blood been displayed or a culmination of such desperate character threatened." [21]

By the time the county-to-county campaign had entered its second month, it was evident to most observers that Tillman, despite the cool perseverance of Earle, had most of the crowds behind him. At Florence on July 10 he gave graphic demonstration of this by adopting a device which thereafter was to be a familiar part of his strategy. This was the so-called hand primary. "Those of you who are for Bratton," he cried, "hold up your hands." A few went up. When he plied the same question concerning Earle, there was a greater response. When asked concerning himself, there was a veritable sea of hands.[22]

The one-sided nature of the canvass, as it moved toward its closing weeks, tended to divest it of popular interest. As if to counteract this influence the indefatigable agitator emphasized the one of his many campaign devices most calculated to goad his adversaries. This was the reading of the list of "perjured" state senators who had failed to vote for the carrying out of the constitutional mandate for legislative reapportionment. There were nineteen names on this list, and one can conceive the reaction when "the invader

20 Charleston *News and Courier*, July 3, 1890.
21 Augusta *Chronicle*, July 2, 1890.   22 *Ibid.*, July 11, 1890.

from Edgefield," on his visit to the home community of each such influential man, read his name. Already at Union, the accuser had been forced by the local senator, on threat of dire consequences, to swallow his words.[23] The procedure was repeated with sensational consequences at Barnwell, the home of Senator Youmans. As the list was being read, a brother of Youmans cried: "Captain Tillman, you are a liar, a black liar. You can't prove the charge of perjury." In the resulting confusion both Tillman and Youmans' brother were threatened with violence.[24] The provocation of such scenes was not highly dangerous to Tillman personally. Had his hot words led to actual strife, the people's hero was so well protected by an unofficial bodyguard that there was almost every chance that he would have avoided hurt.

The canvass, which closed at Walterboro on August 5, had been a triumph for Tillman and his cause. Only at Columbia, Winnsboro, Sumter, Charleston, and perhaps a few other places, were majorities against him. The matchless manner in which he met his opponents served to render him a veritable idol of the white democracy. He was loved for his wit, his aggressiveness in the face of opposition, and his ability to ridicule his foes. Little attention was paid to program and principles; his noisy cohorts preferred banter and personalities. He was content usually to hold his constructive program in reserve.

Recognizing Tillman's nomination as probable, the Conservative leaders met in council a month before the campaign concluded.[25] An element in this assembly favored a declaration not to support Tillman in case he won the nomination. But the majority requested a state primary and contented itself with the ambiguous announcement that it

---

[23] See correspondence between Tillman and William Munro, in Charleston *News and Courier,* June 24, 1890.

[24] August Kohn, *ibid.,* August 2, 1890.

[25] As early as the tenth of June, 108 delegates favorable to Tillman had been elected. Compilation from *ibid.,* June 23, 1890.

wished the election of officers "who would favor the state and not themselves." [26] The answer of the Tillman organization was obvious. "The campaign," said William Christie Benet, "was begun on the basis of a nominating convention, and it is not to be expected that Tillman and his friends will consent to surrender that which they have already gained and fight the battle over again in the primaries." [27]

The procedure scheduled for the Democratic party provided that on August 10, one week before the closing of the canvass, there should be a state convention to make the rules of the party, to be followed in September by a nominating convention. The anti-Tillman majority of the state executive committee, foreseeing that if this procedure were followed the nomination of Tillman was certain, tried to force a primary for the election of delegates to the nominating convention by declaring that the August convention was called "for the sole and exclusive purpose of determining whether or not delegates to the state nominating convention . . . be elected by primary." When the August convention, by a majority of two hundred, exercised its undoubted sovereign right of overriding the instructions of its executive committee, the anti-Tillman delegates in that convention—those from Richland, Charleston, Sumter, and Beaufort—withdrew. Under the leadership of Irby, the convention then created a new executive committee headed by that Laurens politician. It also provided for the election of delegates to the September convention by the same county conventions which had elected it. Thus were the traditional leaders of the Democratic party supplanted by Tillmanites. It was a revolution. [28]

The anti-Tillman Democrats were confronted with mortifying alternatives. If they re-entered the house of their fathers they must be under the authority of the hated Till-

[26] Augusta *Chronicle,* July 12, 1890.   [27] Cited, *ibid.*
[28] Proceedings, *ibid.,* August 12–14, 1890; Charleston *News and Courier,* August 12–14, 1890; Charleston *World,* August 12–14, 1890.

manites; if they stayed out, they must wander in the wilderness alone, a forlorn minority, or join the traditional enemy, the Negroes and the Republicans. No wonder they hesitated, and in the interval between the two conventions adopted a policy of circumlocution. They declared that the proceedings of the August convention were illegal. The chairman of the old executive committee denied that his organization had been superseded and continued to issue manifestoes in its name.[29] The same men who had petitioned for a primary, in a second conference, unanimously condemned the actions of the August convention, and a bold minority of this group, behind closed doors, gave notice that there were white men in South Carolina who would bolt the party if Tillman were nominated.[30]

The nominating convention met on September 15 with the Tillmanites in even greater majority than at the August convention.[31] The Edgefield farmer and his entire ticket were nominated without opposition. The minority, however, protested strongly against the unseating of the contested Fairfield and Sumter delegations—a protest ominous of the fact that the struggle for the control of the state government had another phase. A delegate declared the proceedings of the convention "null and void," and the unseated men from Fairfield, when extended the courtesy of the floor, indignantly rejected the offer and marched out of the hall amid cheering galleries, with the red jacket borne high, symbolic of their claim to represent the Hampton Democracy of 1876.[32]

The logical sequel was the organization of an independent movement pretending to be the legal Democratic party. The leader of the bolt was Alexander C. Haskell. Although he acted against the advice of his brother and the wiser anti-

[29] Charleston *News and Courier*, August 22, 1890.
[30] Charleston *World*, August 27, 1890.
[31] There were 269 Tillmanites to 40 anti-Tillmanites.
[32] Proceedings of convention, in Charleston *News and Courier*, September 11, 12, 1890; Charleston *World*, September 11, 12, 1890.

Tillman leaders, he sincerely believed that circumstances justified his action. A distinguished veteran of the Confederate army, a lawyer and a bank president, a zealot of his class, and a devout Christian, he hated the profane man who had scoffed at the traditional and favored laws against the interests of lawyers and businessmen. "I do pray very hard, and I am not doing this for fun," Haskell wrote.[33]

"I will not vote for Mr. Tillman," he declared in his famous manifesto, "and I contend that no Democrat should vote for him." The March convention had gone outside the recognized forms of the Democratic party; Tillman had falsely charged the state government with "dishonesty, corruption and perjury"; and the September convention had violated the constitution of the party. "Technically, therefore, as a true Democrat," Haskell summarized, "I cannot vote for Mr. Tillman. Legally, I should not vote for Mr. Tillman. From self-respect I will not vote for him. Morally I cannot vote for him. Not only not vote for him, but a ticket should be run against him." As a practical aid to a possible victory he appealed to the Negro vote. "When the white race divides," he said, "it is a question with the colored race which party will govern the State." In case of success, however, he did not promise the Negro office. He only gave him the vague assurance of "government in the interest of both races." Hampton in 1876, he reminded the public, had made a similar appeal. He closed with a call for a nominating convention.[34]

The Haskell convention met on October 9 with twenty of the thirty-five counties represented by men of high social position.[35] With a cheering throng of men and women in

[33] Alexander C. Haskell to Hinson, October 13, 1890, in Hinson Papers.
[34] Charleston *News and Courier,* September 30, 1890.
[35] The most notable persons listed as delegates were: Alfred P. Aldrich, Barnwell; James D. Peterkin, Orangeburg; A. Foster McKissick, T. Bothwell Butler, and John M. R. Jeter, Union; Robert W. Shand, Richard S. Desportes, Richard Singleton, and Allen J. Green, Richland; William D. Johnson, Edwin A. Bethea, and William Hamer, Marion; Thomas W. Woodward and John W. Brice, Fairfield; James J. Lucas, Darlington; William A.

the galleries, the work of the assembly was accomplished in one hour and twenty minutes. It was the haste of conservative white South Carolinians conscious of performing the disagreeable duty of acting in opposition to the majority of their race. To give the proceedings some of the dignity of the traditional, the attempt was made to clothe the convention in the mantle of 1876. The red jacket that the Fairfield delegation had borne from the convention which nominated Tillman was ostentatiously displayed; General William W. Harllee, the chairman of the convention which nominated Hampton, was chairman of this one; Haskell himself had been a zealous Hampton leader; and the Haskell party was christened the Straightout Democracy, the name of the Hampton party in 1876. A full ticket headed by Haskell was agreed upon and an address to the people published.

This address illustrated the passionate moral hatred of its authors for Tillman. He was accused of resorting to secret council and class appeal in order to secure his nomination; of causing a popular turbulence which prevented "decent and grave" discussion, and of having driven ladies from the campaign meetings by his profane language. His speeches, it was affirmed, had been of such nature as to cause their condemnation by "every man who respects the truths of religion." The conclusion was as follows: "We further solemnly allege that B. R. Tillman and his associates . . . have done more harm and brought greater sorrow on the State than the sword or fire or the hand of man in any shape has ever before effected. . . . We do unhesitantly pledge ourselves as men and citizens . . . to war unceasingly

---

Ancrum, James Cantey, and Alexander H. Boykin, Kershaw; Edmund Bacon and Samuel McGowan, Jr., Spartanburg; Iredell Jones, York; Joseph W. Barnwell, Charleston; William W. Harllee, Florence; and James D. Blanding, John Singleton, and Ellison D. Smith, Sumter. Smith, during his many successful candidacies for the United States Senate, has frequently denied that he attended the Haskell Convention. Yet his name appeared on the list of delegates published in the Charleston *News and Courier*, October 10, 1890, and he, at that time, made no public attempt to correct this record.

against such unworthy men and methods as have thus ruthlessly torn the heart of our State in twain, to feed upon it for
their personal gain." [36]

The anti-Tillman leaders who did not attend this convention gave the Haskell Movement little open support.
Although they felt as much contempt for the cantankerous
farmer as did the Haskellites, they were not willing to sacrifice white unity. In their opinion, Tillmanism was much
better than Negroism and Radicalism. "A ticket," the *News
and Courier* prudently averred, "might have been nominated in protest and dropped if Republican opposition developed." [37] Since Haskell was adjudged not to have followed this course, this newspaper put the Tillman ticket
at the head of its editorial column. "Captain Tillman," ran
a typical expression of Conservative opinion, "was not our
choice for Governor, but he was the choice of a large majority of the Democratic party. Every Democrat is pledged in
honor to vote for him." [38] Only four or five newspapers
espoused the Haskell cause.[39] Senator Hampton and the
other officeholders signified their intention of voting for
Tillman. Yet when asked by the official Democrats to address a meeting organized in opposition to Haskell, Hampton, although his political future lay in the hands of a pro-
Tillman legislature, said with sacrificial gallantry: "I shall
not denounce the man [Haskell] who was my comrade in
war . . . and my trusted friend in 1876." [40]

The Negroes had sound reasons for showing little enthusiasm for Haskell. In return for their votes he promised
only fair play without a share of the public offices. They
remembered how extreme had been his anti-Negro actions

[36] Proceedings of Haskell Convention, *ibid.;* Charleston *World,* October
10, 1890.

[37] Charleston *News and Courier,* October 11, 1890.

[38] Lancaster *Ledger,* cited *ibid.,* October 9, 1890.

[39] Among them were the Darlington *Herald* and the Sumter *Watchman
and Southron.*

[40] Hampton to Irby, October 23, 1890, in Charleston *News and Courier,*
October 25, 1890.

in 1876 and noted that he was attempting to revive the spirit
of that year. They believed his new promises as empty as his
and Hampton's definite assurances to protect Negro rights
in 1876. A meeting of Richland County blacks reminded
the anti-Tillman leader that he had raided their meetings
in 1876; a convention of black educators advised their race
to take no part in the canvass; and in the person of Richard
Carroll, a rising leader, there arose a sort of colored Tillmanite, who said: "Tillman has done more good than any
living man since the War." [41]

Nevertheless, the executive committee of the Republican
party endorsed the Democratic bolter, giving as its reason
Tillman's desire to call a disfranchising convention and
Haskell's promise of "a free and fair vote." [42] The masses of
the blacks, either politically indifferent or fearful of a return to terrorism, evinced little interest in the contest and
made few attempts to vote on election day. They believed
that the Tillmanites would draw Negro blood if Negroes
attempted to vote. [43]

Tillman himself, amid a torrent of expletives, declared:
"There are counties in the State where there will be trouble
of the most serious kind if there is an attempt to vote the
negro for the bolters' ticket. Take my county Edgefield.
There the people will resort to any means rather than allow
the negro to vote for this ticket." [44]

The Tillman leaders were conscious of the support of an
overwhelming majority of the voters and never regarded
the Haskell Movement seriously. Tillman himself quoted
Hampton's words in 1876: "Such Independents are worse
than the vilest Radicals"; and he added that although many
of the Haskellites were "leading South Carolinians" they
were only "representatives of themselves and themselves
alone." [45]

[41] *Ibid.*, October 16, 17, 1890.   [42] *Ibid.*, October 26, 1890.
[43] Wallace, *History of South Carolina*, III, 349–50.
[44] Charleston *News and Courier*, October 10, 1890.
[45] *Ibid.*, October 10, 11, 1890.

The Edgefield leader won the November election by a majority too great to have been achieved without the support of anti-Tillman Democrats. Nevertheless, many of the latter group—some ten thousand—voted against him, for Haskell carried Berkeley and Beaufort counties and received more than 20 per cent of the vote in twelve additional counties.[46] That so many white South Carolinians voted for Haskell despite the stigma of Negroism and independentism, is proof of the avid disesteem in which Tillman was held in certain circles.

[46] The vote was: Tillman, 59,159; Haskell, 14,828. South Carolina *Reports and Resolutions,* 1890, I, 604. Probably 5,000 Haskell voters were Negroes.

Chapter XIII

THE FIRST ADMINISTRATION

ON December 4, 1890, the largest crowd ever to gather on the front plaza of the State House since the inauguration of Hampton witnessed the installation of Benjamin Ryan Tillman as governor of South Carolina. Spectators perched on surrounding trees and monuments. It was the same picnic crowd which in the previous summer, before fifty rural platforms, had yelled for Tillman and against his enemies. But on this day of their hero's formal triumph, all present wore their Sunday clothes, cheered decorously, and abstained from drinking. Among those invited to sit on the platform were few from Columbia and Charleston, few of the aristocrats accustomed to grace such an occasion. The politically dominant group was significantly changed.

Even more significant was the change in the type of man who rose to address the multitude before taking the oath of office. In place of the flowing hair, pleasing face, and graceful movements of the traditional governor of South Carolina were short hair, grimy complexion, a blankness of expression caused by the empty left eye socket, and a certain awkwardness of movement. The speaker was dressed unobtrusively in the long coat and high collar of the country gentleman. He drew about himself none of the staginess of the conventional leader of the people, and if, as some declared, he were a Southern demagogue, he wore none of the trappings of that estate. He may have been, as some claimed, an egotist and a potential tyrant, but signs of personal vanity were absent. He seemed his real self: a plain farmer trying to look respectable. The unusual qualities hidden beneath a stolid appearance were revealed when he spoke. Then the sparkle of the single eye, the clever gestures, the expressive but shrill voice, divulged strong feelings; the blending of generalities with concrete realities, expressed in the careful style of the essayist, demonstrated his understanding of the movement he was leading.

As befitted a man studiously unpretentious, he opened his address by denying himself the right to utter the trivialities characteristic of formal occasions. He would not, he said, "win applause by flights of what some call eloquence, but which sensible people concede as 'glittering generalities,' the tinsel and brass buttons of a dress parade, meaning nothing and worth nothing"; he would not "evolve beautiful theories or discuss ideal government." Of him was demanded "the display of practical statesmanship and business methods." "We come," he professed, "as reformers, claiming that many things in the government are wrong," and he presented a long list of suggested reforms. But this plain-looking man was not just a practical businessman; he was a thinker who, as the result of study, had given South Carolina a revolutionary idea; and now in his moment of triumph he was not too practical to give philosophical definition to the forces he led. He indulged to a greater extent than his predecessors in generalizations, even if they did not "glitter" with the old saws and congratulations and even if the tinsel was tarnished with realities. With the constructive revolutionist's appreciation of history, he put his victory into its proper setting as the third important change in the management of South Carolina affairs in twenty years. He dogmatized: "The citizens of this great commonwealth have for the first time in its history demanded and obtained for themselves the right to choose her Governor; and I, as the exponent and leader of the revolution which brought about the change, am here to take the solemn oath of office. . . . Democracy, the rule of the people, has won a victory unparalleled in its magnitude and importance. . . . The triumph of democracy and white supremacy over mongrelism and anarchy, of civilization over barbarism, has been most complete."

The defense of white democracy was supplemented by a frank explanation of what he felt should be the position of the element of the state's population in whose interest the first important change in the management of its affairs was attempted. This was the Negroes. In three sentences the defender of Reconstruction violence swept away the justification of the universal democracy to which most South Carolina leaders for twenty-five years had rendered lip service. He said, "The whites have absolute control of the State government, and we intend at any and all hazards to retain it. The intelligent exercise of the right of suffrage . . . is as yet beyond the capacity of the vast majority of colored men. We deny, without regard to color, that 'all men are created equal'; it is not true now, and was not true when Jefferson wrote it." There followed an eloquent plea for a constructive benevolence toward the blacks. Since "the carpet-bag vampires and native base traitors" had disappeared, he felt that retaliation for the wrongs of the past should cease and that the two races should live together in peace. Specifically, he asked for the abolition of lynching so that the finger of scorn could no longer be pointed at South Carolina.

The larger portion of the address was concerned with specific administrative reforms. First, the new governor called for the remedy of the "absolute retrogression" in education which he believed was due to the neglect of the public schools and to the costly battle between the friends of the state university and Clemson College. The verdict of the people in favor of his reforming higher education was interpreted as a call for compromise. "The people have decided," he said, "that there is no use for a grand University at Columbia, but they are equally determined that the South Carolina College as a school of liberal education in the classics, in the theoretical sciences and in literature, 'shall be liberally supported.' " Its mechanical appliances should be transferred to Clemson and its experimental station abolished. Again he voiced the opinion that The Citadel had outlived its usefulness, but because of a "conservative regard for the rights and wishes of even a small minority" he refused to ask for the destruction of this "landmark of the old *regime*." The building of Clemson College of course received much attention. This was fittingly accompanied by the restatement of a previous suggestion that the advisability of establishing a normal and industrial school for girls be investigated.

Numerous other reforms were advocated. A commission should be appointed to examine the management of the lunatic asylum. The state penitentiary should be self-supporting and, to further this end, restrictions on the hiring out of convicts should be loosened without surrendering state regulation of this labor. He repeated old demands for a constitutional convention, the reapportionment of seats in the legislature, the abolition of one of Charleston's two seats in the Senate, and the establishment of a uniform control of the administration of local justice. He declared that the assessment of taxes by popularly elected officials was "an absolute and pitiable failure" and recommended centralization of this function. There should be an immediate reorganization of the railroad commission and the granting to it of adequate authority to control the carriers, without, however, crippling corporate efforts.

At great length the governor advanced his idea of what disposition should be made of the state's rights in the Coosaw River phosphate deposits when, on March 1, 1891, the contract that had been granted the Coosaw Mining Company expired. He believed that the stockholders of this "octopus" had grown rich under their dollar-a-ton lease, and demanded a survey of the Coosaw deposits and the immediate raising of the royalty to two dollars a ton. "This cuttlefish," he maintained, "must be grasped with a mailed hand."

Many of the governor's recommendations were directed toward fulfilling his pledges to reduce the tax burdens of the people. Such obviously was the object of projected reforms in the administration of the asylum, the penitentiary, and the railroad commission; the proposed increase in the phosphate royalty; and the reassessment of taxes on corporate and other forms of wealth. These suggestions were supplemented by the more difficult demand that useless offices be abolished and salaries reduced in proportion to the increased purchasing power of the dollar consequent upon the prevailing "hard times." [1]

Tillman's inaugural address received the enthusiastic approval of the governor's friends and the respect of his enemies. To say that it was the ablest and most significant utterance of any South Carolina official since the great days when South Carolinians made American history, is faint praise beside that which some of his opponents gave it when it was delivered. It was commended for its vigor and clarity of statement and for its multitude of concrete suggestions. "We cannot help saying," wrote an Edgefield antagonist, "that his inaugural address is perhaps the strongest paper we have ever read. His utterances are bold, brave, striking, startling, but never revolutionary or incendiary. . . . A man who can think and labor as B. R. Tillman must have thought and labored on this great address must be a man of phenomenal force." [2] Indeed, it exhibited the governor at his best; it was a harbinger of an administration of achievements.

The governor's zeal for effective enforcement of laws against lynching was expressed in the proposal that the

[1] Tillman Inaugural, in South Carolina *House Journal*, 1890, pp. 130–54.
[2] James T. Bacon, in Edgefield *Chronicle*, cited in Charleston *News and Courier*, December 18, 1890.

legislature give him authority to remove sheriffs guilty of failure to protect prisoners against mobs. But this bill failed to pass at both the 1890 and 1891 sessions of the legislature because the anti-Tillman minority convinced the majority that the purpose of the measure was to gratify a tyrant's lust for power.[3] Despite this setback, the first year of the Tillman administration was not disgraced by a single lynching, a pleasant contrast to the twelve in one year (1889) of the previous administration. There can be little doubt that Tillman's vigorous attitude toward law enforcement had something to do with the improvement. "The law in South Carolina," he wrote in support of a sheriff from whom a lynching mob had failed to take a prisoner, "must be respected and the lynch law will not be tolerated." [4] When the first of the six lynchings of the following year occurred, that of Dick Lundy, who had murdered the son of the sheriff of Edgefield, the governor reprimanded that official for neglect of duty.[5] He attributed the five additional lynchings of the year to the legislature's refusal to give him power to discipline sheriffs.[6]

This plea for justice was not extended to other fields of interracial relations. Tillman, as his words frankly prove, was a convinced reactionary; and he accompanied his progressive attitude toward lynching with attempts to bind the blacks more rigidly within the bonds of caste. A bill was introduced to separate the two races on railroad cars.

[3] South Carolina *House Journal*, 1891, pp. 16–17.

[4] Tillman to John M. Nicholls, September 29, 1891, in Governor Tillman's Letter Books (South Caroliniana Library). The two volumes in this collection have been carried away since the writer used them in 1938.

[5] Charleston *News and Courier*, December 16, 1891; Tillman to Captain William W. Adams, December 7, 1891, in Governor's Letter Books (Library of the South Carolina Historical Commission); *id.* to Solicitor Nelson, December 7, 1891, *ibid.*; *id.* to Sheriff William H. Ouzts, December 7, 1891, *ibid.*

[6] For a list of South Carolina lynchings, see National Association for the Advancement of Colored People, *Thirty Years of Lynching in the United States, 1889–1918* (New York, 1919), 88.

Over the protests of the Negro members from Beaufort and of the railroad companies, the proposal passed the House by a great majority but failed in the Senate.[7] The sentiment for race segregation had not as yet developed sufficiently to overcome the opposition to the inconvenience of providing a double system of passenger facilities. Conversely, Tillman's oft-repeated demand for a constitutional convention to disfranchise the blacks failed to get the necessary two-thirds vote of the House after it had passed the Senate.[8] The governor's effort to abolish the gerrymander through which the greater portion of the Negro voters were concentrated in one Congressional district met with failure at the hands of a legislature reluctant to interfere with established race relations. The ostensible purpose of the measure was to prevent the state from being "held up to scorn" before the nation for the construction of "a district the like of which has never been seen before"; the real motive was to redistribute Negro political power in such a way as to prevent the return of even a single black congressman.[9] The only successful attempt of the first Tillman administration to restrict the freedom of the blacks was the imposition of a prohibitive tax upon the operation of labor agents who induced farm hands to emigrate.[10]

Following Tillman's advice, the legislature altered radically the organization of the University of South Carolina. Its agricultural and mechanical departments were abolished, and a new board of trustees composed of the governor and his friends were elected and authorized to reorganize it, under the name of the South Carolina College,

[7] South Carolina *House Journal*, 1891, pp. 276–77; Charleston *News and Courier*, December 16, 22, 1891.

[8] South Carolina *House Journal*, 1891, p. 567; South Carolina *Senate Journal*, 1891, pp. 102–103.

[9] South Carolina *House Journal*, 1891, p. 56; South Carolina *Senate Journal*, 1891, p. 34.

[10] South Carolina *Acts*, 1891, p. 1084.

into a school of "theoretical science, law, literature and art." The teaching staff was reduced from twenty-five to thirteen.[11]

Tillmanism struck this historic institution a stunning blow which has been an important factor in preventing its holding the position of leadership to which it is entitled. Tillman, who understood better than his contemporaries how to exploit popular prejudices, in his letters to the *News and Courier,* broadcast the conviction that the university was a center of foppery and snobbery. To this he added searching criticisms of the inadequacies of the school's standards and procedures. He exhibited the scorn of a self-educated man for an institution which, in the intellectual doldrums of the 1880's, was not doing its full educational duty. He chided the school for not nourishing the qualities which had given it distinction before the Civil War. Inevitably, the accusations of this vivid fault-finder created warm resentment among the friends of the university. The students had hissed him at the March convention, and he was snubbed when he appeared officially among them at the 1891 commencement.[12] Such conduct, said Tillman, "has soured me," and was evidence of "the narrow prejudice and bitter partisan feeling."

The school fell into a bad condition. "There is dilapidation everywhere about the institution," wrote the observant governor in 1891,[13] "and a woeful lack of modern books in the library." At that time there were only ninety-eight students, a number which fell to seventy in 1892. This pitiful condition, Tillman admitted, was due "almost wholly to the political and social antagonisms which exist in the State." The Tillmanites felt little inclination to

[11] *Ibid.,* 687–91; the number of professors listed in South Carolina *Reports and Resolutions,* 1891, I, 328–30.

[12] Tillman to Robert Moorman, June 1, 1892, in Governor Tillman's Letter Books.

[13] South Carolina *House Journal,* 1891, p. 42.

patronize it because of "the inhospitable atmosphere surrounding it," and the adherents of the old regime were resentful because they had lost control of the board of trustees.[14] The inability of the school to attract students led to a movement among the Tillmanites to abolish it. Its seventy students, said the state superintendent of education, did not justify the annual appropriation of $41,500; its buildings should be used for a normal school.[15]

Tillman expressed the popular conviction inherited from the time of Thomas Cooper that the college should not tolerate professors with religious views at variance with those of a majority of South Carolinians. This attitude was illustrated in the case of William J. Alexander, a Unitarian professor of philosophy who was dismissed when the faculty was reduced. The discharged teacher believed he had been a victim of bigotry, basing his contention on the fact that the trustees had questioned him on religious matters and that the governor had specifically called for a declaration concerning the divinity of Christ. The professor frankly admitted his skepticism on many of the details of the great Christian affirmations. Tillman, personally as unorthodox as Alexander, the day after the meeting of the trustees wrote the convicted heretic commiserating over the fact that unjust circumstances called for the dismissal. The governor sentimentally affirmed: "I do not share in the slightest in the feeling which causes men to cry out against you. . . . The seeker after truth, the man who in the vale of tears honestly strives to know and do what is right without pandering to the prejudices . . . of the multitude, must, like the meek and lowly Jesus, expect persecution and sorrow as his lot. . . . The masses of mankind inherit their religions." [16]

[14] Tillman, in South Carolina *Senate Journal*, 1892, pp. 12–14.
[15] Mayfield, in Charleston *News and Courier*, November 22, 1892.
[16] Tillman to William J. Alexander, April 22, 1891, in Governor Tillman's Letter Books.

Alexander naturally was not inclined to view a matter so personal as the fate of his livelihood with such a philosophical but cynical recognition of the inevitable. He protested his fate on the grounds of academic freedom, and by publishing Tillman's letter convicted him of a willingness to allow a man to be punished for holding views for which the governor had sympathy. The publication of his letter forced Tillman to proclaim a doctrine nearer to his fate and destiny than his vapid musings in favor of freedom of the mind. "There is a vast difference," he wrote Alexander, "between allowing a man perfect religious freedom and putting him in a position to teach his dogmas." [17] Most certainly it would have been imprudent for the chief politician of a religious people to make a fight in behalf of a Unitarian, and thereby to bring his own views in discomforting contrast with those of the multitude inclined to "bigotry" and "ignorant clamor." Making no pretense to be other than a political and social innovator, he wisely kept to himself his views on matters intellectual and religious.[18]

Tillman's attitude toward the college was not altogether immoderate. His respect for literary education, even when conducted by his enemies, insured his adherence to the pledge of the March convention that the school not be abolished. Lenient always toward those whom he could control or humble, he did not let his hate long survive his triumph. He tried to allay the suspicions against the college which his agitations had aroused. His messages bristle with tributes to its past services and with suggestions which he hoped would result in its prosperity. He saw no reason why it and Clemson College should remain permanently antagonistic. Perhaps he would have received popular applause had he endorsed the suggestion that the older institution be abolished. But he sharply rejected such "mut-

17 Id. to id., May 20, 1891, ibid.
18 Id. to id., May 19, 1891, ibid.

terings of discontent," believing that the legislature was "too enlightened" to listen.[19]

As foreshadowed in the address before the first Farmers' Convention, Governor Tillman used his position to achieve noteworthy results in the field of normal and industrial education for white women. His insistence upon this idea encountered none of the opposition which Clemson College had experienced. The ground had already been prepared by others. In 1886, David B. Johnson, a young Tennesseean who was superintendent of Columbia graded schools, had organized in that town the Winthrop Training School to meet a need for competent teachers. To aid in the project an annual subsidy of $2,000 had been secured from the George Peabody Fund through the influence of Robert C. Winthrop of Massachusetts, after whom the school was named. In 1887 the institution was given a statewide significance through the establishment by the legislature of a Winthrop scholarship worth $150 for each county. This was followed by an offer from the school's trustees to put it under state control. The wisdom of this last suggestion made a favorable impression on Tillman, and in his Inaugural he praised the work of the Winthrop experiment and spoke of "the imperative need of an industrial school for girls."

The fruit of his advice was the appointment of a commission consisting of Johnson and two women to visit schools in other states and report on the type of institution deemed advisable. A favorable report from the commission enabled Tillman to ask the legislature to establish a college. Accordingly, a bill prepared jointly by Tillman and Johnson was enacted in 1891, creating the South Carolina Industrial and Winthrop Normal College. The project called for the establishment of "a first-class institution for the thorough education of 'white girls'" in the practice

[19] *Id.*, in South Carolina *House Journal*, 1891, p. 42; 1892, pp. 18–19; 1893, pp. 47–48.

of teaching, cooking, dressmaking, and so on. Provision was made for the absorption of Winthrop Training School by the new institution.[20]

Governor Tillman, as the leading trustee of the project, gave some of his best efforts to its realization. He carefully scrutinized the bids of various towns in the state for its location and heartily concurred in the selection of Rock Hill. This progressive town on the North Carolina border offered liberal subsidies of lands and building materials and $60,000 in cash. The governor furthered all details connected with the construction of the plant, securing moderate state appropriations to supplement those of Rock Hill, and the use of Negro convicts as laborers on the buildings. He consulted with architects and contractors over plans and supplies, and roundly scored the members of the school's trustees for alleged extravagances and inadequate supervision.[21] He became a friend and supporter of the man who as president of the new college was most responsible for its success. Tillman was "struck with Johnson's genius for managing things."[22] His confidence was not misplaced; Johnson combined great zeal for the college's welfare with Machiavellian tactics in accomplishing this unselfish objective.

Tillman had cause for congratulating both himself and the state when, in May, 1894, he presided at the laying of the cornerstone of the main building of Winthrop College. Factionalism was set aside while he presented his lively concepts of the education of women. "There had not been one dissenting voice," said the partisan turned moderate, "against the building and equipment of this college.. . . . It is the one thing and the only thing upon which the men of South Carolina are at present united."[23]

[20] South Carolina *Acts,* 1891, pp. 1102–1107.
[21] Tillman to Bruce and Morgan (Atlanta architects), December 30, 1893, in Governor's Letter Books; *id.* to William J. Roddy, March 24, 1894, *ibid.*
[22] *Id.* to Professor Edward S. Joynes, December 28, 1912, in Tillman Papers.
[23] Charleston *News and Courier,* May 13, 1894.

Winthrop College fulfilled all his predictions. It opened its doors October 15, 1895, with 304 students, and has since that time given professional instruction to thousands of young women who have had no small part in what Tillman called the hard task of guiding South Carolina "out of the wilderness of poverty, ignorance and stagnation." It has been one of the most constructive legacies of Tillmanism.[24]

The nonpartisan atmosphere which enveloped the execution of the Winthrop idea was possible because Tillman consented to a compromise he would not accept for the agricultural college: the combination of two distinct types of education on the same campus. In order to avoid a repetition of the Clemson College controversy, he yielded to Johnson's arguments in favor of combining industrial education with normal education; and then, by the use of the same arguments used to confute the separate agricultural college idea, tried to convince himself that the combination would work.[25] The history of Winthrop, however, shows that the same fate has overtaken industrial education when combined with normal and literary instruction which Tillman said would overtake agricultural education under similar circumstances. Industrial education was crowded out by traditional subjects and was not attractive to the type of young women who attended Winthrop. They were of the upper and middle classes to whom teaching and stenography were the lowest professions to which they would aspire.[26]

Ill-feeling was engendered by the assiduity with which Tillman pursued his resolution to reform the administra-

[24] Adequate histories of Winthrop College are Edward S. Joynes, *The Origin and Early History of Winthrop* (n.p., n.d.); Ira B. Jones, *Winthrop Cornerstone Day Address, May 12, 1894* (Lancaster, S. C., 1894); Milton L. Orr, *The State-Supported Colleges for Women* (Nashville, 1930), 104–28.

[25] "It is our intention," he said, "to teach everything and have the students practice every industrial art that will lead to independence." Charleston *News and Courier*, May 13, 1894.

[26] Orr, *State-Supported Colleges*, 114–24.

tion of the lunatic asylum. His demand that its board of
regents be reduced from nine to five by the drawing of
lots caused the entire board to resign;[27] and when he took
charge of an investigation of alleged irregularities in the
management of the institution, its superintendent, Dr.
Peter Griffin, assumed a defiant attitude. The governor,
nevertheless, proved enough carelessness in Griffin's conduct to justify his dismissal. Amid countercharges that he
had acted to make room for a political friend, he wisely
selected for "the most important office of the State"[28] Dr.
James W. Babcock, a South Carolinian and a Harvard
graduate who became an efficient administrator, the intimate friend and personal physician of the man who
brought him to South Carolina, and a distinguished authority on pellagra.[29]

On the advice of the governor, the legislature reapportioned the 124 seats in the House of Representatives according to the census of 1890. This resulted in the decrease
of the Charleston delegation from twelve to eight, and of
several low-country counties by one each, all to the advantage of the upcountry.[30]

The royalty on phosphate mining in the waters of the
state was increased from one to two dollars a ton (this
applied to marine deposits only, since the state exacted no
royalty from phosphates mined from land), and a commission, with the governor as chairman, was authorized to
take charge of the Coosaw River mining operations and
make a survey of the marine deposits. On March 1, 1891,
the date of the expiration of the Coosaw contract, the
commission issued licenses for three new companies to un-
dertake the mining. This plan was interrupted when the
Coosaw Mining Company obtained an injunction from
Judge Charles H. Simonton of the United States Circuit

[27] Tillman to Jones and others, March 10, 1892, in Governor's Letter Books.
[28] Id. to Dr. Peter E. Griffin, May 5, 9, 20, 1891, ibid.
[29] Columbia Record, August 11, 1910.
[30] South Carolina Acts, 1891, p. 1070.

Court which stopped operations for more than a year.[31] When the United States Supreme Court in April, 1892,[32] finally allowed the licensees of the state to begin operations, some $68,000 in revenue had been lost and opportunity had been given for the newly discovered phosphate mines of Florida to gain markets at South Carolina's expense. The phosphate commission failed to make its projected survey of the deposits because of meager funds and because the Edgefield farmer and his agents were no better equipped for the task than their predecessors.

Although the state had increased the royalty, its phosphate revenue declined rapidly after 1893. With the approval of Tillman, the royalty of the sick business was in 1894 reduced to fifty cents a ton. The industry was doomed because of the competition of superior deposits in Florida and elsewhere; the inept interference of the farmer-governor hastened the process. Tillman admitted that his criticism of his predecessors' administration of the phosphates was irresponsible. In 1891 he said, "I did a good deal of blowing last summer." [33]

A prolonged struggle grew out of the governor's desire to reorganize the railroad commission. A bill was introduced giving him power to appoint and suspend members of that body and authorizing it to fix "fair and reasonable" rates without the right of the railroads to appeal to the courts.[34] The legislature, however, objected to giving the governor the power of appointment and dismissal, and the railroad companies objected to the prohibition of court appeals. The result was that when the bill finally passed, it provided for the election of the railroad commission by

[31] State *ex rel.* Tillman *et al. v.* Coosaw Mining Company, 47 Federal Reporter 225.

[32] Coosaw Mining Company *v.* South Carolina, 144 U.S. Reports 550.

[33] Charleston *News and Courier*, December 16, 1891. For history of the phosphate case, see Tillman, in South Carolina *House Journal*, 1891, pp. 12–14, 39–41; Charleston *News and Courier*, June 8, 1897; South Carolina *Reports and Resolutions*, 1892, I, 240–45; 1890–1904, *passim.*

[34] Text of bill, in Columbia *Daily Register*, December 30, 1890.

the legislature and did not deny the right of court review. Tillman, angered, vetoed the measure. The bill failed again at the next session because of a filibuster.[35]

Likewise, the legislature failed to effect the governor's oft-repeated hint that public expenditures be reduced. The reform program necessitated actual increases; public functions were already very limited, and the budgets of state institutions and salaries of public officials very small. Consequently, Tillman and his legislature could effect only minor savings. The contingent fund of certain officials was reduced; the completion of Clemson College was delayed; subsidies for fairs were withheld. The governor quibbled with sheriffs and others over expense accounts. He told the phosphate commissioner: "Your food must come out of your salary. . . . You had better carry cold victuals on your travels." [36] As the situation developed, the total expenditures of neither the first nor the second year of the Tillman administration were as low as the average for the ten years of the Conservative administration.[37]

The governor was more successful in his efforts to equalize tax burdens by increasing corporate assessments, especially those of railroads and banks. The increase was from $150,000,000 to $168,000,000.[38] This was a move in the right direction, one tending to put upon the shoulders of the more profitable forms of wealth a greater share of the tax burden. But, as Tillman made clear, this was only a beginning toward the achievement of the ideal of assess-

[35] "Piedmont," in Charleston *News and Courier,* January 2, 1892.

[36] Tillman to Adolphus W. Jones, June 22, 1891, in Governor Tillman's Letter Books.

[37] For the last year of the Richardson administration the expenditures were $1,112,092; for the first year of the Tillman administration, $1,151,038, and for the second year, $1,125,038. Under Republican rule (1868–1876) the average annual expenditures were $1,886,557; for ten years of Conservative rule (1877–1887) this figure was $1,026,946.

[38] Report of State Treasurer Bates, in South Carolina *Reports and Resolutions,* 1891, I, 192–96; Tillman, in South Carolina *Senate Journal,* 1891, p. 10.

ment of all property at actual value, and this bare beginning was soon checked by the willingness of the courts to
protect complaining banks and railroad companies against
the tax decrees.[39]

To the indignation of the governor's opponents, Tillmanites were elected to every vacant office. Irby became
speaker of the House; John L. McLaurin, attorney general; Young J. Pope, a justice of the Supreme Court; and
the offices in the State House were cleared of anti-Tillmanites, even of insignificant clerks. Very disconcerting to Conservatives was the failure of the legislature to elevate William H. Wallace to the Supreme Court vacancy given
Pope. Wallace had been speaker of the famous body which
had in 1877 contested with the Republicans for the control of the State House, and had long served as a circuit
judge. His doom as an officeholder, however, was sealed
when he incurred the anger of Tillman by denying the
governor's right to remove a minor official while the Senate was not in session to confirm the change.[40] Conservatives bewailed a noble leader of the past victimized by an
upstart tyrant.

The ultimate affront to Conservatives was the defeat of
Wade Hampton for re-election to the United States Senate. As soon as it was evident that Tillman's friends would
control the legislature, there were pleas that the state's
aged leader in war and peace be spared. The memories of
1861 were recalled, and Generals Butler and Johnson Hagood begged for their comrade in arms. Policy might have
prompted the Tillmanites to heed these outbursts. They
could not have, says the state's historian,[41] "better honored
themselves and mollified the passions whose subsidence
was essential to normal political life than by his [Hamp-

39 Tillman, in South Carolina *Senate Journal,* 1892, pp. 19–23.
40 *Ibid.,* 1891, pp. 26–29.
41 Wallace, *History of South Carolina,* III, 355–56.

ton's] reëlection." But the passions of the times were "very
bitter and malignant," [42] and the unpleasant memories of
the recent past impressed Tillman more than recollections
of 1861 and 1876. He spoke of Hampton's attempt to humiliate him at Columbia during the previous summer; of
the senator's refusal to ride in the same carriage with him
at the Aiken campaign meeting; of the senator's comparison of Tillmanism with Mahoneism; and of his refusal
to condemn Haskell or to speak against that bolter. "Our
senator, if not elected," concluded Tillman ominously,
"can attribute his defeat to his own acts." [43] The Tillman
leaders planned definitely to give the senatorship to Irby.
The Conservatives then grew angry. "God grant," said a
Charleston senator, "that some revolution will come that
will hurl those from power who forget their duty to Wade
Hampton." An attempt was made to stem the tide by having the old hero appear in the State House lobby in hope
that the sight of him might revive old loyalties; but he refused to humble himself.[44] He was defeated overwhelmingly, receiving only 43 of a total of 157 votes.[45]

"It was a hard thing to do to retire Hampton," wrote
Tillman on the day of this defeat, "but justice demanded
it. . . . Fully half of those who voted against him were
old Confederate soldiers and they echoed the sentiments
of three fourths of our people." [46] But to future generations of South Carolinians, Tillman's act was a ruthless
violation of cherished traditions of which Hampton was
a living symbol. For his services and tragic losses he had
been given the people's highest award, the emoluments
and honors of what was expected to be a lifetime career

[42] Kirkland, "Tillman and I," in Columbia *State*, July 7, 1929.
[43] Charleston *News and Courier*, November 29, 1890.
[44] Ball, *State that Forgot*, 232.
[45] South Carolina *House Journal*, 1890, pp. 207–208, 221–23, 242–49.
[46] Tillman to Martin V. Collins, December 11, 1890, in Governor Tillman's Letter Books.

in the national Senate. "Blot out Wade Hampton from the history of South Carolina for the past thirty years," said a truthful interpreter of this symbolism,[47] "and you blot out South Carolina." No wonder the verdict of the patriotic historian has been: "No single act of ruthless power by the greedy victors was more discreditable . . . than turning out the leader of 1876."[48]

A very unhappy and unheroic circumstance accentuated the bitterness caused by Hampton's retirement. He fitted perfectly Tillman's definition of the "broken-down aristocrat." Careless living had prevented the retrieval of material fortunes lost in war; he was a poor man dependent upon his salary as senator for the maintenance of his social position. And now ungrateful South Carolina literally forced him at the age of seventy-two on the charity of his friends.[49]

The Tillmanites partly justified the retirement of Hampton by truthfully saying that he had displayed only commonplace abilities. But the force of this argument was vitiated by a consideration of the qualities of his successor. Irby's virtues were only those of the hack politician. He was handsome and commanding, a warm and jovial friend, and an able political organizer. Tillman considered himself and Irby as an invincible team. But Irby's virtues were overshadowed by sensational vices. Indeed, the story of his early career reads like a Wild-West melodrama. In fits of drunken violence he sometimes terrorized his Laurens fellow citizens. He threatened or whipped inoffensive neighbors for fancied wrongs as he went about cursing, armed with a Winchester rifle. On one occasion he had stood by while his Negro servant attacked a white man, and on another it had taken an armed posse to subdue this

[47] D. E. Huger Smith, in Charleston *News and Courier*, December 8, 1890.
[48] Wallace, *History of South Carolina*, III, 356.
[49] Ball, *State that Forgot*, 232; Edward L. Wells, *Hampton and Reconstruction* (Columbia, 1907), 211–12.

berserk drunk. Once, charged with murder, he had hidden
in a remote section of Edgefield County,[50] but had gone
unpunished because of his popularity and family influence.
That Tillman tolerated his elevation to the United States
Senate can be explained only on the grounds that the
Edgefield leader could be insensitive to crimes of violence
committed by members of his own group.

Gary's and Tillman's charge that the Hampton clique
controlled public office for the selfish benefit of themselves and their friends can with equal justice be made
against the clique which surrounded Tillman. Blatantly
the Tillmanites appropriated the spoils of office. Even the
heads of judges fell. Talk of "rotation in office" was forgotten. Tillman himself, once in office, was never willing
to retire in favor of another and was content for two members of his family to hold positions concurrently. Later he
justified this "selfishness" of his by saying, "In fact all the
world is naturally that way." [51]

"Don't let there be any cornering of offices in South
Carolina. . . . This is a contest of officeholders against
the people," said a nephew of Martin W. Gary in 1890.[52]
Yet this man and three other members of the Gary family,
lawyers all,[53] probably secured more offices for themselves
than any other one family in the history of South Carolina, and Hugh L. Farley, relative and intimate friend of
Mart Gary, became adjutant general. The people perhaps
felt that this was proper reward for the "wrong" done

[50] See Charleston *News and Courier,* August 1, 1885; July 31, 1897; Laurens-
ville *Herald,* August 7, 1885.

[51] Tillman to Henry C. Tillman, October 14, 1913, in Tillman Papers.
The two other members of the Tillman family who held office were George
D. Tillman and George's son-in-law, Osmund W. Buchanan, congressman
and circuit judge respectively. Later George's son, James H. Tillman, was
lieutenant governor.

[52] Eugene B. Gary, in Charleston *News and Courier,* December 31, 1890.

[53] Eugene B. Gary, lieutenant governor and justice of the state supreme
court; Frank B. Gary, circuit judge and *ad interim* United States senator;
John Gary Evans, state senator and governor; Ernest Gary, member of the
legislature and circuit judge.

Mart Gary, but Ben Tillman was not so charitable. To give others opportunity for office, he wrote in later life, "is not the Gary way. They are always watching for the main chance for themselves." [54]

There was talk of an "Edgefield ring." "Edgefield," wrote Tillman, "has so many men holding high office that the other counties are complaining and kicking like mules." [55] Only about fifty of the seven hundred lawyers in the state espoused Tillmanism, a movement which its enemies said was directed against the legal profession; but, says a critic of Tillmanism, "if anyone of these fifty was not seeking public office at the hands of the 'movement' no trace of him has ever yet been discovered." [56]

While it is true that new men came into office with Tillman, they were not "the common people," "the wool-hat boys," whose fortunes Tillman was supposed to make. Farmers who won office under Tillman usually belonged to his own landholding group. Before long many of the new placemen were claiming aristocratic pedigrees.[57]

Tillmanism, however, was not merely a conspiracy to seize the spoils of office. Its object was to revolutionize certain aspects of the political life of South Carolina, and this object could be secured only by supplanting hostile with friendly agents. Governor Tillman was severely criticized for tampering with the judiciary, but, as he repeatedly made clear, this was necessary in order to remove judges determined to negate his major policies. Moreover, in extenuation of the fact that Tillmanism did not bring about a more democratic distribution of offices, this can be said: It was not a proletarian movement designed to reward the lower rungs of society, and if it did not succeed

[54] Tillman to Henry C. Tillman, October 14, 1913, in Tillman Papers.
[55] *Id.* to F. T. Walton, February 13, 1893, in Governor Tillman's Letter Books.
[56] McGhee, "Tillman, Smasher of Traditions," *loc. cit.*, 8018.
[57] Edward McGrady and Samuel Ashe (eds.), *Cyclopedia of Eminent and Representative Men of the Carolinas* (Madison, Wis., 1892), I, *passim.*

in dispossessing the lawyers, it merely failed where similar reform movements in other states have failed.

How much of his program had Tillman, after two years in office, forced through his legislature? The construction of Winthrop and Clemson colleges had been promoted and the South Carolina College reorganized; the governor had triumphed in dealing with the phosphate interests and with the lunatic asylum, and in filling the offices. Legislative representation had been reapportioned; the tax assessments of corporate wealth had been increased; and a prohibitive tax imposed upon the activities of emigrant agents. When it is remembered that most of the legislators had had no previous experience as lawmakers and that precedent decreed legislative sessions of only one month, this was a fair record of accomplishment. The self-confident governor, with unprecedented popular support behind him, had presented his plans with startling emphasis. He had reminded the legislators that they had been chosen by the people because they had expressed devotion to himself and his principles. Harshly, even profanely, he had disciplined refractory members, summoning them, one by one, into his office to demand that they change their votes. "The boss down stairs" was known to talk angrily when measures went against him.

Such tactics had their limitations even in dealing with men who knew that the governor held their political fates in his hands. The solitary farmer who had blasted his way into power was not as yet master of the arts of negotiation and diplomacy. He was patient enough to present precise explanations of his policies, but was unable to supplement reason with tact. Honorable gentlemen who were not immediately responsive to his will were called "damned fools" and roundly reprimanded. Many Tillmanites willingly listened to John C. Haskell and other experienced minority members who told them that Tillman was a tyrant whom the true patriot should try to curb. At the end of the second legislative session an observer wrote: "Men who a year ago seemed to take pleasure in doing all he wanted done now apparently find pleasure in going against him." [58]

The result of this estrangement was the defeat or neglect of many administrative measures. There had been failures in the promises to call the constitutional convention; to require each county to support its own patients in the lunatic asylum; to adopt a new railroad law; to revise the Congressional districts; and to reorganize county governments. Resentment against the notorious "Tillman dictation" had borne bitter fruit.

The revolt of the Tillman legislature took a sharp personal turn in the so-called free-pass incident. It became generally known in the summer of 1891 that the man who just twelve months before had accused his predecessors in office of having been "bamboozled and debauched" and "tamed, so to speak" by the railroad companies when they received free passes on the trains, had himself accepted the same favors from the same companies. Tillman saw both the humor and the danger of the exposé. He admitted that he, like the hated Bourbons, had some of the old Adam in him. And was he not a stingy man in debt who was attempting to live on a small salary? Did he not know that free passes were the greatest conveniences imaginable? He accepted them, succumbing, as he slyly put it, to "the irresistible nature of the passes and the luxury of such travel." [59]

Of course, there were the usual protective reservations. The passes, the honest farmer carefully informed his benefactors, would not influence his official conduct. "I take it of course that you extended these courtesies," he wrote a railroad official, "to the Governor of South Carolina and

[58] Orangeburg *Times and Democrat,* in Tillman Scrapbooks.
[59] Tillman to L. M. Moon, June 27, 1891, in Governor Tillman's Letter Books.

not to the individual, and as such I accept and thank you for them." [60] In other words, Honest Ben was not going to demonstrate personal gratitude for a very, very personal favor, a favor which relieved an impecunious pocketbook. Later, as the records demonstrate, he was proud of the fact that these gifts had no effect upon the battles he actually waged against the railroads. His feelings were not too delicate to allow his smiting the hand which once fed him! And when his enemies contrasted his possession of the passes with his previous criticism of others, he argued fatuously: "My office has no connection with the railroads and I never criticized state officers about taking free passes, but I scored the members of the General Assembly who allowed their votes to be influenced by this means." [61]

Others naturally saw the matter differently. His many critics commented on "the cold nerve" of this lusty Pharisee; [62] while at least one Tillman leader was so thunderstruck that he wondered whether his idol had feet of clay. [63] As soon as the matter became public, Tillman stopped using the passes and frankly admitted that he had made a mistake; [64] nor could he offer resistance when the Tillmanite majority spitefully joined the minority to prohibit public officials from accepting free passes. [65]

The hostility toward the governor among his own partisans was not accompanied by any lessening of the aversion of the Conservatives for him. Columbia developed into "the most ardent Tillmanhating place in the State." Prominent citizens ostentatiously avoided him in the streets. "I meet scowling faces when I walk up Main

[60] *Id*. to C. W. Ward, February 20, 1891, in Governor's Letter Books.

[61] *Id*. to John Murphy, April 19, 1892, in Governor Tillman's Letter Books.

[62] George R. Koester, "Bleaseism," Chap. II. This series of twenty-four articles, appearing originally in the Greenville *Piedmont* in 1916, is available in Tillman Scrapbooks. Cited hereafter by author, title, and chapter.

[63] Kirkland, "Tillman and I," in Columbia *State*, July 7, 1929.

[64] Tillman to Captain Samuel M. Mays, April 6, 1892, in Governor Tillman's Letter Books.

[65] South Carolina *Acts*, 1891, pp. 1046–47.

Street," Tillman confessed. At official celebrations he was embarrassed by the snubs of his opponents.[66] The Tillman family was not invited to the balls and other parties given by Columbia society, and the wives of the aristocracy dropped their custom of calling on the mistress of the governor's mansion. This conduct was caused in part by sincere anger, but it also had a sinister objective, the social annihilation of a large and not unambitious family of proud South Carolinians. Fortunately, however, the Tillman girls and their mother were not sharply touched by such matters. They did not attempt to develop social pretensions; their intense pride confuted the snobbery of their self-styled superiors.

Tillman himself, aside from the discharge of official obligations, made no effort to bridge the chasm between Tillmanism and anti-Tillmanism. "The policy of the administration," ran a mild characterization of the situation,[67] "does not seem to have been cast with any view of winning friends from the opposition." Indeed, Tillman took gratuitous delight in the fact that "the snarls and barbs of defeated and base ingrates" did not destroy his equanimity,[68] and he openly alluded to his Conservative opponents as "the curs of Haskellism" and "the bloodhounds of envy and personal malignity." [69]

The untoward circumstances of the first Tillman administration lead to the conclusion that the impolitic conduct of the chief had accentuated the hatred of enemies, had antagonized friends, had needlessly sacrificed many of the promised fruits of Tillmanism. Seemingly, the backbone of the administration had been broken by quarrels centering around the inept conduct of the governor. Was it

[66] Tillman to John D. M. Shaw, April 6, 1891, in Governor Tillman's Letter Books.
[67] Thad E. Horton, in Atlanta *Journal*, May 10, 1891.
[68] Tillman to unidentified friend, n.d., in Governor Tillman's Letter Books.
[69] Greenville *Echo*, n.d., in Tillman Scrapbooks.

not a truism that a politician in order to succeed must be politic? But had not the leopard been unable to keep the promise of the March convention that he would change his spots? Did not the situation call for another "retirement"; another fit of paralyzing misgiving, like those which had afflicted Tillman in 1887 and 1888? Would not his retirement banish the war of brothers and enable patriotic South Carolina to resume the even ways of the past?

Chapter XIV

THE RETURN TO POWER

GOVERNOR TILLMAN answered with a platitude those who predicted his overthrow at the end of his first term. "In our government," he wrote, "the people are the source of power and the people can always be trusted." [1] This declaration was a statement of his actually strong position; for he knew that "the people," by which he meant a majority of the white voters of South Carolina, were a mighty shield against the lieutenants who were "ready to stab me in the back if opportunity offers." [2] He understood that he enjoyed an undiminished popularity, that he was as capable in 1892 as in 1890 of arousing popular enthusiasm, and that wayward friends could be forced to obey his orders or suffer the fatal penalties of his burning addresses to the people.

He appreciated the effectiveness of his Caesarian influence over the people, glorying in the fact that Brave Ben Tillman needed no political machine and none of the tricks of political intrigue. He ruled as the tribune of the people, by the exercise of simple and direct oratory. The common people believed that he could do no wrong. They did not even resent so obvious a misdeed as the free pass incident. The tale went the rounds that a Tillmanite declared that if he caught Tillman stealing his sheep he would, nevertheless, vote for the governor. [3] Yet Tillman

---

[1] Undated statement, in Governor's Letter Books.
[2] Tillman to W. P. Addison, January 16, 1892, *ibid.*
[3] Koester, "Bleaseism," Chap. IX.

realized that his talents were not merely those of the demagogue. He knew that he possessed a moderate and statesmanlike program worthy of the applause of the intelligent.
He believed that he wielded powers of persuasion capable
of convincing the most critical.

He passionately shared the race, class, and provincial
prejudices of the average white South Carolinian, but at
the same time he possessed the ability to appraise with almost scholarly objectivity the nature of these prejudices.
He was able to give calculated direction to the passions
which moved him; he executed his plans, he said, "cold-
bloodedly." To a man of such feelings and such clear understanding it was easy to adopt a simple yet infallible
strategy. Profiting by Dawson's truthful characterization of
him as the leader of the Adullamites, he set the rustic majority against the genteel minority. He marshaled the upcountry against the low country; championed the poor
against the rich; the country people against the townsmen;
the "outs" against the "ins"; the rest of the state against
Columbia and Charleston; and finally inflamed the en-
franchised whites against the disfranchised blacks. All that
was needed for him to predict certain victory was the use
of a little simple arithmetic.

So it was a supremely confident Ben Tillman who, on
the evening of December 28, 1891, spoke to a "cheering
throng" from the front porch of Senator Irby's "palatial
home" at Laurens. He announced his candidacy for governor, boldly appealing to the people over the heads of
the politicians. He asked them to give him a new legislature. The tidal wave of Tillmanism which in 1890 had
swept from the mountains to the sea, he said, had deposited
in the State House "much dead driftwood." This "driftwood" should be supplanted by legislators more willing
to do his and the people's will.[4]

4 Summary of Tillman speech at Laurens, in Charleston *News and Courier*,
December 30, 1891, and in Greenville *Echo*, n.d., in Tillman Scrapbooks.

The Conservative best able to measure the strength of Tillman recommended that he be unopposed for re-election. This was Joseph H. Earle, who through the thirty-odd debates of the 1890 canvass had observed Tillman's powers as a vote getter. "My deliberate judgment," said this analyst, "is that Governor Tillman is at present as strong with the farmers as he ever was, and I believe that he will be re-elected over anyone who will probably take the field against him." "The more quietly and gracefully that they [the Conservatives] yield to the will of the majority," Earle continued, "the better it is for all concerned." [5] This advice, however wise in perspective, was impossible in the passion-dominated days of 1892. Gentlemen of pride could not be told that they must deal "quietly and gracefully" with the noisy and graceless Tillman! There must be a fight against "the rude traducer" and "the brutal tyrant" to save honor and pride if nothing else. Conservative opinion was more intense in its dynamic hatred of Tillman in 1892 than it had been two years before. He was the man who had caused the defeat of Hampton and Wallace, assaulted the sacred judiciary, set class against class, advocated laws against corporate wealth, and remained untamed under the sobering influence of responsible position.[6]

Blind passion, however, did not dominate in the council of the anti-Tillman leaders. Already men of long experience in the management of political affairs, they gleaned wisdom from their mistakes in 1890. They frowned upon the attempt to revive Haskellism,[7] and by offers of doctrinal compromise wooed many Farmers' Movement leaders whom Tillman had estranged. Only those whose past conduct proved that they were willing to submit to

[5] Charleston *News and Courier*, February 24, 1892.
[6] See letter of the resourceful Thomas W. Woodward, in Winnsboro *Herald and News*, February 2, 1892.
[7] See Charleston *News and Courier's* condemnation, February 26, 1892, of what may have been a second Haskell manifesto.

the verdicts of the Democratic party, whether pro-Tillman or anti-Tillman, were given positions of leadership.

Under such intelligent control, the Conservatives met in Columbia on March 24, 1892, in what they called the Peace and Harmony Convention, or in what their enemies derisively called a second March convention. There were 272 delegates present, representing all but one county. Most conspicuous among the delegates were former Senator Hampton and Sheppard and Richardson, former governors. "The head of our present State administration" was accused of conspiring to keep alive strife and discord, and of wishing to create a servile legislature and a timid judiciary. Sheppard, a man of moderation who had been stirred into action by the defeat of his father-in-law, Judge Wallace, sounded the keynote of the assembly when he said that it was necessary to "fight for the elimination of a Governor who usurps the function of the judiciary." Yet in doctrine this body agreed with the Tillmanites almost to the point of surrender. It pledged obedience to the verdict of the Democratic party and resolved not "to stir up passion by general accusations which we cannot prove." After James L. Orr, an upcountry cotton mill executive and the son of a distinguished politician of the same name, refused the gubernatorial nomination, that honor was given Sheppard. His aides in the scheduled forensic battle were Orr, who consented to run for lieutenant governor, and Lawrence W. Youmans, who became candidate for secretary of state. With Samuel Dibble as state chairman, the Conservatives perfected a strong organization in every county.[8]

They were less fortunate in the selection of candidates than they had been in 1890. Sheppard was admirably fitted to be governor of South Carolina—he was a man of honor, an experienced public servant, and an impressive orator of the bombastic type dear to Southerners. But he could not successfully conduct a series of debates on the plane

[8] *Ibid.*, March 24, 25, 1892; Ball, *State that Forgot*, 234.

Tillman prescribed. He lacked personal magnetism, was somewhat uncertain in his convictions, and was too dignified to evoke the sympathy of crowds accustomed to the irony and banter of his opponent. Unable and unwilling to play the clown, he was made into one by Tillman and the unruly crowds. Moreover, the fact that he was a banker and a lawyer and a former officeholder gave the Tillman editors opportunity to label him the enemy of the class-conscious farmers. Since he had failed Tillman in 1886, he was vulnerable to the slander that he had played traitor to the Farmers' Movement. Tillman's private estimate of him was devastatingly significant: "I prefer him to any man the Conservatives can put up." [9]

The qualities which Sheppard lacked were supposed to be supplied by Orr and Youmans, men of force and vivid speech. Orr, a broad-shouldered giant, was not of the old officeholding clique, but the fact that he was president of a cotton mill was a telling point against him before the class-conscious multitudes, and his size lent color to the accusation that he wished to bully Tillman. Youmans had been among Tillman's most effective antagonists in the newspaper war of the 1880's, but he was a "mustachioed strutter," so much in earnest that he was easily ridiculed by his impious opponent.[10]

In opposition to this combination Tillman, with characteristic energy, marshaled his forces. The thought that perhaps there might be no effective opposition made him apprehensive. Under such circumstances, he said, "the canvass will lag and lose interest and the Conservatives may elect men to the General Assembly opposed to us." [11] The considerable opposition which actually developed created in him a joyous longing for the fray. He busied himself with selecting candidates to take the place of rejected

[9] Tillman to Irby, February 8, 1892, in Governor Tillman's Letter Books.
[10] Estimate based on Koester, "Bleaseism," Chap. XIII.
[11] Tillman to Asbury C. Latimer, March 2, 1892, in Governor Tillman's Letter Books.

members of the "driftwood legislature." The tribune of
the people threatened verbal broadsides against the state
senators who had forgotten pledges.[12] But in actual practice he was not as ruthless as his general statements seemed
to threaten, making room on the Tillman wagon for wayward followers who had made "errors of the head and not
the heart." [13] He likewise bent his energies toward controlling the approaching May convention of the Democratic party, warning his partisans against compromise with
the Conservatives. To a lieutenant who wished to divide
a county delegation with the opposition he sternly wrote:
"The people are not going to submit to any such trade,
and if you have any regard for my wishes you will stop this
foolishness." [14] He designated fieldworkers to manipulate
matters in his favor,[15] and he was especially anxious to control Edgefield—"to show the state how Sheppard stands
at home when he opposes me." [16]

Tillman concerned himself with loading his "basket"
with the "rocks" he expected to hurl at his opponents in
the approaching county-to-county canvass. Would the
phosphate commissioner furnish information that the Coosaw Mining Company had swindled the state? [17] Would a
Washington friend furnish evidence of Hampton's bankruptcy and of Youmans' having asked the Republicans to
give him a judgeship? [18] Would a Greenville friend furnish
the evidence with which to "blast" Orr? The hours of
labor in Orr's mill and the price of its stock? [19] "I have
no fear after . . . I get on the stump," he wrote confidently. "I shall make the fur fly and present such facts

[12] *Id.* to Charles Crosland, April 27, 1892, *ibid.*
[13] *Id.* to John M. Waddell, May 30, 1892, ibid.
[14] *Id.* to J. H. Delyens, April 12, 1892, *ibid.*
[15] *Id.* to Henry H. Townes, March 18, 1892, *ibid.*
[16] *Id.* to M. B. Davenport, April 6, 1892, *ibid.*
[17] *Id.* to Adolphus W. Jones, July 11, 1892, *ibid.*
[18] *Id.* to Rollin H. Kirk, September 3, 1892, *ibid.*
[19] *Id.* to H. B. Buist, April 4, 1892, *ibid.*

and arguments as will hold my old friends if they are not blinded by prejudice." [20]

Meanwhile, the executive committee of the Democratic party modified the rules of that organization to suit the governor's taste. It prescribed, early in January, that Democrats who bolted the party in 1890 could not vote again in the primaries unless they took formal oaths to support all party nominees. Negroes who had been allowed to vote in the primary because they had supported Hampton in 1876 were to continue to exercise this privilege only on condition that they could get ten white men to vouch for their loyalty in that critical year. When the Conservatives asked that a primary be substituted for the convention method, Tillman and Irby objected. Such a reform, said these erstwhile champions of democratic methods, would be unfair to the counties of the low country which possessed small white populations. They did, however, consent to the election of delegates to the state nominating convention by primary. This was an important advance toward the full application of the primary principle. [21]

In the canvass of 1892 two new forces in the form of anti-Tillman and pro-Tillman newspapers played an important part. The first of these was the Columbia *State* which made its debut on February 8, 1891, under Gonzales' editorship. This well-known newsgatherer had left his position as the Columbia correspondent of the *News and Courier* to war against Tillman unrestrained by the conservatism of the Charleston journal. Although the son of an exiled Cuban patriot, he was as intensely South Carolinian in his prejudices and ideals as Tillman. But as a self-made man who had risen from the lowly occupation of telegraph operator to a position of prominence in a rising city of the New South, Gonzales was the fearless enemy

20 *Id.* to Townes, March 18, 1892, *ibid.*
21 Charleston *News and Courier,* January 6, 18, 23, April 7, 1892.

of dueling, murder, lynching, and other forms of barbarism characteristic of South Carolina rural life. Ben Tillman was, of course, the friend of barbaric eccentricities. This rustic's tolerance of violence conflicted with the businessman-editor's vision of a progressive commonwealth. Gonzales developed an almost uncanny knowledge of his enemy's faults, presenting them in the public prints with tactless veracity. And despite his preachments against lawlessness, he was too spirited a South Carolinian not to back brave words with an occasional fight.[22]

Gonzales was South Carolina's ablest editor after the untimely removal of Dawson in 1889.[23] The Columbia *State,* Tillman admitted, was "a bold, dashing, spicy and aggressive sheet, edited with spirit and ability." [24] But its influence in the campaign of 1892 was not as Gonzales intended. In that year it contributed unwittingly to the triumph of Tillman. The editor was too opinionated to develop the realistic tactics through which voters are won from the enemy; by raising issues he gave Tillman opportunity to strike back; and by his vehemence he foolishly accentuated the division between businessman and farmer. Although actually he was as provincial in his loyalties as Tillman, the fact that his father had been a Cuban was an Achilles' heel in the view of the nativist multitudes. The Tillmanites with impunity called him "the treacherous Spaniard."

Early in 1892 Tillman induced the Columbia *Daily Register,* an old journal which had developed into a friend of the farmers' cause, to become a militant supporter of Tillmanism. He took this action because he was without a champion among the daily newspapers to combat the influence of the *News and Courier,* the Greenville *Daily News,* and the Columbia *State.* He wished to have, he said,

[22] See autobiographical statement, in Columbia *State,* April 15, 1892.
[23] He was murdered by a Charleston physician.
[24] Tillman to Charles A. Calvo, Jr., January 30, 1892, in Governor Tillman's Letter Books.

a journalistic friend "with an aggressive and dashing policy" like the *State,* one that could "fight the devil with fire." He promised the *Register* increased subscription lists and the public printing.[25]

To give the newspaper a dynamic pro-Tillman bias, T. Larry Gantt was imported from Georgia [26] where he had made a reputation as a champion of the Farmers' Alliance. In appearance and manners the new editor conformed to the caricaturist's conception of the agricultural agitator of his day. "He wore," said a commentator, "a coarse woolen shirt and soft collar with the remnant of a tie, never properly adjusted. On his head was a faded woolen hat of many summers, brown with the dust of all of them. His baggy trousers stopped where the tops of his unpolished brogan shoes began, and his black coat, worn only in winter, was brown with age." His writings were nervously scratched on scraps of paper or were improvised as he set them in type. He had come to South Carolina, he said, for the purpose of "running a rough-and-tumble campaign." "There's no use for you fellows to begin telling lies on this thing, now," he announced to the enemy with a twinkle in his bright eyes, "for I give you fair warning that I kin beat any man in South Carolina in the lying business." [27] To which Tillman replied with the same twinkle in the single eye, "The newspapers all lie and even the *Register* stretches the blanket once in a while." [28]

Such a person as T. Larry Gantt could not last long; he was a mere apparition in a storm. But while he existed, he was a beacon before whom the more stable Gonzales paled. He had humor and an unaffected plainness in contrast with Gonzales' unimaginative earnestness. Endowed with all the prejudices of the current agrarianism and violently

[25] *Ibid.*
[26] Tillman to Irby, February 8, 1892, *ibid.*
[27] McGhee, "Tillman, Smasher of Traditions," *loc. cit.,* 8019.
[28] Charleston *News and Courier,* July 28, 1892.

partisan if never bitter, Gantt was the very man to second
Tillman's campaign of country against town. He paraded
private affairs of the opposition and gave dignified gentlemen ridiculous nicknames. When threatened with violence
if he did not leave the state, he showed courage: "If we
leave South Carolina before our mission is ended," said
the editor, "it will be in a casket with feet foremost." [29]

As Ben Tillman was preparing for the county-to-county
canvass of 1892, he was confronted with dissensions within
his own ranks more ominous than the combined opposition of Sheppard, Gonzales, and the other Conservatives.
There had developed a clash of principles which went beyond antipathy for Tillman's despotic personality. The
new conflict centered around the Farmers' Alliance.[30] Tillman from the very beginning of the Alliance had resented
its presence in South Carolina as a possible rival of the
Tillman-conceived Farmers' Movement, and he became a
member of it only from expediency. The Alliance tried
to center the interest of the South Carolina farmers in national affairs, while Tillman felt that they should be primarily concerned with the state. He suspected the Alliance
of third-partyism and believed that the organization's flare
for state socialism was neither just nor wise. The pro-
agrarian character of the platform of the Peace and Harmony Convention was obviously a Conservative attempt
to drive a wedge between Alliance members and the cantankerous leader of the farmers. Further, there was specific
antagonism toward Tillman among Alliance leaders for
having engineered the defeat of Milton L. Donaldson, the
Alliance candidate for the United States Senate in 1890.

The anti-Tillman wing of the Alliance brought Ben
Terrell of Texas, a prominent leader of the order, to South
Carolina to debate with Tillman in the summer of 1891.
The scene of this encounter was a closed conclave of the

[29] Columbia *Daily Register*, April 10, 1892.
[30] See above, pp. 147–48.

organization in the old opera house at Spartanburg. The issue was a semisocialistic Subtreasury Plan dear to ortho-dox Alliance members. Under this scheme farmers would be allowed to deposit their staple in Federal warehouses and receive in return loans equal to 80 per cent of the value of the deposits. This project was expected to benefit the farmers by increasing the volume of currency and by enabling them to hold their crops for higher prices.[31] Till-man let it be known before the debate that he opposed the plan. But he also revealed that he would not be defiant if the decision went against him. "After hearing me," he explained, "if they [the Alliance members] are not con-vinced, I will quietly submit and get out of the way. We cannot afford to divide in the face of the bitter and ac-tive opposition right here in South Carolina, and I have preached unity and the rule of the majority too long to change my tactics now."[32] With customary bravado he be-gan the debate by declaring that the Subtreasury Plan was "socialistic," promoted "special privilege," and was out of keeping with the traditions of the Democratic party. But when he did not win the sympathy of the majority of the Alliance delegates, he diplomatically agreed to support the plan. He had, said the correspondent of the Columbia *Daily Register,* "been made to eat a good, large slice of humble pie. He had to tell the farmers that if they would not go with him, he would go with them."[33]

Tillman's acquiescence did not quiet opposition within the ranks of the farmers. There were rumors that some wise Conservatives, despairing of the hope of defeating Tillman singlehanded, were searching for a dissatisfied Tillmanite to run against the chief. They decided on W.

[31] Buck, *Agrarian Crusade,* 130–31.
[32] Tillman to W. N. Wilder, June 8, 1892, in Tillman Papers. *Cf. id.* to George C. Ward, May 19, 1891, in Governor Tillman's Letter Books; *id.* to R. L. Beall, June 8, 1891, *ibid.*
[33] Columbia *Daily Register,* July 25, 1891; Charleston *News and Courier,* July 25, 1891; Koester, "Bleaseism," Chap. VI.

Jasper Talbert, a high official of the Alliance and fiery Tillman lieutenant who had a personal dislike for the leader and was not afraid to meet him on the stump. Tillman was alarmed. He called Talbert "my political enemy and would-be rival" who had been slandering him since 1891, and spoke of a possible "alliance between Gonzales and the Sub-Treasury men" which might cause his defeat.[34] To forestall such a scheme he agreed to the incorporation of the Subtreasury Plan in the platform of the state Democratic party. "Well, I 'went and done it,' " he wrote Irby on making this concession, "and my Alliance brethren are as happy as the father of the prodigal son." [35] Already, with Irby, he had bought stock in the *Cotton Plant,* the official organ of the Alliance. Tillman hoped that this would "exert a restraining influence on the paper" and forestall criticisms of him.[36]

Accordingly, the Tillman-dominated Democratic convention of May, 1892, espoused the Subtreasury Plan along with principles of the Alliance with which the chief had no quarrel; elected Tillman as the head of the state's delegation to the national convention; and carried out the expressed desire of both Tillman and the Alliance that Cleveland's nomination be opposed in the national assembly. But, at Tillman's suggestion, there was no instruction to bolt in case Cleveland won the nomination.[37]

Out of the bargainings and adjustments necessary to harmonize the Tillman and the Alliance forces resulted an event very distasteful to Tillman personally. This was the defeat of George D. Tillman, now a candidate for an eighth term in Congress, at the hands of Talbert. The two Tillman brothers had, through the years, remained personal friends, and George had lent the younger brother

---

[34] Tillman to James H. Tillman, February 14, 1893. *Cf. id.* to William A. Neal, February 15, 1892, in Governor Tillman's Letter Books.
[35] *Id.* to Irby, April 9, 1892, *ibid.*
[36] *Id.* to *id.,* February 8, 1892, *ibid.*
[37] Columbia *Daily Register,* May 19, 1892.

money with which to pursue political ambitions. But they were in no sense political allies. Rumors were afloat that Ben in 1890 checkmated George's ambition to be United States senator because the younger man felt one Tillman brother in that position would have made anomalous his own expected candidacy for the second senatorship in 1894.[38] George, in retaliation, assumed a patronizing attitude toward the political successes of his younger brother. He ostentatiously informed the public that he was not a member of the Farmers' Association, and he was often seen in the company of Senator Butler, Ben's expected rival for the senatorship in 1894. When asked, "Whom do you favor for governor, Tillman or Sheppard?" he replied evasively, "I am a George Tillman man and tote my own skillet." [39] Unlike Ben, he refused to give expediency precedence over principle on the Subtreasury issue. This gave Talbert his opportunity. He declared George unworthy of membership in the Alliance, and the obstinate old eccentric replied with reckless attacks on the order, thereby, as Ben later said, "driving off hundreds of his life-long friends" and making his defeat inevitable.[40]

This defeat caused George to develop a hatred for Ben from which he never recovered. Because Ben did not quixotically follow his example of antagonizing the Alliance, George concluded that his brother was in collusion with Talbert. He was especially indignant because Ben subscribed to the stock of the *Cotton Plant* and because he advised his upcountry hearers, "Hew to the line and vote against your brother if he is opposed to us in this contest." [41] George threatened the Farmers' Association and

[38] Wallace, *History of South Carolina*, III, 358.

[39] Cited in Tillman to James H. Tillman, February 14, 1893, in Governor Tillman's Letter Books.

[40] *Id.* to James B. McKie, December 24, 1914, in Tillman Papers. See also, account of George D. Tillman-Talbert debate, in Charleston *World*, August 24, 1891.

[41] Tillman to James H. Tillman, February 14, 1893, in Governor Tillman's Letter Books.

allowed rumors that he was supporting Sheppard to go unrefuted. Ben was disturbed over this "display of temper," this "unreasonable and unjust attitude," and tried hard to correct his erring brother. "We must," he wrote Irby, "bear with him and convince him of his error both as to our attitude toward him and his attitude toward the Alliance." [42] Although Ben's advice went unheeded, he did what he could to save George.[43] Certainly no evidence has ever been produced to prove that Ben was false to a once-beloved brother. The extent of his "betrayal" had been that he had refused to jeopardize his own political fortunes for the sake of one who persisted in being very foolish.

George's obstinate nursing of his grievance made Ben melancholy—a despondency which might have weakened one of less tenacity. The burden of the accusation led him to declare: "I had almost rather quietly go home than to permit him so to disgrace himself." [44] And when the full weight of George's resentment fell upon him, he cried, "It is a bitter, bitter thought that my only brother, to whom I have always turned as a father, . . . in his old age has come to consider me a traitor and a scoundrel. I am as badly hurt by the suspicion as if my wife or one of my children should put the poisoned chalice to my lips." Ben Tillman, however, did not let the morbid suspicions of an unreasoning person unnerve him. He reminded George that he, too, was not free from the suspicion of unbrotherly conduct, and that if there must be fratricidal war, George must take the initiative. Ben had been true. "My conscience is clear," he said, "and I can meet my dead mother

---

[42] *Id.* to Irby, February 8, 1892, *ibid.*

[43] *Id.* to James H. Tillman, September 12, 1892, in Tillman Papers. "I saw plenty of evidence," the correspondent of the Columbia *Daily Register* later wrote, "that Ben Tillman, in a quiet way, was trying to aid his brother without coming out in the open." Koester, "Bleaseism," Chap. VI.

[44] Tillman to Irby, February 8, 1892, in Governor Tillman's Letter Books.

when the time comes and say: 'I have been a true son and brother.' " [45]

The first of the joint debates of the canvass of 1892 was held at Greenville on April 16. Before five thousand listeners Tillman demonstrated the same tactics he had used two years before. The familiar mob was once more delighted by his coarse wit, his sparkling repartee, his confessions of virtues, and his hectoring challenges to adversaries. "I am here," he began, "to meet my traducers face to face, and let God and justice decide between us." Amid derisive laughter he attacked the "peace and harmony" policy of his opponents, ridiculing them for having called a March convention of their own and for putting in their platform some of the principles of the famous Tillman assembly of March, 1890. The only reason, he asserted, why there would not be another bolt from the Democratic party was that "the enemy had [in 1890] tried the negro and failed." Gonzales' new newspaper was called the "organ founded by the Haskellites to keep alive prejudices and malice." A hand primary proved that the greater portion of the crowd was in his favor.

The treatment of Tillman's opponents in 1892 indicated that the spirit of bitterness was even sharper than in 1890. Class consciousness had become a dominant motive for hate. The "impressive eloquence" of Sheppard was greeted by so many of what the *News and Courier* called "senseless yells" that he was forced to be apologetic. This modest gentleman was asked rude personal questions: "Are you a member of the Columbia Club?" "Are you president of a bank?" "What percent do farmers pay for money at your bank?" The retaliatory howls of the Conservatives caused Tillman, in rebuttal, to speak with unusual fierceness. He answered Sheppard's assertion that he (Sheppard) would carry Edgefield in the primary with the

[45] *Id.* to James H. Tillman, February 14, 1893, *ibid.*

boast, "I will go home, make three speeches, and if I can't win in the primaries I will withdraw from the race. . . . I have gone through hell to become Governor, and have been told that no other man could make the movement a success." He expressed his contempt for his adversaries in a historic epigram: "I had rather follow the majority to hell than these men to heaven." Offended because Orr had said he was "not fit to unlatch the shoes of Judge Wallace," he accused the candidate for lieutenant governor of being "the president of a factory that is making men and women work thirteen hours a day." Finally, he struck at the unfaithful within his own ranks. The "driftwood legislature," he said, had been "bamboozled and controlled by demagogues"; he would make the candidates for the next legislature "swear on Bibles" that they would support him.[46]

The dauntless speaker next went to Edgefield to ask his neighbors for vindication of the charges against his character. There he said: "I have a rough outside. God did not make me of that silken kind that enables me to bamboozle men, to give them lip-service or pretend to serve them; but my heart beats warm for the people of South Carolina and those who know me love me most. . . . Although I make no pretensions to religion or being a churchman, is there a man here who ever knew me to do an act of dishonor or dishonesty?" [47] Edgefield responded a few days later with the election of a delegation of Tillmanites to the Democratic State Convention headed by Honest Ben.[48]

"Only the mercy of God," wrote one who was present at the debates of the canvass of 1892, "averted bloodshed that year. Several times it seemed that the meetings would break up in murderous riots." Neither Tillman nor his

---

[46] Charleston *News and Courier*, April 17–19, 1892; Columbia *State*, April 17–19, 1892; Columbia *Daily Register*, April 17–19, 1892.
[47] Charleston *News and Courier*, April 25, 1892.
[48] *Ibid.*, May 8, 1892.

opponents would mitigate the caustic characterizations of
each other, and candidates on both sides were known to be
armed. The crowds, inflamed by whiskey or the words of
the speakers, grew more and more turbulent. Their wild-
ness reached a climax at Walterboro. There the profane
yells were so deafening that Youmans was "howled down,"
and no speaker on either side was able to secure an uninterrupted hearing. The conduct of the rowdies, said an
observer, "was such as would have been a reproach to a
negro bedlam." [49]

The experiences of 1888 and 1890 were re-enacted in
Charleston. James C. Hemphill, who had succeeded Dawson as editor of the *News and Courier,* emulated Dawson
when he called the Edgefield farmer the chief of the Adullamites. Tillman's speech, Hemphill predicted, "is likely
to prove a trying ordeal for any self-respecting Charleston-
ian to hear him. He spoke here once before and denounced the people as cowards. . . . Governor Sheppard
is a gentleman, while Governor Tillman makes no pretense at being one. He scorns refinement of manners and
speech and prefers 'damn you' to 'if you please.' " [50] These
insulting words stirred the Edgefield rustic to speak as
defiantly in 1892 as he had done in 1888. The editor, he
said, who denied him the title of gentleman was the "upcountry ragamuffin who used to 'go around in copperas
breeches around Long Cane," [51] and his newspaper was
accused of trying to win the governor to its side by giving
him an aristocratic pedigree.[52] Defiantly the proud com-
moner exclaimed in the words of John Dryden, "I am one

[49] *Ibid.,* June 11, 1892; Koester, "Bleaseism," Chap. XII; *id.,* in Columbia
Daily Register, June 11, 1892.
[50] Charleston *News and Courier,* June 14, 1892.
[51] Hemphill, like Calhoun and other adopted leaders of Charleston's
upper class, was a native of the upcountry. He was born at Due West,
Abbeville District, the son of a Presbyterian minister.
[52] Charleston *News and Courier,* September 11, 1890, had published a
sketch of Tillman asserting, perhaps through the ignorance of the writer,
Matthew F. Teague, that the governor was descended from the aristocratic
Maryland family of Tilghmans.

of God Almighty's gentlemen." [53] This boast, replied
Hemphill, was evidence of "the malice, the conceit, the
vulgarity of the man." [54] The quotation was not given its
proper figurative meaning.

The meeting at Florence on June 30 was "the wildest
and the roughest of the campaign," and "a bloody riot
seemed imminent several times." The disorders of the day
began when Tillman was greeted at the railroad station
by three groups of glowering rowdies. Next, a delegation
from the near-by town of Timmonsville hoisted above the
speaker's stand a banner depicting Tillman as "The Great
Bamboozler Running away from Our Youmanry." When
the bearers of the lampoon refused to remove it, the Tillmanites rushed to the platform with drawn pistols. Bloodshed was avoided by Youmans' insistence that the banner
be removed. This incident was followed by that candidate's
attempt to force Tillman to recant a previous assertion
that "Earle was a more honorable man than Youmans."
Tillman's tart response was, "Not a damn bit." When a
minister of the town tried to force an apology for the use
of the expletive, the speaker refused amid a scene of ter-
rifying disorder.[55]

Conduct even worse than that at Florence prevailed at
Edgefield a week later, where the candidates had gone for
a return engagement. The trouble began when the howls
and hoots of Tillman's friends prevented Youmans from
being heard. When McLaurin, the Tillman candidate for
attorney general, arose to speak, he was met by retributive
shouts from a mob of Sheppard's friends under the leadership of one of the reputedly dangerous men of "bloody
Edgefield," who told McLaurin that if he attempted to
speak he would be shot. To end the impasse, Tillman or-

[53] "His tribe were God Almighty's gentlemen." *Absalom and Achitophel*,
Pt. I, 645.
[54] Charleston *News and Courier*, June 15, 1892.
[55] *Ibid.*, July 1, 1892; Columbia *Daily Register*, July 1, 1892.

dered adjournment. After this was accomplished, the Tillmanites bore Tillman and McLaurin to the porch of the
near-by Village Academy, where they prepared to speak.
Enraged by the apparent defeat of their purpose, the anti-
Tillmanites advanced in mass formation upon Tillman
and McLaurin. Pistols were drawn and a pitched battle
seemed inevitable; but this unhappy eventuality was prevented by the sheriff and some women who rushed between the two groups, and by the retreat of the Tillmanites to the county courthouse, with Tillman and McLaurin
on their shoulders. There, behind a guard of sentinels,
both speakers had their say.[56]

The scenes of the Walterboro, Charleston, Florence, and
Edgefield meetings were repeated only once at the remaining meetings of the canvass. Alarmed authorities of the
towns closed the saloons; partisans saw the folly of "howling down" candidates while the opposition learned to conduct themselves with greater equanimity. The only remaining incident of near-violence occurred at Union when
the giant Orr said that the ministers of the state were
against Tillman because the governor cursed and boasted
of not going to church. "I do curse sometimes," said Tillman frankly, "but there is not a drop of hypocrite in me.
. . . Any preacher or anybody else who says that I boasted
of not going to church, lies." Face to face, Tillman and
Orr stood tense, while the crowd, with pistols ready,
massed on the platform. Orr did not strike. "Had Orr laid
one of his burly hands on Tillman," said the correspondent of the *Register*, "there would not have been enough of
his huge body left to bury." [57]

The canvass of 1892 was disappointing to those interested in such forms as a means of public enlightenment.

[56] Columbia *Daily Register*, July 8, 1892; Charleston *News and Courier*,
July 8, 1892; Koester, "Bleaseism," Chap. XIII.

[57] Columbia *Daily Register*, August 5, 1892; Columbia *State*, August 5,
1892.

Instead of a calm discussion of differences of opinion, through which plain men might arrive at intelligent decisions, there was resort to personalities, groundless accusations, and private revelations unseeming in candidates for responsible public office. The crowds, instead of listening open-mindedly to opposing arguments, spent most of their time yelling. There can be no doubt that Tillman, as the individual who organized public opinion and who profited most by these disturbances, was largely responsible for the ugly tempers displayed.[58]

Tillman's opponents, on the other hand, cannot be acquitted of partial responsibility for the turmoil. Aware that they could not defeat their powerful rival by ordinary methods of political discussion, they sought extreme stratagems. Orr and Youmans tried to bully Tillman by display of their physical courage and by the threat of physical force. That there was no bloodshed was due more to Tillman's prudence than to theirs. They tried to discredit him personally through indictments of irreligion and blasphemy. These were grave slanders in a religious commonwealth like South Carolina.

There was something more than clownishness and demagoguery in Tillman's tactics in 1892. He constantly kept the unrealized portions of the program of his first administration in the public eye; he stressed the necessity of having a sympathetic legislature in order to realize this program. He made the farmers realize more clearly than ever that they had certain class interests opposed to those of town and business. His attack on Orr as a cotton mill executive activated the dormant political consciousness of the cotton mill workers. Tillman was teaching two large

[58] The late Dr. C. Prescott DeVore, an Edgefield planter and friend of the Tillmans, told the author in 1923 that he asked Ben: "Why do you raise so much hell?" "Well," replied Tillman, "if I didn't, the damn fools would not vote for me." Tillman actually had written DeVore's father: "I appreciate your good advice about speaking irreverently and will endeavor to guard against it. . . . I only speak thus for emphasis." Tillman to Dr. James A. DeVore, May 12, 1892, in Governor Tillman's Letter Books.

underprivileged classes to demand some of the privileges of an imperfectly realized democracy. This was a phase of the main constructive achievement of his whole career, the arousal of the political consciousness of the white masses.

Chapter XV

THE SECOND ADMINISTRATION

THE elections of 1892 returned Governor Tillman to office with greatly increased power and prestige. In the primary of August 27 he received a majority of 22,000 out of a total popular vote of 87,000 and won 264 of the 320 delegates to the nominating convention.[1] The Sheppard ticket carried only 4 of the 35 counties. Tillman won Edgefield by a majority of 1,500. Five of the 7 congressmen elected were Tillmanites. The people had obeyed the injunction "to kill off the race of fence straddlers" by electing new men to take the place of the "driftwood" legislature and its Conservative allies. Only 8 of the 36 senators and 22 of the 124 representatives were anti-Tillmanites. Of the 102 Tillmanites of the new House, only 27 had sat in the old, and most of these had records satisfactory to the governor. The new members were ready to execute the orders of their "political daddy," acting through Cole L. Blease as House leader and John Gary Evans as Senate leader. The Conservatives, true to their promise of the previous spring, made no efforts in the general election to nullify the decision of the primary. Tillman, for his part, loyally supported Cleveland after the New Yorker became the Democratic Presidential nominee. James B. Weaver, the Populist candidate for President, received only one thirtieth of the South Carolina vote.[2]

Tillman, during his last two years in office, ruled abso-

[1] Charleston *News and Courier*, September 1, 1892.
[2] South Carolina *Reports and Resolutions*, 1892, I, 546–49.

lutely by using his control of public opinion to discipline legislators and officials. He moved toward his objectives without respect for the feelings of either supporters or enemies. He was severe toward friends. "You don't know what you are talking about," he wrote an obstreperous follower. "Why don't you join the anti-Tillmanites anyhow? You have been talking sometimes like you wanted to." [3] He was even more harsh toward enemies. He protested against officials' retaining clerks who had voted for Sheppard,[4] and ordered public money removed from the Bank of Charleston because its head was also president of the company which published "the lying editorials" of the *News and Courier*.[5] Lieutenants, he felt, should not recommend "half and half men" to him for appointments, but those "obnoxious to the ring." [6] He even wished "somebody would lynch" one or more editors who "slander and misrepresent men and distort facts." [7] No wonder he continued to meet scowling faces in the streets of Columbia and that his subordinates obeyed him more from fear than from love. Yet the secretary of this hard-fibered man was able to write: "He is accustomed to criticism and thrives on it." [8]

Inevitably he was accused of tyranny. "Since Mr. Tillman's advent into politics," wrote a thoughtful critic, "there has been no such thing in the State as free speech and free thought. We have all been under a kind of bondage, both his friends and his foes, and Mr. Tillman had the monopoly." [9] Admittedly, he represented a majority of the recognized voters of the state as opposed to what he

[3] Tillman to Joshua W. Ashley, February 8, 1894, in Governor's Letter Books.

[4] *Id.* to John S. McKie, September 26, 1892, in Governor Tillman's Letter Books.

[5] *Id.* to John ———, January 21, 1893, in Governor's Letter Books.

[6] *Id.* to J. Elmore Martin, November 1, 1893, *ibid.*

[7] *Id.* to F. H. Richardson, January 15, 1894, *ibid.*

[8] Tompkins to T. F. King, July 14, 1893, *ibid.*

[9] Prosperity *Press and Reporter,* cited in Charleston *News and Courier,* March 25, 1895.

called "aristocratic privilege and the claim of inheritance by divine right"; [10] but, as the most famous of South Carolinians had pointed out long before, the will of a majority could be as burdensome as that of a hereditary aristocracy or monarchy. Moreover, only according to the orthodox Southern definition was Tillmanism the rule of the majority of South Carolinians. Out of a white voting strength of approximately 100,000, Tillman was the voice of 60,000. This was a clear majority of 20,000. But what of the 120,-000 potential Negro voters who, if combined with the 40,000 Conservative voters, would very likely have made a total of 160,000 anti-Tillmanites? From the viewpoint of this 160,000 the rule of the 60,000 Tillmanites was the tyranny of a minority. And if Tillman was severe toward Conservative whites, he was savage toward the blacks. Of course, he denied them political privileges, and, as we shall see, justified lynching under certain conditions. He even discouraged Northern relief to Negro storm sufferers, fearing "the collection of lazy, idle crowds to draw rations as they did in the days of the Freedman's Bureau. . . . They cannot be treated as we would white people." [11]

Yet when one asserts that Tillman was a tyrant, he indulges more in hyperbole than in an accurate use of that term. This democrat regarded the white majority as his master, knowing as well how to follow public opinion as how to lead it. He was careful in most cases to advance only measures considered moderate and reasonable by his majority. Although he sought objectives with much bluff and bluster, his aims were never erratic. He realized that he did not possess the right to be the absolute ruler of a sovereign state. His powers were limited by the Federal government and by the whole hierarchy of courts and legislatures. Although he assumed all the prerogatives which the law gave

[10] Tillman, in South Carolina *House Journal,* 1894, p. 20.
[11] *Id.* to John E. Russell, September 12, 1893, in Governor's Letter Books.

him, he had an honest respect for the restraints it imposed upon him.

Governor Tillman, in his first message in 1892 to the newly elected legislature, forgot the passions of the previous summer and contented himself with a statement of concrete reforms he wished accomplished. The first demand, naturally enough, was the fulfillment of objectives frustrated by the previous legislature. He was concerned because both state and Federal courts had interfered with his attempts to evaluate railroad and bank properties. "The power to levy and collect taxes," he declared, "lies at the very root of government," and for the judiciary to override this right of legislature and executive was dangerous tyranny. The proper procedure, he believed, was for the corporations to be forced to appeal to juries instead of irresponsible judges, who were pictured as agents of plutocracy seeking to destroy popular authority. While South Carolina was powerless to resist the encroachments of the Federal courts, he believed the state judges could be brought to terms.[12]

The new legislature docilely presented the governor with the two-thirds majority necessary for a vote of the people on the constitutional convention issue.[13] The efforts of the Conservatives to have the proposed constitution submitted to a popular referendum were unsuccessful.[14] Tillman feared the possible opposition of the 40,000 Conservatives combined with the 120,000 Negroes.

The revived railroad regulation bill met with furious Conservative opposition. The new project provided for a railroad commission of three to be elected initially by the legislature and subsequently by the people. In fixing rates, the commission was authorized to examine the books and

[12] South Carolina *Senate Journal*, 1892, pp. 19–23.
[13] South Carolina *Acts*, 1892, pp. 6–7.
[14] Columbia *Daily Register*, December 9, 1892.

schedules of the railroad companies. The *News and Courier* declaimed, "The monstrous injustice of this bill toward the largest and most important interest of the State will drive out capital." A railroad official asserted, "It puts property rights and interests at the mercy of three men who can ruin us and wipe out values of millions of dollars of property from a whim of their own, or in obedience to a temporary gust of public wrath." The railroad workers, fearing injury to their wages, added their protests to those of their employers.[15] But Tillman and the legislature remained obdurate. "The opposition of eight or ten thousand railroad employees," said the governor, "does not amount to a damn compared with fifty to sixty thousand farmers demanding the passage of this bill." [16] It became law.[17] The predictions of the alarmists did not come true. Conservative men were put on the commission, and capital was not driven from the state. South Carolina had merely been given a railroad law like that already possessed by progressive Western states.

The governor, acting through the state board of equalization, levied tax assessments upon railroad properties based on higher evaluations; but the companies, insisting that the assessments were unjust, refused to pay the increment. They took refuge behind injunctions granted by the Federal courts. The sum of $208,600 was involved. In the judicial battle to secure this amount, the governor won a victory when the United States Supreme Court, in January, 1893, denied the lower Federal courts jurisdiction over county assessments under $2,000.

But when tax executions were placed in the hands of the county sheriffs, another judicial obstacle appeared. It was discovered that 1,410 of the state's 2,552 miles of railroads were in the hands of receivers, and Federal Judge Charles H. Simonton issued an injunction restraining sheriffs from

15 Charleston *News and Courier*, December 13, 14, 16, 1892.
16 Columbia *State*, December 23, 1892.
17 South Carolina *Acts*, 1892, pp. 8–17.

levying upon property in this category. Tillman was furious against "the unholy alliance between the dignity of the Federal courts and these harlot corporations." He resolved to test the validity of this action by ordering the sheriffs to hold railroad property to satisfy tax claims.[18] The state, he said, could not afford to back down in so important a matter. But the court struck back with dispatch. Judge Simonton, with the aid of Judge Nathan Goff, sustained the injunction by fining the sheriffs $500 each, or imprisonment until they paid their fines or purged themselves. When the United States Supreme Court sustained this action, the governor surrendered by paying the fines.

Although defeated, Tillman published a trenchant denunciation of the "unholy marriage" between the railroads and the courts. In an argument of twelve pages, he effectively sustained the thesis that by its high-handed action the Federal court had denied the sovereignty of the state in the vital matter of taxation and had placed railroads in receiverships in a privileged position. This "fungoid growth of modern judicial precedent" was an outrage upon the historic priority of the tax claims of the state. It had "spread and grown with the rapidity of a banyan tree in the tropical jungles of Asia, until it now overshadows the land and blights the sovereignty of the States." The railroads, he continued, had become bankrupt because of mismanagement, the watering of stock, and the desire of the majority stockholders to steal property. The courts were "instruments to carry out this robbery." Former Governor Chamberlain, the Carpetbagger, was now receiver of the South Carolina Railroad and thus was the representative of Northern wealth in conspiracy against the freedom of South Carolina. He was aided by Federal Judge Goff, a Carpetbagger who once "did his utmost to throttle Anglo-Saxon civilization," and now, after fifteen years' absence, returned to South Carolina to gloat over the fresh humiliations he was able to

[18] Tillman orders to sheriffs, January 28, 1893, in Governor's Letter Books.

impose. Chamberlain's and Goff's allies were native Bourbons, the friends of Wade Hampton. There was Judge Simonton, a Charleston gentleman "who sucked State's rights with his mother's milk, and now plants his dagger in the State's breast." What a fantastic revolution in the whirligig of time! concluded Tillman without perhaps realizing how easy it was for Bourbons to subordinate political principles to economic opportunities.[19]

Despite the opposition of business interests, the Tillman legislature made a beginning in social legislation. It limited the hours of labor in cotton mills. This measure, introduced by "Citizen Josh" Ashley, a clownish but sagacious representative of the upcountry democracy, reflected the growing importance of the poorer whites who were being concentrated in the mill villages. Tillman, although he had not yet developed interest in the social uplift of "the damned factory class," was willing to champion legislation opposed by mill executives of Orr's type. The original measure, which would have imposed a sixty-hour week for mill operatives, was described by the *News and Courier* [20] "as a bill to discourage manufacturing." A mill president declared, "A ten-hour a day law would ruin every mill in the State." But he got a vehement answer from a Tillmanite who was destined to become the most notable political leader of the mill laborers. "If you have to buy any capital by murdering women and children," declared Blease, "for God's sake let it go, let it go!" The bill passed after a compromise under which the maximum hours per week were extended to sixty-six.[21] Thus South Carolina made a beginning in a type of legislation sanctioned by the progressive thought of the age.

Perhaps the project of Tillman's second administration which created most rancor was the proposal that the existing Congressional districts, under which Charleston was

[19] Tillman, in South Carolina *House Journal*, 1893, pp. 15–34.
[20] Charleston *News and Courier*, November 25, 1892.
[21] South Carolina *Acts*, 1892, pp. 90–91.

placed in an area of considerable white population, be abolished in favor of an apportionment which consigned that city to a district of coastal counties with huge black majorities. This was interpreted by Conservatives "as a plan of devilish ingenuity designed to give Charleston a black congressman." In deference to a proud city, the bill was abandoned in 1892.[22] It was revived at the next session in a modified form, and Charleston was actually placed in a district with a black majority of 68,000.[23] Yet the prediction that a black congressman would represent the city did not become true because of the prevailing suffrage discriminations.

Governor Tillman was proud of his success in refunding the state debt of $5,250,000 at an interest rate of 4½ per cent in place of the former 6 per cent. At first the governor tried to sell his new issue of bonds at 4 per cent, but a visit to New York City taught him the necessity of an increase of ½ per cent.[24] There was a general stringency of money and rumors were afloat that the Tillman administration was "incompetent and inimical to capital." [25] The actual reduction in interest rate resulted in an annual saving to the state of $78,000. This somewhat modest sum was proof that a hardheaded farmer could play finances successfully and that the critical investors of Wall Street recognized the stability of the South Carolina ruler.[26]

Tillman again tried to redeem his pledge to cut public expenses. The governor's and the judges' salaries were reduced $500 each, and those of state officers $200 each. Seven thousand dollars was saved, but such a minor economy was not significant. Under Tillman, colleges were being opened and experiments undertaken that meant increased rather than decreased expenditures. The governor sought reve-

[22] Charleston *News and Courier*, December 6, 1892.
[23] South Carolina *Acts*, 1892, pp. 90–91; 1893, pp. 413–14.
[24] Tillman to George W. Williams, August 28, 1891, in Governor Tillman's Letter Books; *id.* to William H. Brawley, September 28, 1892, *ibid.*
[25] *Id.* to J. M. Gaines, March 1, 1892, *ibid.*
[26] *Id.*, in South Carolina *House Journal*, 1893, p. 8; 1894, p. 20; Alfred B. Williams, in New York *Times*, June 4, 1896.

nues beyond the general tax levy—a special tax on fertilizer and income from a state liquor monopoly; this enabled him to cut the general property levy one-half mill. But the new collections were as truly tax burdens as were the traditional sources. At the end of twelve years of Tillmanism the per capita state tax was $1.91, which was low; but it was not as low as the $1.50 per capita rate of 1870 or the $1.63 of 1890.[27]

The zeal with which Tillman had opposed lynching during his first administration was changed to the opposite policy during his second. He returned to ideas he had professed during the Reconstruction period. During the canvass of 1892 he said, "There is only one crime that warrants lynching, and Governor as I am, I would lead a mob to lynch the negro who ravishes a white woman." [28] When the first lynching of the second administration did occur, that of John Peterson at Denmark in Barnwell County, who was charged with an attempted rape upon a fourteen-year-old white girl, the governor had his secretary write a Barnwell officer: "The villain deserves lynching and he [the governor] has been hoping to hear that you have caught and lynched him." Tillman preferred that the alleged felon be lynched "before the officers of the law get possession of him," because the legal punishment for attempted rape was not death as Tillman believed it should be. The only precaution he asked of the Barnwell officer was "to preserve the proprieties." [29] Peterson, after capture, asked for and received the governor's protection; but he was later surrendered to Barnwell officers, from whom he was taken and lynched. A Columbia mass meeting led by Gonzales and John C. Haskell accused the governor of connivance in this

[27] Ball, *State that Forgot,* 224–25; August Kohn exhaustive analysis of state tax policies, in Charleston *News and Courier,* May 15, 1897.

[28] At Aiken, cited in Charleston *News and Courier,* July 7, 1892. This statement was frequently repeated. *Cf.* Tillman to Hall, June 1, 1894, in Governor's Letter Books; *id.* to William J. McPherson, July 1, 1892, *ibid.*

[29] Tompkins to Stanwix G. Mayfield, April 18, 1892, in Governor Tillman's Letter Books.

lawless act.[30] This protest merely aroused the fury of the race-prejudiced Tillman masses. The Conservatives were charged with seeking Negro votes by encouraging black men to defile white women. An informal Barnwell jury of five hundred declared that Gonzales was "an outlaw to society, a fit prey to fall at the hands of an outraged people, and is blacker at heart than the rapist and is worthy of a worse fate than John Peterson." [31] Tillman, for his part, calmly asserted that an investigation would serve no useful purpose, which was doubtless true.[32] The investigation which he did authorize came to nought, like hundreds of similar procedures in all sections of the South.

Tillman's words about lynching and his attitude in the Peterson case were reprehensible. Although the five lynchings during his first administration contrasted singularly with the thirteen such tragedies of his second term,[33] he speciously insisted that the legislature was to blame because it had refused to give him power to remove sheriffs who surrendered prisoners to the lynching mobs.[34] Yet his justification of lynching was correlated with the actual Southern view of proper interracial relations: white blood must not be defiled with black blood; a summary vengeance must be visited upon the black man who attempted the crime. Tillman had contempt for those Southerners who reprehended lynching as lawlessness, for he believed that "those who so loudly denounce the course of the Denmark lynchers would be the first to demand speedy vengeance were some fiend to ravish one who was dear to them." [35]

Allegations of graft embarrassed Tillman throughout his second administration. Many charges were born of the jaundiced imagination of enemies and were without foun-

[30] Columbia State, April 26, 1893.
[31] Columbia Daily Register, April 28, 1893.
[32] Charleston News and Courier, April 27, 1893.
[33] Wallace, History of South Carolina, III, 400, gives a partial list of lynchings.
[34] Tillman to Hall, June 1, 1894, in Governor's Letter Books.
[35] Columbia Daily Register, April 28, 1893.

dation. Such, for example, were the allegations concerning whiskey rebates.[36] Such also was the slander that a piano he honestly purchased in 1891 was given for official favors.[37] In other cases Tillman's guilt was assumed by his enemies until he was able to disprove the charges. This was giving Tillman, the officeholder, a dose of the same medicine Tillman, the agitator, had forced upon his predecessors. Unfortunately, he was sometimes unable to defend himself. He was notoriously careless in his accounts and his memory of private transactions was short. So when the "character assassins" confronted him with charges of financial irregularities, months or even years after the alleged transactions, he did not always have at hand the data necessary for perfect refutations.

His conduct was not always above valid criticism. As the free-pass incident of his first administration proved, the integrity of Honest Ben was not invariably of the unbending variety. With a salary of only $3,500,[38] he experienced difficulty in making ends meet. This led him to participate in a species of pilfering. He received from the superintendent of the penitentiary certain valuables without proper inquiry into the authority of that official, the genial Colonel William A. Neal, to make these alleged gifts or sales. Neal gave Tillman, among other things, a carload of twelve thousand bricks, convict labor and a mule for the operation of a small farm near the governor's mansion, a certain inexpensive bookcase, ten tons of cottonseed meal, and weekly supplies of vegetables, wood and coal, and a little hay, oats, and molasses.

These examples of what Tillman in his more vigilant days would have called "official debauchery" came to light four years after he had left the governor's office. It was proved Neal had made Tillman gifts of state property, and

[36] See below, pp. 245-46.
[37] See the explanation by the merchant, M. A. Malone, in Columbia *State*, April 10, 1906.
[38] Reduced to $3,000 in 1893.

the former governor was bluntly asked to pay $109.06, a modest estimate of the value of the goods.[39] Tillman paid the bill, saying in a display of almost unbelievable credulity, "I never dreamed that the articles were not charged to his [Neal's] account and settled for. Since I have discovered that the State is the loser, I, of course, am willing to pay for each and all of these things." [40]

This was not an important episode in Tillman's career. To only a small degree did he benefit from Neal's laxities. He was too well disciplined to participate in "the high old time" and "good cheer" of this official's "debauchery." [41] A man so basically honest as Tillman could not be dishonest or even careless in matters of large moment. When, in later life, an enemy recalled the Neal transactions, Tillman brushed the accusation aside. "Oh, pshaw! it is a waste of good soap to shave an ass," he said of his accuser. "I feel disgusted that I have had to travel all the way from Washington to wash off the dirt and filth and manure that this man has been spouting. . . . If I had wanted to sell out, I could have gotten enough to have feathered my nest without bothering about potatoes and oats." [42]

Among his major achievements the governor placed the primary system of nominating Democratic candidates for office. Yet, as part of a general conspiracy to reduce the importance of Tillman in the annals of the state, the most competent students of the subject deny him this honor. They point out that this agency of democracy emerged from sectional, class, and racial circumstances which existed before Tillman. Under the convention system representation was apportioned according to population, which meant that "the silent negro vote of the parishes" gave disproportion-

[39] He had already paid the Southern Oil Company $180 in June, 1899, for the cottonseed meal. Columbia State, August 27, 1906.

[40] William F. Stevenson to Tillman, May 20, 1899, in Tillman Papers; Tillman to Stevenson, May 6, 1899, ibid. See also, Charleston News and Courier, March 14, 24, September 30, 1899.

[41] Charleston News and Courier, August 10, 1899.

[42] Columbia State, August 27, 1906.

ate strength to the white minority of the low-country counties. Under the primary system the power of the white voter in all sections of the state would be equal; the supremacy of the upcountry, where the greater portion of the whites lived, would be assured. The lower classes desired the primary as a means of regaining the direct participation in government they had experienced in ante-bellum days before the principle of white unity destroyed the individual's freedom of suffrage. Under the convention system, the plain voter could not directly and secretly express his choice, but attended open club meetings where he was subjected to the machinations of influential people. The direct primary, as the least hampered means for expression of the public will, offered minimum opportunity for discontent within the party, and for that reason was the best means of preventing bolts endangering white supremacy.

Agitations for the primary antedated Tillmanism. Pickens County in 1876 adopted it in the nominations of local officers, as did eight additional counties by 1878, and nearly all the counties by the time the Edgefield leader made his influence felt. As early as 1878 the newspapers of Edgefield and Anderson criticized the alleged overrepresentation of the low country in state conventions, and in 1882 the "Greenville idea," calling for the apportionment in this body according to white population, was an important issue.

The critics of the Tillman thesis supplement the proof that Tillman was a late advocate of the primary by stating that after he had proclaimed its virtues, he was not always its consistent friend. He favored it when it served his purposes and opposed it when it did not. "Tillman," Professor David D. Wallace sapiently observes, "believed in the primary no more than did Calhoun in state sovereignty for its own sake, but only as a means to an end." As we have seen, he refused in 1890, 1892, and 1894 to allow state-wide primaries at the request of the Conservatives, this for the practical reason that his control of scheduled nominating conventions was already assured.[43] He justified these reversals of principle by saying that the primary device would be unjust to the coastal counties whose votes "would be overwhelmingly crushed by the votes of the Piedmont counties." [44] This was, as Professor Wallace avers, the setting aside of an abstraction to use a disapproved means of holding power. The much-denounced ring methods were used to triumph over the ring.

Despite these facts, assertions concerning "the groundlessness of claiming Tillman as the father of the primary system" have not been demonstrated. If Tillman did not create the sectional, class, and racial issues which made the primary likely, he, more than any other South Carolinian gave most effective expression to these issues. By the exercise of his peerless gifts of popular appeal, he undermined the confidence of the voters in the rings and manipulations which he said were the essence of the convention system. After winning popular prestige, he selected the primary as the most satisfactory means of allaying discontent within the Democratic ranks and of reducing the danger of political appeal to the Negro.

His opposition to the primary in 1890, 1892, and 1894 needs explanation. The Conservatives favored it in those years as the only alternative to their certain defeat. They quite unreasonably asked Tillman to change accepted rules of the game at the very moment of victory and to replay the game under new rules. Considering the late dates at which these requests were made, it would have been quixotic for Tillman to grant them.

As a matter of actual record, he advanced the cause of the primary in two of the three years in question. The nominating convention of 1890 provided that subsequent nominating conventions be chosen by county primaries instead of

[43] See above, pp. 161, 201, 267.
[44] Tillman, in Charleston *World*, May 12, 1890; *id.*, in Charleston *News and Courier*, April 18, 1892; July 25, 1894.

by the prevailing practice of county conventions. This convention also created adequate rules for the conduct of the primaries which have not since been radically changed. The Tillman-dominated convention of 1894, if it refused to make immediate application of the state-wide primary, provided for this in 1896 and in subsequent years.[45]

Practical reasons as well as principle impelled Tillman in championing the primary. A promise was thereby kept; increased strength was given the white masses, this politician's main support; and there was fear that a continuation of the convention system, which Tillman had thrown into disrepute, would give voters adequate pretext to appeal to the blacks. Having secured the adoption of the primary, Tillman lent the influence of his guiding hand to protect it against irregularities and restrictions.[46]

Perhaps of greater significance than providing an adequate instrument of public expression was Tillman's teaching the people to exercise the political power they already had. He won a greater victory for popular government when he forced the convention of 1888 to inaugurate joint debates than he would have won had he been successful in forcing that same convention to adopt the state primary. The joint debates were the device through which he marshaled the people to decisive action in elections. Today, some fifty years after he first aroused the white voters, they still exercise the political opportunity he taught them to use in such lively fashion.[47]

First on the list of his constructive achievements Governor Tillman placed Clemson College, the principal ideal of his early agitations. In the realization of this ideal he presided

---

[45] Charleston *News and Courier*, September 20, 1894.

[46] Tillman to S. M. Porter, May 14, 1912, in Tillman Papers.

[47] For example, in South Carolina in 1912, 140,326 males out of a total white population of 679,161 voted in the primary, or 21 per cent; in the same year 15,036,542 persons in the United States out of a total population of 91,972,266 voted in Presidential election, or only 16 per cent. Columbia *State*, August 30, 1912; *World Almanac and Encyclopedia*, 1912 (New York, 1912), 674, 680, 725.

in the dual capacity of governor and life trustee. He enthusiastically endorsed the suggestion that a plant originally
intended for 250 students be expanded to accommodate
600, and noted exultantly that the college promised to become "one of the grandest schools of applied science in the
Union." [48] He shrewdly arranged for its adequate support
without doing direct violence to his promise that general
taxes should not be increased. The legislature in 1891, he
boasted, did not "give a cent" of the general tax funds for
Clemson, but the college got the Federal aid for agricultural and industrial education, the so-called privilege tax
on fertilizer, and the labor of Negro convicts; subsequent
appropriations asked of the legislature were small.[49]

The ubiquitous chief executive took an active part in the
construction and organization of the college. In selecting
professors, he sought the advice of college presidents instead
of politicians; he even wrote that, while a Democrat was
preferable, a qualified Republican was acceptable for the
professorship of agriculture.[50]

To the 424 students assembled on July 6, 1893, for the
opening of the new institution, the governor explained the
purpose of the Clemson experiment. "We do not propose,"
he said, "to make any one-sided, one-horse men of you, but
you must work." [51] The dairy, shops, farm, and laboratories
which he inspected that day were proof that the young men
were to be taught to work and study intelligently at a minimum cost to their parents and to the state. With pardonable
boastfulness the governor was able to assert that this child
of his emotions and brains was a more valuable investment
to the state than the university which he had partly dis-
mantled.[52] With expanded plant and augmented curric-

[48] Tillman to the President of Michigan Agricultural College, June 8,
1891, in Governor's Letter Books.
[49] Id., in South Carolina House Journal, 1892, pp. 11–12.
[50] Id. to President of Michigan Agricultural College, June 8, 1891, in
Governor's Letter Books.
[51] Charleston News and Courier, July 7, 1893.
[52] Tillman to W. E. H. Searcy, April 18, 1894, in Governor's Letter Books.

ulum, the enrollment in later years was thrice that of 1893; and the institution, through its extension department, was able to supply the farmers with the very information Tillman so keenly felt they needed in the 1880's. A college hatched amid the partisan strife of Tillmanism became an institution broad enough in its services to meet the approval of all white South Carolinians.

When Tillman left the governor's office in November, 1894, he had just experienced the triumphs of the election of 1894 and of the successful maintenance of the Dispensary. Influenced by these victories, his valedictory was a mixture of angry thrusts at opponents and of exultation over constructive achievements. His prediction that his road as chief executive would be "long, rough, rocky and stumpy" had come true, because he had experienced "dogged opposition," "severe adverse criticism," "a malignant and slanderous warfare," "the darts of envy and malice," and an opposition of "Machiavellian cunning and unscrupulous political methods." "I am glad," he confessed, "to be relieved of the burden [of the governorship], which has pressed upon me at times with a weight, which no man living can conceive who has not been similarly situated." [53] In the passions of the moment he did not realize that his own irascible disposition was in a large measure responsible for these burdens. "My enemies . . . have hated me, I know not why," he said.

The other side of the valedictory was less emotional. The governor asserted that he had met "complex questions of grave consequences" with a heroic devotion to duty and a clear conscience. "I have worked harder for the State than I have ever worked for myself." His comforts had been faith in his integrity and the knowledge that he had the support

[53] Already in the previous August he had told the people of Columbia that "a peculiar condition of affairs" there had led his friends to be regarded as "dark lanternites, men unfit to associate with their fellows." "In three months," he had then said, "I will leave your city, and thank God because I am glad of it." Charleston *News and Courier*, August 21, 1894.

of the sovereign majority of South Carolina. Thus sustained, he had accomplished signal reforms. As listed by him they were: the establishment of Winthrop and Clemson colleges, taxation reforms, the victory over the phosphate interests, the Dispensary law, the refunding of the state debt, the empowering of the railroad commission to fix rates, and the establishment of a greater degree of white democracy by the inauguration of the state primary. To this list should be added the limiting of the hours of labor in cotton mills, the reapportionment of legislative and Congressional representation, economies in public expenditures, and the preparation of a way for a constitutional convention.

Critics of the retiring governor have often said that the bitterness and strife he evoked outweighed the constructive good he accomplished; that his conception of social and political uplift were too narrow to have actually effected improvements in the lives of the many humble men who followed him. The agricultural distress largely responsible for his emergence was more severe at his going than at his coming. But critics must estimate Tillman in the light of his times. "The just historian of the future," to whom he plaintively appealed to sustain his good name, must recognize this fact. Tillman cannot be judged according to the standards of social and economic amelioration prevailing in more recent times in more progressive communities; he came before socialist practices. Measured according to the standards of his day, he was the most successful governor South Carolina has ever had. Compared with this man of intelligence and energy, those who have followed him, and most of those who preceded him, seem pigmies. His governorship, he predicted in a spirit short of immodesty, "will mark an epoch in our annals to which the future historian of the State must devote more than a passing glance." [54]

[54] Tillman, November 28, 1894, in South Carolina *House Journal*, 1894, pp. 19–20, 45–49, 58–59.

Chapter XVI

THE DISPENSARY ESTABLISHED

THE writers who have assigned Governor Tillman minor roles in the creation of Clemson and Winthrop colleges, the Democratic primary, the constitution of 1895, and other innovations of his times, freely acknowledge that he was the father of the public monopoly in the sale of alcoholic liquors. The establishment of the Dispensary was the Edgefield governor's most original contribution to both the theory and the practice of government. It brilliantly exemplified the adaptation of a strange idea to the actual needs of a conservative commonwealth. Nothing within the attainable could have been more radical than the imposition of a public monopoly upon an important branch of the business life of individualistic South Carolina. Yet the Dispensary proved to be a practical solution of a vital problem. It was a reasoned compromise between unrestrained drinking and the impracticalities of total Prohibition.

Ben Tillman concentrated his great energies upon the solution of the liquor problem and pressed his plans with effective political strategy. So great was his interest in the Dispensary that it became almost an obsession with him. He proved so well that it could be successfully applied in an American state that it has since become one of the most widely accepted solutions of the problem of liquor control. That it did not, like the agricultural college, become a permanent South Carolina institution was due not to lack of statesmanship on the part of its creator but to the development of religious and moral opposition over which Ben Tillman had no control.

Governor Tillman's espousal of the Dispensary idea ran counter to the remedy for the evils of drink which South Carolina was trying to apply. This remedy was Prohibition. Before the Civil War temperance societies had flourished, and two communities had prohibited saloons. In 1880 the sale of liquor was outlawed in rural areas,[1] and two years later the voters of individual communities were given authority for local option. Seventy-eight areas adopted Prohibition by 1891. In that year the enemies of liquor forced through the House a state-wide Prohibition measure, but it failed in the Senate. Encouraged, the Prohibitionists asked that it be made an issue in the canvass of 1892. The alarmed political managers, whether pro-Tillman or anti-Tillman, for there were Wets and Drys in both factions, tacitly agreed that the county-to-county canvassers should not mention the liquor issue, but that separate boxes should be placed at the polling places to register the vote on Prohibition. Although but 68,515 of the 88,474 voters troubled to express their sentiments on this issue, the majority in favor of Prohibition was nearly 10,000.[2] A pious people had indicated its disgust with the grogshops.

Three months after the referendum Tillman mildly advised the legislature against the threatened enactment of Prohibition. He first admitted the menace of alcoholism. "Liquor drinking," he declared, "is the cause, directly or indirectly, of most of the crimes committed in our country. It also produces much of the poverty and misery among certain classes." Nevertheless, he believed that Prohibition was impractical. "The human family," he asserted tritely, "cannot be legislated into morality." "All classes, men and women alike, feel, at times, the need of stimulants, and many who are never guilty of excess in their use resent any law infringing upon personal liberty." These hoary arguments were supplemented by the assertion that the August

[1] South Carolina *Acts*, 1880, pp. 459–61.
[2] Columbia *State*, September 8, 1892.

vote was not a mandate for Prohibition. It had been submitted, Tillman speciously claimed, "as an abstract proposition, without any definite legislation being indicated";
the majority which it received was not a majority of the
votes cast in the accompanying gubernatorial contest.

These arguments against Prohibition were an introduction to Tillman's own solution of the liquor problem. "I
would call your attention," he told the legislature, "to the
law now in force at Athens, Ga., by which a dispensary for
the sale of liquors is provided, and which, after trial, is
pronounced a success by the prohibitionists themselves."
This was the nucleus of what would grow into a dominant
idea, but which as yet had not reached the center of the
Tillman consciousness. At this time the boss was even willing that the legislature exercise its own discretion in the
matter of liquor regulation. "I will leave it with you," he
said, "and will cheerfully approve any law you may enact." [3]

With clear majorities in both houses of the legislature,
the Prohibitionists, early in the 1892 session, introduced a
stringent Prohibition bill. They had the verdict of the
people on their side and seemingly only the philosophical
opposition of Governor Tillman. The measure passed the
House by the good majority of 66 to 42, the Tillmanites
voting overwhelmingly in the affirmative.[4] The bill reached
the Senate a week before the scheduled time of adjournment; its sponsors wore smiles of triumph; they anticipated
the enactment of their cherished scheme with "the cheerful
approval" the governor had promised.

But had they been closer observers, they would have seen
clouds on the horizon. T. Larry Gantt, in his influential
newspaper, supplemented with arguments and details Governor Tillman's vague endorsement of the Athens experiment,[5] and, after the House had passed the Prohibition

[3] Tillman, in South Carolina *Senate Journal*, 1892, pp. 24–28.
[4] Charleston *News and Courier*, December 14, 1892.
[5] Columbia *Daily Register*, November 30, 1892.

bill, that editor professed to believe that its enactment would destroy the Tillman Movement.[6] Tillman was known to cast ominous frowns at the course of events.[7] Among the many proposed solutions of the liquor problem, fantastic and otherwise, was Senator John Gary Evans' version of the Athens idea. Yet, supposedly competent observers were satisfied that the Senate would pass the Prohibition bill. Good South Carolinians could not believe that the directors of public affairs actually planned to embark the conservative old commonwealth in the liquor business. Newspaper reporters refused to subject themselves to the tedium of reading the Evans Dispensary bill, contenting themselves with Evans' enigmatic explanation: "Damn it, that's just a bill to give us pure liquor."

The opposition underestimated the fertile Tillman imagination. Convinced of the impracticability of Prohibition, the governor listened to Gantt's exposition of the Athens liquor monopoly. The editor glowingly recounted how he and a certain Captain John W. Brumby had read of the Gothenburg system, under which the Swedish city had established a private liquor monopoly under rigid municipal control; and how this system had been established in the Georgia town in the altered form of a municipally owned monopoly. It was, affirmed Gantt, a compromise measure designed to destroy the differences between the Wets and the Drys. The governor was also told that the Athens experiment was a financial success, a means of securing revenues without additional taxes. Tillman was deeply impressed, and Gantt telegraphed the mayor of Athens for a copy of the ordinance.[8]

"Tillman," said Gantt, "jumped on this bill like a duck on a June bug." This meant that the governor, with Napoleonic dispatch, resorted to highhanded tactics to secure

---

[6] Ibid., December 14, 1892.

[7] Charleston News and Courier, December 12, 1892.

[8] Gantt's part is explained by items in T. Larry Gantt Scrapbook (in possession of Robert J. Gantt, Spartanburg).

the enactment of this novel legislation. His open-minded attitude on the liquor question was abandoned. "After three days of anxious consultation and discussion," the Dispensary bill was prepared by him and his legal advisers, and five days before the adjournment of the legislature it became known that orders "from the lower region of the State House" had decreed its passage. Evans made it the special order of the Senate for eight o'clock on December 22. It was offered as an amendment to the Prohibition bill to obviate the necessity of the three required readings of a new bill. Ten senators argued that the "amendment" was not germane to the original bill, and when they were overruled, they filibustered. They did not surrender until seven o'clock of the following morning when the measure was allowed to pass by a vote of 18 to 10. The governor, through admonitions administered in the strongest language, had cowed reluctant Prohibitionist senators.

The following evening, the last of the session, the so-called amendment was sent to the House with the information that it or nothing must be taken. After a confused debate lasting several hours, the measure passed the House by vote of 47 to 30 a few minutes before the 1892 session of the South Carolina legislature closed. "The House," the governor explained, "had no time to examine or alter the bill. It was accepted and amended in title to suit its new purpose, becoming an 'Act to prohibit the manufacture and sale of intoxicating liquors as a beverage within this State, except as herein provided.' " Lifelong Prohibitionists were persuaded, by Tillman's forceful casuistry, that in supporting this measure they were not abandoning principle. Did it not provide for the closing of saloons? [9]

When on Christmas Eve, 1892, South Carolinians read the text of this so-called Prohibition Act in their *News and*

[9] Charleston *News and Courier*, December 18–26, 1892; Columbia *State*, December 18–26, 1892; Columbia *Daily Register*, December 18–26, 1892; Tillman, "The South Carolina Liquor Law," in *North American Review* (Boston), CLVIII (1894), 140–41; Ball, *State that Forgot*, 246–48.

Courier they were astounded to discover that the most important portion of its title was the "except as herein provided." In fact, the law did not create Prohibition but a public monopoly of the liquor trade. A state board of control, composed of the governor and two other state officials, was given supervision of the Dispensary, and a Dispensary commissioner was provided for active administration. County boards of control were created with authority to appoint the dispensers and their assistants. To be eligible for one of these appointments, one had to prove that he did not drink and was not privately interested in the liquor business. A majority of the electors of any township could prevent the establishment of a dispensary in their midst. In a county which had previously prohibited the sale of intoxicants, a petition of one fourth of its citizens and the affirmative vote of its electors could effect the establishment of a branch of the institution.

A person wishing to purchase liquor was required to file an application with the dispenser stating the quantity and the kind of liquor wanted. If the applicant was intoxicated or addicted to the use of liquor in excess, he was to be denied the right to purchase. The liquor had to be sold between the hours of sunrise and sunset in sealed packages, which were not to be opened on the Dispensary premises. Constables, appointed by the governor, were charged with the prevention of private sales. The profits of the retail trade were to be divided evenly between the counties and the municipalities, and those accruing from wholesale transactions were to go to the state. If the state board of control felt that a municipality was negligent in the enforcement of the law against private sales, it could withdraw the municipality's share of the Dispensary revenue. The law was to go in effect July 1, 1893.[10]

Governor Tillman undertook the administration of this law with the fondest hopes for its success. "I think," he

[10] South Carolina *Acts*, 1892, pp. 62–76.

wrote a friend, "the Dispensary law will work well and the goose will hang higher next year." [11] He did not offer, he said, an ideal solution of an involved problem, but "the best method of controlling the evils which are inherent and inseparable from the intemperate use of liquors" under any circumstances. Fifty dispensaries would displace the more than 613 saloons and the 400 drugstores selling liquor. The element of profit was destroyed, thereby removing the most powerful motive for stimulating sales. Pure and unadulterated products would be insured by a system of chemical analysis. There would be no sales to minors or drunkards. The prohibition of sales by the drink, with "the concomitants of ice, sugar, lemons, etc.," would destroy "the enticements and seductions" of saloon life. Men compelled to buy liquor during the day and "go elsewhere to consume it will be likely to go home and be within the restraining influence of that charmed circle." Whiskey was to be sold for cash only, and there would be no more "chalking up" of daily drinks against pay day. Saloons as centers of gambling and prostitution would be destroyed, as would the political influence of the "whiskey rings." The modest prices demanded—twenty cents a half pint instead of fifty cents—meant the discouragement of illicit sales and the keeping of thirty cents in the pocket of the consumer for the support of his family. Extremely low prices, however, were avoided so as not to encourage the consumption of alcohol in unwholesome quantities or to destroy the profits of the state.

Some critics have been unkind enough to say that the desire for profits was the principal cause of Tillman's conversion to the public monopoly idea. It was "an easy way of spinning straw into gold," of meeting the state's financial obligations without violating pledges to reduce taxes.[12]

---

[11] Tillman to John D. M. Shaw, January 23, 1893, in Governor Tillman's Letter Books.
[12] Ball, *State that Forgot*, 243.

Tillman was the first to admit that so practical a consideration was "not to be despised." In place of the annual license fees of $215,000 which the municipalities exacted
from the saloons, there would be the ever-expanding revenues of the public monopoly, which the local divisions of
government were required to share with the state. In answer to those "fanatical, unreasonable people who cry
aloud against the iniquity of a government's sharing in the
'blood money'" from husbands and fathers addicted to
whiskey, Tillman quite logically pointed out that all
branches of government, including the United States, had
for decades shared, through the high license system, in the
profits of strong drink. "It is," he asserted, "far-fetched, unreasonable, then—hypocritical in fact—to pretend that any
disgrace can attach to the revenue feature." Indeed, the
governor was enough of an economic determinist to hope
that he could effect a union between God and Mammon.
He believed that the croakings of the Prohibitionists might
be silenced through sharp reductions of taxes made possible
by Dispensary revenues.[13]

It was well for the success of the experiment that the
governor was able to speak enthusiastically in its behalf.
So socialistic a measure, adopted in a welter of partisan
passions, provoked determined opposition. Tillman himself commented wryly on "some comical alignments and
alliances" among his enemies. He noted that anti-Prohibition newspapers and whiskey merchants united with Prohibitionists, divines, and "cranks." The effectiveness of
this opposition was greatly increased by the fact that the
dispensaries were placed in the towns, the foci of anti-
Tillmanism. Mere partisanship might have been overcome
in the course of time in the same manner as opposition to
Clemson College. But there were more fundamental barriers to the acceptance of the Dispensary. One was the re-

[13] Tillman, in South Carolina *House Journal*, 1893, pp. 34–41; *id.*,
"The South Carolina Liquor Law," *loc. cit.*, 141–49.

sentment of a traditionally individualistic people against being told that they must drink liquor under police regulation and give into the public treasury profits which had previously gone to private persons. The law was interpreted as an invasion of private rights and as a ruthless destroyer of businesses. Another barrier was the growing popular conviction that to convert the commonwealth of South Carolina into a barkeeper was a disgrace. The liquor bottle, even after Tillman ingeniously blew the Palmetto coat of arms into it, could not be made respectable.

The Dispensary law was not dry upon the books before its critics spoke. The Columbia *State* immediately began a fourteen-year labor of doing the liquor monopoly to death. It was pictured as a destroyer of personal liberties; it was a "foolish and fanatical" scheme; it placed the personal habits of a proud people in the hollow of a tyrant's hands.[14] The *News and Courier* predicted that the law would never go into effect,[15] and the municipal authorities of Charleston and several other towns licensed saloons to operate for six months after the date the law demanded that they be closed. A convention of seventy barkeepers pledged themselves to do all in their power to frustrate the law,[16] while the most influential of the Prohibition organs called it "a just ground for lamentation," [17] and a Baptist congregation expelled from its membership the dispensary commissioner.[18] Truly there was "a comical alliance" between the saints and the sinners.

But Tillman, stirred by opposition, boldly planned to execute the law. "The barrooms of the State," he warned, "will be closed after July 1, and the law will be enforced to the limit." [19] Anti-Prohibition cities were told that he

[14] Columbia *State*, December 24, 1892.
[15] Charleston *News and Courier*, January 3, 1893.
[16] *Ibid.*, January 25, 1893.
[17] *Baptist Courier*, cited *ibid.*, January 6, 1893.
[18] *Ibid.*, October 23, 1893.
[19] Tillman to W. P. Russell, January 5, 1893, in Governor Tillman's Letter Books.

would make them "as dry as a powder house after the first of July unless there were dispensaries." [20] He warned the "friends of temperance" who refused to sign petitions for local dispensaries that they were "playing into the hands of the whiskey man." [21] Believing that the Dispensary constabulary was "the life of the law, its very backbone," he made careful inquiries into the qualifications of the prospective members of this force, stressing sobriety and courage.[22]

He personally directed what he called "the herculean task" of equipping and stocking the dispensaries. This work soon exhausted the meager $50,000 which the legislature provided for the inauguration of the institution. Agricultural Hall, a three-story building in Columbia, was converted into the Dispensary warehouse and fifty-four persons were employed to bottle the liquor. "I haunted the building," Tillman later recounted, "until I got the business to working. . . . I had my fighting blood up, and I said: 'I'll make it go,' and I did. I stayed around there and watched everything and organized the whole machine, and I didn't go away until I got it running."

Desiring to get "pure whiskey, good whiskey" as cheaply as possible, he spent two weeks at Louisville and Pittsburgh where he informed himself concerning the methods of the distilling business. But he found the distillers "very skittish" when he told them that he had no cash. They did not wish to credit a man who could offer as security only his word of honor as the head of an unpopular experiment. He next went to Cincinnati, where he met a man who liked him personally and offered ample credit. This was George Hubbell of the Mill Creek Distilling Company. "Will you trust me?" asked the governor. "Yes," replied the merchant; "I have enough faith in the people of South

---

[20] *Id.* to J. H. Steinmeyer, May 19, 1893, *ibid.*
[21] *Id.* to Charles Purcell, January 25, 1893, *ibid.*
[22] *Id.* to W. H. Snead, June 29, 1893, in Governor's Letter Books.

Carolina and their confidence in you, that if you say I will be paid, I will go ahead and furnish the liquor on credit." Before Tillman left Hubbell's office, the distiller informed him that, under the policy of the Whiskey Trust to which the Mill Creek Distilling Company belonged, he was entitled to rebates on purchases. "I don't want any dealings with rebates," said Tillman simply; "you keep that as a bonus for the accommodation you have given me in selling me liquor at a fair price."

The governor disposed of another complex phase of liquor purchasing with the same simple directness. This was the grading of whiskeys in the face of possible swindles through adulterations. He naïvely confessed to Hubbell his complete ignorance of such matters. "I haven't drunk enough liquor to tell what it is. One is as good to me as another because I don't drink enough to get my tongue educated." The prudent solution of this difficulty would have been the purchase of bottled goods. But he wanted the lower prices of barrel-lot purchases and had the temerity to devise a grading system all his own. This was the famous X, XX, and XXX system practiced during the whole history of the Dispensary. This audacious amateur chemist explained to Hubbell: "You put me one barrel of two stamp whiskey one year old and one barrel of cologne spirits and mix it and ship it to me as X. You put me one barrel of cologne spirits with the two year old and ship it to me as XX; and you put me the same except that it shall be three years old and ship it to me as XXX." To insure honesty he firmly admonished the dealer: "If I catch you monkeying with your agreement, I will quit you, and won't buy a gallon."

This manner of doing business had one great advantage. It enabled the inexperienced and impecunious governor to secure sufficient liquors for the scheduled opening of his business. But such simple tactics provoked suspicions and criticisms which lasted as long as the Dispensary. Because

Tillman refused rebates which rightly belonged to the state of South Carolina, he was accused of secretly taking these funds for himself. He freely admitted: "There is no doubt that if I was corrupt and wanted to make money out of my position of buying liquor, I could have done it." As usual, he took refuge against the accusation in the confidence of the white majority of South Carolina.

His enemies were not satisfied with so irrelevant a defense. When they discovered that in 1894 he had purchased a farm at Trenton for $6,000, they concluded that the money came from whiskey rebates. Unfortunately, he could not easily prove his innocence because of careless business practices. He had traded with a member of the notorious Whiskey Trust without the protection of competitive bids, expert chemical analysis, or comprehensive bookkeeping! But carelessness did not prove guilt, and a resort to the records of Edgefield County proved that he was no richer after the establishment of the Dispensary than before. These records showed that he had borrowed $6,105.60 with which to make the Trenton purchase and that long-standing mortgages against his properties had not been retired.[23]

With the actual opening of the dispensaries on July 1,

[23] Statements of James B. Hill, clerk of the court of Edgefield County, and of Washington Clark, president of the Carolina National Bank, Columbia, in Charleston *News and Courier*, December 10, 1894. Tillman explained his part in the inauguration of the Dispensary in "Testimony Taken . . . by the Committee to Investigate the Dispensary," in South Carolina *Reports and Resolutions*, 1906, III, 432–36. George Hubbell wrote Tillman's Dispensary commissioner: "Before you bought any goods of us we obtained permission of the Distilling and Cattle Feeding Company (so-called Trust) to sell to the state of South Carolina without rebate voucher, which called for seven cents a proof gallon payable six months after the date. . . . If we had not obtained the above mentioned privilege from the Trust for you . . . , you would have paid seven cents a proof gallon more. . . . All that was thoroughly understood by the governor." Hubbell wrote Tillman: "The writer took in the situation, believing that the state would make a success of it [the Dispensary experiment]. . . . As luck would have it we got all our money according to agreement and you got your goods. . . . You could not have bought from any one house or any other five houses when you first started, and no doubt that is the reason you bought them from us." Hubbell to David H. Traxler, May 28, 1897, in Tillman Papers; *id.* to Tillman, June 12, 1897, *ibid.*

1894, prophecies about the inability of the governor to put the law into effect vanished. He ominously gathered the badges and arms necessary for the use of the constables he planned to dispatch to places where the experiment did not run smoothly. "I will make the places that won't accept the Dispensary," he declared, "dry enough to burn. I will send special constables if I have to cover every city block with a separate man." [24] At the end of the first month there were twenty-nine local dispensaries in operation; by the end of November this number had increased to fifty. The governor was able to report financial success at the end of the first four months of operation. The revenue had been $166,043 and the profits to the state government alone totaled $32,198.[25] "There can be no doubt," the *News and Courier* admitted, "that everything about the Dispensary is done in the most improved and business-like fashion." [26]

[24] Cited in New York *Sun*, July 9, 1893.
[25] South Carolina *House Journal*, 1893, p. 36.
[26] Charleston *News and Courier*, July 16, 1893.

Chapter XVII

THE DISPENSARY FACES STORMS

DESPITE elation over the financial success of the Dispensary, Tillman conceded that it had one important weakness—the difficulty of prohibiting private sales of liquors. There were flagrant violations of the law in every section of the state, especially in Columbia and Charleston. Municipal authorities stood idly by while the law was defied; judges and juries refused to convict notorious offenders; the newspapers "heaped every possible abuse on the [Dispensary] Constables," calling them "spies" and "sneaks"; the Federal authorities between July and November, 1893, issued no less than 235 liquor licenses in South Carolina. Yet not for a moment did Tillman falter. He resolved "to exert my whole power as Governor" to stop illegal traffic. He recommended "drastic measures" to the legislature of 1893,[1] and that body responded by amending the Dispensary Act of 1892 so as to give the Dispensary constables extensive powers of search.[2]

Although the governor pursued the enforcement of the Dispensary law energetically, it is not true, as some have alleged, that he counseled the constables to be arbitrary and irresponsible. He demanded that they be "intelligent, brave, honest and sober," and courteous to all persons.[3] "You must behave yourself," he wrote a Greenville constable, "and not go to cursing and swearing like a black-

[1] South Carolina *House Journal,* 1893, pp. 41–45.
[2] South Carolina *Acts,* 1893, pp. 430–50.
[3] Tillman to Theo S. Gaillard, October 1, 1893, in Governor's Letter Books; *id.* to Howard M. Stackhouse, January 17, 1894, *ibid.*

guard." He dismissed many constables guilty of drunken-ness.[4]

But Tillman was more intent upon securing obedience to his law than in demanding that his agents have good manners. He believed that there existed against the Dispensary a conspiracy which must be counteracted resolutely. There was, he explained, "a swarm of gad flies, mosquitoes and gnats exerting themselves to the utmost to sting me to death, all of whom I pushed aside with the same feeling and spirit which they displayed. . . . I met partisanship and unfairness with partisanship and unfairness." [5] Only Tillmanites were appointed to the constabulary,[6] and in good South Carolina style the constables were told to "shoot to kill" if necessary.[7] In the face of deep prejudices in favor of an independent judiciary, the governor roundly lectured magistrates deemed derelict in enforcement of the law. Failure to convict provoked threats of dismissal or transference of cases to more sympathetic courts.[8] Towns remiss in enforcements were threatened with the withholding of their share of the monopoly's revenues,[9] and constables convicted of lawlessness by hostile courts were promised speedy pardons.

So stern and so frequent were Tillman's admonitions to his constables that many of those harassed officers must have felt that the chief was not satisfied unless they went to extremes. The chief seemed aware of every failure, however petty, to enforce the law. He wished to know why express shipments were not examined for whiskey; why Jack Fisher

[4] *Id.* to S. T. Dagnoff, November 13, 1893, *ibid.; id.* to H. B. Mayson, October 14, 1893, *ibid.; id.* to David A. Dickett, March 15, 1894, *ibid.; id.* to Mrs. Emma Gaines Padgett, March 24, 1894, *ibid.*

[5] *Id.* to J. C. Garlington, November 6, 1893, in Governor Tillman's Letter Books.

[6] *Id.* to Leon F. Bamberg, July 17, 1894, in Governor's Letter Books.

[7] *Id.* to Chief Constable J. R. Fant, August 4, 1893, *ibid.*

[8] *Id.* to M. S. Carroll, September 30, 1893, *ibid.; id.* to Buist, October 23, 1893, *ibid.*

[9] *Id.* to Mayor and Town Council of Anderson, S. C., February 19, 1894, *ibid.*

and his gang of Hell Hole Swamp blockaders had not been caught; why whiskey selling was allowed "almost openly" in Greenville, Spartanburg, Gaffney, and other places; why a certain W. N. Bates was not frustrated in his attempt to sell liquors; and why searches were not made "for wagons from North Carolina selling whiskey." [10] Rioters against the law, he warned, "must be promptly and sternly punished," [11] and constables menaced by mobs were told, "Threatened men live long." [12] The chief constable while at Spartanburg was ordered to "get a gimlet and long steel rod and prod into some of the suspicious barrels and boxes at the depot"; [13] for the governor preferred that twenty innocent barrels be searched than that one containing contraband liquors escape. [14]

The irregular manner of appointment along with secrecy of operations bred intense hatred of Governor Tillman's "spies." To save money, the governor believed that a goodly portion of the population of the state should act as amateur detectives in the enforcement of his favorite law. He freely appointed so-called "local constables," who were asked to spy out violations of the law for specified fees. He paid from $10 to $25 for evidence leading to the conviction of an individual, $50 for the capture of a wagonload of illicit spirits, and 25 cents a gallon for captures in lesser quantities. [15]

He was a strong believer in secret service, telling his constables that they would be "perfectly useless" if their iden-

[10] *Id.* to H. M. Limberger, August 4, 1893, *ibid.; id.* to Fant, October 18, 1893, *ibid.; id.* to W. G. Weston, July 22, 1893, *ibid.; id.* to J. W. Butler, July 18, 1893, *ibid.; id.* to M. E. Jordon, July 22, 1893, *ibid.; id.* to Edward P. Waring, July 21, 1893, *ibid.*

[11] *Id.* to John S. Wilson, February 28, 1893, in Governor Tillman's Letter Books.

[12] *Id.* to Jordon, July 18, 1893, in Governor's Letter Books.

[13] *Id.* to Fant, Ja   ry 16, 1894, *ibid.*

[14] *Id.* to P. P. Meekins, February 13, 1894, *ibid.*

[15] *Id.* to Dr. Henry P. Goodwin, July 13, 1893, in Governor Tillman's Letter Books; *id.* to Snead, June 29, 1893, in Governor's Letter Books; *id.* to Gaillard, February 3, 1894, *ibid.*

tity became known.[16] Race prejudice did not prevent him from employing Negroes for detective work,[17] or from ordering white detectives to disguise themselves as blacks.[18] He ordered one constable to "dress like a gentleman of leisure," enter a carriage at the Charleston railroad station, and then register at a hotel as a Northerner in order to discover if illicit drinks were sold.[19] A Greenville constable was enjoined to "put on some store clothes and a stiff hat" and see what he could discover among the upper classes.[20]

The highhanded methods of the governor aggravated the resentment against the law. The newspapers, in the name of personal liberty, excited the people to resist searches of their dwellings. Mobs gathered in Sumter, Charleston, Greenville, and other places to resist raids on "blind tigers," and juries refused to convict on evidence of constables.[21] The "spies" were pictured as "monsters," and casualties incurred in their efforts to enforce the law were called "murders." "Our bloody Governor" was portrayed as presiding over stores of ammunition to be used against the defenders of the public liberties.[22] "The people," said the Columbia *State*,[23] "will know if the Governor's armed spies shall choose to enter their homes, insult their women and shoot down themselves, their sons or brothers, they will be promptly pardoned." "I'll be damned," said the brother of the governor,[24] "if I don't shoot the first spy that enters my residence or opens a package of my goods sneaking around hunting liquor." "So intense is the feeling," prophesied a reporter of the Atlanta *Constitution* in February, 1894, "that an outbreak is imminent at any minute." [25]

[16] *Id.* to Martin, July 18, 1893, *ibid.; id.* to Weston, July 22, 1893, *ibid.*
[17] *Id.* to Gaillard, October 30, 1893, *ibid.*
[18] *Id.* to D. D. Brunson, August 11, 1893, *ibid.*
[19] *Id.* to Gaillard, October 30, 1893, *ibid.*
[20] *Id.* to C. C. Cunningham, December 22, 1893, *ibid.*
[21] Charleston *News and Courier*, February 5, 6, 1894.
[22] Columbia *State*, January 1, 1894.   [23] *Ibid.*, January 28, 1894.
[24] George D. Tillman, in Charleston *News and Courier*, January 16, 1894.
[25] E. C. Bruffy, cited *ibid.*, February 14, 1894.

Less than two months after these words were written, the eruption came at Darlington, a county seat in the Pee Dee section. The men of the town, despising Tillman and his methods, refused to patronize the Dispensary and protected blind tigers. The governor retaliated by threatening to withdraw the offending municipality's share of the monopoly's revenue,[26] and by sending four constables to the scene with instructions to act vigorously. When they attempted to execute search warrants, they were "guyed, cursed and abused" by armed mobs and forced to retire from the streets. Tillman dispatched reinforcements of eighteen constables to the obdurate town. The citizens seized the arms of the local militia company and solemnly resolved to resist the execution of the odious search warrants. The governor then dispatched the Sumter militia. After a night's observation, it retired under the assumption that quiet had been restored. Later in that day, March 30, 1894, the constables themselves, after timid attempts to execute the warrants, sought to withdraw. Four of them went to one of the town's two railroad stations to await a train, while the remaining eighteen repaired to the other station for the same purpose. Both retreating parties were followed by angry citizens. Only a spark was needed to start trouble.

The spark came when Paul Rogers, one of the citizens, exhibited a face bloodied by Billy Floyd, a person accused of carrying tales to the constables. What ordinarily would have been regarded as a common street brawl assumed ominous significance when the injured man asserted that his assailant had been helped by one of the constables. "Well, Rogers," said the Darlington chief of police, "point out the man and I will arrest him." Rogers pointed out John B. McLendon, the chief constable. After a curt exchange of abusive language, McLendon suddenly drew his pistol and killed Frank E. Norment, a citizen. Immediately

[26] Tillman to Mayor William F. Dargan, January 29, 1894, in Governor's Letter Books.

there followed a rapid exchange of shots by which another
citizen and a constable were killed, and two citizens and
two constables were wounded. The surviving constables fled
before the citizens, who were incited to fury by Norment's
wife covered with blood from the dead man. The town
bell was rung, and the citizens, heavily armed and rein-
forced by sympathizers from the near-by towns of Florence
and Sumter, began to search woods and swamps for the
escaped agents of the Dispensary. A wholesale lynching
seemed imminent. The train of the four constables who had
escaped from the other station was riddled with bullets as
it retreated toward Charleston.

That afternoon the news of "the terrible tragedy" at
Darlington reached Columbia in the form of incendiary
bulletins to the *State*. The Dispensary spies, these notices
related, had provoked a conflict, shot down innocent citizens in cold blood, and were being pursued by infuriated
citizens. The people of the capital city, already excited by
the *State*'s interpretation of the governor's Dispensary
policies, massed on the street, threatening the vindictive
acts of which a Southern mob is capable. Tillman, convinced that there was a state-wide conspiracy to massacre
the constabulary, overthrow the Dispensary, and create a
state of insurrection which would force Federal intervention, moved decisively.[27] He commandeered a special train
and ordered the three Columbia militia companies to Darlington.

The Richland Volunteers refused to assemble; the
Zouaves threw down their arms; the Governor's Guards,
who seemingly wished to obey the orders of their legal
commander-in-chief, were induced by mob leaders to dis-
obey. Ellison Capers, the revered bishop of the Episcopal
Church who, three years before, had come to the rescue of
Tillman under similar circumstances, told the militiamen
that were he an officer of their company he would surrender

[27] *Id.* to J. B. Tree, April 13, 1894, *ibid.*

his commission and refuse to move. There were threats of burning the Dispensary warehouse, and the governor, with many fearful for his safety, retreated to the governor's mansion. There he received news that the companies of Manning and Sumter had followed the example of their Columbia comrades. He ordered out the entire militia brigade at Charleston, only to receive from its commander the following ringing rebuff: "The brigade will uphold and defend the honor of the State, but it will not lend itself to foment civil war among our brethren." Other companies of what the governor sarcastically called "our boasted militia" adopted the same behavior, and the sheriff of Darlington telegraphed that he could not protect the hunted constables. It seemed as if Tillman was helpless.

He was not, however, without resources. Uncowed, he vented his feelings in defiant words while he acted with coolness and deliberation. Before reporters representing the newspapers of the whole nation who were interested in what was called the Dispensary War, he denounced his enemies as he strode the floors of the governor's mansion. The editors of the Columbia *State,* the *News and Courier,* and the Greenville *News,* he said as he pointed in the direction of Darlington, "are the murderers of those shot down over yonder." To the enraged men pursuing the constables in the Darlington woods he imputed cowardice: "They are careful not to come close to them." At the same time he declared the counties of Darlington and Florence in a state of insurrection and seized telegraph and railroad lines to prevent additional sensational news dispatches and the further concentration of vengeful bands. To take the place of the disobedient militia, he called for volunteers among the "sturdy farmers, mechanics and clerks" of the rural areas. "If we can't get the city companies to enforce the law," he said, "their arms will be taken from them and given to those in the country who will see that they are properly cared for."

These "wool-hat boys," these Tillmanites from the
country, who were as capable of fighting as the most valiant
Charleston company, took their horses from the plow and
shouldered shotguns. The news that the first of these contingents, the Salley Rifles of Newberry, was about to arrive
brought a threatening mob to the railroad station; and
when the company debarked before its train reached the
station and took refuge in the penitentiary, the mobs gathered before the gates while John C. Haskell regaled it with
a venomous harangue. Other companies were furtively concentrated behind the penitentiary walls; but the three
Edgefield companies, among them Tillman's old command,
the Edgefield Huzzars, openly braved the mob by marching
through the main streets. During Saturday and Sunday,
March 31 and April 1, the second and third days of the
disturbance, 19 companies of organized militia and 8 companies of volunteers—500 men in all—gathered in the penitentiary. Other hundreds and even thousands were preparing to move when the governor gave word that his forces
were sufficient. The entire rural masses of white South
Carolina were ready to fight for a beloved chieftain.

The Edgefield Rifles and the Salley Rifles were detailed
to guard the Dispensary warehouse and the State House,
while to the Edgefield Huzzars went the post of honor, the
guarding of the person of the governor at the mansion.
Sunday afternoon two hundred men of the organized militia were sent to Darlington. There they learned that all
members of the pursuing posse had returned home after
vain attempts to catch the constables. After an uneventful
residence of five days at the scene of the riot, the troops were
sent home; Tillman was assured that the Darlington Dispensary could be reopened without fear of violence.[28] Soon
the fugitive constables reported unharmed to the governor,
and Columbia became quiet. The five or six days of excitement known as the Darlington Riot were over.

[28] *Id.* to General R. N. Richbourg, April 5, 1894, *ibid.*

Governor Tillman dealt as sternly as possible with the disobedient militia. He did not attempt court-martial procedure because he felt that would be "a costly farce." Instead, he dismissed his "bandbox soldiers" from the service of the state.[29] The Governor's Guards were singled out for special reproof. On Sunday morning, April 1, they were summoned to the governor's mansion for a rebuke which Tillman hoped would bring repentance. Pale with anger, this master of the burning phrase let fall words "of a character as to blanch the face of every man who stood in the ranks." "When my right arm," he said, "was stretched forth night before last to command the peace . . . , you, representing that right arm, were paralyzed by a mob. . . . You stand before the State as a disgrace, as men who have refused to obey the orders of their superior officer." Then he said that he would restore the men to the service of the state if they promised to obey him in the future. But instead of making the expected pledge, the men, in a dudgeon, threw down their arms and left the old militia captain standing alone. He was "cut to the heart."

The Dispensary disturbance, despite its troubles, ended in triumph for the determined governor. In a message to the legislature flaming with passion he effectively justified every step he had taken in the crisis. The Conservative newspapers, not the constables, he said, were responsible for the bloodshed. He firmly believed, without being able to give definite proof, that there had been a state-wide conspiracy to overthrow his administration by violence. Certainly the situation he faced was similar to that which had resulted in the destruction of the Chamberlain regime. In this crisis, as in all crises of his career, he appealed to the white masses and was made safe by their sending the armed volunteers to Columbia. Actual and threatened violence was effectively met by force.

The farmers, said the governor, should be organized

[29] *Id.* to General Thomas A. Huguenin, April 5, 1894, *ibid.*

"into shotgun companies for use in future emergencies. If such a state of affairs happens again the only salvation will be to show the opposition that we are ready for them." [30] The result was the enlistment of over one hundred new militia companies. Not since the days of the Confederacy, commented Tillman, "had South Carolina showed such a martial spirit." The common people demonstrated that they were willing, if necessary, to sustain the verdict of the ballot box with organized force. The result was that both Tillman and the Dispensary emerged from the Darlington crisis stronger than before. The governor was able to write his best friend a week afterwards: "Everything is quiet except the wool-hat boys are organizing militia companies all over the State. We are in the saddle more firmly than ever." [31]

The governor's conduct was sustained not only by his constituency but also by the outside world. For the first time in his career he was a sort of national hero; the press of the English-speaking world was filled with compliments of his handling of the menace of mobs and mutineers. A magazine as far afield as the London *Spectator* commended the resolute manner in which the governor met the crisis.[32] The South Carolina Conservatives had put themselves in an absurd position. This presumably most civilized element of the state's population had invoked against a legal institution the very spirit of lawlessness of which only the less civilized Tillmanites were supposed to be capable. The habitual denouncers of Tillmanite lynchers for rape had encouraged "a property-destroying mob of man-hunters." [33] Tillman was not amiss of the truth when he wrote an English bishop a week after the riot: "My enemies and the enemies of the law are now confessing failure and defeat

---

[30] *Id.* to W. I. Carr, April 9, 1894, *ibid.*
[31] *Id.* to Irby, April 13, 1894, *ibid.*
[32] *Spectator* (London), LXXII (1894), 459–60.
[33] Wallace, *History of South Carolina,* III, 362.

and are sorely chagrined over their blunders." [34] Indeed, no less bitter an enemy of Tillman than the editor of the Greenville *News* prefaced an attack on the Dispensary by saying on April 8: "Governor Tillman's acts during the trying and memorable week just past have been sensible, conciliatory, and in all respects proper." [35]

After weathering the Darlington storm, the governor fancied that "the fight was won, and men were ready to yield obedience to the law." Satisfactory agreements over law enforcement problems were effected, and illicit liquor dealers prepared to leave the state. But on April 19, three weeks after the Darlington disturbance, the Dispensary received a blow more deadly than denunciation and riot. The state supreme court, by vote of two anti-Tillmanite justices to one Tillmanite justice, declared the Dispensary sections of the so-called Prohibition Act of 1892 unconstitutional on the ground that the state had no right to establish a monopoly for profit. The right of the state to prohibit private sales was sustained. In other words, Prohibition was legally established. [36]

Tillman, in order not to be embarrassed by an injunction, was forced to obey the court. On April 21 he closed the dispensaries, locked up their stock of $200,000 worth of liquors, and dismissed his constables. "As I had put forth all my energies to force men to obey the law," he said with apparent meekness, "I felt compelled to obey it myself." He would let the state have a taste of what he ironically

[34] Tillman to the Right Reverend F. J. Cester [?], Bishop of Chester, April 13, 1894, in Governor's Letter Books.

[35] Alfred B. Williams, in Greenville *News*, April 8, 1894. Tillman, accounts of the Darlington Riot, in South Carolina *House Journal*, 1894, pp. 22-35; *id.*, "Our Whiskey Rebellion," in *North American Review*, CLVIII (1894), 513-19; *id.*, "The Darlington Riot," in Tillman Papers. See also, Benjamin F. Taylor, *The Darlington Riot* (Columbia, 1910); Ball, *State that Forgot*, 231, 250-51; Wallace, *History of South Carolina*, III, 361-62; Columbia *State*, March 30-April 10, 1894; Columbia *Daily Register*, March 30-April 10, 1894; Charleston *News and Courier*, March 30-April 10, 1894.

[36] McCullough *v.* Brown, 41 South Carolina 220.

called "Prohibition, rock-ribbed and steel-hooped," a type
of temperance which would fill true moderates with disgust.
It was, he added bitterly, not an angel of light, "but an
abortion, a jubilant demon, who jeered and laughed as he
polished his bar glasses and cried, 'What are you going to
do about it?'" Declaring that he was left with no power
with which to enforce the law, he said he could do nothing
about it.[37] The barkeepers reopened their establishments
"in grand style." Charlestonians lit bonfires, and bore
a whiskey barrel garlanded with flowers triumphantly
through the streets. The United States government issued
licenses to 1,174 retail liquor dealers, twice as many as in
pre-Dispensary days. Men who had never previously sold
liquor went into the business and whiskey could be purchased openly in every hamlet.[38]

Yet the governor did not surrender before what he called
an "illogical and strained" and "muddy" court decision. In
fact, before the court acted he had stacked the cards in
favor of the Dispensary. At the 1893 sessions of the legislature he had secured the passage of a revised Dispensary act
to replace the one the supreme court had under review and
secured the election to the court of Eugene B. Gary, a
Tillmanite, in place of Justice Samuel McGowan, a Conservative. This change, of course, did not prevent the adverse decision of the court upon the act of 1892, as Mc-
Gowan's term of office did not expire until August 1, 1894;
but it did make certain that after that date a decision favorable to the act of 1893 could be exacted by a court two to
one in Tillman's favor. "I knew," the governor explained,
"the same general principles underlay both Acts, and that
if one was unconstitutional the other must be also. . . .
But . . . I resolved to thwart the Court if I could."[39]

Tillman suspended the act of 1893 until after McGowan

---

[37] Charleston *News and Courier*, May 9, 1894.
[38] Tillman, in South Carolina *House Journal*, 1894, pp. 35–36.
[39] *Id., ibid.*, 35–37.

went out of office,[40] ordering trial justices not to hear cases
under the law until that time.[41] As he expressed the situation: "I took the act of 1893 and went into the bushes
with it and they [the members of the court] have not been
able to touch it since." [42] Later, after hand primaries proved
that the voters sanctioned his program,[43] he ordered the
dispensaries reopened on August 1.[44] He next insisted that
the reconstituted court pass upon the new act. "A speedy
determination of the issue," he wrote the chief justice, was
necessary to prevent "friction and possible bloodshed." [45]
Obediently the court acted on October 8, 1894. The law
was declared constitutional by a vote of two Tillmanites
to one Conservative. The state, affirmed the majority, had
under its police power the right to establish a public monopoly in a commodity as dangerous as whiskey.[46] It was true,
as the *News and Courier* asserted, that the law had been
interpreted "in a biased atmosphere," but this was also
true of the opposite decision given six months earlier. A
man of action felt justified in combating partisanship with
partisanship.

For the remaining three months of his term of office, the
governor applied the same tactics he had used during the
first nine months of the Dispensary system. "I propose,"
he declared, "to make the enemies of the Dispensary get
out of the road and obey the law. . . . It has come to stay,
and the sooner this fact is recognized by the whiskey people
and the other opponents the better it is for them." [47] Once
more he prodded the constables into inquisitorial actions.[48]
Once more he used both threats and persuasion to secure

[40] *Id.* to T. N. Rhodes, June 13, 1894, in Governor's Letter Books.
[41] *Id.*, at Orangeburg, in Charleston *News and Courier*, July 27, 1894.
[42] *Id.* at Holly's Ferry, *ibid.*, July 22, 1894.
[43] *Id.* to K. R. Bougham, August 2, 1894, in Governor's Letter Books.
[44] Charleston *News and Courier*, July 24, 1894.
[45] Tillman to Chief Justice Henry McIver, August 20, 1894, in Governor's
Letter Books.
[46] State *ex rel.* George *v.* Aiken, 42 South Carolina 222.
[47] Charleston *News and Courier*, October 9, 1894.
[48] Tillman to John Griffen, August 13, 1894, in Governor's Letter Books.

the co-operation of municipal authorities in enforcement problems.[49] Experience had not taught him to be less high-handed. This was evidenced by the pardoning of a constable convicted by a jury of ten Tillmanites of shooting a Negro in the back. It was, said the prosecuting attorney, a clear case of murder; but to Tillman, conviction had only been possible because the jury was "a terrible lot of fools" who were "corrupt and crazy." To let this decision stand would have been "too sweet a morsel to his enemies." [50] Such procedure was effective. It did not lessen the popularity of the governor, and it daunted the opponents of the law.

When "the head barkeeper," a sobriquet which Tillman good-humoredly accepted, left office in November, 1894, he could speak with satisfaction of "his very large and complex business." Of course the Dispensary still had fundamental weaknesses,[51] but for the time being they were overshadowed by evidences of success. The menace of mob violence had been overcome, and difficult judicial snags had been removed. The gravest immediate problem, that of enforcement, was being met vigorously. A critical outsider reported: "The closing of all the saloons and public bars in the state has unquestionably broken up the practice of 'treating' and diminished the number of arrests for drunkenness and disorderly conduct." [52]

The net profits of the Dispensary for the first months of its existence were $97,694.93 for the state and $76,775.25 for the counties. Tillman's prediction that in time these profits would increase proved true.[53] During the thirteen and one-half years of the existence of the state Dispensary, the profits were $9,751,181.48, distributed annually in such

[49] *Id.* to W. P. Hursey, October 12, 1894, *ibid.; id.* to C. C. Townsend, September 13, 1894, *ibid.*

[50] *Id.* to Stanyarne Wilson, October 22, 1894, *ibid.*

[51] See p. 460.

[52] "I.N.F." in New York *Tribune,* cited in Charleston *News and Courier,* December 28, 1894.

[53] Tillman, in South Carolina *House Journal,* 1894, pp. 41–43.

a way as to rise from $100,000 in 1895 to $414,000 in 1899 and to $870,000 in 1905. This was an excellent increase over the $215,000 which the saloons yielded the public treasury in 1892.[54]

Obviously, the Dispensary was a practical success. A compromise solution of one of South Carolina's most difficult problems, its establishment showed Ben Tillman's statesmanship in its most original and most constructive aspects. That it was not destined to be a permanent institution was no fault of his.

[54] Leonard S. Blakey, *The Sale of Liquor in the South,* in Columbia University *Studies in History, Economics, and Public Law,* LI (New York, 1912), 18, 46.

Chapter XVIII

THE GOVERNOR BECOMES SENATOR

BEN TILLMAN had no cause for dissent from the customary opinion that the reward of a successful governor should be a seat in the United States Senate. The experiences of position and power had long since destroyed earlier inhibitions against office-seeking; in fact, he was scarcely governor before he was scheming for the national office.[1] The senatorship was more permanent and better salaried than the governorship. To desire it, in preference to returning to the Edgefield plantation, where debts were burdensome and income declining, required the exercise of only minimum selfishness. Confidence in his own ability to win the senatorship had been stimulated by his experiences in the 1892 campaign and in the Dispensary difficulties. The people were behind him. They felt that his trials and triumphs entitled him to the highest office in their gift.

Another reason why Tillman took an active part in the political discussions of 1894 was to consolidate his position in South Carolina affairs. A governor and a legislature must be elected who would protect the Dispensary and sponsor the constitutional convention. These objectives doubtless could have been attained through quiet manipulations, but that was not the Tillman way. The governor must arouse enthusiasm for his person; the people must demand that the politicians carry out his will. This could be accom-

[1] "You may divide our forces and prevent my becoming your colleague," he had written Senator Irby in 1892. Tillman to Irby, December 5, 1892, in Governor Tillman's Letter Books. *Cf.* Wallace, *History of South Carolina,* III, 356, 358.

plished only by a repetition of the canvasses of 1890 and 1892. He must visit every county in the state and launch his sallies of wit, ridicule, and billingsgate. The mobs would cry with delight; he would be elected, and his ideas would win.

Fresh issues were arising in Tillman's mind to give a renewed fervor and variety to what he was going to say in the coming canvass. He was gradually developing into a prominent champion of free silver and the other Populist projects. Moreover, there came to his attention an individual against whom he could indulge his penchant for wordy assaults. This person was no mere South Carolinian, but Grover Cleveland himself, the President of the United States and the chosen chief of the Democratic party. The South Carolinian was convinced that the President was not only wrong in policies but was also personally dishonest. He longed for an opportunity to attack so eminent a culprit.[2]

Tillman's opponent in the senatorial canvass was Matthew C. Butler, a leader endowed with qualities which traditionally made for political success in South Carolina. By birth and by marriage to the daughter of Governor Francis W. Pickens, he belonged to the two most distinguished Edgefield families. In war and peace he had lived up to the reputation of his forebears. As a Confederate cavalry general he had demonstrated consummate fearlessness. At Hamburg and elsewhere during the Reconstruction, his boldness had won the applause of the white masses. His reward was election to the United States Senate in 1877. There his winsome manners won modest favors for his constituents from Republican majorities. Commanding in appearance and possessed of a fine head and symmetrical features, he was adjudged "the handsomest man in South

[2] "I would give five thousand dollars if I had it," he wrote Irby concerning that senator's opportunity to attack Cleveland. Tillman to Irby, July 22, 1894, in Governor Tillman's Letter Books.

Carolina, if not in the country." [3] To good looks were added a sense of humor, an inexhaustible fund of anecdote, and an almost phenomenal memory for faces and names. He was enviably popular.[4]

Butler was too good a politician not to understand that after 1890 leadership in South Carolina had passed to a man whose qualities differed radically from his. Realizing the folly of crossing swords with Tillman, and lacking the heroic timber necessary to organize a counterrevolution, he cautiously decided to play a double role. He would retain Conservative support and at the same time would discreetly avoid the wrath of Tillman, or if that proved impossible, he would espouse agrarian principles in the hope of winning the support of Tillmanites estranged from their disagreeable chief. Inconspicuous in state affairs after the rise of Tillman, he was not among the many Conservatives who debated the fiery farmer.[5] He had no personal quarrel with the governor, who had been his neighbor during the many years both men had been planters in the southern section of Edgefield. Without affiliating with the organizations of the Tillmanites, Butler shifted his position on national affairs from that of a Bourbon Democrat to one favoring many of the measures of the Populists and the Farmers' Alliance.

Actually, however, the senator was in an impossible position. His ambition to retain the senatorship conflicted with that of a determined man leading invincible forces. His reputation would have been better served had he, like Hampton, recognized fate and gone to the political block with head erect. That was the way of the gallant gentleman he was supposed to be. Tillman, with ruthless insight, pre-

[3] Ball, *State that Forgot*, 241.

[4] Characterization of New York *Times,* cited in Charleston *News and Courier,* November 8, 1894.

[5] During the canvass of 1892, complained a Conservative, Butler "did not lift a finger or utter a word" in favor of Tillman's opponents. Greenville *News,* cited in Charleston *News and Courier,* July 5, 1894.

pared to tear the mask from Butler's face and disclose what lay behind. He hinted happenings in his opponent's "private life that are notoriously current." [6] He knew that Butler, despite congeniality, was innately an aristocrat; that the Butler family did not exchange social calls with their Tillman neighbors; that, as Tillman told an audience of plain people, Butler "doesn't realize your needs as one who sprung from you"; [7] and that Butler, loving polite society, had lost intimate touch with the common people.[8] Moreover, much was wanting in the senator's attitude toward the agrarian movement. Tillman recalled that Butler had engaged in a bitter quarrel with Gary, the farmer's patron saint, under circumstances not free from slander and scandal; that the senator, in a debate with Tom Watson of Georgia, had uttered sentiments heretical among orthodox agrarians; that he had approved of Sheppard's candidacy in 1892; [9] that, despite his growing willingness to champion anti-Cleveland measures, he was sufficiently cordial toward the President to be allowed to dispense Federal patronage.[10] He was, therefore, disqualified to engage in the sort of personal attack upon the President which Tillman would make popular.

Despite these facts, Butler persisted in his attempt to alienate Tillman's agrarian followers. He eagerly embraced an opportunity given him by the Farmers' Alliance to declare himself on the famous Ocala Demands of that order, acceding to all the demands except government ownership of railroads and the Subtreasury Plan. He favored the free coinage of silver, a Federal income tax, and the repeal of the tax on circulations of state banks.[11] Tillman, however, prevented the senator from proving himself the better

[6] See Tillman's speech at Lancaster, *ibid.*, June 22, 1894.

[7] *Id.* at Chester, *ibid.*, June 21, 1894.

[8] *Id.*, at Bennettsville, *ibid.*, June 28, 1894.

[9] *Id.* to Thomas W. Crews, June 12, 1894, in Governor Tillman's Letter Books.

[10] *Id.*, at Kingstree, in Charleston *News and Courier*, July 8, 1894.

[11] *Ibid.*, May 21, 1894.

friend of the Alliance by answering the inquiry in almost identical terms. The resemblance between the statements of the two candidates, said the *News and Courier,* was "so remarkable that they might have been written after consultation between their respective writers." [12] The only important difference was that Tillman used the bolder rhetoric in condemning portions of the Alliance program. He spoke as one who believed his strength was greater than that of his questioners.[13] The Alliance did not see fit to endorse Butler.

The senator's sudden cordiality toward agrarianism, on the other hand, cost him the active support of the Conservatives. The press said that he was "pandering to what he considers the larger side," [14] and that there was no reason why "any Anti of the Old Guard of 1892 should trouble himself seriously to serve Butler now." [15] John C. Haskell declared that "a splendid chance to down Tillman and his cohorts" was "absolutely thrown away" by Butler's attempt "to get on the same platform with Tillman." [16] The result was that the Conservatives generally absented themselves from the campaign meetings and failed, except in a few counties, to present candidates for the legislature, the body which selected the senator.[17] Actually, Butler was defeated before the canvass of 1894 began.

The Alliance leaders were no better pleased with Tillman's partial endorsement of their platform than were the Conservatives with Butler. But they dared not oppose the governor because they knew that he was stronger with the people than they. The Alliance became completely subdued when Tillman began to give direction to the popular en-

[12] *Ibid.*
[13] Tillman to Thomas P. Mitchell, April 28, May 15, 1894, in Governor Tillman's Letter Books.
[14] Charleston *News and Courier,* May 21, June 4, 1894.
[15] Greenville *News,* cited *ibid.,* July 5, 1894.
[16] Interview, Washington *Post,* cited *ibid.,* August 6, 1894.
[17] *Ibid.,* August 3, 1894.

thusiasm in his favor.[18] With the aid of Irby for the state at large and of Gantt for the populous Piedmont, he revived the Tillman organization in each of the counties; pro-Tillman committees were constituted to promote legislative candidacies; [19] influential friends were personally urged to make the race; [20] and county leaders were ordered to limit the number of Tillmanite candidates to the number of vacant seats.[21] He firmly urged Irby, Gantt, and other impetuous friends not to engage in intrafactional fights; [22] appointed spies to discover whether or not candidates who professed loyalty to him were sincere; [23] and tolerated no division of strength in face of the opposition.

Butler, in despair over Tillman's strength, proposed that the contest be decided by a nominating primary made binding on all Democratic candidates for the legislature. Undoubtedly the governor would have won under this or any other method of expressing the popular will, but he rejected the proposal. His plans for capturing the Senate seat through the legislature were already perfected.[24]

Had Senator Butler been a man of ordinary prudence and courage he would have given up the contest before the first meeting of the joint canvass was held on June 18. But he fatuously believed he could stem the tide of Tillmanism by appealing to the sensibilities of his audiences. At the worst, this former Confederate general knew that he could not be frightened by the pyrotechnics of the Great Bamboozler or the howls of the Tillman mobs. Too often he had stood calm under Federal fire. Indeed, he himself might

[18] Charlotte *Observer*, cited *ibid.*, August 2, 1894.

[19] *Ibid.*, June 24, July 2, 1894.

[20] Tillman to Robert B. Watson, March 17, 1894, in Governor Tillman's Letter Books.

[21] *Id.* to Thomas H. Rainsford, April 28, 1894, *ibid.*

[22] *Id.* to T. Larry Gantt, May 28, July 15, 1894, *ibid.; id.* to Shaw, December 9, 1892, *ibid.*

[23] *Id.* to Luther Reese, February 9, 1894, *ibid.*

[24] Tompkins to D. B. Durisoe, July 25, 1894, *ibid.*

browbeat Tillman and thereby discredit the demagogue before his own crowds.

Since the chance to defeat Tillman through enlightened appeal never presented itself, the brave and reckless Butler adopted bullying tactics early in the canvass. Opportunity for such behavior came when the governor, at the second meeting, hinted that Butler's partisans were traveling on free passes and that a "corrupting fund" had been raised on Wall Street in behalf of the senator's candidacy.[25] Enraged by these accusations, Butler, the next day, loosed a flood of vituperation. Advancing upon the governor, the senator cried: "He must take his punishment like a man. . . . If Governor Tillman or anyone else makes charges of a corruption fund against me, he is an infamous liar. . . . Governor Tillman may go to the Senate, but he shall not go there slandering me. Let him go there on his own merits and not by vilifying, lampooning, and misrepresenting better men than he is." Then he attacked the governor's war record, asserted that he had fled from Hamburg when the shooting began, recalled the free pass incident, and implied that he had accepted Dispensary bribes. In other words, Tillman was told that he was a coward, a bulldozer, a liar, and a bribetaker! It was a series of insults which thousands of South Carolinians believed could be honorably met only by bloodshed.[26]

Yet there was no bloodshed. While Butler was speaking, Tillman suppressed his great anger and listened quietly. At the meeting the next day, he remained cool, merely reproaching Butler for making charges which "were fouler and blacker than had been made against any man" and which were unworthy of an Edgefield man. When a member of the audience asked why he did not meet the insults with violence, his answer was vehement but peace-assuring: "Yes, I tell you, you cowardly hound, why I took them,

[25] Kohn, in Charleston *News and Courier*, June 20, 1894.
[26] *Id., ibid.*, June 21, 1894.

and I'll meet you wherever you want to. I took them because I, as Governor of the State, could not afford to create a row in a public gathering and have our people murder each other like dogs." [27]

At the next few meetings of the canvass the governor acted to minimize possible disorder resulting from Butler's aggressiveness. He avoided dangerous personalities and demonstrated by hand primaries that his antagonist stood almost alone in his attempts to revive the partisan feelings of 1890 and 1892. Tillman did not fear the accusation of personal cowardice for not resorting to physical assault. It was generally known that he was surrounded by an informal group of determined men who protected him as effectively as the formal bodyguards of presidents and kings. "The man who hurts Ben Tillman," declared the chairman of the Bennettsville gathering, "would be lynched before sundown." [28]

Prudence resulted favorably for Tillman. The campaign gradually assumed more the character of a rural festival in honor of a hero than a contest between two candidates. Butler, seeing the futility of aggressiveness, began to ignore Tillman in his speeches, an example which Tillman was not slow to follow. The enmity between the two men reached such a low ebb that they rode in the same carriage at the Conway meeting of July 4. The Conservative press, two weeks after the beginning of the canvass, acknowledged that Tillman's election was "a foregone conclusion." [29] The governor, who thrived on spirited opposition, wrote dolefully, "The canvass is so one-sided between Butler and myself it is almost devoid of interest." [30]

During the last two weeks of the contest, some of the old personal bitterness between the candidates was revived. The prelude was the reception given Tillman when, on

27 *Id., ibid.,* June 22, 1894.
28 William D. Evans, *ibid.,* June 28, 1894.
29 Kohn, *ibid.,* June 24, July 2, 5, 1894.
30 Tillman to Gantt, July 15, 1894, in Governor Tillman's Letter Books.

July 12, he made the fifth speech of his career in Charleston. He opened with the none too philosophical inquiry: "Why do Charlestonians hate me anyhow?" He answered himself with customary rudeness: "Because they are behind the times and because their street cars are run by mules instead of electricity. They are cut off from the whole State in progress, in sympathy and in politics; they can go to the devil in their own way if they want to." There were jeers from the audience, and the speaker, disgusted, sat down with this passing shot: "I am going to have the Dispensary down here whether you want it or not." The *News and Courier* declared with reason: "He has no right to appeal for courteous treatment from a city he has treated with discourtesy for years." [31]

The revival of the dispute between the two candidates concerned their respective parts in the Hamburg Riot. The outside, unacquainted with the peculiarities of South Carolina social ethics, might assume that the controversy would have involved accusations of killing some of the eleven who fell in that affair. But white South Carolina looked on Hamburg as an event in honorable warfare and on its participants as heroes. It, therefore, became the duty of the seeker of popular favor to emphasize his part in the riot at the expense of the part of his opponent. Thus Tillman and Butler accused each other of *not* killing Negroes, and each boasted of a hand in that activity.

Tillman answered Butler's assertion that the governor was not active at Hamburg by claiming that his opponent, while his seat in the Senate was under contest, had denied that honor to himself. This was followed by the collection of affidavits from well-known Hamburg rioters solemnly affirming or denying that Ben Tillman was "seen by anyone of us when the firing began." The controversy naturally came to a head at Edgefield. "It's a lie," cried Butler when a member of the audience said that he had minimized his

[31] Charleston *News and Courier,* July 13, 14, 1894.

part in the riot to secure the Senate seat. Immediately "a most dangerous scene" developed. Partisans of both candidates rushed to the speaker's stand cursing and with pistols half drawn. Trouble was prevented only by the intervention of the two contestants.[32]

At Union, where Butler was howled down after Tillman imputed that he did not pay his debts and was "allowing his mouth to be used as a sewer," the senator rushed at Tillman as the governor sat on a departing train. "You know," cried Butler, "you put those hoodlums up to howling me, and you know that you perpetrated a damned fraud and a lie when you did so." The governor tried to turn wrath away with a humorous answer: "Now, General Butler, you are old and one-legged." But when Butler continued to revile "the blackguards" who had insulted him, Tillman reproached him for having championed the antidueling law making it impossible "for a gentleman to get redress for an insult." Other advances by Butler were met by Tillman's repeated declaration that he did not wish to fight. Finally the unseemly quarrel was ended by the intervention of the conductor. "Governor Tillman," said the *News and Courier*'s report, "was remarkably calm during the entire spat." [33] Butler had failed in his final attempt to reckon directly with his opponent.

The verdict of the press on the Tillman-Butler contest was that "not a single sentence" had been uttered contributing to "the elevation and instruction of the people" and that "the disgraceful sparring" between the two men had "contributed nothing to their reputations." [34] It was nevertheless true that Tillman's commendable coolness had prevented Butler's blustering tactics from leading to riot. It was also true that Butler, despite his foolhardiness, demonstrated a reckless bravery worthy of the gallant Confederate he was. Deserted by Conservatives in the leadership of a

[32] Kohn, *ibid.*, July 20, 1894.   [33] *Id., ibid.*, August 1, 1894.
[34] *Ibid.*, August 9, 1894.

forlorn hope, he won the partial respect of hostile crowds by the utterly fearless manner in which he attacked their hero.[35]

Butler did not surrender when the August primary resulted in the choice of a legislature pledged overwhelmingly to Tillman. He withdrew his pledge to abide by the primary, declaring that the Democratic organization was controlled by "a handful of selfish, corrupt ringsters." [36] His object was to capitalize the resentment which many persons felt toward Tillman because of the governor's Populistic tendencies, his administration of the Dispensary, and his tactics in controlling the gubernatorial nomination. But a majority of the Conservatives were in no humor to venture upon the dangerous paths of independentism. They knew that the Tillmanites were in a great majority among the whites and that the undemocratic registration laws which they had helped make rendered an appeal to the Negro majority impractical. Gestures in the direction of insurgency, said Tillman caustically, were "so much insolence and idiocy and blind rage" of persons "sick nigh unto death after the long fast since they were turned out of power in 1890." [37] Consequently Butler did not lead a bolt.

Still he was not ready to give up the fight. In blind passion he swore against election laws which had made possible his holding a Senate seat for eighteen years. He threatened to appeal to the courts and to the privileges committee of the Senate, but the Democratic leaders in the Senate let it be known that Tillman was acceptable to them.[38] On December 11, 1894, the South Carolina legislature, by a majority of better than 5 to 1, elevated Tillman to the Senate of the United States.[39]

[35] Hugh L. Farley, *ibid.*, August 19, 1894.

[36] *Ibid.*, August 15, 1894.

[37] Atlanta *Constitution*, September 17, 1894, in Tillman Scrapbooks.

[38] "I.N.F.," in New York *Tribune*, cited in Charleston *News and Courier*, December 28, 1894.

[39] Tillman's vote was 102; Butler and William D. Crum, the Republican candidate, polled 19. *Ibid.*, December 12, 1894.

Chapter XIX

THE SUCCESSION TO THE
GOVERNORSHIP

MEANWHILE, Tillman was battling with another problem almost as dear to him as his own election to the Senate. He wished to secure a successor as governor to whom he could safely entrust the continuation of his policies. To complicate his plans, five loyal Tillmanites aspired to this trust. The situation was further complicated by the weakness of the Conservatives. Lacking an aggressive leader to pit against the crafty Tillman, and discouraged by the defeats of 1890 and 1892, they presented no gubernatorial candidates in 1894. With the enemy in the open field, Tillman could have forced the Tillmanites to support a single candidate and then, by the sheer weight of numbers, could have won an easy victory. But the Conservatives played a subtle game. They knew that there were bitter jealousies among the Tillmanites and that the reigning tyrant was hated by many. They saw the possibility of combination with the disaffected.

The difficulties of Tillman's position were partly solved by the virtual self-elimination of three of the five gubernatorial aspirants because of personal weaknesses. The first of these was Dr. Sampson Pope, who was ruled out of the race in all but name when it was evident that he was too hot-tempered and erratic to deserve the support of either chief or people. The second candidate was Hugh L. Farley, an impecunious gentleman whose claim to distinction was his amusing talk and his friendship for General Gary.[1] Till-

---

[1] Tillman Scrapbooks.

man dismissed him as "a wit and a clown" who had eschewed "all chances of being intrusted with weighty and responsible matters." [2] He withdrew from the race. The third aspirant was James E. Tindal, a cultured planter who had been since 1885 a consistent advocate of the more constructive phases of Tillmanism.[3] Had Tillman been a statesman ruling over a broad-visioned people, he would have done well to select Tindal as his successor; but such was not the case. Tindal was too academic in utterance, too much given "to a Sunday-school, Alliance philosophy," to be effective on the stump. The two candidates taken seriously were William H. Ellerbe and John Gary Evans.

Ellerbe was a successful farmer who had served as comptroller general under Tillman. His principal strength was his subservience to Tillman's will. By profession a farmer, he was acceptable to a movement presumably in the interest of that calling. His major drawback was that he was "halting and inexperienced in speech." [4]

Evans was a lawyer of thirty, "in appearance and manner as much like a woolhat as any youngster stepping out of a dinner dance at Delmonico's might have been." He was well dressed, a graduate of a Northern college, and as proud of a distinguished ancestry as any low-country Bourbon. He was the nephew of Martin W. Gary and the son of another Confederate general.[5] His strength lay in his dedication to the peculiar doctrines of South Carolina; [6] in his efficient championship in the legislature of the Dispensary and other administration measures; and in his ability to stir audiences by a sprightly advocacy of Tillmanism. But as an aristocrat and a lawyer he belonged to a class and profession that Tillman, at least in his more demagogic moments, professed to despise.

---

[2] Tillman to Irby, December 5, 1892, in Governor Tillman's Letter Books.
[3] Tillman Scrapbooks.   [4] Koester, "Bleaseism," Chap. VII.
[5] Ball, *State that Forgot*, 239–40.
[6] See his confession of faith, in South Carolina *House Journal*, 1894, pp. 127–39.

The boss of South Carolina could not conveniently solve the problem of the two candidates by forcing one to withdraw. A principle of political ethics to which he consistently adhered was to show no favor between candidates deemed competent and loyal. "I cannot," he often wrote those who asked for his support, "take sides between 'good' reformers who are aspiring for place at the hands of the General Assembly or the people." [7] He believed that both Ellerbe and Evans were worthy and loyal and therefore felt obligated to condemn neither. "Our policy," he wrote with the rivalries of 1894 in mind, "should be to allay and prevent hostility rather than to get up fights in our ranks." [8]

Commentators upon the campaign of 1894 believe that Tillman did not uphold this principle. They assert that he covertly favored Evans at the expense of Ellerbe.[9] Sufficient evidence proves this to be inaccurate. In the first place, it is clear that before Evans entered the race, the governor actually favored Ellerbe. "I was put in office by the Farmers' Movement and my successor ought to be a farmer," he explained in defense of this position.[10] In the second place, he discouraged Evans' candidacy, writing to a confidant: "I honestly believe Evans could come nearer getting place . . . as Lt. Gov. than he can as Gov." [11] But when Evans, on his own initiative, decided to enter the race, Tillman accorded him this privilege, and then publicly and privately assumed an attitude of neutrality.

Three circumstances refute the belief that this attitude was insincere. Tillman repeatedly asserted his neutrality

[7] Tillman to Eugene B. Gary, October 27, 1893, in Governor Tillman's Letter Books. Cf. id. to Jefferson A. Sligh, November 24, 1894, ibid.

[8] Id. to Shaw, December 9, 1892, ibid.

[9] Wallace, History of South Carolina, III, 363; Ball, State that Forgot, 239; Kirkland, "Tillman and I," in Columbia State, July 21, 1929.

[10] Koester, "Bleaseism," Chap. VII; Tillman's and Ellerbe's speeches at Barnwell and Winnsboro, in Charleston News and Courier, July 18, 25, 1894.

[11] Tillman to unidentified sheriff, February 13, 1894, in Governor Tillman's Letter Books.

and the searchlights of investigators have not revealed that he was lying; he never used his main weapon, the address to the people in behalf of Evans. Finally, in perfect confirmation of his impartiality, he wrote Larry Gantt begging him to desist from his efforts to consolidate the Tillman forces behind Evans. He admonished the fiery editor: "If you treat all Reformers who disagree with you in supporting Evans as traitors, . . . you will inevitably drive off enough men and counties to join the Antis in the next campaign to defeat the man nominated that year. You are hard and unreasonable in your attacks on our friends as you were in '92 on the Sheppardites, and it won't do. Stop it or I will force you to open up the whole subject and tell all I know. It is no sin to oppose Evans or Ellerbe. Allow every Reformer to do so without charging bad motive. . . . Evans and Ellerbe are as good friends as I have." [12]

Realizing that Tillman's attitude was the key to the governorship, both Evans and Ellerbe, through secret intrigue and through public declaration, vied with each other in trying to snuggle close to the boss. They favored the doctrines he favored; they rejected those he rejected; and they imitated as best they could his methods of public speech. The Conservative press jeeringly called them "coattail swingers." Tillman, half amused and half irritated, joined in the derision of his self-styled friends. They, he said playfully, "ought to be spanked for quarreling about who is the closest friend of Tillman." [13] Quoting Captain McHeath in the play, he declared, "How happy would I be with either, were t'other dear charmer away." When a questioner pressed for a declaration of preference, he answered, "Well, sir, you can vote for either as you like best, but you must not say I told you to do so." [14]

[12] *Id.* to Gantt, July 15, 1894, *ibid.*
[13] Charleston *News and Courier,* July 25, 1894; Augusta *Chronicle,* July 25, 1894.
[14] At Barnwell, in Charleston *News and Courier,* July 18, 1894.

Before the summer canvass was very old, it was evident that Evans was running ahead of his rival. He manifested both the ability and the willingness to denounce the enemies of Tillmanism as bitterly as the chief had ever done. By skillfully seconding every position Tillman assumed, he gradually convinced the mass of Tillmanites that he, and only he, was Tillman's political heir. The fact that his utterances aroused the hate of the Conservatives served but to endear him to the Tillmanite mobs.[15] Ellerbe, on the other hand steadily lost ground with the campaign crowds. His dull speeches failed to excite enthusiasm. Falsely interpreting popular apathy as evidence that Tillman was secretly favoring Evans, he pursued an antagonistic policy. At first he grovelingly begged the chief to designate him as the favorite, thereby creating the belief that he was taking unfair advantage of Tillman. Then, to capitalize the rising tide of Conservative sympathy for him, Ellerbe, at the Fairfield meeting, committed the cardinal sin of criticizing the administration of the Dispensary.[16] Tillman's comment shortly afterwards is significant: "Ellerbe ruined himself by attacking me for reopening the Dispensary. . . . It was nip and tuck with them [Ellerbe and Evans] until after the Fairfield meeting."[17]

Whatever hope Ellerbe had of winning the Democratic nomination by a combination of his friends with the Conservatives was negated by an intrigue of Evans' friends. They devised the so-called Colleton Plan of holding a convention of Tillmanites to "suggest," in the manner of the March convention of 1890, a candidate for governor to the regular Democratic nominating convention. The initiator of this scheme was Irby. At first Tillman opposed it. It would cause, he wrote Irby, a split between the Farmers'

---

[15] Philadelphia *Press*, cited *ibid.*, September 21, 1894.

[16] *Ibid.*, July 18, 25, 1894.

[17] Tillman to James K. Henry, September 13, 1894, in Governor Tillman's Letter Books.

Alliance and the Farmers' Movement and consequently result in the defeat of the suggested candidate.[18] With emphasis he publicly declared, "To return to the convention system, after proclaiming our belief in the ability and right of the people to govern themselves, is like a dog returning to its vomit, and I would be ashamed to go on the stump as the nominee of such a convention." [19]

But the dog did return to its vomit. Tillman learned to endorse such a nominee. While on an unheralded trip to Washington, he was "tamed by the mysterious hypnotic influence" of the ingratiating Irby, acquiescing in the Colleton Plan. As a consequence, the executive committee of the Farmers' Association set August 16 as the date of a suggesting convention.[20] This return to the highhanded methods of ring rule created a howl among Conservatives and the moderate Tillmanites, a furor which grew into a mighty chorus when, as the summer canvass progressed, it became evident that the hated Evans was besting the more moderate Ellerbe. Now Tillman spoke as vigorously in favor of the project as he had previously spoken against it. "If the committee," he said, "should prove so treacherous as to call off the convention, and let all the candidates go into a general primary, you had better watch and pray that Reform measures are not destroyed." [21]

Tillman in this instance repudiated principles of popular sovereignty because he was a good politician who put self-preservation above doctrine. "I thought," he explained, "it unwise and extremely dangerous to change front in the face of the enemy." The calling off of the suggesting convention would have given "great aid and comfort to the Antis" who were intriguing for the friendship of El-

---

[18] *Id.* to Irby, February 6, 1894, *ibid.; id.* to H. M. Edwards, February 11, 1894, *ibid.*

[19] Columbia *Daily Register,* August 7, 1894.

[20] Philadelphia *Press,* cited in Charleston *News and Courier,* September 21, 1894; Farley, *ibid.,* August 19, 1894.

[21] Columbia *Daily Register,* August 7, 1894.

lerbe.[22] For the sake of principle he could not risk turning over the command of the Tillman citadel to a lieutenant suspected of treasonable relations with the enemy. Moreover, this repudiation of an accepted principle of free elections was more technical than actual. Tillman did not invalidate the doctrine of majority rule; he merely prevented the possibility of the Conservative minority holding the balance of power between factions of the Tillmanite majority. Finally it should be made clear that Tillman did not attempt to dictate, as has frequently been asserted, the Tillmanite choice for governor. He left his friends as free to choose between Evans and Ellerbe as they had been before he endorsed the suggesting convention. The fact that Evans won over his rival was due to Evans' personal superiorities.

The program of the Tillman faction moved according to schedule. Twenty-three thousand Tillmanites gathered in Reform Clubs to elect delegates to the state convention. This body, by vote of 262 to 58, "suggested" Evans to the Democratic party. Indeed, this vote was made unanimous when Ellerbe agreed to support the winner on promise of the governorship at a later date.[23]

Conservatives threatened appeal to the general election, realizing that the elimination of discord in the ranks of the Tillmanites presaged their victory in the regular primary. Resentment against Tillman was at a white heat. Gonzales asserted that he was not a true Democrat because of his repudiation of Cleveland; Senator Butler withdrew his pledge to abide by the results of the Democratic primary; Sampson Pope, whose spirited canvass for governor under the Tillman banner failed to win him a single vote in the suggesting convention, announced himself an independent candidate in the general election.[24]

[22] Tillman to Henry, September 13, 1894, in Governor Tillman's Letter Books.
[23] Charleston *News and Courier*, August 11–17, 1894; Philadelphia *Press*, cited *ibid.*, September 21, 1894.
[24] Charleston *News and Courier*, August 24, 1894.

Despite this opposition Tillman was able to direct events toward the desired goals. Only Charleston and Beaufort elected anti-Evans delegates to the nominating convention. Tillman issued a characteristic warning to Butler, Pope, and others who were threatening bolts. "The cry of a ring," he said, "is not going to scare anybody or muster any votes. I give notice now that we are not going to have any Alabama business [25] in South Carolina. If these people want to warm this black snake into life,[26] . . . we are ready to meet them and give them the worst drubbing they have ever had in their lives. The defeated politicians who cannot get a majority white vote had better understand this." [27]

The nominating convention of September 19 acted with the firm but moderate expediency of which Tillman was always capable in moments of crisis. It resolutely answered the attempt to impugn its loyalty to the Democratic party by adopting a platform which avoided personal denunciation of President Cleveland and which pledged allegiance to the national party. At the same time it gave the gubernatorial nomination to Evans and ambiguously endorsed the Ocala Demands of the Farmers' Alliance. To prevent the control of the state by the manipulations of cliques, the convention abolished the convention method of making nominations for state offices; thereafter all candidates, including those for governor and the United States Senate and House, would be chosen by direct primary. The convention, said the *News and Courier*,[28] "had guided its course with great judgment and steered clear of stones and stumps in the way." It was Tillman's object to forestall the greatest of his fears, the appeal of the anti-Tillmanites to the potential Negro majority.

The tactics of Tillman had destroyed the chances of an

[25] Alludes to the independent movement in that state led by Reuben F. Kolb.

[26] Reference is to a possible calling of the Negro into politics.

[27] Charleston *News and Courier*, August 29, 1894.

[28] *Ibid.*, September 21, 1894.

effective bolt. The erratic Pope alone among the dissatisfied Democrats acted, fighting bravely against the Tillman-
dominated election machinery for Negro participation in
government. He was defeated by Evans by vote of 39,507
to 17,278.[29] His considerable strength was proof of the continued unpopularity of Tillman in certain quarters.

While achieving two of his 1894 objectives, the senatorship for himself and the governorship for a friend, Tillman
did not forget his third ambition of that year. This was the
securing of popular sanction for a constitutional convention. He had induced the legislature to order a referendum
on this issue at the November election. This assembly was
needed, he said grandiloquently, to erect "a fitting capstone
to the triumphal arch which the common people have
erected to liberty, progress and Anglo-Saxon civilization
since 1890." [30]

Tillman's normal desire for this confessed means of destroying the Negro's political rights became fanatical when
Pope called on the blacks to fight against the convention.
In October the aroused Negrophobe spoke of the "crisis
which is upon us more serious than any circumstances since
1861" because of "the unfortunate divisions" among the
whites. "When I consider the fact that the opposition may
defeat the calling of the constitutional convention," he
added in alarm, "I shudder to think what will inevitably
follow in the next political campaign." As the time for the
vote drew near, his apprehension increased. The opposition, he asserted, "will stop at nothing." There was "an
unholy alliance between the independents and negroes." [31]
Under the circumstances Tillman felt that summary expedients were justified. Through threats and discriminatory
questions imposed by Tillman-directed officials, all but 10,-
000 of a potential Negro-voting strength of 130,000 were

[29] South Carolina *Reports and Resolutions*, 1894, II, 470.
[30] Tillman, in South Carolina *House Journal*, 1894, pp. 21–22.
[31] Charleston *News and Courier*, October 30, November 4, 1894.

prevented from registering, and the managers of elections were instructed to intimidate and defraud Negroes who attempted to vote.[32]

Despite Tillman's precautions, the opposition to the convention proved formidable. To the hostility of the ten thousand Negroes was added that of thousands of white Conservatives who failed to share the governor's alarms. They were more disturbed over the likelihood that the bitter fruits of Tillmanism would be grafted in the fundamental law of the state. The obligation which many of them felt to vote for Evans as the regular party nominee did not apply to the convention issue; they could vote against it without being adjudged bolters. Moreover, a large number of Tillmanites in Spartanburg and other Piedmont counties refused to follow their leader on this issue. They believed that in his plans to disfranchise the Negro was hidden a conspiracy to disfranchise "thousands of honest but poor and uneducated Anglo-Saxon voters." How, asked Larry Gantt, could there be suffrage discriminations which did not also discriminate against whites without violating the national Constitution's prohibition of suffrage restrictions on grounds of race? When Tillman refused to reveal the details of a plan which was supposed to accomplish this purpose, the resistance of Gantt and his upcountry followers stiffened.[33]

The opposition to the constitutional convention polled 29,523 out of a total of 60,925. The governor had carried his point by the narrow margin of 1,879.[34]

Tillman's personal triumph in respect to his three aims of 1894 had been so decisive that for many years his place in the United States Senate could not be seriously challenged. But the results in other respects did not reveal the best auguries

[32] Complaints of the Republicans, *ibid.*, November 7, 1894; February 7, 1895.

[33] See Gantt editorial, in Spartanburg *Piedmont Headlight*, cited *ibid.*, October 13, 1894.

[34] South Carolina *Reports and Resolutions*, 1894, II, 472.

for Tillmanism. In an election "saturated with trickery and fraud" on the part of his agents,[35] the powerful opposition to his convention idea had ominous meaning. Thereafter neither Tillman measures nor Tillman lieutenants would enjoy the popular support Tillman himself could command. Thousands were outraged over the methods of the Tillman machine. Evans, its chief beneficiary in 1894, was never again to be elected to an office on a state-wide poll, and the Dispensary, the Tillman measure with which Evans' name was most prominently linked, was ultimately to be undone. Seemingly it was possible for Tillman to remain personally popular without exercising unchallenged authority in South Carolina affairs.

The senator-elect, however, was satisfied with his position. A seat in the Senate belonged to him; the new governor was cordial to the Dispensary; the constitutional convention was assured. The fact that he was called tyrant and political trickster by many caused him little worry. He was accustomed to the lashings of enemies and was grateful that his hide was thick. The vitriol poured on his head was in a sense neutralized by the vitriol he continued to pour on the heads of others. He knew that he had the approval of a majority of the white voters, a circumstance which always gave him comfort. Moreover, this thoughtful man foresaw escape from provincial bickerings and recriminations by devoting himself to national issues, with the possibility of winning the approval of all white South Carolinians. This possibility became a probability when it was realized that he shared equally with his Conservative opponents the peculiar traditions of his state. There was within him the faculty of forgetting and forgiving; beneath a rude exterior was much kindness, humor, and good sense.

Tillman relinquished the governorship in November, 1894. The ten months' respite before his assumption of the

[35] "I.N.F.," in New York *Tribune,* cited in Charleston *News and Courier,* December 27, 1894.

duties of the constitutional convention and the Senate was a period of happy relaxation. He returned to his first loves, his family and his farm. He was still as devoted to his wife as before he became governor; his manners and his dress were still informal and careless; he was still passionately fond of farming. But this time he did not return to the ancestral acres on Horne's Creek. As a senator he felt the necessity of being near railroad and telegraph facilities. He wanted a large house and the luxury of rich acres. With funds borrowed from a Columbia bank, he purchased a plantation at Trenton in Edgefield County some ten miles from his old home. He spent several enjoyable months of his vacation putting his house and acres in order.

Chapter XX

THE CONSTITUTIONAL CONVENTION

THE South Carolina constitution of 1868 remained in force for nineteen years after the whites recovered control of the government. Why this instrument, like other relics of Negro rule, was not sooner abolished needs explanation. Theoretically, this handiwork of the Negro, Carpetbagger, and Scalawag was an excellent document, being largely modeled on the constitutions of Northern states. As part of the New South Movement, influential persons were gradually reconciled to progressive principles in it to which they had once been adverse. Such, for example, was their acceptance of universal education and representation according to population. Moreover, they feared a reversion to the punishments of Reconstruction if they destroyed a major feature of Republicanism. Finally, after 1885, the Conservative legislators refused to give the two-thirds vote necessary for a constitutional convention. They preferred the old constitution to one made by Tillmanites.

But the triumph of Tillmanism in 1890 made a new constitution inevitable. Impelled by a race prejudice which seemed almost instinctive, the white masses demanded a fundamental law made only with white hands, a law which would recognize restrictions on Negro suffrage in a manner to put that question beyond future argument.

No South Carolinian was better equipped than Tillman to effect this demand. Sharing fully the race prejudices of the average white South Carolinian, he had long since repudiated the illusion of political and social equality. He

deprecated predictions of Republican intervention in South
Carolina politics, knowing that the right of South Carolinians to manage their internal affairs would not suffer
infringement. If another Reconstruction were attempted,
it would be met by the same violence used against the post-
bellum experiment. Liberal rationalizations concerning
race equality meant no more to Tillman than to the veriest
backwoodsman. In his inaugural address he had renounced
Jeffersonian philosophizing about the equality of man.
When confronted with the fact that such equality, in its
political and civil aspects, was embodied in the Federal constitution, he produced his bag of tricks, his Machiavellian
guile, by which the Fourteenth and Fifteenth amendments
could be circumvented.

After winning popular approval for the making of a
new constitution, Tillman's task was to have the convention so composed as to do his bidding. To accomplish this
purpose he solicited the co-operation of the anti-Tillmanites on a broad program of anti-Negroism. He wisely sought
the aid of the best legal talent, which was in the Conservative ranks, knowing that a constitution drawn in a nonpartisan atmosphere was most likely to have permanent value.
Moreover, he feared that the Conservatives, if not treated
fairly, would seek the co-operation of Negro voters.

But in calling the Conservatives to his side, Tillman was
also motivated by considerations other than such "farseeing
statesmanship." He was attempting to mend his political
fences. At this stage of his career there were as many Tillmanite members of the legislature who secretly disliked
him as there had been in 1892. These dissatisfied solons—
the so-called Forty—came to an understanding with the
Conservatives for an equal division of the convention seats.
This action was hailed as "the first break in the clouds of
partisan confusion and mutual distrust which has swathed
the State like a shroud for the last four years." [1] A biparti-

[1] Charleston *News and Courier*, December 6, 7, 1894.

san conference was called for March 26, 1895. Tillman, resentful of the plans of the Forty, countered with the calling of a bipartisan conference of his own. So great was his influence over both friends and enemies that the plan of the Forty immediately collapsed. If compromise was to come, it must come at Tillman's dictation.[2]

To effect compromise on his own terms, Tillman and Governor Evans, on the evening of February 15, 1895, met a group of influential Conservatives headed by Joseph W. Barnwell and James C. Hemphill. They were the men who Tillman said "had persecuted and opposed me with all the vigor and malignity of which they were capable." Yet personal feelings were subordinated to political needs. It was agreed that there should be an equal division of convention delegates between the two factions under conditions suggested by Tillman: that only general principles be embodied in the fundamental law; that the homestead act be guaranteed; that the completed document not be submitted to a vote of the people; and that, most important, no suffrage provision be adopted which disfranchised any white man except for crime. The degree, however, to which the agreement was binding upon its signers was not precisely stated. The Conservatives asserted that all persons involved were obligated to an unconditional advocacy of an equal division of the delegates; while Tillman claimed that they were merely obligated to suggest this equal division to the various counties, and that from the standpoint of his faction the acceptance of the plan was dependent upon its adoption by Charleston, Richland, and other Conservative counties.[3]

A few Conservatives hailed with enthusiasm this first friendly conference between Tillman and leaders of the

[2] *Ibid.*, March 27, 28, 1895.

[3] Text of agreement, *ibid.*, March 2, 1895. See Tillman interview with Kohn, *ibid.*, February 23, 1895; Tillman speech, in *Journal of the Constitutional Convention of the State of South Carolina* (Columbia, 1895), 466–72. Cited hereafter as *Journal of the Constitutional Convention.*

opposition since his meeting with Dawson at Augusta in 1886.[4] But the lying down of the lion with the lamb was too good to be above suspicion. The Conservative conferees were violently attacked by the major portion of the press for making an agreement with the hated farmer. These criticisms were overshadowed by Tillmanite opposition to the action of their chief. Senator Irby, troubled by threats against his re-election and hurt by the fact that he was not invited to the conference, took the offensive. In a bitter letter he accused Tillman of folly and treachery. Tillman had walked into the spider's parlor; he would make it possible for the Conservatives to destroy the fruits of Tillmanism. Irby let it be known that he would oppose an equal division of delegates.[5]

Tillman replied with unaccustomed mildness to the onslaught of his erstwhile friend. "We must make concessions and due allowances for prejudices and feelings that have been so deeply aroused." [6] The truth was that he was defeated by Irby and was ready to make any concession short of acknowledging this fact. It was clear that the Tillmanite majority was unwilling to concede equality with their opponents. Might not the possible Conservative control of the convention result in the disfranchisement of thousands of poor white men? How could this be prevented while staying within the limits of the Federal Constitution?

With logic and numbers against him, Tillman revoked his agreement with Barnwell and Hemphill. It would lead, he said, to the disfranchisement of "illiterate and poor white men" and to "the supremacy of the whole crowd who have been left out in the cold for the past four years." The Conservatives with justice accused him of breach of faith.

---

[4] "Senator Tillman," declared Hemphill, "is admirable in the role of peacemaker." Charleston *News and Courier*, February 25, 1895. Others declared he was "generous in concessions," ready to abate selfish interests in favor of a policy of moderation. William W. Ball, in Columbia *Evening News*, cited *ibid.*, February 25, 1895.

[5] *Ibid.*, February 27, 1895.   [6] *Ibid.*, March 2, 1895.

"He will not keep his word. He will not let those of his own political way of thinking keep their word," complained Hemphill.[7] He himself later admitted: "I repudiated it [the agreement] because I saw from the temper of the people who were backing Goff,[8] that we could not depend on them and trust the Conservatives with equal representation." He asserted that his ability to control the opinion of his own faction had been overestimated.[9]

The repudiation of the agreement, however, did not prevent the concession of substantial representation to the Conservatives. At Tillman's suggestion Edgefield returned two Conservatives on its delegation of six. This idea was taken up by other pro-Tillman counties, and Conservative Richland gave representation to Tillmanites. Although Charleston refused to follow this example, it did elect a delegation of very moderate men. The compromises actually effected resulted in the election of 43 Conservatives to 113 Tillmanites. Had the delegates been chosen strictly on a partisan basis, the minority faction would have controlled only Charleston and Richland. Beaufort, the only other county in which the anti-Tillmanites controlled the Democratic organization, returned a Negro delegation.[10]

Tillman now addressed himself to the task of preventing the Negro from wielding influence in the approaching gathering. This was not a difficult problem, but it loomed large in Tillman's pronouncements because he was an alarmist concerning the black man's political potentialities. To achieve his purpose he first secured the enactment of the registration law of 1894. It provided that persons who had registered since the Eight Box Law, which included most whites, were to be allowed to vote with little trouble;

[7] *Ibid.,* July 2, 1895.

[8] The Federal judge who was trying to frustrate the meeting of the convention. See p. 291.

[9] Tillman, in colloquy with William C. McGowan, in *Journal of the Constitutional Convention,* 472.

[10] Charleston *News and Courier,* July 25, 30, 31, August 1, 1895.

those who had registered previous to that law, or who were unregistered, were subjected to such baffling rules that most Negroes would be excluded.[11] He then instructed election officials to refuse to issue registration blanks to Negro applicants. The attorney general explained that this was done because the election law did not provide for the printing of the blanks, but the Republican state chairman clearly demonstrated "a general conspiracy" to withhold the desired papers.[12] Governor Evans revoked the commissions of notaries who took the registration affidavits of Negroes, and there were reports of blacks crowding registration offices vainly trying to get their names on the polling lists.[13]

A convention of some one hundred Negro and white Republicans denounced Tillman's purposes and called on the Negroes "to register to a man." [14] But only ten thousand succeeded in this ambition. "One hundred thousand," said a Republican complaint, "after unparelleled exposure, suffering and sacrifice, remained unregistered." [15] The outcome was the election of only six Negro delegates, five from Beaufort and one from Georgetown. "Outside of a few white men and so-called colored leaders," said a correspondent of the New York *Evening Post,* "the negroes have no one to guide them and neither courage nor intelligence sufficient to make themselves felt of any political importance." [16]

A greater menace to Tillman's plan was the efforts to have the election of the delegates declared illegal. Federal Judge Nathan Goff ruled that the registration laws violated the constitutional prohibition of suffrage restrictions on racial grounds. This "second emancipation" caused "humble rejoicing" among certain Negroes.[17] Their ela-

---

11 South Carolina *Acts,* 1894, pp. 804–805.
12 Charleston *News and Courier,* March 5, 7, 1895.
13 *Ibid.,* March 8, 9, 1895.   14 *Ibid.,* February 7, May 4–9, 1895.
15 *Ibid.,* March 15, 1895.   16 Cited *ibid.,* March 25, 1895.
17 Mills *v.* Green, 67 Federal Reporter 818; Charleston *News and Courier,* May 9, 1895.

tion, however, was premature, for Tillman warned that the convention would be held regardless of the decree of "this dirty Republican, Judge Goff," who was "brought from his home in West Virginia . . . to overthrow the rule of the people in our State." He reminded those who were tempted to appeal to the Negro vote: "The devil forgot that while the registration law may go and the eight-box law may amount to nothing, that the shotgun has gone nowhere." [18] And when John J. Dargan, a lone Conservative, tried to organize the Negroes of Tillman's home county, he was told by the Edgefield mob, "We have got the negro down, and, by God, we are going to keep him down." When the visitor tried to speak, he was driven away by the mob who told him that if he resented its curses his "damned heart" would be cut out.[19]

Happily, if questionably, the United States circuit court of appeals overruled Judge Goff,[20] thus removing the last judicial snag in the way of the election of the delegates. White sentiment was now solidly united behind Tillman's anti-Negro objectives. He was able, said the Negro delegates, to hypnotize the whites of both factions with "the scarecrow of white supremacy." [21]

On September 10, 1895, the people of South Carolina assembled in convention for the third time since the Civil War to make a fundamental law. The leaders were men of considerable distinction. Outstanding among the Conservatives were George D. Tillman and John C. Sheppard of Edgefield; George Johnstone of Newberry; Daniel S. Henderson of Aiken; and Theodore G. Barker and John P. K. Bryan of Charleston. Three of the Negro delegates, Thomas E. Miller, Robert Smalls, and William J. Whipper, upheld the cause of their race with ability and con-

---

[18] Charleston *News and Courier*, May 11, July 28, 1895.
[19] Dargan, *ibid.*, June 28, 1895.
[20] Mills *v.* Green, 69 Federal Reporter 852.
[21] New York *World*, cited in Charleston *News and Courier*, October 3, 1895.

ducted themselves with a dignity which usually won polite treatment. But they were hopelessly outnumbered, and for the most part merely served to remind their race-conscious opponents of a past record to be avoided.

Of course, the actual leadership of the body devolved upon Ben Tillman. A New Yorker described him as sitting in the heart of the assembly, his feet at times resting on the top of his desk and "his one fierce eye watching the six negro delegates." He carried his points neither by persuasion nor kindness, but by inspiring fear in both friend and foe, whom he lashed with sharp words and forceful arguments. He always evinced a calculating conservatism which put no strains upon his premiership.[22] As leader of the sovereign body of South Carolina he was as completely the state's master as any individual has ever been. The other Tillmanite leaders were Governor Evans, president of the convention, and Irby, whose opposition stirred Tillman most effectively.

Tillman studiously tried to avoid partisanship, declaring that the delegates "should discountenance the first attempt at drawing factional lines." [23] This time he had not come to Columbia, as on previous occasions, with the work of the assembly "in his pocket." He listened to the arguments of others and was voted down on some issues.[24] Conservative lawyers were allowed such an active part in the deliberations that one historian fancies they had "fully as much to do with framing the suffrage clause" as had the leader and his majority.[25] "It has been demonstrated on this floor," Tillman himself declared, "that . . . we vote here as free men and equals, at no man's dictation." [26] But such liberalism was the delusive tolerance of the true master. An obvious tyranny would have been evidence of

[22] Creelman, in New York *World*, cited in Charleston *News and Courier*, October 2, 3, 1895.

[23] *Ibid.*, September 16, 1895.   [24] Kohn, *ibid.*, October 21, 1895.

[25] Ball, *State that Forgot*, 229.

[26] *Journal of the Constitutional Convention*, 468.

weakness. His was the self-effacement in small matters of the well-established ruler. In matters of policy Tillman's tyranny could be as flagrant as ever.

A vivid illustration of his power came early in the history of the convention. George D. Tillman, the chronic advocate of small units of government, asked the creation of as many new counties as individual communities might elect. After he was brought to reason by the adoption of his brother's suggestion that minimum limitations of size, population, and wealth be imposed,[27] the convention, contrary to the usual practice of such assemblies, passed a specific act of legislation to please the Tillman brothers. A new county was created out of the Saluda River section of Edgefield.[28] While Ben was absent at the bedside of a sick daughter, George D. induced the convention, by vote of 76 to 64, to name it Butler County in honor of the Edgefield family of that name.[29] He paid tribute to former Senator Matthew C. Butler, expressing the fear that "it would be a long time before his equal in ability, eloquence and influence" would be a South Carolina senator, and asserting that Mart Gary had failed to have a monument erected in his honor because of "the suspicion of independentism." [30]

Ben, who wished the new county called Saluda, was angered when he read in the newspapers that his brother George had cast aspersions upon him and Gary in the interest of his rival in the 1894 canvass. Savagely he arose in the convention two days after George had spoken to demand that the name Saluda be substituted for Butler. "I am simply attempting," he stormed, "to prevent the convention from stultifying itself and sending the news abroad that the Reform constitutional convention of South Carolina has rebuked the legislature that retired Butler. . . .

[27] *Constitution of the State of South Carolina . . . 1895* (Columbia, 1904), Art. VII.
[28] *Ibid.*, Sec. 12.
[29] *Journal of the Constitutional Convention,* 95–96.
[30] Charleston *News and Courier,* September, 15, 1895.

This last representative has disgraced the name of Butler and made it a stench in the nostrils of every man of South Carolina."

He next launched into an odious comparison between Butler and Gary. He spoke of "an eagle too noble to win success by picking at flies," of a hero whose ambitions had been frustrated by Butler. "It is a sense of righteous indignation and wounded sentiment," he affirmed, "which called down the wrath of the people on Butler's head." He then reproached his brother for his disparaging remarks, and censured Irby, who had voted for Butler County, for accepting the inference that he as a senator from South Carolina was likewise inferior to Butler. Finally, he warned the Conservatives: "Those of you who have blundered into this movement take warning. If you give us the point of the sword, you will receive it back."

The reaction of the convention to this speech demonstrated the remarkable personal influence of Tillman. The Conservative delegates, with the exception of George himself, could not muster enough courage to reply. George dared reproach Ben for his unfairness and asked the delegates if they "were going to act like jumping jacks when the master pulls the cord in a Punch and Judy show." Irby, shaking his fist at Ben, said what he pleased. "I throw it back in your teeth," he cried, "that nothing M. C. Butler may do will ever disgrace the name of Butler in South Carolina. It will live when yours is dead and forgotten. . . . He was ignominiously defeated by you, sir, and you should have magnanimity enough to let this man [Butler] pass." But the convention, acting like George's jumping jacks, reversed its previous decision by vote of 80 to 54.[31]

Three days later Tillman gave another rude manifestation of his strength. The question was whether or not Gonzales should be censured for an editorial accusing President

---

[31] *Journal of the Constitutional Convention*, 112–14; the debate, in Charleston *News and Courier*, September 17, 1895.

Evans of misinterpreting the vote on the Saluda County issue. After Conservative lawyers had spoken in the editor's defense, Tillman demanded action. He said that the lawyers' arguments were "sophistical and intended to deceive" and that Gonzales "could be sued for libel or flayed with a stick." In a display of feeling which was violently unparliamentary, he asserted that the editor had "dished out more malice and hatred than any other man in the State except himself," and shaking his fists at the Conservatives, he warned them that he would "chunk them with rocks" if they allowed the insult to Evans to go unrebuked. Many of them took warning, for the resolution of censure was carried by vote of 123 to 23.[32]

Strengthened by such examples of supremacy, the director of the convention could devote himself to what he said was "the sole cause of our being here," namely, the writing of the franchise provision of the constitution. For several reasons this was a difficult task. To improve upon the existing methods of excluding Negroes from voting, the new provision must be free from the "fraud and intimidation" which Tillman admitted was a part "of the bog and mire that we have been wallowing in for the past twenty-five years." [33] The elimination of Negroes of all degrees of wealth and intelligence from the suffrage must be effected without breaking the pledge not to disfranchise 13,242 illiterate and mostly landless whites. A simple literacy test would have eliminated 58,086 Negroes and given the whites a voting majority of 11,758 without the necessity of "fraud and violence"; but it would have excluded the white illiterates and admitted 74,851 Negro literates. The exclusion of so many whites would probably have caused violence. "Our ballot box," said a friend of the uneducated whites, "would be saturated with blood." [34] The proposal

[32] *Journal of the Constitutional Convention*, 156–58; the debate, in Charleston *News and Courier*, September 20, 1895.
[33] Charleston *News and Courier*, October 31, 1895.
[34] Irby, *ibid.*, October 10, 1895.

of Robert Aldrich of Barnwell that Negroes be made ineligible for public office was rejected as obviously unconstitutional. It would make the delegates, commented Tillman, "the laughing stock of the country and write them down as a set of idiots." [35] A so-called "grandfather clause" was proposed by a group of Conservatives. It would have given the suffrage to those unable to qualify under a literacy or property test who had served in the Confederate or Union army or were descendants of such veterans. This was an obvious means of discriminating against blacks without the necessity of resorting to the "discretion" of election officials. Its proponents feared that the "discretionary clause" offered as an alternative would be used by Tillmanite officials against whites as well as blacks. But at Tillman's dictation the "grandfather clause" was defeated by vote of 117 to 20. He said that it was unconstitutional, a contention which was sustained by the highest court in 1915 in the case of a state which applied it. [36]

The plan considered as best fulfilling the requirements of the situation was presented by Tillman in his capacity as chairman of the convention's suffrage committee. The "consummate skill" with which it evaded direct violations of the Fifteenth Amendment [37] was due to John P. K. Bryan, the lawyer on the suffrage committee whose expert advice Tillman sought; but the essentials of the plan had been evolved months before by the crafty farmer-politician from Edgefield. In general it was like a provision of the Mississippi constitution of 1890. [38] It gave the suffrage to every male adult in South Carolina if he fulfilled the follow-

[35] The vote was 102 to 25. *Journal of the Constitutional Convention*, 270.

[36] It was presented by Henry C. Patton of Richland. *Ibid.*, 424–25, 429; Charleston *News and Courier*, March 15, October 30, 31, 1895. See Tillman's discussion of its constitutionality, in Columbia *State*, September 28, 1900. The Supreme Court decision is Guinn and Beal *v.* United States, 238 U.S. Reports 347.

[37] New York *Tribune*, cited in Charleston *News and Courier*, October 7, 1895.

[38] "Nothing else under high heaven would do except the Mississippi plan," Tillman had declared in July. *Ibid.*, July 28, 1895.

ing qualifications: he must have lived in the state for two years, the county for one year, and the voting precinct for four months; he must have paid his poll tax six months before election and must not have been guilty of any one of a specified list of crimes. Up to January 1, 1898, a man who fulfilled these requirements, and who could read any section of the constitution, or could "understand and explain it when read" to him, was to be a lifetime voter. After that date the person who fulfilled the aforementioned residence, tax, and court qualifications, and could read and write any section of the constitution submitted to him by the registration officer, or who had paid taxes the previous year on property assessed at $300, could become a voter. The board of registration in each county should be composed of "three discreet persons"; no provision was made for bipartisan management.[39]

It is not difficult to perceive how these elaborate regulations were designed to discriminate against the Negro. Among the disqualifying crimes were those to which he was especially prone: thievery, adultery, arson, wife-beating, housebreaking, and attempted rape. Such crimes as murder and fighting, to which the white man was as disposed as the Negro, were significantly omitted from the list. The rigid residence and poll tax provisions struck at the migratory and improvident habits of a poor race. Tillman, with a malicious smile, reminded the convention that its failure to provide minority representation on the registration boards was the reason why it was "twitted by Northerners with proposing to perpetuate trickery and fraud and strike down the free American voter." But a Conservative delegate, without understanding Tillman's irony, suggested that partisan administration was the keystone of the whole suffrage structure; that South Carolina need not be more honest than other states.[40] It was assumed that the "three

[39] *Constitution of the State of South Carolina . . . 1895*, Art. II.
[40] Debate, in Charleston *News and Courier*, November 9, 1895.

discreet persons" would apply the "understanding" and the "reading and writing tests" with "discretion" sufficient to exclude the great mass of Negro illiterates from the polls while allowing this privilege to the corresponding class of whites. In other words, a strong barrier was erected against universal suffrage, but that barrier had a gate and its key was given to friendly white men "who will know what is expected of them." [41] The law's notorious delay was regarded as a protection against the scheme's being declared unconstitutional. "It would go from court to court," declared its author, and by the time the United States Supreme Court acted the whole body of illiterate whites would have been registered.

This continuation of the chicanery practiced by the whites since Reconstruction was defended by its sponsor as a temporary expedient. "I only swallow enough of it," he declared, "to protect the ballot of the poor white men. Then I am for one ready to cast the poisoned chalice from my lips and afterwards put elections on a high plane." The elevation of the ballot was supposed to be secured by the literacy or property test applicable in 1896. The property alternative, the leader explained, "does not restrict one single ballot. . . . You simply reach out and take in a few more white and a few more colored men." He asserted that a reading test would not work unreasonable hardships, for an adequate school system would be provided for all self-respecting persons who came of age after 1897. But "the poisoned chalice" has been a significant part of the election law of South Carolina ever since Ben first quaffed of it. Delegate Henry C. Patton of Richland forced the Edgefield casuist into an admission from which there was no escape: that the reduction of Negro suffrage to a minimum without violating the pledge not to take this privilege from white men was impossible, within the necessary limits of the

[41] *Ibid.*, November 2, 1895.

Federal Constitution, unless there was "fraud and discrimination"—the old evils.[42]

Tillman vainly tried to extricate himself from this awkward position by a statement so filled with a conflicting mixture of frankness and hypocrisy that his hearers laughed. He said: "Some have said there is fraud in this understanding clause. Some poisons in small doses are very salutary and valuable medicines. If you put it in here that a man must understand, and you vest the right to judge whether he understands in an officer, it is a constitutional act. That officer is responsible to his conscience and his God, he is responsible to nobody else. There is no particle of fraud or illegality in it. It is just simply showing partiality, perhaps [laughter], or discriminating. Ah, you grin, [turning to Mr. Patton], you of all men to get up here and wrap your Pharisaical robes around you." [43]

Confronted with this flagrant attempt to eliminate their race from politics, four of the Negro delegates—Miller, Whipper, Smalls, and James Wigg—spoke against the impending calamity. It was a momentous occasion—the last time the rulers of South Carolina vouchsafed even hostile attention to pleas for the political rights of their submerged majority. The Negroes brought into play all weapons of debate; begging, arguing, and mildly threatening by turns. Flights of eloquence were interspersed with sallies of humor and sarcasm. Yet there was moderation; a return to the political supremacy of the black race was not asked, merely an impartial administration of an educational test which would give the more cultured race a substantial majority without depriving the literate portion of the colored race of a voice in the government. The proposal was defended by an appeal to the rights of man against those "who were striking at the very roots of universal liberty." The doctrine

42 See debate, *ibid.*, October 30, 31, 1895.
43 Tillman, in *Journal of the Constitutional Convention*, 469.

of the innate inferiority of the black man was repudiated, and his superiority to the Indian was affirmed. Indeed, the Negro was said to have been useful in establishing civilization in the American wilderness. "It was the brawny arm of the negro," said Whipper to his white auditors, "that has cared for you in your cradle, made your harvests, protected you in your homes, and yet this is the man you propose to rob of his right to vote."

The sordid aspects of Negro history were said to have been caused more by the white man than by the black. The whites, cried Whipper, were held by the chains of slavery and "the iron rust of these chains is still in the hearts of the white people." The mistakes of the dominant race were paraded. "It was your love of power and your arrogance," said Miller to the opposition, "which brought Reconstruction on you. Your hatred has been centered and the negro is the sufferer of your spleen." At one moment the constructive achievements of Reconstruction were extolled, while at the next the scandals of that period were said to be the work of white rascals not under Negro control. Attempts were made to ally the underprivileged whites with the blacks by asserting that the disfranchisement of the second group would affect the first group in the same manner. Tillman was reminded of the fact that, despite his boasted democracy, he had never received the endorsement of more than one fourth of the potential voters of both races.[44]

The speeches of the Negro delegates were heard with undisguised interest by attentive crowds. "What oppressed people," said a Darlington delegate, "ever sent a delegation who could surpass in ability the colored delegates from Beaufort?" [45] They presented, said the *News and Courier*, "the claims of the unfortunate people whom they represent

[44] Speeches of the Negro delegates, in Charleston *News and Courier*, October 27, 29, November 2, 1895; Mary J. Miller (ed.), *The Suffrage Speeches by Negroes in the Constitutional Convention* (n.p., n.d.), *passim*.
[45] Miller (ed.), *Suffrage Speeches by Negroes*, 3.

in part as strongly, as fully, and as eloquently as they could be presented." [46] Tillman himself admitted that Whipper was "the ablest colored man I ever met." So considerate was the convention of the feelings of the Negroes that it enjoyed the rebuke that one of them imposed upon an impolite white delegate.[47] But their arguments had no practical results. This was demonstrated when Whipper offered a simple property and educational test as a substitute for Tillman's intricate measure. He asked the supposedly more intelligent race to permit its superiority to be tested by standards other than mere color of the skin. A Conservative newspaper admitted that he had the better of the argument.[48] No logic, however, could prevail against deeply rooted prejudices of race, against what another Conservative newspaper called "an inexorable determination not to accede to his [Whipper's] plea, a determination born of stern necessity." [49] The six Negro delegates alone voted for the substitute.[50] Their prediction that the whites would have remorse of conscience because of this repudiation of democracy has not come true. White South Carolina has learned to regard Negro disfranchisement as complacently as a law of nature. Since 1895 no ear has even been given to arguments of the question.

Tillman, knowing that the words of the Negro delegates had been broadcast to the nation, wisely saw the need of a reply. He began with a portrayal of the horrors of the times when the Negroes voted freely. He retold the story of Reconstruction—"the hellish purpose" of "Thad. Stevens and his gang," the State House "filled with minions of Black Republicanism," the "eight years of misgovernment and robbery," and the aftermath in which "fraud and corrup-

---

[46] Charleston *News and Courier*, October 29, 1895.
[47] Koester, "Bleaseism," Chap. XXIV.
[48] Sumter *Watchman and Southron*, November 2, 1895.
[49] Columbia *State*, October 27, 1895.
[50] *Journal of the Constitutional Convention*, 412–13, 420–21; Charleston *News and Courier*, October 29, 1895.

tion" were exposed. During Reconstruction, according to the inflamed imagination of this interpreter, everyone went armed, "fearful of robbery," and "the sky was lit almost every night by the glare of burning dwellings and gin houses." In reply to the assertion that the Negroes were not responsible for these iniquities, he said, "The negroes put the little pieces of paper in the box that gave the commission to these white scoundrels who were their leaders." This connection between black voters and white corruption, he affirmed, "must be our justification, our vindication and our excuse to the world that we are met in Convention openly, boldly, without any pretense of secrecy . . . to so restrict the suffrage . . . that this infamy can never come about again."

Smalls and Whipper, the only survivors of the Reconstruction regime on the floor, were exposed as illustrations of the venality of Negro politicians. The attack upon their characters was so unparliamentary that it can be fully explained only as an example of the contempt a white South Carolinian had for the Negro in politics. Ben Tillman was never so ungenerously incriminating in his attacks upon white enemies. The two colored delegates, the speaker explained, by trying to prove that the blacks were not guilty of the crimes of Reconstruction, forced him to unearth proofs that they "perpetrated these damnable robberies." He proved that Smalls was involved in "printing steals," and that Whipper, after being absolved of one act of corruption, was guilty of financial irregularities as grotesque as they were sordid.[51]

Tillman had greater difficulty in overcoming opposition to his suffrage proposals among his own followers than among the Conservatives or the Negroes. The Tillmanite attack was led by Irby, who nursed a personal grievance as

[51] Tillman address, October 31, 1895, together with John C. Sheppard's and George D. Tillman's supplements and Robert Smalls's reply, in *Journal of the Constitutional Convention*, 443–81.

well as a principle. The personal grievance was Tillman's opposition to giving him a second term in the Senate. The principle was that there should be no restriction, educational or otherwise, upon the common white man's exercise of the suffrage.[52] But his position was hopeless. Sharing with Tillman the conviction that the main task of the convention was to reduce the Negro vote, he was unable to supplement his protest with a practical anti-Negro plan. "How do you propose," he was asked by the leader, "to get around the Chinese wall, the impassable bulwark which the Fifteenth Amendment throws around the negroes, except by an educational or property qualification?" The only answer was that things should be left as they were. This admission enabled Tillman to unite the whole body of white sentiment behind his plan to withstand the Negro peril. Irby was twice voted down when he protested against Tillman's "gag law," and when the Tillman suffrage measure came up for final vote there was nothing for him to do except to join the tide of approval.[53]

The principle of disfranchisement was extended to the school provisions of the new constitution. Tillman said he did not intend to erect an educational barrier to the Negro with one hand and tear it down with the other. So without too great violence to the American principle of universal education, he made possible educational discrimination against the blacks. Separate schools for the two races were continued; the local school officials were not required to apportion funds equally between the two systems; and no provision was made for compulsory education.[54] These provisions have made possible a steady decline in the proportion of funds given Negro schools—from about 29 per cent

[52] Charleston *News and Courier,* October 10, 1895.

[53] *Journal of the Constitutional Convention,* 440–41, 464–69; Charleston *News and Courier,* November 1, 2, 1895.

[54] Creelman, in New York *World,* cited in Charleston *News and Courier,* October 2, 1895; *Constitution of the State of South Carolina . . . 1895,* Art. XI, Sec. 5.

in 1899 to slightly over 10 per cent in 1920. Actual administration demonstrates, as Tillman intended, that the schools of South Carolina exist primarily for white children. Yet the generally progressive tendencies of the educational parts of the constitution have been of absolute benefit to the Negro schools. The principle of universal education has not been abandoned, and it is a fact that almost twice as much was spent for Negro education in 1920 as for all education in 1899.[55]

When it became known that the convention was going to give attention to the already existing statutory prohibition of interracial marriages, Smalls suggested a provision declaring that a white man guilty of cohabiting with a Negro woman be disqualified for officeholding and that the offspring of such a union take the name of the father and enjoy the right of inheritance. Tillman agreed with the Negro leader to the extent of wishing to make the offense a misdemeanor. He said that he sought to "protect negro women against the debauchery of white men degrading themselves to the level of black women." But neither proposal was adopted. The majority preferred a simple declaration against miscegenation.[56]

As a substitute for a simple proposal to penalize sheriffs from whom the victims of lynchings were taken, Tillman secured the passage of a measure providing for the removal on conviction of such officials and the penalization of counties in which lynchings occurred, on the judgment of a local court, to the extent in each case of not less than $2,000 in favor of relatives of the victim.[57] "If you want to stop lynching," said the erstwhile justifier of the deed, "we must prick the conscience of the taxpayer." It was indeed a clever idea to make the community as a whole responsible for a com-

[55] See reports of the state superintendent of education, in South Carolina *Reports and Resolutions*, 1920, *passim*.
[56] *Journal of the Constitutional Convention*, 319, 324; the debate, in Charleston *News and Courier*, October 4, November 23, 1895.
[57] *Constitution of the State of South Carolina . . . 1895*, Art. VI, Sec. 6.

munity crime. Perhaps this was the most hopeful legal remedy conceivable; its principle is the core of the Federal antilynching proposals of four decades later.[58]

The number of judgments, however, in consequence of the hundred-odd lynchings since 1895, have been few. It has been considered wise to appeal to the courts only when the victim of the mob has been guilty of no wanton crime. Perhaps lynching is a community custom for which there is no legislative remedy, and perhaps it is foolish to expect a South Carolina county to condemn through its courts what it actually approves.[59]

The various distinctions which the constitution drew between the two races necessitated a definition of a person of color. George Johnstone, voicing rising prejudices of race, argued that any degree of Negro blood sufficed to define a Negro. But the Tillman brothers were more realistic. "There are families now," said Ben, "who are received [socially by whites] that have negro blood." [60] George, after an academic discussion of the alleged scarcity of persons of pure Caucasian blood, said that if Johnstone's definition were adopted, "respectable families in Aiken, Barnwell, Colleton and Orangeburg would be denied the right to intermarry among the people with whom they are now associated." [61] The words of the Tillman brothers carried weight, for when Johnstone's proposal was returned from its committee, it defined a person of color as one "with one eighth or more negro blood." In this form it was adopted.[62]

Ben Tillman had his way concerning the recognition he wished given the Dispensary. The legislature was author-

[58] Charleston *News and Courier*, November 11, 12, 1895.

[59] Congressman Fred H. Dominick of South Carolina said in 1922 of this law: "I think possibly three actions have been brought in South Carolina since that time [1895] under that law. . . . That provision in the Constitution has no more to do in preventing it [lynching] than if it were not there." *Cong. Record*, 67 Cong., 2 Sess., 1345.

[60] Charleston *News and Courier*, October 4, 1895.

[61] *Ibid.*, October 17, 1895.

[62] *Journal of the Constitutional Convention*, 324–25.

ized to follow one of three courses: continue the state monopoly, establish Prohibition, or inaugurate a private dispensary monopoly like the original Gothenburg Plan. Tillman's first choice, of course, was the continuation of the Dispensary. But he feared an adverse United States Supreme Court decision and wanted to insure against barrooms. "We may have," he explained to James Creelman, "Prohibition, or we may have state dispensaries, or dispensaries in private hands, but there will never again be a regular barroom open in the State. That principle is as permanent as the fixed stars." [63]

Apart from race or alcohol, Tillman guided the convention in channels of wholesome progress. "We have come here," he said on that memorable day in November when he pushed his educational plans through the assembly, "to take a new departure. Are we to move forward, upward, onward?" He effected the raising of the general educational tax from two to three mills, to be distributed among the counties in proportion to enrollments. Poll tax and state Dispensary revenues also accrued to the schools. Higher education was not neglected; the South Carolina College and The Citadel were remembered as well as Winthrop and Clemson, and state subsidies to private colleges were prohibited. Estimating his educational achievements, the *News and Courier* said, "Tillman has shown a broad, liberal and genuine interest in the schools and colleges of the State." [64]

The proposal that South Carolina should abandon its unique position of not granting divorces, making adultery the one ground for such action, was defeated by the opposition of the religious and chivalric sentiments of the people. South Carolinians insisted that no divorce law was needed because their virtues were superior to those of any other

[63] New York *World*, cited in Charleston *News and Courier*, October 4, 1895.

[64] Educational debate, *ibid.*, November 15, 16, 19, 1895; votes in *Journal of the Constitutional Convention*, 560–65, 573.

people in the civilized world.[65] Even the influence of Tillman could not force the recognition of the divorce decrees of other states.[66]

The convention, after a session of twelve weeks, adjourned on December 4, 1895, with provision for the constitution to go into effect the following New Year's without a popular referendum. The document perpetuates some of the chronic evils of American state government. The executive powers are so divided that the governor is largely denied the power to execute the laws he is sworn to uphold. The judiciary is shackled by devices which delay the law and protect criminals, and the legislature is burdened by unreasonable restrictions and by the necessity of passing local legislation.[67] Nevertheless, the convention discharged its duties with reasonable intelligence. It had been united by the serious purpose of restricting the suffrage and bringing the fundamental law in line with the progress of the times. Its handiwork is about as good as the average state constitution. That the new document registered the desires of the ruling element of South Carolina is proved by the fact that it has not been rewritten in more than forty-five years. Tillman, for once, had won the admiration of the entire white population of the state.[68]

To what extent have the suffrage provisions of the constitution been successful? The main purpose of keeping the Negroes away from the polls has been most certainly accomplished. Since 1895 the colored vote has been negligible.[69] Negroes no longer sit in the legislature or in Congress, no longer contest the elections even of Beaufort. The election

[65] Creelman, in New York *World*, cited in Charleston *News and Courier*, October 4, 1895.

[66] This has since been done by the state supreme court. Debate on divorce, *ibid.*, October 1, 2, November 23, 1895. See also, *Journal of the Constitutional Convention*, 258.

[67] Wallace, *History of South Carolina*, III, 374.

[68] *Cf.* Barnwell *Sentinel*, cited in Charleston *News and Courier*, December 2, 1895.

[69] The Republican vote in 1896 was 9,313; in 1900 it was 3,579; in 1920 it was 1,646. Some of these votes were white.

officials have done with thoroughness the work Tillman
outlined for them. The constitution defined the attitude of
white South Carolina toward Negro suffrage. Yet this proc-
lamation did not change in any vital particular the political
status of the blacks. Legal subterfuges and the threat or
practice of force had kept them away from the polls before
1895. Since that time, though the terms have been altered,
many incidents testify that lawless force remains the ultimate arbiter of South Carolina color politics.[70]

Tillman's prediction that the additional suffrage restrictions were necessary because political rifts among the
whites and political restlessness among the blacks would
increase has not been substantiated by events. Since 1895
white minorities have been more submissive to the Democratic party than before that date, and the Negroes have
been forced to make political inactivity a habit. On the
other hand, Tillman's hope that two white political parties
protected from black pollution by an educational test
might animate and elevate South Carolina politics has not
been realized. This is largely true because of the maintenance of the Democratic primary as the real election and the
consequent making into a mere formality the general election operating under the constitution. The primary oper-
ates under extralegal rules of its own, of which the most
important is a radical application of the doctrine of white
supremacy. No Negro may vote; [71] all whites may do so:
illiterates, and in some cases paupers, criminals, and the
mentally weak. "Whiteness of skin," writes a patriotic historian cynical over the possibility of improvement, "suf-
fices to cover every blackness of character." [72]

[70] At Phoenix, Greenwood County, 1898, a political riot resulted in the
lynching of six Negroes. Charleston *News and Courier,* November 9–12,
1898. At Columbia in 1920 force was used against prospective Negro women
voters. William Pickens, "The Woman Voter Hits the Color Line," in
Nation, CXI (1920), 372–73.

[71] In 1938 the rule exempting from this proscription the few surviving
blacks who had voted for Hampton in 1876 was rescinded.

[72] Wallace, *History of South Carolina,* III, 371.

That the conditions are such is largely due to the influence of Tillman himself. He condoned the use of violence against the Negro's political activities,[73] and, as will be shown, it was not long before he was, in speeches which attracted national attention, glorifying force and an unfair application of the "understanding clause." Moreover, he learned to repudiate the dogma that two political parties are necessary for political health.

[73] Charleston *News and Courier,* November 14, 1898.

Chapter XXI

EMERGENCE OF A NATIONAL LEADER

BEN TILLMAN'S genius lay in the explosive energy with which he converted his convictions into actions. He was neither a profound nor an original thinker; his mental processes moved deliberately; the significance of social concepts impressed him slowly but with cumulative clarity. When his contemplations ultimately flowered into an idea, he clung to it with the tenacity of an obsession, wringing out of it every vestige of logical and emotional value. The reader of his many speeches and letters is fatigued by his wearing away of an idea until it was threadbare. But this overemphasis had its uses. It prevented that discursiveness fatal to effectiveness, impressing fundamentals upon the minds of even the most unsophisticated. Tillman pounded, he ejaculated, he mimicked, he exaggerated. Yet beneath the sound and the fury was a constructive principle, which gave a foundation of doctrine to the enthusiasms of his followers.

In his youth Tillman's one absorption was the achievement of a literary education. Then came preoccupation in the task of making a living out of his red lands. When this effort brought partial failure, he stormed and calculated and developed another absorption—agricultural education, an idea relentlessly carried forward to triumph. His next dominant interest was election to the governorship and the enactment of proclaimed policies. These objectives achieved, he looked around for new interests. They came in the form of the national problems of the 1890's, and for the first time in his life the South Carolinian allowed state issues to slip into the background.

The new idea was the least original of the several which had held the center of Tillman's attention. He merely imbibed the pro-silver and the anti-Cleveland doctrines current on a thousand Populist platforms. Such an uncritical acceptance of the oft-repeated teachings of others did not presage a future either as revolutionary or as initiatory as had been his South Carolina career. Much that he was going to say had been worn thin.

Yet in a certain sense his national career promised to be as successful as his state career had been. He brought to it the same willingness to concentrate upon the problem at hand. Having saved national issues for the time when he could do something about them, he attacked with almost dramatic suddenness, proving that he was more than an obtuse provincial.

His refusal to be concerned prematurely with nonstate issues is illustrated by his attitude toward Grover Cleveland. In 1892, when the New Yorker won the Presidential nomination, the South Carolinian submitted to his leadership. He tied the hands of the Farmers' Alliance directors who were toying with Populism and prevented South Carolinians from voting for the Populist candidate, saying that it was "simply infamous for any true Tillmanite" to violate pledges to the Democratic party.[1] But, though Tillman was not yet ready to risk complications which might endanger his local leadership, he had let it be known that he believed in free silver, a national income tax, the direct election of senators, and other measures of the agrarians. Moreover, he was not without a national reputation. Articles about him had appeared in the Northern press. Many of these were caricatures; but, when for once he made the front

[1] Tillman to John M. Norris, February 15, 1892, in Governor Tillman's Letter Books; *id.* to Augusta *Chronicle*, February 13, 1892, *ibid.; id.* to Asbury C. Latimer, September 1, 1892, *ibid.; id.* to William S. McAlister, September 8, 1892, *ibid.* See also, *id.,* in *Cong. Record,* 55 Cong., 1 Sess., 2123.

page, he was praised for his conduct in the Darlington disturbance.

So he was received expectantly when, at the Bimetallic convention in St. Louis in October, 1893, he made his first appearance before a national audience. He was presented as one who "played in time with the popular apprehensions of his section." He did not disappoint, stimulating a heretofore listless meeting to enthusiasm by uttering the convictions of a silverite in phrases that struck like shot. He was adjudged the very embodiment of the agrarian forces organizing to capture the Democratic party.[2]

Tillman, in the months before his canvass for the Senate, became possessed of just the passion he needed to motivate him in national politics. His personal hatred for Cleveland was born of the conviction that the New Yorker had entered into a corrupt bargain with the sugar refiners. He gave the following interpretation of a conference of Democratic leaders he had witnessed at party headquarters in 1893: "It was clearly brought out that the sugar refiners were ready to contribute to the Democratic campaign fund if it could be understood that the industry would be fostered and not destroyed by the Democratic tariff policy, and I received the impression which became indelibly fixed on my mind . . . that President Cleveland understood the situation and was willing to acquiesce in it."[3]

But distrust of Cleveland's morality was not the determining factor in Tillman's attitude toward him. The true explanation was the President's refusal to give him the Federal patronage to which he felt he was entitled as Democratic boss of his state. At first he listened for some intimation of the President-elect's favor. "My purpose," he wrote applicants for Federal office, "is to sign no man's application for any office until I know that the President will con-

[2] St. Louis *Republic* and "E.B.C.," in Charleston *News and Courier,* October 7, 8, 1893.

[3] Tillman, in *Cong. Record,* 59 Cong., 2 Sess., 2090.

sider it as adding strength. I intend to preserve my self-respect." [4] Actually, however, he sacrificed his self-respect to the extent of prodding Cleveland indirectly. He tried to get assurances from the President-elect through Irby and Congressman McLaurin. When this failed to bring results,[5] he tried to interview the President at the time of Cleveland's second inauguration, but he was forced to stand "out in the cold" because of the "jollification and glorification" incident upon the occasion.[6]

Ultimately, he broke his promise of no direct intervention. He wrote Cleveland a letter asking for the patronage. "If I can help you," he wrote four days after the inauguration, "in giving an absolutely unbiased opinion of the fitness and character of applicants I will do so and will eschew personal and political prejudice in answering your inquiries." Although he named no persons for whom he wanted office, he begged the President to give no favors to Gonzales and Hemphill, whom the South Carolina boss described as "personally obnoxious to me by reason of their malignant and outrageous assaults upon my personal and political character." [7] Naturally Cleveland did not seek "the unbiased opinion" of one who could not rightly claim lack of bias among his virtues. He made the Tillman letter public without answering it, and he showed where his sympathies lay by giving appointments to the friends of the hated editors. Tillman, outraged, felt there would be a reaction in his favor. "I would want nothing better to club Butler with and to keep our men all in line," he wrote Irby, "than to be able to show that he [Cleveland] has joined Hemphill and Gonzales in the charge that we are not Democrats." [8]

[4] Id. to John G. Motley, January 21, 1893, in Governor Tillman's Letter Books; id. to S. E. Holley, January 17, 1893, ibid.; id. to S. S. Crittenden, February 25, 1893, ibid.
[5] Id. to McLaurin, January 27, 1893, ibid.
[6] Cong. Record, 54 Cong., 1 Sess., 1075.
[7] Tillman to Grover Cleveland, March 8, 1893, in Governor Tillman's Letter Books.   [8] Id. to Irby, April 1, 1893, ibid.

Tillman resolved to submit no longer to the Cleveland control of the Democratic party. His hope, of course, was that the anti-Cleveland element within that organization could dominate in 1896 and thereby obviate the necessity of having to decide between disloyalty to party and loyalty to Cleveland. An idea took shape in his mind. The agricultural West and the agricultural South should combine against the industrial and commercial East. This was characteristic Tillman strategy: the setting of the rural classes against the less numerous industrial and commercial classes.

The idea gradually evolved. Through letters and personal urgings, the South Carolinian tried to organize the South and the West against the coalition which he said existed between the Cleveland Democrats and the conservative Republicans.[9] Conventions of silver advocates, he proposed, should meet simultaneously in January, 1894, at Atlanta and Omaha or Topeka. Close co-operation should be established between the two bodies without actual union. He believed that such an agrarian coalition might win the Presidency from the two old parties. "It is another Farmers' Movement on a national scale," commented its promoter exultantly.[10]

The plan for the silver conventions did not materialize. Tillman was preoccupied with South Carolina affairs and was made cautious by the possible perils of deserting the traditional party. He was soon writing a friend: "Our people love the name of Democracy and will not change it lightly or easily." [11] Perhaps it was best, he added, to sit steadfast in the Democratic boat so that Cleveland might the more readily be pushed out of it. He believed that this might be hastened if bolting Democrats returned to the

9 *Id.* to M. E. Crosham, October 31, 1893, *ibid.*

10 *Id.* to Irby, October 26, 1893, *ibid. Cf. id.* to A. C. Fisk, October 23, 1893, *ibid.*

11 *Id.* to Harry Skinner, May 4, 1894, *ibid.*

traditional allegiance.[12] He urged Irby to strike the President: " 'Cry havoc and let slip the dogs of war,' and plant your dagger as close to his vitals as you know how. He is a public enemy oblivious of the rights and interests of the people south of the Potomac and west of the Mississippi and we can better afford to do without any tariff legislation than to allow him to consummate the corrupt bargains said to exist." [13]

In this frame of mind the South Carolinian began his 1894 canvass for the Senate. He had found the enemy, and he struck with the full force of his brutal rhetoric. The public was amazed by the savage irreverence with which a Democratic state boss attacked the only Democratic President since the Civil War. At the first meeting of the canvass Tillman called the corpulent Cleveland "that old bag of beef." [14] In Marlboro the President was declared to be "either dishonest or the most damnable traitor ever known." [15] At Winnsboro the speaker said that he would give $5,000 to be able to go to the Senate so that he could "tell the old scoundrel in the White House what I think of him." The campaign of denunciation culminated at Lexington on July 20. "When Judas betrayed Christ," Tillman told his applauding followers, "his heart was not blacker than this scoundrel, Cleveland, in deceiving the Democracy. . . . He is an old bag of beef and I am going to Washington with a pitchfork and prod him in his old fat ribs." [16]

[12] *Id.* to Marion Butler, May 8, 1894, *ibid.; id.* to Thomas Gaines, May 7, 1894, *ibid.*

[13] *Id.* to Irby, July 22, 1894, *ibid.*

[14] Charleston *News and Courier*, July 19, 1894.

[15] *Ibid.*, June 28, 1894.

[16] A combination of words, cited *ibid.*, July 23, 1894; Philadelphia *Press, ibid.*, September 21, 1894. Tillman had used the somewhat obvious imagery of the pitchfork as early as his speech at Marion, November 5, 1887: "If these gentlemen [the lawyers] desire that I shall give them the handle of the pitchfork, let them turn their peaceful end to me. If they come at me as they have been coming, if they continue to misrepresent me as they

The symbolism of the pitchfork adopted by the farmer-politician was apt. To his agrarian disciples he was a simple but brave farmer using a favorite tool to attack the vipers that infested the road of civic advance; to his urban enemies he was wielding the favorite weapon of the devil to impale honest statesmen. Whichever interpretation is adopted, Tillman spoke the truth when he pictured himself as the brandisher of the Pitchfork. The press was quick to call him Pitchfork Ben or Pitchfork Tillman, and soon the cartoonists were representing him as holding the famous tool. His friends took up the idea. They presented him with silver or gilt pitchforks, and miniature ones appeared on coat lapels. Thereafter the sobriquet of Pitchfork was always associated with his name.[17]

In the interval between election to the Senate and assuming his seat, Tillman found time for national affairs. He warned Western leaders that "the country is not yet ready to sink to the servitude of money. Ballots or bullets will bring relief."[18] Before a bimetallic convention at Memphis he urged the union of the South and the West with "a one plank platform demanding the free coinage of silver at sixteen to one."[19] At the Atlanta Exposition he proclaimed the new sectionalism in answer to the nationalist platitudes of Cleveland and others. Concerning his enemies among Southern business interests he uttered the

---

have been doing, I shall give them the pitchfork end every time." Davis Scrapbooks. United States Senator James F. Byrnes, who for many years was intimately acquainted with Tillman, gives the following version of the term: "He told the story of a farmer with a pitchfork in his hand walking by the side of a wagon loaded with hay. As he passed a neighbor's place a savage-looking bulldog attacked him and, just in the nick of time, the farmer stuck him with the pitchfork. The owner of the dog yelled, 'Why didn't you use the other end?' To which the farmer replied, 'Why didn't your dog use the other end?' The illustration delighted the farmers." *Cong. Record*, 76 Cong., 3 Sess., 8397.

[17] Tillman, in Washington *Post*, cited in Spartanburg *Herald*, November 22, 1906.

[18] *Id.* to Thomas F. Bryan, cited in Charleston *News and Courier*, January 24, 1895.

[19] *Ibid.*, June 22, 25, 1895.

following: "There are some so infatuated that they think
that all the financial wisdom of the country is monopolized
by the East, and they say 'Me too' everytime the New York
World speaks or Grover Cleveland grunts." [20]

His activities won the hostile interest of the American
press. A Buffalo newspaper said, "Tillman is ignorant and
uncouth, his language is vulgar and profane, and his head
is full of dangerous and visionary ideas regarding the function of government." [21] The Springfield *Republican* said
that his election to the Senate was "an awful come-down for
South Carolina"; Colonel Henry Watterson, the famous
Louisville editor, spoke of his Memphis utterances as "the
silly braggadocio" of a demagogue; and the directors of
the Atlanta Exposition said that his Atlanta speech was
"devoid of reason, sense and patriotism." [22]

Despite its derogatory tone, the press did not attempt to
minimize the importance of the new senator from South
Carolina. He was called the great harsh voice of the dissatisfied portion of the nation; the New York *Press* said that he
expressed the sentiments of "the masses of the people of
South Carolina far more faithfully than did the Bourbon
politician Butler"; and the Washington *Post* affirmed that,
despite his "crankiness and eccentricity," he was "nobody's
fool." [23] Tillman, knowing from experience that the opposition of the newspapers was not without advantages,
contemplated the great audiences allowed him through
their columns and was conscious of substantial, even enthusiastic, sympathy. On the reception the Atlanta audience
gave him and Governor Evans, he commented: "It did my
heart good to hear the Governor of Georgia say that two
crank Reformers from South Carolina had evoked more
applause than the President of the United States." [24]

[20] *Ibid.*, November 29, 30, 1895.
[21] Buffalo *Enquirer*, cited *ibid.*, September 28, 1894.
[22] These and other comments, cited *ibid.*, December 22, 1894; December
6, 1895.
[23] Cited *ibid.*, December 22, 1894.   [24] Cited *ibid.*, November 29, 1895.

Tillman, on taking his seat in the Senate, joined the Democratic caucus, resented being called a Populist, and inaugurated his legislative career by the conventional act of attempting to extract $15,000 from the Treasury for damages done Newberry College during the Civil War.[25] Some predicted that his ambitions had been satisfied by election to high office and that he would become a party hack. "He has discovered," said a close observer, "that there is a sort of freemasonry among the leading members of the Senate, and that unless the new member is taken in the fold and taught the signs he is like the poor boy at the fair." [26] But the new senator was not taken in the fold; he was not satisfied; he chafed under the restraints of the Senate rules and prepared "to kick over the traces." He formulated a bold speech designed to attract national attention. Although tradition frowned on long speeches by novices, the gentleman from South Carolina made his maiden effort on January 29, 1896, less than two months after his arrival in Washington.

There was an air of expectancy when the new senator arose ostensibly to speak in favor of a free coinage of silver substitute for a House bill. Only one or two senators were absent; the members of the House crowded around the walls; and the galleries were thronged with those eager to catch the first words of a picturesque new figure. The speaker was heralded as a demagogue, a man of unbridled tongue, an advocate of dangerous economic principles. He was said to be a mixture of a circus clown and boisterous incendiary.

Those who expected that he would turn the occasion into an effort to conciliate his Senate colleagues did not know the man. Sensing the unsympathetic atmosphere, he reacted as he had often done under similar circumstances in South Carolina. Opposition always incited him to audacity; nor could the rules of the Senate restrain him. His delivery and

[25] *Ibid.*, December 3, 4, 21, 1895.   [26] *Ibid.*, January 21, 1896.

his words were those that had brought him success on a hundred rural stumps. The only evidence of change was in the superficial matter of dress. In place of the farmer's garb he wore a standing collar and a fashionable Prince Albert coat with trousers to match.

His manner of speech startled the audience. His stern face pale with excitement, Tillman rose from his seat, threw his head back, lifted his lips in mocking sneers, flung his hands in the violent manner peculiar to this left-handed man. At the same time he wheeled furiously in a circle, facing the galleries more often than he did the presiding officer; and for two hours loosed a fire of virulent rhetoric that blazed into a riot of emotion. The strident tones reverberated in the narrow Senate chamber. They echoed through the corridors of the Capitol, attracting additional auditors.

The speaker's introductory remarks enhanced the startling effects of his peculiar elocution. He told his hearers what to expect. His forensic experiences, he explained, had been "out in the open air under the trees, before the common masses of the country, where men are allowed, if they feel disposed, to applaud . . . the orator." He described the difficulties of a farmer conforming to the decorum of the Senate. But instead of attempting the adjustment, Farmer Ben, with characteristic humor, tossed "Senatorial dignity" on the prongs of his pitchfork. He sneered at the set essays with which the solons were supposed to be edified; he sneered at the monotony with which these essays were read; at the empty chairs to which they were addressed; at the "Senatorial stare" designed to "Gorgonize" speakers; at the party discipline which prevented freedom of expression. "How much of this so-called Senatorial dignity . . . ," he cried, "is worthy of preservation? It hangs over this Chamber like a wet blanket; it smothers down independent action; it obliterates the man, and we are here the puppets, the cogs in the wheel of party, to do the bidding of the manipulators of the party machines." He called the people in the galleries "muzzled automatons" because they were not supposed to applaud, and while the gavel tapped for order when one of his sallies provoked a violation of this rule, he shouted derisively, "if you will just let me down into the bog and quagmire of Senatorial dignity gently—of nobody saying anything while I speak—I will get used to it after a while."

The egotist boasted of his unique position. He was "the only farmer, pure and simple," among the ninety senators and therefore on him rested the responsibility "of giving utterance to the sense of wrong" of that half of the American people who were farmers. "I speak plainly and bluntly," he affirmed, "and use Anglo-Saxon, the vernacular, the language of the common people; for I am one of them and I expect to tell you how they feel, and what they think, and what they want." Free silver, he admitted, was "old straw," but he would discuss it in his own way. "It has been thrashed, sir, by lawyers; it has been thrashed by railroad magnates; it has been thrashed by the president of this corporation and the attorney of that corporation. It has not been handled on the pitchfork of a farmer. . . . Farmers use a pitchfork in handling straw. . . . They also use pitchforks to handle manure, and perhaps I shall find some of that in my pathway before I get through."

The body of the address was merely a hackneyed restatement of silverite criticisms of the financial policies of the Cleveland administration. But, as was promised, "the old straw" was pitched on the now famous Tillman Pitchfork with unique energy. The Cleveland policy was "more bonds, no increase of revenue, . . . contraction, lower prices, harder times" for the purpose of sinking "deeper in the bog of pauperism and poverty the sweating, toiling masses, the farmers and other laborers." Those who wished to maintain the gold standard were "insatiate cormorants, the shylocks" whose "damnable scheme of robbery" was to give corporations a monopoly on the issuance of money so that the burden of paying the interest on the public debt would rest heavily on the masses. The drop of the price of silver below the ratio of sixteen to one was not due to economic law but to the machinations of the monometalists. The country was "atrophied, palsied in its extremities" for want of a plentiful supply of money, and yet Cleveland was callous to this need. The fall in prices caused "disaster and ruin" among the farmers and made it impossible for them to discharge debts. The remedy proposed was familiar: free coinage of silver at sixteen to one and liberal issuance of greenbacks.

Once more the South Carolinian urged the union of the agricultural sections to fight uncompromisingly the battle of free silver. "Self-preservation and patriotism," he adjured, "should bind the South and West in equally strong bonds of union. We can not afford to longer put party above country." Then he expressed happiness over the union he believed was forming. "We of the South," he said to the Westerners, ". . . are glad to find that west of the Mississippi the 'galled jade winces,' and that the collar of servitude which has been fastened around our necks . . . is beginning to make your shoulders raw."

Interest languished as the speaker repeated the formal arguments of the silver advocates. But his auditors were astounded when, departing from set notes, he indulged in his favorite devices of personal abuse and sinister interpretation of motives. The victim was Cleveland. Never in the memory of living newspaper reporters was the President of the United States attacked so systematically and so violently on the Senate floor.

The first charge was that the President had conspired with "the gold ring of New York" to secure his nomination in 1892. These financiers had spent money lavishly at the national convention, keeping "up such a noise . . . that one would have thought that pandemonium had broken

loose and all the demons of hell had collected in one group
to shout for 'Grover.' " The platform of the party had been
"cunningly drafted" so as to afford "an excuse to the elastic
conscience of the bull-headed and self-idolatrous man who
holds the reins of power" to further a gold policy. The
President had contradicted his published pledges, betrayed
his party, and effected its disunion and defeat.

Major accusations were that Cleveland paid out gold instead of silver when there was a demand for the redemption
of United States notes, and issued bonds to buy more gold
when the Treasury's supply of that metal approached de-
pletion. Both acts, said Tillman, were the unlawful behavior of a "besotted tyrant" heedless of the interests of
anyone except his moneyed friends. "This arrogant and
obstinate ruler" had issued bonds "secretly, with his law
partner as a witness to the contract," and thereby had
created "suspicion in the minds of millions of his country-
men that a President of the United States can use his high
office for private gain." Cleveland, the South Carolinian
concluded, "will go down in history as the most gigantic
failure of any man who ever occupied the White House, all
because of his vanity and obstinacy."

In a dramatic peroration the senator described the doom
he felt would overtake the country if the wrongs done by
Cleveland were not righted. The money-changers had been
able to impose a sad plight upon the laboring classes. The
working classes were "working out a hopeless existence of
toil year in and year out, the women 'stitching in poverty,
hunger and dirt,' . . . the men bearing their hopeless
burdens of debt." Among the industrial workers there
were "millions now on the march, and they tramp, tramp,
tramp; tramp the sidewalks hunting work and tramp the
highways begging bread." The country could not be saved
from "the miseries of revolution and internecine strife"
unless citizens should desert party and organize to restore
the Republic of the Founding Fathers. A menacing paral-

lel was drawn between 1861 and 1896. In the earlier year the land was drenched with blood to emancipate four million blacks; in the latter year "ten times that many white slaves" were having the collar of industrial servitude put around their necks. If they could not get liberty by the ballot, they should try bullets. A new Mason and Dixon's line "will sooner or later bring together . . . the toiling and now downtrodden masses" of the city and country; "agrarianism and communism will join hands." The industrial workers might "some day take a notion to tramp to Washington with rifles in their hands," while the farmers "will lift no hand to stay the march, but join it." [27]

The Senate reacted most unfavorably to the speech. Not a member dignified it by endorsement or answer. Only two, William M. Stewart, the Nevada silverite, and James H. Kyle, the South Dakota Populist, bestowed the congratulations usually given a major effort. There was talk of expunging the harangue from the *Congressional Record,* but the idea was not pushed for fear of martyrizing the speaker. The friends of the President were outraged, and such protagonists of parliamentary decorum as Justin S. Morrill of Vermont and George F. Hoar of Massachusetts felt wounded that public manners had decayed to the extent of enabling the senator of a conservative state to speak as Tillman had done.

The press of the country denounced the South Carolinian in language as unrestrained as his own. The New York *Times* called him "a filthy baboon, accidentally seated in the Senate chamber"; the Springfield *Republican* termed him "a slang-whanging buffoon and demagogue"; and the Philadelphia *Record* said he was a Jack Cade determined to start a bloody slaughter. The last-mentioned journal cited his presence in the Senate as South Carolina's

[27] Text of speech, *Cong. Record,* 54 Cong., 1 Sess., 1072–80; atmosphere is elaborately described in Charleston *News and Courier,* January 30, 31, February 1, 1896; New York *Tribune,* New York *Herald,* and Philadelphia *Record,* cited *ibid.,* February 6, 9, 1896.

expiation for the sins of aristocracy and slavery; from him oozed the "ignorance, intolerance and violence of the State's mean white trash" suffering from previous oppression and the low price of cotton.[28] More philosophical editors saw in the "diatribe" of this "spokesman of the new and degenerate South" cause for "melancholy reflection" on the decadence of a once august legislative assembly. Tillman's "outbreak of blackguardism and incendiarism" demonstrated that "in the lowest deep" into which others had degraded the Senate there was still "a lower deep . . . left to be touched." [29]

Despite the severity of these judgments, Tillman had reasons to be satisfied with his bold bid for national fame. For some time his speech was "the chief topic of both Houses." [30] The offense of some senators was more simulated than real; their enmity for the President was great enough for them secretly to enjoy the strictures. They sent thousands of copies of the speech to their constituents.[31] If cultured people reacted unfavorably, the vivid exposure of what the press was pleased to call his vices made Tillman the hero of "the common people," and his desk was piled high with letters of commendation.[32] He had demonstrated what the Washington correspondent of the London *Times* called "his Jacobin genius." [33] By a single speech he had aroused more interest than all the agitations of "Sockless Jerry" Simpson, William A. Peffer, Kyle, and the other contemporary agrarians.[34]

The hostility of the press caused Tillman no heartache. He carefully collected the clippings, knowing that the bitter

[28] Cited in Charleston *News and Courier*, February 1, 5, 9, 1896.

[29] *Nation*, LXII (1896), 110.

[30] New York *Herald*, cited in Charleston *News and Courier*, February 6, 1896.

[31] *Ibid.*, January 30, 1896; Galveston *News*, cited *ibid.*, February 16, 1896.

[32] R. M. Larner, *ibid.*, February 11, 1896.

[33] London *Times*, January 30, 1896.

[34] New York *Tribune*, cited in Charleston *News and Courier*, February 6, 1896.

mouthings of the journalists were the substance on which he had often fed.[35] Then he struck back at "the hireling editors and reporters who now degrade the so-called freedom of the press to so despicable a level." He wrote that he had ample compensation for their abuse in "thousands of letters" in which the people informed him "that truth, bravely told, had a sweet and wholesome sound." [36]

Paradoxically enough, the prestige Tillman won from his speech of January 29 was due partly to the essential moderation of his views. The newspapers had mistaken lurid language for radicalism. Actually he advocated only one measure which could be defined as radical. This was the free coinage of silver, the minimum demand of the agrarians. He did not favor a third party; he ignored many of the reforms demanded by the Populists; his bid for Western support did not violate Southern prejudices. The President, in his opinion, was corrupt because he had abandoned the sound principles of the Democratic party to woo Republican heresies. The peroration was an admonition not to revolution but to a return to the agrarian idyl of the Early Republic. Indeed, the orator kept close to native shores. His long career as the boss of a conservative commonwealth differentiated him from the Utopian theorists who in many states led the agrarian revolt. He was prudent to the point of unoriginality.

To illustrate his notion of the struggle of the agrarian South and West against the Eastern "money power," Tillman directed the drawing of the famous allegorical cows which appeared as cartoons in the New York *World*. An enormous cow was shown bestriding the United States; her maw was in the West being fed by the products of the agricultural states; her udder was over Manhattan Island being drained of its substance by the men of Wall Street. Congress, so the second cartoon undertook to illustrate,

[35] Larner, *ibid.*, January 31, 1896.
[36] Tillman to New York *World*, February 14, 17, 1896.

through the enactment of a Federal income tax, had turned the cow around, putting her mouth over Wall Street and her udder over the West. But the Supreme Court had declared the income tax unconstitutional. This was symbolized by a third cartoon in which the judges were grabbing the cow by the throat to prevent her from eating while the farmers tugged away at the empty udder. The question asked was, How long will the farmers submit to this cruel appropriation of their resources? [37]

Fortified by a speaking tour of the West on which he observed the "hatred and anger" of the people for the "bond-holding, bloodsucking East," [38] Tillman, on May 1, delivered his second speech in the Senate. His broad objective was to "discuss the general conditions and the diseases at work in this country." His specific purpose was to answer Senator David B. Hill's defense of the financial policies of the Cleveland administration. He merely repeated the substance of his earlier effort, not because of lack of enterprise, but rather because Tillman knew that the best way to win the general public is to express again and again a few simple ideas. That Hill, the quick-witted representative of New York capital, deigned to have words with the farmer-senator was recognition of Tillman as an equal, which gave him opportunity to exercise his peculiar talent for running debate.

The maledictions of the farmer fell upon Hill and the great city he represented. The New Yorker was accused of being the senator of "the bondholders, the bankers of New York City, and nobody else." The people of that city through the stock-speculating agencies were said to "gamble in the products of the labor of this country, based on nothing, and when the laborers and farmers . . . ask to have this stopped by law the attorneys of corporations, the bond-

[37] For interview and cartoons as reprinted in 1913 from New York *World*, March 1, 1896, see *Cong. Record*, 60 Cong., 1 Sess., 5382–85.
[38] Charleston *News and Courier*, May 7, 1896.

holders, the bankers, and the money sharks of New York have more influence here than 35,000,000 of us." When Hill reminded the speaker that all New Yorkers were not millionaire speculators, Tillman in accepting the correction said: "You have more white slaves in sight of the Statue of Liberty, or within 10 miles of it, than are to be found in any other area on the American continent."

The possible consequences of the injustices imposed upon the agricultural half of the people were described in menacing terms. "If you force the people to bloodshed," cried the South Carolinian to the New Yorker, "let the blood be on your hands, not on mine. . . . I tell you we are desperate . . . and before we starve we will make somebody else desperate. . . . There is to-day more hatred and anger in the hearts of the people of west of the Mississippi for . . . the bloodsucking East than ever they had for the South."

Hill's charge that he was a Populist led Tillman to declare himself concerning the approaching canvass of 1896. He denied the charge of Populism, identifying himself as a Democrat of the school of Jefferson and Jackson who was going to his party's convention to call it "out of the woods of" Republican rottenness. But if "the New York boodlers" secured enough delegates to endorse Cleveland and sound money, Tillman said, "I will take my hat and bid the Senator from New York and all the Democrats like him a long farewell." He did not explain precisely what would be the nature of the "long farewell," merely talking vaguely about "a new party." [39]

When Congress adjourned in the spring of 1896, Tillman was ready to contend for control of the Democratic National Convention. His two speeches had caused cold shudders down the backs of conservatives, but had riveted the admiration of millions upon him. Through constant reiteration he had made perfectly clear his faith in the

[39] *Cong. Record*, 54 Cong., 1 Sess., 4657-72.

liberal monetary policies of his agrarian associates and his aversion for Cleveland, the villain of the piece. Although, as Hill and other thoughtful conservatives proved, his program of a few financial reforms was too simple a remedy for great evils, this program had its uses. It was arrayed in enough inflammatory rhetoric to startle without disturbing too greatly the fundamentally conservative instincts of the multitude.

Without doubt Tillman could induce South Carolina to remain faithful to his program and person. In reply to one of Hill's taunts he had boastfully but truthfully said, "I know I represent a State, and I represent it so thoroughly and so fully that I can . . . claim to give its voice and say where its vote is going." [40] Of course, he was likely to play an important part in the national convention, but it was extremely doubtful that he could control that body. Probably the wielder of the Pitchfork could not accustom his rough hands to the rapier of diplomacy. Moreover, he was too shrewd an analyst to think that the representative of a traditionally poor and unpopular commonwealth had much chance of capturing control of a great organization aspiring to the confidence of the nation.

[40] *Ibid.*, 4659.

Chapter XXII

1896

A RENEWED demonstration of Tillman's strength in South Carolina augmented his prestige prior to the national convention. His objectives were to control the May convention of the state party; to secure a sympathetic governor and legislature; and to designate a senatorial colleague to replace Irby. The Dispensary was the chief local issue.

Why Tillman turned on Irby is not difficult to explain. The young senator's conduct in Washington had been thoroughly disreputable. Spending much of his time in drunken pleasures, he had not even discharged perfunctory duties. Out of the 795 roll calls while he was in office, he had voted on only 240; he had made only two short speeches and had failed to push the few measures he introduced. An editor was not exaggerating when he wrote: "This is the worst record that can be found against any sound, healthy man who ever sat in the Senate of the United States." [1]

Such criticism naturally made Irby sensitive and contentious. He engaged in a bitter controversy with Shell and Farley of the Laurens coterie of Tillmanites. Because Tillman refused to participate in this difficulty, Irby became unreasonably suspicious of the loyalty of the man whose political fortunes he had helped make. He listened to the gossip of enemies, and engaged in the expensive luxury of talking freely about disagreements with his chief.

---

[1] Yorkville *Yeoman*, cited in Charleston *News and Courier*, August 30, 1897. See compilation of Irby's record, made in 1906, from the *Senate Journals* and *Cong. Record*, in Tillman Papers.

Tillman was exceptionally patient with the wayward senator. He loved the magnetic young man like a brother and appreciated his effectiveness as a political organizer. But he believed that his first duty was to himself and to his state, not to a besotted friend. He gave the derelict full and sound advice, outlined a program of rehabilitation, and warned against the delusion that Irby could dictate policies to him. "If our political and personal friendship is broken," Tillman wrote, "you alone will be the blame. While lacking in power of combination which you possess, I have managed very .well thus far. . . . You may divide our forces, but I cannot surrender my independence and individuality even to you. My strength lies with the people, yours with the politicians; together we are invincible; apart I may hold my grip, you cannot." [2]

By 1895 Irby was too far gone along the road of self-destruction to mend his ways. In that year he and Tillman publicly parted company, and it was clear to observers that Tillman wanted another Senate colleague. He accepted Irby's charge of ingratitude and bad manners with composure, believing that the people would confirm his opinion that Irby was not worthy of re-election.

Tillman's choice of John Gary Evans as Irby's successor was justified from the leader's viewpoint. The young governor had proved a competent tool and an aggressive advocate of the Tillman dogmas.[3] He subordinated gentlemanly inclinations to his chief's stern resolve to maintain the Dispensary against all odds.[4] His efficient if moderate enforcement of the controverted liquor law rendered him, with

[2] The story of the Tillman-Irby relations is fully told in Tillman to Irby, December 5, 1891; July 21, 1892; August 2, 1893; February 13, July 15, 1894, in Governor Tillman's Letter Books; id. to Shaw, December 9, 1892; July 29, 1894, ibid.

[3] His views in South Carolina House Journal, 1894, pp. 127–39; New York Tribune, cited in Charleston News and Courier, December 28, 1894.

[4] See the comparison between Evans and Tillman views, in Charleston News and Courier, February 11, 1896.

the possible exception of Tillman, the most hated man in the state.[5] The leader wished to reward a loyal servant who had suffered in his behalf.

In the first skirmish with Irby, Tillman won easily. The former asked the Democratic Executive Committee to declare no one eligible for membership in the state party unless he would abide by all the decisions of the national party. But Tillman, working behind the scenes, carried his point that the matter be decided at the approaching state convention.[6]

The state convention was as completely dominated by Tillman as any similar body had ever been. As in the past, he brought the platform to Columbia "in his pocket" and read it with "that peculiar force and impressiveness" of which he was capable. It authorized the South Carolina delegates to the national convention to withdraw from that body if they did not approve its action, in order to await additional instructions from the state convention. This was a clever subterfuge designed to evade the issue of bolting. Irby countered with resolutions demanding unconditional obedience to the national party. In an impassioned harangue he accused Tillman of being a bolter and of attempting to use the South Carolina party for the promotion of his Presidential ambitions. Tillman replied, "There is no obligation, moral or otherwise, to stand by a party that does not adhere to principles." Toward Irby he was pointedly personal: "We have had the man who has been honored a great deal more than he had honored himself twit you with not representing anyone. Great God! You sunburned delegates, who represent the bone and sinews of the country, said not to represent anybody!" The Irby resolutions were voted down by 253 to 67, and he was re-

[5] Ball, *State that Forgot*, 240; Kirkland, "Tillman and I," in Columbia *State*, July 21, 1929; Tillman to Martin, October 25, 1893, in Governor Tillman's Letter Books.

[6] Charleston *News and Courier*, April 7, 8, 9, 1896.

moved as state chairman of the party. Tillman headed a delegation sent to Chicago with instructions to vote for its leader.[7]

A sequel to Tillman's victory was the inglorious ending of Irby's senatorial candidacy. The people followed the suggestion to discard a man whom they had honored more than he had honored himself.[8] "My motives and my official acts for the past year," this harassed man confessed, "have been misunderstood by the faction of which I was a charter member. . . . The entire machinery of the party government has been organized to humiliate, defeat and destroy me." With this explanation he withdrew from the Senate contest.[9]

On the way to the Chicago convention, Tillman added to his national importance by repeating in a dozen states what he had said in the Senate. Declaring his intention to bolt the party if it did not adopt his favorite idea, he shouted: "If the Democratic party doesn't adopt free silver, it ought to die, and I have a knife with which I'll cut its throat." [10] He did not, however, in these addresses attempt to push the Presidential candidacy which the South Carolina convention had sought to confer upon him, asserting that the platform should be above personalities.

The Tillman candidacy in truth did not develop the popularity for which his South Carolina friends hoped. The Carolinian's uncouth appearance, his abuse of Cleveland, and his rehearsing of silver doctrines in their crudest form, excited much applause but failed to inspire the confidence demanded of an aspirant for the highest American office.[11]

[7] Kohn, *ibid.*, May 21, 1896.   [8] *Ibid.*, June 5, 1896.

[9] *Ibid.*, June 18, 1896. There were also personal reasons not directly mentioned in the newspapers. It was rumored that Irby was involved in a scandal. "There is evidently something hidden under those saintly sentences," commented the Darlington *News*, cited *ibid.*, June 30, 1896.

[10] See dispatch from Lebanon, Indiana, to unidentified newspaper, June 14, 1896, in Tillman Scrapbooks; Charleston *News and Courier*, May 26, June 26, 30, 1896.

[11] Unidentified Indianapolis newspaper, June 14, 1896, in Tillman Scrapbooks.

The silver leaders in Congress were not impressed by his financial insight; [12] no delegation except his own was instructed in his favor. [13] No attempt was made to organize a Tillman boom; the South Carolinians at Chicago had no money for so expensive an undertaking. [14]

Nevertheless, the energetic Southerner was a man of importance among the delegates who gathered in Chicago the second week in July. He was called "one of the four most conspicuous men in the convention." [15] His rustic appearance and manners seemed to make him the true enemy of the Eastern plutocracy the convention was preparing to condemn. His clothes were described as wrinkled, his hat as a dilapidated relic of his gubernatorial days, his manners as so bad that he soiled the counterpane on the bed of his hotel room as he rolled in his boots. [16]

He found time to be other than picturesque. Ringleader in the move to organize the free silver majority against the "gold bugs," he warned that intriguing conservatives might force compromise "by playing on the vanity of men by putting the [Presidential] bee to buzzing." [17] He bent his efforts toward making certain that Senator John W. Daniel, a silverite, would supplant as temporary chairman Senator Hill, the choice of the Democratic National Committee. The South Carolinian said confidently, "The silver men are running this affair, and they propose to run it in their own fashion. If the gold men don't like it, let them bolt. I hope they will." Daniel won over Hill.

The next step in the party revolution was the writing of the platform along pro-silver lines. Tillman was an energetic member of the subcommittee charged with this task.

[12] Larner, in Charleston *News and Courier,* May 23, 1896.

[13] The New York *Times,* in a preconvention survey of the sentiments of the delegates, did not mention him as one of the favorite candidates. Cited *ibid.,* June 8, 1896.

[14] Kohn, *ibid.,* July 5, 1896.

[15] *American Review of Reviews* (New York), XIV (1896), 135.

[16] Larner, in Charleston *News and Courier,* July 4, 1896.

[17] Kohn, *ibid.,* July 7, 1896.

He witnessed the adoption of his free silver and anti-Cleveland notions, but saw the failure of his attempt to have the President condemned by name.[18]

Through negotiations of Tillman with Hill and William J. Bryan, the two other scheduled speakers, it was agreed that the silver and gold factions should each have an hour and a quarter of the convention's time for the presentation of their views. Tillman asked for fifty minutes of the majority's time and the right to close the debate. Bryan and Hill felt that this was too long for a closing speech. Wishing to have the most time he could get, Tillman agreed to open the debate with the desired fifty minutes at his disposal.[19]

This was undoubtedly the greatest opportunity of Tillman's life. He was allowed to make the longest address of the convention in favor of a platform which the overwhelming majority approved at a time when this majority had not definitely decided on a Presidential candidate. The delegates were sympathetic toward his views and were highly interested in his personality. The press promised him "a good show," while he expressed the hope that he could dispel prejudices against his personality.[20]

But the speaker mistook his audience. He seemed to think that the fifteen thousand persons before whom he arose at eleven-thirty on the morning of July 9 were but a magnified replica of his South Carolina audiences. There was the same disorder and informality, the same enthusiasms about the men and measures he liked or disliked, and the same spirited opposition to arouse the force of his forensic powers. So he reacted in the manner of the rural stump. His hair was unkempt, his dark features flushed, his one eye gleamed, and his voice was ready to ring like a

[18] *Id., ibid.,* July 9, 10, 1896; Tillman, in *Cong. Record,* 63 Cong., 1 Sess., 30.

[19] William J. Bryan and Mary B. Bryan, *Memoirs of William Jennings Bryan* (Chicago, 1925), 110–11.

[20] Kohn, in Charleston *News and Courier,* July 11, 1896.

clarion. He looked the very "incarnation of the mob, vengeful and defiant," one who scorned tact and moderation. He would proclaim the truth in unvarnished phrases. He would announce the reality of the division between the agricultural and the commercial sections. He would accompany the attack on the "sin" of the gold standard by attacks on Cleveland and other "sinners." In other words, the speech which he had made twice in the Senate and a dozen times in his preconvention tour would be made again. There was no consideration for the change in audience and atmosphere.

He began the assault in the most infelicitous manner. A man who knew how to invoke historical prejudices in his favor now invoked one of these prejudices to his hurt. He made the ghost of secession walk! He drew a parallel between 1861 and 1896, saying that the first movement had disrupted the union of states for the liberation of black slaves, and that the second was destroying the union of Democrats for the liberation of white slaves. "We are willing to see the Democratic party disrupt again to accomplish that result. . . . That if those who hold the contrary opinion . . . choose to imitate the old slaveholders and go out, we say let them go." Then, as a prelude to a long statistical analysis designed to prove that New York and other Eastern areas were sucking the substance of agriculture, he blurted out the following: "Some of my friends from the South and elsewhere have said that this is not a sectional issue. I say it is a sectional issue."

Although the speaker was of course not actually trying to provoke the recurrence of events of 1861, his use of such words as "secession," "disruption," and "sectional" was too much for even so radical a body as the Democratic convention of 1896. The leaders felt that the strength of their party lay in its ability to gather votes in all sections of the country; that actually there was little hope of winning the Presidency unless New York and other Eastern states could be won.[21] The fact that Tillman was telling the truth in asserting that the issue was sectional was quite aside from the point; it was the duty of all good Democrats, pro-silver and pro-gold, to drown, if possible, the sectional monster in waves of patriotic platitudes. When Tillman attempted the opposite, one can well imagine the reaction of both the floor and the galleries. His first reference to secession provoked a continuous hiss mingled with disapproving shouts. His description of the process of secession brought forth cries of "No! No!" and "Time! Time!" Neither the Southern nor the Western radicals applauded his attack on the East. Half his time had scarcely expired before it seemed he would be compelled to do what he had often forced his South Carolina opponents to do: sit down. His eye was bloodshot, his face was haggard, and he paced the platform nervously.

But Ben Tillman was not the man to yield. Like the good warrior he was, he met strenuous opposition with vigorous assault. Thoroughly angry, he alternately wagged his head in derision and shook his fists defiantly. The passion that possessed him caused his words to become furiously personal. He asked Hill to explain the "inscrutable reason" for his changing from an enemy to a friend of Cleveland. Then came the assault upon the President. Should the convention endorse this pro-gold leader, its members would write themselves down as "asses and liars." To call him "courageous" would be to endorse a man who had "the courage to over-ride the Constitution." To commend his "fidelity" was to approve a man who had been "faithful . . . unto the death of the Democratic party." The Republicans were certain to win in November unless the Democratic party declared itself by "express repudiation of this man." Amid howls and hisses, Tillman closed with resolutions embodying his opinions.

He had overshot the mark. James K. Jones and Hill, the

21 See analysis, in *Nation*, LXIII (1896), 43–44.

leaders respectively of the majority and minority factions, jumped to their feet to deny what had been said. Jones cried, "The great cause in which I and those who feel as I do are engaged in is not sectional. . . . I utterly repudiate the charge that this question is sectional." Hill let Tillman know that the representative of the state of secession was not going to drive him and his state out of the party. The press declared the Tillman speech "a grievous failure," and his friends mourned the sacrifice of a great opportunity. Catching the temper of the convention, he, after its refusal to endorse Cleveland, withdrew his resolutions of condemnation, explaining, "the failure to indorse an express resolution . . . carries with it the converse of the proposition. No brave man strikes a fallen foe."

The Tillman failure was followed by two other bids for the favor of the convention. The first of these, Hill's, failed for precisely opposite reasons. The New Yorker's clear but unexcited exposition of the minority views on silver did not impress the impassioned multitude.

The second bid came from Bryan, who previously was not so well known as Tillman. His oration, like the South Carolinian's, was a rehash of the arguments of the silverites. But here the similarities ended. In place of Tillman's sinister face and startling voice was a handsome and serene countenance and a musical voice. Instead of rashly presenting hard truths, Bryan avoided harsh realities and used the unctuous expressions necessary for a trying situation. To avoid indiscriminate repetitions, an oft-repeated speech was adapted extemporaneously to meet the changing humors of the audience. Instead of invoking sectionalism and personalities to support silver doctrines, those same doctrines were carried forward by the passionate conviction that their adoption would benefit all men of all sections. The consequence was that Tillman's effort must be recorded as one of the great failures in the annals of American oratory and Bryan's as one of the supreme triumphs.

The sequel can be told briefly. Tillman got the hisses of the convention while Bryan received a prodigious ovation. Tillman's name was withdrawn from the list of Presidential nominees after the first ballot showed that he possessed only South Carolina's seventeen votes. Bryan won the nomination with the South Carolinians voting for him.[22]

Tillman's discomfiture was mitigated by the triumph of his principles. He was delighted with the defeat of the Cleveland faction and found nothing objectionable in the views and personality of the kindly Bryan. He had not been forced to abandon party to vindicate principle. As a member of the majority faction of the national party, he became the most consistent of regular Democrats, a blind champion of the decrees of the dominant organization, a foe of anyone who threatened a division of the party of the white man.

After Bryan's nomination the Carolinian turned his savage rhetoric in two directions. To the right he thundered against the small group of white South Carolinians who refused to accept Bryanism. To his left he "gave hell" to the Populists and Democrats of North Carolina, who were conspiring with Negroes and Republicans to win the Democratic organization of that state.[23] He toured thirty states, speaking for Bryan; he drew large crowds. Yet his speeches were not of great significance. He was merely one of the many orators trailing after the Democratic candidate. The party organization did not regard him as an asset. His record in the Senate and at Chicago arose to smite him, and

[22] The debate is fully reported in *Official Proceedings of the Democratic National Convention, . . . 1896* (Logansport, Ind., 1896), 198–249, 303–16. The fairest account of Tillman's speech is Kohn, in Charleston *News and Courier*, July 10–11, 1896. See also, accounts of Amos J. Cummings and Henry George, *ibid.*, July 12, 1896; Chicago *Record-Herald*, n.d., in Tillman Scrapbooks; *American Review of Reviews*, XIV (1896), 135–36; Bryan and Bryan, *Memoirs*, 113; Harry T. Peck, *Twenty Years of the Republic, 1885–1905* (New York, 1907), 496–97. On the first ballot 17 South Carolinians voted for Tillman, 1 not voting. All 18 voted for Bryan on the second ballot.

[23] Charleston *News and Courier*, September 26, 1896.

the "pure cussedness" of his "cyclone powers" lent color to the Republican charge that lawlessness was the ruling element in the Democratic party. Tillman unwittingly had a small part in bringing about Bryan's defeat.[24]

In the meantime, all was not well with the Evans candidacy for the Senate. The elimination of Irby from the race had been the signal for the entrance of Joseph H. Earle, the man whom Tillman had defeated in 1890. But the Earle of 1896 was not the Earle of six years before. Without sacrificing the respect of the Conservatives, he had won the gratitude of the Tillmanites by advising that Tillman be not opposed in 1892; and when he asked for a judgeship, they gave it to him.[25] As a senatorial candidate he promised to co-operate with Tillman on national policies, asserted that he was nonpartisan concerning state affairs, and refused to indulge in invective. This shrewd opportunism caught Conservative voters. Without a candidate of their own, they quietly rallied to the man who drank only moderately at the fountain of Tillmanism.

Evans could not effectively resist the Earle strategy. He was unpopular because of the intrigues through which he had become governor and because of his Dispensary policies. And the fates put in the path of this luckless politician an unexpected antagonist who was in a sense more formidable than the prudent Earle. John T. Duncan, an eccentric lawyer, entered the lists for the sole purpose of destroying Evans, pursuing this objective with the persistence of a clever man who was partly insane. He accused his antagonist of having accepted while state senator a fee for influencing the enactment of a bond issue. Although the accused had been guilty of nothing but legitimate services as attorney for a broker, this "bond scandal" was magnified into a crime by the newspapers and was eagerly believed by many. Evans

[24] Washington *Star* and Spartanburg *Herald*, cited *ibid.*, August 10, November 23, 1896.

[25] See Tillman and McLaurin eulogies of Earle, in *Cong. Record*, 55 Cong., 2 Sess., 3302–3305, 3309–11.

allowed himself to become involved in confusing verbal altercations with Duncan as well as in undignified attacks on Earle.[26]

At first, Tillman did not take active part in the contest. But when his friend seemed to be weakening under the Duncan attack, Evans was allowed to read a testimonial from Honest Ben denying the truth of the "bond steal" and assuring him that if he behaved with common prudence his fight was won.[27]

Evidently Evans did not behave with common prudence because the combined vote of Earle and Duncan exceeded his by the small margin of six hundred. The Tillman favorite was forced into a second primary,[28] and the Conservatives, heartened at Earle's unexpected strength, resolved to give the hated Evans a death blow.

Aroused by his friend's peril, Tillman, in the two weeks between the primaries, energetically espoused his cause. He publicly declared, "I regard the election of Governor Evans to the Senate now as a political necessity. . . . With his defeat would go the defeat of the Tillman party." [29] The statement was circulated among the voters, and the senator personally visited his Edgefield neighbors asking for their votes. But these efforts were in vain. Earle won the second primary by a majority of 3,348. Edgefield joined Charleston in securing the result.[30]

Tillman was defeated only in the sense that it was proved that he could not impose upon the voters an inept candidate who was odious to thousands. Evans' campaign, Tillman explained, "was the worst bungled affair I ever saw." [31] Earle could never have won had he not adroitly sacrificed principles by bending under the yoke of Tillmanism. The Tillmanites who voted for him said that he was the better of the two Tillmanite candidates. At the same time, they

[26] Charleston *News and Courier,* July 18–August 18, 1896.
[27] *Ibid.,* July 23, September 6, 1896.
[28] *Ibid.,* August 30, 1896.   [29] *Ibid.,* September 3, 1896.
[30] *Ibid.,* September 12, 1896.   [31] *Ibid.,* September 26, 1896.

elected a pro-Tillman legislature and a pro-Tillman governor in the person of Ellerbe. The Edgefield leader personally remained as popular as ever. This was proved when
he appeared among the people at Gaffney a few months
after Evans' defeat. Hundreds trudged through the snow
to hear him indulge in the old familiarities and review his
activities in national politics. "There can be no question,"
remarked a truthful reporter, "about the continued hold
Tillman has on some people and the confidence put in his
expressions." [32]

The death of Earle shortly after he entered the Senate
gave Tillman opportunity to demonstrate that he was still
a power in state politics. The Conservatives, aware of his
continued hold, refused to qualify a candidate. The three
who presented themselves in the special primary were
Evans, Irby, and Congressman John L. McLaurin, all of
whom vied in championing the Dispensary and other Tillman principles. Irby professed reconciliation; Evans again
implored the boss's support; McLaurin apologized for past
criticisms.[33] McLaurin was elected by a vote almost twice
as great as the combined votes of his opponents.[34] Evans had
failed to recover from his previous defeat, and whatever
chances Irby may have had were shattered when, a few days
before the primary, he accused Tillman of secret partiality
for McLaurin.[35]

The elevation of McLaurin to the junior senatorship
pleased the senior senator. The two men had long been
close friends, and the new senator, as a member of the
House Committee on Ways and Means, had proved to be
the only Tillmanite congressman of more than average
ability.

Tillman in 1897 found himself supreme. The government of South Carolina was in friendly hands, and the senator's personal popularity was so great that no one dared

---

[32] Kohn, *ibid.*, December 6, 1896.   [33] *Ibid.*, June 7, August 25, 1897.
[34] *Ibid.*, September 2, 1897.   [35] *Ibid.*, August 29, 1897.

raise a hand against him. He was in harmony with the leaders and principles of the national party and was recognized as a distinguished politician. Without hope of ever being able to dominate the national Democratic party, he could devote himself freely to augmenting his prestige as a member of the Senate.

Chapter XXIII

A SENATOR FINDS HIS PLACE

TILLMAN'S position in the Senate after settlement of the issues of 1896 and 1897 was not one of greatest significance. His first speeches had not quelled initial suspicions. As a Democrat he must face the opposition of a Republican majority likely to stifle his suggestions. He could not demonstrate his talents for constructive legislative and administrative achievements, could not repeat in Washington what he had done in Columbia.

Moreover, there was no opportunity to play the role of great minority leader in the manner of his distinguished predecessor, Calhoun. The spokesman of South Carolina at the end of the nineteenth century had no vital issue to present. The state had long since retired from national or sectional leadership; its people had no original national policies and were controlled by unanimous adherence to dead issues. The broad national programs were concocted in the North and did not greatly stir South Carolina. Therefore, when Tillman discussed these programs, he did so more as a thoughtful individual than as the reflector of the will of the constituency he was supposed to represent. Although his utterances gained in freedom and detachment, the roots of his senatorial career were implanted in shallow soil; for he represented no great interest bidding for control in the national councils in the sense that Calhoun expressed the viewpoint of the planter South, or Nelson W. Aldrich, in Tillman's time, that of the industrial East. Tillman for the most part had to be critical and academic; only in minor matters was he able to be intelligently selfish.

The new senator brought to Washington certain virtues overlooked by those who emphasized his blatancy. The chief of these was willingness to perform routine duties. "He likes senatorial life," said one critic, "and is rapidly becoming accustomed to the limits to which senatorial courtesy and social requirements may extend." [1] His lack of obstructiveness for a year following his speech of May 1, 1896, even led to the prediction that he would sink into obscurity, following "the fate of those evangelists of disorder who come and go from time to time, flying fiercely across the heavens and then disappearing." [2]

The prophet did not know the man. The South Carolinian's long silence merely indicated that he was busy establishing a solid reputation for hard work and stability which was going to make him a fixture in the Senate. He had no intention of becoming a conventional gentleman who happened to wear the toga. He retained his savagery and his prejudices; all that was needed for him to flail and roar was a significant occasion.

Such an occasion arose when President McKinley called Congress in extra session in 1897 to revise the tariff according to the pleasure of the triumphant Republicans. Here was an issue rich with dramatic possibilities: Big Business, triumphant and corrupt, against the agricultural masses. The agrarian senator whetted his Pitchfork. The old arguments against the tariff were given new life by blending them, in a somewhat contradictory fashion, with the Tillman banter and sarcasm. Herod was out-Heroded by demands for protection for South Carolina industries. These demands, like true satire, served a double purpose. By being ridiculous they made still more ridiculous Republican demands for protection, and at the same time possibly conferred a few tariff benefits on nascent South Carolina indus-

[1] Larner, in Charleston *News and Courier*, May 22, 1897.
[2] Memphis *Commercial-Appeal*, cited *ibid.*, May 4, 1897.

tries. Thus Tillman added merriment and venom to a hackneyed subject.

The South Carolinian entered the tariff debate with conventional Democratic arguments. The protective principle was "robbery," a cruel imposition upon the agricultural South, "the Ishmaelite section, which . . . never has had any rights since the war." This "mother of trusts" eliminated foreign competition so that the great manufacturing combines might exploit the consuming public.[3] In this spirit he bitterly protested against duties on fertilizers, cotton bagging, and cotton ties, articles used by Southern farmers. "He [the farmer] is 'the forgotten man' who is never cared for in your legislation," he complained. After he was gratified by the elimination of the tax on fertilizer, he vainly threatened to filibuster "until December" if bagging and ties were not put on the free list along with commodities used by Western farmers.[4]

The spectacular senator went beyond other Democrats in attacking the sugar schedule. On May 13, while the Senate was discussing in dull fashion what to do with one Elverton R. Chapman, who had refused to testify concerning the sugar speculations of senators in 1894, Tillman blurted that the purpose of the original investigation was not to punish Chapman but to determine whether any member of the Senate Finance Committee had abused his official position to profit from sugar speculations. Certain newspapers, he explained, were at that moment accusing three unnamed senators of this activity. The Senate was not inclined to be interested in this supposed irrelevancy,[5] but Tillman was not the person to let a matter of this character rest. Two weeks later he asked that a committee of five senators be appointed to examine the charges. "If we have,"

[3] *Cong. Record,* 55 Cong., 1 Sess., 1623–27.
[4] *Ibid.,* 1857–58, 1860, 2772; Charleston *News and Courier,* July 21, 1897.
[5] *Cong. Record,* 55 Cong., 1 Sess., 1054; Charleston *News and Courier,* May 14, 19, 1897.

he said, "corrupt and debauched men in here owned by trusts and corporations, we ought to find out who they are." [6]

The Senate responded quickly to this reflection on the honor of its members. Senator Aldrich explained that the "ungracious" task of preparing tariff schedules always provoked newspaper charges of unworthy motives. As chairman of the Finance Committee he denied as "absolutely and utterly false" that any of the members of his group were guilty of speculations in sugar stocks. Edmund W. Pettus, a Democrat, pointedly asked the South Carolina senator to abandon insinuations against the Senate as a whole in favor of naming guilty individuals. But Tillman was unable to do this; instead, he was given a dose of his own medicine, the rehearsing of old charges of Dispensary corruption. His proposed investigation was voted down by the decisive majority of 35 to 15.[7]

Tillman supplemented these agitations by declaring that although protection was unrighteous, it should be utilized by Southerners. They should "take care of the local interests of our States in the general game of grab and stealing." Later, he added, "if we are to have this stealing from the people by protected interests, I want my share for South Carolina, and I am not ashamed to say it." [8] Although other Democrats did not follow his example, he voted for duties on lumber, rice, cotton, corn, and other Southern products, and regretted that his section of the nation did not have a more diversified industrial life over which the principle of protection could be extended.[9]

Because he felt that any tariff policy necessarily discriminated against agriculture, the South Carolinian championed another idea which was heresy among Democrats. He favored a Federal bounty on agricultural exports: ten

---

[6] *Cong. Record*, 55 Cong., 1 Sess., 1310–14.
[7] *Ibid.*, 1435–38, 2845.　　　　　[8] *Ibid.*, 57 Cong., 1 Sess., 1801, 2574.
[9] *Ibid.*, 55 Cong., 1 Sess., 1577, 1587–89, 1627, 1800–1801.

cents a bushel on wheat, two cents a pound on tobacco, one cent a pound on cotton, with proportionate payments on rye, hops, and corn. His purpose, he said, was to give the farmers privileges in return for privileges given manufacturers by the tariff. The tariff on manufactures, he contended, was in effect a bounty since it raised prices. On the other hand, it was an insult to the farmers to pretend to give tariff protection to agricultural commodities not imported while on the free list.

With plea and threat, Tillman sought support of his proposal. The Republican cry for protection of American labor against the pauper labor of Europe should be extended to the American farmer as well. The alternative was the vengeance of the agrarians, nine million strong. "You gentlemen who are pressing madly onward, imagining that you can hold your farmer vote," he cried amid a shaking of heads, ". . . must explain why you refuse to give the farmer equality and justice in this scheme of protection."

Neither Republican nor Democratic senators in considerable numbers were impressed by the warnings of the fiery South Carolinian. The agricultural bounty amendment was defeated by vote of 59 to 10.[10] Tillman was at least twenty years ahead of his time. Today the principle of direct Federal aid to agriculture has become a fixed policy.

In the meantime, Tillman discovered an opportunity to expand his somewhat fruitless critical role by advocating constructive legislation. An interest in the navy resulting from his membership on the Senate naval committee prompted him, in 1896, to join hands with William E. Chandler, Republican chairman of the committee, in an effort to establish a government-owned plant to manufacture armor plate for battleships.

To supply the plates for the new ironclads begun in 1887, the secretary of the navy induced Bethlehem Steel Company to erect an armor-plate factory on the understanding

[10] *Ibid.*, 1623–34.

that this company would be given contracts at compensatory rates. The first price agreed upon was the high figure of $604 a ton. At a later date the secretary induced Carnegie, Phipps and Company to compete with Bethlehem. Soon, however, dissatisfaction arose in naval circles with the conduct of the two companies. In 1893 it was discovered that the Carnegie company was fraudulently imposing inferior armor upon the navy. In retaliation, a House committee scathingly denounced and fined the company. Resentment over this incident had scarcely subsided when it was disclosed that Carnegie and Bethlehem had effected price-fixing agreements and that Bethlehem was charging the United States $310 more a ton than it was charging the Russian government.

This situation gave Tillman opportunity to raise his voice. In his emphatic way he told the Senate that the interests of the government and the Armor Trust were diametrically opposed; he accused the manufacturers of extortion and urged the establishment of a government-owned armor plant.[11] A Senate committee composed of Tillman, Chandler, and two others investigated the price of armor plate, while the secretary of the navy made an independent inquiry into the problem. The Senate committee recommended $300 a ton as a just price and the secretary recommended $400. The two armor-making companies, frightened by the exposure of their own chicanery, agreed to furnish armor for the vessels constructed in 1897 at the secretary's price plus a twelve-dollar royalty.[12]

Firmly convinced that $300 was as much as the government should pay for armor, Tillman, in 1897, pushed an amendment reducing the price to that level. With characteristic violence, he denounced the armor makers as monopolists engaged in the "grab game of looting the Treasury

---

[11] *Ibid.*, 54 Cong., 1 Sess., 4470–74.

[12] See history of this question as told by Senators Chandler and Eugene Hale, *ibid.*, 55 Cong., 3 Sess., 2629; 56 Cong., 1 Sess., 5311.

at will." He poured verbal vitriol upon the heads of the senators who refused to regard his proposed price as just. The Armor Trust, he said, had " 'friends' in this Chamber" who were willing to grovel "in the mire of corruption and rottenness." When he was accused of being "insulting and slanderous," he replied that no senator could frighten him into not interpreting the facts as he saw them. Surprisingly enough, a Republican Senate was convinced by the arguments of the vehement Democrat. The maximum price for armor was placed at $300 a ton. In this the House concurred.

But this meant the success of only half of the strategy necessary to bring the hated Armor Trust to terms. If both Bethlehem and Carnegie carried out their threats of refusing to sell at the stipulated price, the naval expansion program would be obstructed. Foreseeing this, Tillman and his allies demanded a simple provision, the building of a government plant in case the price was not accepted. He heaped scorn upon senators who conjured up the specter of state socialism, upon those who would "not have the government do anything on its own hook except to sit down here as the agent and tool of these corporations and trusts." To the assertion that the government could not conduct a great business economically, he replied ingeniously: better that expenditures go in the pockets of overpaid civil servants than into those of a greedy trust. But, as Tillman predicted, the prejudices of the Senate against state competition with private business was too great. His project was voted down.[13]

Of course the Armor Trust refused to furnish its product at $300 a ton. Consequently the government in 1898, confronted with the emergency of the Spanish-American War, was forced to accept the $400 maximum. Even this price was a saving of $500,000 on each battleship over charges prevailing before the armor-plate question was agitated.

[13] *Ibid.*, 54 Cong., 2 Sess., 2556–63; 55 Cong., 1 Sess., 2555–59.

Not wishing to cripple the navy in time of war, Tillman acquiesced in the acceptance of the trust's price while joining Senator Marion Butler of North Carolina in the renewal of the fight for a public armor plant. This time Chandler, the old enemy of the Armor Trust, deserted the Tillman cause; and Eugene Hale of Maine, in behalf of the naval committee, flatly declared that government manufacture was "the most expensive way of making armor that the wit of man can devise." The Tillman proposal was, on April 25, 1898, tabled by the decisive majority of 36 to 14.[14]

The persistent senator from South Carolina did not let renewed defeat discourage him. On March 1, 1899, he reintroduced the project of 1898. He reminded the Senate that it had twice expressed the conviction that $300 was a just price for armor, but had been forced, under pressure of war, to meet the price of the Armor Trust. An amendment embodying Tillman's ideas was introduced by Marion Butler and passed the Senate by vote of 39 to 27. The House agreed, as it had done before, to accept the Tillman price but refused to authorize the factory. Thus the situation was just as it had been the previous year, and Tillman expressed keen disappointment.[15]

At the 1900 session of Congress, Tillman made his fifth and final fight against the Armor Trust. By this time he had mastered all but the more technical details of armor manufacture and was able to answer questions with authority. The steel magnates were now asking $545 a ton for armor in place of the $412 previously accepted. They justified the increase on the grounds that the improved product of the new Krupp process raised the cost of manufacture. The majority of the Senate Committee on Naval Affairs, realizing that the naval program was three years behind because of the haggle over prices, agreed to pay the $545 for the

14 *Ibid.*, 55 Cong., 2 Sess., 4234–42.
15 *Ibid.*, 3 Sess., 2623–36, 2844–51, 2862–66.

armor immediately needed for the three ships under construction, but provided for the construction of the government plant should the manufacturers refuse $445 for future
orders. Tillman surrendered once more, but demanded that
the price of future orders be placed at $300.

He made a heroic last stand in defense of his position, but
was overwhelmed by an invincible combination of Republican senators. Hale, new chairman of the naval committee,
told the South Carolinian that he "must not charge his
atmosphere with suspicion" since senators as honest as he
were opposed to paternalism. Henry Cabot Lodge, naval
expansionist, joined hands with Marcus A. Hanna, patron
of private business, in asserting that the delay in ship construction was caused by Tillman's insistence on impossible
armor prices. Boies Penrose of Pennsylvania and Davis Elkins of West Virginia hinted that the farmer-senator was
ignorant of the actualities of armor making. Endorsing
these arguments, the Senate rejected Tillman's plan in
favor of that of the naval committee.[16]

This was a partial victory for the persistent senator—
the serving of notice on the Armor Trust that the government would erect a plant unless prices were lowered. But
unfortunately the House refused to accept the $445 price as
the alternative to the plant, demanding instead that the
alternative be a price deemed "reasonable and equitable"
by the secretary of the navy. Tillman cried furiously that
he had rather see the naval appropriations bill fail than
witness Senate submission to the trust-dominated branch of
Congress. By a vote of 63 to 0 the Senate refused to yield to
the House. But that body was obdurate, and the Senate,
fearing the failure of the naval bill, surrendered. The vote
was 39 to 35.[17] Thus ended a brave fight.

[16] Hale, *ibid.*, 56 Cong., 1 Sess., 5318; Henry C. Lodge, *ibid.*, 5401; Marcus
A. Hanna, *ibid.*, 6360; Boies Penrose, *ibid.*, 5413–14; Davis Elkins, *ibid.*, 5417.
[17] *Ibid.*, 6263–65, 6369, 6700–6705, 6798.

The struggle had not been in all respects a defeat. The agitation of the armor question had caused important reductions in prices, which saved several million dollars for the government. Likewise, the long pursuit of a single question had proved Tillman's worth as legislator and champion of popular rights. The soundness of his position was several times recognized by the vote of both Democrats and Republicans. On the other hand, he interrupted the rapid expansion of the navy, a cause dearer to the average American than thwarting the harpies of the Armor Trust. Moreover, as Penrose argued, a government armor plant under existing circumstances was probably impractical. The Tillman idea clashed with the sacrosanct dictum of the ruling capitalists against public competition with private business. Somewhat out of touch with the dominant forces of the nation, he was slow to understand the prodigious power of American plutocracy.

Long before the South Carolinian gave up his fight against the armor companies, he was participating in debates of great importance growing out of the war with Spain. Although his attitude was generally indistinguishable from that of other Democratic senators, he had some special prejudices to contribute, prejudices reflecting the views of a Southern farmer unwilling to adjust inherited convictions to the new imperialism of the Republicans. Frequently he injected his views in the discussions. It was of little consequence to him whether or not his remarks were adjudged relevant or irrelevant; he would have his say regardless of the opinions of others.

Tillman joined the popular demand for the war with Spain, talking belligerently even before the President and Congress were disposed to act. In March, 1898, he exulted that the people of South Carolina were moved to "the highest pitch of excitement over the war situation." Later he added that the blood of Revolutionary sires demanded vengeance for the sinking of the *Maine* and that the Republican administration should be supported in liberating Cuba.[18] He told the Senate that he did not object to the planting of "the American flag wherever it is possible to carry it until Spain sues for peace." [19]

Such views were not strange to Tillman. He was ever a fervent patriot when patriotism did not interfere with his still more fervent sectionalism. He eagerly joined all South Carolina in embracing this first opportunity since 1860 to participate in a great national emotion and to share in the emergency expenditures. South Carolinians were given army commissions, and camps were established in the state.

Tillman's enthusiasm for a war directed by a Republican President did not, however, lead to his acceptance of the Republican solution of the resultant territorial problems. The war gave the nation Cuba, Hawaii, Puerto Rico, and the Philippines, in which the Republicans erected governments with many of the privileges of American citizenship but distinctly without the equality of statehood. Tillman countered this imperialistic solution by suggesting a narrowly nationalistic policy. He said that the conquered regions should not be annexed to the United States, first, because it was unethical to subjugate one people to the will of another; second, because attaching people of alien culture and inferior races to the United States would contaminate the national customs and blood. These two reasons appear again and again in Tillman's discourses on the colonial issue. Obviously they were somewhat contradictory, but the Democratic senator, in his rush to be critical of the Republicans, did not always iron out anomalies.

His speech of April 15, 1898, in favor of unconditional recognition of Cuban independence, was his first blast against the alleged desire of the imperialists to exploit a weak people for selfish purposes. For Americans to attempt to govern Cuba would bring accusations of greed from

[18] Charleston *News and Courier*, March 5, April 16, 1898.
[19] *Cong. Record*, 55 Cong., 2 Sess., 6530.

other nations and unleash the evils of carpetbaggery. Such a government would only mean "some species of pseudo-independence or autonomy or some other humbug" as a disguise for the financial tutelage of Wall Street.[20]

The protracted discussion in the Senate over the annexation of the Philippines gave the South Carolinian opportunity to express most completely his sympathy for a people he believed were maltreated by the Republicans. The American people, he said, were at a turning point in their destiny: they could become greedy conquerors or they could bestow on the Filipinos the self-determination for which the Revolutionary Fathers fought. To follow the first course would mean untold misery for both Filipinos and Americans, the sacrifice of freedom on the altar of selfish aggression; to apply the second alternative would signify the attainment of "the honor of having fought a war for the love of liberty and humanity." He would not "carry the Christian religion to the people on the point of a bayonet." He would have the United States involved in Philippine affairs only to the extent of establishing a protectorate which would prevent intervention by a third power but would allow the natives to manage their own affairs.[21]

Tillman at times loudly asserted that the extension of American sovereignty should automatically entail the conferring of American rights and laws. The Democratic party's endorsement of this viewpoint, he said, meant that descendants of slaveholders "have changed places with the Republicans of 1860" and were contending "for liberty as represented by the flag and the Constitution," while the Republicans were contending "for the power of Congress to limit the citizen's rights." Specific acts of Republican repression were eagerly cited: Hawaii was being turned over to an oligarchy of white men endowed with authority to inflict "enormities and outrages" on the colored races of those islands; the tariff discriminations against Puerto Rico pro-

20 *Ibid.*, 3888–92.   21 *Ibid.*, 3 Sess., 1529–34.

moted the interests of American sugar barons; and the plan to have Americans participate in the government of that island was carpetbaggery. He scorned the "hypocrisy and namby-pamby philanthropy" of those who would foster a blighting paternalism reminiscent of the Freedmen's Bureau.[22]

The senator used these abuses to justify discriminations against the Negroes in the South. "I want to call attention," he often said to the Republican senators, "to the remarkable change that has come over the spirit of the dream of the Republicans. . . . Your slogans of the past—brotherhood of man and the fatherhood of God—have gone glimmering down through the ages." The disgrace of the situation, he added, was that the leaders against colonial equality were those who for twenty-five years had clung to the principle "that all men, including the negro, are free and equal." [23]

Despite his frequent expressions to the contrary, Tillman was too firm a believer in the inherent superiority of the Anglo-Saxon to remain truly discontented with the restrictions that the Republicans imposed upon the colonials, provided, of course, that one admitted the necessity of their coming under American control. Sometimes he said that no people of Spanish or Negro blood were capable of self-government [24] and that he would vote for the annexation of Hawaii if only persons of white blood should participate in the government.[25] His grievance, the real motive for his opposition, was the refusal of the Republicans to admit inconsistencies in their views of colored people.[26] He wanted the Republicans to confess their conduct toward the colonials as frankly as he was confessing his toward the blacks. "I do not object to those white men in Hawaii being protected," he said to the senators, "but do not protect them with hypocrisy and cant. Be men! Stand up! Come out and

22 *Ibid.*, 56 Cong., 1 Sess., 2974, 2977, 3624, 4650, 5898.
23 *Ibid.*, 55 Cong., 2 Sess., 6533; 56 Cong., 1 Sess., 2185, 2242–44, 2651.
24 *Ibid.*, 55 Cong., 2 Sess., 6531.
25 *Ibid.*, 6534.   26 *Ibid.*, 56 Cong., 1 Sess., 2244.

say why you do this thing." [27] Such a confession would have satisfied a yearning near Tillman's heart. It would have been, at least by inference, a justification of the attitude of the white South toward the Negro.

Of course, the Republican senators made no such admission. Like the discreet Southern gentlemen who preceded Tillman in the Senate, they saw no reason why undemocratic practices born of necessity should be confessed. They answered the South Carolinian's proddings by asserting suavely that they were giving liberal government to the colonials and that the injection of the American Negro into the debate was irrelevant.[28] But Tillman's arguments concerning Republican inconsistency could not be refuted; [29] indeed, he had made a significant point. His failure to cause a modification of the colonial policies was an implied justification of a policy toward the Negroes as illiberal as that toward the Hawaiians, Puerto Ricans, and Filipinos.

In the absence of a firsthand acquaintance with the people of the colonies, it was easy for Tillman's imagination to endow them with the same weaknesses and vices he ascribed to the American Negro. He affirmed that the colonials were a "heterogeneous mass of ignorant and debased specimens of mankind"; that the Spanish Americans were mongrels incapable of self-government; that the Filipinos were unregenerate Asiatics. He felt that the Negro was trouble enough without patriots wishing to bring home other race problems by deliberately incorporating Malays, Negritos, Japanese, Chinese, Spaniards, and mulattoes in the body politic. This was his explanation of why a majority of Southern senators voted against the Philippine treaty. "It was not because we are Democrats," he said, "but be-

27 *Ibid.,* 2184.

28 Replies of Senators Shelby M. Cullom, John C. Spooner, and Knute Nelson, *ibid.,* 55 Cong., 3 Sess., 837; 56 Cong., 1 Sess., 2242–44.

29 George F. Hoar, *Autobiography of Seventy Years* (New York, 1903), II, 305.

cause we understand and realize what it is to have two races side by side that can not mix or mingle without deterioration and injury to both." This was why, when it was evident that the Republicans would not heed his admonitions, he rashly declared that he wished a hurricane would destroy the newly acquired islands.[30]

By the time the Presidential contest of 1900 rolled around, the South Carolina senator had sufficiently recovered the prestige lost at Chicago in 1896 to play a conspicuous part in the councils of his party. He was in harmony with Bryan and other majority Democratic leaders who appreciated his industry no less than his picturesque demagoguery. Early he welcomed imperialism as an issue for the canvass of 1900; indeed, Senator John C. Spooner was unkind enough to insinuate that the South Carolinian's participation in the debates on this subject was "to do the 'dirty' work of a political party . . . as a Presidential election is approaching." [31] At the same time the desire of certain Democrats to eliminate the silver issue from the canvass did not get his support. He, like Bryan, was convinced that a principle for which they had fought valiantly in 1896 was not dead four years later.

As a member of the platform committee at the Kansas City convention of 1900 Tillman kept the silver issue from being shelved in the interest of expediency. Yet he willingly agreed with those who wished to make imperialism the "paramount issue" of the canvass so that the anti-silver Democrats supporting Bryan could have some platform on which to stand.[32]

Because the South Carolina senator was regarded as "the very lungs, throat, tongue and megaphone of Bryanism," he was given the honor of reading the platform before the

[30] *Cong. Record,* 55 Cong., 2 Sess., 6531–33; 3 Sess., 1532; 56 Cong., 1 Sess., 2977, 5898–99.

[31] Spooner, *ibid.,* 3219.

[32] New York *Tribune,* cited in Charleston *News and Courier,* August 20, 1900; Democratic staff correspondent, in *Outlook,* LXV (1900), 623–28.

fifteen thousand assembled in convention. His penetrating tones commanded the far reaches of the great hall as he strode up and down the rostrum gesturing in the approved Tillman manner. To arraign the Republicans, the speaker adopted a sepulchral voice that conveyed perfectly a sense of scorn. With clenched fists or great swings of the arms, he verbally consigned all Republican nonsense into oblivion. There was great applause when he commended free silver and denounced the trusts. But the demonstration of the hour came when the stentorian South Carolinian declared that imperialism was "the paramount issue of the campaign." The delegates sprang to their feet, waving hats, flags, and umbrellas. A second reading of this declaration provoked another and greater demonstration as a huge American flag was lowered upon the rostrum bearing the legend: "The Flag of the Republic Forever; of Empire, Never." During the outburst, which lasted eighteen minutes, Tillman beamingly surveyed the scene, perhaps in thought contrasting it with the reception given him by the same Democrats four years before. As he resumed the reading, he could not resist the temptation of a chuckling aside. "If Mark Hanna had been here a few minutes ago he would have thought hell had broken loose in Missouri." [33]

Tillman enlivened the Presidential canvass with arduous "pitchforking" in Western states against imperialism, an issue which gradually overshadowed the money question. The question of the hour, he asserted, "is whether the country shall remain a republic in fact or in name, whether our government shall undergo a change, and an Empire, resting on force and military power, shall take its place?" [34] He could not withstand the temptation of hauling in the

[33] *Official Proceedings of the National Democratic Convention, 1900* (Chicago, 1900), 130–31; *Outlook*, LXV (1900), 626: Charleston *News and Courier*, July 6, 1900; Charleston *Evening Post*, cited in Columbia *State*, August 20, 1900.

[34] Benjamin R. Tillman, "Causes of Southern Opposition to Imperialism," in *North American Review*, CLXXI (1900), 439–46.

Negro issue. His audiences were interested in this issue, but his critics said that he was playing into the hands of the Republicans,[35] and the electorate failed to heed his warning about imperialism. Bryan was more decisively beaten in 1900 than in 1896.

The year 1900 marked the end of Tillman's first term as senator. In those six years he had demonstrated that he was a bold if not always successful critic of the majority party, an advocate of constructive principles, and a statesman with ideas, a leader of the minority.

[35] Columbia *State*, September 28, 1900.

Chapter XXIV

A SENATOR RETAINS HIS CONSTITUENCY

SOUTH CAROLINIANS approved almost unanimously the views of their senator on national issues. They shared fully his anti-Republican prejudices, and even such personal enemies as Alexander C. Haskell and Gonzales believed as he did on free silver, imperialism, and Big Business. But this approval did not lead Tillman to neglect other means of ingratiating himself with his constituency. He consciously strove to attune himself to their sentiments. His plain living and dress and his unparliamentary diction confirmed better than a hundred doctrinal speeches that he was truly their representative. He always found time for South Carolinians who came to Washington, receiving them in the unaffected manner of the plain farmer. Each summer he went among the people to discover their thoughts and to give an account of his stewardship. They were delighted to learn that his head had not been turned by the allurements of the national capital; that he was still Honest Ben, as capable as ever of the half-vituperative, half-humorous oratory with which he had long regaled them. Although he had become "muffle jawed," Ben said that he had not grown "too big for his breeches," but was trying to destroy the atmosphere of corruption which surrounded him in the political Babylon.[1] He reported that he had done his duty, answered the people's letters, visited the departments in their behalf, and performed many other functions

[1] At Moffettsville, in Columbia *State*, July 6, 1898.

besides drawing his salary. He had plied his pitchfork, prodding Republicans and their evil cohorts.[2]

He gratified deeply-ingrained prejudices against Northerners and Republicans. "I have the biggest time in the
world," he said humorously, "throwing rocks at the Republicans and watchin' 'em dodge." [3] He had called them
"damnable hypocrites" because of the inconsistency between their Negro and colonial policies in particular,[4] and
because of their political depravity in general. The North
was "trust ridden, corrupt, decadent," dominated by the
vote-selling "foreign element." "The people there are not
free, and the men sent to Congress are the puppets of the
bosses." His audiences, satisfied, subjected him to "belaud-
ing and bepraising and buttering." [5]

Tillman was too much of a realist to allow his devotion
to his constituents to express itself only in sentiment and
prejudice. As their agent in Washington, he felt bound to
gratify their desire for a share of the material benefits of a
wealthy government. He would secure for South Carolinians as many offices and appropriations as possible. He
tackled this task in the manner of the average Congressional
hack, becoming a hardened practitioner of "pork-barrel"
politics.

He pursued this sordid occupation without any sacrifice
of self-righteousness. From the bottom of his heart he felt
that the South, and especially South Carolina, was due
material compensation for the many wrongs which the
North had imposed upon it. Reconstruction and Negroism,
the tariff, Civil War pensions to Union veterans, and the
Civil War debt, were means through which the South had
contributed "at least two and one half billion dollars." The
North had exploited Southerners as "a conquered people,"
from whom every possible dollar must be squeezed to meet

[2] At Orangeburg, in Charleston *News and Courier*, June 15, 1900.
[3] At Union, in unidentified newspaper, in Tillman Scrapbooks.
[4] New York *Sun*, cited *ibid.*
[5] Charleston *News and Courier*, August 5, 1899.

unfair appropriations. "There has not been a day since 1860," he added, "when South Carolina could receive any consideration in Congress." [6]

Although Tillman was as willing as any member of Congress to justify pork-barrel appropriations by sophistical arguments, he frankly admitted that many of his claims on the government largess had no intrinsic merit, but were warranted because similar appropriations were going to other states. "You tickle me and I will tickle you" was the Congressional policy. After admitting that it was unwise to spend millions dredging rivers, he crassly declared when Senator Augustus O. Bacon protested, "Oh, I am going to help you get any money for any Georgia river you can, and I am going to ask you to help me to get some for the little creeks and hollows and wallows down in my State." [7] Only Tillman dared phrase this masterpiece of unscrupulous honesty: "The whole scheme of river improvement is a humbug and a steal; but if you are going to steal, let us divide it out, and do not go to complaining." [8] He asked a senatorial critic if the senator were aware that his state was being robbed by dishonest taxation, "would he not be willing to get almost any kind of an appropriation for his State, even though it was a little tainted sometimes with lack of public utility?" [9]

When Southern colleagues told him that one wrong did not justify another, that such an ethic was the cause of the continuation of a vicious circle, he cried, "I am tired of so much sentimentality in the South and no practicability. I think if we have got to have these iniquities we should have our share of the benefits." [10] "If you were one of the heirs to a cow," he told Joseph W. Bailey, when that Texas sena-

6 *Cong. Record,* 56 Cong., 1 Sess., 6283; 57 Cong., 1 Sess., 5102.
7 *Ibid.,* 57 Cong., 1 Sess., 2280–81.
8 *Ibid.,* 56 Cong., 2 Sess., 3527. *Cf. ibid.,* 55 Cong., 3 Sess., 2627; Charleston *News and Courier,* May 17, 1900.
9 *Cong. Record,* 56 Cong., 2 Sess., 2394.
10 Reply to Marion Butler, *ibid.,* 54 Cong., 2 Sess., 2448.

tor reproached him for getting a portion of the Federal appropriations for the Charleston Exposition, "and all the other heirs were sitting down to supper and eating the beef and you had to stand by—my friend, you lean too far backward, you had better get your conscience straightened." [11]

All Tillman's energy was invoked in quest of special grants for South Carolina. He threatened filibusters, argued at tedious length, solicited the friendships of Presidents McKinley and Taft and influential Republican senators with a diplomacy not apparent in his surface manners. A tireless suppliant at the offices of departmental and bureau heads, there was no limit to his avidity for material favors for his constituents. But he was personally honest, seeking no appropriations from which he could himself profit. He was content to live modestly on his salary and on the limited revenues of his farms and lecture tours.

The Spanish-American War gave Pitchfork Ben his first good opportunity to spear appropriations for his state. The government was distributing appointments and expenditures without considerations of party; South Carolinians in hordes sought the aid of their senator to secure army appointments. "Everybody down there [in South Carolina]," he wryly commented, "wants to be a general or a captain or a major or something else." [12] He was satisfied with the number of commissions granted from a list he submitted to President McKinley. After the war was over, he sought compensation for damages done by soldiers encamped in Southern states. Soldiers, he said, had run over crops and perhaps "stole some man's fruit or some little odds and ends like that." The aggrieved farmers were "poor people. . . . They need this money." [13]

As a patriot who fully appreciated war services, he zealously championed military pensions. Convinced of Republican abuse, he pushed war claims of his own, however re-

[11] *Ibid.*, 58 Cong., 2 Sess., 2355. [12] *Ibid.*, 55 Cong., 2 Sess., 6534.
[13] *Ibid.*, 56 Cong., 1 Sess., 4974.

mote. The most noteworthy case of this type concerned James A. Thomas, a Mexican War veteran who had, under act of Congress, been deprived of a pension because he had enlisted in the Confederate army. Tillman was outraged. All veterans of the Mexican War, he believed, "should have the same opportunity to draw Uncle Sam's money and suck the sweet milk of the Treasury as any other ex-soldiers have." In 1900 he maneuvered a bill through the Senate providing Thomas a monthly stipend of $45, but the measure was delayed by the House Pensions Committee. He then resolved to "act in the only way left for me to attract attention to the injustice of the case." This meant a filibuster against the House pension bill. But he later changed his mind, unsuccessfully appealing to the House's sense of fairness to get justice for his man.[14] The following year when he was at first unable to get results, he declared: "I swear by the Almighty God I will never let another pension bill pass here, if by objecting and obstructing I can do it, until this old man gets justice." Thomas got the pension.[15]

Of greater value to South Carolina was the revival of claims for reimbursement of expenditures in no less than four wars. In 1858 John A. Black, an agent of the state, had presented evidence to sustain Revolutionary War claims of $316,947, War of 1812 claims of $202,230, and Seminole and Mexican War claims of $57,000. These demands had not been adjudicated at the time because of the Civil War, and they were almost forgotten. But Tillman revived them in 1900 and secured the appointment of an investigator to re-establish their validity.[16] Centering his energies on the 1812 claim, the senator struggled three years for its redemption. The government countered with the demand that South Carolina pay $125,000 in State House bonds which had been held in Washington since 1856. Tillman subtracted part of this amount from the 1812 claim, leaving a

14 *Ibid.*, 678–81, 6134, 6372; 2 Sess., 2185.   15 *Ibid.*, 2 Sess., 2185, 3019.
16 Kohn, in Charleston *News and Courier*, May 28, 1900.

balance of nearly $100,000 due South Carolina, and piled his desk high with books preparatory for a filibuster. "I simply shut my jaws down on the proposition," he said, "that I would have that money or I would have an extra session." The Senate yielded to this species of blackmail, and the senator had the satisfaction of tendering the governor of South Carolina a United States treasury check for $89,137.86, together with the canceled $125,000 obligation.[17]

During his first years in Washington, the senator "pleaded, begged, and quarreled," as he expressed it, "to get a few crumbs" for the "little orphan of a naval station" which had been established at Port Royal in 1883 through the influence of Senator Butler. Tillman's efforts bore fruit in the erection of two new buildings and in the installation of machinery for the repair of ships.[18] But the Port Royal establishment did not prosper. Senator Hale of the naval committee said that its docks were "absolutely useless" and that but for the adroitness of Butler, the station would never have been established.[19] Tillman could not induce the Navy Department to send vessels there except "some old trash or other that the other yards did not care to have." Port Royal lacked adequate railroad facilities and labor supply, and the navy personnel was reluctant to go to so isolated a place.[20]

The failure of Port Royal caused a shift in Tillman's interest which made possible his greatest pork-barrel triumph. In 1900 the mayor of Charleston informed him that Port Royal was likely to be abandoned and solicited his services in behalf of a larger station at Charleston. Accompanied by the mayor, the senator won the interest of naval authorities, and a board of experts recommended the trans-

[17] Tillman reminiscences, in *Cong. Record,* 65 Cong., 2 Sess., 7728; Wallace, *History of South Carolina,* III, 417–19.

[18] *Cong. Record,* 55 Cong., 3 Sess., 2627–28; 56 Cong., 1 Sess., 5491.

[19] *Ibid.,* 56 Cong., 1 Sess., 5490.

[20] *Ibid.,* 5491.

fer.[21] Tillman next enlisted the powerful aid of Senators Hale and Chandler of the naval committee and forestalled the opposition of North Carolina and Georgia congressmen who wanted the transfer made to Wilmington or Savannah.[22] His measure passed the Senate with ease, and after some difficulty ran the hurdle of the House.[23] The mayor of Charleston wrote Tillman: "Your name will be inseparably associated with this great navy yard, whose location here has been largely due to your wise and efficient counsel." [24]

For never a moment thereafter did the South Carolina senator forget the Charleston navy yard. It occupied a place in his consciousness comparable to that held by Clemson College or the Dispensary during earlier years. He defended it on all occasions against all critics; he haggled constantly over funds for its maintenance and expansion; he even interfered with its internal administration, once reprimanding the President of the United States for refusing to remove a commandant of whom the senator disapproved. "You have treated me shabbily," he wrote Taft. "I do not understand why unless it is because I am a Democrat." [25] Convinced that naval authorities were conspiring to wreck his favorite project, he himself became party to a cabal consisting of the ten members of the Senate naval committee in whose states were located navy yards. These gentlemen supported the needs of each other's projects; and when this device failed there remained the threat of filibuster. Senator Penrose once declared, "I have never failed in 18 years to vote for the appropriations for the Charleston Navy Yard, knowing all the time that I could not get an adjournment of Congress until I did so." [26] Tillman succeeded in having

[21] James A. Smyth to Tillman, October 2, 1902, in Tillman Papers; R. Goodwin Rhett, in *Cong. Record*, 64 Cong., 1 Sess., 4450–51.

[22] *Cong. Record*, 56 Cong., 1 Sess., 5492–93.

[23] Larner, in Charleston *News and Courier*, May 30, 1900.

[24] James A. Smyth to Tillman, July 21, 1902, in Tillman Papers.

[25] Tillman to William H. Taft, June 15, 1912, *ibid.*

[26] *Cong. Record*, 63 Cong., 3 Sess., 4713.

a dry dock, a machine shop, and other equipment of a first-class navy yard placed at Charleston. He complained that over a period of twenty years the Charleston expenditures amounted to only $5,727,687.39.[27]

Magazine writers protested the success of the navy-yard junto. In 1909 these criticisms were introduced in the Senate debates by Joseph M. Dixon of Colorado and Robert M. La Follette of Wisconsin. It was maintained that the location of yards should be determined by naval experts instead of senators who "vie with each other in a struggle to secure the largest appropriations possible under all circumstances for the States from which they come." The naval committee's insistence on a chain of yards scattered along the Atlantic coast was several times more expensive than the concentration of naval repair work at two or three convenient points. It was specifically charged that Charleston was unsuited for a first-class yard because of its lack of trained mechanics, the shallowness of its waters, and its isolation.[28]

Tillman's answer revealed his determination to protect Charleston at all cost. He asserted sweepingly that the magazine articles were "the lies" and "the trash" of muckrakers hostile to the South. It was absurd for Dixon to recommend for the navy because he was "a man from the Rocky Mountains." Naval experts should not determine navy-yard policies because already too many commissions were usurping the powers of Congress, and because the Navy Department was dominated by a political machine bent on sacrificing Charleston in favor of Boston and New York. The Charleston navy yard, the senator was sure, had great natural advantages. Its waters were sufficiently deep; in fact, there was room in Charleston Harbor for a hundred battleships; and there was strategic need of a navy yard south of Norfolk. Finally, under La Follette's proddings, the South Caro-

---

[27] *Ibid.*, 3553.

[28] Joseph M. Dixon and Robert M. La Follette speeches, *ibid.*, 60 Cong., 2 Sess., 2378–79, 2434–36, 2550–53.

linian admitted that the Charleston development was justified as part of the appropriations the national government
owed the South.[29]

Another Tillman triumph was the securing of $250,000
for the Charleston Exposition of 1902. "The little pitiful
sum," said the senator, was justified because Buffalo and
St. Louis expositions were receiving larger amounts. The
appropriation passed the Senate but "the watchdogs of the
Treasury" held it up in the House.[30] Tillman flitted nervously about the Senate charging discrimination. With the
aid of such powerful leaders as Lodge, Spooner, Chandler,
and Hoar, the Charleston appropriation was attached to the
St. Louis measure in such a manner that one could not live
without the other. Under this protection the favor for
Charleston slipped through the House. Tillman, his heart
welling with patriotic pride, invited the senators to visit the
Charleston show where they would find "a high-spirited,
noble, and chivalrous people" and an environment in
which they could "drink history by the quart, or by the
gallon, or by the barrel." [31]

This unexpected victory led to the accusation that Tillman and other Democratic senators had been rewarded to
withdraw their opposition to Republican bills for the government of Cuba and the Philippines. Tillman's expressed
intention of filibustering against these measures never ma-
terialized. The newspapers said that all but one of the
Democratic senators had been "fixed" by rivers and harbors
appropriations; and that one, who was Tillman himself,
had been "fixed" by the Charleston grant. For several days,
said one newspaper, "the fiery Tillman was in great distress,
but soon he 'made good' on Cuba and the Philippines and
all his troubles disappeared." The South Carolinian called
the accusation "a lie." "No man," he declared, "has ever
dared approach me with any hint that I could be seduced

29 *Ibid.*, 2434-36, 2551-53.   30 *Ibid.*, 56 Cong., 2 Sess., 3292-94, 3541-43.
31 *Ibid.*, 57 Cong., 1 Sess., 1119.

or induced to cast any votes here because of money that my State was getting." The filibuster had been abandoned, he affirmed, because the Democrats could not agree concerning its wisdom, and Republicans could have accomplished their purpose through an extra session. His denial of collusion should be accepted, for he was not a liar; but on other occasions he had openly favored "log-rolling" conspiracies. Perhaps he unconsciously deferred to the Republicans in gratitude for the favor granted the chief city of his beloved state.[32]

The manner in which the South Carolina senator distributed the Federal patronage and the offices at his disposal augmented his popularity at home. It is true that his first consideration was his family and his personal friends. He secured a sinecure for his eldest son [33] and himself confessed that he enjoyed "taking public pap." [34] But, generally, the historic division of South Carolinians into Tillmanites and anti-Tillmanites did not influence his distribution of public plums. Later in life he could truthfully write, "Since I have been senator I have never asked a man from South Carolina who came to me for favors whether he voted for me or not." [35] The only requirements were that the suppliant be a white Democrat who had not recently behaved in a manner personally obnoxious. Indeed, the senator sometimes bent backward to favor opponents of his more turbulent years. He endorsed Earle's candidacy for the Federal attorneyship [36] and Butler's application for a major generalship of volunteers during the War with Spain. He asked President McKinley not to remove the enfeebled and impoverished Wade Hampton from the sinecure to which President Cleveland had appointed him. This "graceful

[32] Accusation against Tillman summarized, in Columbia *State*, March 6, 10, 1901; his answer, in *Cong. Record*, 56 Cong., 2 Sess., 3541–42.

[33] As clerk of the Committee on Five Civilized Tribes. Columbia *State*, February 3, 1910.

[34] Kohn, in Charleston *News and Courier*, July 4, 1918.

[35] Tillman to Columbia *State*, March 16, 1916.

[36] *Id.* to Earle, November 23, 1892, in Tillman Papers.

act" was done without any sort of personal or political understanding between the two men.[37] To the once-hated city of Charleston went the two most important pork-barrel appropriations of Tillman's career.

Why was he so generous toward former enemies? His anger, although sharp and sudden, was seldom lasting; behind it lay the saving graces of generosity and humor. His hates were more often political than personal, and even when personal, they were not nurtured by those deep moral emotions which sustain undying passions. There were elements of the superficial and the theatrical in the Tillman anger.

Furthermore, as the senator became absorbed in the larger affairs of the nation, the animosities of his South Carolina days appeared less important, subjects for kindly reminiscences instead of brooding. There was a positive reason why this very rational man wished to forget the conflicts of the past. Chief deputy of a beloved state in Washington, he felt that it was his duty to forget factionalism so that he might faithfully represent all white Democrats of South Carolina. This was the stand of the civic moralist, not merely a politician's vote-getting intrigue. In 1903 he said in all sincerity to newly-won Conservative friends: "If I helped Charleston it was from duty and not because I wished to change your attitude toward me." [38]

Tillman's appeals to the prejudices of South Carolinians, his championship of their doctrines, and his distribution of national favors inevitably won to his side the majority of his former enemies. He was snuggled to as a powerful man who had expressed the South Carolina viewpoint better than anyone since 1860, and as one who had a realistic conception of his duty toward his constituents. "I am glad," he told a group of former enemies, "you are willing to acknowledge that I am not a nonentity in the United States

[37] Charleston *News and Courier*, June 10, 1897.
[38] *Ibid.*, April 3, 1903.

Senate, and I am glad that you are willing to honor me. . . . Let the past bury its dead." [39] Only a small minority of the anti-Tillmanites refused to give him either sincere or simulated support.

This change of attitude is strikingly illustrated by the conduct of the ruling element of Charleston after they realized that he could be used for material benefit. In 1898 the mayor of the city gave him a public banquet to enlist his influence to have troops for Cuba embark there.[40] In 1900 the opposition of Charleston to his re-election to the Senate melted away amidst acknowledgment that but for his "splendid management" the navy yard would not have been won.[41] In 1903, after the navy yard and the exposition appropriations had become established facts, he was lionized at a second banquet.[42] Thereafter, the senator found the Charleston atmosphere most congenial. After a visit there in 1912 he wrote, "The treatment of me by the citizens of the city was so geniune and kindly that I could not help realizing that at last I have won their love." [43]

The Columbia and Greenville newspapers derided Charleston for honoring him even though he was "a very useful man in Washington and could ill be spared by venerable cities desiring to appropriate the naval stations of their neighbors." [44] But the two intractable towns soon fell in line. In 1899 the senator was enthusiastically received as the principal guest of a Columbia banquet. The town wherein "deep oaths were sworn of eternal hatred to Tillman" had had "her heart melted to gentleness by the touch" of a Federal appropriation for the Congaree River. Gonzales

[39] Columbia *State*, March 9, 1899.

[40] Charleston *News and Courier*, October 6, 11, 1898; Columbia *State*, October 10, 1898.

[41] Charleston *News and Courier*, May 30, 1900.

[42] Wallace, *History of South Carolina*, III, 416; James A. Smyth to Tillman, March 16, 1903, in Tillman Papers.

[43] Tillman to Mrs. Henry P. Williams, November 25, 1912, *ibid.*

[44] Columbia *State*, October 10, 1898; August 27, 1900; Greenville *News*, cited in Charleston *News and Courier*, October 11, 1898.

absented himself from the dinner, but he "could not condemn the feeling of gratitude" toward Columbia's benefactor. In Greenville, too, there was a Tillman dinner.[45]

Such developments made the re-election of Tillman in 1900 a foregone conclusion. The winning of Conservative applause had not diminished his popularity with the rural masses.[46] Absolute master of the May convention of his party, he directed that body toward national issues on which all South Carolinians were agreed. When a single delegate opposed the move to endorse the senator's conduct in Washington, the convention rose as one man to squelch the dissenter by expressing gratitude for the manner in which the senator "exposed and condemned the hypocritical imperialistic policy" of the Republicans.[47] He was too popular to provoke organized opposition in the August primary. Nevertheless, 18,213 voters scratched his name from the ballot. This was not due so much to personal dislike of the candidate as to his injection of the Dispensary issue into the gubernatorial contest.[48]

[45] Columbia *State,* March 9, 10, 17, 1899.
[46] Jones to Tillman, October 3, 1899, in Tillman Papers.
[47] Charleston *News and Courier,* May 17, 1900.
[48] Wallace, *History of South Carolina,* III, 392.

Chapter XXV

SOUTH CAROLINA POLITICS 1901–1906

IT should not be assumed that Tillman's triumphant re-election in 1900 indicated full and sincere support by the elements that had opposed him in the past. Resentment still burned in the memories of those from whom he had taken political power. This group, while numerically in the minority, was still powerful. It was composed of bankers, merchants, editors, the educated, and the aristocrats; those who were best organized politically and socially and who had formerly regarded South Carolina as a sort of personal monopoly. To them Tillman was still the crude rustic who had usurped their power and repaid courtesies with insolence. Many of them, despite public professions of affection for the man who had good things to give, detested him as avidly as ever. "The Conservative party," a Tillman lieutenant wrote his chief in 1899, "hate you in their hearts as bitterly as they ever did and will continue to hate you until you are crushed." [1] Subdued by his repeated victories, leaderless to stem his irresistible effectiveness with the voters, they continued to attack him at vulnerable points. They criticized his betrayal of the traditions of the Southern gentleman on the Senate floor. They called attention to his unorthodox views on the tariff. They deplored his instigation of race prejudice and objected to his chronic interference in state politics. Without attempting a frontal attack, they awaited the day when the passions of Tillmanism would cool. Then, perhaps, would it be possible to return

[1] Judge D. A. Townsend to Tillman, May 31, 1899, in Tillman Papers.

to the "normal," to the resumption of political control by
the faction Tillman had unhorsed in 1890. There was hope
that Tillman himself might eventually yield. Assurance of
security in the Senate might induce him to surrender the
control of matters strictly South Carolinian in favor of a
happy isolation in Washington!

Contributory to this latent Conservative protest was the
dissatisfaction among the Tillman leaders themselves. They
had never loved the blustering chief who exacted efficient
public service according to his peculiar standards; who
would not tolerate the loafer, the drunkard, the dishonest,
the erratic; and who degraded those more conservative or
more radical than he. They courted him for a time, knowing
that his disfavor spelled their downfall; but one by one
they quarreled with him, and with his maledictions upon
them they passed into obscurity. Most prominent among the
fallen lieutenants were Shell, Irby, Donaldson, Norris,
Farley, and Gantt.[2] Their only consolation was the conviction, however unjust, that personal success had changed a
once hungry reformer into a fat aristocrat no longer interested in the common man.

Drawing recruits from both the Tillmanites and the
Conservatives was another group inimical to Tillman: the
Prohibitionists. They continued to reject the Tillman contention that the Dispensary was an admirable substitute for
the saloon. The fact that the Palmetto Tree had been literally blown into the whiskey bottle evoked lurid denunciations. "The proud emblem of a proud State adorns the
pockets of every drunkard in the street. . . . It is hurled
by the drunken husband at his trembling wife and children,
and in short has become the coat of arms of Satan in his
worst form." [3]

The strength of the agitation against the Dispensary was

[2] Kirkland, "Tillman and I," in Columbia *State*, July 31, 1929; Ball, *State
that Forgot*, 230.
[3] President of the South Carolina branch of the Woman's Christian Temperance Union, in Charleston *News and Courier*, November 1, 1897.

enhanced by Tillman's misunderstanding of the motives of the Prohibitionists. He continued to regard the state monopoly as acceptable merely because it was practical. To him it represented moderation; it yielded generous revenues; it could be perfected by the elimination of administrative inefficiencies and dishonesties. As a man who personally had never bowed before the temptation of Demon Rum, he saw no reason why the attempt to drive the demon from the state should be made. He did not understand why such common sense did not appeal to the Prohibitionists. But this was a fact: Many of them had been drunkards, or had husbands, brothers, or fathers victimized by liquor, and as a consequence they reacted from strong drink with the moral fervor of religious fanatics. Their emotions were the same as those of medieval saints fleeing from sex. Tillman's pro-Dispensary arguments left them cold. They had been injured by a vice, betrayed by a sin, against which practical expedients were futile. They would banish Demon Rum from the commonwealth. When Tillman, uncomprehending, questioned their motives, they returned denunciation with anathema.

The forces opposed to Tillman—the Conservatives, the dissatisfied Tillmanites, and the Prohibitionists—found an unexpected ally in Judge Charles H. Simonton of the United States district court, who, on May 31, 1897, issued an injunction annulling that portion of the Dispensary act forbidding the sale of liquors not removed from the containers in which they were brought into the state. In other words, the court held that the public authorities could not forbid private persons from selling liquors under the same regulations as the Dispensary. Immediately, carloads of loose packages were imported, numerous "original package" stores were opened, and it was freely predicted that this competition would force the dispensaries to close. The Dispensary constables, fearing imprisonment for contempt, were unable to interfere with "original package" sales, but kept the Dispensary alive by arresting merchants who allowed the contents of the packages to be drunk on the premises.[4]

These attacks on his "pet institution" gave Tillman sound reason to ignore the suggestion that he eschew state affairs. On the floor of the Senate he proved that the Simonton decision was defective, and secured the passage of a bill giving states the right to regulate the liquor traffic as they saw fit. But this measure failed in the House where "Czar" Thomas B. Reed would not let it come to a vote.[5]

Tillman appealed to his highest tribunal, the South Carolina voters. During the summer of 1897 he appeared at barbecues, taking "hand primaries" and even suggesting the possibility of his resigning from the Senate to run for governor on a Dispensary platform. Before hilarious picnic audiences he called Simonton a tyrant whose "dirty hand" he promised to take from the throat of South Carolina. As for Prohibition, he asserted that the drinking of alcohol was not forbidden by Scripture and that it was beneficial to certain "pure Christian men" he knew.[6]

The obstacle of the Simonton decree was removed by a decision of the United States Supreme Court on May 9, 1898, declaring that the state, in the exercise of its police powers, could take entire control of the sale of liquors and prohibit their sale except by authorized agents.[7] This gave the Dispensary a new start and made possible a more efficient suppression of illegal sales.[8]

Tillman threw himself energetically into the gubernatorial canvass of 1898 as a champion of Governor Ellerbe, the Dispensary candidate. The other candidates were Claudius C. Featherstone, Prohibitionist, and George D.

[4] Wallace, *History of South Carolina*, III, 380–81; *Outlook*, LXI (1899), 8; New York *Times*, August 19, 1899.

[5] *Cong. Record*, 55 Cong., 1 Sess., 858, 1405–1406, 2612; Charleston *News and Courier*, July 13, 1897.

[6] Tillman, in Charleston *News and Courier*, August 7, 10, 19, 1897.

[7] Vance *v.* W. A. Vandercook Company, 170 U.S. Reports 438.

[8] *Outlook*, LXI (1899), 8.

Tillman, who demanded that the state Dispensary be replaced by county option. When Ben announced that, if necessary, he would stump the state to save the Dispensary, he was accused of seeking primarily to humiliate his estranged brother. The Spartanburg *Herald* said that his hatred of George was "somewhat fiendish," a statement which the Columbia *State* modified to merely "selfish, not fiendish." Infuriated by this public galling of an old sore, Ben roared that the two newspaper articles were "double-distilled essence of falsehood and 'fiendish' malignity," motivated by a hatred born of the fact that he had retired the two editors from the control of the state. "The treacherous Spaniard [Gonzales], who makes the charges of betrayal and unbrotherly conduct against me, only advertises his own depravity and blackness of heart." [9]

After the elimination of George D. Tillman in the first primary, the strength of the Prohibitionist Featherstone seemed so menacing that Ellerbe, fearing defeat, entered into an agreement with Gonzales, who opposed both Prohibition and the Dispensary. In return for the editor's support, Ellerbe secretly promised to abandon the Dispensary in favor of George D. Tillman's plan of county option.[10] Ellerbe defeated Featherstone by the narrow margin of 5,000 votes. If it is true that Gonzales turned as many as 2,600 votes, his influence determined the result. But the governor did not keep his promise to the editor. Under the formidable compulsion of Tillman, he repudiated local option in favor of the Dispensary, and thus Tillman's favorite institution weathered the storms of 1898.[11]

The pugnacious senator prepared early for the fight the Prohibitionists planned against the Dispensary in 1900. Miles B. McSweeney, who became governor when Ellerbe died in 1899, was willing to administer the law according to

9 Tillman, in Columbia *State*, January 2, 1898.
10 *Ibid.*, January 11, 1899.
11 Wallace, *History of South Carolina*, III, 392.

Tillman's specifications.[12] To prevent enemies from "fly-blowing and distorting facts," Tillman demanded an investigation of the "full financial showing" of the Dispensary, with nothing "cloaked or hidden." [13] He favored revision of the Dispensary act and drafted a bill embodying suggested changes.[14] These actions were supplemented by the declaration that some Prohibition leaders were "cowards and hypocrites" seeking "an impractical and undesirable ideal." "I am proud to believe," he wrote a Methodist minister, "the Dispensary law is much better in its practical results than Prohibition could possibly be." [15] Then he announced that he was willing to canvass the state once more in defense of this conviction.[16]

The Prohibitionists nominated James A. Hoyt, a Baptist editor, as their candidate for governor.[17] McSweeney, with the Tillman endorsement, was the Dispensary candidate.

The tone of the campaign of 1900 was pitched by Tillman. In a half-jocular manner he told delighted audiences: "Prohibition will not do because of the Old Adam in us. . . . You love your liquor just like you do your girls." Liquor drinking, he again asserted, was justified by Holy Scripture. The inevitable opposition such talk aroused led him to declare: "There is an unholy alliance of preachers and barkeepers led by Colonel Hoyt." [18] A remark so suggestive of slander was instantly contested. Bishop William W. Duncan said that this "reckless statement of Tillman was an outrage and disgraceful," and the Reverend Charles S. Gardner of the leading Baptist church at Greenville contended that it was "a mean and contemptible effort to break the force of the almost unanimous advocacy of Prohibition

[12] Miles B. McSweeney to Tillman, August 15, November 22, 1899, in Tillman Papers.
[13] Tillman to Robert Aldrich, December 18, 1899, *ibid.*
[14] *Id.* to D. A. G. Ouzts, December 11, 1899, *ibid.; id.* to J. S. Drakeford, December 12, 1899, *ibid.*
[15] *Id.* to John O. Willson, August 11, 1899, *ibid.*
[16] Charleston *News and Courier,* August 5, 1899.
[17] *Ibid.,* May 24, 1900.   [18] *Ibid.,* July 19, 21, 27, 1900.

by the preachers, and served its author as a good occasion also to throw contempt upon a class of men for whom he has in many other ways expressed contempt." [19] The state Baptist weekly submitted that Tillman's use of the Bible to justify drinking "puts him down as a far worse man than his most ardent enemies have ever branded him. . . . We do not believe His Satanic Majesty is capable of handling God's Word more perversely and irreverently than Senator Tillman does." [20]

Tillman was content to let the people judge between him and the preachers.[21] In a tour of the state his "red hot" attacks on the ministers were received "with the old-time whoops," [22] and at Greenville the Reverend Mr. Gardner's sermon was refuted point by point amid a raising of hands which proved that the accusation about "an unholy alliance" between clergy and barkeepers was widely believed.[23]

McSweeney defeated Hoyt by the decisive majority of 14,000; for the time being, the Dispensary was safe. Although the strenuous efforts of its founder saved it, the great strength of the Prohibitionists was attested by the fact that so many voters scratched his name from the ballot in his unopposed candidacy for the Senate.[24]

That the friendship established between the senator and the citizens of Charleston was not based on the most solid foundations is demonstrated by an incident connected with the Charleston Exposition. President Roosevelt was invited to visit the fair, and subscriptions were taken to purchase a sword to be presented by the President while in Charleston to Major Micah Jenkins, a gallant member of Roosevelt's Rough Riders. Lieutenant Governor James H. Tillman, George D. Tillman's son, directed the taking of the sub-

[19] *Ibid.*, July 25, 1900.
[20] *South Carolina Baptist*, cited in Columbia *State*, August 16, 1900.
[21] Tillman to Willson, July 23, 1900, in Tillman Papers.
[22] Charleston *News and Courier*, July 27–31, 1900.
[23] *Ibid.*, August 7, 1900.
[24] The voters who did this numbered 18,213. Wallace, *History of South Carolina*, III, 392.

scriptions and the senator was among the subscribers. The attitude of the Tillmans toward Roosevelt's part in the proposed ceremonies changed, however, when in February, 1902, the President withdrew a dinner invitation to the senator.[25] James H. Tillman, without consulting a majority of those who had subscribed to the sword fund, rudely withdrew the invitation to the President. Naturally, Charleston and responsible state officials were alarmed, fearing that Roosevelt would refuse to pay the expected visit. There was a rush to create a new sword fund and a committee was sent to Washington to assure the President that the Tillman nephew was not the keeper of South Carolina hospitality. Roosevelt came to Charleston and was received with all the cordiality a loyal city usually bestows upon the head of the nation.[26]

Ben Tillman had tried to frighten Roosevelt into staying away from Charleston. In an interview published in a New York newspaper he said that in South Carolina "there is a very intense feeling against the President" and that his presence there might provoke "some drunken fool" to insult him.[27] When the President refused to heed this warning, the senator was furious over the reception given the distinguished guest. It was, he said, "an anti-Tillman demonstration." It was a mercenary city's repudiation of its benefactor to put "a few paltry dollars" in the treasury of the exposition. Charleston "occupied the pitiful attitude of a beggar asking alms from the man who insulted her friend." [28]

A more serious cause of continued ill-feeling between the senator and his enemies was the tragic feud between Gonzales and James H. Tillman, a man who represented the Tillmans and Tillmanism at their worst. Jim Tillman, as he was familiarly known, had many qualities necessary for success in the politics of his day. His tall consumptive frame,

[25] See p. 410.
[26] Charleston *News and Courier*, February 28, 1902.
[27] New York *Tribune*, cited in Columbia *State*, March 5, 1902.
[28] Tillman to James A. Smyth, May 7, 1902, in Tillman Papers.

his feverish black eyes, his well-chiseled face, and his long raven hair gave him a striking appearance. Reckless but affable, he was popular with the rough element his uncle had aroused into political consciousness. Moreover, he was ambitious and scheming; he capitalized effectively on Ben's popularity to increase his own. By loud professions of willingness to engage in physical encounters, he appealed to the strain of violence close to the heart of Tillmanism. He outdid his uncle in conjuring up anti-Negro prejudices, and by clever demagoguery effectively attached the growing population of the cotton-mill villages to his standard. "He had," the uncle wrote, "as many brains as any Tillman I ever knew."

But, as the uncle significantly added, Jim Tillman "could not control his passions." [29] Unlike Ben, he was a free spender of his own and other people's money, a gambler, a drinker, a rascal who sometimes tried to wear the cloak of righteousness. His erratic conduct was that of a man tortured by consumption. He was "pulled in an Augusta dive for gambling" and was accused of attending cock-fights.[30] As lieutenant colonel of a regiment during the Spanish-American War he was threatened with court-martial because he insulted a superior officer and ordered the flogging of two Negroes.[31] When at Gaffney in 1900 he publicly posed as "a consistent member of the Presbyterian church," his uncle ejaculated, "What makes you tell such a God-damned lie as that, Jim?" [32]

Despite his faults Jim Tillman's political star steadily rose. Beginning as a journalistic defender of his uncle, he soon became a fairly prominent politician. In 1900 the people of the state made him lieutenant governor, the result

[29] *Id.* to Lehman Johnson, August 21, 28, 1914, *ibid.*

[30] Columbia *State*, October 7, 29, November 16, 1900. The manner in which Jim Tillman was "pulled" is not known. There is no record of his being arrested or fined.

[31] *Ibid.*, October 6, 8, 15, 16, 1898.

[32] Yorkville *Enquirer*, cited *ibid.*, September 6, 1900.

of his championing the Dispensary, parading his services for his uncle, and appealing to the anti-Negro prejudices of the cotton-mill operatives. He favored the closing of Negro schools by denying licenses to Negro teachers.[33]

The feud between Gonzales and Jim Tillman began in 1890 when Jim, writing in a Winnsboro newspaper, accused the "wily Spaniard" of falsely reporting his uncle's words at the March convention. Gonzales, at a meeting of the social club which gave the State Ball, cried that Jim was "unfit for association with gentlemen," and that if his name were presented for membership in the club, the editor would blackball him. He ignored Tillman's challenge to a duel, explaining that "so contemptible an object as this callow fellow" was beneath his notice.[34] For a decade the feud smoldered. When in 1900 the Edgefield man offered for the lieutenant-governorship, Gonzales warned the people that "it would be a calamity" to give him an office which would put him in line for the governorship.[35]

When Jim's success in 1900 gave him a good chance to win the higher office in 1902, Gonzales acted with decision. The honest and fanatically self-righteous editor assumed the perilous role of exposing falsehood grown formidable. His task in this case was not difficult. In editorial after editorial he charged that Tillman was "a proven liar, defaulter, gambler and drunkard." As lieutenant governor he had falsified the records of the Senate; as a commander of a regiment he had "disgraced himself by his conduct"; as president of the Edgefield Monument Association he had embezzled sacred money. He was "this rogue," "a disgrace to his uncle, a double disgrace to his father," a second Franklin J. Moses headed for prison.[36] The terrible fact about these onslaughts was that they were not slanders; they were largely

33 Charleston *News and Courier*, June 15–22, 1900.
34 Charleston *World*, January 9, 1891.
35 Columbia *State*, August 30, 1900.
36 Columbia *State*'s editorials of March–April, 1902, conveniently summarized, in Charleston *News and Courier*, October 2, 1903.

the unvarnished truth and had the result Gonzales intended. Jim Tillman was disgraced before the people and was defeated in his candidacy for governor. He declared: "But for the brutal, false and malicious newspaper attacks headed by N. G. Gonzales, I believe I would have been elected." [37]

The sequel was the assassination of Gonzales at Columbia on January 15, 1903. Four months had elapsed since the election of 1902 and the defeated candidate had been brooding over the Gonzales editorials. Fresh from his duties as presiding officer of the Senate, he met his defamer in broad daylight and mortally wounded the unarmed man. State and national press cried out in indignation, but a majority of South Carolinians justified the killing. A change of venue was secured to Lexington, strong in its pro-Tillman sentiments; the inclination of the jury panel was secured in advance; [38] a farcical plea of self-defense was evolved by skilled lawyers; irrelevant political matters were introduced in evidence. The jury returned a verdict of acquittal. The assassin of Gonzales, as of Dawson, the other great anti-Tillman editor, went legally unpunished; but the Gonzales family experienced a ghastly vengeance. The ghost of the dead man pursued Jim Tillman the rest of his unhappy days.

Ben Tillman was in no way responsible for the crime of his unfortunate nephew. Jim's political rise was due as much to his unique characteristics as to the prestige of the Tillman name. Ben understood the nephew's weaknesses

---

[37] James H. Tillman circular, Edgefield, South Carolina, August 29, 1902, in Tillman Scrapbooks.

[38] B. L. Caughman, a political ally, wrote Tillman on July 11, 1903: "It is very important we should get men we can trust in every section of the county [Lexington] to organize the forces [in favor of Jim]." Tillman Papers. George W. Croft, second in command among the defense lawyers, wrote Tillman on September 16, 1903: "We [the lawyers] canvassed thoroughly the jurors of both weeks and many of the jurors have been sounded." *Ibid.* There is a persistent tradition unconfirmed by documentary evidence that the Jim Tillman defense hired Ben Covar, an Edgefield stalwart, to sell pictures of the two principals among prospective Lexington jurors. The reaction of each man was carefully noted by Covar as this salesman-detective successively displayed the likenesses of Gonzales and Tillman.

and was careful not to endorse his ambitions. The enmity between the uncle and the venomous journalist was more political than personal; Ben sincerely deplored the murder.[39]

But, regardless of his personal will, the uncle was involved in Jim's affairs. Jim was a close relative whose political prestige was in part a reflection of Ben's; the man Jim murdered had spent a goodly portion of his energies criticizing the senator. For this reason many people failed to make fine distinctions and held Ben indirectly responsible for the tragedy. When Jim was put on trial for his life, the uncle came to the rescue with the loyalty every South Carolinian expected of a kinsman. "Jim Tillman," he explained, "was my nephew, and blood is thicker than water." [40] He co-operated with Jim's lawyers in securing a change of venue.[41] He tried to influence the verdict by attempting to create the belief that an acquittal was inevitable and by unsuccessfully attempting to insert in a newspaper a fictitious interview by what he called "a supposititious citizen." [42] He assisted in paying the expenses of the case and at the trial sat among the defense lawyers; [43] and he allowed them to link together the dead man's hatred of the two Tillmans.[44]

[39] Tillman to D. W. McLaurin, February 22, 1916, *ibid. Cf.* McGhee, "Tillman, Smasher of Traditions," *loc. cit.*, 8020.

[40] Tillman to A. W. Sims, October 11, 1916, in Tillman Papers.

[41] Croft wrote Tillman on June 9, 1903: "There are several persons here [in Columbia] whose affidavits we very much desire. So far we have been unable to get them; but believe you can be the means of securing them." *Ibid. Cf.* Altheus Johnson to Tillman, April 30, 1903, *ibid.*; Patrick H. Nelson to *id.*, June 24, 1903, *ibid.*

[42] Croft to *id.*, September 24, 1903, *ibid.*; Tillman to Colonel E. B. Hoak, of the Augusta *Chronicle*, July 24, 1903, *ibid.* Thomas W. Loyless, editor of this newspaper, wrote Tillman in reply to the request for the publication of the article on July 30, 1903: "While *The Chronicle* can sympathize with Senator Tillman personally over the unpleasant position in which he has been placed, it must decline to publish a fake interview in its columns in order to aid him or his nephew or any other man." *Ibid.*

[43] Croft to *id.*, June 24, September 24, 1903, *ibid.*; Charleston *News and Courier*, October 16, 1903.

[44] Columbia *State*, October 16, 1903.

Most South Carolinians learned to forget or even to justify the murder; the Conservatives became politically so reconciled to Ben Tillman that he believed the brother of the dead editor voted for him in 1912. Nevertheless, the assassination created a chasm deeper than that engendered by the contentions of the 1890's. The anger of the earlier period was expressed only in words; that of the later period in blood. Deep in their hearts the friends of Gonzales never absolved the uncle and defender of the editor's murderer. They erected an imposing monument to Gonzales' memory; to them he was the valorous patriot who died struggling to redeem the state from the violence and bloodshed of Tillmanism.[45]

The aversion felt for the senator by some of the Tillmanites was manifest in the controversy between Tillman and his erstwhile lieutenant John L. McLaurin. The friendship between the two men had begun at Bennettsville in 1885 when McLaurin had entertained "the backwoodsman from Edgefield" and imbibed his doctrines.[46] "Curly-headed Johnny" was after Tillman the most effective of the Tillmanite orators and was among the chief's most trusted advisers. His reward had been the attorney-generalship in 1891 and a seat in Congress in 1892. In 1897 he became Tillman's colleague in the Senate.

There were reasons, however, why the South Carolina senators quarreled. McLaurin had ideas of his own and would not give his imperious colleague the blind obedience he demanded of those whose fortunes he had made. Furthermore, McLaurin was inherently weak. He was able to create issues but he lacked the physical strength and the tenacity of purpose necessary to realize them. He was so changeable in his views and disposition that his integrity, even his rationality, were at times questioned. Forever grasping after

[45] Tillman to D. W. McLaurin, February 22, 1916, in Tillman Papers; Wallace, *History of South Carolina*, III, 412.

[46] John L. McLaurin, in Charleston *News and Courier*, October 30, 1913.

opportunities to serve his personal or political advantage, the junior senator became tainted with Republicanism. Before he became senator he suffered criticism by favoring "a just and fair reciprocity" in protective duties to benefit the South.[47] Such views were so like those of Tillman that they did not prevent McLaurin's elevation to the Senate; but, secretly resentful of Tillman, who, he believed, preferred Evans as his colleague, McLaurin veered further toward Republicanism. He became so friendly with President McKinley that in 1898 he said the President should be re-elected without opposition, and surprised his colleagues by casting the deciding vote in favor of the annexation of the Philippines.[48]

His conduct in the Philippine matter had been incredible. After delivering an eloquent speech against ratification (in part a plagiarization of an address by Henry Van Dyke), he suddenly changed his mind and voted with the Republicans. Despite a lame explanation,[49] his vacillating and disloyal behavior aroused indignation in Democratic circles. Tillman led the chorus of criticism that resulted in McLaurin's expulsion from the Democratic caucus.

The estrangement between the South Carolina senators was intensified by a struggle over the disposition of the patronage. Tillman sought McKinley's friendship and solicited offices for his friends without sacrificing his anti-Republican principles; but McLaurin was willing even to vote Republican, and the patronage consequently was put in his hands. The postmasterships and the district-attorneyship went to his friends over Tillman's protests, and he was offered membership on the Philippine Commission. It needs little imagination to realize how this antagonized Tillman, always a seeker after the loaves and

[47] *Cong. Record,* 55 Cong., 1 Sess., 182.
[48] Charleston *News and Courier,* February 7, 1899.
[49] McLaurin statement, 1893, in Tillman Scrapbooks.

the fishes.[50] Personal exasperation was implied in all his denunciations of McLaurin's alleged betrayal of the party.[51]

After his vote on the Philippine treaty the junior senator elaborated his pro-Republican principles into a philosophy designed to regenerate both the Democratic party and the South. He called his system Commercial Democracy. In addresses before leaders of the textile industry he brilliantly phrased the objectives of Southern businessmen, advocating the gold standard, the protective tariff, a larger army, ship subsidies, and colonial expansion. He urged South Carolina to abandon a narrow sectionalism, the ghost of Calhoun, "the vagaries of Bryan Democracy," and the partisan tyranny of Tillman, in order to enjoy a fairer measure of the national prosperity. He had created an issue, an opportunity to rally progressive businessmen and others who favored the abandonment of fanatical traditionalism and the one-party system.[52]

Yet McLaurin had no chance. He had evolved a situation beyond the power of his inconsistent personality. It was feared that he might betray Commercial Democracy as readily as he had surrendered on the Philippine issue. The great majority of South Carolinians were too immersed in traditions to tolerate a movement that threatened party unity. There was talk that the search for votes would bring "the niggers to the polls and the shooting will begin." [53]

Tillman, profoundly alarmed over a possible break in the state's political unity, imagined that "many good men had their grips packed" to march after the golden calf of industrial progress.[54] With all his vindictiveness he ar-

[50] This was frankly expressed in the Gaffney speech. Columbia *State*, May 26, 1901.

[51] McLaurin, in Tillman Scrapbooks; *id.*, in *Cong. Record*, 57 Cong., 1 Sess., 219.

[52] Columbia *State*, April 19, 20, 23, May 22, 1901; McLaurin, in *Cong. Record*, 57 Cong., 1 Sess., 218–19.

[53] William E. Curtis, cited in Columbia *State*, May 22, 24, 1901.

[54] Tillman, *Struggles of 1876*, 4–5.

raigned the former lieutenant who dared to differ from him. McLaurin, cried, Tillman, had betrayed his party and his people; he had "no conscience or principle." [55] McLaurin, replying in kind, said Tillman was "an intellectual who disgusted the Senate in order to please the gallery loafers." [56]

At Gaffney, May 25, 1901, Tillman invaded a public appearance of the junior senator and demanded a division of time. Apparently, here was opportunity for debate unlike "the conventional clap-trap of mummified one-party oratory" South Carolina had endured for fifty years. There was a chance for a combat of ideas, which a two-party system makes possible, between able and prepared antagonists. [57] But Tillman, seeking to secure the one-party system rather than to respect a principle of political science, jammed the Pitchfork to the hilt into McLaurin. He simply accused him of selling out to the Republicans "for a mess of pottage." McLaurin, shaken by the assault, entreated the sympathy of the audience against a man who had "no more mercy or pity than a tiger over its prey," and asserted his right to vote on national issues without saying "Yes, massa," every time the tyrannical Tillman beckoned.

The junior senator was suffering from an illness which made him unfit for further forensic efforts. When Tillman suggested that he should resign in order to test his principles before the people, McLaurin replied that Tillman wanted others to take a risk he would not take himself. The senior senator shot back that he would resign if McLaurin would. The junior senator was trapped. He was forced to consent to a joint resignation, and before the day was over, that document, to take effect September 15, was on its way to Governor McSweeney. [58]

[55] Tillman interview, in Columbia *State*, April 21, 1901.
[56] McLaurin interview, *ibid.*, April 21, 1901.
[57] Wallace, *History of South Carolina*, III, 388.
[58] Columbia *State*, May 26, 29, 1901; Tillman, in *Cong. Record*, 57 Cong., 1 Sess., 221–22.

This was virtually political suicide. In a series of joint debates, Tillman would have torn the last shreds of political prestige from McLaurin's person and left him bare to the pitiless gaze of an electorate which had nothing but contempt for a leader disloyal to the tribal party; fortunately, a malady described as "brain fever" prevented him from debating. Desperate for aid, he was guilty of an act which, had it been known, would have completed the humiliation. Four days after the Gaffney encounter, he wrote John D. Archbold, notorious Standard Oil agent who specialized in bribing congressmen, saying, "I can beat Tillman if properly and generously supported." Archbold expressed "my great admiration for his [McLaurin's] wise and courageous course" and signified his willingness to confer with him.[59] But any support the agent might have given the erratic senator was forestalled when the governor refused to accept the resignations, explaining that he wished to spare the state a heated political contest. In reality McLaurin's friends had brought pressure to bear upon McSweeney so that the junior senator might be relieved.[60]

Tillman continued the attack on his unhappy colleague before the state Democratic committee where he sponsored a resolution asking McLaurin to resign. With eye flashing and lips quivering, he yelled, "Peace and harmony won't come when there are sneaks and thieves and traitors going around and hiring Hessians and distributing gold and buying up newspapers." The Tillman resolution was carried by a majority of 21 to 5.[61] McLaurin rejected the resolution;[62] Tillman again challenged joint resignation;[63] the junior senator once more refused to act; and the hatred between the two senators continued to glow until it burst into flames

[59] McLaurin to John D. Archbold, May 21, 1901; Archbold to Congressman Joseph Sibley, of Pennsylvania, June 6, 1901, first published in *Hearst's Magazine*, cited in Charleston *News and Courier*, January 8, 1913.
[60] Columbia *State*, June 1, 2, 4, 7, 1901; Tillman, in *Cong. Record*, 57 Cong., 1 Sess., 221–22.
[61] Columbia *State*, July 26, 1901.   [62] *Ibid.*, August 7, 1901.
[63] *Cong. Record*, 57 Cong., 1 Sess., 222–23.

in the physical encounter already related.[64] One final act was needed to annihilate McLaurin completely: denial of the right to be a candidate in the Democratic primary. This was done, with Tillman's connivance, by the executive committee of the party. An independent thinker had been declared an outlaw.

The elimination of McLaurin made it possible for Tillman to win victories in both 1902 and 1904 without the usual sound and fury. He quietly dominated the 1902 convention of the state party, forcing stringent pledges of party loyalty and insuring the subordination of the Commercial Democrats.[65] He viewed with satisfaction the elevation of Asbury C. Latimer, an inoffensive Tillmanite, to McLaurin's seat, and of Duncan C. Heyward, a low-country aristocrat who favored the Dispensary, to the governorship.

Pleased with the trend of party politics, the South Carolina boss in 1904 played the part of harmonizer. He approved the return of the eminently nonpartisan Heyward to the governorship. Sensing the trend of Democratic sentiment, he early emphasized that Bryan and free silver were impossibilities for the Presidential canvass. For years an uncompromising advocate of principles, he was prepared now to repudiate principles for expediency. The South Carolina delegation, with Tillman its chief, went uninstructed to the national convention,[66] so that it might "smell around for the strongest candidate." [67] On the eve of the convention, Tillman opposed putting "last year's eggs in a new nest," meaning that Bryan should not be the candidate or free silver the issue.[68] As a member of the resolutions committee he labored successfully through sleepless nights to prevent

[64] See p. 8.

[65] Charleston *News and Courier*, May 22, 1902; Tillman to James A. Hoyt, May 17, 1902, in Tillman Papers.

[66] Columbia *State*, May 19, 1904; New York *American*, May 19, 1904.

[67] Tillman interview, at Washington, in Charleston *News and Courier*, April 13, 1904.

[68] *Ibid.*, July 5, 1904.

the commitment of the party to either side of the historic silver issue. He agreed that "nothing should be put in the campaign which was a campaign issue." [69] This accomplished, he voted the South Carolina delegation for Alton B. Parker, justifying his action on the grounds that Eastern money and influence were necessary to win, despite a previous declaration that "the grinning, cold-blooded, selfish face of Hill smiling on one side and August Belmont, the representative of Wall Street, had Parker's hands leading him." [70]

The master stroke of the convention was the South Carolina leader's defense of Parker's nomination after the nominee had telegraphed the convention that the gold standard was "irrevocably established," and that if his views on the subject were not satisfactory to the majority someone else should be nominated. To cap the excitement, word was passed that the nominee had telegraphed Senator Edward W. Carmack refusing the nomination unless the party platform specifically endorsed the gold standard. Tillman, "in a towering rage," pounced upon Senator John W. Daniel, who had influenced him in favor of Parker, shouting that "he had been deceived, seduced, maltreated, and hornswoggled." The Virginian tried to mollify the South Carolinian, but Tillman "continued his red-hot tirade, swearing and shedding floods of tears by turns" and wiping off "his tears and other effluvia" with his sleeve.[71] But when it became known that Parker had not asked a modification of the platform, the South Carolinian's wrath subsided as rapidly as it had risen, and he accepted John Sharp Williams' invitation to read and defend a telegram to Parker acquiescing in the nominee's decision on the gold standard.

After recounting his natural if unfounded indignation, Tillman asserted that "the only escape from some great

[69] *Official Proceedings of the Democratic National Convention, 1904* (New York, 1904), 278–80.   [70] Charleston *News and Courier,* July 7, 1904.
[71] Champ Clark, *My Quarter Century of American Politics* (New York, 1920), II, 150.

disaster to the party" was to let the nomination stand. He believed that the Parker telegram revealed "a highly honorable and sensitive nature unwilling to sail under false colors." He explained that it was no new knowledge that the nominee was a gold man and that the gold standard should be recognized as *res adjudicata*. Despite the objections to Parker, he concluded, "the national Democracy has spoken. It has put this man on a platform which was reported unanimously." There should be no turning back.[72] The convention by a great majority accepted this masterly bid for reconciliation.[73] The general opinion was that "Mr. Tillman never did better work in his life." [74] The fact that he had once won notoriety as a destroyer of the meaningless harmonies of the politicians was forgotten.

With this triumph to his credit, the senator returned in the summer of 1904 to a politically quiet South Carolina. For the first time in his public career there was scarcely a cloud on the horizon. Although sores reopened by the crime of Jim Tillman were not healed, and although the Prohibition element was dissatisfied with Ben's solution of the liquor problem, a governor more acceptable to all factions than any since 1885 was being re-elected without opposition. Not for two years, since the annihilation of McLaurin, had Tillman burst into fury against a South Carolina politician. The Dispensary controversy was in abeyance, and the ill will created by Charleston's reception of Theodore Roosevelt in 1902 had been counterbalanced by the city's banquet for Tillman in 1903. The senator's conduct in Washington continued to satisfy his constituents; his second re-election to the Senate in 1906 appeared inevitable. He had seemingly assumed the role once played by Wade Hampton, that of Grand Old Man of South Carolina who frowned down division among his people on important issues and who would not take part in their petty contentions.

[72] *Official Proceedings of the Democratic National Convention*, 1904, p. 318.
    [73] *Ibid.*   [74] Charleston *News and Courier*, July 12, 1904.

Chapter XXVI

THE NEGRO ISSUE

Ben Tillman had too broad a vision of his functions as a senator to allow state politics and the details of routine legislation to absorb his entire attention. He in fact appreciated the advantages of making himself the center of agitations which transcended the boundaries of the little state he represented. Since leadership in most matters was closed to him because of membership in the minority party, he created important issues. One of these was the status of the Negro. He defended before the American people the extremely reactionary views of South Carolinians on this great national question in a manner to excite universal interest and more than a little sympathy.

Tillman was dissatisfied with the contradictory and unrealistic exposition of South Carolina's attitude toward its Negro majority as rendered by his predecessors in the Senate. Hampton and Butler had given lip service to the prevailing democratic doctrines while glossing over the fact that the South Carolina blacks were bound in political and social servitude. As fervently convinced as the two Bourbons that the Negro should be held in subjugation, their successor was too honest intellectually, too "brutally frank," too eager to be startling, to ignore realities in the interest of racial and sectional harmony. He told the nation, in brutal language, that white South Carolina had triumphed over black South Carolina with shotguns, election frauds, and intimidations, and that white South Carolinians were determined, if necessary, to maintain its supremacy by these methods. He boldly repudiated the liberalistic clichés of his day so far as they applied to the blacks. He declared them incapable of exercising the higher functions of civilization. This position of course was not original with Tillman; but he was the first responsible Southerner after Reconstruction to proclaim it elaborately.

Between 1898 and 1909 he won the attention of the American public by countless speeches on the race question. Almost every conceivable pretext was utilized to impose this issue upon the usually unwilling ears of the senators, and from 1901 to 1909 he spent the greater part of the Senate recesses reiterating his views before Chautauqua audiences in every section of the United States. His emphatic manner of speech, and his frequent invocation of the vulgarities of the South Carolina hustings, always attracted large and interested crowds.

The major premise from which Tillman drew his conclusions was that the African was biologically inferior to the white man. Although he admitted that Negroes were men and not baboons, he qualified this statement by saying that "it took something else besides having the shape of a man to make a man" and that some of the Negroes were "so near akin to the monkey that scientists are yet looking for the missing link." [1] The record of this "ignorant and debased and debauched race" in its African environment was one of "barbarism, savagery, cannibalism and everything which is low and degrading." It was "the quintessence of folly" to suppose that the Negro could emulate the Anglo-Saxon in progressive civilization.

Long years of intimate contact with Negroes had convinced Tillman that newly arrived Africans were naturally savages, and that the freedmen on the farms and in politics were innately lazy, cowardly, and corrupt. In the final analysis he did not depend on his reading of current books on the race question for his views. That was not necessary,

[1] *Cong. Record*, 59 Cong., 2 Sess., 1440.

for he knew that all sensible Southerners believed as he did.
Outsiders with contrary opinions were ignorant of the
realities of Negro life; they would revise their views were
they to visit the Black Belt.[2]

Belief in the innate inferiority of the blacks logically
led to the conclusion that they should remain an inferior
caste. Neither in theory nor in practice should they be
given the same economic, social, or political opportunities
as the whites. Tillman rejected President Roosevelt's injunction to "deal with each man on his merit as a man." A
Negro should not have the same treatment as a white man
"for the simple reason that God Almighty made him colored
and did not make him white." It was neither possible nor
desirable that racial antagonisms should "disappear in the
universal brotherhood of man." "Feelings of revulsion," he
felt, arose in the breast of every white man when such a
program was suggested.[3]

He held that "the mysterious influence of race antagonism
and caste feeling" was as universal as the division of mankind into inferior and superior races. He never tired of
answering criticism of Southern racial attitudes with examples of the inflexibility and even cruelty of Northern
discriminations. The "Northern people," he said wither-
ingly, "have no more use for the colored man at close quarters than we have. . . . They love him according to the
square of the distance" from him. They would not marry
him, allow him freedom in seeking employment, or permit
him to enter their theaters and restaurants. The riots which
occurred in Northern cities were examples of race prejudice
more cruel than similar events in the South. "Northern
white men vent their anger upon the blacks indiscriminately, and their race hatred is so intense that the innocent
and the unoffending are made to suffer. In the South, on
the other hand, the mob hunts down the man who is guilty

2 Ibid., 57 Cong., 2 Sess., 2515, 2564.
3 Ibid., 59 Cong., 2 Sess., 1032, 1039–40.

or supposed to be guilty, and innocent negroes are not molested." The unsoundest of motives, Tillman claimed, prevented a frank confession by Northerners of this fact: a mistaken philanthropy born of ignorance of the blacks, and the desire to curry favor with the Negro voters of the border states.[4]

Prejudices of caste prevented the foulest social disaster of which Tillman could conceive: the amalgamation of races. The elimination of "the caste feeling and race antagonisms of centuries" would mean that the Caucasian, the "highest and noblest of the five races," would disappear in an orgy of miscegenation. He even imputed that the purpose of those who would give civic and social opportunity to the blacks was to convert the South into a mulatto state. Roosevelt and other contemporaries would not admit this, he said; but an older and franker generation of advocates of Negro rights had admitted that race mixture was implied in their theories. Wendell Phillips and Theodore Tilton had openly advocated it and Thaddeus Stevens had practiced it.[5]

Tillman's astounding contribution to the race controversy was his justification of lynching for rape. He bluntly declared to startled senators: "As governor of South Carolina I proclaimed that, although I had taken the oath of office to support the law and enforce it, I would lead a mob to lynch any man, black or white, who ravished a woman, black or white. This is my attitude calmly and deliberately taken, and justified by my conscience in the sight of God." On another occasion he declared that his views were, "To hell with the Constitution" when it stood in the way of mob justice to rapists. Thousands, of course, agreed with this judgment, but only a few Southern leaders of Tillman's generation were willing to acknowledge such radical views.

---

[4] *Ibid.*, 57 Cong., 2 Sess., 2558–64; Tillman, "Causes of Southern Opposition to Imperialism," *loc. cit.*, 443.

[5] *Cong. Record*, 57 Cong., 2 Sess., 2564; 59 Cong., 2 Sess., 1040.

The moralistic Tillman was intolerant of sexual promiscuity and scorned as a coward the man who refused to shoot on sight the seducer of a wife or daughter. But when a Negro violated a white woman, even death by torture was too gentle a fate. It was his belief that by the act of rape the Negro expressed in boldest and most horrible form his desire to shatter the walls of caste and effect racial amalgamation. Rape resulted from the universal refusal of the white woman to accept the advances of Negroes inoculated with the virus of equality. The white women of the rural South were represented as "in a state of siege" by black brutes who roamed freely in regions inadequately policed, their breasts pulsating with the desire to sate their passions upon white maidens and wives. No Southerner could return home without the uneasy fear that his wife or daughter had been victimized. From forty to a hundred Southern maidens were annually offered as a sacrifice to the African Minotaur, and no Theseus had arisen to rid the land of this terror.[6]

The fate of the ravished woman was painted in ghastly colors by the South Carolina senator. She was choked or beaten by the black savage, her body prostituted, and her brain branded as by a red-hot iron with a memory which haunted her as long as she lived. Tillman declared in all sincerity: "I have three daughters, but, so help me God, I had rather find either one of them killed by a tiger or a bear and gather up her bones and bury them, conscious that she had died in the purity of her maidenhood, than to have her crawl to me and tell me the horrid story that she had been robbed of the jewel of her womanhood by a black fiend."

With emotional intensity the Southern leader portrayed the reaction of white men when they discovered that the black deed had been imposed upon one of their women.

[6] *Ibid.*, 59 Cong., 2 Sess., 1441; Tillman to New York *Sun*, November 4, 1913. *Cf. Cong. Record*, 57 Cong., 1 Sess., 5102.

"The young girl thus blighted and brutalized drags herself to her father and tells him what has happened. . . . Our brains reel under the staggering blow and hot blood surges to the heart. . . . we revert to the original savage." The whole countryside rises and condign punishment is imposed upon the villain. To designate such an occasion as a "lynching bee," a festive occasion, was a misnomer. "There is more of the feeling of participating as mourner at a funeral" among the men who, "with set, stern faces," avenge "the greatest wrong, the blackest crime in all the category of crimes."

The senator faced resolutely the allegation that lynching was an act of lawlessness. Shall men, he asked, allow a rapist trial according to the forms of law? His answer was an emphatic *No!* The culprit had put himself outside both human and divine law. The courts forced the victim of the rape to undergo "the second crucifixion" of publicly testifying against the deflowerer. The lynching simply involved the bringing of suspects before the victim who identified her assailant in unmistakable terms so that "death, speedy and fearful" might be meted out to him.

The senator's justification of lynching was the most effective reply ever made to those who condemned illegal justice under any circumstances. His address was carefully prepared, free from extemporaneous ranting, ornamented with literary quotations, and eloquent without sacrifice of the "brutal frankness" which gave force to the speaker's words. If passion was stronger than logic in this speech, it was passion born of the conviction that men should be ruthless in protecting the virtue of their women.[7]

Tillman denied the assertion of Henry W. Grady, Booker T. Washington, and others that the Negro race had made signal progress since emancipation. It had retrograded. Under slavery the Negro was exceedingly well behaved.

[7] Authority for Tillman's utterances on lynching, except where otherwise noted, is his speech, in *Cong. Record*, 59 Cong., 2 Sess., 1440–43.

The uplifting influence of that institution was so marked that there were "more good Christian men and women and ladies and gentlemen" among the Southern slaves than in all Africa. But these conditions were suddenly reversed when, as a consequence of emancipation, the Negro was "inoculated with the virus of equality." Then "the poor African" became "a fiend, a wild beast, seeking whom he may devour"; then he inaugurated "misrule and anarchy and robbery" by voting for "the carpetbag horde of thieves and scoundrels and their scalawag allies, the native born rapscallions." Horizons were lit with the fires of white men's houses and Negroes planned to kill all the white men, marry their women, and use white children as servants. Tillman was firmly convinced that Reconstruction was one of the most horrible experiences recorded in history. It had so demoralized the Negro that he could never recover the virtues of the slave.[8]

He ridiculed the attempt of the black man to achieve some of the nonpolitical objectives of Reconstruction. The worth of the Negro was in inverse ratio to the degree he aspired after higher standards of civilization. Many among the older generation who retained the attitude of slaves were orderly and moderately industrious; but the younger generation with progressive aspirations were degenerate vagabonds "who are doing all the devilment of which we read every day." They were being taught by their leaders to lie and steal as compensation for the wrongs of slavery.[9]

Against Negro education Tillman was especially bitter. The "little smattering of education" which the blacks absorbed was "enervating and destructive of the original virtues of the negro race." "Over education," on the other hand, by stimulating ambitions impossible of attainment, created discontent which resulted in crime, as in the city

---

[8] *Ibid.*, 57 Cong., 2 Sess., 2562–64; Tillman to Benjamin R. Tillman, Jr., November 17, 1913, in Tillman Papers.

[9] *Cong. Record*, 57 Cong., 2 Sess., 2562; Tillman to Benjamin R. Tillman, Jr., November 17, 1913, in Tillman Papers.

of Washington, where intensive efforts were made to educate the blacks. There the Negro criminal and illegitimacy rates were high and Negro public opinion did not frown upon open violations of the moral law.[10] Booker T. Washington, the outstanding example of the educated colored man of the times, was declared "a humbug" whom a German was forced to chastise because Washington "had been making goo-goo eyes" at the German's wife.[11]

Such views led Tillman to justify the use of the fraud and violence by which the white South rid itself of Negro rule. In 1900 he told the Senate: "We [the white South Carolinians] took the government away. We stuffed ballot boxes. We shot them [the Negroes]. We are not ashamed of it." And two years later: "We will not submit to negro domination under any conditions that you may prescribe. Now you have got it. The sooner you understand it fully and thoroughly, the better off this country will be." [12]

With equal frankness the South Carolinian confessed his part in reducing Negro suffrage to a minimum by nullifying the Fifteenth Amendment. The *"understanding clause"* of the South Carolina constitution, he told a Baltimore audience, was "the most charming piece of mechanism ever invented." He explained how Negroes were rejected through difficult questions and whites accepted through easy ones. By this experience the Negro discovered that *"it was not healthy* [for him] *to go to the polls."* [13]

Tillman was incensed over Roosevelt's appointment of Negroes to office in the South. Such appointments were a challenge to the social fabric, an entering wedge for reversion to the horrors of Reconstruction. It made no difference that the appointees were competent and honest; they

[10] *Cong. Record,* 57 Cong., 2 Sess., 2564; 60 Cong., 1 Sess., 2195.

[11] Tillman to D. G. Ambler, March 24, 1911, in Tillman Papers.

[12] *Cong. Record,* 56 Cong., 1 Sess., 2245; 57 Cong., 1 Sess., 5102.

[13] Baltimore *American,* January 5, 1907, cited *ibid.,* 59 Cong., 2 Sess., 1044. *Cf. ibid.,* 55 Cong., 2 Sess., 6532; 56 Cong., 1 Sess., 3223–24; Chicago *Examiner,* November 28, 1906, in Tillman Scrapbooks.

must be kept out of office to prevent "ever so little a trickle of race equality to break through the dam." He invoked all the parliamentary skill at his command to prevent senatorial confirmation of Roosevelt's colored appointees. When legal remedies failed, he favored mob violence as a means of driving colored men out of office. In such emergencies, he said, "our instincts as white men" provoked unlawful acts "which we feel it necessary to do." [14]

Throughout Tillman's career he believed that the race problem harbored consequences of the most sinister purport. He decided that the traditional friendship between the races was being supplanted by hate and predicted that the blacks would soon attempt to capture political control of areas in which they possessed majorities. This combination of hate and ambition would inevitably create "conditions more threatening in some of their aspects than they were in 1861," the inauguration of a war of races. The South was "on the edge of a volcano," and he thanked God that marriage had carried his daughters to areas without large Negro populations. [15]

Apprehensively he urged the arming of Southern whites. The presence of the Negro, he told a militia officer, was "almost the only reason why men should continue to give their time and money to maintain military organizations." He advised those unable to effect such organizations to secure "buck-shot cartridges for your bird and duck guns." [16]

He cried out against the fates for failing to solve the race question. The Civil War, he said, had settled only two issues, slavery and nationalism. After that struggle a false idealism had combined with sordid political ambitions to

[14] Tillman's views on this issue are best stated in the debates over the appointment of the postmistress at Indianola, Mississippi, in *Cong. Record,* 57 Cong., 2 Sess., 2511–15, 2559.

[15] *Ibid.,* 2564–65; 59 Cong., 2 Sess., 1440–42; Tillman to Chandler, November 25, 1911, in Tillman Papers; *id.* to Sophia Tillman Hughes, May 4, 1916, *ibid.*

[16] *Id.* to A. W. Leland, December 8, 1911, in Tillman Papers; *id.* to Captain Moorer, March 4, 1912, *ibid.*

tie the putrid "carcass of slavery" to the South. The race question was still causing "more sorrow, more misery, more loss of life, more expenditure of treasure" than any other American problem. "It is like Banquo's ghost, and will not down." [17]

Believing that any removal of this incubus must come from the dominant section of the country, he earnestly asked Northerners to present a plan. But Republican opponents replied with the suggestion that he take the initiative. On one occasion Senator Albert J. Beveridge, after listening for two hours to Tillman's lurid oratory, said he would be willing to listen for two hours more if the South Carolinian would advance a solution. But Tillman was more productive of criticism than of remedies. He confessed, "I do not know what to do about it [the race question]. I do not know what to tell you to do about it. I see no end to it." [18]

Occasionally he professed to see the solution in the migration or expulsion of the blacks from the South. But on other occasions, and with more emphasis, he opposed their removal. "It would simply mean their [the Negroes'] destruction; and I do not want to destroy them." Their natural increase would be greater than the number who could be moved. They did not wish to leave the South and no law of Congress could make them do so. Moreover, he admitted that the whites did not want the blacks to leave because it would cause derangement of labor and other economic ills. "We have some selfish and greedy men down there [in the South] who want to hold on to the negroes as laborers," said Tillman. But he hoped he would not be placed among that number. [19]

The most tangible reform he could suggest was that the Fifteenth—and sometimes the Fourteenth—Amendment be

[17] *Cong. Record*, 56 Cong., 1 Sess., 3223; 59 Cong., 2 Sess., 1443–44.
[18] *Ibid.*, 57 Cong., 1 Sess., 5102; 59 Cong., 2 Sess., 1040.
[19] Correspondence with Bishop Henry M. Turner, *ibid.*, 57 Cong., 2 Sess., 2465–66; 59 Cong., 2 Sess., 1042.

repealed. He believed that such a formal declaration of surrender in the struggle to give the Negro political and civil equality would confirm the black man in his inferior position and pave the way for greater harmony between the races. But he rightly concluded that the time was not ripe for so drastic a reform. In his opinion Northern leaders were not ready to acknowledge the prodigious Republican error, nor would timid politicians of both parties accede to the proposal. In later years he waited hopefully for opportunity to suggest it, but the proper moment did not come in his lifetime.[20] He had to content himself with the tacit assurance that the North was permitting the South to solve its race problem on its own terms.

Of course, there were "good" Negroes; Tillman was too thorough a Southerner not to appreciate the servility and subordination of the Southern blacks as a whole. No Southerner was more effusive than he in praising those Negroes who accepted the stigma of inferiority imposed by the whites. He denied that his words against Negro aspirations were "for the sinister purpose of belittling the negro race—of dooming them to obloquy and mistreatment." He would allow them equality before the law and the right to property and happiness, provided, of course, they did not seek political and social equality.[21]

He never tired of presenting the example of his servant Joe Gibson and Joe's wife Kitty, who served the Tillman family for forty-odd years. Both were illiterate ex-slaves without political ambitions or social aspirations, resigned to the primitive living standards of Southern Negroes. Tillman showed his confidence in Joe by putting him in charge of his plantation during the senator's absences. "A more loyal friend," said the master, "no man ever had. Every child that I have would share his last crust with that negro

---

[20] Tillman, *Struggles of 1876*, 12–13; *id.* to D. M. Taylor, May 22, 1911, in Tillman Papers; *id.* to Senator James K. Vardaman, October 3, 1913, *ibid.*
[21] *Cong. Record*, 57 Cong., 2 Sess., 2562; 59 Cong., 2 Sess., 1443.

tomorrow." On another occasion the senator added, "I do not know whether I belong to Joe or Joe belongs to me. . . . we have agreed to live together until one or both of us die, and when I go away, if I go first, I know he will shed as sincere tears as anybody. I would die to protect him from injustice and wrong." [22] Joe died first and his master proved his affection by providing for the funeral and erecting a monument over his grave.[23]

The significance of Tillman's anti-Negro views does not lie in their originality or scientific accuracy. Except for the justification of lynching, his arguments were merely emphatic repetitions of words heard wherever Southerners foregathered. His thoughts were too morbidly extravagant for anyone but the most fanatic believer in the doctrine of superior and inferior races. Moreover, he failed to expound his views in an orderly fashion; with the unlimited time allowed the Senate forum and the Chautauqua platform at his command, he said what he pleased in a hit and miss fashion, disregarding logical classifications and heedless of repetitions.

But these views revealed bluntly and truthfully to an interested North what the majority of Southerners actually felt concerning the Negro. Since the Civil War, Southern leaders had evaded the subject; yet the average Southerner was thinking in Tillman's terms. It was therefore inevitable when Tillman expounded these views in the North, among a supposedly hostile people, that waves of applause passed from the Potomac to the Rio Grande. Enlightened Southerners said that the words of the South Carolinian were harsh and imprudent; but to the white masses of the South they were all wisdom, all a courageous flinging of irrefutable doctrines in the face of the enemy. The savagery of the

---

[22] *Ibid.*, 57 Cong., 2 Sess., 2562, 2566; 59 Cong., 2 Sess., 1443.
[23] Tillman to Sophia Tillman Hughes, February 20, 1913, in Tillman Papers; *id.* to Nick Chiles, April 12, 1913, *ibid.*

arguments, the defiance of supposed adversaries, stimulated a popular interest which would not have been evoked by less demagogic tactics.

Tillman's Southern colleagues signified their disapproval by a stonelike silence or by withdrawing from the floor of the Senate during his anti-Negro tirades.[24] But no Southern senator dared reply to his arguments; no Southern politician dared make the race question a campaign issue against the South Carolina leader. They knew that his words made him popular throughout the South, that he received thousands of approving letters, that roaring crowds greeted him whenever he appeared in Dixie. Tillman himself believed that his views on lynching voiced "the feeling and purpose of 95 per cent of the true white men of the Southern States." [25] Such popularity made him contemptuous of the "negro-loving newspapers of the South," [26] and won to his side, during the last phases of his agitations, the voices of two eminent Southern demagogues, Senators James K. Vardaman and Hoke Smith.

The effects of Tillman's agitations on Northern audiences are more difficult to measure. Published opinions of his speeches were often violently denunciatory. He was called "the vulgar, profane, coarse, murder-glorifying, treason-uttering, scowling, vicious and uncultured Tillman"; and a minister in whose church he spoke said he was unworthy to touch the shoelaces of Negroes like Frederick Douglass and Booker T. Washington.[27] Republican senators condemned him as one who can "defend slavery . . . and even boast of committing murder," and his justification of lynching was termed a "retrogression to the brutal days of tyranny." [28]

[24] Senators Spooner and Joseph R. Burton noted this, in *Cong. Record*, 57 Cong., 1 Sess., 5103; 59 Cong., 2 Sess., 1445–46.

[25] *Ibid.*, 1442.   [26] Tillman, *Struggles of 1876*, 13.

[27] Binghamton (N.Y.) *Evening Herald*, unidentified date, in Tillman Scrapbooks.

[28] Senators Spooner and Burton, in *Cong. Record*, 57 Cong., 1 Sess., 5103; 59 Cong., 2 Sess., 1445.

Thomas M. Patterson of Colorado, the only Democratic senator who answered the Negrophobe, said that the South Carolinian attempted to create the impression that Democratic supremacy in the South depended on fraud and violence, and that were his views to dominate in the councils of the Democratic party it would forfeit Northern support.[29]

Tillman answered these attacks by indicating that his words harmonized with changing Northern attitudes toward the race question. The North was growing less prejudiced against the South and its attitude toward the blacks, partly because of better sectional understanding since the War with Spain, partly because the Republicans themselves were discriminating against the colored races of the newly acquired colonial possessions, but primarily because the Northern migration of Negroes was provoking race riots and a disposition to treat blacks in the Southern fashion. Tillman believed that all white Americans had an instinctive aversion for fraternal relations with blacks. In order to bring the North to the Southern viewpoint, he felt that it was necessary to dispel ignorance or indifference toward Southern actualities.

His "campaign of education" had some of the desired effects. Wherever he went in the North great audiences "applauded every sentence which fell from his lips." [30] Toward the end of his career he was able to write: "I was never received more kindly and enthusiastically in the South than I was in almost every place I spoke in the North." [31] If the war amendments were not formally repealed as the result of his agitations, they were nullified during his times. This development was surreptitiously under way before he entered the national arena, but his was the vital role of clarifying and stabilizing an ill-defined social trend. "I have no doubt," he himself wrote, "that I have been instrumental

[29] *Ibid.*, 59 Cong., 2 Sess., 1040–45.
[30] Chicago *Examiner*, November 28, 1906.
[31] Tillman to William F. Barton, February 16, 1916, in Tillman Papers.

in causing the Northern people . . . to have a much saner view of the negro question and in some respects understand the dismal, dangerous aspects of it." [32] Ben Tillman fostered the modern reaction against the Negro. This achievement was one of his most significant influences on American life.

[32] *Id.* to Taylor, May 22, 1911, *ibid.*

Chapter XXVII

THE ATTACK ON ROOSEVELT

THE most durable of Ben Tillman's many animosities
was his hatred of Theodore Roosevelt. This grew out of
the President's withdrawal of an invitation to attend the
White House banquet of February 24, 1902, in honor of
Prince Henry of Prussia, a naval officer. The South Carolinian was invited because he was a member of the Senate
naval committee, but between the invitation and the dinner occurred the Tillman-McLaurin brawl. The morning
before the dinner the President let it be known in the newspapers that Tillman's presence was not desired. "In view
of the contempt proceedings," the White House explained,
"Senator Tillman's presence would not only be an affront
to the Senate, but a discourtesy to Prince Henry." The
President commissioned Senator Francis M. Cockrell of
Missouri to ask the South Carolinian to decline the invitation. Tillman refused because Roosevelt had, without previous notice, aired his intent in the press.[1] "Of course I
would not withdraw under such a threat as that," the proud
senator explained. "Had the President sent a mutual friend
in a *quiet way* suggesting that it would be an awkward situation, any man who knows me at all knows how quickly I
would have relieved him of his obligation to me." [2] The
President heard Tillman's answer from Cockrell at noon
and immediately ordered his secretary to write the senator
as follows: "The President regrets that he is compelled to

[1] Washington *Post*, February 24, 1902.
[2] Tillman to Magill, March 3, 1902, in Tillman Papers.

withdraw the invitation to you to dine to-night at the White House." [3]

Long before Roosevelt came to the White House he had learned to suspect Tillman. In 1896 the New York aristocrat had classed the South Carolina agrarian with those who deeply mistrusted "a taste for learning and cultivated friends, and a tendency to bathe freely." Tillman possessed "an untrammelled tongue" and had a brother who had "been frequently elected to Congress upon the issue that he never wore either an overcoat or an undershirt." [4] The South Carolina senator and two other agrarian leaders of 1896, added Roosevelt, "have not the power to rival the deeds of Marat, Barrère, and Robespierre, but they are strikingly like the leaders of the Terror of France in mental and moral attitude." [5] In subsequent years the opinionated Republican leader did not modify his characterizations; and when the senator committed a misdeed which seemed to confirm previous judgments, Roosevelt, with characteristic impulsiveness, publicly turned the culprit away from his table.

Tillman was utterly humiliated. The rebuke of the most popular man in the United States had been added to the reprehension which the attack upon McLaurin had provoked. The worst aspect of the situation was that the senator could do little. Heretofore, his main antagonists had been South Carolinians, men whom he could denounce and then relegate to oblivion; but a denunciation of the great man in the White House would scarcely be noticed or remembered. He had to be content with strong but largely ineffective words. He let it be known that he considered the President's implications indecent and insulting and that he was willing to abide by the judgment of "all brave and self-

[3] George B. Cortelyou to Tillman, February 24, 1902, *ibid.*

[4] Roosevelt to his sister, September, 1896, cited in Mark Sullivan, *Our Times: The United States, 1900–1925* (New York, 1926–1935), II, 387–88.

[5] Henry F. Pringle, *Theodore Roosevelt: A Biography* (New York, 1931), 153.

respecting men" concerning who was more the gentleman.[6] Privately he declared that he had been treated "in a cowardly and ungentlemanly way" by "this ill-bred creature who is accidentally President." [7] He swore never to enter the White House until it was occupied by another. To the end of his days Roosevelt was to him "unspeakably base," "a 'S.O.B.' " [8] Tillman nagged the President on every possible occasion; verbal assaults upon Roosevelt and the Roosevelt policies became almost a monomania with him.

Earlier attacks upon imperialist policies were intensified when Roosevelt became responsible for them. The South Carolinian's first foray was against efforts to subjugate the Filipinos. While the President insisted that for "every guilty act committed by our troops . . . a hundred acts of far greater atrocity have been committed by the hostile natives," [9] Tillman questioned the conduct of the American soldiers. Were they not "occupying the attitude of butchers and practicing cruelties that would disgrace the Inquisition"? [10] Behind the administration's plan of government for the Philippines he saw "the desire of some men to get ungodly and indecent wealth." [11] The President's agents were given "the same autocratic power the Czar exercises in Russia" and were frustrating plans for local self-government.[12]

The coup by which Roosevelt secured Panama was of a startling character like that by which Tillman had imposed the Dispensary upon South Carolina. In both instances men of deeds acted unconventionally in pursuit of desirable objectives. When pressed in debate concerning what he would have done had he been in the President's place, the South Carolinian admitted that as a last resort—after the consent

[6] Charleston *News and Courier*, February 25, 1902.
[7] Tillman to James A. Smyth, May 7, 1902, in Tillman Papers.
[8] *Id.* to Judge Annis, January 9, 1917, *ibid.*
[9] Pringle, *Theodore Roosevelt*, 296.
[10] *Cong. Record*, 57 Cong., 1 Sess., 4811.
[11] *Ibid.*, 5103.   [12] *Ibid.*, 58 Cong., 3 Sess., 349.

of the Senate had been obtained—he would have said to the recalcitrant Colombians: "You are a mangy lot; you are dickering with us and attempting to rob us and obstructing the progress of civilization and commerce; get off the face of the earth; we will take the Isthmus and build a canal and own the country." [13]

But Tillman hated Roosevelt too hotly not to find fault with the Panama policy. It would have been preferable, he asserted, for the President, "as the advance agent of civilization," to have taken Panama openly rather than intrigue "in the disreputable, dishonorable creation of a so-called republic in a back room." If it was true that the President had used the method of the "sneak-thief" and the "bully," he ought to be impeached.[14] When Roosevelt denied complicity in the Panama Revolution, Tillman said that the circumstantial evidence against the President was such that he should reveal all facts before the Senate ratified the treaty. This was a fair and simple demand.[15] But the Republican majority, brushing constitutional sophistries aside, acquiesced in what the President had done.[16] To this day the mystery of the Panama Revolution remains unsolved. Tillman had aided in impressing upon his contemporaries the suspicion that Roosevelt had not been honorable in dealing with Colombia.

Too patriotic to disapprove the construction of the canal, Tillman did assail Roosevelt's methods of executing the huge project. He characterized as "this miserable humbug of graft" "the enormous salaries" paid the agents of the canal commission. Its members were so fearful of yellow fever that they did not adequately inspect the work; its chairman was perhaps incompetent; its secretary was a press agent "hypnotizing public opinion" by spreading "slander and abuse and misrepresentation and lying." He condemned the power over canal activities which Congress gave

13 *Ibid.*, 2 Sess., 714.   14 *Ibid.*, 710, 715, 801.
15 *Ibid.*, 715, 965, 1305, 1310, 1315, 2143.   16 *Ibid.*, 1305, 1309–10, 1315.

the President and the license of the secretary of war to let contracts without guarantee that these agreements would result in the completion of the canal. Congress should make specific grants or negotiate a general contract obligating its holders to execute the entire task.[17] He injected the Negro issue, giving authority to the canard that an American ship had been sent to Martinique for women to be distributed among the West Indian Negroes working on the canal. He opposed an eight-hour day for these laborers, wanting no "philanthropic, humanitarian, . . . canting policy" toward tropical colored men at the expense of the American taxpayer.[18]

Roosevelt's establishment of American control of the customs of the Dominican Republic after the Senate had refused to ratify a treaty sanctioning this act brought vigorous objections from the South Carolina senator. Turning the full force of his vicious logic against the White House, he demanded that the rights of the Senate be defended against this "strenuous man, fond of his own way." "We have got to say 'No,' and say it in loud words, to Theodore Roosevelt, or he will not hear it at all." Was the Senate sunk so low as to allow this man to hector and threaten it for "a pound or two of pork"? Senators should stand on their feet and say to Roosevelt, "You have got to obey the law or we will take you by the throat, sir." Roosevelt was sustaining in the "mulatto republic" a government of "assassins, cutthroats, robbers, murderers, libertines, everything that the English language can give you in the way of debauchery, degradation, beastly, and brutal" for the benefit of "shylocks and sharks." The intervention of the United States government in behalf of these bondholders indicated that "the microbe of graft and stealing" had possessed persons connected with the Roosevelt administration.[19]

[17] *Ibid.*, 59 Cong., 1 Sess., 282, 396, 439, 441.
[18] *Ibid.*, 447–48, 2338.   [19] *Ibid.*, 1173–79.

The most obvious weakness in the President's armor was the imputation that his re-election in 1904 was facilitated by contributions of the identical "malefactors of great wealth" he was supposed to reform. Later investigations proved the allegation substantially correct. "Either Roosevelt closed his eyes to the facts deliberately, or elaborate precautions were taken" by crafty lieutenants "to keep him in ignorance." [20] Hoping to catch him in a scandal, Tillman introduced a resolution asking the secretary of the treasury for information concerning the campaign contributions of national banks. Revelations of such contributions by insurance companies led the senator to assume that the banks had been guilty of the same practice.[21] The secretary of the treasury asserted that an examination of one thousand reports of bank examiners revealed only $500 contributed by two small banks. Tillman, disappointed, asserted that either the reports were fraudulent or that relevant facts had been overlooked.[22]

The dissatisfied South Carolinian next pressed for an investigation by the Senate Committee on Privileges and Elections. At the hearing this body gave him he was ill prepared to sustain his accusations. His only evidence consisted of fragmentary information furnished by James W. Breen of the New York *Herald,* and the committee concluded that the charges were not well enough sustained to justify further investigation. But it did appoint a subcommittee to prepare legislation to prevent malpractices in campaign contributions.

Tillman loudly protested against this procedure, saying that favorable legislative action could not be secured because of the desire of the ruling forces in Congress to protect corporate contributions for the campaign of 1906. He was right; there were interminable delays. He expressed himself as "a little astonished" that, though the "crime" of

[20] Pringle, *Theodore Roosevelt,* 356–58.
[21] *Cong. Record,* 59 Cong., 1 Sess., 223–29.   [22] *Ibid.,* 5371.

campaign contributions "was acknowledged by everybody," the Senate committee "seemed to pooh-pooh the idea of an investigation"; he believed the report that certain representatives of Big Business, under threat of telling all they knew, had coerced Roosevelt into using his influence against investigation.[23] Tillman was no longer an active member of the Senate when the truth of the 1904 campaign became known and remedial legislation was enacted.

Tillman was a constant critic of Roosevelt's failure to live up to promises of trust-busting. He complained that the insincerity of the administration was manifested by prominent officials who left the employment of the government to enter the service of corporations and other supposed enemies of the Rooseveltian theory of control.[24] Attorney General John W. Griggs, after learning secrets of the Department of Justice, resigned his office to become the attorney of the very monopolies he had prosecuted. The senator affirmed that never had he known a former official who "was so brazen, had so much impudence, had so little regard for the decencies and proprieties of life."[25] The government, instead of prosecuting the men actually guilty of forming monopolies in violation of law, merely attempted to grapple with impersonal corporations. The absurd doctrine had been pronounced that the corporation could be punished, while its members, "the eyes, the head and the hands," were "dipped in the immunity bath."[26] Further, the government seemed helpless to prevent dissolved trusts from reorganizing. "They go right around," said Tillman, "and transfer or swap about or work up some chicanery or trickery" in order to resume forbidden practices. The only way to stop "this devilment" was to put "some millionaire in prison with stripes on him." This was not done because Roosevelt was "monstrously persuaded

23 *Ibid.*, 4322–28, 5365–71.   24 *Ibid.*, 282, 439, 441, 5369.
25 *Ibid.*, 57 Cong., 2 Sess., 768–69.   26 *Ibid.*, 59 Cong., 1 Sess., 4322–23.

by some people who get around him and honeyfugle him with flattery." [27]

Tillman even opposed notable constructive reforms of the President. He joined other senators in voting against the Pure Food and Drug Act and the Eight Hour law for Federal employees.[28] He subjected the reforestation program to carping criticism, found no relation between the scheme and agricultural improvement, and saw in it only the machinations of the lumber barons. As a practical man Tillman thought it was foolish for the government to purchase and preserve timber with no hope of revenue from cuttings.[29]

The Republican President and the Democratic senator clashed savagely over the eternal Negro question. Roosevelt's extremely Northern attitude toward the black man seemed especially designed to inflame men of the Tillman type. The President expressed contempt for Charleston gentlemen who complained about Reconstruction but exploited and defrauded Negroes. As a protest against injustice, he felt he should try in some small way to help the Negro. He would not ask that the average black be allowed to vote, but merely that the better type be occasionally recognized by Presidential appointments—that they "be given the pitiful chance to have a little reward, a little respect, a little regard, if they can by earnest, useful work succeed in winning it." [30]

Any efforts to give Negroes office was bound to incur the animosity of the Southern senator. When the President in 1903 ordered the post office at Indianola, Mississippi, closed after "a brutal and lawless element" of the town had forced the colored postmistress to resign, Tillman asserted that the

---

[27] *Ibid.*, 2428–30.   [28] *Ibid.*, 2756, 5773; 55 Cong., 3 Sess., 1596.
[29] *Ibid.*, 56 Cong., 2 Sess., 2451; 59 Cong., 2 Sess., 3200, 3205.
[30] Theodore Roosevelt to Owen Wister, April 27, 1906, cited in Owen Wister, *Roosevelt: The Story of a Friendship, 1880–1919* (New York, 1930), 252–56.

appointment of a Negro to even a minor post was "the match which has touched off an electrical line of thought, reaching to the remotest bounds of this country." Such an opening of the door of hope to the colored people closed that door to the white people because "ever so little a trickle of race equality" would mean a return to Reconstruction. Protests by Southern whites were treated "with contumely and contempt" by the President. Venal motives underlay this action. The Republican machine desired to secure the Negro vote in the border states and to control the Southern Republican delegates in the national conventions. Such conditions accounted for the fact that outraged Southerners "rush to do an unjust and improper thing." [31]

The storm gained fury when Roosevelt sent to the Senate the name of a colored man as collector of the port of Charleston. This man, Dr. William D. Crum, enjoyed the respect of Charleston because he deferred to Southern race convictions. When, for example, the daughter of William Wilberforce, the English abolitionist, visited him, he allowed her to ride alone in his carriage while he walked.[32] Roosevelt said that while at the Charleston Exposition leading citizens assured him "that Crum was one of the best citizens of Charleston, a very admirable man in every way, and while they protested that negroes ought not to be appointed as postmasters, they said there was no objection to appointing them in other places, and specifically mentioned the then colored collector of the customs at Savannah as a case in point." [33] December 31, 1902, he nominated Crum as the Charleston collector to succeed a white man who had died.

Despite the fact that the position was unimportant, the very Charlestonians who had praised Crum now went into hysterics. A mulatto was placed in a position of official

[31] *Cong. Record,* 57 Cong., 2 Sess., 2511–15, 2560.
[32] Authority for this statement is the late Professor Yates Snowden, University of South Carolina.
[33] Roosevelt to Wister, cited in Wister, *Roosevelt,* 254.

superiority to white lady clerks—Charleston aristocrats! This made white Charleston shudder. Mayor James A. Smyth and the trade bodies of the city protested to Roosevelt and enlisted Tillman's services to prevent confirmation of the appointment.[34]

The fight between the senator and the President over Crum was long and stubborn. It began on January 5, 1903, when the mulatto's name was first sent to the Senate, and did not end until six years later when Roosevelt went out of office. With solid support from white South Carolina, Tillman, by threatening filibuster, saw the Senate adjourn on March 4, 1903, without a confirmation. Under the law Crum immediately went out of office. But the President on the next day presented his name through recess appointment to a special session of the Senate. When Tillman again succeeded in blocking confirmation, Roosevelt made a second recess appointment the day after the adjournment of the special session. Confirmation was blocked for the third time by Tillman when the Senate again met in special session in November and December, 1903. Once more the President was equal to the occasion, giving Crum another recess appointment "precisely at . . . noon" of the first Monday in December, 1903, during "the constructive recess" which was said to exist at the moment between the special session of the Senate and the regular session of Congress which immediately followed.[35]

Tillman welcomed the opportunity to turn his oft-repeated arguments on the Negro question into a constitutional debate. He challenged the President's theory of recess appointments, especially his theory of "constructive recess," declaring that Crum's appointment was "a very slight, insignificant incident" compared with the "great constitutional question" involved in the application of the Senate's

[34] Columbia *State*, January 10, 1903.
[35] A precise history of the Crum appointments is given by Secretary of the Treasury Leslie M. Shaw, in *Cong. Record*, 58 Cong., 2 Sess., 1108.

right to confirm Presidential appointments. He demanded that the Senate take Roosevelt "by the throat as a predecessor of his was taken by the throat" and "stop dawdling around here neglecting its duty." [36] The Senate passed his resolution asking the secretary of the treasury to report on the legality of the Crum appointment.[37] When this official answered evasively,[38] Tillman introduced a sweeping resolution asking the Senate Judiciary Committee to report on the question.[39] This was followed by the fifth blocking of the Crum appointment and by a report from the Judiciary Committee condemning the theory of the "constructive recess." Roosevelt had been reprimanded.[40]

After 1904 the struggle over Crum dragged on at weary length. Finally the question was settled with Tillman triumphant just as Roosevelt was going out of office. On February 6, 1909, the President presented the mulatto's name for the last time, and Tillman filibustered for three days. As a consequence the Republican senator sponsoring the nomination, under pressure from leaders anxious to consider more important matters, withdrew Crum's name. Then William H. Taft, the conciliatory President-elect, let it be known that he would not appoint Negroes to Southern office, and Crum resigned, effective March 4, the day Roosevelt retired.[41]

[36] *Ibid.*, 1106.   [37] *Ibid.*, 1109.
[38] Letter of Secretary of the Treasury Shaw, with Tillman comments, *ibid.*, 1365–66.
[39] *Ibid.*, 1549.
[40] Charleston *News and Courier*, April 28, 1904; Tillman, *Struggles of 1876*, 9–10.
[41] Spartanburg *Herald*, February 10, 1909; Tillman, *Struggles of 1876*, 9–12.

Chapter XXVIII

THE RAILROAD RATE BILL INTERLUDE

BEN TILLMAN, like most successful politicians, could sit at the council table with enemies. His hatreds, for all their fuss and fury, were largely impulsive outcroppings of surface emotions. One even suspects that his denunciations of Roosevelt were in part born of subconscious jealousy of the Tillmanesque qualities the President demonstrated so consummately. Roosevelt was more spectacular than Tillman, more adept in coining telling phrases, more strenuous in action, more dramatic with the Big Stick than the senator with the Pitchfork. Had there been political accord between the two men, the South Carolinian would have been among the President's ardent admirers.

Tillman esteemed Roosevelt's virtuous family life; he favored the President's trust-busting program and shared with him prejudices against the courts; he studied Roosevelt's theory of governmental regulation of business, in his heart applauding the efforts to put it in operation. Both men hid moderate opinions behind vehement utterances. Tillman was as strongly opposed as Roosevelt to some of the more radical phases of Bryanism and agrarianism. Like the President, he desired "rational and patriotic legislation" which would eliminate the "spectre" of public ownership of great industries. So when an opportunity came to co-operate in furthering an important phase of Roosevelt's program of government regulation, Tillman assumed the obligation with alacrity.

The Congress which met in December, 1905, had as its

objective the most important measure of the Roosevelt program of business reform. This was the Hepburn rate bill, a very complicated and technical measure prepared by the experts of the Interstate Commerce Commission for relieving shippers of the irregular and extortionate rates which inadequate regulative legislation enabled the railroads to charge. Despite ambiguities regarding the courts' powers of review, the bill was clear in the essential purpose to give the commerce commission powers to determine and prescribe "just and reasonable" railroad charges and to exercise detailed supervision over its prescriptions. The measure was an assault upon the manner in which the railroads had acquired great wealth: the taking of profits without the restraints of Federal regulation. It embodied the ambition of the small businessmen and the masses of the people to be freed from injustices in railroad charges.

The proposed reform was the most important move in Roosevelt's ambition to shift the influence of the Republican party from the side of great wealth to that of the Progressives. He had explained it in his messages and partly expressed it in the Elkins Act of 1903 prohibiting rebates to favored shippers. The Hepburn bill, proudly called an administration measure, passed the House by a great majority. This seemed to presage easy sailing through the Senate. But that body was ruled by an able group of conservative Republicans ready to use their skill to defeat the proposal.

While the bill was being given preliminary consideration, Tillman made it clear that he favored its principles. It harmonized with his frequently expressed theory that the government should deal positively with combinations of great wealth.[1] Before Congress met in 1905 he wrote Chairman Elkins of the Senate Interstate Commerce Committee that he was "with Roosevelt in the fight." "If he means business on the rate-making programme he laid down last year, we Democrats—all the patriots who are left—will have an

1 *Cong. Record*, 57 Cong., 1 Sess., 2281.

opportunity to help him use the big stick on recalcitrant Republican heads." [2] Although he opposed "anything like radical or ultra legislation," he favored rigid regulation of rates to protect the people from "oppressive and exacting and tyrannical and outrageous robberies by the railways," and he wished to contribute "toward a proper and just solution of this vexed problem." [3]

Still, no one could have predicted that Roosevelt's most turbulent critic would play a leading role in the enactment of the President's measure. Despite his eleven years on the Senate Interstate Commerce Committee, Tillman admitted that he was poorly informed on railroad problems,[4] and had failed to attend the committee's investigation of the rate question.[5] Naïvely asserting that a law adequately covering this complex problem did not require a "thousand or more phrases and lines, all doubled and twisted and muddled up," he tried to "get to the kernel of the proposition" by introducing a bill of one paragraph simply giving the Interstate Commerce Commission power to fix rates.[6]

In a lengthy speech endorsing regulation he embodied a multitude of carping criticisms of the Hepburn bill. Its sponsor, "Pete" Hepburn himself, did not understand its "mass of words." There were loopholes in the measure through which the Supreme Court might "drive not only an automobile, but a whole freight train." The President's tactics were dictatorial. The bill was a "stupendous farce" because it was prepared by railroad lawyers. "I would sniff less at the meat . . . to see if there was not some poison in it if it had not had such cooks." [7]

No wonder the country was bewildered when on February 23, 1906, it was announced that the Senate Committee

[2] Tillman to William E. Chandler, June 4, October 19, 1905, cited in Nathaniel W. Stephenson, *Nelson W. Aldrich: A Leader in American Politics* (New York, 1930), 274, 279.

[3] *Cong. Record.*, 59 Cong., 1 Sess., 2425.   [4] *Ibid.*

[5] Tillman to Chandler, June 4, 1905, cited in Stephenson, *Nelson W. Aldrich,* 274.

[6] *Cong. Record,* 59 Cong., 1 Sess., 272–78, 2428.   [7] *Ibid.*, 2424–31.

on Interstate Commerce had imposed upon the utterer of these extravagances the obligation of piloting the Hepburn bill through the Senate. The action was unprecedented. A Republican committee had placed the President's favorite measure in the hands of a Democratic senator who was a sworn enemy of the Chief Executive and had openly questioned the bill's wisdom. The appointment seemed unbelievable, a paradox, a weird practical joke; but it was a fact. Tillman on February 26, before a crowded Senate, formally announced that the obligation had been imposed upon him.

This denouement resulted from a subtle intrigue not uncommon in politics. The Committee on Interstate Commerce was dominated by the so-called railroad senators. After an unsuccessful attempt to induce Roosevelt to eliminate the rate-making provisions of the bill, the committee refused to sponsor it. Aldrich, the leader, privately denounced it; Elkins, the chairman who ordinarily would have given it his name and guidance, disavowed it. Shelby M. Cullom, ranking Republican member, should have sponsored the nameless orphan, but was incapacitated by illness. The logical person to fill the gap was Jonathan P. Dolliver of Iowa, a Republican who was eager to assume the obligation. But the astute Aldrich carried his contention that the bill be reported without approval or disapproval, thereby throwing the whole discussion back to the Senate. Then, affirming that he was against the bill, "in his best ironical vein" he "remarked that as it stood, it was more a Democratic measure than a Republican measure" and should go before the Senate under Democratic auspices. He therefore moved that Tillman, the ranking Democrat of the committee, be given that honor. Dolliver was greatly disappointed, but "Aldrich stood to his guns" and Tillman was elected.[8]

With a sly dig at Aldrich, the Southerner commented, "Somebody, by some hocus-pocus—I really hardly know

[8] Stephenson, *Nelson W. Aldrich*, 293–96.

how it happened—came to us unexpectedly and in a great hurry dumped this baby in my arms." [9] The Rhode Islander explained some weeks later with unctuous flattery: "I voted to place the bill in charge of the Senator from South Carolina, having great confidence in his judgment, intelligence, and discretion." [10]

The masterful Aldrich had wisely calculated that the time had passed for a direct rejection of the rate bill. The spirited drive of the President, the propaganda of the radical journalists, the united front of the Western and Southern senators, had aroused public opinion to the point of mandate. So the strategy was, not to destroy, but to temper or emasculate. By putting Tillman in charge, Republican senators were released from obligation to support the bill and a degree of disharmony was established between the President and its sponsorship. The fact that Tillman was the bitterest adversary of the President seemed to forestall the co-operation necessary to pilot the bill to success. Washington and the country laughed heartily over the stratagem; Roosevelt's enemies jeered at his predicament; the radical press interpreted the incident as an example of the Machiavellian nature of Aldrich. [11]

Perhaps the Rhode Island senator had a too-accurate knowledge of his Democratic associate to believe, as his critics said he did, that Tillman would bungle the responsibility. The opportunity for positive service so unexpectedly thrust upon the South Carolinian aroused his long-hidden but ample talents for constructive achievement. As a member of the Senate minority he had never been near the springs of power. Given for once the opportunity, he earnestly strove to be a positive force. With the true statesman's willingness to compromise he discarded previous misgivings concerning the Hepburn bill, expressing his intention

[9] *Cong. Record*, 59 Cong., 1 Sess., 3797.   [10] *Ibid.*, 4852.
[11] Julian Hawthorne, in New York *American*, February 27, 1906; Henry B. Needham, "Railroad Senators Unmask," in *Collier's Magazine* (New York), XXXVI (1906), 19–20; Sullivan, *Our Times*, III, 229–33.

to be serious the day he took charge of the measure. "I don't propose," he said, "that this thing shall be turned into a circus with me as a clown."

The friends of the bill exhorted him to high effort. Here was a chance, they said, for "the noble Roman from South Carolina 'to improve his reputation' " through the proper execution of "the greatest responsibility that has rested on Mr. Tillman's shoulders." He was pictured as "an example of the might of non-partisanship" and as one in whom "the diplomacy of sound maturity had supplanted mere verbal ebullience." [12] Flattery was pleasing to a man accustomed to opprobrium, flattery accompanied by an olive branch from his enemy in high place, the President himself.[13]

Roosevelt rose artfully to the embarrassing circumstances of the Tillman leadership. Although he interpreted Aldrich's behavior as "simply childish" and as evidence that that shrewd legislator had for once " 'completely lost both his head and his temper,' " he was willing for Tillman to have charge of the bill provided the Southerner would co-operate.[14] To preclude the possibility of a rebuff the President avoided direct communication with Tillman. Instead he waved flirtatious newspaper signals in the South Carolinian's direction. "He was quoted as saying that Tillman was 'an honest man and a hard fighter,' " and an inspired article in the New York *Sun* read: " 'The President will be ready to see Mr. Tillman if the South Carolina Senator should call at the White House.' " [15] Later, Roosevelt was saying that he was "delighted with the way Senator Tillman handles the rate bill." Tillman's phrase "corn-field law" was said to be a favorite at the White House, and the

---

[12] Hawthorne, in New York *American*, February 12, 1906; New York *Press*, March 17, 1906; Detroit *Free Press*, February 27, 1906; *Literary Digest*, XXXII (1906), 355.

[13] Savannah *Morning News*, cited in Spartanburg *Herald*, March 3, 1906.

[14] Theodore Roosevelt, *An Autobiography* (New York, 1920), 435–36; Roosevelt to Whitelaw Reid, March 1, 1906, cited in Joseph B. Bishop, *Theodore Roosevelt and His Times* (New York, 1920), II, 2.

[15] Sullivan, *Our Times*, III, 233.

President publicly enjoined the Republican senators to aid the South Carolinian.[16]

Tillman, however, would not budge from his resolution not to enter the White House as long as Roosevelt was there. Nothing short of an apology for the withdrawal of the dinner invitation would induce him to change his mind. He replied gruffly to the invitation of the New York *Sun*. " 'Senator Tillman showed some impatience this evening when asked if he had seen the President. He replied that he had not been to the White House since the bill was committed to his keeping, and saw no necessity for going.' " [17] It seemed that the President would have to be content with a general with whom he could communicate only through the public prints, an awkward situation that must have given Aldrich pleasure.

But the difficulty was obviated when Henry B. Needham, a magazine writer friendly to Roosevelt, suggested to him that William E. Chandler, the one Republican "who had Tillman's utmost confidence," "serve . . . as a liaison" between Roosevelt and Tillman. Chandler was an ardent enemy of the railroads because the Boston and Maine Company had been responsible for his retirement from the Senate. In 1906 he held an obscure sinecure as member of the Spanish-American Claims Commission, a position that Tillman had helped him secure. Roosevelt, with the impulsive energy with which he seized opportunities, at once had a conference with Chandler at the White House. The President explained "slowly and carefully" what he wanted communicated to Tillman. After the interview with Roosevelt, Chandler hurried to the South Carolinian who was "distrustful and suspicious" and questioned his visitor "closely as to what the President had said." Assured by Chandler that the President stood with him on the controversial phases of the rate bill, he finally consented to co-operate.

[16] New York *Times*, March 25, 1906.
[17] Sullivan, *Our Times*, III, 233–34.

"I thought very seriously . . . before I would consent to pocket my pride, and lay aside my just indignation for a past wrong," he explained, ". . . but having regard for my duty, in charge of a great legislative bill, affecting the rights of the entire country, I decided it to be necessary for me to cooperate and help Theodore Roosevelt pass a good railroad law."

The following day, which was April 1, Tillman's disquiet over the wisdom of his decision made him glad to share the responsibility of his alliance with Joseph W. Bailey. "He reported to Chandler" that he and Senator Bailey "did not believe there would be any difficulty in coming to an understanding on the basis propos[e]d by the President." "This message Chandler immediately carried to Roosevelt" and returned to Tillman with the intelligence that the President was satisfied with the arrangement. Thus was the alliance perfected. Daily for more than a month Chandler played messenger between the White House and the senator. By April 15 the machinations of what Tillman playfully called "the conspirators" had been seemingly so successful that they believed they could muster a positive majority in the Senate.[18]

It was well for their peace of mind that they were so self-confident because the opposition to the rate bill was formidable. Though public opinion was overwhelmingly in its favor, senators were not necessarily responsive to that influence. They were protected by long terms, indirect election, and the power of great wealth. The opposition included all senators who carried weight with the Republican majority: the Senate's boss, Aldrich; Philander C. Knox of Pennsylvania and Spooner, both of whom used vast legal learning to question the constitutionality of the measure; Lodge, who was Roosevelt's intimate friend; and Lodge's

[18] Tillman and Chandler accounts of these negotiations, in *Cong. Record*, 59 Cong., 1 Sess., 6775–76, 6885–86, 6938. See also, Sullivan, *Our Times*, III, 251–56; Richardson, *William E. Chandler, Republican*, 662–70, 674.

colleague Winthrop M. Crane. These men tried to befuddle less learned colleagues by exaggerating the complexities of the bill which by its very nature was difficult to understand.

To combat these men, Roosevelt controlled a few Republicans and a portion of the Democratic minority of thirty-three. Some of the Democrats were as definitely "railroad senators" as were the Republican leaders; others cherished state rights traditions and feared administrative tyranny. Moreover, the friends of the bill were seriously divided over "broad court review" versus "narrow court review" of the decisions of the Interstate Commerce Commission, and they lacked the legal training to cope with this involved issue.

Tillman's invocation of corn-field law, while picturesque, was scarcely a match for the sophistries of his erudite opponents. He confessed that he was bewildered by the fog of phrases and that he was not master of the technique of steering a bill. "This is," he confessed, "the first baby I have ever had to nurse and guide through the labyrinth of senatorial legislation, and therefore I am green." [19] When Aldrich asked him whether the bill gave jurisdiction to the Interstate Commerce Commission on the question of rate differentials between localities, Tillman admitted his ignorance of what the Rhode Islander called "the most vital point in this bill." [20]

Despite his limitations, the South Carolinian tugged heroically at the measure for eleven weary weeks. He listened attentively to what learned observers called "one of the grandest battles of forensic eloquence witnessed in a generation" over "the most important measure" of legislation "since the civil war." [21] He tried to curb the loquaciousness

[19] *Cong. Record,* 59 Cong., 1 Sess., 4279.
[20] *Ibid.,* 4338.
[21] Sullivan, *Our Times,* III, 242; Albert J. Beveridge, in *Cong. Record,* 59 Cong., 1 Sess., 6612–13.

of the very men who on other occasions had tried to restrain him. The rate bill, he explained, was "a matter of too great importance for us to have the appearance of dawdling or paltering with it, or losing unnecessary time." He asked senators to show promptness in presenting the set speeches each felt obligated to deliver; complained against "the mere waste of time" in considering amendments which "have been discussed and discussed and killed and killed and killed and killed, and yet we go on repeating, repeating, repeating." But such impatience did not lead to a desire to prevent debate. He felt that "this important legislation is something that requires a great deal of discussion," and he always thanked God that "any Senator who has got anything to say can always get a hearing here." [22] After May 3 he was able to limit speeches to fifteen minutes, and could guarantee final vote for May 18.[23]

Only occasionally did Tillman relapse into rudeness. Once his good friend Spooner felt obligated to admonish him for saying that the opponents of the bill were "controlled." [24] Already, Elkins had scolded him for this tendency: "The Senator takes the dear people out of his vest pocket every morning and puts them down on his desk and says, 'Dear things, I will have charge of you and not allow the bad corporations and railroads to get you this day of our Lord.' " [25] On another occasion his frankness served a useful purpose. He blurted out in the open Senate the monstrous secret of the whole procedure. It was that Aldrich "seems to be by common consent in the control of those who are opposing this bill, or guiding or managing it for that side." Such an exposure may have shocked the shy undercover man, but he remained evasive and composed, still unready to reveal the actual extent of his power.[26]

The crux of the debate was the degree to which the rail-

[22] *Cong. Record*, 59 Cong., 1 Sess., 3725, 4330, 6791–92.
[23] *Ibid.*, 6131.   [24] *Ibid.*, 4852.
[25] *Ibid.*, 4834.   [26] *Ibid.*, 4851.

roads should be permitted to appeal to the Federal courts from the rate-fixing activities of the commerce commission. The conservative senators wished to amend the Hepburn bill so that all rates designated by the commission should be subject to broad and all-inclusive court review. They took refuge in the "heritage of the Common Law"—that the determination of what was "just and reasonable" should be finally determined not by an administrative or legislative body but by the courts. The progressive senators, while admitting the right of the courts to some powers of review, strove to limit this function to the veto of acts adjudged confiscatory. They "believed that the Constitution of the United States had released" Congress from respecting the traditional legal privileges of property except the prohibition against confiscation. This in substance was the issue between the "broad review" and the "narrow review" senators. The distinctions made by the constitutional lawyers between "jurisdiction" and "judicial power," and between "unrestricted review" and "review with limitation," were merely subsidiary.[27]

Our corn-field lawyer had neither the ability nor the patience to participate freely in drawing these refined distinctions. He was content to announce that he stood with the more radical wing of the "narrow review" party. Heralding the bill as an attack on "the great accumulations of wealth in the hands of the few" before which "the honest patriot stands appalled," he wanted a revolutionary measure effectively putting the railroads under Federal regulation. His distrust of administrative tyranny melted before fears of a greater tyranny, the power of courts unrestrained by law. Day after day he valiantly mustered all the facts and arguments at his command to sustain the conviction that the Federal courts were incapable of administering railroad law on a "reasonable and just basis."

[27] Sullivan, *Our Times,* III, 249–50; Stephenson, *Nelson W. Aldrich,* 286–87.

Tillman's indictment of the Federal courts was his most pertinent contribution to the debates. While "my capitalistic friends and my lawyer friends" shook their heads, he derided the notion that "these judicial high priests" were more infallible than administrative officials. They were indeed often quite fallible. "They have changed front or reversed themselves and wobbled about a little on certain important questions." Changes of opinion might be induced by nothing more godlike than a disordered stomach. Some judges had been guilty "of some very questionable and discreditable acts." One judge got drunk at a banquet; others ran "into temptation" by riding on the "private cars of railroad magnates"; some were "judicial tyrants" who for as long as six years suspended the orders of rate-making agencies. "These judges, . . . clothed in authority for life," exemplified "the prophecy of Jefferson, that they would reach out and sneak over the fields of jurisdiction, here a little and there a little, like a thief in the night." [28]

To prevent these unscrupulous agents of wealth and privilege from negating the authority of the Interstate Commerce Commission, Tillman naturally demanded the narrowest possible court review. He contended that Congress had as much right to prohibit judicial intermeddling with railroad rates as it had to prevent such interferences in collecting taxes or issuing fraud orders by the Post Office Department. This line of reasoning was sound, but, as Spooner made clear, such intermeddling had not been the practice of the courts. And Tillman had neither the ingenuity nor the revolutionary courage to suggest means by which the courts' traditional power of saying the last word in such matters could be nullified. [29]

Tillman's most pronounced point was the desire to prevent the courts from suspending rates fixed by the Inter-

[28] Stephenson, *Nelson W. Aldrich*, 296; *Cong. Record*, 59 Cong., 1 Sess., 3796, 6301–10.
[29] *Cong. Record*, 59 Cong., 1 Sess., 4561, 4566, 4569, 4843.

state Commerce Commission pending review proceedings. In other words, he wished preliminary or interlocutory injunctions prohibited, contending that the courts, after "the flimsiest and slightest kind of a hearing," were in the habit of stopping the enforcement of rates and then "take their own time to settle the issues." He cited cases in which such suspensions lasted from seven to seventeen years while the shippers waited vainly for relief. He scorned the contention that his proposal was anarchistic, saying that it was merely a bid for simple justice.[30]

The South Carolinian's acceptance of the Roosevelt alliance was conditioned upon the President's endorsement of his views on judicial review. In the Chandler conversations, Roosevelt reiterated his pledges in favor of narrow review and against interlocutory injunctions.[31] He told Chandler that he was in "complete disagreement" with the Republican Senate leaders, three of whom, Knox, Spooner and Foraker, he mentioned by name, saying that they "were trying to injure or defeat the bill by ingenious constitutional arguments." Then he "slowly and carefully" told Chandler the basis on which "there should be co-operation . . . : an amendment expressly granting a court review, but limiting it to two points; (1) an inquiry whether the Commission had acted beyond its authority—ultra vires was his expression—and (2) whether it had violated the constitutional rights of the carrier." The President's exposition of the "narrow review" doctrine was said by him to be "a final decision." Chandler believed that this would be acceptable to Tillman, but called attention to the Southerner's views on interlocutory injunctions. Chandler quoted the President as saying that the former senator need not explain further because he (Roosevelt) was warmly in favor of some such restriction of injunction.

[30] Ibid., 3449, 3789–90, 6301–6302, 6306.
[31] Sam H. Acheson, Joe Bailey: The Last Democrat (New York, 1932), 190–91; Stephenson, Nelson W. Aldrich, 303.

The accord between the senator and the President seemed so perfect that Roosevelt arranged, through Chandler, for Bailey and the South Carolinian to confer with Attorney General William H. Moody, "as a representative of the President and his trusted adviser in the law points involved." The two senators found the attorney general in "absolute accord" with them except as to how long injunctions should be prohibited. He told them, "I will send you what I understand to be the kind of an [narrow review] amendment we can agree on, and which I think he [Roosevelt] will accept." At two subsequent conferences the three men perfected the substance of this amendment which the two senators were informed had Roosevelt's approval. Tillman notified Moody that he thought he could "get 26 [Democratic] votes, and possibly 1 or 2 more, for the proposed amendment, and if the President was certain of 20 Republican votes it was a sure thing." [32] Accordingly, on May 3 Tillman introduced this "narrow review" amendment in the Senate. It read: "If such court shall find that the order was beyond the authority of the Commission or was in violation of the constitutional rights of the carrier it shall issue an injunction against the enforcement thereof: *Provided, however,* That no such injunction shall be issued as a preliminary or interlocutory proceeding."

But on the evening of the following day Tillman was apprised that the passage of his amendment was not certain. Chandler shocked him at dinner with the intelligence that Roosevelt had, at a press conference that afternoon, abandoned the Tillman amendment in favor of the so-called Allison amendment. Immediately, Chandler and Tillman rushed to Bailey, who "was equally innocent of any knowledge, except what he had heard on the street." The three dismayed conspirators now hurried to Moody. When they revealed the tale of Roosevelt's treason they found him, ac-

---

[32] Tillman, Bailey, and Chandler accounts, which are almost identical, in *Cong. Record,* 59 Cong., 1 Sess., 6775–78, 6885–86, 6881, 6938.

cording to Tillman, "absolutely innocent of any knowledge of any such purpose on the part of the President." [33]

Naturally, Tillman was exasperated. Aldrich's biographer flatteringly calls him "the last American expression of the age of the code of honor," with "its rigid notions of obligation, its scrupulous ideas of what gentlemen committed themselves to when they agreed upon joint action." Although the student knows that there were times in Ben Tillman's career when he did not adhere to so romantic a notion of honor,[34] the Aldrich biographer was right in saying that "it was inconceivable that" this particular "coalition could be dissolved without formal notice to all participants." [35] But the fact remained that the President had abandoned the main point of a bill Tillman had loyally piloted for weeks, in favor of an amendment bearing a Republican's name so that laurels of victory were plucked from Democratic brows. More important, the acceptance of this amendment meant the abandonment of "narrow review" in favor of powers of review acceptable to the Republican conservatives.[36]

Why had Roosevelt forsaken his allies? A contributing cause was that Tillman was not able to deliver the 26 or more Democrats he had said he could. A party caucus of April 18 proved that not all Democrats were behind him. Charles A. Culberson of Texas expressed the views of the dissenters when he said that the adoption of the anti-injunction provisions "would be unwise, even if it were not unconstitutional." [37] But the genius behind the change was the insidious Aldrich who undermined Roosevelt's support. This crafty statesman, with public opinion against him, reasserted his momentarily imperiled leadership of the Senate in a brilliant demonstration of his power to appraise and

[33] Tillman narrative, *ibid.*, 6776; text of amendment, *ibid.*, 6299.

[34] For example, the breaking of the pledge over the division of delegates to the constitutional convention of 1895. See p. 288.

[35] Stephenson, *Nelson W. Aldrich*, 314.

[36] *Cong. Record*, 59 Cong., 1 Sess., 6886.   [37] Acheson, *Joe Bailey*, 201.

influence men. By a few evasive strokes he frustrated Tillman's desire to bring the rate bill to a speedy vote until he
secured his position. Saying little, he encouraged his lawyers
to confuse the debate with legal technicalities. Next he approached Tillman and Bailey with a generous offer of compromise. But the two Democrats rejected the proffered
peace because they felt they could win in an open fight and
"because they looked with suspicion on gifts from the
Greeks." [38]

With "a subtle magic" Aldrich reconciled the irrecon-
cilable. He assembled his party colleagues, convinced them
of the advantages of re-establishing party harmony and of
satisfying their constituents with some kind of rate bill, and
gained consent to his "compromise" officially called the
Allison amendment. It was framed in a manner to grant
the courts "the final decision as to whether" they should
pass not only on "the confiscatoriness but on the reasonable-
ness of the orders of the [Interstate Commerce] Commission." Injunctions were expressly allowed. This outright
victory for the "broad review" faction was obviously no
compromise at all. But the intrigue was executed so cleverly
that the "average eye" could discern little divergence between the Allison amendment and the Roosevelt principles.[39]

"With his majority securely in hand, Aldrich went to the
President" and secured his capitulation. Roosevelt again
illustrated his faculty for swift rearrangement, called the
press to the White House and announced his adherence to
the Allison plan. In his "quite labored" explanation he tried
to prove that it was the Senate rather than he who had
yielded. " 'But, Mr. President,' " interrupted a warm ad-
mirer, " 'what we want to know is why you surrendered?' "
"This was a body blow and quite took Roosevelt's breath

[38] *Ibid.*, 199; Tillman, in *Cong. Record,* 59 Cong., 1 Sess., 6937.
[39] Stephenson, *Nelson W. Aldrich,* 306–12; text of Allison amendment,
in Sullivan, *Our Times,* III, 257.

away," commented an eyewitness.[40] Recovering his composure, Roosevelt defended the necessity of compromise in order to get a rate bill which satisfied even his somewhat indefinite notions of progress and reform. If his dubious conduct left compunctions of conscience, that could be easily forgotten in what Tillman called the "great hurrah and furor" under cover of which this versatile man shifted from one project to another.[41]

The Democrats raged long and mightily over their betrayal. Almost daily for two weeks Southern senators jeered at the "trimmer" or the "quitter" whose mind was like "an unadjusted kaleidoscope." While Aldrich smiled blandly or gave evasive answers they said, amid laughter, that that crafty senator had trapped the President of the United States. All the while the Republican senators protested that there had been no surrender. William B. Allison even asserted that his amendment, "properly construed conceded nothing of the narrow review" doctrines he had originally held. This last statement was "a sad strategic blunder"; for Bacon of Georgia immediately phrased an amendment stating Allison's original position. Aldrich was now compelled to reveal his hand by forcing the Republican majority to reject the Bacon proposal. This was followed by Thomas H. Carter's unctuously admitting that the Allison amendment was a constructive reconciliation of Republican differences.[42]

For eight days following the Roosevelt betrayal Tillman maintained a curious silence. Seemingly it took Carter's "earnest defense and eulogium of the President" to open the flood gates of his pent-up wrath. Never in his long career in the Senate did the Carolinian speak more effectively. "In order that" he "might be careful to misstate nothing," he adhered to a prepared manuscript. For his accustomed

[40] From MS. of Richard Hooker, of Springfield (Mass.) *Republican*, cited in Stephenson, *Nelson W. Aldrich*, 314–15.

[41] Tillman, in *Cong. Record*, 59 Cong., 1 Sess., 9641.

[42] Sullivan, *Our Times*, III, 259–64; Stephenson, *Nelson W. Aldrich*, 317.

violence of speech he substituted the attitude of one amused at his own folly. He admitted that he had been foolish enough to enter into a "conspiracy" with the leader of the opposition—the man of uncertain convictions—and the inevitable had happened. Amid laughter he "confessed" his part in the Roosevelt-Chandler negotiations. Then came his "inside history of recent events." He meticulously cited names, dates, and places to prove that Roosevelt was guilty of sheer duplicity; and to demonstrate that Aldrich was the cause of the President's change of mind, he flatly declared: "The Senator from Rhode Island has resumed control of the Republicans. He shakes his head. That may be due to his modesty, or the fact that he has come nearer being unhorsed and thrown into the ditch in this struggle than ever before since I have been here." Yes, the "grand old Republican party" was "united absolutely," said Tillman with a shrug, as he withdrew his amendment embodying his conception of narrow review.[43]

Roosevelt's wrathful reply to the Tillman accusations tested to the breaking point the public's faith in his facile veracity. Tillman's assertion that the President had imputed chicanery to Senators Knox, Foraker, and Spooner was immediately telephoned to Roosevelt by his intimate friend Lodge. The reply from the White House was that it "was a deliberate and unqualified falsehood." [44] This was the beginning of what the newspapers playfully called the Ananias club.

Tillman, without resorting to ugly language, calmly laid the evidence on the table in order that "the thoughtful and honorable men of the country" might sit in judgment. The evidence consisted of a reaffirmation by Chandler that the unflattering words about the three senators had been uttered by the President and made "emphatic by repetition." Chandler possessed an excellent reputation for truthfulness and his memory of the event was fortified by a

[43] *Cong. Record,* 59 Cong., 1 Sess., 6774–77, 6780.   [44] *Ibid.,* 6787.

diary. Certainly he was in a better position to give evidence than one who did not have a high reputation for exact reporting.[45] What Roosevelt was accused of saying was an accurate description of the machinations of the three senators,[46] and was in keeping with the private judgments he frequently passed on those who offended him. When Tillman, with malicious intent, exposed Roosevelt's opinion of three important members of his own group, did not good policy prompt a little lying? [47]

The President took an even rasher step in his efforts to placate the critics of his double-dealing. He asserted that Tillman initiated the Chandler negotiations and denied that in these conversations he was bound by a precise policy. He had Attorney General Moody write him that "There was nothing in the conversations between the Senators [Bailey and Tillman] and me which in any way bound you to any particular amendment." [48]

Both Chandler and Tillman effectively refuted the allegation that either had initiated the conversations. Chandler said, "A friend of mine [Needham] . . . told me that the President wished to get into communication with the Democrats and would shortly ask me to come and see him." While the two men were talking, Chandler received a note from the President asking him to come to the White House. "I did not go to the White House as a representative of Senator

---

[45] Sullivan, *Our Times*, III, 266. Roosevelt confessed privately at the time: "I cannot remember the details of the conversation." Roosevelt to Lodge, May 19, 1906, cited in Henry C. Lodge (ed.), *Selections from the Correspondence of Theodore Roosevelt and Henry Cabot Lodge, 1884–1918* (New York, 1925), II, 216.

[46] "I thought the action of those Senators who were led by Aldrich in the committee jeoparded the bill," wrote Roosevelt. *Ibid.*, II, 217.

[47] *Cong. Record*, 59 Cong., 1 Sess., 6885–86, 6938. The scholar best acquainted with the faults of Roosevelt writes, "In all probability, despite his denials, Roosevelt had used derogatory terms in talking with Chandler about the opponents of his bill. It was his invariable custom to do so." Pringle, *Theodore Roosevelt*, 424.

[48] *Cong. Record*, 59 Cong., 1 Sess., 6886-87. *Cf.* Roosevelt to Lodge, May 19, 1906, cited in Lodge (ed.), *Correspondence of Theodore Roosevelt and Henry Cabot Lodge*, II, 215-19.

Tillman," he added with clarifying emphasis, "but solely because the President summoned me there by a letter from Mr. Loeb, and I waited for him [Roosevelt] to express his object." Neither Roosevelt nor Needham attacked this unfortunately irrefragable statement.

Tillman branded as "absurd on its face" the theory that he had sent Chandler to Roosevelt. "I . . . declare most emphatically that to no human being have I ever given authority or even expressed a wish to have any conference with Theodore Roosevelt in regard to the bill now under consideration." It was generally known that he had regarded personal contact with the President as distasteful and that Roosevelt had said that the latchstrings of the White House were on the outside for him. Moody's statement was simply the fable of a faithful servant. He said that his writing of the narrow-review amendment was an attempt "to adopt phraseology which would effect the intention of the two Senators." In other words, the attorney general of the United States was acting not as an agent of the President but as a clerk of Bailey and Tillman! The most charitable explanation of the whole charge is that the President was seeking to bluster his way through a muddle.[49]

Roosevelt's imprudence went to even greater extremes. Newspaper articles inspired by the White House explained that the agreement was broken because Tillman "could not control the real [Democratic] party leader in the Senate, Joe Bailey, of Texas." He was said to suspect "Senator Bailey of holding secret conferences with Mr. Aldrich." It was even asserted that "documentary proof of this" was in the possession of "a distinguished member of the administration." [50] The "proof" was a memorandum sent by Chandler to Roosevelt on April 11, saying, "The game of the railroad Senators is to support Bailey's amendment and induce him to agree

---

[49] *Cong. Record*, 59 Cong., 1 Sess., 6885–87, 6938.
[50] Chicago *Tribune*, May 15, 1906, in *Cong. Record*, 59 Cong., 1 Sess., 6936–37; New York *Times*, May 16, 1906, *ibid.*, 7010–11.

to a broad right of review. . . . Mr. Tillman, however, considers himself as acting with the President to pass the review clause with the minimum amount of court power and will not enter into any such game." Bailey, as subsequent events proved, was not above secret understandings with oil and railroad interests, but, as Chandler made clear, there was nothing in the memorandum to justify suspicions of his disloyalty to the rate bill. Apparently, Roosevelt's doubts concerning him were dissolved, less than twelve hours after the sending of the memorandum, by Chandler's assurance to the President that Tillman was satisfied the Texan was not playing "the game of the railroad senators." The next day Roosevelt invited Bailey to confer with the attorney general.[51]

The two Southern senators excoriated the man who had circulated this dangerous insinuation against their friendship. The big Texan called the statement "an unqualified, a deliberate, and a malicious lie"; the man who inspired it "an unqualified, deliberate, and malicious liar . . . however high the office which he holds." Tillman called the author of the story "a muck rake" whose narrative was "concocted . . . by the cuckoos and hirelings of the Republican machine to muddy the waters." "There has never been," he affirmed, "the slightest suspicion on my part in the good faith of the Senator from Texas."[52]

Tillman was not one of the three senators who voted against the Hepburn bill when, on May 18, it finally passed. Despite "bitter memories" he was too wise an opportunist, too highly endowed with the statesman's appreciation of the necessity of compromise, to refuse half a loaf when the whole was unavailable. "I will vote for it," he explained, "because it is the best I can get." In a final estimate he said wistfully: "The big stick and the pitchfork, which had been . . . fighting together, then separated. The pitchfork, while on

[51] Acheson, *Joe Bailey,* 197–99.
[52] *Cong. Record,* 59 Cong., 1 Sess., 6936–37.

duty on the firing line . . . looking around for the ally, saw the tail of his coat hustling to the rear, and . . . the last seen of him he was sliding toward the Allison base, trying . . . to reach the home base." But generously he added: ". . . but for the work of Theodore Roosevelt, in bringing this matter to the attention of the country and proclaiming in and out of season his desire and purpose or hope to get effective rate legislation, we would not have any bill at all. . . . whatever success may come from it will be due largely to him." [53]

Except for his fine sense of modesty, the South Carolinian might have admitted a measure of pride in the supreme legislative achievement of the Roosevelt administration. Beyond the irrelevance of personal hates and conflicts, he was fundamentally satisfied with the law, joining the President in believing that it was good. The recognition which he refused to arrogate was bountifully conferred by others. For once in his long career he was a national celebrity, the subject of flattering sketches in newspapers and magazines. His part in the railroad rate legislation has been amply recognized by the general historians of the United States.

[53] *Ibid.*, 7087, 9641.

Chapter XXIX

RENEWAL OF THE ATTACK
ON ROOSEVELT

THE thirty-four days of Tillman's co-operation with the President were merely a short if significant interlude in his almost continuous bombardment of the administration. An opportunity, perfect from Tillman's viewpoint, shortly arose for another assault. The senator's two pet abominations, the Negro and Roosevelt, were caught at their worst. This was the so-called Brownsville Riot.

On the night of August 13, 1906, members of the three companies of the Twenty-fifth United States Infantry, Colored, stationed at Fort Brown, Texas, made an assault upon the town of Brownsville which resulted in the killing of one white man and the wounding of another. The soldiers had been angered by indignities imposed upon them by whites who resented their presence. Diligent official investigation fixed the responsibility upon members of the three companies and ascribed knowledge of the outrages to the men as a whole, but failed to determine individual responsibility. After warning the men that summary action would be taken unless the names of the guilty were revealed, the President, on November 5, 1906, ordered the three companies discharged from the service. About 160 men were affected, among them soldiers who had won military honors. The order meant the forfeiture of pensions, the denial of entrance to soldiers' homes, and in some cases destitution. Roosevelt justified his course with the assertiveness of one who was absolutely certain he was right. The participation of the soldiers in the "horrible atrocity" was, by "the testimony of scores of witnesses," established "beyond chance of successful contradiction," and there was "no doubt" that many of the men were privy to the conduct of their guilty fellows.[1]

On December 20, 1906, Senator Foraker introduced a resolution asking an investigation of the Brownsville affair. In the discussion which followed, the Ohio senator, who was a friend of the Negro in the traditional Republican sense, argued incisively that the blacks had been unjustly treated by Roosevelt. Southern senators like Daniel of Virginia and Culberson of Texas joined such friends of the President as Lodge of Massachusetts in approving the dismissal of the troops. Tillman arrayed himself on neither side, dexterously attacking two enemies who were simultaneously hostile to each other. There was, he admitted, "an element of incongruity and of the ridiculous almost" in the position he and other senators took in the debate, but he justified a seeming inconsistency by turning it into a general discussion of the race question.

Following the line of argument advanced by Foraker, the Carolinian protested against the injustice of punishing 167 men when only 20 of them had even been accused of crime. The President had been guilty of a procedure more summary and unjust than that of a Southern lynching mob which did not kill the innocent along with the guilty. Roosevelt's contention that the men had broken the oath of enlistment was subjected to a searching analysis. After reading the oath Tillman declared with telling effect, "I see nothing in this oath which makes it obligatory upon a man . . . to tell something that he does not know or to tell something that might incriminate himself." As a student of Negro character he knew that blacks "will bear torture with stoicism in defense of one another rather than act as traitors."

[1] Pringle, *Theodore Roosevelt*, 458–61.

Why punish a poor black because he is true to his nature and color?

Criticism of the particular punishment did not mean that Tillman held the men of the Twenty-fifth Regiment guilt-less. Unlike Foraker, he shared Roosevelt's conviction that some had been guilty of murder, merely taking exception to the condemnation of the innocent. The President had been careful not to indict black soldiers in general or to repudiate previous words of racial encouragement. Tillman sweepingly condemned this attitude. This regiment, he said, was "a lawless brutal, murderous set of cutthroats" who were guilty of such offenses against the Southern code of race relations as pushing ladies off sidewalks and attempting to drink at the same bar with white men. Imbued with hatred for the white race in general, they had invaded Browns-ville, and "shot it up, doing murder." No punishment was too severe for the actual murderers, were it possible to detect them. He warned that if one of the suspected men, Sergeant Mingo Sanders by name, returned to his native South Caro-lina, he would encounter an "unhealthy" situation.

Yet, contended Tillman, these blacks were not basically responsible for their misconduct. Ultimate blame rested with white leaders who had inoculated them with doctrines of social equality and then sent them, despite protests, into Southern communities. The chief offender was of course Roosevelt, who had proclaimed that each man should be dealt with on his merits regardless of color, and specifically that black enlisted men should enjoy indiscriminately the privilege of entering hotels, theaters, cars, and other public places. Encouraged by a President who "stood sponsor for the doctrine of absolute equality anywhere," the soldiers were naturally angered when "the bitter, vindictive, nigger-hating Texans" refused to accord them this equality. Roose-velt should have felt "happy and proud" that his favorites had attempted energetic action when their ambitions were frustrated by white foes of social equality. This was a clever *reductio ad absurdum* of the President's position, a pointed proof that the New York aristocrat was ignorant of the realities of the Negro problem, an effective refutation of the convenient contention of both Northern and Southern senators that the Brownsville clash had nothing to do with the race question.[2]

A skillful marshaling of the evidence by Foraker forced the President to recede from his rash stand, and individual soldiers who could prove their innocence were allowed to re-enlist.[3] Tillman, equal to any possible emergency, now abandoned previously enunciated arguments to oppose the cause for which he had formerly pleaded. The Senate, he said, by its reversal had "stultified itself," and he, who had impugned the original discharge of the innocent along with the guilty, now decried the re-enlistment of the guilty along with the innocent.[4]

Of his conduct toward the President in 1908 Tillman declared, amid laughter, "If anybody wants any more in the way of criticism than I have indulged in this session, he is a very big glutton." Senator Beveridge was not uttering idle compliments when he said that the Southerner occupied "with great ability and brilliancy . . . the role of complainer" and that the Senate audience was entertained by his "picturesque phrases and Carlylean diction." But he was something more than an irresponsible scold. As Beveridge slyly suggested, he was cleverly "playing politics" in the face of an approaching Presidential election. Roosevelt was experiencing the inevitable eclipse which comes as a President ends his term of office. The senators were learning to resent his ceaseless stream of admonitions. Tillman essayed to give expression to this reality, probing with his Pitchfork the infinitesimal rift in Republican ranks.[5]

[2] Tillman, in *Cong. Record*, 59 Cong., 2 Sess., 1030–40.
[3] *Ibid.*, 60 Cong., 1 Sess., 3124.   [4] *Ibid.*, 2 Sess., 2948.
[5] See Tillman and Beveridge interchanges, *ibid.*, 1 Sess., 3365–72.

On March 16, 1908, the Carolinian made the bitterest attack upon Roosevelt which ever fell from his lips. Before crowded galleries who frequently applauded the peculiar vividness of his utterances, he cited "cold-blooded facts" to demonstrate that the Executive was "keeping the words of promise to the ear and breaking them to the hope." There were "sins of omission and commission." The President had allowed the Hepburn bill to be crippled; he had refused to sanction the prosecution of Paul Morton, "a malefactor of great wealth in his own council"; he had failed to press "to a successful issue" the personal-punishment clause of corporation-control legislation. He clamored against combinations of capital while advocating the formation of railroad trade associations. Under the guise of freeing organized labor from prohibitions against combinations, he planned amnesty to trust offenders. He had called stock gamblers "pernicious to the body politic," but failed to enforce existing laws against this "running sore and cancer." The speaker had touched the President at his weakest point, the discrepancy between promises and achievements, and he appealed once more to "the future historian" to sustain his contention. "Achievement was remarkably small, when reckoned in terms of the promises publicly made," that individual wrote.[6]

This was Tillman's last general attack on Roosevelt. Three days later, just six years after the White House invitation was withdrawn, the Southern senator was the victim of illness which forever deprived him of his powers of forensic aggressiveness.[7]

The President was to have the last word. In his letter of January 5, 1909, to Senator Eugene Hale he accused Tillman of improprieties in a certain land deal, presently to be explained. Until then Roosevelt had never publicly expressed

<hr/>

[6] Louis M. Hacker and Benjamin B. Kendrick, *The United States Since 1865* (New York, 1932), 386; debate, in *Cong. Record*, 60 Cong., 1 Sess., 3359–76.

[7] See p. 462.

his opinion of his most outspoken enemy in the Senate. Perhaps he did not want to dignify the Tillman attacks with notice. The Greater Man in the White House privately felt a condescending contempt for the Lesser Man in the Senate, which stung Tillman more than the open hatred of an equal. In a letter in 1908 to Lincoln Steffens, Roosevelt had delivered a patronizing opinion of the senator. Tillman and Senator Robert M. La Follette, said the President, had "advertised" themselves so that they were "very popular in the Chautauquas where the people listen to them both, sometimes getting ideas that are right, more often getting ideas that are wrong, and on the whole not getting any ideas at all . . . and simply feeling the kind of pleasurable excitement that they would at the sight of a two-headed calf, or a trick performed on a spotted circus horse." [8]

If this was trivial, the Hale letter, seven months later, proved that Roosevelt knew how to impart crushing force to the Big Stick. South Carolinians knew that their frugal senator would exceed the strictly ethical to improve his modest estate, but no voice weighty enough to be heard by the nation had ever questioned the general belief that the corn-field lawyer was too ruggedly honest ever to deviate from the narrowest path of rectitude. When the Man with the Big Stick discovered that this was not entirely true, he struck with decision. He proved that the hankering after the things of Mammon which Tillman so graphically ascribed to the wicked lawyers and corporations was the one sin of the flesh from which the farmer-senator was not free. Roosevelt immolated the chronic corrector of others on the altar of his own morality.

Tillman's involvement in the scheme to acquire advantageous wealth for himself was an outgrowth of his indignation over the acquisitions of vast Western acreages

[8] Roosevelt to Lincoln Steffens, June 5, 1908, cited in Pringle, *Theodore Roosevelt*, 418.

by railroads.[9] This lover of the soil learned to appreciate the value of these lands while on his lecture tours and wanted them cleared and farmed as his ancestors had exploited the South Carolina wooded regions.[10] In fact, he thought of himself as participating in the development of Western lands by making inquiries with possible purchases in view.[11]

With such an idea in mind, he introduced in the Senate on January 31, 1908, a resolution inquiring whether or not railroad companies were selling Western lands to actual settlers at the $2.50 an acre required by Congress when it made the grants. His suspicions that the law was being evaded were confirmed when the Senate Judiciary Committee reported the substance of his resolution.[12] Then, February 19, he directed the attention of the Senate to what he called "a scheme of swindling in which my name is used rather unpleasantly and without the slightest warrant." It was a real estate circular issued by Bryan R. Dorr of Portland, Oregon, soliciting subscribers to join a syndicate to acquire land. It said: "The illegal and outrageous robbery on the part of the Southern Oregon Company is notorious in this State, but until now it has been impossible to secure the necessary concerted action. That the right men are behind this movement will be appreciated at once when I state that among those who have spoken through our attorneys for part of this land is *Senator Tillman of South Carolina, the leader of the Democratic party in the United States Senate,* a man who usually gets what he goes after. So sure is Senator Tillman of our success that he has subscribed and paid the necessary fees for a quarter section for himself and *ten other quarter sections for ten of his nearest relatives.*"

Seemingly to set at rest the implication that he was using

---

[9] *Cong. Record,* 59 Cong., 2 Sess., 3200, 3205.
[10] *Ibid.,* 56 Cong., 2 Sess., 2451.   [11] *Ibid.,* 60 Cong., 1 Sess., 2215.
[12] *Ibid.,* 1366–67, 2112.

his influence as a senator for his personal gain, Tillman ordered the Dorr circular printed in the *Congressional Record* and made the following apparently unambiguous denial of the truth of its assertions: "I have not bought any land anywhere in the West nor undertaken to buy any. I have made some inquiries, as one naturally would in roaming through the West. I simply want the people of the country to be put on notice that this swindler at Portland has no warrant whatever for endeavoring to inveigle others into his game." The Senator put the facts of the case in the hands of the Post Office Department "to block this rascal as much as I can." [13]

At the opening of the next session of Congress the South Carolinian joined the other senators in censuring Roosevelt for criticizing Congressional restriction of the secret service. Their chief argument, replied the President confidently, "was that the Congressmen did not themselves wish to be investigated by Secret Service men." "Was this not an insult?" cried Tillman. Were congressmen accused of withholding an appropriation because it might be used to bring "a lot of rascals and scoundrels" among them to justice? "There may be men here who feel that way, but God knows I do not." [14]

Then suddenly on the head of the man who denied implication in Western land deals, who had asked for an investigation of these deals, who had loudly protested his personal integrity, there fell with a thud the Roosevelt letter to Hale.

A case had just arisen, said the President, which illustrated "in striking fashion" that the much-abused secret agents of the government may discover, "in the strict line of their duty," facts which "ought not to be hidden or sup-

[13] *Ibid.*, 2215-17.
[14] Roosevelt, cited in Pringle, *Theodore Roosevelt*, 483; Tillman, in *Cong. Record*, 60 Cong., 2 Sess., 311-14.

pressed." Post office inspectors, at the request of Senator Tillman, had investigated the actions of land dealers whose circular he had exhibited and they had discovered, despite the senator's assertion, "I have not bought any land anywhere in the West nor undertaken to buy any," that he was at that time negotiating the purchase of Oregon lands through the agency of the attorneys who were also the agents of Dorr, the land dealer whom Tillman had denounced. Four months before his denial of undertaking to buy lands, the senator had written these attorneys, Reeder and Watkins of Marshfield, Oregon, as follows:

"I wired you from Wausau, Wis., as follows, and write to confirm it: 'Wm. E. Lee, my agent, will see you about land. I want nine quarters reserved. Will forward signed applications and money at once. Members of my family are entrymen. Letter follows. (Signed) B.R.T.' I write now to say that I wired Mr. Lee . . . to go at once to Marshfield and see you about the land, to locate quarters for seven members of my family who are of age and one for my private secretary. . . .

"When Lee writes me he has completed the locations I instructed him to draw for the money needed to make the payment of $21 on each application & I have sent the blank applications to my home to be filled out & forwarded to Mr. Lee at Marshfield."

On December 7 following, this agent wrote to Reeder and Watkins that he had advised Tillman that his proposed purchases were "a good gamble," and added: "In case Senator Tillman gets in on this deal with some good land in the eight quarters we want, I am satisfied that he can be of great help in getting matters started from Washington, and cause the Government to get busy and do something along the line you desire. He will set up such a howl that it will be impossible to do otherwise. This will be very important for your whole scheme to have a man of his influence here to aid you at this end of the line. By all means save a lot of good land for us, as we intend to be of more value than any of the others in this matter."

Fifteen days after the introduction of the resolution asking investigation of landholdings, and three days before his denial of a prospective purchase, Tillman began to retreat. To Reeder and Watkins he assumed the attitude he had taken in the railroad pass incident while governor. "What I have done here in stirring up the question of Oregon land grants to railroads, etc.," he explained, "has been done entirely apart from any personal interest I have in the matter." As though frightened by the doubtful ethics of his position he added an *although* and an *if:* "Although I never would have had my attention called to it but for the investigation I set on foot in connection with the proposed purchase by me of some of the timber land in question. . . . If I can succeed in causing the Government to institute suit for the recovery of the land and make it easy for others as *well as myself* [15] to obtain some of it. . . ." [16]

These letters had been secured by post office inspectors when they visited Dorr to investigate Tillman's accusation. Dorr exhibited a letter from his agent in Marshfield claiming that Tillman had made application to purchase lands. The inspectors went to the Oregon town, visited Reeder and Watkins, made copies of the Tillman letters, and reported their discoveries to their official superiors.[17] This report was brought to the attention of the President who immediately ordered the original Tillman letters or photostatic copies. On January 4, 1909, the inspectors supplied Roosevelt with photostatic copies.[18]

There was no proof of Tillman's suspicions that the in-

[15] Italics are Roosevelt's.

[16] Roosevelt to Eugene Hale, January 5, 1909, with exhibits, in *Cong. Record*, 60 Cong., 2 Sess., 720–39.

[17] Report of Post Office Inspectors O. C. Riches and E. C. Clement to G. D. Linn, inspector in charge, July 27, 1908, *ibid.*, 731–34.

[18] Postmaster General George von L. Meyer statement, *ibid.*, 889–90.

vestigation had been started for the purpose of discrediting him and that in pursuit of this object secret service agents in the employ of the President rifled the senator's desk at the Capitol.[19] Nevertheless Roosevelt, once he had the damaging evidence in his hands, eagerly used it to expose an old enemy. He waited only a day after he received the photostats to relay his discovery, in resounding terms, to the Senate and the nation.

The President's accusation brought a chorus of jeers to the South Carolinian. Ironically enough, he who had elected Roosevelt to the Ananias club three years before, was now himself elected to that unenviable organization by the President. The fact that the lands Tillman proposed to buy were exempt from the law requiring sale to "actual settlers" was interpreted as acquitting him of a plot to violate the law but not of a conspiracy to use his official position for personal profit. It was argued that no equitable purpose was served by a law requiring land companies to disgorge holdings worth perhaps a hundred dollars an acre so that the senator from South Carolina and the members of his family could buy some of these acres at $2.50. If the companies must surrender the land, it was adjudged the duty of the senator to promote the forfeiture to the government so that it might be sold at its actual value or allocated to homesteaders.[20]

Tillman's friends were alarmed over his predicament. "Expressions of regrets" over revelations of "some ugly matters" were in the air, and "the news of his possible undoing" was said to be "astonishing." Newspaper admirers said they hated like the devil to send the story.[21]

Never before in his long experience of spectacular appearances before the Senate did Tillman attract more attention than when he arose, a few minutes past twelve on

[19] *Ibid.,* 889.
[20] See comments, in *American Review of Reviews,* XXXIX (1909), 136–37.
[21] "T. H. D.," in Spartanburg *Herald,* January 8, 1909.

January 11, 1909, to defend himself against the Roosevelt charges. Because of the seriousness of the occasion and the precarious condition of his health, the speaker resolved not to allow stress of feeling to lure him from his prepared manuscript. Yet occasionally he exceeded restraints to indulge in the ancient expletives. His voice remained strong, and the initial difficulties of ill-health were soon dissipated in the recovery of old-time fluency. He was heard for the most part in intense silence. Once or twice there was applause when he spoke of the Big Stick trying to put the Pitchfork out of business. The atmosphere was fittingly judicial, for as Tillman said, a member of the Senate "for the first time in history" was "brought to the bar of public opinion, before the Senate itself, to be judged under indictment by no less a person than the President of the United States."

Half of the speech was disappointing; it was a labored and shopworn assault upon the President. He was accused of hiding behind a hypocritical veil of righteousness in order "to blacken my name and destroy my character" by striking "below the belt." The judicial appraiser of this sorry business was not interested in this manifestation of the Tillman spleen. Theodore Roosevelt, despite his many faults, was not on trial before the great and attentive audience crowding the Senate chamber on that January day. Ben Tillman was on trial.

Fortunately for his reputation, after the slings at the hated occupant of the White House, the senator addressed himself to the indictment. Indeed, he answered the charges against him so boldly and so ably that he saved himself from disgrace. Wisely attempting explanation rather than denial, he admitted the authenticity of the letters Roosevelt published. Yet he insisted that he was guiltless of wrong motives in trying to purchase lands, and that this was evident in his having, "without any compulsion from any source and with nothing to conceal," called for an investigation by the Post

Office Department. As for his statement that he "had not undertaken to buy any land," Tillman said everything hinged on the meaning of the word "undertaken" and his use of it. He explained: "I was perhaps not as full and explicit in my statement as I should have been . . . ; but a moment's thought will convince any honest-minded man that—as I had not signed any papers, had not paid any money, had taken nobody's receipt, the usual process by which one 'undertakes' to buy land—I was speaking accurately and not falsely." If he "had told the Senate of the entire transaction," he claimed that "it would have made no difference whatever," and that he would have been charged with "intruding" his private affairs in a public discussion. "I declare most emphatically," he said, "I have never concealed my efforts to buy land. . . . I explained to the Attorney-General my effort. . . .[22] I explained to the agent of the Secret Service the whole transaction when I gave him the Dorr circular and the letters which have been sent to me concerning it." His official position did not legally or morally debar him from the citizen's right to purchase land. It was not his intention, he admitted, to become an "actual settler" upon the land he wished to purchase, but this land was not subject by law to the actual settler provision of the homestead legislation. Effectively he used the point that he did not attempt purchases at a lower figure than any other citizen would have had to pay and that his action involved no violation of the rights of other citizens.

This explanation was a worthy example of Ben Tillman's willingness manfully to confess unsavory details of his private conduct and was a masterful demonstration of his ability at self-defense. It was held acceptable by the Senate.[23]

The verdict of the contemporary press was sound enough to be adopted by the historian. It was the universal opinion

[22] This was denied by Attorney General Charles J. Bonaparte, in *Cong. Record*, 60 Cong., 2 Sess., 887–88.
[23] Tillman, *ibid.*, 740–43; his second defense, *ibid.*, 887–93.

that Tillman had not been guilty of a crime though his conduct had been at least "censurable"; that he had been indiscreet and "disingenuous," if not dishonest; that, although the object he wished to secure by official action was proper, he failed "to perceive that the highest standards of" parliamentary ethics required "a senator to divorce any possible personal pecuniary" gain from official deeds; that if he had not been guilty of outright lying, he was guilty of evasion and suppression; and that he had committed a blunder he would have been the first to condemn in others.[24]

The Oregon land controversy ended the long warfare Tillman waged against President Roosevelt. The Republican leader retired from office two months after the Hale letter, and illness had already deprived Tillman of aggressive inclinations. For the most part the battle had been a one-sided affair. The Pitchfork had often been brandished without retaliatory gesture from the giant who reserved the Big Stick for opponents more formidable than the representative of a small state. But Tillman persisted. Although he could not destroy the adversary, he occasionally pricked the giant's hide and evoked a roar of wrath. In one instance, the controversy over the accuracy of Chandler's report of Roosevelt's words, the Carolinian was the victor. In another, the Oregon land controversy, the President gained the victory. He had struck the last and most effective blow. But more significant was the truce of 1906 when both the Pitchfork and the Big Stick co-operated to achieve one of the most constructive measures of Roosevelt's brilliant regime. Tillman will be remembered for that, not for the petty triumphs and failures of his assaults on the President.

[24] See summaries, in *Current Literature*, XLVI (1909), 120; London *Times*, January 12, 1909.

Chapter XXX

GROWING CONSERVATIVE

IT is popularly assumed that the satisfactions of successful public service gradually molded Ben Tillman into a wiser, mellower, and more conservative man. This belief, like most generalizations concerning an individual of many contradictory emotions and thoughts, is subject to qualifications. It has been most tenaciously held by those who contrast the belligerent harangues of the earlier years with the platitudinous essays delivered after 1910 by a broken old man. Such a reduction of a complex career to simple blacks and whites involves the neglect of irrefutable facts. It is not possible to paint Tillman entirely black during his earlier years. He was never an unadulterated radical or reformer; his program was always moderate and often emerged from conservative or reactionary convictions. Behind his barbarian exterior were hidden the graces of good humor, lack of fanaticism, and respect for traditions. On the other hand, it is a mistake to paint his quieter years entirely white. Ben Tillman never became the perfect gentleman and politician of the Southern idyl. To the end of his days he remained the Edgefield rustic of unpretentious manners, of voluble profanity, of dynamic emotional outbursts. That his last years were not characterized by startling public appearances was due to no fundamental change in his nature; he was not a dead lion, but one caged by physical infirmities.

To claim that age brought a profound change for the better in the South Carolina firebrand is the most derogatory of the many unflattering remarks made about him. This assertion carries the implication that he was a deluded rascal during his so-called demagogic years and that his greatest virtue was the ability to conform in the elevating company of gentlemen. Such a patronizing attitude was properly resented by Tillman whose pride in the achievements of his earlier years remained unabated. He knew that his title to fame rested largely upon those years; that to have repudiated the Ben Tillman who hurled Bourbons from power and brandished the Pitchfork would have reduced him to the level of a nonentity.[1]

The later years of Tillman's life did bring changes but they should not be interpreted as a *volte-face*. They can be most accurately described as the gradual subordination of nonconformist and radical tendencies to an already existing but often latent conservatism. The transformation was not psychological, emotional, or subjective; it was objective. The senator still cherished the principles of the nineties, but to the objective world they were no longer radical.

No more constructive reforms evolved from his tired imagination. He was more interested in past achievements than in future innovations. He thrashed old straw, shunned issues which disturbed the emotions, acquiesced peacefully in the proposals of younger leaders. As his once radical ideas came to be regarded as moderate they merged into his inherently conservative traits to render him, in the opinion of the objective world, an unadulterated conservative. "When I came to Washington," he wrote in 1912, "I was considered an ultra radical. I am now, according to the papers, a reactionary. I do not think I have changed at all, but the country has caught up with me and passed by." [2]

The first striking example of this passivity was Tillman's submission to the destruction of the Dispensary, the unique innovation of his productive years. He had protected it

---

[1] Tillman to R. M. Little, May 13, 1912, in Tillman Papers.
[2] *Id.* to Norman S. Richards, May 30, 1912, *ibid.*

for more than ten years against its many enemies, but it was abolished by the South Carolina legislature in 1907. Tillman, it is true, fought for its retention with some of his accustomed vigor, but when he saw that the cards were stacked against him he submitted to its extinction, experiencing no poignant regrets over what had happened.

The check which the senator was able in 1900 to impose upon the enemies of the state monopoly was temporary. The influential anti-Tillman minority continued the battle against Tillman's "baby." Newspapers ridiculed "the Great Moral Institution." Prohibitionists, led by the Baptist and Methodist clergy and by the Woman's Christian Temperance Union, refused to accept Tillman's thesis that his experiment was a step in the direction of Prohibition. Added to this organized opposition was the powerful conviction among South Carolinians in general that it was immoral for the proud Palmetto state to engage in the liquor business, scandalous for the schools to be supported in part from liquor revenue.[3]

The unpopularity of the Dispensary was justified by its internal weaknesses. It failed to impose the restraints upon the use of alcohol which had been promised. The streets remained unsafe for ladies on Saturdays and sales days. "Blind tigers" continued to flourish; in Charleston "the tiger and the law lay down together."[4] Standing rumors of corruption finally became undisputed actualities. Petty irregularities developed into deliberate grafting on a large scale. In 1896 provision was made for the election of the state board of control by the legislature, and shortly afterwards members of the board were supplementing their $400-a-year salaries by bribes from liquor houses. It was the custom of the distilling trade to allow rebates on prompt payments. These discounts were not returned to the state but were divided between salesmen and the members of

---

[3] Ball, *State that Forgot*, 253–55.
[4] Wallace, *History of South Carolina*, III, 419–20.

the board. The fact that no accurate standards of quality were ever established made possible extensive adulterations with the connivance of the board.

By 1904 conditions in official circles were reminiscent of Reconstruction days. The State House and the Columbia hotels swarmed with whiskey lobbyists, and officials on modest salaries lived in bizarre affluence. "Ice," says an observer, "clinked in cut-glass bottles, champagne corks popped and twenty-dollar bills fluttered about." There was "corruption in the form of 'samples' of fine liquors and handsome presents," and "easy 'winnings' at cards." A Dispensary director boasted that he could buy the doors off the State House.[5]

Public disgust hastened the destruction of the Dispensary. The Brice Act of 1904 permitted counties to adopt Prohibition by popular vote. Representative J. Fraser Lyon of Abbeville, and State Senator Neils Christensen of Beaufort, leaders of an investigating committee, gathered information to prove that the Dispensary was "one of the most elaborate systems of grafting in modern times."[6] And in 1906 the anti-Dispensary forces prepared to capture the state government.

Tillman rose to the defense of the Dispensary. As in 1900, he made it the chief issue of his 1906 campaign for re-election. Still convinced that his pet was the best solution of the liquor problem, he scorned as "cowardly" the suggestion of certain newspapers that he stay in Washington and allow others to direct state affairs.[7] He prevented the legislature in February, 1906, from passing an anti-Dispensary bill[8] and wielded the Pitchfork with almost the old-time zest: "The enemies of the Dispensary, who for

[5] Ball, *State that Forgot*, 250–52. See also, Wallace, *History of South Carolina*, III, 376; Will Irwin, cited in Spartanburg *Herald*, April 12, 1908.
[6] Ball, *State that Forgot*, 256–59; Wallace, *History of South Carolina*, III, 420–22; *Literary Digest*, XXXI (1905), 406.
[7] Spartanburg *Herald*, April 1, 1906.
[8] *Ibid.*, January 18, March 6, 1906; John Gary Evans to Tillman, February 11, 1906, in Tillman Papers.

years have controlled the State, have been putting men in charge of it who have mismanaged it, stolen from it, brought it into bad repute." Called to Columbia to substantiate this charge, he appeared before the legislative committee investigating the Dispensary and offered constructive proposals for reform.[9]

Tillman was a leader of irresistible popularity in 1906. The May convention of that year endorsed as a matter of course the man who had just won the laurels of the railroad rate bill,[10] and the Columbia *State* ruefully admitted, "There is no denying that Benjamin R. Tillman manages to represent with accuracy the sentiment of a majority of South Carolina Democrats on nearly all national issues." William W. Lumpkin had the temerity to offer as the opposition candidate, but soon discovered the folly of his position and withdrew from the canvass. The senator proved to be the same "Ole Ben" to the affectionate crowds of "wool-hat, one-gallus boys." He gesticulated and grimaced and hit his enemies "straight from the shoulders." Lyon, the anti-Dispensary candidate for attorney general, was called "a liar, a cur, and a malicious slanderer"; the editor of the Columbia *State* was accused of a conspiracy to lead the people around with a ring in their noses; "the shameless straddlers" who would not commit themselves on the Dispensary question were "howdy-doing, hand-shaking, baby-kissing, woman-loving politicians." To free the Dispensary from scandal the speaker proposed that liquor bids be deposited in triplicate once a year with the chief justice of the state, the speaker of the House, and the board of control, and opened in the presence of the Dispensary committees of both houses.[11]

[9] Tillman, February 13, 1906, in "Testimony Taken . . . by the Committee to Investigate the Dispensary," in South Carolina *Reports and Resolutions,* 1906, III, 424–34.

[10] Spartanburg *Herald,* May 17, 1906.

[11] Accounts of the campaign of 1906, in Columbia *State,* June 19, 21, July 6, 8, 10, 12, 1906; Charleston *News and Courier,* June 19, 21, July 6, 8, 10, 12, 1906; Spartanburg *Herald,* June 19, 21, July 6, 8, 10, 12, 1906; unidentified out-of-state newspaper, September 2, 6, 1906, in Tillman Scrapbooks.

The primary of 1906 was a signal personal triumph for Tillman and a decisive defeat for his "pet." Lyon was elected attorney general; Martin F. Ansel, a Prohibitionist, defeated Richard I. Manning and Cole L. Blease, friends of the Dispensary, for governor. A legislature pledged to the abolition of the Dispensary was elected. This pledge was redeemed in 1907 when the counties were given the option of Prohibition or the establishment of dispensaries under county control. The Dispensary as a state institution was dead.

The apparent contradiction between the triumph of Tillman and the defeat of the Dispensary is explained by the fact that the captain was willing to abandon the sinking ship without deep regrets. Absorbed by national interests, he admitted not only indifference but ignorance of Dispensary affairs. "I have," he told the 1906 investigating committee, "been paying slight attention to the Dispensary law for a long time. . . . I was deputized by the people to look after their business as a Senator, and I haven't been about it [the Dispensary], except in a very vague and indefinite way, until the last twelve months." [12] In fact, he had already reconciled himself to its doom. "I am very much disgusted," he had written in 1904, "with the present situation in Dispensary matters and do not feel very much confidence in seeing things bettered at the coming session of the legislature. If we cannot lift the system to a better level and restore confidence among the people, it is doomed." [13] His 1906 fight for the institution had significant qualifications. He did not oppose its abolition if its administration could not be reformed and if the people decided against it.

No longer the heroic Tillman who would have wagered his fate on the survival of the Dispensary, he surrendered as soon as the people decided against him. Compensation for defeat was his own re-election to the Senate and the com-

[12] Tillman, February 13, 1906, in "Testimony Taken . . . by the Committee to Investigate the Dispensary," in South Carolina *Reports and Resolutions,* 1906, III, 426.
[13] *Id.* to Theodore D. Jervey, December 26, 1904, in Tillman Papers.

forting belief that the legislature, not Tillman, was responsible for the disgrace brought on South Carolina by the Dispensary scandals.[14]

With the Dispensary thorn removed from his side, the
South Carolina senator addressed himself to measures in
keeping with his conservative tendencies. His fulminations
during the campaign of 1906 against those progressive
South Carolinians who advocated compulsory education
were almost as great as against the Prohibitionists. Without
favoring mass ignorance, he feared Negro education. "It
always seems to me," he wrote a protesting schoolmistress,
"not only idiotic but criminal to strain every nerve . . .
to disfranchise the negroes and then turn right around and
provide means to undo our work." [15]

Tillman's conservatism was likewise manifest in his opposition to Federal child labor legislation as proposed by
Senator Beveridge. He listened attentively to the Indianian's
lurid descriptions of child labor conditions in the cotton
mills of the South, mourned for the exploited children, suggested crusades against this "very great evil," but opined
that Federal regulation was an unconstitutional invasion
of state affairs. When the Indiana senator demonstrated
that labor regulation could not be handled by individual
states, Tillman refused to be practical, remaining an old-
fashioned state rights South Carolinian unmoved by realities more recent than those of Reconstruction. He feared
that pickaninnies picking cotton might be bothered! [16]

More shocking to liberal sentiment was Tillman's demand that South Carolina be allowed to import European
immigrants under contract. In 1906 some five hundred
Belgian, Dutch, and German laborers were actually induced
to come to the state under contract to work in cotton mills
and to give a stipulated share of their wages in return for

[14] Id., "The Story of the Dispensary and How It Bred Corruption," ibid.
[15] Id. to Miss F. M. Earle, April 29, 1912, ibid. Cf. id to James C. Derieux,
September 16, 1913, ibid.
[16] Debate, in Cong. Record, 59 Cong., 2 Sess., 1801–1808.

previously paid steamer fares.[17] Fortunately, the House had inserted in the immigration law of 1907 a provision designed to destroy the contract labor scheme. Lodge pointed out the danger of allowing manufacturers to import laborers obligated to work for passage money in such large numbers as to lower disastrously the wage and living standards of American labor.[18]

The patriot who represented South Carolina in the Senate reacted strongly against this indictment of a plan to advance the material welfare of his state. The South, he affirmed, was able only by special inducements to attract foreigners because of the presence of the Negro and of "worn out and plowed and skinned" lands. He believed that Lodge was actuated by a desire to keep all selected immigration out of the South and denied that the contract labor plan would debase native white labor. Its object was to rid South Carolina of a "grave and dangerous situation" caused by the presence of a Negro majority. He wished, he said, to use foreigners to supplement black farm labor, not to work in cotton mills in competition with native whites. The plan was fatuous and was made doubly so by the passage of the House proviso.[19]

On March 19, 1908, occurred an event which fundamentally altered Tillman's career for the ten remaining years of his life. On the night of that date, while at home in Trenton, he suffered a stroke of paralysis. His affliction took the form of a slight interference with his speech, "a numbness and a tingling in the left side," and the loss of the use of his left arm and leg. It was a severe recurrence of slight paralytic symptoms he had experienced in 1905. He ascribed his trouble "to hard mental labor, intense nervous strain for twenty years, and to overeating." The fact that he had never known how to rest, coupled with his sixty-

---

17 *Ibid.*, 2946–47.   18 *Ibid.*, 3020–21.
19 *Ibid.*, 2940–52, 3017–36, 3084–85, 3090, 3099.

one years, was having the inevitable effect. His strenuous oratory taxed his strength so heavily that only an iron constitution fostered by the simple life of his early years had prevented him from reaching the breaking point sooner. Especially exhausting were his long lecture tours. Less than a year before his collapse he described the devastating effect of having, within a short span of two months, traveled eleven thousand miles to deliver fifty lectures. "I reached home on the 3rd of May as nearly 'played out' as I ever remember to have been in my life, and after a week's rest still feel fatigued, but I have to start again today to meet engagements made by the Chicago Lecture Bureau." [20]

A week after the paralytic stroke he had recovered his spirits and was able to walk and talk without faltering. But he was told that his was a progressive paralysis from which there would never be complete recovery. He was advised not to return to Washington for the remainder of the session and to make a recreational tour of Europe.[21]

The European tour lasted from May to October, 1908, in the company of Mrs. Tillman and a close friend and personal physician, Dr. James W. Babcock. The thoughts of Farmer Ben among the mellow splendors of the Old World may seem incongruous. Certainly he did not go abroad to have his American prejudices destroyed. "The thing that impressed me most on my trip to Europe," he wrote, "was the poverty of the people and the horrible lack of pride." The frugal farmer did not like the European tipping system. The antiplutocrat deplored the fact that "some rich fellow owned Abbotsford" and placed restrictions upon visitors to that residence of a beloved novelist. The son of the sunny South detested the "perpetual mist, or shower, or some precipitation of water" which characterized the

[20] Tillman to M. C. Turner, May 11, 1907, in Tillman Papers.
[21] See Dr. James W. Babcock's account of Tillman's first illness, in Spartanburg *Herald,* May 22–27, 1908; Tillman to John H. Allen, May 22, 1911, in Tillman Papers.

climate of Scotland. In Spain he lamented the absence of light, which he said the priests kept from both their cathedrals and the minds of their people.

Yet the pilgrim did not conform in all respects to the satirist's portrait of the successful American in Europe. His sound, if limited, literary experiences found expression in lively appraisals of many European monuments. He had read enough romantic poetry to appreciate the beauties of Switzerland and the Rhine. As he moved through Holland, John L. Motley's phrases about Dutch heroes and battles ran through his head. In Florence he was impressed by Cellini's "Perseus," and in Seville he made an intelligent comparison between the women of Murillo's canvases and those he saw on the streets. But his principal delight was Scotland, where had been enacted the scenes of Scott's novels. The characters in these books were as real to him "as those I meet on the street every day." He was careful to visit the Saut Market made immortal in *Rob Roy*. "I imagined," he said, "I could see the picture of Bailie Jarvie dangling from the thorn bush in the mountains and Helen MacGregor's sour visage; then too I could see Rob Roy towering over the cowering merchant and hear him thundering forth." If the South Carolina senator was not able to experience reactions as refined as those of such cosmopolite colleagues as Aldrich or Bacon, he certainly was no Goth recently emerged from the backwoods.[22]

Tillman reaped the promised reward of his withdrawal from politics. When Congress reconvened in December, 1908, he was back in his seat strengthened and refreshed, exhibiting much of his old-time fire. "Uncle Benjamin," a Washington correspondent observed, "is right back on the job in the old form that made him famous." He soon proved this in several ways. He rebuked Roosevelt for the activities

22 Tillman to Judge Annis, April 29, 1914, in Tillman Papers; *id.* to Senator Augustus O. Bacon, October 28, 1911, *ibid.; id.* to Dr. Babcock, June 11, 17, 1918, *ibid.*

of the secret service, twitted Republican leaders in good style,[23] defended himself on the Oregon land issue, and participated aggressively in the debates on the Payne-Aldrich tariff.

In this debate the South Carolina senator exhibited almost to perfection his peculiar powers of argumentation. He ran the whole gamut of forensic strategy, sometimes even striving for polish and elegance. Conventional attacks upon the justice of the protective system were mingled with attempts to reap the benefits of protection for his state. His motive was to portray the absurdity of protection by carrying it to logical extremes while cannily securing tariff "steals" for his own people. He joyously exposed inconsistencies in the tariff views of senators: Republicans who prated about the welfare of workingmen but sought protection for every selfish interest in their states; Democrats who repeated ancient free-trade platitudes and then hastened to gather all the crumbs Republicans let fall. The cream of the jest was his admission of being one of the guilty Democrats. In the rough and tumble of debate he mixed indignation, the imputation of motives, and what he called "self-idolatry," with boisterous wit and sarcasm. Never was Ben Tillman more brilliant than in this his last assault upon the Republican oligarchy. He hurled his shaft at the mighty Aldrich, often forcing that crafty leader out of his elusive silence. The Rhode Islander had his way as usual, but Tillman's frequent prediction that the people would rise in wrath against the direction of legislation in reactionary channels was soundly prophetic. Aldrich was never again to play the dictator and was making his last stand for the privileges of the rich.

Losing patience when Aldrich refused to lift protection from items used by Southern farmers, the South Carolinian delivered a classic rebuke: "It does seem to me very singular

[23] Unidentified Washington newspaper, cited in Spartanburg *Herald*, December 20, 1908.

that the Senator's heart always hardens toward that poor fellow who walks behind the plow handle, while it gets as soft and as generous in dealing with some manufacturers as if they were made of different clay from the man who farms." [24] That senators could be sentimental and windy in defense of selfish and sordid interests appealed to Tillman's sense of the ridiculous. These emotionalists regarded protection as "a glorious goddess" who must be praised in words which outdid "the American eagle in flying up in the skies." Why, he asked amid peals of laughter, did not Aldrich, "the astute manager who is in control of this bill," put a stop to this flood of words so that the benefits of the goddess could be had as soon as possible? [25]

One of the reasons why the debate seemed so absurd to Tillman was that he regarded it as a perfect illustration of the innate selfishness of man. Senators were protectionists toward home industries, and free traders when other states' industries were concerned. He even suggested that the usually impeccable Democrats were not sinless. While Republicans were making free trade speeches, the Democrats were wanting everything their states produced protected. "We are getting very badly mixed here," said Tillman to continued laughter, "and it is pretty hard to tell the sheep from the goats. . . . I am afraid, before we get through, there will not be trough enough for all the hogs to get their snouts into it." [26]

The senator knew that South Carolina was so constituted industrially that it could not get a fair share of the protection "steal." But there was such a thing as a *reductio ad absurdum* of the whole protective argument, and there were the crumbs under the table. So, in a mocking vein he asked that the fostering principle of protection be thrown around a South Carolina industry which was both interesting and

[24] *Cong. Record*, 61 Cong., 1 Sess., 1918, 3904, 3917, 3871. *Cf. ibid.*, 1439, 2218, 2712, 3891–93.
[25] *Ibid.*, 2234.
[26] *Ibid.*, 1635. *Cf. ibid.*, 2234, 2316, 3395.

infantile. He demanded a duty of ten cents a pound on the one hundred million pounds of tea imported each year in order that a single tea grower on an experimental farm at Summerville, South Carolina, might enjoy a rise in the price of the twelve thousand pounds of tea he produced annually.

With infinite irony Tillman invoked the argument for protection. He described the Summerville tea farm as "a poor, little puling infant industry out in the piny woods . . . begging the United States for help." To give it the protection of a high tariff, he said, would improve the quality of the article through eliminating the competition of low-grade teas from foreign countries without increasing prices to the consumer. He begged Aldrich to harken to his plea, for, asserted the Carolinian, the Rhode Islander "is not only the Committee on Finance, but to all intents and purposes he is the Senate of the United States, in the making of this law, and he knows it." Amid disclaimers from the self-effacing boss, the speaker mock-heroically confronted him with his own arguments. When Aldrich admitted that the protection of a promising infant industry was sound Republicanism, Tillman proved that the South Carolina industry was "a lusty little baby and can cry" by offering the Republican senator the gift of some native tea "that will cool his 'inwards.' " Then, intimating that "the cohesive power of public plunder" was what held the Aldrich gang together, he asked the senator to give the tea industry $1,200 worth of protection through a duty that would yield nine million dollars in revenue! Half serious in his desire to protect the tea industry, but with no notion that his huge joke would succeed, Tillman gloated over putting the protectionists "in a very uncomfortable position." "I feel," he said, "we are very near the devil's kitchen and the fumes from below are coming up." [27]

The Senate of course did not take the Tillman sugges-

[27] *Ibid.*, 3900–3904, 3919–21.

tion seriously. Aldrich told him that such a tax was unjustified in the absence of assurance that tea could become a
prosperous American industry. Tillman himself rejected as
unsound the proposal of certain Republicans that a bounty
be substituted for the proposed duty. The Democrats were
not impressed by the proposal that they abandon antipro-
tectionist traditions in favor of a dubious experiment. Tillman could muster only eighteen votes for his idea. Bailey
of Texas was the only Democrat in this number.[28]

As soon as the tea project failed, the Carolinian abandoned Washington to resume his habit of "preaching . . .
the gospel of white supremacy" before Northern audiences.
After spending a month in Ohio he returned home where
he told an Anderson gathering that he marveled over his
good health.[29] But his recovery was largely illusory. The
paralytic stroke of March, 1908, had left him in some respects a permanent invalid, and on February 16, 1910,
came a far more serious illness which began with a collapse
on the steps of the Capitol. At first his condition was reported as "not serious," but during the second and third
days his affliction was such "as to thoroughly alarm his
friends." A cerebral hemorrhage rendered him speechless
and caused asphasia and a paralysis of his entire right side.
On the fourth day, however, he began to improve, and
within two days the change for the better was so pronounced
that his case was considered almost miraculous. His memory cleared; he soon regained partially his powers of speech
and the use of his right arm and leg.[30] Within three weeks
he was well enough to go home so that, as he expressed it,
he might see his flowers, direct the building of a cattle barn,
and hear the June bugs.[31] At Trenton he was able to walk
about his farm with the aid of a stick and he had hopes of

[28] *Ibid.*, 3934. [29] Tillman, *Struggles of 1876*, 1.
[30] Washington dispatches to Spartanburg *Herald*, February 17–24, 1910.
[31] Columbia *State*, March 17, 1910.

being able to resume his seat in the Senate in December.[32]

When Congress convened in December, 1910, he was in his seat looking well and cheerful. But as he walked it was noticed that the once vigorous man leaned heavily on a cane,[33] and he privately confessed that his well-being was more apparent than real. "I have no strength," he wrote. "When I look into the glass and see the old Tillman, and when I try to put him through his stunts, things that used to be easy are beyond my strength. I feel like I ought to be arrested as a fraud." [34]

[32] Tillman to Senator Morgan G. Bulkeley, May 14, 1910, in Tillman Papers.

[33] Spartanburg *Herald*, December 3, 8, 1910.

[34] Tillman to John R. Abney, February 11, 1911, in Tillman Papers.

Chapter XXXI

PARTIAL RETIREMENT

THE senator from South Carolina was forced to recognize the radical alterations of ill-health. Regrets for impaired physical strength were followed by complaints over loss of mental alertness, over inability to remember recent events or to control tears when sensibilities were touched.[1] Most tragic, however, was the failure of forensic powers. In the spring of 1911 Tillman tried, before an audience of Edgefield friends, to rehearse in his traditional manner, but after a few harmless words, the labor became so great that he was forced to sit down. Bitterly he concluded that he must take his seat among the "has-beens."[2] Thereafter he confined the expression of his ideas to private conversation, letters, or short written addresses on subjects of little current interest. The day when he stirred the Senate with strident oratory and rapid questioning was passed. He admitted as accurate the report that "age and bodily infirmities have taken the fight out of him. He no longer uses the pitchfork, but crutches."[3]

He became unable or unwilling to continue his habit of executing routine duties vigorously, complained of their tediousness, and studiously turned his feeble energies into less important activities. He directed his farm and wrote many letters, but gave scant attention to the main problems of Congress except to answer roll calls. He was absent from

[1] Tillman to Senator Bacon, October 28, 1911, in Tillman Papers; *id.* to W. L. Tallman, September 26, 1911, *ibid.*
[2] *Id.* to J. H. Claffy, May 19, 1911, *ibid.*
[3] *Id.* to Judge Annis, June 21, 1914, *ibid.*

Washington for long intervals. In his own mind this neglect was justified. Did he not arrange to be paired with a Republican senator when absent? Was he not able to convince himself that Congress was "doing nothing gloriously" even during the extra session of 1913 which enacted the major achievements of the Wilson administration? [4]

Despite his shortcomings, Tillman remained mentally competent after his illnesses. Ideas continued to germinate in his mind, his emotions were still fiery, his opinions and prejudices were still strong. His intelligence, if less agile and original, was still solid; he continued to express himself firmly and rationally in many animated letters and conversations.[5] Yet these means of communication were not adequate for one accustomed to public speech, and he loudly mourned his deterioration. "When I contemplate," he wrote in 1912, "the weak and trembling figure I now cut, tottering on the brink of the grave, and unable to make a speech, I am compelled to feel sorry for myself." [6] Time and again he longed to be "uproarious," to "blow off," and not to have to content himself with being "a spectator in Venice," unable to "put in some licks for Democracy" by delivering speeches against Republican scandals "that would reverberate throughout the country." [7]

The senator's infirmities led him to take great interest in the improvement of his health. He became his own doctor to prove that the physicians were wrong in diagnosing progressive paralysis. "Since my illness four years ago," he told the Senate in 1914, "I have learned more about the human body than during all the balance of my life." [8] His

[4] Id. to Senator Bacon, June 17, 1911, ibid.; id. to Riggs, August 29, 1913, ibid.; id. to James M. Baker, October 4, 1914, ibid.; id. to Senator Isaac Stephenson, March 10, 1917, ibid.

[5] "K. F. M.," in Charleston News and Courier, May 11, 1912.

[6] Tillman to J. W. Gregory, September 1, 1912, in Tillman Papers.

[7] Id. to J. L. Hewitt, June 29, 1914, ibid.; id. to J. M. Miller, June 17, 1916, ibid.; id. to Henry C. Tillman, January 19, 1912, ibid.; id. to D. T. Gettys, March 8, 1912, ibid.

[8] Cong. Record, 63 Cong., 2 Sess., 4532.

health practices revealed courageous self-discipline and created a satisfying hopefulness, but gave further evidence of his abandonment of the objective interests on which fame usually rests. Tillman had become just another old man concerned with his ailments and vainly fighting the inevitable effects of senility. It goes without saying that his health practices were not sufficiently useful or original to be regarded as other than quackery by those of critical intelligence. Physicians, he was forced to recognize, laughed at his nostrums.[9]

The captain of the ship on which the invalid returned from Europe impressed him with the wisdom of physical culture; after some necessary reading he equipped himself with dumbbells and outlined an elaborate system of exercises consisting of no less than seventeen intricate movements. Every morning and evening for the remaining years of his life, except when he was prostrated by illness, a strange scene occurred in the Tillman bedroom. An old man could be observed studiously kicking his feet and twisting his body in every possible way as he whirled dumbbells through the air. The object was to bend every joint and to exercise every muscle.[10]

There were other health devices. One was the drinking of more than a gallon of water each day. Another was "deep breathing and the holding of the breath long enough to count ten." A third was a remedy no more unconventional than Lady Webster's Pills, a cathartic recommended by Isaac Stephenson, the aged millionaire senator from Wisconsin. A fourth was *Agua Nova Vitae,* a medicine sent by an unknown Pennsylvania friend, which gave Tillman a ravenous appetite. A fifth was the avoidance of the supposed evil effects of tobacco.[11] His favorite panacea was dieting.

[9] Tillman to Augustine T. Smythe, July 8, 1912, in Tillman Papers; *id.* to Judge A. W. Whitfield, January 19, 1915, *ibid.*

[10] Tillman statement, June 17, 1911, *ibid.*

[11] *Id.* to Riggs, August 1, 1912, *ibid.; id.* to unidentified senator, May 16, 1914, *ibid.*

In 1912 he wrote, "I have cut out all meat except white meat, and am a vegetarian so much so that I claim to belong to the Nebuchadnezzar brigade." [12] He became so enamored of an onion diet that a newspaper declared, "Perhaps the most noted advocate of the onion in America is Senator Tillman of South Carolina." [13] At this time his breakfast consisted of raw onions and raw tomatoes; his dinner of buttermilk, bread and butter, and six or eight boiled onions; his evening meal of cheese, tomatoes and raw onions. The onions, he said, helped his digestion and kept his liver and kidneys in order.[14]

The senator did not find his restoratives as helpful as he hoped. In his opinion *Agua Nova Vitae* soon lost its vital properties,[15] and he frequently violated his dietary rules. The Christmas season especially found him once more the normal South Carolinian who relished turkey, jowl, collards, chitterlings, pig's feet, and fruitcake. The summer vacation offered fried chicken and so many garden delicacies that he could not restrain his appetite.[16]

These defections did not prevent a continued enthusiasm for his remedies. To the end of his days he babbled about the uselessness of physicians and medicine, and how his own health practices would preserve his life for another fifteen years.[17] Naturally, he wished to share his supposedly valuable experiences with others. He urged the senators to follow his example, quaintly described the evils of tobacco, and successfully introduced a resolution to prohibit smoking in the Senate Chamber.[18] He published in Bernarr MacFadden's *Physical Culture Magazine* an outline of his physical

---

[12] *Id.* to Mrs. Henry L. Smeltz, May 13, 1912, *ibid.*

[13] Unidentified editorial, in Tillman Scrapbooks.

[14] Tillman to Mrs. Charles S. Moore (Lona Tillman), October 29, 1913, in Tillman Papers.

[15] *Id.* to Ferdinand Muckley, October 22, 1912, *ibid.*

[16] *Id.* to Mrs. Smeltz, January 13, 1913, *ibid.; id.* to Dr. Babcock, January 15, 1914, *ibid.; id.* to Mrs. Moore, July 27, 1917, *ibid.*

[17] *Id.* to S. E. McAdoo, July 22, 1914, *ibid.;* statement, August, 1914, *ibid.*

[18] *Cong. Record,* 63 Cong., 2 Sess., 4531–32.

exercises [19] and he discussed, "for the benefit of mankind," the possible preparation of a moving picture showing him "kicking and cavorting in my B.V.D's." [20] This publicity brought him many letters asking for prescriptions. For a time his healing services were in such great demand that he was advising as many ill people as a popular physician.

It had always been Tillman's habit, even during the busiest years of his senatorship, to steal away frequently from public business in order to dictate long and intricate letters to the manager of his farm.[21] At Trenton it was his practice to spend whole days riding and walking over his lands. Politicians and newspapermen could only interview him by following his rapid movements about the fields.[22] His partial retirement naturally led to the accentuation of these practices.

"Why do you spend so much valuable time at such work?" he was asked by a visitor in 1908. "Well, now, maybe," was the reply, "because I find this pastime fully as interesting—if not as remunerative—as some folks find horse-racing." [23] But farming was to him more than a mere hobby. His boasts on the Senate floor of his devotion to it were utterly sincere; for farming had been his earliest passion, and the mystery and beauty of growing things fascinated him to the end of his life. The fact that his farming was not a financial success—his investments in agriculture were probably greater than his returns—was not an unusual experience for one of his environment. Thousands of farm-bred Southerners allowed the profits of other activities to be absorbed by farms. Although he was too closefisted to enjoy losing money, the pleasure he derived from observ-

[19] Reprinted, *ibid.*, 4945–46.
[20] Tillman to Carl E. Williams, February 12, 1917, in Tillman Papers.
[21] See Dexter Marshall, in Nashville *Banner*, September 8, 1906, in Tillman Scrapbooks.
[22] Tillman to A. K. Smoak, September 14, 1916, in Tillman Papers.
[23] Broughton Brandenburg, "At Home with Big Americans: With 'Pitchfork' Ben Tillman in Edgefield, S. C.," in *Delineator* (New York), LXXI (1908), 238.

ing sleek cattle and lush fields was sufficient to blind him to financial losses revealed by complex plantation books. Moreover, a special circumstance ameliorated the burden of supposed losses. Part of his farm expenses was borne by a wealthy and generous friend, the Federal government.

Federal support of his farm took the form of a continuation of the types of petty graft he had practiced while governor. He received gifts of seed and plants from the Bureau of Plant Industry. Among the items for which he begged were sorghum and cotton seed, velvet beans, enough privet for a hedge 750 feet long, asparagus crowns, as well as many varieties of flower seeds and plants. To satisfy Tillman's varied demands, the Department of Agriculture, when it could not fill his orders, was willing to make purchases for him.[24]

A more substantial and more unusual Federal aid to the senator's farming operations was the furnishing of labor. He required the clerks and other persons to whom he gave office to spend the Congressional recesses working on his Trenton estate. "I have been in the habit," he confessed, "always of having the stenographers or messengers or other appointees of the naval committee . . . help me in the farm or the garden. Jones did it, Harris did it, Wyche did it, and Pollard is doing it." J. Broadus Knight, his most valued clerk, "not only did it but he kept all my machinery in order and cut my oats and wheat and other grains." Thomas B. Greneker took "hold of the farm work like a lion," and Jake Smith, in the intervals between desultory duties as a Senate doorkeeper, was the veteran handyman of the Tillman establishment.[25]

The senator was an exacting taskmaster, ordering his

[24] Tillman to Dr. Beverly T. Galloway, March 28, 30, April 15, October 15, 1912, in Tillman Papers; *id.* to James E. Jones, January 15, 1913; February 17, 27, 1917, *ibid.; id.* to Benjamin R. Tillman, Jr., March 6, 1916, *ibid.; id.* to William A. Taylor, March 9, 1916, *ibid.*

[25] *Id.* to Benjamin R. Tillman, Jr., April 15, 1916, *ibid.; id.* to Luther N. Jones, September 10, 1916, *ibid.; id.* to Kohn, August 13, 1917, *ibid.* The clerks mentioned in this and the following paragraph were Luther N. Jones,

subordinates to report for farm duty at a moment's notice and jerking them out of bed at ungodly hours. No respecter of persons, he demanded of palefaced office men the same standards of achievement he imposed on black veterans of many seasons and harvests. The unfortunate novices suffered grievous blisters and sore muscles while the taskmaster, with stick in hand and curses on his lips, urged them to their labors. "Wyche, Patton and Knight," he wrote concerning a harvest of pea-vines, "are doing all they can, but, poor things, they know nothing about how to do it easily and their hands are so tender that it is pitiful to see the blisters." He said to David, the colored laborer who was working with the trio, that were the Negro a college graduate there would be four such distinguished persons in the field. But David, while the eye of the unacademic boss twinkled, looked at the hands of the college graduates and said that he preferred "graduation in field work." [26]

The farmer-senator dismissed from his services the clerical assistants who did not accept the Tillman version of their duties. No clerk, he wrote a dissatisfied one, had previously objected to this type of work, and he added, "Whether the government pays those I employ or whether I pay them myself is not a matter of importance. I employ them and the government furnishes me the help to do the amount of work I have." [27] He reminded a friend of the clerk that if he "had stuck it out until we got to Washington," he would have had "a pleasant job and a good salary." There the senator allowed his overnumerous employees to attend law school during the ample recess hours. This aiding of impecunious South Carolinians to gain education at public expense gave him almost as much impish satisfaction as his ability to compel them to work on his farm.

C. Granville Wyche, Richard Pollard, J. Broadus Knight, Thomas B. Greneker, Leon W. Harris, and Grover C. Patton. The doorkeeper was Jake S. Smith.

[26] Tillman to Benjamin R. Tillman, Jr., September 20, 1914, *ibid.*

[27] *Id.* to S. L. Pender, August 19, 1917, *ibid.*

"Every boy," he said proudly, "who has graduated from my office has made a success of life." One became the mayor of a town, a second a court official, a third a state senator, and a fourth a naval officer.[28]

The old taskmaster taught his clerks to write correctly and to farm intelligently. These were skills which Tillman not unwisely felt were parts of a wholesome education. And they were achievements which his clerks, although usually college graduates and sons of farmers, did not possess. If, however, they submitted to the conscientious tyranny of their employer-teacher, bad syntax and spelling were corrected, and indifference to the problems of the soil gave way to a lively participation in the traditional occupation of South Carolinians.[29]

Partial retirement, Federal aid, and a liberal income allowed Tillman during his last years to indulge freely in experimental farming. He felt that his mission was to teach the people how to grow crops best suited for their soil and climate.[30] The list of his agricultural experiments was long. He always seemed to believe that a new crop was better than an old one.[31] As early as 1899 he was not too busy with politics to rush home and "demonstrate that tobacco is a cheaper and better paying crop than cotton," [32] and in 1908 he proudly showed visitors "some little patches of ground back of the house" where he grew several kinds of alfalfa, pecan trees, and *figa d'India*.[33] Later, his experiments included peanuts for hogs, bur clover, Irish potatoes, and pepper. He even contemplated a pond for "growing fish profitably and cheaply by feeding them." [34] From 1910 to 1912 he carried on an elaborate experiment in the winter feeding of cattle. He was a successful pioneer in the growing

[28] *Ibid.*   [29] *Id.* to Wyche, August 30, 1912, *ibid.*
[30] *Id.* to Ruth Berry, October 30, 1917, *ibid.*
[31] *Id.* to Dr. William J. Murray, March 10, 1913, *ibid.*
[32] Charleston *News and Courier*, July 7, 1899.
[33] Brandenburg, "At Home with Big Americans," *loc. cit.*, 238.
[34] Tillman to H. M. Smith, May 11, 1915, in Tillman Papers.

of asparagus in Edgefield County. His fifteen acres of this vegetable set the pace for the establishment of a thriving neighborhood industry. During the last years of his life when Negro labor became demoralized by World War prosperity, he tried the innovation of engaging white farm laborers.[35]

The most elaborate Tillman experiment was concerned with an important farm problem, the provision of adequate fencing. The senator thought he saw a solution in hedges of *citrus trifoliata,* or hardy lemon. He planted a half mile of this thorny bush, claiming that it was "not only idiotic but criminally extravagant to build fences with posts and wire" when "a living fence that will not rot down" could be had for the planting. Such a fence, he added, was "bull-strong, horse-high, and pig-tight." [36]

The attention which the farmer-senator gave "money crops" did not prevent indulgence in flower-growing, a passion akin to his appreciation of poetry. "The screen of rare blossoms around the Tillman veranda," said an enthusiastic visitor, "was a feast for the eyes." [37] There were orchids, gentians, dwarf lilies, amarillas, japonicas, narcissi, and a profusion of roses. He possessed almost two hundred varieties of the last plant.[38]

Tillman's contributions to horticultural knowledge were no more significant than his experiments in self-medication. In moments of self-criticism he acknowledged that "he himself is not much of a farmer; in fact that his farming is usually considered something of a joke." [39] The only crop he succeeded in introducing was asparagus. Tobacco and pepper plantations, fish ponds and cattle raising, did not

[35] *Id.* to Benjamin R. Tillman, Jr., March 23, 1918, *ibid.*

[36] *Id.* to Riggs, November 25, December 6, 1911, *ibid.;* Tillman statement, 1918, *ibid.*

[37] Brandenburg, "At Home with Big Americans," *loc. cit.,* 238–39.

[38] Tillman to Good and Rease (firm of florists), February 8, 1913, in Tillman Papers.

[39] Chester speech, cited in Columbia *State,* August 18, 1909.

supplant cotton and corn; white labor failed; the citrus hedge developed fatal breaks; nearly $2,000 was lost on the cattle-feeding experiment. Dreams of arresting the decay of the old home place did not come true; Bermuda grass and cattle raising could not halt such relentless causes of decay as gully washing and the desire of tenants to seek their fortunes in more prosperous areas.[40] The flower garden at Trenton lacked artistry. It had the jumbled effect of a too liberal use of the resources of the National Botanical Garden, presenting more the appearance of an experimental station than the unassumed splendor of the genuinely successful Southern garden. Lack of order and adaptation defeated his strivings for floral charm.

The senator was more successful in nonagricultural ventures than in farming. His and his wife's frugality made possible a generally wise use of his considerable income. His salary, during his twenty-three years in Washington, amounted to about $160,000.[41] These earnings were in a small measure augmented by petty graft in the form of supplies, services, and the junketing trips which are available to senators. The most profitable undertaking of his life was his ten years of lecturing. The returns from this endeavor rose in 1906 to $20,000, and the following year to $27,000. He used part of his income for the retirement of debts remaining from his early farming and political activities. Other sums were judicially used in the purchase of $10,000 worth of oil stocks and in real estate investments at Augusta, Georgia, and High Point, North Carolina. However, the loss of $10,000 through cotton speculations, the extravagance of farm operations, and the necessity of supporting and educating a large family, prevented Tillman from building a fortune. His income in 1915, one of his most

[40] Tillman statement, 1911, in Tillman Papers; *id.* to Riggs, November 25, December 16, 1911; October 21, 1912, *ibid.; id.* to Benjamin R. Tillman, Jr., March 23, 28, 1918, *ibid.*

[41] Estimate of Columbia *State,* August 3, 1911.

prosperous years, amounted to only $5,795 in addition to
his salary of $7,500.[42] At that time he could say with satis-
faction: "I am not wealthy at all, but I have sufficient of
the world's goods to be independent." [43]

The most satisfying phase of Tillman's later years, as it
had been of his early and middle years, was his happy domestic life. He continued to adore his wife. "You do not
know, dear," he wrote in 1913, "how much you are to me.
. . . You have always been so beautiful and had such a
sacred regard for what you consider your duty." [44] His children venerated him, regarding his sense of justice as fault-
less.[45] He returned their esteem in ample measure, giving
them full support of means and wisdom.

In Washington the senator lived modestly in an inconspicuous hotel and welcomed every opportunity to return
to the simple spaciousness of his Edgefield County house.
There he was his natural self, could farm and garden, and
eat without stint generous portions of native viands. There
he received all visitors with an unplanned cordiality which
always included an invitation to the table. "At our house,"
he explained, "we make company of nobody, but everybody
takes pot luck." [46]

His private life was, however, marred by some of the unhappy vicissitudes of fortune. He had scarcely entered the
Senate before he learned in July, 1896, "what it is to have
a beloved child leave full of life and be brought back home
a corpse." Addie, his oldest daughter, a bright-eyed lass of
nineteen, was killed, along with a young Episcopal minister, by lightning when the couple halted their horses under
the shelter of a tree in the North Carolina mountains during a sudden shower. "I shall never forget," the father later

[42] Tillman statement, February 24, 1915, in Tillman Papers.
[43] Id. to Judge Annis, February 2, 1917, ibid.
[44] Id. to Mrs. Tillman, September 5, 1913, ibid.
[45] Brandenburg, "At Home with Big Americans," loc. cit., 237.
[46] Tillman to Ebbie J. Watson, December 19, 1911, in Tillman Papers; id.
to Mrs. Moore, June 6, 1912, ibid.

wrote, "my wife's agonized screams when a neighbor brought her the news early next morning." [47]

A second misfortune came at the end of Tillman's active period in the Senate. On December 29, 1903, Benjamin R. Tillman, Jr., aged twenty-five, had married Lucy Frances Dugas, whom the groom's father described as "a beautiful and winning young woman of twenty-one." She was more than that. She was the heir of Edgefield's most aristocratic family, the granddaughter of Francis W. Pickens and Lucy Petway Holcombe, a glamorous Texan whom Pickens met at a Virginia watering place. Her mother was Douschka, an almost legendary figure born in Russia where Pickens was American minister. Her inheritance consisted of a large cotton plantation, Edgewood, a house surrounded by a beautiful garden and a great forest, and family jewels and household furnishings more splendid than those of any other Edgefield family. The youthful couple established themselves at Edgewood. B. R., as young Tillman was familiarly known, was madly in love with his wife, and because of the influence of his father and his Clemson education was equipped to manage the Pickens acres. Two children, Douschka Pickens and Sarah Starke, were born to the union. There were hopes of a successful household.

But it would have been well had the couple accepted the advice of their elders against marriage. The aristocratic young lady was warned of the folly of attempting to mix the blue Pickens blood with the red blood of the Tillmans; of the possible lack of congeniality between the family reared amid the rude austerities of the Horne's Creek plantation and a woman accustomed to the polished convivialities of the Edgewood house; of the anomaly of a marriage between the daughter of Edgefield's most Bourbon family and the son of one whose mission was to destroy Bourbonism. Senator Tillman, on the other hand, warned

[47] Charleston, *News and Courier*, July 17, 1896; Tillman to R. B. Dixon, September 7, 1912, in Tillman Papers.

his son of the peril of marriage into a family of aristocratic
pride whose glamour was in his opinion no fit substitute for
the plain virtues of the Tillman household. The marriage
resulted, as might have been expected, in what the senator
ruefully described as "six years of strife and unhappiness."
A temporary separation in November, 1908, was followed
by permanent separation a year later. Unfortunately the
elder Tillman injected himself too pointedly into his son's
private affairs, allowing his "suspicious nature" to lead him
into accusations against his daughter-in-law. She in turn
learned to distrust and to hate her father-in-law and the
whole Tillman family. The proud patrician had little respect for the senator's virtues and fame; she saw in him
only a meddlesome and dictatorial old man as rude as he
was tactless.

The inevitable sequel was a battle for possession of the
two Tillman children, who were five and three years old
in 1909. While the younger Mrs. Tillman was ill in Washington, her husband took the children to his mother's apartment. Immediately the elder Mrs. Tillman, without their
mother's knowledge, carried them to Trenton. At Edgefield courthouse, a few days later, their father, at the suggestion of Senator Tillman, deeded them to his parents
under an old statute giving a father arbitrary authority over
his offspring.[48]

The senator's decisiveness had for once been imprudent.
He was challenging a sentiment over which the veteran
political boss had no more control than the most obscure
citizen. This sentiment was the public's conviction, the law
to the contrary, that a mother had first claim on her children. Senator and Mrs. Tillman were accused of "kidnap-
ing" their grandchildren; the law under which the deed
was executed was declared "barbarous . . . and enough to

---

[48] Recorded December 1, 1909, Edgefield County, South Carolina, Deed
Book, XXI, 517.

make the blood of every true man boil."[49] A movement was inaugurated which led to the repeal of the obnoxious statute,[50] and Lucy Dugas Tillman brought suit before the South Carolina supreme court for the repossession of her children. Though Senator Tillman contested the case with spirit before a court composed of former political lieutenants, the state of public opinion tolerated but one verdict. By unanimous decision the children were given the mother "until it be otherwise adjudged."[51] Had the decision been against the mother, popular demonstrations would have been made against the grandfather. There was talk of forcibly taking the children from him or of tearing down his portrait over the speaker's desk in the State House.[52] Earlier situations had been reversed; instead of threats of force in Tillman's favor there were threats of force against him.

This public defeat over an issue of intimate concern grieved Tillman greatly. Two days after the publication of the decision he suffered his second stroke of paralysis.[53] When he recovered somewhat he busied himself with securing modification of the decision.[54] In December, 1912, this came in the form of a decree giving the father custody of the two children for two months of the year and for half the Christmas holidays.[55] But there were circumstances which judges, Tillmanite or otherwise, could not control. They could not make the Tillman children love their grandfather. In fact, the two girls learned to despise him. In despair he confessed to the chief justice of the state: "I

[49] Opinions of different persons, in Spartanburg *Herald,* January 30, February 6, 1910; Columbia *State,* February 13, 1910.

[50] South Carolina *Acts,* 1910, pp. 704–705.

[51] Columbia *State,* February 1, 16, 1910. The hearing was January 31, 1910; the decision, February 15, 1910. *Ex parte* Tillman, 84 South Carolina 552.

[52] Spartanburg *Herald,* February 16, 1910.

[53] See p. 468.

[54] Tillman to Dr. E. F. Pickford, November 16, 1912, in Tillman Papers; *id.* to Benjamin R. Tillman, Jr., December 7, 1912, *ibid.*

[55] Tillman *v.* Tillman, 93 South Carolina 281.

have no idea the little girls will ever do other than hate me." [56] Sent to the Tillman home in obedience to the orders of the court, the little girls, after ugly and distressing scenes, marched away, and there was nothing that could be done about it. The old man was grieved.[57]

Ill-health compelled Ben Tillman to devote much of the time of his last years to private concerns. This gave him much pleasure. There were his farm and its absorbing labor problems. There was the satisfaction of husbanding his substantial if not great financial resources. The management of the affairs of his numerous family was an obligation eagerly assumed. Even the management of his shaky health gave him a pleasure which was not entirely morbid. The unhappiness caused by the breakup of his son's marriage was amply compensated by the happiness of his domestic circle. But public troubles at times interrupted the quiet scene at Trenton. The chief of these centered around a personality as vivid as the Ben of the 1890's, Cole L. Blease.

[56] Tillman to Eugene B. Gary, July 13, 1914, in Tillman Papers.
[57] Mrs. Tillman to Henry C. Tillman, July 1, 1914, *ibid.;* Tillman to *id.,* July 1, 1914, *ibid.; id.* to Benjamin R. Tillman, Jr., July 4, 11, 1914, *ibid.*

Chapter XXXII

BLEASE

THE senator's retirement from active leadership of the democratic movement in South Carolina called for another Tillman to advance the American dream of human equality. It is true that the Edgefield farmer had taken steps in this direction, and had taught the white masses to exercise political power and had given them beneficial reforms; but he had not fulfilled all his promises of mass liberation. Many felt that the sum total of Tillmanism was the giving of offices to Tillman and his friends. This was too extreme a judgment, but Tillmanism had more features of the superficial than of a truly radical attempt to uplift the masses. There had been no material improvement, no spiritual awakening, real or illusory. Tillman lacked the fervor or the fanaticism of the great evangelist.

He had aroused certain classes without satisfying them. The tenant farmers and the small landowners were hopping the same clods they had hopped before they heard of Tillman. Tillman's "damned factory class" multiplied with the expansion of cotton manufacturing but did not develop the economic and cultural resources necessary to use the colleges and the other shining achievements of Tillmanism. Their restlessness was answered by the resurgence of Bourbonism, the election of Governors Duncan C. Heyward and Martin F. Ansel, and eight quiet years characterized by no significant reforms and by the growth of social scorn for the mill hands.[1]

[1] Koester, "Bleaseism," Chap. I; Wallace, *History of South Carolina*, III, 425–26.

Tillman, with the insight which never deserted him, recognized the need of a second Tillman. "Conditions are such in South Carolina," he wrote in 1912, "that some honest, brave man is almost a necessity to arouse the people and start another reform movement." [2] This second Tillman had to be as Tillman had been, a genuine South Carolinian adaptable to changing popular demands, ardent in adherence to the extreme individualism of a provincially narrow state, reactionary toward the Negro, and a friend of the small farmer and mill hand to whom he must exhibit a sympathetic personality and friendly heart.

Such a leader emerged in flaming colors during the years of Tillman's quiescence. He was Cole L. Blease. Unlike Tillman, Blease was not nurtured in rural isolation but in the highly social environment of his father's hotel and livery stable in the upcountry town of Newberry. His father, says the son, was more a man of "charity than any other man who lived in his county" and "fed many and many a man and his stock without charging a cent." The younger Blease made friends among those who entered these hospitable doors. He learned to imbibe freely of the convivial cup and developed gracious manners. Warm emotions rather than troublous thoughts dominated his personality. He possessed none of Tillman's aloofness or hardness; he was indiscriminately sociable.

Yet Cole L. Blease was no mere livery stable loafer. He combined the characteristics of cavalier and barkeeper, both of which in a sense he was. In appearance he was striking if not handsome. He possessed heavy raven hair and moustache, dark fierce eyes, carried his well-formed body with an air of assurance, and wore an ostentatiously large wool hat and the gaudy insignia of fraternal orders. About him, said an acute observer, was "a touch of consciousness, almost staginess." [3] Blease was ambitious. Possessed of an

[2] Tillman to John G. Richards, January 11, 1912, in Tillman Papers.

[3] Ludwig Lewisohn, "South Carolina: A Lingering Fragrance," in *Nation*, CXV (1922), 37–38.

egotism which exceeded Tillman's self-confidence, he wanted to be a lawyer and a politician. He won the prize of a gold watch for oratory at Newberry College and completed a law course at Georgetown University. In the memorable canvass of 1890 he appeared in Newberry as Tillmanite candidate for the legislature. "If you want to do something for me," his father told the voters, "send my son to the legislature." This they cheerfully did.[4]

Unlike Tillman, Blease did not succeed through the somewhat sudden execution of well-laid plans; he did not win the governorship until twenty years after he first entered politics. He advanced himself through the humble virtue of persistence. Re-elected to the legislature in 1892, he was defeated for that office in 1894 and 1896. Encouraged by election to the state Senate in 1904, he ran for governor in 1906 and 1908. Though twice defeated, his canvasses of the state gave him experience and won him many friends. Gradually he became the best-known man in South Carolina, one who was hated and loved as Tillman had been.

The Newberry politician followed the well-marked path of his Edgefield predecessor. Beginning as a Tillman leader in the legislature, he was one of the group who, at Helena, saved the chief from harm at the hands of men supposedly bent on assassination.[5] He was "the poor man's friend," avoiding aristocratic aloofness as easily as did the one-eyed farmer. He imitated the older man's forensic style, compelled attention with Tillmanesque mannerisms, gestures, and accusations; and like the master, created a chronic atmosphere of suspense and was as interesting to his enemies as to his friends. Abundantly endowed with the Tillman gift of ridicule and power to envelop issues in irrelevant personalities, he took the same unctuous pride in being utterly frank.

[4] His interesting autobiography is Cole L. Blease, *Annual Message, January 12, 1915* (Columbia, 1915), 36–43.
[5] Tillman to Victor B. Cheshire, March 10, 1916, in Tillman Papers; *id.* to A. W. Sims, October 11, 1916, *ibid.*

Blease inherited Tillman's enemies—the corporations, the aristocrats, the newspapers, the preachers, the political rings—all who by reason of superior culture or craft had made themselves into the better classes. The younger Gonzales [6] and the Columbia *State* became the center of the Blease invective. The inarticulate masses loved him, as they had loved Tillman, because he was "the worst abused man in South Carolina." There must be good in one whom the self-righteous cursed.

Blease, despite the violence of his language, was not as radical as Tillman. He was too devoted to the South Carolina tradition to approve progressive ideas.[7] If Tillman's program of reform lacked comprehensiveness, Blease scarcely had any program whatever. Yet he voiced the feelings of the common people in their own language and made them think he was one of them. About him was none of the reserve of the upper-class politician seeking votes. This satisfied the ordinary man more completely than a program of social reform.[8]

This most effective of the Tillman imitators did not get all his inspiration from the older man. Bleaseism, as Tillman once angrily declared, was "the incestuous child of unscrupulous ambition on the body of Tillmanism." [9] To be more specific, Bleaseism was the darker phase of Tillmanism, or what Tillman himself called "Jim Tillmanism." Because he was an intimate friend of the baneful Tillman nephew, Blease believed that the hostility of the Gonzales family was induced by his friendship for the murderer. He shared in the atmosphere of recklessness and rowdyism which enveloped Jim, and when murder destroyed Jim's future, Blease was his political heir. From this Tillman he learned how to carry the reaction against Ne-

---

[6] After the murder of Narciso G. Gonzales in 1903, it was his brother, William E. Gonzales, who was the butt.

[7] Cited in Spartanburg *Herald*, July 31, 1908.

[8] James B. Smith, in Columbia *State*, September 5, 1910.

[9] Tillman, in Augusta *Chronicle*, November 2, 1913.

groism further than the elder Tillman and how to stimu-
late the political consciousness of the white mill operatives.

Jim Tillman, because of frailties of character and body,
did not last long. Blease, on the other hand, was possessed
of such iron constitution and such iron persistence that he
remained a factor in South Carolina politics for five decades. It was never proved that he was a criminal. The grave
accusation of receiving Dispensary graft rested on the
doubtful authority of a dead distiller.[10] The most serious
dereliction of which there is proof was the plagiarism of an
essay while a twenty-year-old student at the University of
South Carolina. He appropriated some sophomoric platitudes so unoriginal that in a sense they belonged to him as
much as to their first compiler. But the university, profess-
ing an austere sense of honor, expelled the offender from
a debating society, and he quit the institution in a huff.[11]
Certainly this petty offense did not convict him of depravity
or destroy his political chances.

Blease was no mere swinger on Tillman's coattails. Tillman was intellectual, harsh, ascetic, careless in dress; Blease
was unread, affable, intemperate, meticulous. Only in fields
where similarities were portents of conflict were the two
alike. Both were self-centered, dictatorial, and potentially
jealous of each other. Tillman always believed that Blease
"never did become a reformer until he was quite sure which
way the cat was going to jump." [12] Blease welcomed the
support of the South Carolina arbiter, but he saw no reason
why he should retire from the lists if Tillman became antagonistic.

While Tillman was absent in Europe, Blease gave the

[10] Lewis W. Parker's report of Samuel J. Lanahan's conversation, in Columbia *State,* February 14, 19, 1908.
[11] The essay, "The Resources and Pleasures of a Cultivated Mind," in
South Carolina Collegian (Columbia), VI (1888), 11–13. For the exposure of
Blease and proof that the essay first appeared under the name of J. M. Bo-
land in the *Davidson Monthly* (Davidson College, N. C.), III (1871), 3–10,
see editorial in *South Carolina Collegian,* VI (1888), 15–16.
[12] Tillman to Sims, October 11, 1916, in Tillman Papers.

gubernatorial contest of 1908 the flavor of 1890. He called his inoffensive opponent, Governor Ansel, a "nigger lover" because he had made "an infernal nigger" into a notary.[13] He opposed the state's support of higher education for Negroes, advocated the vigorous application of vagrancy laws against blacks, and let his passion for "cussing niggers" lead him to call them "baboons and apes." He called William E. Gonzales "a Cuban Ananias, who controls a Spanish bureau at Columbia." [14] In a special appeal to the cotton mill operatives he favored the enforcement of health and child labor regulations and opposed Tillman's plan of importing labor under contract [15] on the grounds that foreigners were "worse than negroes" and threatened to "underbid our people." He answered attacks on his private life by indelicately calling on the pastors of the Newberry churches to testify in his behalf.[16]

The opposition answered in full measure the insults and boasts of the speaker. The Columbia *State* republished the stories of the candidate's plagiarism and of his alleged Dispensary graft, represented him in a cartoon standing between a grafter and a "blind tiger," [17] and, in a clever bid for the anti-Negro sentiment, proved that he had advanced the welfare of the Negro state college.[18] Newberry pastors were induced to declare, "We do not directly or indirectly endorse his candidacy," and in many sermons he was accused of "insulting and impugning the Christian ministry." [19]

The defamation of Blease was a tactical error that converted its victim into a popular martyr. Especially effective was his appeal to the popular conviction that "the church folks have no business meddling in politics." [20] "If all the

---

[13] Columbia *State,* July 29, 1908.

[14] Cited in Spartanburg *Herald,* August 22, 1908.   [15] See p. 461.

[16] Columbia *State,* June 21, August 8, 1908; Spartanburg *Herald,* July 31, 1908.

[17] Columbia *State,* August 23, 1908.   [18] *Ibid.,* August 24, 1908.

[19] *Ibid.,* August 9, 1908.   [20] "A Lexington Man," *ibid.,* August 18, 1908.

rascals were turned out of the church, there would not be a quorum next Sunday." [21] He was unable to overcome the precedent which demanded a second term for Ansel but did poll 40,000 votes, twice his strength in 1906.[22]

The valiant demagogue entered the 1910 canvass with advantage. His opponents underestimated his strength, fatuously asserting that his 1908 vote had been due to the unpopularity of Ansel.[23] When the lead which Blease achieved in the first primary proved the falsity of this surmise, the opposition stupidly repeated old slanders and circulated "incredible falsehoods, often easily proved untrue." [24] Emphasis was placed on the contrast between "the impurity" of Blease and "the purity" of Claudius C. Featherstone, his second primary opponent. "The issue," said the Columbia *State,* "is one of men, not measures. . . . No one had run for Governor since 1876 for whose defeat reasons are so strong." [25] A few days before the election this newspaper published the notorious Buzzard Cartoon. Blease's head was attached to the body of the loathsome bird on whose pinions were written Dispensary Grafters, Ignorance, Race Prejudice, Lawlessness, Blind Tigers, Injustice, Class Prejudice.[26]

The harassed candidate took refuge in race and class prejudice. He opposed the schooling of Negro children at the expense of white taxpayers and denounced compulsory education by implying that the poor and uneducated who did not send their children to school were as virtuous as those who did. He appealed to religious bigotry by attacking state support of higher education. He defied his enemies to prove that he was a grafter and proved himself no hypocrite by confessing that he drank whiskey when he liked. He triumphed over Featherstone by 5,000 votes.[27]

[21] Speech at Prosperity, *ibid.,* August 9, 1908.
[22] *Ibid.,* August 28, 1908.   [23] *Ibid.,* August 4, 1910.
[24] Wallace, *History of South Carolina,* III, 426.
[25] Columbia *State,* September 3, 10, 1910.
[26] *Ibid.,* September 8, 1910.   [27] *Ibid.,* September 1–15, 1910.

Tillman took a friendly if inactive interest in the victory of this second Tillman. He felt that the indignation aroused against the upper classes was the just retribution of the common people against aristocratic snobbery.[28] Featherstone was the type of Prohibitionist the senator had denounced since the inception of the Dispensary, and had incurred the animosity of the Tillman family by disparaging them in the controversy over the Tillman grandchildren.[29]

These circumstances induced Tillman to prepare a paper "endorsing Blease as against Featherstone." But, as he later explained, he was "bamboozled and debauched" by friends into suppressing this statement.[30] When the election was over he telegraphed the victor his congratulations,[31] and he publicly rejoiced over the humiliation of old enemies. Concerning the governor-elect he spoke with hopeful reserve: "I expect Governor Blease to disappoint his enemies. . . . No one can dispute that he has brains, and while he had faults, like the devil, he is not as black as he has been painted." [32]

Unfortunately, the new governor did not disappoint his enemies. In the face of criticism and social snubs more cruel than those visited upon Governor Tillman, he threw discretion to the winds, pardoning a large number of convicts and hurling impudent words at men and institutions. "In vetoing a bill to modify the severe libel law, he used the word 'lie' thirty-three times, 'liar' eight times," and added "cowardly," "slime," and "scurrilous blackguard." He called the newspaper fraternity "a dirty set of liars" and glorified Jim Tillman for the murder. He declared shortly after assuming office: "A large majority of the people of South Carolina elected me Governor, . . . and I expect to see that my

[28] Tillman's farewell address, August, 1914, in Tillman Papers.

[29] Spartanburg *Herald*, February 16, 1916; Tillman to Leon M. Harris, October 10, 1911, in Tillman Papers.

[30] Tillman to Harris, October 10, 1911, in Tillman Papers; *id.* to Kohn, October 12, 1911, *ibid.*

[31] Spartanburg *Herald*, September 25, 1910.

[32] Tillman, in Columbia *State*, September 15, 1910.

friends receive at least some consideration from this Administration." This tactless declaration of official partisanship was followed by singularly little of constructive benefit for the underprivileged whites who had voted for him. He "opposed factory inspection, compulsory education, and the medical examination of school children. . . . He would telegraph a pardon, he declared, to any man who killed a doctor violating his daughter's modesty." [33]

Tillman gave the governor kindly advice which he hoped would quiet suspicions. In July, 1911, he spoke at Orangeburg from the same platform as Blease, wishing him success and asking some friendly questions about his pardon record. In return for Blease's assurance that he would not oppose Tillman's candidacy for re-election in 1912, the senator promised (according to Blease) to remain neutral when the governor offered for re-election at the same time.[34] But there were also ominous words of warning. The senator advised the governor against strong drink and loose talk and asked him to clear up charges of official corruption.[35]

The truth was that Tillman, although he did not tell Blease, had decided that the governor should not be re-elected. One reason for this decision was that the Newberry man was the politician least amenable to the famous "Tillman dictation." Blease knew he had a constituency among whom the name of Benjamin was not always magic. He dared to be independent, even ignoring the senator's request for the formation of a new county,[36] scolding him for holding two offices at the same time,[37] and openly declaring that Tillman's support was not essential for his re-election.[38]

Another cause of Tillman's misgiving was the belief that

[33] Wallace, *History of South Carolina*, III, 427, 429–30.
[34] Blease and Tillman statements, in Charleston *News and Courier*, August 25, 26, 1912.
[35] Tillman to Blease, October 15, 1911, in Tillman Papers.
[36] *Id.* to Luther Reese, March 11, 1911, *ibid.*
[37] Columbia *State*, February 4, 1911.
[38] *Ibid.*, October 25, 1911.

the governor was morally unworthy of high trust. As early as September, 1911, he wrote a friend that Ira B. Jones, a supreme court justice who had announced his candidacy in opposition to Blease, "will make a far better governor than Blease has made." [39] Thereafter a constant refrain ran through the Tillman letters—the contrast between his own moral worth and Blease's supposed depravity. "My spotless character and purity of private life" were set against the belief that Blease "gets drunk, is a gambler and unless reports are untrue is bad after women." The contest was one of "State pride, decency, honesty, and truth" on one side against all that is evil and bad on the other.[40]

But our moralist understood a difficult political situation too well to believe that condemnation of Blease on personal grounds necessarily made expedient a condemnation of his public ambitions. He knew that, although South Carolinians were moralistic, they were unwilling to let mere individual sin destroy their faith in one who promised victories in the battle for greater democracy. Blease, they wrote the senator, "is not the kind of man we admire at all, but we will be damned if we haven't got to beat that Haskell gang and the Columbia *State*. . . . We have got to whip a certain crowd and we will have to do it with Blease—that damned crowd who think they ought to rule in some damn way." [41] Moreover, Tillman knew that the old Tillmanites were aligned with Blease. "His warmest friends," the older man explained, "are my warm friends and have always been." [42] He felt that the old Haskellites were still against him; that they, "if they thought they could do it with impunity, would not only stab me in the back but would stab me in front and rejoice in the opportunity." [43]

---

[39] Tillman to William H. Glenn, September 25, 1911, in Tillman Papers.
[40] *Id.* to John G. Richards, February 12, 1912, *ibid.; id.* to Henry C. Folk, August 1, 1912, *ibid.; id.* to John J. McMahan, August 13, 1912, *ibid.;* Tillman statement, August 9, 1912, *ibid.*
[41] J. Neil Brown to Tillman, August 9, 1912, *ibid.*
[42] Tillman to Howard M. Stackhouse, May 24, 1912, *ibid.*
[43] *Id.* to Olin Sawyer, February 17, 1912, *ibid.*

He was certain that he would not find an alliance with Blease's enemies congenial. "If I thought," he wrote, "that Gonzales was going to vote for me as senator, I would write him and ask him not to do it." [44]

Such thoughts were supplemented by admiration of the governor's election methods and disapproval of those of his opponents. "Blease," he wrote the manager of the anti-Blease campaign, "has enough Tillman in him to have learned how to fight. He . . . is a good stump speaker and fine organizer." [45] Personal dislike for Jones was accompanied by contempt for the conduct of the anti-Blease candidate in the county-to-county canvass. "Every day," wrote Tillman, "something comes up which makes me lament that Jones ever entered the race at all, for he is absolutely a child in Blease's hands." [46] The senator deplored the circulation of accusations against Blease which could not be proved. "Felder's dictograph, Nicholl's drunken bragging, and now Grace's unspeakably vulgar and indecent story about the negro girl," he warned, "are making him [Blease] stronger every day." [47] His deeply engrained instincts of chivalry were outraged when the opposition circulated slanderous canards about Blease's wife.[48]

A very practical reason why Tillman hesitated to condemn Blease openly was that the senator himself was a candidate for re-election. Many, especially among his old enemies, thought that the old warrior, after eighteen years in Washington, should retire to make room for a more active senator. But such was not his intention. A year before the primary he began writing that he wished "to die in harness." He felt that he was able to discharge the routine duties of his office, win the chairmanship of an important Senate committee, and enlist Federal support for South Carolina

[44] *Id.* to W. J. Stackhouse, August 17, 1912, *ibid.*
[45] *Id.* to J. William Thurmond, February 19, 1912, *ibid.*
[46] *Id.* to *id.*, August 12, 1912, *ibid.*
[47] *Id.* to G. Heyward Mahon, August 3, 1912, *ibid.*
[48] *Id.* to Howard M. Stackhouse, May 24, 1912, *ibid.*

projects. Neither age nor illness had lessened his greed for office. "I am anxious," he confessed, "to go back to the Senate because I have won such an enviable place there that it is worth my while to live a little longer to enjoy it." [49]

He pushed his candidacy with all the old Tillman tactics except the principal one, the public harangue. He corresponded vigorously with friends and analyzed local political trends as accurately as ever. He correctly surmised that, barring unforeseen developments, his re-election would be easy. He knew that many former enemies would support him. But because of his disabilities he did not, as formerly, welcome opposition, intriguing to ward off possible rivals.[50] He tried to convince himself and others of the wisdom of a stay-at-home campaign.[51]

The most publicized man in South Carolina history now feared neglect at the hands of the press. He asked for articles explaining why he should be returned to the Senate. "All of us," he admitted lamely, "like to read nice things about ourselves." [52] The man who had so often protested against the methods of the conclave now asked political intriguers to fix the party convention for a preprimary endorsement of his candidacy.[53] Tillman was fast deteriorating.

His formal announcement for re-election was not inaccurately described as "a cry for quarter," a plea for a vote of confidence, not because he could perform as formerly, but because he wanted sympathy in his affliction.[54] The people were willing to gratify him. They appreciated his services, and his two opponents, Nathaniel B. Dial and W.

49 *Id*. to William T. Crews, September 25, 1911, *ibid.; id*. to Dr. N. F. Kirkland, October 28, 1911, *ibid*.

50 *Id*. to Thurmond, February 19, 1912, *ibid*.

51 *Id*. to Henry C. Tillman, May 10, 1912, *ibid.; id*. to I. H. McCalla, May 12, 1912, *ibid*.

52 *Id*. to Thomas M. Raysor, November 25, 1911, *ibid*.

53 *Id*. to Thurmond, May 3, 1912, *ibid.; id*. to Sawyer, April 29, 1912, *ibid.; id*. to Richards, May 4, 1912, *ibid*.

54 Tillman statement, May 4, 1912, *ibid.;* criticism of this statement by New York *Evening Post*, cited in Tillman to this newspaper, May 7, 1912.

Jasper Talbert, were not formidable. No serious complication could develop as long as Tillman avoided crossing swords with Blease.

So the senator hesitated to condemn the governor and sought to preserve a perilous neutrality. Less than three weeks before the primary he wrote his son: "Under no circumstances will I come out for Blease, nor will I come out for Jones unless they [the anti-Bleaseites] prove more than they have on Blease." [55]

Tillman himself, however, conspired against keeping this resolution. He freely revealed his attitude toward Blease in letters to many friends. Naturally, his correspondents talked about what he had written; they were too interested in the issue to keep the injunction of secrecy. The friends of the governor circulated the few complimentary words the senator wrote about their hero, suppressing words of condemnation. The anti-Bleaseites did the opposite. This procedure began with Jones's assertion that Tillman had said he was "eminently qualified to be Governor" and by his offering a hundred-dollar reward to anyone who could get the senator to speak as well of Blease. The answer of the Bleaseites was the production of a letter from Tillman to Harrison Ferguson of Spartanburg declaring: "As far as brains go, Blease is eminently qualified to be Governor." The rest of the letter was a condemnation, but it was not made public. [56]

Tillman was in a dangerous predicament. If the full text of the Ferguson letter was not published, the anti-Blease vote might be alienated. Simultaneously the high command of the Bleaseites knew his actual opinion and were preparing to turn the Blease vote against him. [57] Loss of both contingents would spell the senator's certain defeat. "The people," he cried in panic, "are like mad dogs and are

[55] Id. to Henry C. Tillman, August 7, 1912, in Tillman Papers.
[56] Id. to Harrison Ferguson, August 19, 1912, ibid.
[57] Id. to J. G. Baron, August 17, 1912, ibid.

ready to bite everything in their way." [58] He made a desperate cry for the support of the anti-Tillmanites of old. "I hope my friends," he wrote, "will see to it that for every crazy Tillmanite who votes against me I will get an 'Anti.' " [59]

Continued pressure from anti-Bleaseites convinced Tillman that the situation called for an unambiguous condemnation of the Blease candidacy. He was showered with telegrams asserting that Blease was using the Ferguson letter against him and that the publication of its full text was necessary to rally the full force of the anti-Blease sentiment.[60] Tillman was ready to act, justifying the abandonment of an uncertain neutrality by Ferguson's betrayal of his confidence.[61] But still he hesitated. Mrs. Tillman begged him not to champion Jones, the judge who had given the adverse decision in the case of the Tillman grandchildren. "My judgment," he explained, "was with Jones; my sentiment with Blease." For nights he could not sleep. Finally he let conscience triumph over sentiment. On August 24, three days before the primary, he released the full text of the Ferguson letter. "I have done my duty and the angels can do no more. . . . I expect to lose thirty to forty thousand votes on account of my attitude." [62]

The letter was a characteristic Tillman denunciation of a lieutenant who he believed had betrayed the Tillman principles. It was brutally personal: Blease was foolishly partisan; he had injured the good name of the state; he had not successfully refuted charges that he had accepted bribes for pardons. "I hope for the credit of the State," Tillman summarized curtly, "he will be beaten." [63]

[58] *Id.* to Henry C. Tillman, August 19, 1912, *ibid. Cf. id.* to John Gary Evans, August 21, 1912, *ibid.*

[59] *Id.* to William D. Evans, August 20, 1912, *ibid.*

[60] Telegrams, August 21, 22, 1912, in Tillman Scrapbooks.

[61] Tillman to Charles P. Calvert, August 21, 1912, in Tillman Papers.

[62] *Id.* to Claude Patton, August 26, 1912, *ibid.*

[63] *Id.* to Ferguson, August 19, 1912, in Charleston *News and Courier,* August 24, 1912.

By turning on Blease, Ben Tillman had not literally put his head in a noose. His majority in the primary over his two opponents was 7,263, almost thrice as great as Blease's scant majority of 2,674 over Jones. The people had willed that he die in harness, but had ignored his cry for the execution of his heir-apparent. The singular cycle of Tillman's career was nearing completion. He had joined forces with the very persons it had been his mission in life to teach the common people to despise. In peril, he had frantically asked for Conservative votes and had admitted that they made his election possible.[64] He was grateful to his new-found friends; he regarded the rumor that William E. Gonzales and his brother had voted for him as "a great moral victory." [65] He had, in a sense, surrendered to the Haskellites, to forces as different from Tillmanism as from Bleaseism.

Blease's anger was boundless. Tillman, he said, was driven by "insane jealousy" to make an "infamous eleventh hour stab" at a friend to whom he was pledged. Such treachery was the result of overpersuasion of an enfeebled mind by the malice-inspired Gonzales. "I fear no evil from Senator Tillman's letter except that possibly his mind has become more diseased of late than it was when I had my last talk with his confidential physician." [66] The invalid lion was powerless to annihilate Blease, as he had annihilated others, by haranguing the voters. Blease did not follow Irby, Mc-Laurin, and the other accused lieutenants into oblivion. He, not Tillman, now represented the masses. Had the senator's repudiation of the governor come two or three weeks before the primary, enough former Tillmanites might have voted against the old chief to have defeated him.[67]

He was deeply hurt by the desertion of former friends. Concerning once strong Tillman counties he wrote: "To

[64] Id. to Richards, September 12, 1912, in Tillman Papers.
[65] Id. to Dr. William R. Eve, January 14, 1914, ibid.
[66] Blease, in Charleston, News and Courier, August 25, 1912.
[67] Kirkland, "Tillman and I," in Columbia State, July 21, 1929.

have Laurens, York and Anderson vote against me as they did is the sorest trial I have ever had in political life." [68] He knew that the anti-Tillman votes did not come to him in the traditional Tillman manner. There was none of the old devotion in the new attachment, only gratitude for opposition to a greater evil; the hate for the destroyer of Hampton still smoldered. Honest Ben had not become the leader of the aristocrats, the men of the cities, the anti-Bleaseites.

As soon as their joint triumph in the primary became evident, Tillman tried to reason with Blease. In his blunt fashion he warned the governor against wrongdoing. Tillmanism was described as "noble, high, and elevating"; Bleaseism as "selfish, low, dirty, and revengeful." Tillman had responded sagely to taunts; Blease had reacted in a manner which proved him "too little and too narrow to be Governor of any State." This was followed by ancient but sound advice: "Put a bridle on that unlicensed tongue of yours." [69] This bid for reform was accompanied by conciliatory acts. Tillman warned against attempts to deprive Blease of the party nomination, declaring, amid the anger of new friends, that white men could not afford to cheat each other. He begged the newspapers to restrain themselves until the governor did something infamous and asked Blease's friends to urge him to show self-control. [70]

But the prodigal son of Tillmanism, all impulse and emotion, was too full of pride to repent; there was no room in his stubborn head for Tillman logic. He interpreted Tillman's profession of patriotic impartiality as the hypocrisy of one who had wickedly abandoned a friend in time of

[68] Tillman to J. L. Langston, September 5, 1912, in Tillman Papers. Tillman ran second in Anderson and Laurens, but received 2,099 to Talbert's 1,322 and Dial's 956 in York. See Columbia *State*, August 30, 1912.

[69] Tillman to Blease, August 29, 1912, in Tillman Papers.

[70] *Id.* to A. N. Woods, September 4, 1912, *ibid.*; *id.* to J. R. Desportes, September 4, 1912, *ibid.*; *id.* to J. S. J. Suber, September 9, 1912, *ibid.*; *id.* to John Gary Evans, September 12, 1912, *ibid.*; *id.* to James L. Sims, September 15, 1912, *ibid.*

need. Blease did not reform. His second administration was more disreputable than the first; he tolerated horse racing; and he freed his chauffeur after this Negro was repeatedly convicted of speeding through the Columbia streets. His pardons finally reached the amazing total of 1,708. Rapists and murderers were on the list, and the lawyer-friends of the governor enjoyed a lucrative practice as pardon brokers.[71] In all of this there was only a modicum of downright villainy. If money was passed, the lawyers, not Blease, got it. If some said the pardoning was motivated by sensation mongering, others said it was caused by Christian charity.

What angered the senator most was the ousting of James W. Babcock from the superintendency of the insane asylum. When Blease tried to besmirch the doctor's reputation, Tillman begged Babcock to strike back.[72] When this was not done, the senator became violent. Blease should be impeached; he wished he could drive the villain from the stump; he spoke of the governor's "blind-tiger record, his race-track gambling record, his whore-house record."[73] "How long, oh Lord, how long," cried the senator in anguish, "will it be before some man with nerve and just provocation call Blease's bluff and beat him as he ought to be beaten."[74]

And so it was without hesitation that Tillman in 1914 plunged into the struggle to prevent the governor from becoming his senatorial colleague. True, the senator did not like Blease's opponent, Ellison D. Smith, a farm leader who had won a place in the Senate independent of the Tillman influence.[75] But he recognized Smith's virtues, and after

[71] Wallace, *History of South Carolina*, III, 434–35.
[72] Tillman to Dr. Babcock, January 23, February 25, 1913, in Tillman Papers; *id.* to Kohn, January 23, 25, 27, 1914, *ibid.*
[73] *Id.* to Smoak, February 26, 1914, *ibid.*; *id.* to Richards, May 30, 1914, *ibid.*
[74] *Id.* to Stevenson, March 6, 1914, *ibid.*
[75] *Id.* to Julius D. Dreher, February 23, 1912, *ibid.*; *id.* to Henry C. Tillman, November 23, 1913, *ibid.*; *id.* to W. B. Moore, June 23, 1914, *ibid.*

unsuccessful attempts to induce others to enter the race,[76] became reconciled to the Smith candidacy as a means of checkmating the incorrigible Blease.[77]

Early in the fight Tillman advocated the application to the primary of the complicated suffrage requirements used up to that time only against the Negro.[78] Had this suggestion been accepted the suffrage would have been taken from thousands of poor or illiterate whites. This, because of the fear of Blease, from the erstwhile champion of the common people! He encouraged Langston D. Jennings and William P. Pollock, two independent senatorial candidates, into brow-beating Blease;[79] tried to persuade John G. Richards, a close friend, not to run for governor on the Blease ticket; and failing, gave his support to Richard I. Manning.[80]

Tillman's most effective blow was the alignment of the Wilson administration against Blease. He told the President that the governor in the Senate "would be a very big thorn in his side and far more painful than ever I was to Roosevelt, for Blease would be more unscrupulous than I was."[81] His messages to the White House asserted that the immoral Blease had the use of blind-tiger money.[82] Our political realist did this so that Federal appointments and appropriations might not be used by the man he slandered; for he knew that Blease's chief weakness was not actual or potential corruption but inability to be corrupt according to the rules of the patronage game. After he was certain that he had carried his point he let the voters know "that Blease will have absolutely no influence with the Administration" and

[76] Id. to Henry C. Tillman, September 19, 1913, ibid.; id. to McLaurin, November 8, 1913, ibid.

[77] Id. to W. B. Moore, September 19, 1913, ibid.

[78] Id. to T. M. Dantzler, August 28, 1913, ibid.

[79] Id. to Langston D. Jennings, June 24, 1914, ibid.

[80] Id. to H. B. Ingram, August 12, 1914, ibid.; id. to Richards, August 14, 1914, ibid.; id. to Snowden, October 4, 1914, ibid.

[81] Id. to Henry C. Tillman, September 19, 1913, ibid.

[82] Id. to Joseph P. Tumulty, September 29, 1913, ibid.

that "those men who are thinking deep down in their hearts about getting jobs" should understand "the absurdity of sending a Senator to Washington who is at odds with the Administration." [83]

The underhanded driving of nails into Blease's political coffin was supplemented by a resounding public statement. In his so-called Farewell Letter of 1914 the senator asserted that Blease had done nothing creditable, while Tillman had made a constructive revolution. "For God's sake," he cried, in commenting on his own record, "let those who were formerly Tillmanites, but now Blease shouters, show what Blease had done of similar character." [84] When the voters in 1914 disapproved of Blease by a majority greater than that by which they had approved of him two years earlier, the old chieftain was delighted. It was a triumph of righteousness over sin, a vindication of his faith in the common people. He believed that the Blease type of demagogue was done for.[85]

This last statement was not true, for Blease as a candidate for governor in 1916 was more formidable than he had been in 1914. His opponent was Manning, an unpopular aristocrat who was seeking a second term. He was, in Tillman's opinion, "the worst politician South Carolina had ever produced who became Governor," one among the Bourbons who "still believe they are divinely commissioned to rule the State." [86] This circumstance plus the fact that his son Henry was offering for Congress in pro-Blease counties of the upcountry, might have restrained Tillman from taking a direct part in the 1916 canvass. But his hatred of Blease was too great for him to forbear. Once more he made the "eleventh hour stab" before the primary.[87]

[83] *Id.* to Duncan C. Heyward, November 8, 1913, *ibid.*
[84] Tillman farewell address, August, 1914, *ibid.*
[85] Tillman to L. L. Wagnon, September 1, 1914, *ibid.*
[86] *Id.* to Virgil McGraw, March 7, 1918, *ibid.; id.* to Glenn, September 13, 1916, *ibid.*
[87] *Id.* to Columbia *State,* September 10, 1916.

Despite Tillman's efforts, Blease was defeated only by a narrow vote; a change of 2,343 ballots would have given him the election.[88] Manning's Bourbon friends resorted to questionable tactics. Large sums of money were used against "the poor man's friend" and there was evidence of political coercion.[89] Tillman ignored these circumstances, but he did join Blease's friends in believing that his attacks had much to do with the former governor's defeat.[90] He was aware of the bitter class feelings in the hearts of many of his old followers, and he spoke of the failure of the ruling classes to give them the comradely treatment he believed was the right of every white South Carolinian.[91] He preached to Governor Manning against the snobbery which made Blease possible,[92] yet impatiently rejected as "a damned lie" the charge that he had betrayed the common people.[93]

Thus the aging senator had the satisfaction of seeing Blease's one signal triumph followed by two defeats. He knew that he had played an important part in this outcome. But Bleaseism was not dead. It was destined in 1918 to plague the steps of the dying Tillman. And in a sense it was a more vital force than Tillmanism. The unsuccessful Blease represented that portion of the common people whom a deteriorated Tillman had abandoned.

[88] Wallace, *History of South Carolina*, III, 442.
[89] Koester, "Bleaseism," Chap. I.
[90] Charleston *American*, September 2, 1916; Tillman to John J. McMahan, September 11, 1916, in Tillman Papers.
[91] Tillman to Dr. William B. Patton, September 18, 1916, *ibid.*
[92] *Id.* to Richard I. Manning, September 18, 1916, *ibid.*
[93] *Id.* to Carey D. Chamblee, September 30, 1916, *ibid.*

Chapter XXXIII

WILSON

"I HAVE prayed," wrote Tillman to Woodrow Wilson in the summer of 1912, "to see a real Democrat President before I die. Next March my prayer will be answered." [1] The prophecy was fulfilled, for when the South Carolinian returned to Washington in March, 1913, to begin his fourth term in the Senate, the "real Democrat" in the person of Wilson entered the White House. In fact, the situation in Washington was reminiscent of South Carolina in 1890. There had been a minor revolution in the political life of the country, and the new President had a progressive program for a friendly Congress. Might not the reformer of 1890 give ready aid to the new leader and his program? Was not the Wilson Evangel a moderate yet constructive effort to give reality to the same sort of agrarian democracy Tillman had proclaimed twenty years before? Tillman saw the situation that way and was willing to co-operate.[2]

But, alas, the atrophying effects of his paralytic strokes prevented the Southerner from rendering useful aid to the Wilson program. Senator Tillman, after a fretful wait of eighteen years, now lived to see the day when legislation acceptable to him was possible; but it was cruelly ironic, indeed almost tragic, that personal disabilities prevented his participation in its making. Just enough of the old fire and the old awareness remained for the invalid to realize vividly the uncomfortable paradox of his situation. He

---

[1] Tillman to Woodrow Wilson, July 12, 1912, in Tillman Papers.
[2] *Id.* to William E. Chandler, November 6, 1912, *ibid.*

could not make use of the experience gleaned from long attention to the business of the Senate; an early career of brilliant achievement in South Carolina could not be enhanced by effective aid to a similar program in Washington. The significant portion of his senatorial career was over. Other names previously obscure, those of Carter Glass, Oscar W. Underwood, Robert L. Owen, and so on, were to be linked with the great acts of the Wilson administration. Tillman's name was to appear scarcely at all in the Wilson chronicle. Perhaps his fame would have been better served had he succumbed to his malady in 1910 or been defeated by the Bleaseites in 1912.

Another circumstance not directly connected with his health also militated against his strength as a leader of the Wilson forces. He could not longer say in 1913, as he had been able to say in 1896, that he represented South Carolina and gave it voice.[3] By quarreling with Blease he had alienated a majority of the old Tillmanites. He did not enjoy the leadership of the bulk of those who voted for him, the old anti-Tillmanites, men whose loyalty to him extended no further than his opposition to Blease. Their leader in fact was Woodrow Wilson, a national hero whom South Carolinians could follow because he was a Democrat who had spent his boyhood in Columbia. In a very direct sense South Carolinians were giving Wilson the sort of loyalty they had once given Hampton and Tillman. And Wilson did not belong to the Tillman school of South Carolina ideas; the President was too urbane for that. Indeed, he recognized William E. Gonzales, not Tillman, as his deputy in the state.

Despite physical handicaps and his changed position in South Carolina politics, Tillman tried to play a hand in Wilsonian politics. He began with participation in the Democratic National Convention of 1912, where, as a good party man, he said he was willing to follow any Presidential

3 See p. 328.

candidate likely to win.[4] He was not an initial sponsor of the Wilson candidacy, being too much of an elder states- man to feel fully the emotions of the younger men behind the Wilson crusade. Vexed because Wilson allowed Gon- zales to be his host when the candidate returned to the scenes of his boyhood,[5] the senator proposed that the South Carolina delegates to the national convention go unin- structed, of course with Tillman in his accustomed place at the head of the delegation.[6]

Yet his desire for Democratic success was so great that he veered toward the Wilson candidacy as it became more and more impressive. His jealousy of Gonzales was lessened by the fact that he, too, was able to strike a blow for Wilson which attracted more than local attention. As a sequel to the break between Wilson and Colonel George Harvey and Harvey's friend, Colonel Henry Watterson, Tillman, in an interview, gave authority to the belief that the cause of the break was Harvey's and Watterson's desire to secure the financial support for the Wilson candidacy of Thomas F. Ryan, the supposed representative of the evil element in the Democratic party. Tillman asserted that Wilson had seen through the trick and that this independence would endear him to the people. Watterson asserted that the ac- cusation was "a lie out of the whole cloth." But Tillman refused to withdraw it, saying that Watterson had made "an ass of himself." [7] Wilson's friends were elated.

So when the South Carolina convention of 1912 endorsed the Wilson candidacy without ordering its delegates to vote for anyone, the old veteran was pleased. Actually, it was Gonzales and other anti-Tillmanites who had directed

[4] Tillman to Senator Bacon, June 3, 1911, *ibid.; id.* to Henry C. Tillman, February 15, 1912, *ibid.*

[5] *Id.* to James H. Rice, March 8, 1916, *ibid.*

[6] *Id.* to Richards, February 12, 1912, *ibid.*

[7] Colonel Henry Watterson to Tillman, January 25, 26, 1912, in Tillman Scrapbooks; Tillman to Watterson, January 26, 1912, *ibid.; id.* to Richards, February 3, 1912, in Tillman Papers; *id.* to McMahan, January 29, 1912, *ibid.*

this maneuver, but they did this so tactfully that the old man was not offended. He was made the nominal head of a delegation actually if not technically pledged to vote for Wilson. "It was just as I wished about Wilson," was his comment. "The delegates can consult after they get to Baltimore and vote for Wilson and later change." [8] Consequently he went to Baltimore in good spirits heightened by the fact that he was able to secure appointments for no less than sixteen relatives and friends as officials and attaches of the convention.[9] As he sat in that body a speech rumbled in his brain, but he explained, "I sat dumb . . . lest I might explode and burst a blood vessel or be paralyzed and drop dead." He was delighted to cast the South Carolina vote for Wilson, and when the candidate won the nomination he exultantly predicted that Wilson would sweep the country.[10]

The triumph of the Democrats in the 1912 election seemed to give Tillman great opportunity for statesmanship on a national scale. Under the seniority rule he was entitled to the chairmanship of any one of three major committees of the Senate: Appropriations, Interstate Commerce, and Naval Affairs. The headship of the first-named body was by far the most important position, one which a man of Tillman's experience and love of honors might normally seek. It would have made him one of the most powerful members of Congress, would have allowed him to move from the narrow quarters of the Committee on Five Civilized Tribes into the "three magnificent rooms" of the Appropriations Committee, and would have given him the services of eight clerks instead of three.[11]

Fearing that his health might debar him from this assignment, he wrote the President-elect, ostensibly for advice

[8] *Id.* to Thurmond, May 16, 1912, *ibid.*

[9] Tillman statement, June, 1912, *ibid.*

[10] *Id.* to Professor Joynes, July 2, 1912, *ibid. Cf. id.* to S. P. Verner, July 3, 1912, *ibid.; id.* to William G. McAdoo, August 21, 1912, *ibid.*

[11] *Id.* to Elias Door, March 13, 1913, *ibid.*

concerning what he should do, but actually for support of his ambition. "My strength is limited, as you know," he explained; "my will is equal to any task." Wilson's reply though generally evasive contained one comforting sentence. "Your letter convinced me," he said, "that it [the Appropriations Committee] is also the committee on which your interest chiefly lies and where you can certainly be of the greatest and most constant service." [12] Here was the leeway of which the ambitious invalid took advantage. He informed the Democratic caucus that he wished the chairmanship of the Appropriations Committee, with the proviso that he have second place on the Committee on Naval Affairs so that he could retire to the chairmanship of the less important body if the headship of the Appropriations Committee proved too arduous.[13]

The dominant forces in the Senate refused to adapt their plans to the convenience of the ailing senator from South Carolina. He was firmly told "that age and infirmities would prevent him from giving the necessary services required by the important Appropriations Committee" and was offered the chairmanship of the Committee on Naval Affairs. The progressive Democrats in control believed that he was a reactionary prompted by vanity to attempt duties beyond his strength. The chairmanship of the Appropriations Committee was awarded to Thomas S. Martin, the Virginia boss.[14]

Immediately the fighting spirit of the old veteran flared in a manner recalling the days of Pitchfork Ben. Added to robust anger was the pathos of a neglected old man. He told the President that the senatorial conspirators were like the wild asses: "They were athirst and trampled down the green corn." He declared that the "unwritten law" of making

[12] *Id.* to Wilson, January 21, 1913, in *Cong. Record,* 63 Cong., 1 Sess., 30–31; Wilson to Tillman, January 30, 1913, *ibid.*
[13] Tillman to Senator John W. Kern, March 8, 1913, in Tillman Papers.
[14] See unidentified newspaper, May 10, 1913, in Tillman Scrapbooks; New York *Evening Post,* March 15, 1913.

committee assignments according to seniority was violated only in his case.[15] He threatened to carry his fight to the floor of the Senate and prepared an address for the Democratic caucus "so hot that it almost burnt the paper it was written on." The Democratic leaders were accused of "foul ingratitude" and the President of having acted in a manner "unspeakably mean." [16]

The address was never delivered. After spending a night thinking over his problem, Tillman allowed prudence to triumph over outraged honor. "I thought," said this self-critical man, "how pitiful and contemptible was my fight for my rights and the rights of my State as compared with the great battle to be fought for the rights of the people." Too old and too broken to fight Wilson as he had fought Cleveland, he offered the olive branch instead of the pitchfork, delivering an address to "my fellow Democrats" in which he apologized for his anger and acquitted them of ulterior motives.[17] He imagined that he was "a martyr for the party," was pleased with the "very pleasant letter" which Wilson wrote him, and replied with an apology for his stubbornness.[18] He accepted the chairmanship of the naval committee, forlornly aware that this was ultimate defeat.[19]

In 1913 the chairmanship of the naval committee held no prospects of notable service. In those peaceful days naval expansion was not one of the patriotic shibboleths. The President was supposed to be a pacifist adverse to martial preparations. Tillman wrote: "We have a good enough Navy now, and only need to maintain it at its present degree of efficiency," [20] The following year he was of the same opinion: "We ought to spend some of our millions in the

[15] Memoranda for the President, March 7, 1913, in Tillman Papers.
[16] Proposed address of March 14, 1913, *ibid*.
[17] Tillman, at Democratic caucus, March 14, 1913,.*ibid*.
[18] *Id*. to Smythe, March 24, 1913, *ibid*.; *id*. to Wilson, March 24, 1913, *ibid*.
[19] *Id*. to Charles Crosland, March 22, 1913, *ibid*.
[20] *Id*. to Wilson, January 21, 1913, in *Cong. Record*, 63 Cong., 1 Sess., 31.

arts of peace rather than waste them in preparing for wars which never come." [21] Naval protagonists regarded his acts as unfriendly, particularly his interest in maintaining a safe Democratic majority on the naval committee to thwart the leading navalist on it, the "very adroit" Lodge.[22] Although he had faith in the "fighting end" of the fleet, he was suspicious of the Navy Department which he believed was "a very hell-hole of plotting and conspiracy" and was "filled with spies and curs of low degree," persons friendly to Republicans and unscrupulous business interests.[23] So uninterested was he in the general development of the navy that he entrusted the steering of the naval appropriations bill of 1914 to Senator John R. Thornton.[24]

Extreme and hasty naval construction, such as he felt was advocated by the shipbuilders and the National Security League, Tillman rejected out of respect to the national treasury. Thus in the early months of 1915 he cautioned against great expenditures on battleships pending a test of this type of weapon in an expected battle between the Germans and the English.[25] He resented vigorously the attack by the Big Navy group on Josephus Daniels, admiring the Secretary of the Navy for defending enlisted men against the "officer clique," and saying that he "will go down in history as one of the greatest Secretaries the Navy has ever had." [26]

The South Carolina senator was too good a patriot not to fall in line with the popular demand for naval expansion during the World War. Without endorsing Wilson's declaration that the United States should have "incomparably the greatest navy in the world," Tillman said that he favored for his country the second greatest navy. Within this

21 *Id*. to Reverend C. D. Waller, March 27, 1914, in Tillman Papers.
22 *Id*. to Josephus Daniels, January 27, 1914, *ibid*.
23 *Id*. to Lieutenant Commander Louis Richardson, March 23, 1914, *ibid*.
24 *Id*. to Henry C. Tillman, May 22, 1914, *ibid*.
25 *Cong. Record*, 63 Cong., 3 Sess., 5250; Tillman to Admiral Victor Blue, January 22, 26, 1916, in Tillman Papers.
26 *Cong. Record*, 64 Cong., 1 Sess., 1668.

ample limit he co-operated for the attainment of the naval program of 1916, creating a special subcommittee consisting of himself and Senators Claude A. Swanson and Lodge.[27] The labors of this body resulted in the enactment of a program of naval expansion more extensive than that represented by a board of experts, whose five-year plans were compressed into three years.[28] "Because I believe in peace," wrote Tillman to one who complained of his stand, "is no reason why I should not be prepared to smite the bully who does not." [29] In order to devote all possible funds to the navy, he voted against the $40,000,000 pork-barrel appropriation for rivers and harbors. "I do not want my share of the stealing in this bill," he said. "That forty million would build two battle cruisers." [30] The patriotic press applauded. "Senator Tillman," said the New York *Times,* "has spoken as a sound-hearted, clear-headed American." [31]

The senator worked on the naval bill of 1916 as much as his waning strength would allow,[32] but the brunt of the work had to rest on the shoulders of the stronger men, to whom he generously accorded credit.[33]

The South Carolinian's prestige as chairman of the naval committee allowed him to press to a successful conclusion his twenty-year-old project for the erection of a government-owned armor plant. In 1915 he introduced a bill appropriating for this purpose as much as $11,000,000, advancing the old thesis that the armor makers were engaged in a monopolistic conspiracy.[34] The proposal encountered fa-

[27] Tillman to Claude A. Swanson, January 23, 1916, *ibid.*

[28] Providence (R. I.) *Tribune,* June 28, 1916; *Army and Navy Register,* July 1, 1916, in Tillman Scrapbooks.

[29] Tillman to Charles T. Hallinan, June 30, 1913, in Tillman Papers.

[30] *Cong. Record,* 64 Cong., 1 Sess., 8362.

[31] New York *Times,* May 22, 1916.

[32] "I have never," he wrote during the last stages of its history, "been so busy in all my life." Tillman to Riggs, June 26, 1916, in Tillman Papers.

[33] Lodge to Roosevelt, July 10, 1916, cited in Lodge (ed.), *Selections from the Correspondence of Theodore Roosevelt and Henry Cabot Lodge,* II, 491; Tillman, in *Cong. Record,* 64 Cong., 1 Sess., 11,382.

[34] *Cong. Record,* 64 Cong., 1 Sess., 2566–67.

miliar opposition from the senators of industrial states, but Tillman made no direct reply, pleading ill-health. The defense, however, was adequately upheld by Swanson.[35] The failure of the South Carolinian to debate his measure did not prevent his pushing it in other ways. He urged the President and the secretary of the navy to keep the Senate majority behind it and resolutely refused to yield to Republican efforts to vitiate it through modifications.[36] It passed the Senate by a vote of 58 to 23.[37] "It seems to be poetic justice," commented its elated sponsor, "that I should have lived long enough to see my efforts bear fruit." [38]

This self-congratulation was premature. The bill had to pass the House and the plant had actually to be erected. Within a week of the Senate victory, the senator was frantically writing the President that "a fearful fight" was being made in the House against the bill, and later that Charles M. Schwab, the steel magnate, was, with his "hundreds of millions," "debauching and demoralizing the friends of the bill." [39] Then, after the measure passed the House and became law, there was delay in execution. This delay, said a cynically-minded Republican, was but another illustration of the tendency of the Wilson administration to do nothing.[40] Tillman, in fact, went to his grave complaining about this indecision.[41] After his death the armor plant was located in Charleston, West Virginia, where it had a small but effective share in advancing the great program of national defense during the World War.

The feeble state of his health forced the South Carolina

[35] For debates, see *ibid.*, 4431–61, 4513–53.

[36] Tillman to Daniels, January 11, 1916, in Tillman Papers.

[37] *Id.* to Wilson, January 5, 8, 1916, ibid.; *Cong. Record,* 64 Cong., 1 Sess., 4545–53.

[38] Tillman to Henry C. Tillman, March 22, 1916, in Tillman Papers. *Cf. id.* to James W. Breen, March 22, 1916, *ibid.*

[39] *Id.* to Wilson, March 29, April 21, 1916, *ibid.*

[40] James W. Wadsworth, Jr., of New York, in *Cong. Record,* 64 Cong., 2 Sess., 4607.

[41] Tillman to Daniels, June 8, 1918, in Tillman Papers.

senator to turn over the conduct of the great naval appropriations bills of 1917 and 1918 to Swanson and Lodge.
"Swanson," he declared thankfully in 1917, "can handle
everything connected with the Navy, and he is anxious to
do everything possible for me." [42] When the Virginian was
absent from the Senate, Tillman admitted his inability to
answer questions, saying that his memory and strength were
failing.[43] Yet with a sense of duty not ignoble he clung to
the honor of being one of the nominal directors of the nation's first line of defense. Within a few weeks of his death,
he congratulated the Senate on passing the largest naval appropriations bill in the history of the country; and he assured the people that they need not fear attacks from German submarines, because the navy was able to "hunt down
these damned devils and wipe them off the face of the
earth." [44]

The ailing legislator did little in behalf of the great general measures of the Wilson regime. His speeches concerning them were few and inconsequential. During the first
session of Congress under Wilson, lasting from April 7 to
December 1, 1913, he spoke on only two subjects of consequence: his exclusion from the chairmanship of the Appropriations Committee and his opposition to woman
suffrage. The two other occasions when he raised his voice
were over minor matters: his so-called Reminiscences of
Eighteen Years and his request for the clerk to read Zeb
Vance's doggerel on the wool schedule of 1888 entitled
"A Girl with One Stocking—a Protective Pastoral." [45] His
speaking record for the five remaining years of his life was
about the same. In fact, disinclination or illness kept him
away from Washington for long periods, nor while in Washington was he a regular attendant on the Senate debates. It.
was his habit to spend most of his time in his office, appear-

[42] *Id.* to Benjamin R. Tillman, Jr., April 6, 1917, *ibid.*
[43] *Id.* to Daniels, April 27, 1917, *ibid.; Cong. Record,* 64 Cong., 2 Sess., 4582.
[44] *Cong. Record,* 65 Cong., 2 Sess., 7476.
[45] *Ibid.,* 63 Cong., 1 Sess., index.

ing on the floor only when the bell announced an impending vote. Then he inquired of some Democrat how he
should vote, being frequently ignorant of the issues in
question.[46]

Naturally these absences produced criticisms, especially
from those who desired his seat, but he was fertile in ex-
cuses. "I am paired with Senator Goff," he explained; "my
presence is not absolutely necessary, and younger and
stronger men ought to make the quorum." [47] The senator's
unfeigned belief that he was not neglectful had some justification. If not significantly concerned with general legislation, he was engaged at many small matters of interest to
his constituents. Three or four clerks were busy aiding in
his correspondence and interviews. "I am sometimes astonished at my capacity for work," he was able to write as
late as 1916; "for God knows enough of it piles up here
to keep everyone busy." [48] While in Washington he was
careful to help create quorums and to answer roll calls,
loyally giving one of the forty-odd votes necessary for the
enactment of the great administration measures. The once
chronic critic had become a Wilson rubber stamp.[49]

The groveling old loyalist was thrown into emotional
confusion when the wishes of the President and the platform of the Democratic party conflicted. This happened
most sharply when Wilson urged that American ships passing through the Panama Canal be charged tolls while the
1912 platform of the party demanded free passage. Confronted with this dilemma, Tillman confessed: "The predicament we are now in has caused me more worry than anything that has happened in a long while." He wished the
President had remained silent on the issue. He got peace
of mind, however, by inducing the South Carolina Demo-

[46] Ibid., 64 Cong., 1 Sess., 11,786; Tillman to Riggs, August 29, 1913, in
Tillman Papers.
[47] Tillman to Baker, October 4, 1914, *ibid.*
[48] *Id.* to D. M. Bradham, June 15, 1916, *ibid.*
[49] *Id.* to O. H. Forresman, September 16, 1914, *ibid.*

cratic convention to endorse the President's stand while he voted for the Wilson policy.[50]

The senator's endorsement of the President's policies did not include acceptance of those aspects of Wilsonian progressivism conflicting with Southern tradition. The most notable address of his postparalytic years was that of August 18, 1913, against woman suffrage, a cardinal Wilson tenet. "Weak and feeble by advancing years," as he confessed, he spoke without the old-time violence but with undiminished emotion. He portrayed the evils of woman suffrage; sought to view with epic detachment the headlong rush to destruction into which the folly of modernism was leading virtuous manhood and womanhood. Woman suffrage, he averred, would effect a social revolution. There might be improvement in politics, but at what a price— the encouragement of birth control and free love and divorce, the destruction of usefulness and goodness in woman, the wiping out of the natural distinctions between the sexes, and the establishment of the privilege for man to abandon the wife of his youth to seek "some young and buxom girl who suits his lustful eyes." Woman suffrage would inaugurate social and moral decay like that of ancient Rome—"the world rushing along pell-mell, helter-skelter, 'going to the devil,' so to speak." It were better to "endure the evils of corruption in politics . . . rather than bring about a condition which will mar the beauty and dim the luster of . . . glorious womanhood."

Tillman had exhibited what realists call the chivalric delusions of the traditional Southerner: the glory of an undefiled womanhood of the type South Carolina hallowed.[51] Of course, so sentimental a speech was an easy mark for the

50 Cong. Record, 63 Cong., 2 Sess., 10,064–66.

51 The complement to this faith was the reprinting in Cong. Record, 63 Cong., 1 Sess., 3733–35, of Alfred T. Bledsoe, "The Mission of Women," in Southern Review (Baltimore), IX (1871), 923 ff., containing what Tillman admitted was "an unkind and unjust reference to Northern women." Cong. Record, 63 Cong., 1 Sess., 3459–62.

feminists. The South Carolinian was reminded that his state of such "glorious womanhood" had a low age of consent, no compulsory education, no child or woman labor laws, was the third most illiterate commonwealth, and had inflicted upon the country the "divers woes" of "Pitchfork statesmanship." [52] Tillman took refuge in his usual supports: his moral self-confidence and the knowledge that his judgment was sustained by the voters of South Carolina. "I join you," he wrote an old humanist-friend, " 'in thanking God that South Carolina is safe from the heresy and leprosy,' as we both regard woman suffrage." [53]

South Carolinians were silenced by a logical application of one of the major axioms of Tillmanism. It was, he said, impossible to give white women the suffrage without extending the same privilege to Negro women. This "would be unspeakably dangerous" because black women were "wild and rabid," "far more pestiferous and hard to control than the [Negro] men." It would be "more horrible and terrible" for white men to be compelled to shoot black women who tried to vote than it had been to shoot black men with like ambitions.[54]

In still other respects Tillman opposed Wilson measures in obedience to South Carolina prejudice. Once he had fought for the right to import foreign labor; now he favored immigration restriction to the extent of voting for the literacy test which Wilson disliked. With age the senator grew savage in his hatred of foreigners. The World War brought out "latent deviltry in the minds of foreign-born citizens" and demonstrated that the country should go slowly in adding "any more ingredients to our concoction" lest there be "a hell broth." [55] The early settlers who came from

[52] See New York *Tribune*, Chicago *Tribune*, Dr. Anna Shaw, and others, in Tillman Scrapbooks.

[53] Tillman to Professor Joynes, August 27, 1913, *ibid.*

[54] *Id.* to Mrs. Mary P. Calvert, March 22, 1912, *ibid.*; *id.* to R. Lewin Epstein, November 3, 1913, *ibid.*; *id.* to Mrs. William C. Cathcart, January 10, 1917, *ibid.*

[55] *Id.* to I. J. Davis, June 23, 1916, *ibid.*

abroad were being succeeded by "the riff-raff of Europe
. . . who are festering New York and other Eastern cities
like maggots, committing all manner of crime, hiring themselves as sluggers and assassins and debauching and debas-
ing the ballot." [56]

On child labor, too, the old sophist took refuge in the
faith of his people. In a speech loaded with paradox, he
railed against the selfishness of those who exploited child
labor: "I have been shocked to see men in South Carolina
—rich, intelligent, well-educated men—who were willing
to swell their dividends at the expense of little children";
but in a proposed national child labor law he saw more evil
than good. Its stratagem of controlling indirectly the labor
of children by the application of the interstate commerce
provision of the Constitution was, in the senator's opinion,
a dreadful violation of state rights. Let the doctrine of "government by indirection" prevail and the country would be
commanded from Washington. "The present-day 'professional uplifters of humanity' " supporting the measure were
the counterparts of abolitionists of other days; enemies of
the South: Northern sentimentalists who would enter the
homes of Southern people to tell them how to rear their
children; Northern labor agitators and industrialists who
wished to injure the great Southern textile industry. [57]

All the sins which Tillman may have committed against
the Wilsonian gospel were atoned by the final great act of
his legislative career, his enthusiastic and loyal support of
the President's war policies. At first blush one might en-
visage the once rebel senator as an ally of George W. Norris,
La Follette, Vardaman, and the few other rural congressmen who opposed the great adventure in bloodshed. But
Tillman, an old man trembling on the verge of the grave,
achieved a sort of natural comfort by conforming to the

[56] *Id.* to Frank H. Janiszeski, March 16, 1916, *ibid.*
[57] *Id.* to Margaret I. Hamilton, January 10, 1913, *ibid.; Cong. Record,*
64 Cong., 1 Sess., 12,294–95.

powers that be, especially when they were a Congress and President of his own party. Had he, in 1917, possessed his full faculties he would have taken the same course. He was in no sense a pacifist, but a patriot who had sanctioned the war aims of 1861 and 1898 and given much energy to the building of the navy.[58] Nor was he an enemy of offensive warfare. Uncle Sam should not be prepared to "keep other nations from jumping on him, without at the same time being able, if he chooses, to jump on them." [59] Still, Tillman was neither militarist nor a warmonger. His notions of military preparations were always conservative, and he was not among the first of those who cried for war with Germany. With little insight into foreign affairs, he turned to others for moderate direction.

Inevitably he fell behind Wilson's cautious approach to the baffling problems created by a Europe in arms. For a time he saw no reason for a preference among the war-makers. "England," he declared in 1915, "has acted as badly with us as has Germany." [60] For months he patiently joined Wilson's friends in trusting Presidential letter-writing as a means of protecting the country against dangers from Europe. "The diplomacy of the present Administration," he declared, "is neither 'ridiculed abroad nor condemned at home.' " [61]

Yet like Wilson's, Tillman's professions of neutrality were more apparent than real; in fact, at the very beginning of the conflict he expressed conventional anti-German opinions. Early resentment against British interference with American shipping gave way to fury over submarine warfare against vessels with Americans aboard.[62] Specious moralizations against Germany did not prevent Tillman

[58] Tillman to J. I. Westfelt, October 5, 1912, in Tillman Papers.
[59] *Id.* to W. B. Crouch, January 27, 1916, *ibid.*
[60] *Id.* to Grover Patton, July 12, 1915, *ibid. Cf. Cong. Record,* 64 Cong., 1 Sess., 233–34.
[61] Tillman to Percy L. Edwards, January 5, 1915, in Tillman Papers.
[62] *Id.* to Benjamin R. Tillman, Jr., August 19, 1914, *ibid.; id.* to Admiral Blue, May 15, 1915, *ibid.; id.* to Heinrich Charles, February 23, 1916, *ibid.*

from recognizing that vital economic interests of his section were bound to the Allied cause. At first he hoped that the South could secure prosperity by selling cotton to both groups of belligerents; but when the British blockade swept German shipping from the seas, he found satisfaction in the rising prosperity of trade with England and her Allies. The Southern farmer, said the South Carolina senator, should pray for Allied success and oppose an embargo on shipping to Allied countries.[63]

Such sentiments of course engendered an enthusiastic endorsement of Wilson's preparedness program. The purpose of this activity was to keep the country from being "at the mercy of any marauder or barbarian like the Kaiser" in order that it might not be "mercilessly robbed and Prussianized." No impossible stretch of the imagination was needed to believe that to secure this "protection" it was necessary to use the newly created instruments of war to attack the Prussians. "But, Senator," said the President to Tillman in 1916, "it rests with Germany to say whether we shall remain at peace." The South Carolinian replied eagerly, "You are right, Mr. President, we must not go around with a chip on our shoulder. I am for peace, but I am not for peace at any damn price." [64]

So when, in the early months of 1917, Wilson decided that it was necessary to send armed men to Europe, he had in the South Carolina senator an ardent if inconspicuous supporter. The great speeches in the Senate for and against war were interlarded with a brief statement by Tillman in which he accepted uncritically the Wilsonian version of the causes of American participation in the great conflict. "The Kaiser and his slavish underlings, aiders and abettors" were alone responsible for the war, not the German people. Americans would be untrue to every instinct of patriot-

[63] Id. to J. M. DesChamps, September 16, 1914, ibid.; id. to Professor W. T. Lander, May 19, 1916, ibid.

[64] Id. to Millard F. Snider, December 29, 1916, ibid.; Joseph P. Tumulty, Woodrow Wilson as I Know Him (New York, 1921), 250.

ism did they not accept the challenge of the Hohenzollern autocracy and battle until such wickedness was destroyed.[65]

Private utterances were flavored with the spice of the old Tillman. German-Americans who did not favor war with their fatherland were "shameful mongrels," persons whose sense of decency should compel them to keep their treacherous mouths shut.[66] Concerning the Germans themselves, his diction grew opprobrious. He concluded, "I am glad Uncle Sam is going to take a hand and bring them to their senses." [67] With contempt for a parlor socialist who denounced the war as a manifestation of capitalist greed, he said, "I am sorry for you, and God pity the time when our citizens come to look upon such a question in this way." [68] Those who accused him of abandoning the common people of South Carolina to pursue strange gods were chastened with the assertion that Wilson's war for democracy would achieve the very principle for which Tillman had battled in 1890. "The underdog in South Carolina will be trampled out of sight if we do not wake up and defend our country against invasion by the Germans." [69] Efforts to justify German high-handedness on the sea roused his ire: "Are you willing to let the bloody scoundrel known officially as the Kaiser of Germany murder American men, women and children? . . . If you are, then God have mercy on your puny, mustard-seed of a soul." [70]

"I am in favor of marshaling the vast resources of this republic for the one purpose of killing Germans," wrote Tillman. If necessary, four or five million men should be put in the field. Legislation should be enacted to curb "the pernicious, pusillanimous and treacherous activity" of those who sympathized with "the wanton acts of the Prus-

[65] *Cong. Record*, 65 Cong., 1 Sess., 218–19.
[66] Tillman to Hans Rilsch, February 12, 1917, in Tillman Papers.
[67] *Id*. to Wilie Jones, June 17, 1917, *ibid*.
[68] *Id*. to G. A. Glauss, February 12, 1917, *ibid*.
[69] *Id*. to F. F. Bellinger, February 3, 1917, *ibid*.
[70] *Id*. to F. S. Wilcox, February 6, 1917, *ibid*.

sian military caste." He participated in the popular pastime
of spy hunting, instructing constituents that if they discovered German agents spreading propaganda, such agents
"ought to get lost in the swamps, or be strung up to a tree
as an example." [71] Occasionally he used the spy craze as a
means of creating vacancies in the public service for
friends.[72]

Yet Tillman's innate sense of fairness prevented unrestrained participation in spy hunting. When he was satisfied that "envy and disappointment on the part of some
people" caused rumors against Friedrich Johannes Hugo
von Engelken, the German-born president of the Federal
Land Bank at Columbia, he corrected previously accred-
ited accusations.[73] He advised against hysteria which "would
down the gap against tyranny and injustice" and thereby
permit imitation of "the Kaiser and his brood of devils." [74]
He put this principle into practice by trying to restrain an
overzealous district attorney, pro-English Episcopalians,
and others who were using the cloak of patriotism to perse-
cute Lutherans, Bleaseites, and those with German names.
"We want no persecution in South Carolina," he said to a
distressed suspect, "and you know me too well to imagine
that I would tolerate such a thing." [75]

The senator was so stirred by war emotions that he seemingly forsook old habits of thought. At times the old spoilsman wanted no "political generals," no useless rivers
dredged at Federal expense, and no distinctions made between Democrats and Republicans.[76] The old deist for once
in his life declared his faith in Providence. "The roar of the

[71] Id. to Thomas Dixon, April 27, 1917, ibid.; id. to Daniel B. Johnson,
April 7, 1917, ibid.

[72] Id. to Otto Preager, September 20, 1917, ibid.; id. to M. Manley Hamilton, October 24, 1917, ibid.

[73] Id. to William G. McAdoo, July 31, 1917, ibid.

[74] Id. to P. R. McCain, April 5, 1918, ibid.

[75] Id. to L. B. Folk, February 25, 1918, ibid. Cf. id. to William B. Fitts,
February 25, 1918, ibid.; id. to Thurmond, September 6, 1917, ibid.

[76] Id. to David R. Coker, June 18, 1917, ibid.; id. to T. C. Williams, April
24, 1917, ibid.

Entente cannon," he said, "is the veritable voice of God,
speaking to the Hun nation that has forgotten His existence." [77] The thought of his son Henry assuming the "sacred
duty" of military service led to an unaccustomed expression
of belief in Christian immortality. "If he should be killed,"
he wrote of this son, "I will feel he died in a holy cause,
and . . . will welcome me to the other shores." Lack of
faith in the Resurrection was the cause of the "fiendish and
hellish behavior" of the Germans. Those who died in the
Allied cause were following Christ. "The moving inspiration of the Germans is hatred; Love inspires and upholds
the Allies." [78] The old worldling had been forced to his
knees before the throne of the War God.

[77] *Id.* to Henry Buist, March 21, 1917, *ibid.*
[78] *Id.* to Perriton Maxwell, August 18, 1917, *ibid.*

Chapter XXXIV

PATRONAGE UNDER WILSON

ONE reason why the South Carolina senator gave little attention to general naval problems was that he had a local naval problem of his own. This was the adequate support of the Charleston navy yard. A long-standing hobby had grown into an obsession under the stimulus of opportunities for pork-barrel graft offered by a friendly and free-spending administration. As is sometimes the case with distinguished men growing senile, Tillman became excessively practical, counting as realities not great principles or indirect benefits, but direct handouts, the loaves and the fishes. He would give the people definite evidence that he was not moribund by bringing the money home to Charleston.[1]

Fresh stimulus was given to Tillman's long campaign in favor of the Charleston development by the smashing criticisms of its enemies. The leader of the assault was George von L. Meyer. This former secretary of the navy maintained that the United States had too many navy yards, more than countries with larger fleets. The remedy for this extravagance was concentration of resources in two or three strategically located places. The Charleston navy yard should be abandoned because of its proximity to the more important naval facilities of Norfolk. It was maintained through a pork-barrel conspiracy.[2]

[1] See Senator Penrose, in *Cong. Record,* 63 Cong., 3 Sess., 4713.
[2] George von L. Meyer, "Are Naval Expenditures Wasted?" in *North American Review,* CCI (1915), 248–53, cited in *Cong. Record,* 63 Cong., 3 Sess., 3555–56.

Tillman replied vigorously, denying that there had been "any understanding or dickering," and marshaling all his old arguments in favor of the Charleston establishment. Battleships as well as gunboats and destroyers could be docked there provided the Cooper River was dredged. Expenditure of the $175,000 necessary for this work was "forty times more valuable . . . than the little dry creeks they [the army engineers] are pumping water in in the West." [3]

The fate of such projects was determined through wire-pulling and prodding, techniques at which Tillman was adept. "I am looking out all along the line to get 'my share of the stealing,'" he wrote the mayor of Charleston a few weeks before Wilson took office. [4] After that event he made his wishes known to high officials. He told Assistant Secretary of the Navy Franklin D. Roosevelt that under the Republicans the Charleston navy yard had been "suppressed and discriminated against in every way." [5] Into the ears of Secretary Daniels he poured tales of sectional discrimination. It was a "crying shame" that Northern yards were properly equipped while Charleston was neglected. [6] But he soon realized that it was not Northerners and Republicans who were Charleston's most formidable foe. The true enemy was the Norfolk navy yard, championed by Virginia senators high in the favor of the Wilson administration. At first, the South Carolina senator asserted that the generous revenues of the Norfolk post should be counted in the Northern column in tables designed to show sectional discrimination! When this argument failed, the tactics of the Virginia senators were assaulted. Senators Martin and Swanson, Tillman told Daniels, "are going to be very ingenious in trying to get favor for the Norfolk yard." [7]

[3] Tillman, *ibid.*, 3552–53. *Cf. ibid.*, 4713.
[4] Tillman to John P. Grace, February 22, 1913, in Tillman Papers.
[5] *Id.* to Franklin D. Roosevelt, April 12, 1914, *ibid.*
[6] *Id.* to Daniels, April 7, 1914, *ibid.*
[7] *Id.* to *id.*, June 2, 1914, *ibid.*

The naval appropriations bill of 1916 gave Tillman opportunity to push the Charleston demands. He asked $175,000 for dredging the approaches to the navy yard, and $1,085,000 for lengthening the dry dock. The Charleston project, he declared bitterly, had for years been "a target for misrepresentation and falsehood" by hired writers. It was not true that the navy yard was inaccessible because only a little inexpensive dredging was necessary to give accommodation to the whole fleet. Had he not favored funds for Northern naval stations? Why were men so selfish in their sectionalism that they refused to forget a past which taught them to hate South Carolina? [8] When the secretary of the navy showed reluctance over endorsing Tillman's plans he was threatened with the withdrawal of the senator's support,[9] and "Uncle Joe" Cannon as "an honest partisan" was asked to correct alleged misstatements about Charleston. "I tell you religiously—and I am too old to begin lying, you know," Tillman wrote the veteran Republican leader, "that I have never asked for anything for Charleston that I did not believe for the good of the Navy." [10] But he did not in 1916 get the special appropriation he desired; the House objected.

The next year the indefatigable old man repeated his tedious struggle. "I intend to see that the Charleston navy yard is treated like other yards if possible, and I will raise 'merry hell' if it is not," he wrote a friend.[11] To his demands for the dredging of the channel and the elongation of the dry dock were added requests for an ammunition depot, for the enlargement of a clothing factory, and for the adoption of the policy of constructing vessels in navy yards.[12] The opposition was as searching as ever. Lodge successfully

---

8 *Cong. Record,* 64 Cong., 1 Sess., 4450, 4453, 11,381–82.

9 Tillman to Daniels, June 22, 1916, in Tillman Papers.

10 *Id.* to Joseph G. Cannon, July 31, 1916, *ibid.*

11 *Id.* to Martin, January 10, 1917, *ibid.*

12 *Id.* to W. H. Slayton, February 16, 1917, *ibid.*

raised the specter of socialism against public construction of ships.[13] Hoke Smith sponsored the defeat of the project to enlarge the clothing factory. [14] La Follette wanted to know why the secretary of the navy had raised the estimate for the ammunition depot from $35,000 to $125,000. "This itself," said the Wisconsin senator, "raises in one's mind the query as to whether the Secretary [of the navy] has not been importuned by somebody about something on which to base an appropriation for a particular locality." But this item weathered the objection and became law.[15] Chairman Lemuel P. Padgett of the House naval committee blocked the dry dock appropriation.[16]

Tillman succeeded in having $1,650,000 included for Charleston in the great naval appropriations bill of 1918. Provision was at last made for the dredging and the dry dock extension.[17] But this did not satisfy his avid appetite for spoils. He was "woefully disappointed" when a shipbuilding project went to Wilmington, North Carolina.[18]

Tillman demanded what he called his just share of the offices in the gift of the President. At first he gave lip service to the principle of nonpartisan appointments, expressing the hope that Wilson would abolish "useless offices" and restrain "the greedy horde of officeseekers." [19] He gave the President the following platitudinous advice: "What we need in the United States is more attention to the needs and protection of the taxpayers than to the wishes and desires of the tax-eaters." [20] But he was not willing to practice

[13] Lodge to Roosevelt, February 13, 1917, cited in Lodge (ed.), *Selections from the Correspondence of Theodore Roosevelt and Henry Cabot Lodge*, II, 495.

[14] *Cong. Record*, 64 Cong., 2 Sess., 4583–84.

[15] *Ibid.*, 4608–11.   [16] *Ibid.*, 4919.

[17] *Ibid:*, 65 Cong., 2 Sess., 6908–10.

[18] Tillman to William Banks, April 25, 1918, in Tillman Papers; *id.* to Swanson, April 28, 1918, *ibid.*

[19] Tillman statement, November, 1912, *ibid.*

[20] *Id.* to Wilson, January 23, 1913, *ibid.*

such preachment. Unlike other politicians, he recognized this discrepancy with brutal clarity, explaining that he would in general oppose "a big steal" while doing all he could to win favors for South Carolinians.

He was a most active spoilsman. Were he President, he said, he would "turn out every Republican who was obnoxious and inefficient, and the decent ones I would allow to hold the jobs until their commissions expired." [21] He threatened to desert the Democratic organization when political heads were not readily chopped off to make room for his friends. In his opinion "the only two Democrats in Wilson's cabinet" were Burleson and Daniels because they were the only members of that group who did not hesitate to remove Republicans.[22] He complained bitterly because Byran would not employ his friends in the State Department and because they could not get consideration from the Department of Justice as long as Thomas W. Gregory was at its head.[23]

Dissatisfied by the President's attitude toward his importunities, he cried, "No Democratic President would do me as President Wilson is now doing if I were not old and sick." [24] He informed Wilson personally that all departments and bureaus were filled with Republican partisans who deprived deserving Democrats of office. "Leaving out scientific positions, members of our party ought to be given every place, and any other policy will cause great disappointment and heartburning." [25] When the President did not freely comply with his desires, the senator accused Wilson of the worst political sin. "The President's gratitude

[21] *Id.* to C. M. Heirs, November 11, 1912, *ibid.*
[22] *Id.* to Daniel C. Roper, July 31, 1916, *ibid.*
[23] *Id.* to Bryan, June 28, 1914, *ibid.; id.* to Judge Joseph T. Johnson, December 19, 1916, *ibid.*
[24] *Id.* to Albert S. Burleson, September 24, 1913, with copy to Tumulty, September 26, 1913, *ibid.*
[25] *Id.* to Wilson, March 12, 1913, *ibid. Cf.* Tillman memoranda, July 19, 24, 1916, *ibid.*

is like Tallyrand's maxim, 'A lively sense of favors to come.' " [26]

In the belief of this ambitious placeman the Civil Service Commission was "an arrant humbug" without "common sense and practical experience." [27] The Republicans had used it as "a screen to discriminate against Democrats," and even under Democratic administration it was fraudulent. "I have ocular demonstration," he wrote a civil service commissioner, "of the utter absurdity and folly of some of your clerks and underlings who are marking papers." [28] The commission should be emasculated or even defrauded of its privileges. The postmaster general was asked to violate its rules, and another postal official to falsify the grades of an office seeker so that the applicant might be eligible for civil service appointment.[29] "We must learn to play the game . . . so that Democrats will get all the good jobs." [30]

The standards Tillman required of those he recommended for office were low. He would not commend persons he believed would "not make good up to the handle" or who were not "clean in their habits," [31] but he disregarded the technical requirements of the despised Civil Service Commission. On one occasion he asked the postmaster general to give a friend a clerkship "which does not involve a great amount of learning." This man, the senator explained, "deserves well of his country because when his wife's father died" he cared for the four children of the deceased.[32] In asking for an appointment in the internal revenue service, he expressed ignorance of the applicant's qualifications. "I don't know whether Caughman is a book-

---

[26] Tillman to Henry C. Tillman, July 10, 1913, *ibid.*
[27] *Id.* to W. L. Morgan, January 3, 1912, *ibid.*
[28] *Id.* to Charles M. Galloway, September 10, 1913, *ibid.*
[29] *Id.* to Burleson, March 13, 1916, *ibid.; id.* to Ruskin McArdle, July 21, 1914, *ibid.*
[30] *Id.* to N. B. Moore, November 13, 1912, *ibid.*
[31] *Id.* to William Cooper, November 13, 1913, *ibid.*
[32] *Id.* to Burleson, March 18, 1913, *ibid.*

keeper or not. In fact I don't know much about him except
that he is the son of an old friend." [33] He sought a consul-
ship for a man who knew no foreign language; [34] for the appointment as doorkeeper in the office of the Civil Service
Commission of "a good Confederate soldier" who was "a
little old and takes his toddy once in a while"; [35] for the
retention in the census bureau of "a very old, feeble" lady
of eighty.[36] But there were limits to the senator's tolerance.
He refused to recommend a man broken in health for the
Federal marshalship. "If you go to see the President," this
man was told, "he would consider you crazy and me crazy
if I urged your appointment." [37]

The senator was capable of extreme tactics against those
who prevented his friends' having office. He besmirched
reputations. Herbert Putnam, the distinguished Librarian
of Congress, was a "negro-loving whelp" because he discharged a stenographer who did not wish to sit near blacks.[38]
A postmaster endorsed by a local congressman was "an old
lying Republican, a dyed-in-the-wool, negro-loving one";
and he sought proof of the immorality of a Republican
woman postmistress.[39] He sanctioned violence against Negroes who wished to take postmaster examinations. "If the
negro applicants were to receive the proper kind of notice
from some of the boys at Sellers, they would not turn up
at Florence for the examination on February 22nd," he
wrote.[40]

Tillman felt that he was a public benefactor in securing
as many positions for South Carolinians as possible and
his pride was gratified by the resulting applause. Yet he was

[33] *Id.* to Duncan C. Heyward, July 24, 1916, *ibid.*
[34] *Id.* to Tumulty, March 15, 1913, *ibid.*
[35] *Id.* to Galloway, August 7, 1913, *ibid.*
[36] *Id.* to S. L. Rogers, December 29, 1916, *ibid.*
[37] *Id.* to McCalla, December 7, 1912, *ibid.*
[38] *Id.* to Luke Lea, December 17, 1912, *ibid.*
[39] *Id.* to Burleson, May 9, 1917, *ibid.; id.* to Tompkins, January 12, 1912,
ibid.
[40] *Id.* to James W. Ragsdale, January 22, 1913, *ibid.*

self-seeking enough to wish to bestow a portion of the fruit on his two sons. He wanted his son Henry appointed assistant United States district attorney. But he saw obstacles, fearing that "a howl will go up over the State that 'Old Ben' is fixing his family at public expense," and that such a move would have an unwholesome effect upon the political future of this son. The father felt that Henry's ambition to become a congressman could be better served by his election as state's attorney. So Old Ben moved by indirection. He would remove the incumbent state attorney from Henry's path through Federal appointment.[41] But this was never done, and Henry became an unsuccessful candidate for Congress in 1916 without a previous candidacy for the lesser office.

No such difficulty beset the father's giving office to B. R. The older son had no political ambitions at that time and needed the influence of steady employment to offset his domestic difficulties. He was given a position in the Alaska railroad service, and when so distant an assignment proved distasteful, the father found him employment in Washington as clerk of the Senate Committee on Naval Affairs and as compiler of the *Navy Year Book,* a volume of documents already published in other forms. This son, Tillman admitted to the secretary of the navy, "knows very little about the Navy, never having studied it." [42]

All the worst phases of Tillman's greed for public plunder were illustrated by the struggle over the United States district-attorneyship. He wanted J. William Thurmond to have the position. Thurmond was his personal lawyer and the political boss of Edgefield, but had rashly killed a man in a quarrel over Tillmanism.[43] Senator Smith's candidate was Francis H. Weston, state senator for Richland County. Tillman rightly diagnosed the contest as a

[41] *Id.* to Henry C. Tillman, November 9, December 6, 1912, *ibid.*
[42] *Id.* to William G. McAdoo, March 6, 1915, *ibid.; id.* to Daniels, May 11, 1915, *ibid.*
[43] *Id.* to Richard C. Watts, January 21, 1913, *ibid.*

test of strength between historic forces for the favor of Wilson. Against the Tillman influence were arrayed Smith, Gonzales, and a host of old Haskellites.[44]

No wonder the old senator struggled hard to hit the mark for Thurmond. He trotted out his entire bag of tricks: ridicule and invective, begging letters to the omnipotent Wilson.[45] But the President, unyielding, informed Tillman that he was sending Weston's name to the Senate. The alleged incompetence of the successful applicant was given less weight by Wilson than the conviction that the chief enforcer of Federal law in South Carolina should not be a man who had killed a fellow citizen. There can be no doubt that the President's sympathies lay with the group of upper class Columbians to whom Weston belonged. Tillman was deeply hurt and told the President so. Would not his friends, he wrote Wilson, "consider me as having been thrown on the scrap-heap?" "I regret, Mr. President," he concluded in pathos, "more than I can make you understand that this incident will make me unwilling or at least not very anxious to see you again." [46]

But it was not the Pitchfork Ben of angry outbursts against Cleveland who was speaking, not even the sensitive Ben Tillman of the time of Theodore Roosevelt, the Tillman who kept his resolution not to enter the White House. There were to be as many future visits to the President as the senator's feeble legs and the restricted audiences of Wilson would allow.[47] The decaying spoilsman had already resolved upon a course which would satisfy all South Carolina, including himself, Thurmond, Smith, and Weston. This was to divide South Carolina into two Federal judicial districts with two district-attorneyships, one for Weston and

[44] Id. to James F. Byrnes, May 17, 1913, ibid.

[45] Id. to Thurmond, December 12, 1912, ibid.; id. to Crosland, March 22, 1913, ibid.; id to Ellison D. Smith, September 11, 1913, ibid.; id. to Burleson, September 24, 1913, ibid.; id. to Tumulty, July 25, August 21, September 11, 1913, ibid.

[46] Id. to Wilson, February 11, 1914, ibid.

[47] Id. to Henry C. Tillman, February 14, 1914, ibid.

the other for the frustrated Thurmond. And there would be a new judgeship and a new clerkship, plums for friends and relatives.

The battle for this objective was difficult. The cumbersome machinery of legislation had to be turned to get the necessary bill through Congress. The cause was unworthy: the creation of unneeded offices to satisfy the greed and vanity of an old man. Both the attorney general of the United States and the Federal judge for South Carolina asserted that a new district was unnecessary. Tillman himself admitted that "the facts seem to be against even a district attorney and a marshal." [48] Nevertheless, the senator pursued the intrigue with vicious energy, blustering, cajoling, even supplying "tables and statistics showing the necessity of the move." [49]

His hard labors bore the desired fruit. The South Carolina delegation in Congress endorsed the project and the approval of the administration was secured. The act of Congress creating the new district became law in March, 1915. This was Tillman's moment of great rejoicing, an opportunity to rebuke those who jealously criticized him. "Instead of South Carolinians caviling and carping," he wrote an old enemy, "they ought to be glad that they have a man in Washington who can win the friendship and respect of his colleagues of both parties." [50]

Immediately after this triumph, plans were revealed for the division of the spoils. The conspirators had decided that the judgeship should go to Congressman Joseph T. Johnson, and this plan went through without a hitch. It was of course agreed that Thurmond should have the district-attorneyship, but here vexing difficulties developed. Once

[48] *Id.* to James C. McReynolds, October 8, 1913, *ibid.; id.* to Julius H. Heyward, October 18, 1913, *ibid.; id.* to Henry C. Tillman, October 19, 1913, *ibid.*
[49] *Id.* to Tumulty, September 29, 1913, *ibid.; id.* to Ellison D. Smith, February 5, 1914, *ibid.*
[50] *Id.* to Columbia *State,* March 14, 1915.

more the administration was reluctant to appoint a man-killer. Tillman overcame these scruples with threats and spurious arguments, writing to the attorney general: "I am angry and don't intend to conceal it." He distorted the charge against Thurmond to homicide in self-defense. The Edgefield lawyer, ran the senator's fantastic version, "had to crawl around on his belly and be kicked around rather than kill the man before he did kill him." [51]

After Thurmond's appointment was made secure, Tillman unfolded another petal of his odious rose of spoliation. It was to make his private secretary, J. Broadus Knight, clerk of the new court in order that his son B. R. might have Knight's position. Knight had served Tillman for many years both as secretary and as manager of the Trenton farm; the senator felt it would not be "honorable" to discharge him without offering him another position. Nevertheless, Knight was notified that he must retire regardless of the outcome of the effort to secure him the court position. Room must be made for B. R., whom the senator described as "a new man" deserving of the secretaryship he had held many years before.[52]

When both Knight and B. R. got the coveted positions, the insatiable old man knew peace of soul. Although newspapers howled a gale of protests, all was snug in the well-feathered Tillman nest.[53]

[51] Id. to Thomas W. Gregory, March 24, 1915, in Tillman Papers.
[52] Id. to Johnson, March 18, 1915, ibid.; id. to Benjamin R. Tillman, Jr., March 18, 1915, ibid.; id. to Byrnes, March 25, 1915, ibid.
[53] Id. to Columbia State, March 14, 1915.

Chapter XXXV

DYING IN HARNESS

ALL that remains to be treated of the events of Ben Tillman's seventy-one years is the last activity of his life, his candidacy for the Senate in 1918. Several circumstances made this effort inauspicious. He had said he would not, for the fifth time, seek election, writing in his Farewell Letter of August, 1914, "Should I live to the end of my term I shall be seventy-two years of age, and I now serve notice to all who are interested that I shall not try to succeed myself." [1] To prove that he was not a fickle old man, he repeated to the senators in 1916 what he had said two years earlier; and to check the sneers of these veteran understanders of political pose, he added a declaration which came from the heart: "Senators laugh and do not believe me, but I will tell you it is true. You may be that kind of politicians, but I am not. I have stated to the people of South Carolina that I would not be a candidate, and they can not make me be a candidate." [2] The laughter of the senators was not at this time justified; for Tillman privately repeated his words to one to whom he often revealed his innermost thoughts. "I have told the people," he wrote his son Henry, "that I would not ask for reelection, and I certainly do not intend to do so since I told them that I would not." [3]

Tillman's plans to retire were induced by the precarious

[1] Tillman statement, August, 1914, in Tillman Papers.
[2] *Cong. Record*, 64 Cong., 1 Sess., 8361.
[3] Tillman to Henry C. Tillman, September 14, 1916, *ibid.*

state of his health. Despite the heroic cheerfulness with which he applied his health remedies, his progressive paralysis made him constantly less capable of performing his official duties. In 1917 he suffered from a carbuncle infection which necessitated an operation and a protracted retirement to Trenton.[4] In the early months of 1918 his brave optimism broke down. "You are mistaken about my improvement being progressive," he wrote a former secretary, "for neither physically nor mentally is that true. I notice that my legs are more wobbly than they used to be and my memory less alert." [5] Actually, his condition was much worse. A picture taken at the time revealed a drawn face and unsteady legs held far apart.[6] His family wanted him to retire; they feared that the excitement of another campaign would destroy the little health he had left.[7]

His Conservative friends felt that the situation in South Carolina necessitated the retirement of the invalid senator. The country was in the midst of war; Blease was again a candidate for the Senate; a man of youth and vigor and patriotism was needed to oppose that pugnacious campaigner, and such a person was found in Congressman Asbury F. Lever. The Conservatives did not fear the traditional Tillman vengeance. They knew that he could no longer harangue the multitudes and that he had lost to Blease the bulk of his old following.

The injection of Blease and Lever into the issue was seemingly the final and convincing reason why Tillman should retire. Blease's narrow defeat in 1916 by Manning had enhanced his popularity, for many believed that he had been cheated. He now committed the crowning infamy for a South Carolinian of opposing Woodrow Wilson and the war with Germany. Angered by the refusal of the President to give him and his large following recognition, he cried

[4] *Id.* to L. P. Lipscomb, April 29, 1917, *ibid.*
[5] *Id.* to Grover Patton, February 28, 1918, *ibid.*
[6] Tillman Scrapbooks.
[7] Tillman to Josiah J. Evans, November 17, 1917, in Tillman Papers.

in speeches before rural audiences that Wilson and every congressman who voted for war should be removed and that Manning was a worse governor than the Carpetbaggers because they only stole money while Manning was trying to "steal the souls and bodies of your boys." When Blease discovered that he had misinterpreted public opinion, he tried to recant, but Manning's friends would not let him. They constantly exhibited his antiwar record before a war-inflamed populace while declaring that it was a patriotic duty to prevent his election to the Senate.[8]

The choice of Lever as a means of forestalling Blease was judicious. His ten years in Congress made him as familiar as Tillman with the workings of the Federal government. His loyalty to Wilson and the war aims was unquestioned, and his part in the legislation of the administration had been far more distinguished than that of the invalid senator. Although diminutive in stature, the congressman was well-informed, nimble-witted, and sharp-tongued, in some respects more than a match for the vivid but poorly-informed Blease.[9]

Despite the unpropitious circumstances—his wretched health, his promise to retire, the opposition of both the Blease and the anti-Blease forces, and the availability of Lever—Senator Tillman had little difficulty in persuading himself to offer for re-election in 1918. He did this in a public statement of March 7, with the apology that "everything has been changed by our entry in the war." It was the duty of everyone to serve the country as best he could; of course his greatest usefulness was in the Senate. "Hundreds of letters from patriotic citizens" confirmed this resolution. He occupied a position which could not be attained by a new senator: chairman of the naval committee; sponsor of the Charleston navy yard and the armor plant.

[8] Blease's antiwar speeches, in Tillman Scrapbooks. See also, Wallace, *History of South Carolina*, III, 445-51.

[9] Charleston *Evening Post* editorial, in Tillman Scrapbooks.

He had the "respect and friendship" of officials and could best serve the soldiers and their families before the bureaus. Although he asserted that his health was better, he would not conduct an active campaign but would remain in Washington to uphold the hand of the President in the war. "I do not believe the people of the State are in any humor for unnecessary political agitation this year." [10]

The repudiation of the 1914 promise did not surprise those who knew Tillman well. A careful reading of certain supplementary phrases in his retirement utterances gave the student of the Tillman psychology room for thought. The 1916 statement contained a specific qualification. If the people of South Carolina, he explained, "want to elect me, they can do so." [11] Of course he would not refuse the people; indeed, he said, "I am glad to serve them to the best of my ability." [12]

He was most receptive to the sound of the people calling, frequented those places where the sounds were loudest, and interpreted favorably all that he heard. In October, 1917, he was gratified "over receiving letters and petitions to run" [13] and to be told on a visit to the state fair by two hundred men of influence that his services were needed. It was "the general opinion of everybody," he asserted, that Blease could defeat Lever and that Tillman was needed to save the situation.[14]

The Tillman theory that the Senate seat must be his because the people, not he, so willed, led him to pretend complete detachment. "I do not care," he wrote concerning newspaper attacks on his candidacy, "what they say about me editorially, nor indeed, am I taking any interest

[10] Tillman statement, March 7, 1918, in Tillman Papers.
[11] *Cong. Record,* 64 Cong., 1 Sess., 8361.
[12] Tillman to S. E. Atkins, October 16, 1916, in Tillman Papers.
[13] *Id.* to Edwin W. Robertson, October 14, 1917, *ibid.*
[14] *Id.* to Burleson, November 1, 1917, *ibid. Cf. id.* to H. E. Gray, January 24, 1918, *ibid.; id.* to J. Broadus Knight, February 14, 1918, *ibid.*

in the race at all." [15] He was, he boasted, patriotically attending to the business of the nation at war and not making a single speech for himself on the South Carolina stump. "There are many things," he wrote from Washington, "to do in behalf of those who are actually making war that I feel it more important to stay here than for me to be spending my time trying to get votes in South Carolina." [16]

But he reacted to the discordant voices. Newspaper opponents answered his arguments about Tillman statesmanship and prestige by recalling the fates of Hampton and Butler and by accusing him of "an overweaning personal ambition." [17] Such attacks called forth all of Tillman's defensive devices. Feverishly he wrote letters and engaged in personal interviews. Had he possessed the strength, he would have addressed crowds. His active purpose could not be obscured by declarations of simulated indifference. Both friends and enemies knew what Ben Tillman wanted.

Still he kept up the pretense. "If the people want me to run," he continued to repeat, "they will have to take the initiative and let me know in no unmistakable way." [18] Then he urged the people to entreat him to do what he was dreadfully in earnest about doing. He would not run unless he was "conscripted," he wrote a friend; but to make sure that this would take place he added: "You can have those in Columbia who want me to run . . . begin active steps at once." [19] At his urgent request conferences were held "to get," so he claimed, "the unbiased opinion of my sincere friends" concerning his duty. When the first conference reported that the candidacy was "inadvisable" he dismissed the suggestion as injudicious. "To me," he said, "this advice has the appearance of a frameup by the *State*

[15] *Id.* to Gantt, April 8, 1918, *ibid.*
[16] *Id.* to Charles C. Fuller, June 24, 1918, *ibid.*
[17] Unidentified newspaper clipping, in Tillman Scrapbooks.
[18] *Id.* to Baker, September 10, 1917, in Tillman Papers.
[19] *Id.* to Kohn, September 22, 1917, *ibid.*

newspaper and its editor." [20] He then called another meeting which did as he wished by asking him to become a candidate.[21]

Tillman's pretended indifference to newspaper opinion was actually accompanied by efforts to secure favorable interpretation of his candidacy. He asked an old friend to encourage eulogistic editorials in New York newspapers so that they could be republished in South Carolina; [22] sent anonymous communications to weekly newspapers extolling his virtues; [23] jotted down "some thoughts" which he asked the editor of the Augusta *Chronicle* "to weave into an editorial." [24] That he might win through "a short, sharp and decisive" campaign he strove, through "true and tried friends," to have the Democratic State Convention endorse his candidacy.[25] He even asked the president of Winthrop College to organize the students in his behalf in a quiet way "without injuring the college with the Bleaseites." "It is," he explained, "entirely legitimate for these young women to fight my battles now that I am too old and weak to do it." [26]

The most formidable barrier to the success of the old veteran continued to be the gossip about his health. At first he tried to ignore these rumors by remaining in Washington. "It will not be necessary," he said on April 1, "for me to 'show' myself in order for the people to know that I am not moribund." [27] But the consistency with which he avoided South Carolina caused sinister talk; it was asserted that he was ill mentally as well as physically. To quiet these "lies" he would visit the upcountry towns to show the

[20] *Id.* to Walter F. Stackhouse, November 18, 1917, *ibid.*
[21] *Id.* to Martin, November 21, 1917, *ibid.*; Kirkland, "Tillman and I," in Columbia *State*, July 21, 1929.
[22] Tillman to Edward L. Oldham, March 16, 1918, in Tillman Papers.
[23] *Id.* to McGraw, March 19, 1918, *ibid.*
[24] *Id.* to Loyless, March 19, 1918, *ibid.*
[25] *Id.* to Wilie Jones, May 9, 1918, *ibid.*
[26] *Id.* to David B. Johnson, March 23, 1918, *ibid.*
[27] *Id.* to J. K. Mayfield, April 1, 1918, *ibid.*

people "that I am strong enough to walk about and that I have not lost my mind." [28] But he substituted for this project the less trying one of appearing before the Democratic State Convention of May 15.

With his brain stimulated by black coffee, he walked into that gathering infirmly leaning on the arm of his son Henry, who was in uniform. In an atmosphere teeming with war enthusiasm, he loosed one flash of the old-time invective: "To hell with German sympathizers and thank God for Woodrow Wilson." The rest of the address was a repetition of what he had been saying for months: he was not canvassing the state because the war emergency demanded his remaining in Washington. [29]

He felt that his conduct before the convention assured his re-election; [30] but realities were realities. Tillman was an ill man, and he had difficulty fooling himself to believe otherwise. To combat rumors he secured certificates of health from friends in the Senate. At his dictation James H. Lewis of Illinois wrote an inquiring South Carolinian: "Senator Tillman is not the vigorous debater he once was, nor is his physical strength so great that he should be required to squander it, but he does as much work as any man in the Capitol." [31] Swanson was induced to write in the same vein, and the invalid engineered the publication of both letters in the South Carolina press. [32]

The quondam boss of what was once regarded as the sovereign state of South Carolina took a step which proved that times had changed. He asked the President of the United States to influence the people of South Carolina in

[28] *Id.* to Henry C. Tillman, May 4, 1918, *ibid.*; *id.* to Martin, May 8, 1918, *ibid.*

[29] *Id., Speech Before Democratic Convention,* May 15, 1918 (Columbia, 1918).

[30] *Id.* to Charles S. Moore, May 20, 1918, in Tillman Papers; *id.* to Edwin W. Robertson, May 20, 1918, *ibid.*

[31] See *id.* to James H. Lewis, June 13, 1918, for text of the letter Tillman asked Lewis to write to Lawrence G. Southard, Union, South Carolina. *Ibid.*

[32] *Id.* to Southard, June 27, 1918, *ibid.*; *id.* to Kohn, June 26, 1918, *ibid.*, for proof that both Lewis and Swanson complied with Tillman's request.

his behalf or at least not to influence them in favor of any other senatorial aspirant. This would have been humiliating to the proud Ben Tillman of an earlier day, but in 1918 it was a wise and necessary prerequisite to success; for Woodrow Wilson in World War days bossed South Carolina as effectively as Tillman had ever done, and it was part of the Presidential strategy to designate favorites in Congressional contests.

The senator approached the President through the administration's chief political manipulator, Postmaster General Burleson. The negotiations were tedious. In reply to Tillman's first plea, Burleson gave the unwelcome opinion that if there was one chance in a hundred of defeat Tillman should not risk it.[33] Later, however, the senator's importunities led the postmaster general to promise verbally that he was for Tillman "horse, foot and dragoons." This encouraged the senator to ask him "to 'call off' Manning's crowd," that is, to force Lever's withdrawal from the Senate race.[34] But Burleson refused to do this, and Tillman, apprehensive, beseeched a declaration of neutrality. "Write me a brief letter saying that you or no member of the Administration has ever asked Lever or anybody else to go into the race for the Senate." [35] Burleson's reply was welcome. "It is the fixed policy of the Administration," he said, "to refrain from interference in state political affairs. At no time has the Administration in South Carolina or any other state urged or invited any person to become a candidate for the United States Senate." [36] Even this clear but unspecific language did not quell Tillman's fears. The senator asked the President himself to speak. Lever's friends, he wrote Wilson, were circulating rumors that the President had instructed the congressman to oppose the senator.

[33] *Id.* to Josiah J. Evans, November 17, 1917, *ibid.*
[34] *Id.* to John Gary Evans, March 15, 1918, *ibid.*
[35] *Id.* to Burleson, May 8, 1918, *ibid.*
[36] Burleson to Tillman, May 8, 1918, in Tillman Scrapbooks.

An endorsement of the Burleson statement was asked.[37] The President replied that the Burleson statement "expresses with entire accuracy the attitude which I have assumed in all contests between genuine friends of the Administration." [38]

Tillman, having won the neutrality of Wilson, conjured up enough anger to make possible another of his famous verbal assaults. The villains in the piece were Lever and Governor Manning. Lever, he felt, was guilty of ingratitude.[39] But it was against Manning that the main portion of the Tillman wrath was directed: for Lever was only a Macbeth led into crime by the tempter Manning. Not only had the governor instigated the Lever candidacy, but he had also tried to convince the Wilson administration that the elimination of Tillman was necessary to defeat Blease. "Having been a Haskellite in the long ago," ran Tillman's unkind interpretation of his victim's motives, "he has not outgrown his hatred of Tillman and Tillmanism—although he has pretended to be my friend—and thinks this is the opportune time for getting even and laying the old man away in his last race for a political office." [40]

He prepared for the May convention a speech "with lots of hot stuff" in it designed to make Manning wish he had not courted Lever. But on the advice of friends he decided to keep it "bottled up to distill a little longer" while he wrote the governor for an explanation.[41] Manning in his answer admitted that he was "one of a large number who wrote Mr. Lever to enter the race"; that he had asked Wilson and Burleson to look with favor upon this candidacy; and that Tillman's determination to seek re-election

[37] Tillman to Wilson, May 22, 1918, in Tillman Papers.
[38] Wilson to Tillman, May 24, 1918, in Tillman Scrapbooks.
[39] Tillman to Kohn, May 4, 1918, in Tillman Papers.
[40] Id. to Smoak, May 3, 1918, ibid.
[41] Id. to Charles S. Moore, May 20, 1918, ibid.; id. to Edwin W. Robertson, May 20, 1918, ibid.; id. to Manning, May 22, 1918, ibid.

"caused deep concern to many earnest men in this State."[42]

This confession gave occasion for Tillman's last fiery letter to the South Carolina voters. In it were many flashes which proved that the mental processes of a man actually near death were as lively as ever. Sarcastically he described Manning's "egotism and vanity" in the "business of making a senator for the people of South Carolina to swallow." During the 1916 canvass, Lever, said Tillman in words which provoked laughter, "came to Trenton in hot weather in early September in an automobile with curtains down" to secure the condemnation of Blease.[43]

In the two days between the composition of this article and its release the political situation was radically changed by Wilson's asking Lever to withdraw from the Senate race. The continued services of the congressman, the President explained, were needed in the House. "We are at war," Lever meekly replied; "you are the Commander in Chief of the Army and Navy, and it is the duty of every man to be placed where he can best serve his nation."[44] Perhaps, in abandoning his declaration of neutrality, the President was impressed by Tillman's traditional strength with the South Carolina voters or was goaded into action by the petitions of the persistent old senator. It is known that Tillman was delighted with his triumph and immediately rushed to the support of the Lever candidacy for re-election to the House.[45] He ordered the suppression of his denunciation of Manning and Lever, but his request was not respected by the Charleston *American,* which published a pirated copy in the interest of the Blease candidacy.[46]

Seemingly, now the only barrier to Tillman's return was

[42] Manning to Tillman, June 1, 1918, in Tillman Scrapbooks.

[43] Tillman to the press of South Carolina, June 6, 1918, in Tillman Papers.

[44] Wilson to Asbury F. Lever, June 15, 1918, in Tillman Scrapbooks; Lever to Wilson, June 8, 1918, *ibid.*

[45] Tillman to Lever, June 15, 1918, in Tillman Papers; *id.* to Joe Little, June 17, 1918, *ibid.*

[46] Tillman to the press of South Carolina, June 8, 1918, in Tillman Papers; Charleston *American,* June 10, 1918.

the opposition of Blease. That former governor was still the fond hope of many among the lower classes, and he tried to minimize his antiwar record by purchasing Liberty Bonds and offering to raise a regiment. Tillman struck with the remnant of his energy. Blease's pro-Germanism, said the senator, "ought to be sufficient to damn him in the eyes of all sensible and patriotic men." [47] The vengeful candidate was unwilling to trust the people alone to stifle this insubordinate man. He considered the law—the possible punishment of Blease under the severe espionage act of the war period. The senator listened eagerly to rumors that Federal agents were threatening the former executive with internment unless he silenced himself, and inquired eagerly of friends what would be the effect of Blease's arrest upon his "ignorant followers." [48] Nevertheless, Tillman concluded that the Federal government should not be asked to intervene because the cry of persecution might arise and because Blease was "too smart, perhaps, to go over the line in his speeches." [49]

The date of this cautious letter was June 29, 1918. Two days earlier Tillman had been forced to retire to his Washington apartment "feeling ill," and on the day of the letter he was seized with an illness that was to render Blease, the German war, the candidacy for re-election, and other earthly events of no more consequence to him. He was stricken with a cerebral hemorrhage which caused paralysis of the left side. Two days later paralysis possessed the whole body and he sank into a coma from which there was no hope of recovery. Just before day on July 3 he died, lacking one month and eight days of being seventy-two years of age.

Before an assembly of Congressional notables he was buried in Edgefield soil in the Ebenezer Cemetery less

[47] Tillman to William H. Clark, March 27, 1918, in Tillman Papers; *id.* to C. L. Jones, April 20, 1918, *ibid.*

[48] *Id.* to Martin, June 24, 1918, *ibid.*; *id.* to John F. Weekley, June 24, 1918, *ibid.*; *id.* to James G. Breazeale, June 29, 1918, *ibid.*

[49] *Id.* to John C. Neal, June 29, 1918, *ibid.*

than two miles from his Trenton residence. An imposing monument profusely chronicling his achievements was
placed over his grave. He had served in the Senate twenty-
three years and four months, two years longer than any
other South Carolinian up to that time.[50] Some would say
that after Calhoun he was the greatest public character
South Carolina has ever produced. But if such an assertion
opens a controversy, then surely, no South Carolinian, with
the single exception of Calhoun, has ever made a pro-
founder impression on his generation than Tillman.

[50] A record since exceeded by Ellison D. Smith.

Chapter XXXVI

FINAL ESTIMATE

UNLIKE the statesmen of England and New England, Ben Tillman did not make a systematic collection of letters and reminiscences to illuminate the path of biographers; the man and the civilization he represented were either too ill-disciplined or too reticent for such an orderly procedure. Yet it was inevitable that a man so historically minded should have been sensitive concerning the reputation he was going to leave behind. He quitted the governorship with words for "the just historian," and the reminiscent moods of old age provoked an exaggerated pride in his accomplishments. On his sixty-seventh birthday he let the public know that he had "been the most prominent figure" in South Carolina since 1885 because he was "not a self-seeking politician . . . but a genuine patriot trying to uplift the masses of the people." [1] One reason why he proclaimed his virtues was the belief that there was a conspiracy to steal his fame after his death. "Gonzales," he asserted, "is the arch-devil who is bent on robbing me of everything he can possibly take away." [2] He would, therefore, have his friends take up the cudgels in a newspaper discussion of Tillmanism. He corresponded with a proposed biographer and at times contemplated an autobiography.[3] He wanted his reputation properly appraised but this was never done while he lived.

[1] Tillman birthday address, August, 1914, in Tillman Papers.
[2] *Id.* to J. W. Gregory, September 23, 1912, *ibid.*
[3] *Id.* to Smoak, April 10, 1916, *ibid.*

"Those who attempt to question my motives or accuse me of betraying my principles, or Blease either," the old man wrote less than a year before his death, "can go to hell." [4] His accusers, the followers of the numerous lieutenants he had deposed, were conscious of the betrayal of the common people and were vindictive. Blease himself expressed this hate by decorating with profane epithets his copy of the Congressional eulogies of the dead senator.[5] "You are the property of the old Conservative crowd," a former Tillmanite wrote Tillman in 1917. "You betrayed and ruined every leader who aided you." The ghosts of Shell, Irby, Farley, McLaurin, and others were paraded before him. He was accused of corruption: Dispensary rebates, receiving free passes, Oregon land frauds. "The blood you caused to be shed at Darlington cries out from the grave." He had betrayed a brother and tried to rob a daughter-in-law of her children. "You arrogantly invite anyone who doesn't like your black record to go to hell. Take care, you may meet them there." [6]

Such views were widely current at the time of his death and have survived to dog his memory. They were held by many of the forty thousand who, in the primary of 1918, defied war sentiment to vote for Blease in his unsuccessful bid for Tillman's seat.

More damaging to the reputation of the dead senator than the slanders of the Bleaseites was the cold hostility of the Conservatives. Though they were grateful for the favors he bestowed and for the conservatism of his last years, a host of "arch-devils" besides Gonzales remained to conspire against his fame. They hated his memory and they had reasons for their hate. They remembered the purposeful assault he made upon the institutions of their fathers: he had turned friends out of office and preached a veritable

[4] *Id.* to M. V. Sullivan, November 2, 1917, *ibid.*
[5] Copy belonging to the late John K. Aull, in library of Clinton T. Graydon, Columbia.
[6] M. V. Sullivan to Tillman, November 10, 1917, in Tillman Papers.

jihad against Charleston. They remembered the crude manners, the snarling tongue, the Darlington Riot, the murder of the elder Gonzales by a Tillman. And above all they remembered the defeat of Hampton, the symbol of all that was glorious in the South Carolina tradition.

The Conservatives for the most part refrained from open attacks upon his memory; they knew that such tactics would create resentment among thousands. Instead they engaged in a devastating conspiracy of silence, omitting references to Tillman in the published recollections of the immediate past. Their numerous newspaper articles and occasional books are concerned with almost everyone except the state's second most important figure; the Carpetbaggers are extravagantly attacked, the paladins of the Confederacy and the statesmen great and small of the Hampton era are extravagantly praised. Hampton, in the patriotic legend they have constructed, becomes a foil to the unmentioned Tillman.

Not all the enemies of the Edgefield farmer, however, have adhered to the conspiracy of silence. One editor, in the service of the Columbia *State,* began some years before Tillman's death a newspaper assault later embodied in a treatise.[7] This writer interprets Tillmanism as a malevolent fulfillment of the forces of democracy unloosed by Reconstruction. Point by point Tillman is accused of destroying the aristocratic qualities which gave distinction to the South Carolina of an earlier day. It is claimed that because of Tillman's influence the character of the public service has steadily degenerated; that, with the exception of Tillman himself, no member of Congress from South Carolina has in recent decades figured seriously in the formation of national policies;[8] that the commonwealth has become one of the "backward states," a mighty fall from the time when

[7] Ball, *State that Forgot, passim.*
[8] This was before Byrnes became prominent in the Franklin D. Roosevelt administration.

it "led the South and the South led the nation"; that the
state "Democratic party is without a creed except white
solidarity" and a noncontroversial platform of platitudes.
Ben Tillman, it is admitted, made issues, but he has "no
imitators even among those who" call "him their patron
saint." The state has fallen "into an old, an indurated
apathy" which does not allow public indignation in the
face of public derelictions. Although officials are acquitted
of other than petty stealings, the courts have suffered a
melancholy decline and inefficiency in county government
is common. Tillman's attack on Charleston deprived the
legislature of the city's experienced leadership; "it is hopeless for a Charleston man to be a candidate for a state office." [9] "The state colleges are timid and shrinking"; it
would be disastrous for a professor to criticize "any of the
'sacred cows' of the South Carolina populace and politicians." The newspapers, once militant advocates of reform, are now quiescent.

These evidences of civic decay are largely ascribed to the
manner in which the Tillman-instituted primary and party
rules have worked. The Negro, it is true, has been eliminated completely from politics, but at the cost of white
independence of thought. The illiberal deed against the
blacks, instead of becoming a fading memory, remains as
a sort of contemporary reality. The spirit which maintains
the primary as a racial institution sustains the tradition requiring all primary voters to support Democratic candidates from President to coroner. [10]

That there is truth in this indictment is apparent from
Tillman's own admissions. He freely agreed concerning the
mediocrity of his successors in office, [11] and at times questioned the virtues of the democracy he had created. "The
result of this primary," he said when Blease was re-elected,

---

[9] Ball, *State that Forgot,* 270. The tradition was broken in 1938 by the election of Burnet R. Maybank as governor.

[10] *Ibid.,* 270–84.

[11] Tillman to W. W. Dixon, December 9, 1914, in Tillman Papers.

"makes me doubt the wisdom of ever having emancipated these 'wool-hat, one-gallus' men from the domination of the oligarchy." [12] He deplored the "happy-go-lucky way" of handling the primary and the people's custom of "allowing blackguards to abuse one another at their public meetings." [13] He saw faults of omission in his works. He had come as an agricultural reformer; but at his going he observed "the same blight" which was inherited from his ancestors. Burnt-over fields covered with "ghostly gullies and galls" gave evidence of failure to conquer "ignorance and wastefulness." [14] He had come as a friend of the common people; yet at his going he admitted that the common people had not been given "more sympathy and understanding" by the ruling classes. He conceded that there were legitimate reasons for the class prejudices which made Bleaseism possible.[15]

The critical observer can paint the indictment of Tillmanism in even darker colors than suit the taste of the provincial critic. Tillman capitalized on "the strain of violence" [16] which runs through South Carolina life. Violence or threat of violence underlay the crises of his career—Reconstruction; the suppression of Haskellism; the major political campaigns; the Darlington disturbance; the disfranchisement of the Negroes. Ben Tillman openly justified violence when necessary to enforce the majority sentiment of the South Carolina whites. Such an attitude imposed —indeed still imposes—a dreadful tyranny upon the state. It prevents free and progressive thought among the whites; prevents the development among them of so elementary an institution of liberal democracy as an opposition political party. And of course the chief sufferer is the Negro.

[12] *Id.* to Glenn, August 30, 1912, *ibid.*
[13] *Id.* to Knight, August 1, 1912, *ibid.; id.* to Dantzler, August 28, 1913, *ibid.; id.* to Smythe, January 14, 1913, *ibid.*
[14] *Id.* to Mrs. Cathcart, January 28, 1918, *ibid.*
[15] *Id.* to Dr. William B. Patton, September 18, 1917, *ibid.*
[16] The phrase is Ludwig Lewisohn's in *Up Stream; An American Chronicle* (New York, 1922).

He is deprived of all political privileges and many civil rights and is subjected to hardening forms of caste from which there is no escape short of migration. Tillman endorsed this tyranny to the end of his days. "Whoever doubts that civilization depends on white supremacy is a fool and a knave. . . . Any institution . . . that threatens to destroy the political unity of the white race ought not to be established. . . . Therefore, 'two strong political parties' is an idea that should be frowned upon by all good citizens." [17]

But many of the shortcomings ascribed to the post-Tillman regime can with equal justice be imputed to the regime he supplanted. Tillman's exposure of "incipient rottenness" and "decay" among the Bourbon Democrats was identical with the provincialism, vacuity, and mediocrity his critics attributed to his successors. South Carolina since Appomattox has not been in a position to play a distinguished part in the national life; that was no more Tillman's fault than it was Hampton's. The fact that the Edgefield farmer personally exercised a leadership more distinguished than circumstances warranted is a tribute to his masterful personality; no other post-bellum South Carolinian did as much.

Those closest to the dead leader rightly believed that his memory could be best sustained by a positive statement of his deeds. They recorded his achievements upon his tomb and upon his statue in Columbia. His death amidst the emotions of the World War period naturally led to the inscription of much about his last years. His services as chairman of the Senate Committee on Naval Affairs are emphasized along with a quotation proclaiming a belated conversion to the doctrine of patriotic nationalism. To this might have been added mention of his services in the railroad rate bill contest and of his long years of unremitting criticism of the Republican and Roosevelt policies. But the inscription as it is gives too much attention to senatorial services; for only

[17] Tillman to U. L. Rast, April 23, 1913, in Tillman Papers.

in the case of the rate bill did the senator have a chance for notable constructive legislation. During seventeen of his twenty-three years in the Senate he belonged to the minority party; during his last six years as member of the majority faction, illness prevented significant efforts. Ben Tillman was never a mediocrity; but he did not leave behind him a record of achievement to number him among the great of an illustrious legislative assembly.

The memorialists are on firmer ground when they turn to Tillman's South Carolina career. "To the State steadfast," they write; for Ben Tillman in both his virtues and his vices was a true South Carolinian. Possessed of a penetrating and practical understanding of that singular commonwealth, he made effective use of both its dark and bright potentialities. He played upon the state's race, sectional, and class divisions; and he did this so effectively because he was endowed with two gifts in greater degree than any other South Carolinian. One was the vivid pen of the born pamphleteer; the other was powers of exhortation which made him the greatest Southern agitator of his day. He did not, of course, use these powers altogether for evil. If he conjured up dark prejudices, he also projected plans of democratic progress which were successful because they fell within the provincial framework.

"Loving them, he was the friend and leader of the common people," the memorialists truthfully add. He believed that a majority of the white male voters of South Carolina should determine the state's destiny, and as a man of deeds he gave this conviction a higher degree of function than had prevailed when he started his agitations. With one hand he destroyed the last vestiges of Negro political influence and with the other, as the memorialists assert, "taught them [the common white men] their political power." The Tillman-nurtured white primary, by putting the choice of a multitude of public offices directly in the hands of the voters, confirmed the right of the average white man to rule. And

Tillman discharged a still more important function of democracy by creating among ordinary white men the will to vote; for the creation of this desire is more difficult than the mere giving of the voting privilege. Tillman accomplished this through his vivid agitations. He made South Carolina into an interested democracy. The tradition of popular rule he instituted still lives; no politician not closely in touch with the common white man can win office in South Carolina.

To supply the education necessary for the intelligent exercise of democratic privileges, Tillman created Clemson and Winthrop colleges for the training of the white youth of the state. These colleges were born amid the partisan passions created by him, but they have since come to be regarded as useful institutions by all white South Carolinians. "I do not believe I can be happier than I was at these two colleges," he wrote during his declining years. "They are both doing a grand and noble work and I am proud of my association with their initiation." [18] Tillman cannot be denied honor as the founder of two excellent colleges.

Had his memorialists mentioned the Dispensary on his tomb and statue there would have been critical justification. The state liquor monopoly was Tillman's most unique contribution to American political life. It was too bold and too original an experiment to be permanent in so hidebound a commonwealth as South Carolina; nor with the end of Prohibition did the state return to the Dispensary. But if South Carolina has not been willing a second time to put confidence in the most original idea of its leading post-bellum statesman, commonwealths greater and more progressive have. Virginia, Pennsylvania, and other states find public liquor monopolies satisfactory.

Since Ben Tillman made his imprint upon the destinies of South Carolina there have been many changes tending partly to efface his memory. One has been the dispersion of

[18] *Id.* to Senator Bacon, June 11, 1911, *ibid.*

his family. Both his mother's house and the near-by farm-house of his early married life are today literally falling apart and are surrounded by a waste of gullies and thickets. This is an ironic answer to the dead master's dream of agricultural regeneration. A loving father of a large family who had made a career for himself should normally have founded an influential clan, but this did not happen in Tillman's case. The two Tillman sons, despite the prestige of their name, were unable to make good in candidacies for Congress. No Tillman lives on the family estate at Trenton and no child remains in South Carolina to continue the family tradition.

Memory of Tillman has been dimmed by the gradual concentration of popular interest upon dead heroes of more appealing mold. South Carolinians want their idols to possess obvious virtues. They admire the handsome faces, athletic frames, and flowing oratory of the knights of the Confederacy and of the statesmen of the old regime. The heroism of the man with the single eye, the grim countenance, the lashing speech, and the unpleasant candor, is too subtle for continued admiration.

But the memory of Ben Tillman cannot be effaced from the annals of his state. He was unique, the most forceful personality it has produced since the Civil War; and his measure of greatness has increased in comparison with the mediocrity of his successors. His evil, like his good, is written in heroic terms; he was the founder of the sort of democracy his state cherishes, and he was truly representative of this democracy.

It is fitting that his statue stands on the State House grounds as a complement to Wade Hampton's.[19] Inevitably, the form and features of Pitchfork Ben are not as classical as those of the Great Aristocrat. But there is determination in the expressive face and the rugged strength of a leader of the common people in the lineaments.

[19] The Tillman monument is the work of Frederick C. Hibbard, Chicago.

CRITICAL ESSAY ON AUTHORITIES

Manuscripts

The Benjamin R. Tillman Papers in the South Caroliniana Library, University of South Carolina, consist of 55,800 items in 120 boxes marked "Incoming Mail" and 41,850 items in 54 boxes marked "Outgoing Mail," all carefully arranged chronologically. The collection can be used only with permission of Mr. Benjamin R. Tillman, Jr. Despite its great size it is disappointing. The most valuable portion of the "Incoming Mail" is a few letters written by members of the Tillman family during Ben's childhood. The letters received during his early manhood and his governorship are few. For the years following 1896 they are numerous and consist in a great measure of congratulations and petitions of the type often addressed to a prominent person. There are, however, some communications from confederates revealing secrets. The "Outgoing Mail" consists mostly of letters written by Tillman during the last seven and one half years of his life. This least important period of his career is fully revealed, and there are significant autobiographical materials concerning his more active years. Two boxes are sufficient to contain Tillman's letters for the important fifteen years between 1896 and 1911. No letters are preserved for the years before 1896. Two letter books containing some thousand or more items were examined in 1938 by the author in the South Caroliniana Library but they have since been removed. Called Governor Tillman's Letter Books, they cover the period of the governorship and are the most valuable portion of the Tillman Papers. There is authority for the belief that a great mass of Tillman letters dated prior to 1911 was misplaced or destroyed when Tillman changed his Washington office in 1913.

There are twelve Governor's Letter Books for the Tillman administration in the Library of the South Carolina Historical Commission, Columbia. Most of these communications are of a purely routine character, but some of them contain vital information concerning the Dispensary.

Manuscript materials which give precision to statements concerning the economic status of the Tillman family are these:

Revolutionary Stubs, in Library of the South Carolina Historical Commission; South Carolina Grant Books, in Office of the South Carolina Secretary of State, Columbia; Edgefield County, South Carolina, Records of Wills, Edgefield Courthouse; Edgefield County, South Carolina Deed Books, Edgefield Courthouse; United States Censuses of 1840, 1850, and 1860, South Carolina, Edgefield District, in Bureau of the Census, Washington; United States Censuses of Agriculture, 1850, 1860, and 1880, Edgefield County, South Carolina, in State Library, State House, Columbia.

Of slight value to the Tillman student are the William Godber Hinson Papers, in the Charleston Library Association, Charleston; the John Peter Richardson Letter Books, in Library of the South Carolina Historical Commission; and the Robert Means Davis Papers, in possession of Professor Henry C. Davis, University of South Carolina. The John Gary Evans Papers, South Caroliniana Library, is the only collection of a Tillman leader. The present investigator was denied their use.

Public Documents

Journal of the House of Representatives of the General Assembly of the State of South Carolina (Columbia, 1873—) and *Journal of the Senate of the General Assembly of the State of South Carolina* (Columbia, 1873—) are used for the identification of legislative activities and for governors' messages. *Reports and Resolutions of the General Assembly of the State of South Carolina* (Columbia, 1873—) contains the annual reports of state officials and commissions, together with the testimony taken by the legislative committee that investigated the Dispensary in 1905 and 1906. *Acts and Joint Resolutions of the General Assembly of the State of South Carolina* (Columbia, 1868—) and *Constitution of the State of South Carolina . . . 1895* (Columbia, 1904) contain the laws. The judicial decisions affecting the Dispensary and other Tillman measures are in *Reports of Cases Heard and Determined by the Supreme Court of South Carolina* (Columbia, 1871—); *Federal Reporter* (St. Paul, 1880—); and *Cases Argued and Adjudged in the Supreme Court of the United States* (Boston, 1876—). *Journal of the Constitutional Convention of the State of South Carolina* (Columbia, 1895) is a mere record of events, except for Tillman's and other delegates' speeches on suffrage. *Report of the Joint Investigating Committee on Public Frauds . . . 1877–*

1878 (Columbia, 1878) and *South Carolina Resources and Population, Institutions and Industries* (Charleston, 1883) are informing justifications of the Hampton settlement of South Carolina affairs. *The South Carolina Legislative Times: Being the Debates and Proceedings in the South Carolina Legislature at the Session Commencing November, 1855* (Columbia, 1856), is the only record of this type. It is used for the speeches of George D. Tillman.

The *Congressional Record* (Washington, 1873—) from the 54 Cong., 1 Sess., to the 65 Cong., 2 Sess. (1895–1918), contains a complete record of Tillman's participation in the Senate debates. *The War of the Rebellion: A Compilation of the Official Records of the Union and Confederate Armies,* 129 vols. and index (Washington, 1880–1901), gives the war record of James A. Tillman; *House Miscellaneous Documents* (Washington), 45 Cong., 1 Sess., No. 11, and *Senate Documents* (Washington), 44 Cong., 2 Sess., Nos. 31, 48, give Ben's part in the 1876 election. Census of the United States *Reports* (Washington) are useful for social and economic comparisons.

Official Proceedings of the Democratic National Convention . . . 1896 (Logansport, Ind., 1896); *1900* (Chicago, 1900); and *1904* (New York, 1904), give Tillman's addresses in the three most important national conventions in which he participated.

Newspapers and Periodicals

The Charleston *News and Courier* (1873—), in the absence of adequate private letters, is the principal source of information concerning Tillman. What merits of exposition and interpretation any work on him may possess inevitably rest in large measure on the findings of the editors and reporters of this newspaper. From 1885 until Tillman's death thirty-three years later it chronicled his deeds and utterances with unflagging interest and frankness. Its editors, Francis W. Dawson and James C. Hemphill, were always honest and intelligent even in their most hostile criticisms. Narciso G. Gonzales, its chief reporter, combined stenographic accuracy with interpretations almost always tactless because they were either startlingly unfair or startlingly truthful. His successor, August Kohn, combined accuracy with a studied fairness.

Of second importance among newspapers is the Columbia *State* (1891—), which was founded by Gonzales for the specific purpose of fighting Tillman, unrestrained by the conservatism of the Charleston daily. In its columns the faults of the farmer-politician were exposed with pitiless veracity, while his virtues were scarcely understood. With the growing moderation of Tillman, the *State* turned its wrath successively against James H. Tillman and Cole L. Blease, and it then lost its pamphleteering zeal as it grew colorless and commercial. Of third importance among the anti-Tillman dailies is the Greenville *News* (1874—), ably edited by Alfred B. Williams. The Spartanburg *Herald* (1890—), edited by J. C. Garlington, completes the list of anti-Tillman dailies.

Two pro-Tillman dailies attempted unsuccessfully to challenge the supremacy of the four newspapers just mentioned. The first of these, the Charleston *World* (1887–1901), edited by Octavus Cohen, expired after a quarrel with Tillman. The second, the Columbia *Daily Register* (1875–1898), lost its pro-Tillman bias with the retirement of T. Larry Gantt from the editorship. Toward the end of Tillman's career the *Daily Register*'s spirit of protest was revived by the Charleston *American* (1917–1923), a pro-Blease organ under the able editorship of John P. Grace.

Other newspapers which throw light on Tillman's career are the neutral Augusta (Ga.) *Chronicle* (1785—); the independent Yorkville (York) *Enquirer* (1855—), ably edited by the Grist family; Winnsboro *News and Herald* (1863—); Columbia *Record* (1891—); Sumter *Watchman and Southron* (1850–1932); and Charleston *Evening Post* (1894—). The Edgefield *Advertiser* (1836—) and the Edgefield *Chronicle* (1881–1925), both of which at times were edited by the inimitable James T. Bacon, throw light on the Tillman family. Two college publications have been used: *South Carolina Collegian* (Columbia, 1882—), the student monthly of the University of South Carolina, and *Davidson Monthly* (Davidson College, N. C., 1870—).

The following great national dailies have been consulted: Washington *Post* (1877—); New York *Times* (1851—); New York *Herald* (1835–1924); New York *Tribune* (1841–1924); New York *American* (1882—); New York *Evening Post* (1802–1919); and New York *Sun* (1833—).

The following periodicals were used for comments on Tillman and South Carolina events: *Appleton's Annual Cyclopaedia and Register of Important Events*, N. S. (New York, 1876–1895); *World Almanac and Encyclopedia*, 1912 (New

York, 1912); *Appleton's Magazine* (Philadelphia, New York, 1903–1909); *Spectator* (London, 1828—); *Nation* (New York, 1865—); *World's Work* (New York, 1900–1934); *Collier's, the National Weekly* (New York, 1888—); *Current Literature* (New York, 1888–1912); *American Review of Reviews* (New York, 1890–1937); *Outlook* (New York, 1870–1935); *Literary Digest* (New York, 1890–1938); *North American Review* (Boston, 1815—); *Pearson's Magazine* (New York, 1899–1925); *Independent* (New York, 1848–1928); *South Atlantic Quarterly* (Durham, 1902—); *Success Magazine* (New York, 1897–1911); *Delineator* (New York, 1873—); *Saturday Evening Post* (Philadelphia, 1821—); *Sewanee Review* (Sewanee, Tenn., 1892—); *Atlantic Monthly* (Boston, 1857—).

The Benjamin R. Tillman Scrapbooks in the South Caroliniana Library embrace fourteen volumes (Vol. I missing) of uncensored newspaper and magazine materials arranged in rough chronological order, covering almost every phase of Tillman's career. Much of these data cannot conveniently be found elsewhere. Of limited usefulness are the William Godber Hinson Scrapbooks, in the Charleston Library Association; the Robert Means Davis Scrapbooks, in possession of Professor Henry C. Davis, University of South Carolina; the William Joseph Alexander Scrapbook, in the South Caroliniana Library; and the Thomas Lawrence Gantt Scrapbooks, in possession of Robert J. Gantt, Spartanburg.

Studies in South Carolina History

David D. Wallace, *The History of South Carolina,* 4 vols. (New York, 1934), a monumental work of almost unparalleled importance, contains from the viewpoint of an upcountry Conservative a detailed and comprehensive history of Tillmanism, its antecedents and its effects. The work is courageously critical without the sacrifice of a deeply cherished sense of state pride. One may dissent from some opinions of the author—his prejudices against the strain of violence inherent in Tillmanism and against the Negro, for example—without losing a wholesome respect for everything Professor Wallace writes.

William W. Ball, *The State that Forgot: South Carolina's Surrender to Democracy* (Indianapolis, 1932), is the most important book of reminiscences covering the Tillman period of South Carolina history; it is an entertaining and penetrating

criticism of the worth of the agrarian revolt and as boldly critical as an acceptance of the South Carolina tribal faith allows.
The author avoids mention of Blease despite the fact that the
Blease decade was a part of his mature years. This is an example
of timidity eschewed by Wallace.

George R. Koester, "Bleaseism," which more accurately
should have been designated "Tillmanism," is a series of twenty-
four articles first appearing in the Greenville *Piedmont* in 1916
and later in several county weeklies. They are now available in
a scrapbook among the Tillman Papers. The author, a reporter
on the Columbia *Daily Register* who enjoyed the confidence
of Tillman leaders, writes frankly if disjointedly. Thomas J.
Kirkland, "Tillman and I," a series of articles by a Tillman
leader in the Columbia *State*, June 30, July 7, 14, 21, 28, 1929,
is an all-too-brief chronicle that is penetrating and critical.

Francis B. Simkins, *The Tillman Movement in South Carolina* (Durham, 1926), is a preliminary study which is a partial
basis of this book. Phases of Tillmanism are discussed in Edward S. Joynes, *The Origin and Early History of Winthrop*
(n.p., n.d.); Ira B. Jones, *Winthrop Cornerstone Day Address,
May 12, 1894* (Lancaster, S. C., 1894); Milton L. Orr, *The State-
Supported Colleges for Women* (Nashville, 1930); Benjamin F.
Taylor, *The Darlington Riot* (Columbia, 1910); Leonard S.
Blakey, *The Sale of Liquor in the South,* in Columbia University *Studies in History, Economics and Public Law,* LI (New
York, 1912). A primary source is Mary J. Miller (ed.), *The Suffrage Speeches by Negroes in the Constitutional Convention*
(n.p., n.d.). Among the articles that present phases of Tillmanism are the following: "I.N.F.," in New York *Tribune,* reprinted in Charleston *News and Courier,* December 27, 28,
1894, January 2, 1895; William A. Mabry, "Ben Tillman Disfranchised the Negro," in *South Atlantic Quarterly,* XXXVII
(1938), 170–83; David D. Wallace, "The South Carolina Constitutional Convention of 1895," in *Sewanee Review* (Sewanee,
1892—), IV (1895–1896), 348–60; Amora M. Eaton, "The New
Constitution of South Carolina," in *American Law Review*
(Boston, St. Louis, 1866—), XXXI (1897), 198–212; E. R. L.
Gould, "The Gothenburg System in America," in *Atlantic
Monthly,* LXXII (1893), 538–45; Remsen Crawford, "The State
Dispensary System" in *Saturday Evening Post,* CCI (1928), 5–7;
Benjamin R. Tillman, "The South Carolina Liquor Law," in
North American Review, CLVIII (1894), 140–49; *id.,* "Our

Whiskey Rebellion," *ibid.*, 513–19; *id.* and William F. Dargan, "A Last Word on the South Carolina Liquor Law," *ibid.*, CLIX (1894), 46–60.

Tillman's Edgefield background is discussed in John A. Chapman, *History of Edgefield County from the Earliest Settlements to 1897* (Newberry, S. C., 1897); Mason L. Weems, *The Devil in Petticoats Or, God's Revenge Against Husband Killing* (New Ed., Saluda, S. C., 1935); William A. Sheppard, *Red Shirts Remembered: Southern Brigadiers of the Reconstruction Period* (Spartanburg, S. C., 1940); Benjamin R. Tillman, *Hog Raising in South Carolina* in *Clemson Agricultural College, Extension Work*, V, Bulletin 4 (Clemson College, S. C., 1909). The South Carolina background is discussed in Francis B. Simkins and Robert H. Woody, *South Carolina during Reconstruction* (Chapel Hill, 1932); Francis B. Simkins, "The Election of 1876 in South Carolina," in *South Atlantic Quarterly,* XXI (1922), 225–40; XXII (1923), 35–51; Edward L. Wells, *Hampton and Reconstruction* (Columbia, 1907); Alfred B. Williams, *Hampton and His Red Shirts: South Carolina's Deliverance in 1876* (Charleston, 1935); Hilary A. Herbert (ed.), *Why the Solid South? or, Reconstruction and Its Results* (Baltimore, 1890); Edwin L. Green, *A History of the University of South Carolina* (Columbia, 1916); Ludwig Lewisohn, *Up Stream: An American Chronicle* (New York, 1922); and Sidney Andrews, *The South since the War* (Boston, 1866).

Tillman's view of the Negro is summarized by him in "Causes of Southern Opposition to Imperialism," in *North American Review,* CLXXI (1900), 439–46; "The Race Question," in *Van Norden; The World Mirror* (New York, 1906–1910), II (1907–1908), 19–28; and *The Negro Problem and Immigration Delivered . . . Before the South Carolina House of Representatives, January 24, 1908* (Columbia, 1908). See also, Francis B. Simkins, "Ben Tillman's View of the Negro," in *Journal of Southern History* (Baton Rouge, 1935—), III (1937), 161–74.

Biographical Materials on South Carolinians

The Tillman genealogy is elaborately treated in Stephen F. Tillman, *Records and Genealogy of the Tilghman, Tillman, Tilman, Tilmon Family, 1225–1938* (Ann Arbor, 1939). Ben's maternal ancestors are traced in James E. Saunders, *Early Settlers of Alabama* (New Orleans, 1899). His most notable autobiographical effort is *The Struggles of 1876; How South Carolina Was Delivered from Carpetbag and Negro Rule* (n.p., n.d.), a confession of the author's part in Reconstruction. See also, childhood reminiscences, in Spartanburg *Herald,* November 22, 1906. The only attempt at a biography is Thornwell Haynes, *Biographical Sketch of Gov. B. R. Tillman of South Carolina* (Columbia, 1894), a sophomoric effort consisting of thirty-five pages of narrative and twenty-nine pages of extracts from addresses. The atmosphere of Tillman's earlier and more obscure years is authoritatively reconstructed by Hugh C. Middleton, in Charleston *World,* July 16, 1890, and in an article written in 1896 entitled "Ben Tillman: a Character Sketch," in Tillman Scrapbooks; and by the Reverend Royal G. Shannonhouse, in Columbia *Record,* July 14, 1918. *Benjamin Ryan Tillman, Memorial Addresses Delivered in the Senate and House of Representatives of the United States, 65th Congress* (Washington, 1919), and *Memorial to Benjamin Ryan Tillman . . . Clemson College, S. C., December 10, 1919* (Clemson College, S. C., 1919), contain tributes from official associates, notably the remarks of Senator Henry C. Lodge and President Walter M. Riggs.

Washington journalists wrote numerous descriptions in which accuracy was often sacrificed to effect. The best of these are Zach McGhee, "Tillman, Smasher of Traditions," in *World's Work,* XII (1906), 8013–20; Broughton Brandenburg, "At Home With Big Americans: With 'Pitchfork' Ben Tillman in Edgefield, S. C.," in *Delineator,* LXXI (1908), 235–39; Gilson Gardner, "The Real Senator Tillman," in *Independent,* LXI (1906), 68–70; [anonymous], "The Most Extraordinary Compound in the United States Senate," in *Current Literature,* XLI (1906), 153–55; "Tattler" [pseudonym], "The Broken Pitchfork," in *Nation,* CII (1916), 693–94. Other character sketches conveniently found in Tillman Scrapbooks are Clifford Howard, "Tillman, A Study from the American Soil," in *Appleton's Magazine,* VIII (1906), 348–54; W. A. Lewis, "The Tillman of the Armchair," in *Success Magazine,* IX (1906), 396; James Creelman, "A Defender of the Senate," in *Pearson's Magazine,* XV (1906), 622–29; Dexter Marshall, in Nashville *Banner,* September 8, 1906; [anonymous], "Men & Work—Tillman without the Pitchfork," in *Saturday Evening Post,* CLXXVIII (1906), 15; Charles Warren, in Boston *Herald,* March 27, 1906.

The only serious biography of a South Carolina contemporary is Alester G. Holmes and George R. Sherrill, *Thomas Green*

Clemson: His Life and Work (Richmond, 1937), which gives all the relevant facts about Clemson without adequate understanding of Tillman's part in the founding of the college. Louise P. H. Daly, *Alexander Cheves Haskell, the Portrait of a Man* (privately printed, Norwood, Mass., 1934), is a family memoir which scarcely mentions the most important episode in Haskell's life. David D. Wallace's life of Martin W. Gary was suppressed by the Gary family before publication.

The dearth of biographies finds partial compensation in the wealth of biographical dictionaries of South Carolinians which have appeared in the last seventy years. The only qualifications generally required of their subjects for inclusion are membership in the white race and willingness to pay for space. But the sketches are so numerous and so largely autobiographical that much information is provided. The books are the following: J. Belton O'Neall, *Biographical Sketches of the Bench and Bar of South Carolina,* 2 vols. (Charleston, 1859); *An Historical and Descriptive Review of the State of South Carolina,* 3 vols. (Charleston, 1884); Edward McCrady and Samuel Ashe (eds.), *Cyclopedia of Eminent and Representative Men of the Carolinas,* 2 vols. (Madison, Wis., 1892); J. C. Garlington (ed.), *Men of the Times: Sketches of Living Notables: Biographical Encyclopedia of Contemporaneous South Carolina Leaders* (Spartanburg, 1902); Ulysses R. Brooks (ed.), *South Carolina Bench and Bar* (Columbia, 1908); James C. Hemphill (ed.), *Men of Mark in South Carolina: A Collection of Biographies of Leading Men of the State,* 4 vols. (Washington, 1909); Yates Snowden and Harry G. Cutler (eds.), *History of South Carolina,* 5 vols., of which 3 are biographical (Chicago, 1920); Ralph E. Grier (ed.), *South Carolina and Her Builders* (Columbia, 1930); *Biographical Volume* (New York, 1930), supplement to David D. Wallace, *The History of South Carolina,* 4 vols. (New York, 1934); Walter S. Utsey (ed.), *Who's Who in South Carolina, 1934–1935, a Standard Reference Book of South Carolina* (Columbia, 1935). Additional biographical data are contained in Allen Johnson and Dumas Malone (eds.), *Dictionary of American Biography,* 20 vols. and index (New York, 1928–1937); *Who's Who in America* (Chicago, 1899—); and *Biographical Directory of the American Congress, 1774–1927* (Washington, 1928).

Works Not Especially Concerned with South Carolina

The general history of the United States which gives Tillman most attention is Mark Sullivan, *Our Times: The United States, 1900–1925,* 6 vols. (New York, 1926–1935). Harry T. Peck, *Twenty Years of the Republic, 1885–1905* (New York, 1907), and Louis M. Hacker and Benjamin B. Kendrick, *The United States Since 1865* (New York, 1932), appraise Tillman's accomplishments. The causes of agrarian discontent are adequately explained in Julian A. C. Chandler *et al.* (eds.), *The South in the Building of the Nation,* 13 vols. (Richmond, 1909–1913); Solon J. Buck, *The Granger Movement: A Study of Agricultural Organization and Its Political, Economic, and Social Manifestations, 1870–1880* (Cambridge, 1913); and Charles H. Otken, *The Ills of the South; or, Related Causes Hostile to the General Prosperity of the Southern People* (New York, 1894). The course of the agrarian revolt is traced in Solon J. Buck, *The Agrarian Crusade: A Chronicle of the Farmer in Politics* (New Haven, 1921); W. Scott Morgan, *History of the Wheel and Alliance* (New York, 1891); Henry R. Chamberlain, *The Farmers' Alliance: What It Aims to Accomplish* (New York, 1891); Holland Thompson, *The New South: A Chronicle of Social and Industrial Evolution* (New Haven, 1921); and C. Vann Woodward, *Tom Watson: Agrarian Rebel* (New York, 1938).

The biographies of some of the important figures of the Bryan-Roosevelt period contain discussions of Tillman and his influence. This is especially true of Nathaniel W. Stephenson, *Nelson W. Aldrich: A Leader in American Politics* (New York, 1930); Leon B. Richardson, *William E. Chandler, Republican* (New York, 1940); Sam H. Acheson, *Joe Bailey: The Last Democrat* (New York, 1932); Henry F. Pringle, *Theodore Roosevelt: A Biography* (New York, 1931); and Joseph B. Bishop, *Theodore Roosevelt and His Times,* 2 vols. (New York, 1920). This is true to a less extent of Theodore Roosevelt, *An Autobiography* (New York, 1919); Owen Wister, *Roosevelt: The Story of a Friendship, 1880–1919* (New York, 1930); Henry C. Lodge (ed.), *Selections from the Correspondence of Theodore Roosevelt and Henry Cabot Lodge, 1884–1918,* 2 vols. (New York, 1925); William J. Bryan, *The First Battle, Story of the Campaign of 1896* (Chicago, 1896); *id.* and Mary B. Bryan, *Memoirs of William Jennings Bryan* (Chicago, 1925); Champ Clark, *My*

Quarter Century of American Politics, 2 vols. (New York, 1920); George F. Hoar, *Autobiography of Seventy Years,* 2 vols. (New York, 1903); and Joseph P. Tumulty, *Woodrow Wilson as I Know Him* (New York, 1921).

INDEX

Abbeville, 154

Adams, Dock, 61-62

Adullamites, 180, 196, 211

Agricultural College Bill, 112

Agricultural distress, 78-79

Agricultural Hall, 243

Agricultural Society, 91-92, 98

Aiken, 66; Hamburg trial at, 64; Hampton at, 159-60

Aldrich, Alfred P., 164n

Aldrich, Nelson W., 17, 343, 346, 464; on Hepburn Bill, 422-24, 427-28, 433-39; tariff debate, 464-68

Aldrich, Robert, 295

Alexander, William J., dismissed, 177-78

Allison, William B., 434, 440

Altgeld, John P., 18

Ancrum, William H., 165n

Anderson, 118, 153, 228, 468, 500

Ansel, Martin F., 460, 485, 490

Archbold, John D., 389

Aristocracy, in South Carolina, 70-71; its decline, 72-73

Armor plant, 349-52, 511-13

Arthur, Annie, 41

Ashley Hall, 72

Ashley, "Josh," 222

Asparagus experiment, 477-78

Athens, Ga., 236-37

Atlanta, Ga., 314, 316-17

Atlanta *Constitution*, 250

Augusta, Ga., 43, 54, 61, 107, 228, 479

Augusta *Chronicle*, 540

Babcock, James W., 182, 465, 501-502

Bacon, Augustus O., Tillman's friend, 19, 362, 435

Bacon, Edmund ["Ned Brace"], 24

Bacon, Edmund, 165n

Bacon, James T., on Tillman's inaugural, 173

Bailey, Joseph W., 362-63, 468; lec-

tures Tillman, 6; on Hepburn Bill, 426, 432, 438-39

Ball, William B., on Edgefield, 24; on Tillmanism, 549-51

Bank of Charleston, 217

Baptists, on Dispensary, 242, 457

Barker, Theodore G., 291

Barnwell, 114, 161, 224-25

Barnwell, Joseph W., 165n, 287

Bates, W. N., 249

Bates, W. T. C., 147n

Beaufort, 145, 153, 162, 280, 289-90, 307

Belmont, August, 391

Benet, W. C., 162

Bennettsville, 116, 369; Tillman at, 91-92, 96

Benton, Thomas H., 9

Bethea, Edwin A., 164n

Bethlehem Steel Company, 347-49

Beveridge, Albert J., 402, 444, 461

Bible, influence on Tillman, 83

Bimetallic Convention, 312, 316

Black, John A., 364-65

Blackville, 128

Blanding, James D., 165n

Blease, Cole L., House leader, 216; on Dispensary, 460, 484; origin and nature, 486-87; relations with Tillman, 487-90; wins prestige, 490-91; governor, 492-93; quarrel with Tillman, 493-501; defeated in 1916, pp. 503-504; campaign of 1918, pp. 536-38, 540, 544-45, 548-49

Bonham, James, 24

Bourbons, 78, 80-81, 116, 191, 222, 264, 455, 485, 503, 552

Boykin, Alexander H., 165n

Bratton, John, 68, 149-50, 154, 157, 160

Breen, James W., 413

Brice Act, 458

Brice, John W., 164n